P9-DBT-196

Laos

Andrew Burke
Justine Vaisutis

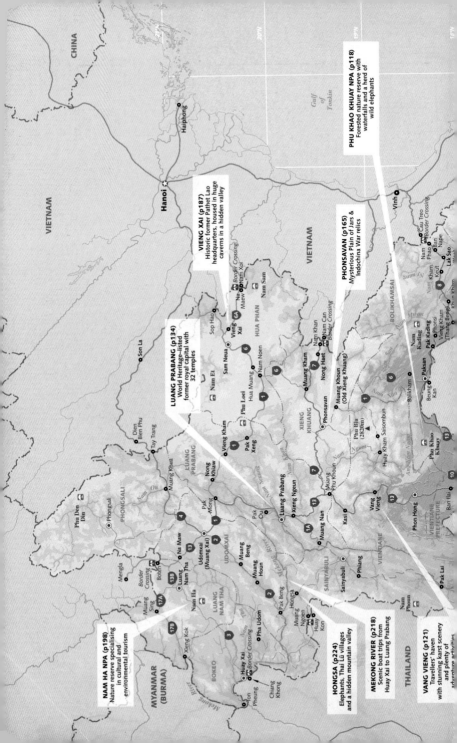

NAM HA NPA (p198)
Nature reserve specialising in cultural and environmental tourism

HONGSA (p224)
Elephants, Thai Lü villages and a hidden mountain valley

MEKONG RIVER (p218)
Scenic boat trips from Huay Xai to Luang Prabang

VANG VIENG (p121)
Travellers' haven with stunning karst scenery and plenty of adventure activities

LUANG PRABANG (p134)
World Heritage–listed former royal capital with 32 temples

VIENG XAI (p187)
Historic former Pathet Lao headquarters, housed in huge caverns in a hidden valley

PHONSAVAN (p165)
Mysterious Plain of Jars & Indochina War relics

PHU KHAO KHUAY NPA (p118)
Forested nature reserve with waterfalls and a herd of wild elephants

CHINA

VIETNAM

Hanoi

Haiphong

Gulf of Tonkin

Vinh

MYANMAR (BURMA)

THAILAND

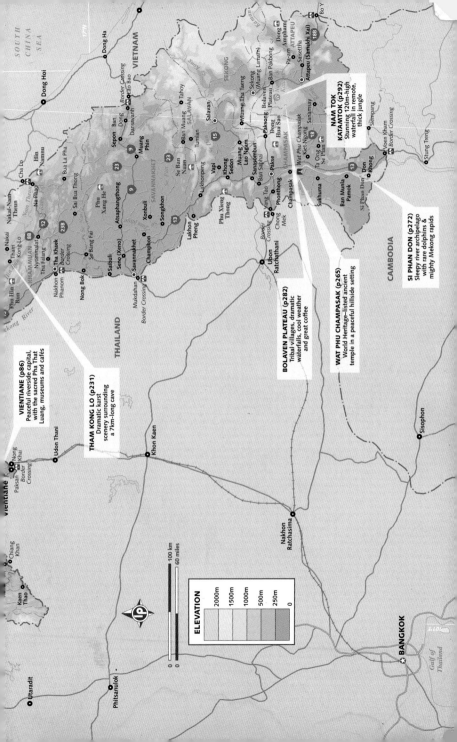

VIENTIANE (p86)
Peaceful riverside capital, with the sacred Pha That Luang, museums and cafés

THAM KONG LO (p231)
Dramatic karst scenery surrounding a 7km-long cave

NAM TOK KATAMTOK (p292)
Stunning 120m-high waterfall in remote, thick jungle

BOLAVEN PLATEAU (p282)
Tribal villages, dramatic waterfalls, cool weather and great coffee

WAT PHU CHAMPASAK (p265)
World Heritage-listed ancient temple in a peaceful hillside setting

SI PHAN DON (p272)
Sleepy river archipelago with rare dolphins & mighty Mekong rapids

ELEVATION

	2000m
	1500m
	1000m
	500m
	250m
	0

100 km
60 miles

Destination Laos

After years of war and isolation, Southeast Asia's most pristine environment, intact cultures and quite possibly the most chilled-out people on earth mean destination Laos is fast earning cult status among travellers.

Laos is developing quickly but still has much of the tradition that has disappeared in a frenzy of bulldozers, concrete and reality TV elsewhere in the region. Village life is refreshingly simple and even in Vientiane it's hard to believe this sort of languid riverfront life exists in a national capital. Then, of course, there is the historic royal city of Luang Prabang, where watching as hundreds of saffron-robed monks move silently among centuries-old monasteries is as romantic a scene as you'll experience anywhere in Asia.

Away from the cities, the rivers that wind dramatically down to the Mekong, the forested mountains of the north, the gothic limestone karsts of central Laos and the 4000 riverine islands of the deep south form one of the most intact ecosystems in Asia. Not surprisingly, this wilderness is drawing travellers looking for nature, adventure or both. Kayaking, rafting, rock-climbing and biking are all available, but it's the community-based trekking that is most popular because it combines spectacular natural attractions with the chance to experience the 'real Laos' with a village homestay – while spending your money where it's needed most.

There is undoubtedly a growing tourist trail in Laos, but that just means there's plenty of roads off Rte 13 where you can make your own trail. After all, half the fun of travelling here is in the travel itself – the people you meet, chickens you share seats with, wrong turns you take and *lào-láo* you drink with the smiling family at the end of the road less travelled.

JULIET COO[...]

Highlights

CLINT LUCAS

Take local transport and the road less travelled, Lao-style

JERRY ALEXANDER

Statues in Wat Xieng Thong (p141), one of the most beautiful intact Buddhist temples in Laos

BERNARD NAPTHINE

Cast your eyes over limestone formations in Phongsali (p210)

Discover Hmong silversmithing (p58), an important part of tribal 'portable wealth'

Cool off at Tat Kuang Si, Luang Prabang Province (p159)

Threads are tied onto wrists to restore equilibrium during a traditional *bqasïi* ceremony (p55)

CRAIG PERSHOUSE

Buddhist doctrine is encoded in the different architectural styles of Pha That Luang (Great Stupa), Vientiane (p94), the most important national monument in Laos

KRAIG LIEB

Seek out stunning traditional textiles (p58)

See the sun set over the ancient Khmer religious complex, Wat Phu Champasak (p265)

ANDERS BLOMQVIST

CAROL WILEY

Elephants dunk their trunks below waterfalls near Tat Lo (p286)

Discover the many faces of Xieng Khuan (Buddha Park; p98), Vientiane

JULIET COOMBE

Rise early to observe the sunrise procession of monks receiving alms in Luang Prabang (p134)

JERRY ALEXA

Marvel at the mysterious Plain of Jars (p170)

ALISON WRIGHT

JOE CUMMINGS

Procession of the week-long Bun Pha That Luang (p307), Vientiane

Kayak down the Nam Song from Vang Vieng (p124)

CAROL WILEY

Fishing, Si Phan Don (Four Thousand Islands; p272)

Play *petang* (p61), a favourite Lao pastime

Hmong people (p50) in traditional headdress, Huay Xai

SARA-JANE CLELAND

Splashing around in the Nam Song, Vang Vieng (p121)

BERNARD NAPTHINE

Small Buddha images in Tham Ting, Pak Ou caves (p158)

Feast on barbecued chicken and sticky rice rolls from street vendors (p75)

KRAIG LIEB

JULIET COO

Spot endangered species including the tiger (p66)

BILL WASSMAN

The ubiquitous Beerlao (p77) is the perfect accompaniment to *làap* (p74), Lao-style salad

Luang Prabang's night market (p155) glows

MARCUS WILSON-SMITH / ALAMY

Contents

The Authors	**15**
Getting Started	**17**
Itineraries	**21**
Snapshot	**26**
History	**27**
The Culture	**46**
Environment	**63**
Food & Drink	**74**

Vientiane & Around   **85**

VIENTIANE	**86**
Orientation	86
Information	87
Dangers & Annoyances	91
Sights	91
Activities	99
Monument to Mekong Walking Tour	100
Courses	101
Festivals & Events	101
Sleeping	102
Eating	105
Drinking	109
Entertainment	110
Shopping	112
Getting There & Away	113
Getting Around	115
AROUND VIENTIANE	**116**
Ban Pako	116
Phu Khao Khuay Npa	118
Vientiane to Ang Nam Ngum	119
Ang Nam Ngum	120
Vang Vieng	121
Vang Vieng to Luang Prabang	129
(Former) Saisombun Special Zone	129

Northern Laos   **132**

LUANG PRABANG PROVINCE	**134**
Luang Prabang	134
Around Luang Prabang	158
Nong Khiaw	160
Muang Ngoi Neua	162
Nam Bak & Pak Mong	164
XIENG KHUANG PROVINCE	**164**
Phonsavan	165
Plain of Jars	169
Phonsavan to Nong Haet	171
Muang Khoun (Old Xieng Khuang)	172
Muang Sui	181
HUA PHAN PROVINCE	**182**
Sam Neua (Xam Neua)	183
Around Sam Neua	185
Sam Neua to Vieng Xai	186
Vieng Xai	187
Nam Noen	188
Nam Noen to Nong Khiaw	189
UDOMXAI PROVINCE	**189**
Udomxai (Muang Xai)	190
Around Udomxai	192
To Luang Prabang Via Pak Beng	192
Pak Beng	192
LUANG NAM THA PROVINCE	**194**
Luang Nam Tha	195
Boten	200
Nam Tha River Trip	201
Luang Nam Tha to Huay Xai	202
Muang Sing	203
Xieng Kok	209
PHONGSALI PROVINCE	**210**
Phongsali	210
Udomxai to Phongsali	213
Muang Khua	213
BOKEO PROVINCE	**214**
Huay Xai	214
Around Huay Xai	219
SAINYABULI PROVINCE	**220**
Sainyabuli	221
Around Sainyabuli	223

Central Laos 226

**BOLIKHAMSAI &
KHAMMUAN PROVINCES** 228
Paksan 228
Paksan to Lak Sao 229
Lak Sao 233
Tha Khaek 234
Around Tha Khaek 238
**SAVANNAKHET
PROVINCE** 242
Savannakhet (Muang
Khanthabuli) 242
Around Savannakhet 247
Dong Phu Vieng Npa 249
Sepon (Xepon) &
the Ho Chi Minh Trail 250

Southern Laos 253

CHAMPASAK PROVINCE 255
Pakse 255
Around Pakse 260
Champasak 262
Wat Phu Champasak 265
Don Daeng 268
Uo Moung
(Tomo Temple) 270
Kiet Ngong &
Ban Phapho 270
Se Pian Npa 271
Si Phan Don
(Four Thousand Islands) 272
Bolaven Plateau 282
SALAVAN PROVINCE 286
Tat Lo 286
Salavan 288
Around Salavan 289
SEKONG PROVINCE 290
Sekong (Muang Lamam) 290
Around Sekong 292
ATTAPEU PROVINCE 293
Attapeu (Samakhi Xai) 293
Around Attapeu 296
Dong Ampham Npa 297

Directory 298

Transport 319

Health 331

Language 342

Glossary 351

Behind the Scenes 353

Index 362

World Time Zones 370

Map Legend 372

Regional Map Contents

Northern Laos p133

Vientiane &
Around p117

Central
Laos p227

Southern
Laos p254

The Authors

ANDREW BURKE

Coordinating Author, Vientiane & Around, Central Laos, Southern Laos, Culture, Environment, Food & Drink

Andrew has lived in Asia since 2001 and in that time he's spent more than six months travelling around Laos. It's the laid-back, simple approach to life that repeatedly draws him back, but he finds the thousands of kilometres of roads less travelled and fascinating photographic subjects just as appealing. This is Andrew's 10th book for Lonely Planet, titles that include *The Asia Book*, *China* and *Hong Kong Citiescape*. When he's not travelling, Andrew works as a journalist and photographer and calls Bangkok home.

My Favourite Trip

Choosing a favourite trip in Laos isn't easy, but during this two months of research I found visiting various villages in the south hugely enjoyable at a cultural level. You could start in Pakse (p255), head north to idyllic Don Kho (p260) for a village homestay and, if you're with enough people, experience the *bqasii* ceremony. Take a boat all the way south to Champasak (p262), and base yourself in an island village on Don Daeng (p268). Cycle out to Wat Phu Champasak (p265) at dawn, then hitch down to Kiet Ngong (p270) and treat yourself to a little comfort in the Kingfisher Eco-Lodge (p271). From here, embark on the sometimes difficult and often very wet trek into the Se Pian NPA (p271), and stay in one of the most remote villages in the south, Ta Ong.

Don Kho Pakse
Kiet Ngong; Champasak
Kingfisher Eco-Lodge; Wat Phu Champasak;
Ta Ong; Se Pian NPA Don Daeng

JUSTINE VAISUTIS

Northern Laos

Justine fell in love with Asia during a year-long stint in South Korea as a tiny tacker. Regular jaunts to the Southeast cemented her yen for all things hot, steamy, spicy and more than a little pungent. Hot on the heels of working on Lonely Planet's *Indonesia* guide, she leapt at the chance to explore Northern Laos for this book. After cycling, trekking, bussing, flying, swimming, sailing and generally losing her way as much as possible, she fell madly in love with the country and its people and plans to return often. This is the 10th Lonely Planet guide Justine has worked on.

My Favourite Trip

Well, one of my favourite trips in Laos would go something like this. Take a few days in Luang Prabang (p134) to acclimatise, indulge in a massage or three and go wat-hopping. Then boat up the Nam Ou, stopping in Nong Khiaw (p160) en route to as north as Laos gets – Phongsali (p210). I'd spend a few days in the surrounding villages for a cultural injection and then catch the ever-lengthening but ever-entertaining bus south to Luang Nam Tha (p195) for several days of ecotrekking in Nam Ha NPA (p198). Then I'd backtrack (a bus fan from way back) to the most beautiful province of all – Hua Phan (p182), and re-acquaint myself with the magical landscape and utterly benevolent people.

Luang Nam Tha; Phongsali
Nam Ha NPA
Nong Khiaw
Hua Phan Province
Luang
Prabang

CONTRIBUTING AUTHORS

Martin Stuart-Fox wrote the History chapter. Martin is Professor Emeritus in the School of History, Philosophy, Religion and Classics at the University of Queensland, Australia. He first worked in Laos from 1963 to 1965 as a journalist, before covering the Vietnam War for two years. On his return to Australia, Martin joined the University of Queensland. He retired in 2005 after five years as Head of History. He has written six books and dozens of articles on Laos, including *A History of Laos* (1997), *The Lao Kingdom of Lan Xang* (1998) and *Buddhist Kingdom, Marxist State* (2nd ed, 2002). His latest book is *Naga Cities of the Mekong* (2006), narrating the histories of Luang Prabang, Vientiane and Champasak.

Steven Schipani wrote the Ecotourism in Laos boxed text (p72). Steven was born in New York City and raised on the Atlantic coast of Long Island, New York. He first went to Asia as a United States Peace Corps volunteer, serving in Thailand from 1994 to 1996. He has worked as a professional guide, fisherman, Thai and Lao language interpreter, and has travelled extensively in Southeast Asia. Since 1999 Steven has been employed by Unesco, the Asian Development Bank, and a number of other international organisations advising on sustainable ecotourism development and heritage management in Laos. His interests include fishing, forest trekking, indigenous knowledge and Lao food. He has one son named Michael.

Dr Trish Batchelor is a general practitioner and travel medicine specialist who works at the CIWEC Clinic in Kathmandu, Nepal, as well as being a Medical Advisor to the Travel Doctor New Zealand clinics. Trish teaches travel medicine through the University of Otago, and is interested in underwater and high-altitude medicine, and in the impact of tourism on host countries. She has travelled extensively through Southeast and East Asia and particularly loves high-altitude trekking in the Himalayas.

LONELY PLANET AUTHORS

Why is our travel information the best in the world? It's simple: our authors are independent, dedicated travellers. They don't research using just the internet or phone, and they don't take freebies in exchange for positive coverage. They travel widely, to all the popular spots and off the beaten track. They personally visit thousands of hotels, restaurants, cafés, bars, galleries, palaces, museums and more – and they take pride in getting all the details right, and telling it how it is. Think you can do it? Find out how at lonelyplanet.com.

Getting Started

With 30-day visas now available to most travellers when they arrive (p315), your most pressing pre-departure concerns are finding good books (p18) to read up on Laos, working out which route to take (p21) and getting enough cash (p309) to last you through the trip. Laos is a low-maintenance destination and an easy place to travel that's most rewarding to those ready to embrace the laid-back Lao way of life. Don't expect everything to be on time; do pack a smile and prepare to slide down a few gears.

WHEN TO GO

The best time for visiting most of Laos is between November and February, when it rains the least and is not too hot. It's also Laos's main season for both national and regional *bun* (festivals; see p19).

If you plan to focus on the mountainous northern provinces, the hot season (from March to May) and early rainy season (around June) is not bad either, as temperatures are moderate at higher elevations. Southern Laos, on the other hand, is best avoided from March to May, when day-time temperatures break into the 40s and nights aren't much cooler.

See Climate Charts p303 for more information.

The rainy season is not as bad as you might think. While it will rain – very heavily – the downpours are often fairly brief and can be bracketed by long periods of sunshine. The rains also clear dust from the skies and land, making everything clearer and brighter. Of course, there are downsides; unsealed roads can become quagmires and extensive travel in remote areas like Salavan, Phongsali and Sainyabuli might be impossible. River travel can be a good alternative during these months. If you intend to travel extensively by river, November is the best; flooding has usually subsided yet river levels are still high enough for maximum navigability. Between January and June, low water can make navigating some rivers difficult.

December to February and August are the peak tourist times. January, in particular, is very busy and booking ahead is advisable.

COSTS & MONEY

Laos is an inexpensive country to visit by almost any standards. Not including transport, a budget of US$15 a day brings with it decent food and comfortable, but basic, accommodation (p298). When you add air-con, hot water and *falang* (Western) food, costs are around US$20 to US$25 per day if you economise, and around US$75 for top-end hotels and food. Of course, you can spend even more if you stay in the best hotels and eat at the most expensive restaurants, although such a scenario exists only in Vientiane and Luang Prabang.

For those on a tight budget, in Vientiane or Luang Prabang you can squeeze by on about $10 a day if you stay in the cheapest guesthouses and eat local food; in remote areas where everything's less expensive you can whittle this figure down to around US$7 or US$8 a day.

Add to these estimates the cost of transport, which varies considerably depending on how fast you're moving. Flying with Lao Airlines (p324) costs from US$40 to US$100 per leg. Most bus trips cost between US$2 and US$13; see p114 for a better idea of costs.

All these costs are paid in a mix of US dollars, Thai baht and Lao kip. Credit cards and other bank cards aren't widely accepted, so pack cash and travellers cheques.

HOW MUCH?

Restaurant meal US$2-10

Budget room with air-con US$6-15

Homestay with Lao family US$2, plus US$1.50 per meal

Internet access per hour US$0.60-$3

Bus Vientiane to Luang Prabang US$9-11.50

READING UP

Relatively little has been written about Laos but there are enough books to keep you interested before you leave and while you're on the road.

Travel Literature

The classic travellers' account of Laos is Norman Lewis' *A Dragon Apparent: Travels In Cambodia, Laos and Vietnam,* written after the author's 1952 trip through French Indochina. It contains this passage on Laos: 'Europeans who come here to live, soon acquire a certain recognisable manner. They develop quiet voices, and gentle, rapt expressions'.

One Foot in Laos (1999) by Dervla Murphy is the veteran Irish writer's account of her lone bicycle trip through off-the-beaten-track Laos, written with passion for the local people and some stinging assessments of travellers and modern ways.

Another Quiet American (2003), Brett Dakin's account of two years working at the National Tourism Authority of Laos, reveals a lot about what drives (or not) people working in Laos, both local and *falang*.

More recent is *In the Naga's Wake* (2006) by Mick O'Shea, the Lao-based adventurer who details his epic kayaking trip down the Mekong River from source to sea.

Several classic travel narratives by 19th-century French visitors to Laos have been translated into English, including Henri Mouhot's *Travels in Siam, Cambodia, and Laos.* The book covers the 1858 to 1860 trip which resulted in the explorer's death – he's buried near Luang Prabang (p159).

Other Books

The vast majority of books on Laos are historical or political works and deal mainly with events of the last century or so.

For well-written, lucid histories it's hard to go past *A History of Laos* by Martin Stuart-Fox, who also wrote the history chapter in this book (p27), and *A Short History of Laos: The Land in Between* (2002) by Grant

---

DON'T LEAVE HOME WITHOUT ...

The range can be limited, but most of what you'll need while travelling can be found in Laos for less than you'd spend at home. There are, however, a few things you shouldn't forget, not least a deep well of patience, your sense of humour and a dose of perspective when a reality check is required. More tangible objects include:

- a sarong (for both women and men) to stay modest while bathing Lao-style
- photos of family to show when language is a barrier
- a phrasebook to make that barrier more surmountable
- contraceptives and tampons if needed
- good sunscreen and mosquito repellent, and a small torch (flashlight) for caves and villages without electricity
- light wash-and-wear clothes
- slip-on shoes or sandals – cool to wear and easy to remove before entering a Lao home or temple
- a Leatherman (or similar) tool, sunglasses and a bandana if you're planning on motorbiking
- a sweater/pullover or light jacket for the cool season, mountainous provinces and overnight buses

TOP 10

FABULOUS FESTIVALS

Laos boasts a couple of festivals (p306) a month, year-round, not to mention public holidays. Here are the most impressive.

1 Makha Busa (Full Moon; national) February (p306)

2 Bun Wat Phu (Champasak) February (p268)

3 Vietnamese Tet & Chinese New Year (Vientiane, Pakse and Savannakhet) February–March (p306)

4 Bun Pha Wet (national) March (p306)

5 Bun Pi Mai Lao (Lao New Year; Luang Prabang) April (p306)

6 Bun Bang Fai (Rocket Festival; national) May (p306)

7 Bun Khao Phansa (national) July (p306)

8 Bun Awk Phansa (national) October (p307)

9 Bun Nam (Boat Racing Festival; Vientiane, Savannakhet, Huay Xai) October (p101)

10 Bun Pha That Luang (Vientiane) October–November (p101)

OUTDOOR THRILLS – INTO THE WILD

There's no better country in Asia to get outside and adventurous.

1 Mounting a week-long expedition to Nong Fa in the Dong Ampham NPA (p297)

2 Boating through the 7km-long Tham Kong Lo cave (p231)

3 Rafting the rapids of the Nam Lik or Nam Ngum (p124)

4 Taking a slow boat up the Nam Ou from Nong Khiaw (p160)

5 Rock-climbing the caves and karsts of Vang Vieng (p125)

6 Scaling a cliff to reach Muang Sui's coffin cave (p181)

7 Trekking in the Nam Ha NPA and staying in local villages (see p198)

8 Trekking into limestone karsts and waterholes of Phu Hin Bun NPA (p230)

9 Riding a motorbike around southern Laos for a week (p263)

10 Climbing Phu Asa by elephant (p270)

LAO-STYLE MÚAN (FUN)

Just saying 'yes' to that weird-sounding dish, drink or experience is fun, Lao style.

1 Bumping along in the back of a *săwngthăew* with loads of Lao people, chickens and rice (p326)

2 Challenging the locals to a game of *petang* (p61)

3 Drinking delicious Beerlao with ice (p77)

4 Eating a full-power *tąm màak-hung* (green papaya salad) with your fingers (p75)

5 Sharing *lào-láo* (whisky) or a jar of *lào-hăi* (jar liquor; home-brewed rice wine; p77)

6 Shopping for coffee and woven silk in the villages of southern Laos (p253)

7 Smiling at everyone you see

8 Taking a wash in the Mekong at Don Daeng (p268)

9 Tucking in to sticky rice and *làap* (meat salad) with your host family in a village homestay (p48)

10 Watching monks collect alms in early morning Luang Prabang (p134)

Evans. Both are wonderfully easy to read and don't require an in-depth foreknowledge of Laos.

Several books have been written about Laos's role in the Second Indochina War. *The Ravens: Pilots of the Secret War of Laos* (1987), by Christopher Robbins, is a fast-paced account of the American pilots hired by the CIA to fly in Laos, where they weren't allowed to wear uniforms because the war didn't officially exist. *Shooting at the Moon: The Story of America's Clandestine War in Laos* (1998), by Roger Warner, and *The Blood Road: The Ho Chi Minh Trail and the Vietnam War* (2000), by John Prados, are well-respected accounts of the war, the CIA and Hmong role in it, and the Ho Chi Minh Trail.

Journalist Christopher Kremmer has written two entertaining books detailing his pursuit of the truth behind the final demise of the Lao monarchy in the late 1970s: *Stalking the Elephant Kings: In Search of Laos* (1998) and *Bamboo Palace: Discovering the Lost Dynasty of Laos* (2003).

Mekong (2000) by Milton Osborne is a more scholarly record of the role of the mighty Mekong River in regional history and modern politics. Anne Fadiman's award-winning *The Spirit Catches You and You Fall Down* (1997) looks at the tragic clash of cultures between a family of Hmong migrants and their American doctors.

There are very few novels set in Laos, the best of them probably being *The Honourable Schoolboy*, John Le Carré's Cold War thriller in which much of the action is set in surreal wartime Vientiane.

Internet Resources

Laos doesn't have a huge web presence, but it is improving. These are the best we've found this time around:

Laos's internet country code is .la

Ecotourism Laos (www.ecotourismlaos.com) Simple but stylish website full of information about the Lao environs, focussing on trekking and other ecotourism activities. Recommended.

Hmong Homepage (www.hmongnet.org) Information about and links to all things Hmong.

Lao National Tourism Authority (www.tourismlaos.gov.la) Mostly up-to-date travel information from the government.

Library of Congress (www.loc.gov) Probably the most complete online resource about Laos, with thorough and regularly updated accounts of history, culture and politics.

Lonely Planet (www.lonelyplanet.com) The Thorn Tree forum is the place to get the latest feedback from the road.

Travelfish (www.travelfish.org) The most consistently updated website for independent travellers in Southeast Asia, including excellent coverage of Lao border crossings.

Vientiane Times (www.vientianetimes.org.la) Website of the country's only English-language newspaper, and operated by the government. In addition to news stories about Laos, it has accurate exchange rates for the Lao kip.

Itineraries

CLASSIC ROUTES

THE NORTH
One to Two Weeks/Huay Xai to Vientiane

Travellers have been following this route since before the 1975 revolution, and it's still one of the best samplers for anyone who wants a good dose of Laos in a relatively short time-span.

Enter Laos via ferry from Chiang Khong in Thailand to **Huay Xai** (p214) and get a taste of the country on a local trek. Heading south, board one of the slow boats that ply the Mekong between Huay Xai and Luang Prabang. This two-day voyage requires an overnight in the small riverside district of **Pak Beng** (p192); the scenery along the Mekong River is a terrific mix of villages, limestone cliffs and intermittent forest.

Boats may stop at **Pak Ou** (p158) so that passengers can visit Buddha-filled caves there. Sightseeing in and around **Luang Prabang** (p139), Laos's atmospheric former royal capital, can easily occupy a week.

From here, continue southward to Vientiane by bus or van along Rte 13, stopping in **Vang Vieng** (p121), a modern-day travellers centre surrounded by craggy, cave-studded limestone peaks. After a few days of river-tubing and cave hikes, head to **Vientiane** (p86), Laos's semibustling capital city.

Pass quiet village ports and rugged gorges on the Mekong to Luang Prabang, then follow Rte 13, which winds high into the mountains between Kasi and Vang Vieng toward Vientiane, to complete this 700km route.

THE SOUTH
One to Three Weeks/Vientiane to Si Phan Don

This classic route takes you through the heartland of lowland Lao culture, a world of broad river plains planted with rice and homemade looms shaded by wooden houses on stilts.

Start in **Vientiane** (p86), the country's capital, and soak up the food, shopping, historical sights and nightlife (it gets quieter from here). Head south to **Tha Khaek** (p234), the archetypal sleepy Mekong riverside town, and go east on Rte 12 to explore the caves of **Khammuan Limestone** (p239) or take The Loop (p240) all the way around, stopping at the incredible **Tham Kong Lo** (p231).

Continue south to **Savannakhet** (p242), where you'll get an architectural taste of how postcolonial Vientiane looked before it was gussied up by the Lao PDR government and international aid. Chowhounds can sniff around for the country's best *fŏe* (rice noodles) and *sĭn sawăn* (literally 'heavenly beef'; dried beef).

Roll on southward to **Pakse** (p255) and, if you don't have enough time to go east, through to tranquil **Champasak** (p262). This town is the base for seeing Laos's most important archaeological site, **Wat Phu Champasak** (p265), Angkor-style temple ruins stepping up the slopes of sacred Phu Pasak.

Make a final short hop to **Si Phan Don** (Four Thousand Islands; p272), an archipelago of idyllic river islands where the farming and fishing life hasn't changed much for a century or more. Swing in a hammock and relax, before moving on to Cambodia or heading to Thailand via Chong Mek.

This route covers about 700km of river plains and rolling hills, bridging clear streams and tracing traditional Lao villages as Rte 13 follows the Mekong south. Expect to move by **bus**, *sǎwngthǎew,* **motorbike** and **boat** as you make your way south. Depending on time, take as many diversions east of Rte 13 as you can.

ROADS LESS TRAVELLED

NORTHERN WILDERNESS

**Two to Three Weeks/
Luang Nam Tha to Xieng Khuang**

This route explores the mountains and plateaus of the north. Start in Luang Nam Tha Province with a trek into the **Nam Ha NPA** (p198) or through hill-tribe villages near **Muang Sing** (p203) and **Muang Long** (p209).

Head from **Luang Nam Tha** (p195) – via **Phongsali** (p210) if you have the time and adventurous spirit – to super-laid-back **Nong Khiaw** (p160), soaking up northern Lao life along the Nam Ou (Ou River) and taking hikes to limestone caves. Crossing the Nam Ou, climb higher into the Annamite Chain through Hmong villages till you reach remote **Sam Neua** (p183). Near here the communist Pathet Lao, with help from the North Vietnamese Army, took shelter in huge caverns in **Vieng Xai** (p187) and mounted a successful campaign to seize control of the country. Sam Neua is also known for intricately patterned hand-woven textiles.

South of Sam Neua, en route to **Nam Noen** (p188), stands **Suan Hin** (p186), where ancient megaliths are arranged in patterns that remain a total enigma to locals and scholars alike.

From Sam Neua a lengthy road trip southwest leads to **Phonsavan** (p165), the fast-growing capital of Xieng Khuang Province. Here one of the main attractions is a large plateau scattered with hundreds of monumental and mysterious lidded stone jars, known as the **Plain of Jars** (p169).

Visit caverns, traditional villages and mysterious relics on this adventure which takes you along 588km of high, winding road and across many rivers and streams. Add 92km for the detour to Sam Neua.

BOLAVEN & BEYOND   10 to 14 days/Pakse to Pakse

This trip into the remote provinces of southern Laos can be done by private
vehicle, including small motorbikes, or more slowly – but more socially – by
public transport. It's best in the dry season.

After a day or two getting organised in **Pakse** (p255), head up onto the
Bolaven Plateau (p282) and to Laos's most impressive waterfall at **Tat Fan** (p283).
At the coffee capital of **Paksong** (p284), you could stop to buy some Java before
continuing on to **Sekong** (p290), passing through Laven, Katang and other
villages en route. If the river is full enough, head down the **Se Kong** (see Down
the Se Kong by Longtail Boat, p292) in a boat for an unforgettable trip into
Attapeu Province (p293). Sleepy **Attapeu** (p293) is an easy place to hang out;
interrupt your sunsets-by-the–Se Kong with a bumpy day trip out to the Ho
Chi Minh Trail (p251) village of **Pa-am** (p296), and an overnight homestay
in the **Se Pian NPA** (p296).

Head back up Rte 16, through Sekong and turn north at Tha Taeng on a
long, downhill laterite road to Beng. Check out **Salavan** (p288) for a day and,
if the season is right, arrange transport along the rarely travelled road to **Tahoy**
(p289), once an important marker on the Ho Chi Minh Trail and now a more
peaceful but thoroughly remote home of the Ta-oy (Tahoy) people.

Beautiful **Tat Lo** (p286) and its inevitable backpackers will be a shock after
days with little, if any, contact with Westerners, and **Utayan Bajiang Champasak**
(p285) makes an attractive lunch spot on the easy trip back to Pakse.

**On this journey
of roughly 650km
you'll climb into
the coffee-grow-
ing districts of the
Bolaven Plateau,
see spectacular
waterfalls, and
visit villages little
changed since the
end of the Second
Indochina War.**

TAILORED TRIPS

ACTION JACKSON TOUR

Laos has plenty on offer for those who like the outdoors. Start with the classic northern trek in the **Nam Ha NPA** (p198), before heading to Luang Prabang and cycling out to **Tat Sae** (p159) or **Tat Kuang Si** (p159) waterfalls. Sit atop a slow bus south to **Vang Vieng** (p121), the activities capital of the country where there are myriad rock-climbing, kayaking and spelunking options and professional guides.

Forget the bus to Vientiane and instead go rafting along the grade five rapids of the Nam Ngum (Ngum River), or kayaking along the Nam Lik (Lik River), part of the way, and complete the trip by minibus. In **Vientiane** (p86) stop long enough for a massage at **Wat Sok Pa Luang** (p96) to work out some of the knots, before trekking into **Phu Khao Khuay NPA** (p118) in search of elephants.

Head south to Tha Khaek by bus or bike and get on a trek into the **Phu Hin Bun NPA** (p230), with its magical waterholes and incredible 7km-long boat ride through the **Tham Kong Lo** (p231) cave. If you fancy more tough trekking, head south to **Pakse** (p255) and get yourself on a trek into the **Se Pian NPA** (p271), before rounding out your stay in Laos with a boat trip around **Si Phan Don** (p272) and a rafting trip from **Don Det** (p283) over the falls to the Cambodian border.

GRAND TEMPLE TOUR

Start in Luang Prabang and head first to the city's showcase temple, **Wat Xieng Thong** (p141), a collection of Buddhist chapels delicately decorated with the best gold stencil work in the country. Virtually every other wat in the old temple district is also worth stopping by, as each is unique, but don't miss the massive bronze seated Buddha image at **Wat Manolom** (p143), the unique watermelon-shaped stupa and faux-lathed windows at **Wat Wisunarat** (p142) and the Buddhist art school at **Wat Xieng Muan** (p144).

Head south to Vientiane for this not-to-be-missed trio: **Pha That Luang** (p91) for its spiky stupa, where Buddhist doctrine is numerologically encoded; **Wat Si Saket** (p94) for the thousands of niches holding tiny Buddhas; and **Haw Pha Kaeo** (p95) for the best collection of Lao Buddhist art in the country.

Saving the most ancient and venerated for last, fly south to the small, unassuming town of **Champasak** (p262). Just 4km outside of town at **Muang Kao** (p267) lie the ruined city walls of Kuruksetra, where the oldest surviving Sanskrit inscription in Southeast Asia was recently found. This defunct kingdom was almost certainly linked to nearby **Wat Phu Champasak** (p265), an Angkor-style temple ruin and the grandest archaeological site in Laos. If you can visit in time for the **Wat Phu Festival** (p268) in February, you'll be treated to one of the country's most visually impressive and spiritually significant festivals.

Snapshot

For centuries Laos was a buffer state, wedged between a pair of bigger neighbours, Thailand and Vietnam, and busy paying tribute to one, the other or both. Forty years ago this balancing act came undone in spectacular fashion when, split down the middle in its role as a Cold War proxy for both American and communist forces, Laos became the most bombed country in history (see p37).

But three decades after the end of the Second Indochina War, Laos is finally growing out of its role as buffer state and becoming a crossroads in an increasingly globalised region.

Western governments, financial institutions such as the World Bank and Asian Development Bank, and NGOs still contribute a large proportion of the money spent on development in this country where poverty is the norm for a huge number of people. For better or worse, however, these contributors are increasingly being replaced by private enterprise and the world's newest superdonor – the People's Republic of China.

The physical signs are increasingly apparent. Just over a decade ago Laos's colonial-era network of roads was a sorry collection of potholed dirt tracks. Today almost all major roads are sealed, and the Chinese are busy finishing off a new highway linking Yunnan with Thailand. Laos will make some incidental money from the traffic on these roads, but the greater effect is in making its long-ignored natural resources more accessible, and thus more open to development, most notably by the mining and energy sectors. If all goes to plan the money expected from a dizzying number of hydroelectric dams (see p65) will allow Laos to help relieve poverty by itself and break the reliance on foreign aid.

The Lao government has recognised that tourism, particularly ecotourism (p72), has grown into a primary source of income and helps channel money to some of the poorest parts of society. And many small-scale projects, such as the Jhai fair-trade coffee cooperative on the Bolaven Plateau (see p285), are improving the deal for the rural poor.

There are, however, a lot of real and potential downsides to this 'progress'. Having China as a major source of funding and as a political role model is unlikely to encourage the Lao government, which is already fearful of the effect opening up to the world will have on its culture and control, to adopt democratic reforms. In short, don't expect basic freedoms like speech, assembly or even uncensored song lyrics (p60) any time soon.

The environment faces alarming threats. Unplanned or illegal logging has been a serious problem for years. But it's the dozens of hydroelectric dams due to be built in the next decade, many by companies with poor reputations for looking after the environment or local communities, that have the potential to change ecosystems dramatically, rapidly and permanently.

The Second Indochina War continues to take its toll. Unexploded ordnance (UXO, see p167) claims scores of lives every year. And many Hmong, who have been fighting with or, more often, running from the Lao military since their American sponsors fled three decades ago, continue to be persecuted. The 'insurgency' (p181) appears to finally be petering out, though reports of atrocities committed by the Lao military continue to emerge.

The challenge for Laos is to balance all these competing interests, to make the most of its opportunities as a conduit of trade without being overwhelmed by the interests of others. For a country with much experience of being squeezed by outsiders, but little in the way of successful outcomes, it won't be an easy road.

FAST FACTS

Area: 236,800 sq km

Border countries: Cambodia, China, Myanmar, Thailand, Vietnam

Population: 5.6 million

Official language: Lao

Literacy: 66.4%

GDP per capita (purchasing power parity): US$2280

Inflation: 6.8%

Original name: Lan Xang Hom Khao (Million Elephants, White Parasol)

Number of elephants in Laos today: around 2000

Laos's share of the Mekong River: 1865km

History Professor Martin Stuart-Fox

PREHISTORY & TAI-LAO MIGRATION

The first modern humans (*Homo sapiens sapiens*) arrived in Southeast Asia around 50,000 years ago. Their stone-age technology remained little changed until a new Neolithic culture evolved about 10,000 years ago. This was the Hoabinhian, named after an archaeological site in northern Vietnam. Hoabinhian hunter-gatherers spread throughout much of Southeast Asia, including Laos. Their descendants produced the first pottery in the region, and later bronze metallurgy. In time they supplemented their hunting, fishing and gathering by horticulture and eventually rice cultivation, introduced down the Mekong River valley from southern China. These people were the ancestors of the present-day upland minorities, collectively known as the Lao Thoeng (Upland Lao), the largest group of which are the Khamu of northern Laos.

> Martin Stuart-Fox is Emeritus Professor at the University of Queensland, Australia. He has written six books and over 50 articles on the politics and history of Laos.

Other Lao Thoeng tribes live in southern Laos, including the Brao and the Katang. Like their northern cousins, they speak Austro-Asiatic languages, a group which includes Khmer. In fact southern Laos is believed to be the birthplace of the Cambodian people, from where they spread further south to establish the kingdom of Funan by the 2nd century CE. The earliest kingdom in southern Laos was identified in Chinese texts as Chenla, dating from the 5th century. Its capital was close to Champasak, near the later Khmer temple of Wat Phu. A little later Mon people (speaking another Austro-Asiatic language) established kingdoms on the middle Mekong – Sri Gotapura (Sikhottabong in Lao) with its capital near Tha Khaek, and Chanthaburi in the vicinity of Viang Chan (Vientiane).

Tai peoples probably began migrating out of southern China about the 8th century. They included the Tai-Lao of Laos, the Tai-Syam and Tai-Yuan of central and northern Thailand, and the Tai-Shan of northeast Burma. They are called Tai to distinguish them from the citizens (Thai) of modern Thailand, though the word is the same. All spoke closely related Tai languages, practised wet-rice cultivation along river valleys, and organised themselves into small principalities, known as *meuang*, each presided over by an hereditary ruler, or *chao meuang* (lord of the *meuang*). The Tai-Lao, or Lao for short, moved slowly down the rivers of northern Laos, like the Nam Ou and the Nam Khan, running roughly from northeast to southwest, until they arrived at the Mekong, the Great River. They worshipped the *ngeuk*, powerful snake deities believed to inhabit these rivers, which if not propitiated could so easily tip frail canoes and drown their occupants. Most Lao peasants still believe that *ngeuk* exist.

> The Lao believe most *ngeuk* have been converted to become serpent protectors of Buddhism, called *naga* (in Lao *nak*). They still require propitiation, however, and annual boat races are held for their amusement. Many Buddhist temples (wat) have protective *naga* balustrades.

The early Lao text known as the *Nithan* (story of) *Khun Borom* recounts the myth of creation of the Lao peoples, their interaction, and the establishment of the first Lao kingdom in the vicinity of Luang Prabang. The creation myth tells how two great gourds grew at Meuang Thaeng (Dien Bien Phu, now in Vietnam) from inside which sounds could be heard. Divine rulers, known as khun, pierced one of the gourds with a hot poker, and out of the charred hole poured the dark-skinned Lao Thoeng. The khun used a knife to cut a hole in the other gourd, through which escaped the lighter-skinned

TIMELINE

1353	1479
Fa Ngum establishes the Lao kingdom of Lan Xang	The Vietnamese emperor La Thanh Tong invades Lan Xang

Tai-Lao (or Lao Loum, Lowland Lao). The gods then sent Khun Borom to rule over both Lao Loum and Lao Thoeng. He had seven sons, whom he sent out to found seven new kingdoms in the regions where Tai peoples settled (in the Tai highlands of Vietnam, the Xishuangbanna of southern China, Shan state in Burma, and in Thailand and Laos). While the youngest son founded the kingdom of Xieng Khuang on the Plain of Jars, the oldest son, Khun Lo, descended the Nam Ou, seized the principality of Meuang Sua from its Lao Thoeng ruler, and named it Xiang Dong Xiang Thong (later renamed Luang Prabang).

THE KINGDOM OF LAN XANG

The first extended Lao kingdom dates from the mid-14th century. It was established in the context of a century of unprecedented political and social change in mainland Southeast Asia. At the beginning of the 13th century, the great Khmer king Jayavarman VII, who had re-established Cambodian power and built the city of Angkor Thom, sent his armies north to extend the Khmer empire to include all of the middle Mekong region and north-central Thailand. But the empire was overstretched, and by the mid-13th century the Khmer were in retreat. At the same time, the Mongol Yuan dynasty in China lost interest in further conquest in Southeast Asia.

This left a political vacuum in central Thailand, into which stepped Ramkhamhaeng, founder of the Tai-Syam kingdom of Sukhothai. To his north, his ally Mangray founded the Tai-Yuan kingdom of Lanna (meaning 'a million rice fields'), with his capital at Chiang Mai. Other smaller Tai kingdoms were established at Phayao and Xiang Dong Xiang Thong. In southern Laos and southern Thailand, however, the Khmer still held on to power.

We know that at this time Viang Chan was tributary to Sukhothai, and it may well be that Xiang Dong Xiang Thong was too. As the power of Sukhothai grew, it exerted more pressure on the Khmer. The Cambodian court looked around for an ally, and found one in the form of a young Lao prince, Fa Ngum, who was being educated at Angkor. Fa Ngum's princely father had been forced to flee Xiang Dong Xiang Thong after he seduced one of his own father's concubines. So Fa Ngum was in direct line for the throne.

The Khmer gave Fa Ngum a Khmer princess and an army, and sent him north to wrest the middle Mekong from the control of Sukhothai, and so divert and weaken the Tai-Syam kingdom. In this he was successful. Sikhottabong acknowledged Fa Ngum's suzerainty. So did Xieng Khuang and a number of other Lao *meuang*. Only Viang Chan held out. Fa Ngum was acclaimed king in Xiang Dong Xiang Thong, then brought Viang Chan into his empire. He named his new kingdom Lan Xang Hom Khao, meaning 'a million elephants and the white parasol'.

Fa Ngum built a fine capital at Xiang Dong Xiang Thong and set about organising his court and kingdom. He appointed his Khmer generals to positions of power, even though this antagonised the local aristocracy. Tributary rulers had to journey to the capital every three years to renew their vows of fealty and present tribute.

Fa Ngum performed sacrifices to the *phii* (traditional spirits) of the kingdom, and to the *ngeuk* of the Mekong. But he also acquiesced to his wife's request to introduce Khmer Theravada Buddhism to Lan Xang. Here, according to the Lao chronicles, he began to run into problems. The Cambodian

By naming his kingdom Lan Xang Hom Khao, Fa Ngum was making a statement about power and kingship. Elephants were the battle tanks of Southeast Asian warfare, so to claim to be the kingdom of a million elephants was to issue a warning to surrounding kingdoms: 'Don't mess with the Lao!' A white parasol was the traditional symbol of kingship.

King Visoun installs the Pha Bang Buddha image in Luang Prabang

King Setthathirat moves the capital to Viang Chan

king despatched a large contingent of monks and craftsmen up the Mekong, but they only got as far as Viang Chan. There the image they were escorting, the famous Pha Bang, magically refused to move, and had to be left behind. Its reason for refusing to go on to the Lao capital was that it knew that Fa Ngum was not morally worthy. And it seems the Pha Bang was right. Fa Ngum began to seduce the wives and daughters of his court nobles, who decided to replace him. Fa Ngum was sent into exile in Nan (now in Thailand), where he died within five years. His legacy, however, stood the test of time. The Kingdom of Lan Xang remained a power in mainland Southeast Asia until early in the 18th century, able to match the power of Siam, Vietnam and Burma.

Fa Ngum was succeeded by his son Un Heuan, who took the throne name Samsenthai, meaning 300,000 Tai, the number of men, his census reported, who could be recruited to serve in the army. He married princesses from the principal Tai kingdoms (Lanna and Ayutthaya, which had replaced Sukhothai), consolidated the kingdom and developed trade. With his wealth he built temples and beautified his capital.

Following Samsenthai's long and stable reign of 42 years, Lan Xang was shaken by succession disputes, a problem faced by all Southeast Asian *mandala* (circles of power). A scheming queen, known only as Mahathevi (Great Queen), is said to have set on the throne, and then killed off, a succession of youthful kings before ruling herself. But she was overthrown by the nobility and sacrificed to the *ngeuk* (by being chained to a rock in the Mekong and drowned). The throne then passed to Samsenthai's youngest son, who took the throne name Xainya Chakkaphat (Universal Ruler). It was an arrogant claim, but he ruled wisely and well.

Tragedy struck at the end of his reign, when Lan Xang suffered its first major invasion. This was by Vietnam, whose emperor wanted revenge for a perceived insult. The story in the Lao chronicles is that a rare white elephant, a symbol of power and kingship throughout Southeast Asia, was captured and presented to Xainya Chakkaphat. Vietnamese emperor Le Thanh Tong asked for proof of its colour, so hairs were despatched in a fine box. Unfortunately, however, it was sent via Xieng Khuang, whose ruler wanted to thumb his nose at the Vietnamese. So he replaced the hairs with a small piece of dung.

Infuriated, the Vietnamese emperor sent a large invasion force against the Lao. After a bitter battle (recounted at length in the Lao chronicles, which even give the names of the principal war elephants), the Vietnamese captured and sacked Xiang Dong Xiang Thong. Xainya Chakkaphat fled and the Lao mounted a guerrilla campaign. Eventually the Vietnamese were forced to withdraw, their forces decimated by malaria and vowing never to invade Lan Xang again.

Consolidation of the Kingdom

The Lao kingdom recovered under one of its greatest rulers, who came to the throne in 1501. This was King Visoun, who had previously been governor of Viang Chan. There he had been an ardent worshipper of the Pha Bang Buddha image, which he brought with him to Xiang Dong Xiang Thong to become the palladium of the kingdom. For it he built the magnificent temple known as Wat Wisunarat (Wat Visoun), which though damaged and repaired over the years, still stands in Luang Prabang.

Southeast Asian kingdoms were not states in the modern sense, with fixed frontiers, but varied in extent depending on the power of the centre. Outlying meuang might transfer their allegiance elsewhere when the centre was weak. That is why scholars prefer the term *mandala*, a Sanskrit word meaning 'circle of power' (in Lao *monthon*).

1641–1642	1707–1713
The first Europeans to write accounts of Lan Xang arrive in Viang Chan	Lan Xang is divided into three smaller and weaker kingdoms – Viang Chan, Luang Prabang, and Champasak

Visoun developed close relations with Chiang Mai, and enticed Lanna monks and craftsmen to his capital. He ordered a new version of the Lao chronicles composed, which he personally edited, and his reign marked a cultural renaissance for Lan Xang. Friendly relations with Lanna continued under Visoun's successor, his son Phothisarat. His grandson, Setthathirat, married a Lanna princess and briefly ruled over both kingdoms. But Lanna wanted its own king, and Setthathirat had trouble enough shoring up support in Lan Xang.

By then a new power had arisen in mainland Southeast Asia, the kingdom of Burma. It was the threat of Burma that in 1560 convinced Setthathirat to move his capital to Viang Chan. Before he did so, he built the most beautiful Buddhist temple surviving in Laos, Wat Xieng Thong. He also left behind the Pha Bang, and renamed Xiang Dong Xiang Thong Luang Prabang in its honour. With him he took what he believed to be an even more powerful Buddha image, the Pha Kaew, or Emerald Buddha, now in Bangkok. Other reasons for the move included population movements (both the Khorat Plateau and southern Laos were by then Lao) and to seek improved trade links.

Setthathirat was the greatest builder in Lao history. Not only did he construct or refurbish several monasteries in Luang Prabang, besides Wat Xieng Thong, but he also did the same in Viang Chan. His most important building projects, apart from a new palace on the banks of the Mekong, were the great That Luang stupa, a temple for the Emerald Buddha (Wat Pha Kaeo), and endowment of a number of royal temples in the vicinity of the palace. The city was surrounded by a substantial wall and moat, 8km long.

The Burmese threat persisted, however. When a Burmese army approached Viang Chan, Setthathirat abandoned the city to mount guerrilla attacks on Burmese supply lines. When the Burmese were forced to withdraw, he returned to celebrate his victory by building yet another temple (Wat Mixai). Burmese hostility disrupted Lao trade routes, so Setthathirat led an expedition down the Mekong to open a new route through Cambodia. But the Cambodians objected. In a great battle the Lao were defeated, and in their chaotic retreat Setthathirat disappeared.

It was over 60 years before another great Lao king came to the throne, a period of division, succession disputes and intermittent Burmese domination. In 1638 Suriya Vongsa was crowned king. He would rule for 57 years, the longest reign in Lao history and the 'golden age' of the kingdom of Lan Xang. During this time, Lan Xang was a powerful kingdom, and Viang Chan was a great centre of Buddhist learning, attracting monks from all over mainland Southeast Asia.

Suriya Vongsa had only been on the throne three years when there arrived in Viang Chan the first European to have left an account of the Lao kingdom. He was a merchant by the name of Gerrit van Wuysthoff, an employee of the Dutch East India Company, who, like Setthathirat, wanted to open a trade route down the Mekong. He and his small party were royally accommodated and entertained during their eight-week stay in the Lao capital.

Van Wuysthoff has more to say about the prices of trade goods than about Lao culture or religion, but he was followed a year later by a much more informative visitor. This was the Jesuit missionary, Giovanni-Maria Leria, who stayed in Viang Chan for five years. During that time he had singularly little success in converting anyone to Christianity, and eventu-

> 'Before Setthathirat moved his capital to Viang Chan, he built the most beautiful Buddhist temple surviving in Laos, Wat Xieng Thong'

1826–1828	1867
Chao Anou of Viang Chan wages war for Lao independence from Siam	Members of the French Mekong expedition reach Luang Prabang

ally gave up in disgust. But he liked the Lao people (if not the monks), and has left a wonderful description of the royal palace and the houses of the nobility. He was also much impressed by the power of the king.

THE KINGDOM DIVIDED

Suriya Vongsa must have been stern and unbending in his old age, because he refused to intervene when his son and heir was found guilty of adultery and condemned to death. As a result, when he died in 1695 another succession dispute wracked the kingdom. This time the result was division of Lan Xang. First the ruler of Luang Prabang declared independence from Viang Chan, followed a few years later by Champasak in the south.

The once great kingdom of Lan Xang was thus fatally weakened. In its place were three (four with Xieng Khuang) weak regional kingdoms, none of which was able to withstand the growing power of the Tai-Syam kingdom of Ayutthaya. The Siamese were distracted, however, over the next half century by renewed threats from Burma. In the end Ayutthaya was taken and sacked by a Burmese army. Chiang Mai was already tributary to Burma, and Luang Prabang also paid tribute.

It did not take the Siamese long to recover, however. The inspiring leadership of a young military commander called Taksin, son of a Chinese father and a Siamese mother, rallied the Siamese and drove the Burmese out not just of central Siam, but from the north too. Chiang Mai became tributary to Siam. After organising his kingdom and building a new capital, Taksin sought new fields of conquest. The Lao kingdoms were obvious targets. By 1779 all three had surrendered to Siamese armies and accepted the suzerainty of Siam. The Emerald Buddha was carried off by the Siamese.

His success went to his head, however, and three years later Taksin, suffering delusions of spiritual grandeur, was deposed by his leading general. The new king, founder of the current Thai Chakri dynasty, titled himself Rama I. He too built a new palace and capital at Bangkok, and quickly consolidated his power over tributary rulers. All Lao kings had to be endorsed by their Siamese overlord before they could assume their thrones, and all had to present regular tribute to Bangkok.

The Lao chafed under these conditions. When Chao Anou succeeded his two older brothers on the throne of Viang Chan, he determined to assert Lao independence. First he made merit by endowing Buddhist monasteries and building his own temple (Wat Si Saket). Then in 1826 he made his move, sending three armies down the Mekong and across the Khorat plateau. The Siamese were taken by surprise, but quickly rallied. Siamese armies drove the Lao back and seized Viang Chan. Chao Anou fled, but was captured when he tried to retake the city a year later. This time the Siamese were ruthless. Viang Chan was thoroughly sacked and its population resettled east of the Mekong. Only Wat Si Saket was spared. Chao Anou died a caged prisoner in Bangkok.

For the next 60 years the Lao *meuang*, from Champasak to Luang Prabang, were tributary to Siam. At first these two remaining small kingdoms retained a degree of independence, but increasingly they were brought under closer Siamese supervision. One reason for this was that Siam itself was threatened by a new power in the region and felt it had to consolidate

Paths to Conflagration: Fifty Years of Diplomacy and Warfare in Laos, Thailand and Vietnam, 1778–1828 (1998) by Mayoury Ngaosyvathn and Pheuiphanh Ngaosyvathn provides the best account of the Lao revolt against Bangkok, from a Lao perspective.

1893	**1907**
France gains sovereignty over all Lao territories east of the Mekong	The present borders of Laos are established by international treaty

its empire. The new power was France, which had declared a protectorate over most of Cambodia in 1863.

Four years later a French expedition sent to explore and map the Mekong River arrived in Luang Prabang, then the largest settlement upstream from Phnom Penh. In the 1880s the town became caught up in a struggle that pitted Siamese, French and roving bands of Chinese brigands (known as Haw) against each other. In 1887 Luang Prabang was looted and burned by a mixed force of Upland Tai and Haw. Only Wat Xieng Thong was spared. The king escaped downstream. With him was a French explorer named Auguste Pavie, who offered him the protection of France.

FRENCH RULE

In the end French rule was imposed through gunboat diplomacy. In 1893 a French warship forced its way up the Menam River to Bangkok and trained its guns on the palace. Under duress, the Siamese agreed to transfer all territory east of the Mekong to France. So Laos became a French colony, with the kingdom of Luang Prabang as a protectorate and the rest of the country directly administered.

The first Frenchman to arrive in Laos was Henri Mouhot, an explorer and naturalist who died of malaria in 1861 near Luang Prabang (where his tomb can still be seen).

In 1900 Viang Chan (which the French spelled as Vientiane) was re-established as the administrative capital of Laos, though real power was exercised from Hanoi, the capital of French Indochina. In 1907 a further treaty was signed with Siam adding two territories west of the Mekong to Laos (Sainyabuli province, and part of Champasak). Siem Reap and Battambang provinces were regained by Cambodia at the same time.

French authorities in Saigon had hoped that their Lao territories would become the springboard for further expansion, to include all of what is today northeast Thailand. This whole area had been settled by Lao and ruled from Vientiane. By the early 20th century, however, French attention had shifted from Indochina to Europe, and from competition with Britain to friendship in the lead-up to WWI. This left up to 80% of all Lao still within the borders of Siam, while in French Laos, ethnic Lao comprised less than half the population. The rest were tribal minorities.

Over the next few years the French put into place the apparatus of colonial control. They built a mansion for the *résident-supérieur* (governor) on the site of the former royal palace, barracks for a small military detachment, a court house, a prison, and housing for interpreters and civil servants, most of whom were Vietnamese. Later came a hospital, covered market and schools. The sites of ancient monasteries were preserved, and in time new temples were constructed by the Lao population. Chinese shopkeepers and Vietnamese artisans arrived, along with a few French merchants. As they took up residence in the downtown area, near the Mekong, Lao villagers were pushed out. Even so, the town grew slowly, and by 1925 the population was still only around 8000.

In other parts of Laos the French presence was less obtrusive. In Luang Prabang, Savannakhet and Pakse town planning and services were slow to be introduced. In time spacious villas were constructed for senior French officials, and the Lao towns were graced by colonial French architecture. A heavily subsidised riverboat service linked the Lao Mekong towns to Phnom Penh and Saigon.

1935	1945
The first two Lao members join the Indochinese Communist Party	The Japanese occupy Laos and force the king to declare independence

Nevertheless Laos remained a backwater. Despite French plans for economic exploitation, Laos was always a drain on the budget of Indochina. Corvée labour was introduced, particularly to build roads, and taxes were heavy, but the colony never paid its own way. Some timber was floated down the Mekong, and tin was discovered in central Laos, but returns were meagre. Coffee was grown in southern Laos, and opium in the north, most of it smuggled into China. The French tried hard to direct trade down the Mekong to Vietnam, but traditional trade routes across the Khorat Plateau to Bangkok were quicker and less costly.

The French introduced a three-tier system of administration into Laos. Ethnic minorities retained traditional links with local Lao leaders, who were supervised by Vietnamese civil servants, who were answerable to French officials. Taxes had traditionally been paid in the form of forest or agricultural products, but the French demanded cash. This introduced a market economy, but caused resentment. A series of anti-French rebellions broke out, first in the south and then in the north, led by traditional leaders who resented loss of authority. It took the French years of military campaigns to suppress them.

In the interwar years the French cast around for ways to make Laos economically productive. One plan was to connect the Lao Mekong towns to coastal Vietnam, by constructing a railway across the mountains separating the two colonies. The idea was to encourage the migration of industrious Vietnamese peasants into Laos to replace what the French saw as the indolent and easy-going Lao. Eventually Vietnamese would outnumber Lao and produce an economic surplus. The railway was surveyed and construction begun from the Vietnamese side, but the Great Depression intervened, money dried up, and the Vietnamisation of Laos never happened. Even so, in all the Mekong towns, with the exception of Luang Prabang, Vietnamese outnumbered Lao until most fled the country after WWII.

The French population in Laos was still only around 600 by 1940, more than half living in Vientiane. Most were officials for whom a posting in Laos was no more than a step on the ladder of promotion. For many their term of service was tedious, if undemanding. They 'kept up appearances', socialised and gossiped. A few succumbed to the charm of the country and made Laos their home.

Nationalism was slower to develop in Laos than in Vietnam. The French justified their colonial rule as protectors of the Lao from aggressive neighbours, particularly the Siamese. Most of the small Lao elite found this interpretation convincing, even though they resented the presence of so many Vietnamese. The Indochinese Communist Party (ICP), founded by Ho Chi Minh in 1930, managed to recruit its first two Lao members only in 1935. Most ICP members in Laos were Vietnamese civil servants or workers in the tin mines.

'The Indochinese Communist Party (ICP), founded by Ho Chi Mnh in 1930, recruited its first two Lao members in 1935'

WORLD WAR II & INDEPENDENCE

The outbreak of war in Europe weakened the French position in Indochina. A new aggressively nationalist government in Bangkok took advantage of this to try to regain territory 'lost' 50 years before. It renamed Siam Thailand, and opened hostilities. A Japanese-brokered peace agreement deprived Laos of its territories west of the Mekong, much to Lao anger.

1946	1949
The French reoccupy Laos, sending the Lao Issara government into exile	France grants Laos partial independence within the Indochinese Federation

To counter pan-Tai propaganda from Bangkok, the French encouraged Lao nationalism. Under an agreement between Japan and the Vichy French administration in Indochina, French rule continued, though Japanese forces had freedom of movement. The Japanese were in place, therefore, when in early 1945 they began to suspect the French of shifting their allegiance to the allies. On 9 March they struck in a lightning coup de force, interning all French military and civilian personnel. Only in Laos did a few French soldiers manage to slip into the jungle to maintain some resistance, along with their Lao allies.

The Japanese ruled Laos for just six months before the atomic bombing of Hiroshima and Nagasaki brought WWII to an end. During this time they forced King Sisavang Vong to declare Lao independence, and a nationalist resistance movement took shape, known as the Lao Issara (Free Lao). When the Japanese surrendered on 15 August, the Lao Issara formed an interim government, under the direction of Prince Phetsarat, a cousin of the king. For the first time since the early 18th century, the country was unified. The king, however, promptly repudiated his declaration of independence, in the belief that Laos still needed French protection. So tension quickly developed between Luang Prabang and Vientiane. The king dismissed Phetsarat as prime minister, so the provisional National Assembly of 45 prominent nationalists passed a motion deposing the king.

Naga Cities of Mekong (2006) by Martin Stuart-Fox provides a narrative account of the founding legends and history of Luang Prabang, Vientiane and Champasak, and a guide to their temples.

Behind these tensions were the French, who were determined to regain their Indochinese empire. After the war's end Chinese forces moved into Indochina north of the 16th parallel and British Indian troops to the south, to accept the surrender of the Japanese. The British soon handed over to the French, who thus were able to occupy southern Laos. In March 1946, while a truce held in Vietnam between the Viet Minh and the French, French forces struck north to seize control of the rest of Laos. The Lao Issara government was forced to flee to exile in Bangkok, leaving the French to sign a modus vivendi with the king reaffirming the unity of Laos and extending the king's rule from Luang Prabang to all of Laos. West bank territories seized by Thailand in 1940 were returned to Laos.

For the next three years the French worked to make up for their previous neglect. The country's first lycée (high school) was built and services improved. The Kingdom of Laos became a member state of the new Indochinese Federation, with its own government and National Assembly. But the French were still very much in control, and those Lao who collaborated were denounced by the Lao Issara in Bangkok, which continued to support armed resistance.

By 1949 something of a stalemate had developed between the French and the Viet Minh in the main theatre of war in Vietnam. In order to shore up their position in Laos, the French granted the Lao greater independence. This partial independence was enough for Laos to gain recognition from Britain and the United States. A promise of amnesty for Issara leaders attracted most back to take part in the political process in Laos. Among the returnees was Souvanna Phouma, a younger brother of Phetsarat, who remained in Thailand. Meanwhile Souphanouvong, a half-brother of the two princes, led his followers to join the Viet Minh and keep up the anticolonial struggle.

1950	1953
Lao communists (the Pathet Lao) form a 'Resistance Government'	Franco-Lao Treaty of Amity and Association grants full independence to Laos

RISE OF THE PATHET LAO

The decisions of the three princes to go their separate ways divided the Lao Issara. Those members who returned to Laos continued to work for complete Lao independence from France, but within the legal framework. Those who joined the Viet Minh did so in pursuit of an altogether different political goal – expulsion of the French and formation of a Marxist regime. Their movement became known as the Pathet Lao (Land of the Lao), after the title of the Resistance Government of Pathet Lao, set up with Viet Minh support in August 1950.

Cooperation between the Lao Issara and the Viet Minh went back to 1945, when, acting on Viet Minh instructions, Vietnamese in Laos backed the Lao Issara government. Joint Lao Issara–Viet Minh forces resisted the French reoccupation. Like the Lao Issara leaders, most Viet Minh in Laos fled the country, leaving the Mekong towns to be repeopled by Lao looking for jobs in the new Lao bureaucracy.

The architect of the Lao Issara–Viet Minh alliance was Prince Souphanouvong. He returned to Laos from Vietnam in time to take part in both the Lao Issara government (as foreign minister, though he would have preferred defence) and in the anti-French resistance. It was Souphanouvong who organised guerrilla resistance from bases in Thailand. He broke with his Issara-in-exile comrades when his close ties with the Viet Minh began to be questioned.

In August 1950 Souphanouvong became the public face of the Resistance Government and president of the Free Laos Front (Naeo Lao Issara), successor to the disbanded Lao Issara. Real power lay, however, with two other men, both of whom were members (as Souphanouvong then was not) of the Indochinese Communist Party. They were Kaysone Phomvihane, in charge of defence, and Nouhak Phoumsavan with the portfolio of economy and finance.

By that time the whole complexion of the First Indochina War had changed with the 1949 victory of communism in China. As Chinese weapons flowed to the Viet Minh, the war widened and the French were forced onto the defensive. In 1953 a Viet Minh force invaded northern Laos heading for Luang Prabang. The French flew in reinforcements, and the Viet Minh withdrew, turning over the whole region to the Pathet Lao. In order to protect Laos from another such invasion, the French established a substantial base in the remote mountain valley of Dien Bien Phu, close to the Lao border.

There was fought the deciding battle of the First Indochina War. The isolated French garrison was surrounded by Viet Minh forces, which pounded the base with artillery hidden in the hills. Supplied only from the air, the French held out for over two months before surrendering on 7 May. The following day a conference opened in Geneva that eventually brought the war to an end.

Kaysone Phomvihane was born in central Laos. As his father was Vietnamese and his mother Lao, he had a Vietnamese surname. He personally adopted the name Phomvihane, which is Lao for Brahmavihara, a series of four Buddhist heavens – an interesting choice for a committed Marxist.

DIVISION & UNITY

As France had already granted full independence to Cambodia and Laos (in October 1953), it was as representatives of a free and independent country that the Lao delegation attended the conference in Geneva. After months of discussion it was agreed to divide Vietnam into north and south, each with a separate administration, but with the instruction to hold free and fair

| Formation of the Lao People's Party (later Lao People's Revolutionary Party) | Formation of the First Coalition Government of National Union |

elections in both zones before the end of 1956. Cambodia was left undivided, but in Laos two northeastern provinces (Hua Phan and Phongsali) were set aside as regroupment areas for Pathet Lao forces. There the Pathet Lao consolidated their political and military organisation, while negotiating with the Royal Lao Government (RLG) to reintegrate the two provinces into a unified Lao state.

The first thing Pathet Lao leaders did was to establish a Lao Marxist political party. Previously Lao communists had been members of the Indochinese Communist Party, but in 1951 the ICP was disbanded and separate parties established for each state. Parties were founded immediately in Vietnam and Cambodia, but there were so few Lao members that it took time to recruit enough to constitute a party. Eventually the Lao People's Party was formed in 1955. (At its Second Congress in 1972 it was renamed the Lao People's Revolutionary Party, LPRP, which is today the ruling party of the Lao PDR.)

In good Marxist fashion, the LPP in 1956 established a broad political front, called the Lao Patriotic Front (LPF), behind which the Party could operate in secrecy. Souphanouvong was president of the Front, while Kaysone was secretary-general of the Party. Together with other members of the 'team' they led the Lao revolution throughout its '30-year struggle' (1945–1975) for power. Over this whole period no factionalism split the movement, which was one of its great strengths compared to the divisions among its opponents.

The first priority for the Royal Lao Government was to reunify the country. This required a political solution to which the Pathet Lao would agree. The tragedy for Laos was that when, after two centuries, an independent Lao state was reborn, it was conceived in the nationalism of WW II, nourished during the agony of the First Indochina War, and born into the Cold War. From its inception, the Lao state was torn by ideological division, which the Lao tried mightily to overcome, but which was continuously exacerbated by outside interference.

In its remote base areas, the Pathet Lao was entirely dependent for weapons and most other kinds of assistance on the North Vietnamese, whose own agenda was the reunification of Vietnam under communist rule. Meanwhile the Royal Lao Government became increasingly dependent on the United States, which soon took over from France as its principal aid donor. Thus Laos became the cockpit for Cold War enmity.

From the Lao perspective, neutrality was the only realistic path for the country. And the only way to restore national unity was to bring the Pathet Lao into some kind of coalition government. To this the US was strongly opposed, seeing it as the thin end of a wedge that would lead to a communist seizure of power.

The Lao politician with the task of finding a way through both ideological differences and foreign interference was Souvanna Phouma. As prime minister of the RLG he negotiated a deal with his half-brother Souphanouvong which saw two Pathet Lao ministers and two deputy ministers included in a coalition government. The Pathet Lao provinces were returned to the royal administration. Elections were held, in which the LPF did surprisingly well. And the US was furious.

Between 1955 and 1958, the US gave Laos US$120 million, or four times what France had provided over the previous eight years. Laos was almost entirely dependent, therefore, on American largesse to survive. When that

Backfire: The CIA's Secret War in Laos and its Link to the War in Vietnam (1995) by Roger Warner provides an informed account of the range of CIA activity in Laos.

1960	1961
Neutralist coup d'état followed by the battle for Vientiane	Orders given to the CIA to form a 'secret army' in northern Laos

aid was withheld, as it was in August 1958 in response to the inclusion of Pathet Lao ministers in the government, Laos was plunged into a financial and political crisis. As a result, the first coalition government collapsed. It had lasted eight months.

With US support a right-wing government was installed in its place, without Pathet Lao representation, and Souvanna Phouma's neutralism was abandoned. Attempts to integrate Pathet Lao units into the Royal Lao Army collapsed, and the civil war resumed. A threatened military coup brought military strongman General Phoumi Nosavan to the Defence Ministry as deputy prime minister, again with American backing. Meanwhile under Kaysone's direction the Pathet Lao began building up their forces, recruiting especially from the tribal minorities in the mountainous areas where the Pathet Lao held power.

As guerrilla warfare resumed over large areas, moral objections began to be raised against Lao killing Lao. On 9 August 1960, the diminutive commanding officer of the elite Second Paratroop Batallion of the Royal Lao Army seized power in Vientiane while almost the entire Lao government was in Luang Prabang making arrangements for the funeral of King Sisavang Vong. Captain Kong Le announced to the world that Laos was returning to a policy of neutrality, and demanded that Souvanna Phouma be reinstated as prime minister. King Sisavang Vatthana acquiesced, but General Phoumi refused to take part, and flew to central Laos where he fomented opposition to the new government.

In this, he had the support of the Thai government and the US Central Intelligence Agency (CIA), which supplied him with cash and weapons. By December he was ready to march on Vientiane. The battle for the city was spirited, but lopsided. Kong Le withdrew to the Plain of Jars, until then garrisoned by the Royal Lao Army, where he joined forces with Pathet Lao units. The neutralist government still claimed to be the legitimate government of Laos, and as such received arms, via Vietnam, from the Soviet Union. Most of these found their way to the Pathet Lao, however. Throughout the country large areas fell under the control of communist forces. Offensives by the Royal Lao Army led to defeat and disaster. The US sent troops to Thailand, in case communist forces should attempt to cross the Mekong, and it looked for a while as if the major commitment of US troops in Southeast Asia would be to Laos rather than Vietnam.

During the Second Indochina War, Chinese military engineers built a network of roads into northern Laos. Though these roads assisted the Pathet Lao, they were never bombed by American aircraft, for fear that Chinese troops might join the war in northern Laos.

THE SECOND COALITION & THE SECOND INDOCHINA WAR

At this point the new US administration of President John F Kennedy had second thoughts about fighting a war in Laos. In an about-face it decided instead to back Lao neutrality. In May 1961 a new conference on Laos was convened in Geneva. Progress was slow, however, because the three Lao factions could not agree on a political compromise that would allow a second coalition government to be formed. The right under General Phoumi was particularly recalcitrant. It took temporary suspension of US aid and a military defeat in northern Laos to convince the right to cooperate.

Eventually the 'three princes' (Souvanna Phouma for the neutralists, Souphanouvong for the Pathet Lao, and Boun Oum, hereditary prince of Champasak and then leader of the right) agreed to the composition of a second coalition government that balanced equal Pathet Lao and rightist

1962	1964
Geneva Agreement on Laos forms Second Coalition Government	US begins air war against ground targets in Laos

---

THE 'SECRET ARMY' & THE HMONG

After Laos gained independence in 1953, the United States trained and supplied the Royal Lao Army, as part of its strategy to combat communism in Southeast Asia. In 1961, CIA agents made contact with the Hmong minority living on and around the Plain of Jars. They spread a simple message: 'Beware of the Vietnamese; they will take your land', handed out weapons and gave basic training. There were also some vague promises of Hmong autonomy. At the time, the plain was in the hands of neutralists and Pathet Lao, backed by North Vietnamese. To protect more vulnerable communities, several thousand Hmong decided to relocate to mountain bases to the south of the plain. Their leader was a young Hmong army officer named Vang Pao.

In October 1961 President John F Kennedy gave the order to recruit a force of 11,000 Hmong under the command of General Vang Pao. They were trained by several hundred US and Thai Special Forces advisors and parachuted arms and food supplies by Air America, all under the supervision of the CIA.

The Hmong were a tough and independent people, who had migrated into Laos in the early 19th century from China, where they had suffered persecution. They preferred to live at high altitudes, where they practised slash-and-burn agriculture and grew opium as a cash crop. In 1918 they rose in rebellion against the French administration, which took the French four years to suppress. In the late 1930s a division occurred within the Hmong leadership over who had the right to represent the community under the French. In the First Indochina War, because of this division, while a majority of Hmong sided with the French (and later the Royal Lao Government), a substantial minority joined the Pathet Lao. The Hmong who formed the 'secret army' were those who had previously fought for the French.

With the neutralisation of Laos and formation of the Second Coalition Government in 1962, US military personnel were officially withdrawn. Even as it signed the 1962 Geneva Agreements, however, the US maintained its covert operations, in particular the supply and training of the

---

representation (with four each), but left the neutralists with a deciding majority (with 11 positions). Delegates of the 14 participating countries reassembled in Geneva in July 1962 to sign the international agreement guaranteeing Lao neutrality and forbidding the presence of all foreign military personnel. In Laos the new coalition government took office buoyed by popular goodwill and hope.

Within months, however, cracks began to appear in the façade of the coalition. The problem was the war in Vietnam. Both the North Vietnamese and the Americans were jockeying for strategic advantage, and neither was going to let Lao neutrality get in the way. Despite the terms of the Geneva Agreements, both continued to provide their respective clients with arms and supplies. But no outside power did the same for the neutralists, who found themselves increasingly squeezed between left and right.

For the Vietnamese, Lao neutrality was designed to maintain existing de facto spheres of military control: the right in the Mekong lowlands; the Pathet Lao in the eastern highlands; with a few neutralist units loyal to Souvanna Phouma in between. Moreover, Hanoi expected the Lao government to turn a blind eye to its use of Lao territory to infiltrate personnel and supplies into South Vietnam along what became known as the Ho Chi Minh Trail – as Cambodia did. For the Americans, Lao neutrality was designed precisely to prevent such infiltration.

1964–1973	1974
The Second Indochina War spills over into Laos	Formation of the Third Coalition Government

'secret army' for guerrilla warfare. The CIA's secret headquarters was at Long Cheng, but the largest Hmong settlement, with a population of several thousand, was at Sam Thong.

Over the next 12 years the Hmong 'secret army' fought a continuous guerrilla campaign against heavily armed North Vietnamese regular army troops occupying the Plain of Jars. They were supported throughout by the United States, an operation kept secret from the American public until 1970. So while American forces fought in Vietnam a 'secret war' was being fought in Laos. The Hmong fought because of their distrust of the communists, and in the hope that the US would support Hmong autonomy, but they paid a high price. In September 1969 a 'secret army' offensive, with heavy US air support, recaptured the Plain of Jars. Within six months a communist counteroffensive drove them back into the mountains, with terrible casualties.

As the war dragged on, so many Hmong were killed that it became difficult to find recruits. Boys as young as 12 were sent to war. The 'secret army' was bolstered by recruits from other minority groups, including Yao (Mien) and Khamu, and by Thai volunteers. By the early 1970s it had grown to more than 30,000 men, about a third of them Thai.

Not until 1970 did heavily censored transcripts of 1969 Congressional Hearings reveal the existence of the 'secret army' to the American people. Though the war in northern Laos was from then on no longer secret, no-one then knew what the war had cost the Hmong. When a ceasefire was signed in 1973, prior to formation of the Third Coalition Government, the 'secret army' was officially disbanded. Thai volunteers returned home and Hmong units were absorbed into the Royal Lao Army. Hmong casualty figures have been put at 12,000 dead and 30,000 more wounded, but could well have been higher.

Years of warfare had bred deep distrust, however, and as many as 120,000 Hmong out of a population of some 300,000 fled Laos after 1975, rather than live under the Lao communist regime. Most were resettled in the United States. It should be noted that of those Hmong who sided with the Pathet Lao, several now hold senior positions in the Lao People's Revolutionary Party (LPRP) and in government.

For both sides the most strategically important area was the Plain of Jars, and this quickly became the principal battleground. As control of the plain would enable the US to threaten North Vietnam, Hanoi moved to prevent this – first by driving out Kong Le's neutralists; then by turning their attention to the CIA-trained Hmong 'secret army' (see opposite) still supplied by the US in the mountains surrounding the plain.

By the end of 1963, as each side denounced the other for violating the Geneva Agreements, the Second Coalition Government had irrevocably broken down. Prime Minister Souvanna Phouma struggled to keep a façade intact, but Pathet Lao ministers had fled Vientiane, and neutralists had been cowered by the assassination of their foreign minister. It was in the interests of all powers, however, to preserve the façade of Lao neutrality, and international diplomatic support was brought to bear for Souvanna Phouma to prevent rightist generals from seizing power in coups mounted in 1964 and 1965.

In 1964 the US began its air war over Laos, with strafing and bombing of communist positions on the Plain of Jars. As North Vietnamese infiltration picked up along the Ho Chi Minh Trail, bombing was extended the length of Laos. According to official figures, the US dropped 2,093,100 tons of bombs on 580,944 sorties. The total cost was US$7.2 billion, or US$2 million a day for nine years. No-one knows how many people died, but one-third of the population of 2.1 million became internal refugees.

The Ravens: Pilots of the Secret War of Laos (1988) by Christopher Robbins tells the story of the volunteer American pilots based in Laos who supplied the 'secret army' and identified targets for US Air Force jets.

1975	1979
Communist seizure of power and declaration of the Lao People's Democratic Republic (PDR)	Agricultural cooperatives abandoned and first economic reforms introduced

US AID-ING & ABETTING

The US had several hundred advisors in Laos, but no ground forces. Advisors were attached to the US embassy, the huge US Agency for International Development, or worked for Air America. Many more US military personnel supported the war from bases in Thailand. In Laos itself, civilians outnumbered the military, especially those working for USAID, which functioned as a parallel government. Their presence generated a demand for housing and other services, including entertainment. Bars and nightclubs sprang up, some renowned for their sexually explicit floor shows, and prostitution was rife.

The promise of employment or adventure attracted other foreigners to Vientiane, which had something of a frontier town feel to it. Drugs were freely available. Marijuana, used by the Lao for flavouring certain soups, could be bought in the markets, along with Lao tobacco. Opium, a traditional medicine, could also be purchased, or smoked in 'dens' across the city. One such was a disused theatre, with the best cubicles on the raised stage – until pressure from the US embassy brought about its closure.

In the Mekong towns, the war seemed far away and hardly intruded on everyday affairs. After all, fighting was not supposed to be happening in a country whose neutrality had been endorsed by international agreement. But war spending and the large American presence did bring some prosperity. New villas were built to rent to foreigners, motor traffic markedly increased and young Lao adopted the latest in American fashions, including flared jeans and long hair.

A substantial amount of American aid found its way into private Lao pockets, to be spent on parties, entertainment and travel abroad. Criticism of the lavish lifestyles of the wealthy was voiced especially by senior monks in the name of Buddhist morality, and was quickly seized upon by Pathet Lao propaganda, which warned that Lao culture and Lao youth were being corrupted by decadent American culture.

During the Second Indochina War, Laos became (and remains) the most heavily bombed country per head of population in the history of warfare. Unexploded ordnance (UXO) still remains a problem along the old Ho Chi Minh Trail, and people, especially children, are still being killed and injured.

During the 1960s both the North Vietnamese and the US presence increased exponentially. By 1968 an estimated 40,000 North Vietnamese regular army troops were based in Laos to keep the Ho Chi Minh Trail open and support some 35,000 Pathet Lao forces. The Royal Lao Army then numbered 60,000 (entirely paid for and equipped by the US), Vang Pao's forces were half that number (still under the direction of the CIA), and Kong Le's neutralists numbered 10,000. Lao forces on both sides were entirely funded by their foreign backers. For five more years this proxy war dragged on, until the ceasefire of 1973.

The turning point for the war in Vietnam was the 1968 Tet Offensive, which brought home to the American people the realisation that the war was unwinnable by military means, and convinced them of the need for a political solution. The effect in Laos, however, was to intensify both the air war and fighting on the Plain of Jars. When bombing was suspended over North Vietnam, the US Air Force concentrated all its efforts on Laos. The Pathet Lao leadership was forced underground, in the caves of Vieng Xai. Though in much of Laos a 'tacit agreement' on spheres of control limited fighting between the two sides, on the Plain of Jars the ground war intensified. Instead of being used in guerrilla operations, units of the 'secret army' fought large-scale battles, in which they suffered heavy casualties.

But all the bombing was unable to staunch the flow of North Vietnamese forces down the Ho Chi Minh Trail (or trails). In January 1971 the one attempt by South Vietnamese forces to cut the Trail in southern Laos ended

1986	1991
The 'New Economic Mechanism' opens the way for a market economy and foreign investment	Promulgation of the constitution of the Lao PDR

in defeat. The Pathet Lao claimed victory, but North Vietnamese forces did the fighting. Thereafter more of southern Laos fell to the Pathet Lao. By mid-1972, when serious peace moves got underway, some four-fifths of the country was under communist control.

In peace as in war, what happened in Laos depended on what happened in Vietnam. Not until a ceasefire came into effect in Vietnam in January 1973 could the fighting end in Laos. Then the political wrangling began. Not until September was an agreement reached on the composition of the Third Coalition Government and how it would operate; and it took another six months before security arrangements were in place for it to take office. The government reflected the changed balance of political power. Souvanna Phouma as prime minister was the sole neutralist, with other ministries equally divided between left and right.

It soon became clear that the Pathet Lao was unified, coordinated and following a well-thought-out plan, formulated at the 1972 Second Congress of the Lao (LPRP). By contrast, the political right was fragmented and demoralised by the withdrawal of its US backer. This gave the communists the initiative, which they never lost.

REVOLUTION & REFORM

In April 1975 first Phnom Penh and then Saigon fell to superior communist forces. Immediately the Pathet Lao brought political pressure to bear on the right in Laos. Escalating street demonstrations forced leading rightist politicians and generals to flee the country. USAID was also targeted and hundreds of Americans began leaving Laos. Throughout the country, town after town was peacefully 'liberated' by Pathet Lao forces, culminating with Vientiane in August.

Souvanna Phouma, who could see the writing on the wall, cooperated with the Pathet Lao in order to prevent further bloodshed. Hundreds of senior military officers and civil servants voluntarily flew off to remote camps for 'political re-education', in the belief that they would be there only months at most. But Pathet Lao leaders had lied, just as they lied in promising to keep the monarchy. Hundreds of these inmates remained in re-education camps for several years.

With the rightist leadership either imprisoned or in Thailand, the Pathet Lao moved to consolidate power. At all levels of government, people's committees took administrative control, at the direction of the LPRP. In November an extraordinary meeting of what was left of the Third Coalition Government bowed to the inevitable and demanded formation of a 'popular democratic regime'. Under pressure, the king agreed to abdicate, and on 2 December a National Congress of People's Representatives assembled by the Party proclaimed the end of the 650-year-old Lao monarchy and the establishment of the Lao People's Democratic Republic (Lao PDR).

The Politics of Ritual and Remembrance: Laos Since 1975 (1998) by Grant Evans provides a penetrating study of Lao political culture, including attitudes to Buddhism and the 'cult' of communist leader Kaysone.

Unlike the military victories of communists in Cambodia and Vietnam, the Lao communists took power by 'quasi-legal' means. Their path to power had always used such means, by entering into coalition governments and demanding strict adherence to agreements, while continually strengthening their revolutionary forces. This strategy was the brainchild of Kaysone Phomvihane, who in addition to leading the LPRP became prime minister in the new Marxist-Leninist government. Souphanouvong was named state president.

1995	1997
Luang Prabang is World Heritage listed	Laos joins the Association of Southeast Asian Nations (Asean)

The new regime was organised in accordance with Soviet and North Vietnamese models. The government and bureaucracy were under the strict direction of the Party and its seven-member Politburo. Immediately the Party moved to restrict liberal freedoms of speech and assembly, and to nationalise the economy. People were forced to attend interminable 'seminars' to be indoctrinated into the Pathet Lao view of the world. As inflation soared, price controls were introduced. In response, those members of the Chinese and Vietnamese communities who still remained crossed the Mekong to Thailand. Thousands of Lao did the same. Eventually around 10% of the population, including virtually all the educated class, fled as refugees, setting Lao development back at least a generation.

The government faced a daunting task. The economy of the rightist zone, particularly in the Mekong towns, had been entirely dependent on the injection of American aid. When this was terminated, the economy collapsed. The situation was aggravated by government policies and Thai closure of the border; and though Soviet, Eastern European and Vietnamese advisors poured in, levels of aid from the communist bloc were insufficient to replace American spending. A badly planned and executed attempt to cooperativise agriculture made things even worse.

Bamboo Palace: Discovering the Lost Dynasty of Laos (2003) by Christopher Kremmer builds on his personal travelogue told in *Stalking the Elephant Kings* (1997) to try to discover the fate of the Lao royal family.

The regime did not persecute Buddhism to anything like the extent the Khmer Rouge did in Cambodia, but it did curtail Buddhist religious life. Younger monks were encouraged to leave the Sangha (monastic order), while those who remained had to work for a living. The people were told not to waste their wealth on Buddhist festivals. Many monks fled to Thailand. The annual rocket festival, held to encourage a copious monsoon, was cancelled. That year there was a drought. People shrugged: the *naga* were annoyed. Subsequently the festival was reinstated.

Though thousands of members of the 'secret army' and their families fled Laos, those who remained still resisted communist control. The Hmong insurgency dragged on for another 30 years. In 1977, fearing the king might escape his virtual house arrest to lead resistance, the authorities arrested him and his family and sent them to Vieng Xai, the old Pathet Lao wartime HQ. There they were forced to labour in the fields. The king, queen and crown prince all eventually died, probably of malaria and malnutrition, though no official statement of their deaths has ever been made.

By 1979 it was clear that policies had to change. Kaysone announced that people could leave cooperatives and farm their own land, and that private enterprise would be permitted. That year Vietnam invaded Cambodia to dispose of the Khmer Rouge, and China invaded northern Vietnam to teach Hanoi a lesson. Laos sided with Vietnam, and relations with China deteriorated. They were no better with Thailand, which was supporting insurgency against the Vietnamese-installed regime in Cambodia.

Reforms were insufficient to improve the Lao economy. Over the next three years a struggle took place within the Party about what to do. The Soviet Union was getting tired of propping up the Lao regime, and was embarking on its own momentous reforms. Meanwhile Vietnam had Cambodia to worry about. Eventually Kaysone convinced the Party to do what the Chinese were doing: open the economy up to market forces, and the country to foreign aid and investment from the West, while retaining a

1998–2000	2000
The Asian economic crisis seriously impacts on the Lao economy	Antigovernment Lao rebels attack a customs post on the Thai border. Five are killed.

RE-EDUCATION

Re-education camps were all in remote areas. Inmates laboured on road construction, helped local villagers, and grew their own vegetables. Food was nevertheless scarce, work hard, and medical attention inadequate or nonexistent. Except for a couple of high-security camps for top officials and army officers, inmates were allowed some freedom of contact with local villagers. Some even took local girls as partners. Escape was all but impossible, however, because of the remoteness of the camps. Only those showing a contrite attitude to past 'crimes' were released, some to work for the regime, but most to leave the country to join families overseas.

---

tight monopoly on political power. The economic reforms were known as the 'new economic mechanism', and were enacted in November 1986.

Economic improvement was slow in coming, partly because relations with Thailand remained strained. In August 1987 the two countries fought a brief border war over disputed territory. The following year relations were patched up, and with China too. The first elections for a National Assembly were held, and a constitution at last promulgated. Slowly a legal framework was put into place, and by the early 1990s foreign direct investment was picking up and the economy was on the mend.

The Economic of Transition in Laos: From Socialism to ASEAN Integration (2000) by Yves Bourdet provides the best account of the 'new economic mechanism' and its results.

In 1992 Kaysone Phomvihane died. He had been the leading figure in Lao communism for more than a quarter of a century. The Party managed the transition to a new leadership with smooth efficiency, much to the disappointment of expatriate Lao communities abroad. General Khamtay Siphandone became both president of the Party and prime minister. Later he relinquished the latter to become state president. His rise signalled control of the Party by the revolutionary generation of military leaders. When Khamtay stepped down in 2006, he was succeeded by his close comrade, General Chummaly Sayasone.

The economic prosperity of the mid-1990s rested on increased investment and foreign aid, on which Laos remained very dependent. The Lao PDR enjoyed friendly relations with all its neighbours. Relations with Vietnam remained particularly close, but were balanced by much improved relations with China. Relations with Bangkok were bumpy at times, but Thailand was a principal source of foreign direct investment. In 1997 Laos joined the Association of Southeast Asian Nations (Asean).

The good times came to end with the Asian economic crisis of the late 1990s. The collapse of the Thai baht led to inflation of the Lao kip, to which it was largely tied through trading relations. The Lao regime took two lessons from this crisis: one was about the dangers of market capitalism; the other was that its real friends were China and Vietnam, both of which came to its aid with loans and advice.

The economic crisis sparked some political unrest. A small student demonstration calling for an end to the monopoly of political power by the LPRP was ruthlessly crushed and its leaders given long prison sentences. Lao dissidents in Thailand attacked a border customs post, provoking a swift Lao military response. A series of small bombings in Vientiane and southern Laos was also blamed on expatriate Lao dissidents, while Hmong 'brigands' attacked transport in the north. The government responded by increasing security, with good effect. By 2004 the Hmong insurgency had all but collapsed.

Post-war Laos: The Politics of Culture, History and Identity (2006) by Vatthana Pholsena expertly examines how ethnicity, history and identity intersect in Laos.

2001	2003
Ten-year development plan unveiled aiming to triple per capita income by 2010	Amended constitution promulgated

PROSPECTS FOR THE 21ST CENTURY

The outlook for Laos as it moved into the 21st century was relatively positive. Despite dissatisfaction over lack of those freedoms (of expression, association, and the press) essential to the development of civil society and overmounting corruption, the LPRP faces minimal internal challenge to its authority. The Party seems set, therefore, to remain in power indefinitely – or at least for as long as it has the support of communist regimes in China and Vietnam.

Feature film making resumed in 1997, after a break of several years when only documentaries were produced, with the release of Than Heng Phongphai *(The Charming Forest) directed by Vithoun Sundara. This was followed in 2001 by* Falang Phon *(Clear Skies After Rain), and in 2004 by* Leum Teua *(Wrongfulness), both by the same director.*

The economic outlook has been helped by major investment projects in hydropower (the US$1.1 billion Nam Theun II dam, plus several smaller dams) and mining (gold, copper and, in the future, bauxite) that will bring a steady income into government coffers. Light industry, including textiles, may face a more uncertain future as the Asean Free Trade Agreement (AFTA) comes into force and Laos joins the World Trade Organisation (WTO), slated for 2010. Forestry is another important resource, but is largely under the control of the military.

A rapidly growing industry is tourism. In 1995 Luang Prabang was placed on the Unesco World Heritage list, and Wat Phu, the ancient Khmer temple near Champasak, followed. Other parts of the country are opening up to ecotourism, including the Bolaven Plateau in the south, the Plain of Jars, and the far north. An added attraction is that many of the country's colourful minority tribes live in these regions. Laos now attracts over a million tourists a year (well over half of them Thai), and the figure is likely to rise.

Laos does not suffer severe population pressure, but there is a steady migration into the cities due to increasing disparities between urban and rural living standards. The government has shown little inclination to address this problem, or the abysmally low education standards, or poor health facilities for a rural population faced with endemic diseases such as malaria, and HIV/AIDS. Some NGOs and foreign aid programs are trying to help, but human resources remain poorly developed.

INTERNET RESOURCES

Official websites with Up-To-Date Information on Laos
Asian Development Bank (www.adb.org/LaoPDR)
CIA Factbook (https://www.cia.gov/cia/publications/factbook/geos/la.html)
International Monetary Fund (www.imf.org/external/country/LAO/index.htm)
United Nations (www.un.int/lao) and (www.undplao.org)
World Bank (www.worldbank.org/la)

Country Profiles
BBC (http://news.bbc.co.uk/1/hi/world/asia-pacific/country_profiles/1154621.stm)
Lao Permanent Mission to the UN (http://www.un.int/lao/)
Library of Congress (http://rs6.loc.gov/frd/cs/latoc.html)

Other Useful Sites
Lao News Agency (www.kplnet.net)
Lao PDR (www.laopdr.com)
Muong Lao (www.muonglao.com/)
Vientiane Times (www.vientianetimes.com)

2004	2005
Laos hosts 10th Asean summit in Vientiane	Ten-yearly census conducted putting population of Laos at 5, 621, 982

Corruption remains a major problem. Far too much of the country's limited resources finds its way into the pockets of a small political-economic elite, who pay little or no taxes. Smuggling of timber and wildlife threatens declared 'bio-diversity areas' (national parks where some people still live). Laws are flouted because the legal system is not independent, but under the control of the Party.

Reforms and new political will are thus both necessary for the country to prosper. The LPRP is now Marxist-Leninist in nothing but name. Rather it exercises a single-party dictatorship, and is becoming increasingly nationalistic. This may appeal to Lowland Lao, but less to the tribal minorities. Care will be needed to maintain social cohesion. It remains to be seen whether the Party has the resourcefulness to meet the challenges ahead.

2005	2006
Construction begins on the Nam Theun II hydropower dam	Eighth Congress of the Lao People's Revolutionary Party and National Assembly elections endorse new political leadership

The Culture

THE NATIONAL PSYCHE

It's hard to think of any other country with a population as laid back as Laos. *Baw pen nyǎng* (no problem) could be the national motto. On the surface at least, nothing seems to faze the Lao and, especially if you're arriving from neighbouring China or Vietnam, the national psyche is both enchanting and beguiling. Of course, it's not as simple as 'people just smiling all the time because they're happy', as we heard one traveller describe it. The Lao national character is a complex combination of culture, environment and religion.

To a large degree 'Lao-ness' is defined by Buddhism, specifically Theravada Buddhism, which emphasises the cooling of the human passions. Thus strong emotions are a taboo in Lao society. *Kamma* (karma), more than devotion, prayer or hard work, is believed to determine one's lot in life, so the Lao tend not to get too worked up over the future. It's a trait often perceived by outsiders as a lack of ambition.

Lao commonly express the notion that 'too much work is bad for your brain' and they often say they feel sorry for people who 'think too much'. Education in general isn't highly valued, although this attitude is changing with modernisation and greater access to opportunities beyond Laos's borders. Avoiding any undue psychological stress, however, remains a cultural norm. From the typical Lao perspective, unless an activity – whether work or play – contains an element of *múan* (fun), it will probably lead to stress.

The contrast between the Lao and the Vietnamese is an example of how the Annamite Chain has served as a cultural fault line dividing Indic and Sinitic zones of influence. The French summed it up as: 'The Vietnamese plant rice, the Cambodians watch it grow and the Lao listen to it grow.' And while this saying wasn't meant as a compliment, a good number of French colonialists found the Lao way too seductive to resist, and stayed on.

The Lao have always been quite receptive to outside assistance and foreign investment, since it promotes a certain degree of economic development without demanding a corresponding increase in productivity. The Lao government wants all the trappings of modern technology – the skyscrapers seen on socialist propaganda billboards – without having to give up Lao traditions, including the *múan* philosophy. The challenge for Laos is to find a balance between cultural preservation and the development of new attitudes that will lead the country towards a measure of self-sufficiency.

LIFESTYLE

Maybe it's because everything closes early, even in the capital, that just about everyone in Laos gets up before 6am. Their day might begin with a quick breakfast, at home or from a local noodle seller, before work. In Lao

Two slim books of *Lao Folktales*, collected by Steve Epstein, retell some of Laos's better-known folklore. They're great for kids and offer an interesting insight into Lao humour and values.

DOS & DON'TS

- Always ask permission before taking photos.
- Don't prop your feet on chairs or tables while sitting.
- Never touch any part of someone else's body with your foot.
- Refrain from touching people on the head.
- Remove your shoes before entering homes or temple buildings.

Loum (lowland Lao, see p50) and other Buddhist areas, the morning also sees monks collecting alms, usually from women who hand out rice and vegetables outside their homes in return for a blessing.

School-age kids will walk to a packed classroom housed in a basic building with one or two teachers. Secondary students often board during the week because there are fewer secondary schools and it can be too far to commute. Almost any family who can afford it pays for their kids to learn English, which is seen as a near-guarantee of future employment.

Given that about 75% of people live in rural communities, work is usually some form of manual labour. Depending on the season, and the person's location and gender (women and men have clearly defined tasks when it comes to farming), work might be planting or harvesting rice or other crops. Unlike neighbouring Vietnam, the Lao usually only harvest one crop of rice each year, meaning there are a couple of busy periods followed by plenty of time when life can seem very laid back.

During these quiet periods, men will fish, hunt and repair the house, while women might gather flora and fauna from the forest, weave fabrics and collect firewood. At these times there's something wonderfully social and uncorrupted about arriving in a village mid-afternoon, sitting in the front of the local 'store' and sharing a *lào-láo* (whisky) or two with the locals, without feeling like you're stealing their time.

Where vices are concerned, *lào-láo* is the drug of choice for most Lao, particularly in rural areas where average incomes are so low that Beerlao is beyond most budgets. Opium is the most high-profile of the other drugs traditionally used – and tolerated – in Laos, though recent crop-clearing has made it less available. In cities, *yaba* (methamphetamine), in particular, is becoming popular among young people.

Because incomes are rock-bottom in Laos – US$100 per month could be considered middle-class – the Lao typically socialise as families, pooling their resources to enjoy a *bun wat* (temple festival) or picnic at the local waterfall together. The Lao tend to live in extended families, with three or more generations sharing one house or compound, and dine together sitting on mats on the floor with rice and dishes shared by all.

Most Lao don some portion of the traditional garb during ceremonies and celebrations – the men a *phàa bịang* (shoulder sash), the women a similar sash, tight-fitting blouse and *phàa nung* (sarong). In everyday life men wear neat but unremarkable shirt-and-trousers combinations. However, it's still normal for women to wear the *phàa nung* or *sin* (sarong). Other ethnicities living in Laos – particularly Chinese and Vietnamese women – will wear the *phàa nung* when they visit a government office, or risk having any civic requests denied.

'there's something wonderfully social and uncorrupted about sitting in the front of the local 'store' and sharing a *lào-láo* with the locals'

POLITICS & THE ECONOMY

At first glance the politics and economy of Laos seem simple enough: a one-party system is controlled by ageing revolutionaries that themselves have become a new elite, who have the power to control the exploitation of the country's natural resources, can squash any dissent and cooperate enough with foreign donors to keep the aid dollars coming in. But this generalisation is just that – the reality is more complex.

Laos is indeed a single party socialist republic, with the only legal political entity being the ruling Lao People's Revolutionary Party (LPRP). President Chummaly Sayasone is both the head of state and the head of the LPRP; the head of government is Prime Minister Bouasone Bouphavanh. Both were appointed to their five-year terms by the 115-member National Assembly in June 2006. The National Assembly itself was elected in April 2006 and

FEELING THE 'REAL LAOS'

A lot of travellers come looking for the 'real Laos', but few know exactly what that is. For about 80% of the population the 'real Laos' is village life, and the best way to really get a feel for how the Lao live is to spend a night or two in a homestay.

A homestay is, as the name suggests, staying with a family in their home, sleeping, eating and living just as they do. So what can you expect? The details vary from place to place, depending on ethnicity, geography and wealth, but the usual experience is described here.

Villages are small, dusty/muddy depending on the season, and full of kids. You'll be billeted with a family, usually with a maximum of two travellers per family. Toilets will be the squat variety, with scoop flush, in a dark hut at the corner of the block. You'll bathe before dinner, either in a nearby stream or river, or by using a scoop to pour water over yourself from a well, 44-gallon drum or concrete reservoir in your family's yard. Bathing is usually a public event, hence the sarong. Don't expect a mirror.

Food will be simple fare, usually two dishes and sticky rice. In our experience it's almost always been delicious, but prepare yourself for a sticky rice extravaganza – during a five-day circuit through homestays in southern Laos we ate sticky rice 14 meals out of 15. Even if the food doesn't appeal, you should eat something or your host will lose face. Dinner is usually served on mats on the floor, so prepare to sit lotus-style or with legs tucked under. Don't sit on cushions as that's bad form, and always take off your shoes before entering the house.

Sleeping will probably be under a mosquito net on a mattress on the floor, and might change to 'waking' once the cocks start crowing outside your window.

It might not be luxurious but homestay is very much the 'real Laos' and is a thoroughly worthwhile and enjoyable experience. Just remember that for most villagers, dealing with *falang* tourists is pretty new and they are sensitive to your reactions. Their enthusiasm will remain as long as their guests engage with them and accept them, and their lifestyle, without undue criticism. To get the most out of it take a phrasebook and photos of your family, and don't forget a torch, flip-flops, a sarong and toilet paper.

consists of 113 LPRP members and two non-partisan independents. There was, and remains, no legal opposition.

Change seems to come slowly in Laos, but when it does most policies and decisions come from a 10-member Politburo and a 52-member Central Committee – two powerful vestiges of the Soviet-style system adopted after the Pathet Lao takeover in 1975. Their decisions are rubber-stamped by the National Assembly.

Few outside the inner sanctum really understand the political scene, but it's accepted that the LPRP is loosely split between an older, more conservative guard and younger members pushing for limited reform. Cynics will tell you the infighting is mainly for the control of the lucrative kickbacks available to those who control the rights to Laos's rich natural resources. Others say the reformers' primary motivation is to alleviate poverty more quickly by speeding up development. The reality most likely lies somewhere between these two extremes.

Economically, Laos is in an interesting period. After the dark times of the Asian financial crisis in the late 1990s the economy is growing at a robust 7% per year. However, other numbers don't look so hot. The World Bank rates Laos as one of the least developed countries in East Asia, with more than 75% of people living on less than US$2 a day. More than three quarters of the population still live as subsistence farmers and gross domestic product was just US$2.9 billion in 2005. Major exports are electricity, garments, timber products and coffee, in that order. In recent years tourism (see p72) has become one of the main earners of foreign income, much of which flows directly into the pockets of those who need it most.

Foreign aid remains a constant of the Laos economy, as it has been since the 1800s. First the French established a basic infrastructure, followed by massive wartime investment by the USA. Soviet and to a lesser extent Vietnamese assistance saw Laos into the 1990s, when the Japanese and Western governments and NGOs started picking up the development tab. Laos's reliance is unsurprising when you consider there is little effective taxation and the country is only now, for the first time, developing notable export capacity (in hydropower). Put simply, the money needed for building roads, bridges, schools, hospitals etc didn't exist at home, so someone else had to foot the bill, or allow Laos to continue languishing in poverty.

In recent years China has started spending some of its enormous surplus in Laos. Apart from the obvious investment in infrastructure such as roads, dams and plantations, this has two significant effects. First, Chinese aid comes with few strings attached, meaning for example that roads, plantations and dams are built by Chinese companies with little or no concern for local people or environments.

This is in contrast to the usual carrot and stick approach of Western donors, who supply aid in various forms that is dependent on the Lao government improving their systems and getting involved in the development, rather than just sitting back and waiting for the dollars to roll in. Of course, not all Western aid programmes are perfect – most are far from it – but most at least pay some attention to factors like governance and environmental impact.

Second, if one of your largest donors, biggest regional political power and enthusiastic investors is a one-party state just like you, it's not the sort of role model that will encourage political or economic reform. Not that significant reform appears to be on the Lao government's agenda anyway, but trying to imitate China won't help get it there.

The overexcited development of hydroelectric and mining operations is expected to reduce Laos's reliance on foreign aid to a certain extent. Mines, such as the gold and copper operation at Sepon, are beginning to contribute to the government coffers. Dams like Nam Theun 2 will do likewise. Just who benefits from these projects, and how many will feel their negative impacts, is debatable. What seems more certain is that while foreign companies extract sizeable profits from their operations in Laos, the taxes and concession fees they pay will take a long time to trickle down to your average Lao family, and most will stay poor for quite some time to come.

POPULATION

Laos has one of the lowest population densities in Asia, but the total population has more than doubled in the last 30 years, and continues to grow quickly. A third of Laos's 5,622,000 inhabitants live in cities in the Mekong River valley, chiefly Vientiane, Luang Prabang, Savannakhet and Pakse. Another third live along other major rivers.

This rapid population growth comes despite the fact that almost one in 10 Lao fled the country after the 1975 communist takeover. Vientiane and Luang Prabang lost the most inhabitants, with approximately a quarter of the population of Luang Prabang going abroad. During the last 10 to 15 years this emigration trend has been reversed so that the influx of immigrants – mostly repatriated Lao, but also Chinese, Vietnamese and other nationalities – now exceeds the number of émigrés.

Most expatriate Westerners living in Laos are temporary employees of multilateral and bilateral aid organisations. A smaller number are employed by foreign companies involved in mining, petroleum and hydropower.

Laos: Culture and Society (2000), by Grant Evans (ed), brings together a dozen essays on Lao culture, among them a profile of a self-exiled Lao family that eventually returned to Laos, and two well-researched studies of the modernisation and politicalisation of the Lao language.

ETHNIC GROUPS

Laos is often described as less a nation state than a conglomeration of tribes and languages. And depending on who you talk with, that conglomeration consists of between 49 and 134 different ethnic groups. (The lower figure is that now used by the government.)

While the tribal groups are many and varied, the Lao traditionally divide themselves into four categories – Lao Loum, Lao Thai, Lao Thoeng and Lao Soung. These classifications loosely reflect the altitudes at which the groups live, and, by implication (not always accurate), their cultural proclivities. To address some of these inaccuracies, the Lao government recently reclassified ethnic groups into three major language families – Austro-Tai, Austro-Asiatic and Sino-Tibetan. However, many people you meet won't know which language family they come from, so we'll stick here with the more commonly understood breakdown.

About half the population are ethnic Lao or Lao Loum, and these are clearly the most dominant group. Of the rest, 10% to 20% are tribal Tai, 20% to 30% are Lao Thoeng ('Upland Lao' or lower-mountain dwellers, mostly of proto-Malay or Mon-Khmer descent) and 10% to 20% are Lao Soung ('Highland Lao', mainly Hmong or Mien tribes who live higher up).

The Lao government has an alternative three-way split, in which the Lao Thai are condensed into the Lao Loum group. This triumvirate is represented on the back of every 1000 kip bill, in national costume, from left to right: Lao Soung, Lao Loum and Lao Thoeng.

Small Tibeto-Burman hill-tribe groups in Laos include the Lisu, Lahu, Lolo, Akha and Phu Noi. They are sometimes classified as Lao Thoeng, but like the Lao Soung they live in the mountains of northern Laos.

> Foreign ethnographers who have carried out field research in Laos have identified anywhere from 94 to 134 different ethnic groups.

Lao Loum

The dominant ethnic group is the Lao Loum (Lowland Lao), who through superior numbers and living conditions – in the fertile plains of the Mekong River valley or lower tributaries of the Mekong – have for centuries dominated the smaller ethnic groups living in Laos. Their language is the national language; their religion, Buddhism, is the national religion; and many of their customs – including the eating of sticky rice and the *bąasii* ceremony (see p55) – are interpreted as those of the Lao nation, even though they play no part in the lives of many other ethnic groups.

Lao Loum culture has traditionally consisted of a sedentary, subsistence lifestyle based on wet-rice cultivation. They live in raised homes and, like all Austro-Thais, are Theravada Buddhists who retain strong elements of animist spirit worship.

The distinction between 'Lao' and 'Thai' is a rather recent historical phenomenon, especially considering that 80% of all those who speak a language recognised as 'Lao' reside in northeastern Thailand. Even Lao living in Laos refer idiomatically to different Lao Loum groups as 'Thai', for example, Thai Luang Phabang (Lao from Luang Prabang). See also Lifestyle (p46).

> Due to Laos's ethnic diversity, 'Lao culture' only exists among the lowland Lao or Lao Loum, who represent about half the population. Lao Loum culture predominates in the cities, towns and villages of the Mekong River valley.

Lao Thai

Although they're closely related to the Lao, these Thai subgroups have resisted absorption into mainstream Lao culture and tend to subdivide themselves according to smaller tribal distinctions. Like the Lao Loum, they live along river valleys, but the Lao Thai have chosen to reside in upland valleys rather than in the lowlands of the Mekong floodplains.

Depending on their location, they cultivate dry or mountain rice as well as wet, or irrigated, rice. The Lao Thai also mix Theravada Buddhism and animism, but tend to place more importance on spirit worship than do the Lao Loum.

Generally speaking, the various Lao Thai groups are distinguished from one another by the predominant colour of their clothing, or by general area of habitation; for example, Thai Dam (Black Thai), Thai Khao (White Thai), Thai Pa (Forest Thai), Thai Neua (Northern Thai) and so on.

Lao Thoeng

The Lao Thoeng (Upland Lao) are a loose affiliation of mostly Austro-Asiatic peoples who live on mid-altitude mountain slopes in northern and southern Laos. The largest group is the Khamu, followed by the Htin, Lamet and smaller numbers of Laven, Katu, Katang, Alak and other Mon-Khmer groups in the south. The Lao Thoeng are also known by the pejorative term *khàa*, which means 'slave' or 'servant'. This is because they were used as indentured labour by migrating Austro-Thai peoples in earlier centuries and more recently by the Lao monarchy. They still often work as labourers for the Lao Soung.

The Lao Thoeng have a much lower standard of living than any of the three other groups described here. Most trade between the Lao Thoeng and other Lao is carried out by barter.

The Htin (also called Lawa) and Khamu languages are closely related, and both groups are thought to have been in Laos long before the arrival of the lowland Lao, tribal Thai or Lao Soung. During the Lao New Year celebrations in Luang Prabang the lowland Lao offer a symbolic tribute to the Khamu as their historical predecessors and as 'guardians of the land'.

Lao Soung

The Lao Soung (High Lao) include the hill tribes who live at the highest altitudes. Of all the peoples of Laos, they are the most recent immigrants, having come from Myanmar, Tibet and southern China within the last 150 years.

The largest group is the Hmong, also called Miao or Meo, who number more than 300,000 in four main subgroups, the White Hmong, Striped Hmong, Red Hmong and Black Hmong (the colours refer to certain clothing details). They are found in the nine provinces of the north plus Bolikhamsai in central Laos.

The agricultural staples of the Hmong are dry rice and corn raised by the slash-and-burn method. They also breed cattle, pigs, water buffalo and chickens, traditionally for barter rather than sale. For years the Hmong's only cash crop was opium and they grew and manufactured more than any other group in Laos. However, an aggressive eradication programme run by the government (with support from the USA), has eliminated most of the crop. The resulting loss of a tradeable commodity has hit many Hmong communities very hard. The Hmong are most numerous in Hua Phan, Xieng Khuang, Luang Prabang and northern Vientiane provinces.

The second-largest group are the Mien (also called Iu Mien, Yao and Man), who live mainly in Luang Nam Tha, Luang Prabang, Bokeo, Udomxai and Phongsali. The Mien, like the Hmong, have traditionally cultivated opium poppies. Replacement crops, including coffee, are taking time to bed in and generate income.

The Mien and Hmong have many ethnic and linguistic similarities, and both groups are predominantly animist. The Hmong are considered more aggressive and warlike than the Mien, however, and as such were perfect for the CIA-trained special Royal Lao Government forces in the 1960s and early 1970s. Large numbers of Hmong-Mien left Laos and fled abroad after 1975.

Ethnic Groups of Laos, Vols 1-3 (2003) by Joachim Schliesinger is a well-respected modern ethnography of Laos. Schliesinger's scheme enumerates and describes 94 ethnicities in detail.

Other Asians

As elsewhere in Southeast Asia, the Chinese have been migrating to Laos for centuries to work as merchants and traders. Most come direct from Yunnan but more recently many have also arrived from Vietnam. Estimates of their presence vary from 2% to 5% of the total population. At least half of all permanent Chinese residents in Laos are said to live in Vientiane and Savannakhet. There are also thousands of Chinese migrant workers in the far north.

Substantial numbers of Vietnamese live in all the provinces bordering Vietnam and in the cities of Vientiane, Savannakhet and Pakse. For the most part, Vietnamese residents in Laos work as traders and own small businesses, although there continues to be a small Vietnamese military presence in Xieng Khuang and Hua Phan Provinces. Small numbers of Cambodians live in southern Laos.

WOMEN IN LAOS

For the women of Laos roles and status vary significantly depending on their ethnicity, but it's fair to say that whatever group they come from they are seen as secondary to men. As you travel around Laos the evidence is overwhelming. While men's work is undoubtedly hard, women always seem to be working harder, for longer, with far less time for relaxing and socialising.

Lao Loum women gain limited benefits from bilateral inheritance patterns, whereby both women and men can inherit land and business ownership. This derives from a matrilocal tradition, where a husband joins the wife's family on marriage. Often the youngest daughter and her husband will live with and care for her parents until they die, when they inherit at least some of their land and business. However, even if a Lao Loum woman inherits her father's farmland, she will have only limited control over how it is used. Instead, her husband will have the final say on most major decisions, while she will be responsible for saving enough money to see the family through any crisis.

This fits with the cultural beliefs associated with Lao Buddhism, which commonly teaches that women must be reborn as men before they can attain nirvana, hence a woman's spiritual status is generally less than that of a man. Still, Lao Loum women enjoy a higher status than women from other ethnic groups, who become part of their husband's clan on marriage and rarely inherit anything.

Women in Laos face several other hurdles: fewer girls go to school than boys; women are relatively poorly represented in government and other senior positions; and although they make up more than half the workforce, pay is often lower than male equivalents. If a Lao woman divorces, no matter how fair her reasons, it's very difficult for her to find another husband unless he is older or foreign.

In the cities, however, things are changing as fast as wealth, education and exposure to foreign ideas allows, and in general women in cities are more confident and willing to engage with foreigners than their rural counterparts. Women are pushing into more responsible positions, particularly in foreign-controlled companies.

RELIGION
Buddhism

About 60% of the people of Laos – mostly lowland Lao, with a sprinkling of tribal Thais – are Theravada Buddhists. Theravada Buddhism was apparently introduced to Luang Prabang (then known as Muang Sawa) in the late 13th or early 14th centuries, though there may have been contact with Mahayana Buddhism during the 8th to 10th centuries and with Tantric Buddhism even earlier.

'About 60% of the people of Laos – mostly lowland Lao, with a sprinkling of tribal Thais – are Theravada Buddhists'

King Visoun – a successor of the first monarch of Lan Xang, King Fa Ngum – declared Buddhism the state religion after accepting the Pha Bang Buddha image from his Khmer sponsors. Today the Pha Bang is kept at Wat Manolom (p143) in Luang Prabang. Buddhism was fairly slow to spread throughout Laos, even among the lowland peoples, who were reluctant to accept the faith instead of, or even alongside, *phii* (earth spirit) worship.

Theravada Buddhism is an earlier and, according to its followers, less corrupted school of Buddhism than the Mahayana schools found in east Asia and the Himalayas. It's sometimes referred to as the 'Southern' school since it took the southern route from India through Sri Lanka and Southeast Asia.

Theravada doctrine stresses the three principal aspects of existence: *dukkha* (suffering, unsatisfactoriness, disease), *anicca* (impermanence, transience of all things) and *anatta* (nonsubstantiality or nonessentiality of reality – no permanent 'soul'). Comprehension of *anicca* reveals that no experience, no state of mind, no physical object lasts. Trying to hold onto experience, states of mind, and objects that are constantly changing creates *dukkha*. *Anatta* is the understanding that there is no part of the changing world we can point to and say 'This is me' or 'This is God' or 'This is the soul'.

The ultimate goal of Theravada Buddhism is *nibbana* (Sanskrit: *nirvana*), which literally means the 'blowing-out' or 'extinction' of all causes of *dukkha*. Effectively it means an end to all corporeal or even heavenly existence, which is forever subject to suffering and which is conditioned from moment to moment by *kamma* (action). In reality, most Lao Buddhists aim for rebirth in a 'better' existence rather than the supra-mundane goal of *nibbana*. By feeding monks, giving donations to temples and performing regular worship at the local wat, Lao Buddhists acquire enough 'merit' (Pali *puñña*; Lao *bun*) for their future lives. And it's in the pursuit of merit that you're most likely to see Lao Buddhism 'in action'. Watching monks walking their neighbourhoods at dawn, collect offerings of food from people kneeling in front of their homes, is a memorable experience.

Lao Buddhists visit the wat on no set day. Most often they'll visit on *wán pha* (literally 'excellent days'), which occur with every full, new and quarter moon, ie roughly every seven days. On such a visit typical activities include the offering of lotus buds, incense and candles at various altars and bone reliquaries, offering food to the monks, meditating, and attending a *thêt* (Dhamma talk) by the abbot.

Lao Buddha: The Image & Its History (2000), by Somkiart Lopetcharat, is a large coffee-table book containing a wealth of information on the Lao interpretation of the Buddha figure.

MONKS & NUNS

Unlike other religions in which priests, nuns, rabbis, imams etc make a lifelong commitment to their religious vocation, being a Buddhist monk or nun can be a much more transient experience. Socially, every Lao Buddhist male is expected to become a *khúu-bạa* (monk) for at least a short period in his life, optimally between the time he finishes school and starts a career or marries. Men or boys under 20 years of age may enter the Sangha (monastic order) as *néhn* (novices) and this is not unusual since a family earns merit when one of its sons takes robe and bowl. Traditionally the length of time spent in the wat is three months, during the *phansǎa* (Buddhist lent), which coincides with the rainy season. However, nowadays men may spend as little as a week or 15 days to accrue merit as monks or novices. There are, of course, some monks who do devote all or most of their lives to the wat.

There is no similar hermetic order for nuns, but women may reside in temples as *náang sǐi* (lay nuns), with shaved heads and white robes.

POST-REVOLUTION BUDDHISM

During the 1964–73 war years, both sides sought to use Buddhism to legitimise their cause. By the early 1970s, the Lao Patriotic Front (LPF) was winning this propaganda war as more and more monks threw their support behind the communists.

Despite this, major changes were in store for the Sangha (monastic order) following the 1975 takeover. Initially, Buddhism was banned as a primary school subject and people were forbidden to make merit by giving food to monks. Monks were also forced to till the land and raise animals in direct violation of their monastic vows.

Mass dissatisfaction among the faithful prompted the government to rescind the ban on the feeding of monks in 1976. By the end of that year, the government was not only allowing traditional alms-giving, it was offering a daily ration of rice directly to the Sangha.

In 1992, in what was perhaps its biggest endorsement of Buddhism since the Revolution, the government replaced the hammer-and-sickle emblem that crowned Laos's national seal with a drawing of Pha That Luang, the country's holiest Buddhist symbol.

Today the Department of Religious Affairs (DRA) controls the Sangha and ensures that Buddhism is taught in accordance with Marxist principles. All monks must undergo political indoctrination as part of their monastic training, and all canonical and extracanonical Buddhist texts have been subject to 'editing' by the DRA. Monks are also forbidden to promote *phĭi* (spirit) worship, which has been officially banned in Laos along with *săinyasqat* (magic). The cult of *khwăn* (the 32 guardian spirits attached to mental/physical functions), however, has not been tampered with.

One major change in Lao Buddhism was the abolition of the Thammayut sect. Formerly, the Sangha in Laos was divided into two sects, the Mahanikai and the Thammayut (as in Thailand). The Thammayut is a minority sect that was begun by Thailand's King Mongkut. The Pathet Lao saw it as a tool of the Thai monarchy (and hence US imperialism) for infiltrating Lao political culture.

For several years all Buddhist literature written in Thai was also banned, severely curtailing the teaching of Buddhism in Laos. This ban has since been lifted and Lao monks are even allowed to study at Buddhist universities throughout Thailand. However, the Thammayut ban remains and has resulted in a much weaker emphasis on meditation, considered the spiritual heart of Buddhist practice in most Theravada countries. Overall, monastic discipline in Laos is far more relaxed than it was before 1975.

Spirit Cults

No matter where you are in Laos the practice of *phĭi* (spirit) worship – sometimes called animism – won't be far away. *Phĭi w*orship pre-dates Buddhism and despite being officially banned it remains the dominant non-Buddhist belief system. But for most Lao it is not a matter of Buddhism *or* spirit worship. Instead established Buddhist beliefs coexist peacefully with respect for the *phĭi* that are believed to inhabit natural objects.

An obvious example of this coexistence is the 'spirit house', which you'll see in or outside almost every home. Spirit houses are often ornately decorated miniature temples, built as a home for the local spirit. Residents must share their space with the spirit and go to great lengths to keep it happy, offering enough incense and food that the spirit won't make trouble for them.

In Vientiane you can see Buddhism and spirit worship side-by-side at Wat Si Muang (p96). The central image at the temple is not a Buddha figure but the *lák méuang* (city pillar), in which the guardian spirit for the city is believed to reside. Many local residents make daily offerings before the pillar, while at the same time praying to a Buddha figure. A form of *phĭi* worship you might actually partake in is the *bąasĭi* ceremony; see opposite.

Outside the Mekong River valley, the *phĭi* cult is particularly strong among the tribal Thai, especially the Thai Dam, who pay special attention to a class of *phĭi* called *then*. The *then* are earth spirits that preside not only over the plants and soil, but over entire districts as well. The Thai Dam also believe

Traditional Khamu houses often have the skulls of domestic animals hanging on a wall with an altar beneath. The skulls are from animals the family has sacrificed to their ancestors, and it is strictly taboo to touch them.

in the 32 *khwǎn* (guardian spirits). *Mǎw* (master/shaman), who are specially trained in the propitiation and exorcism of spirits, preside at important Thai Dam festivals and ceremonies. It is possible to see some of the spiritual beliefs and taboos in action by staying in a Katang village during a trek into the forests of Dong Phu Vieng NPA (p249).

The Hmong-Mien tribes also practise animism, plus ancestral worship. Some Hmong groups recognise a pre-eminent spirit that presides over all earth spirits; others do not. The Akha, Lisu and other Tibeto-Burman groups mix animism and ancestor cults.

Other Religions

A small number of Lao – mostly those of the remaining French-educated elite – are Christians. An even smaller number of Muslims live in Vientiane, mostly Arab and Indian merchants whose ancestry as Laos residents dates as far back as the 17th century. Vientiane also harbours a small community of Chams, Cambodian Muslims who fled Pol Pot's Kampuchea in the 1970s. In Northern Laos there are pockets of Muslim Yunnanese, known among the Lao as *jjin hǎw*.

ARTS

The focus of most traditional art in Lao culture has been religious, specifically Buddhist. Yet, unlike the visual arts of Thailand, Myanmar and Cambodia, Lao art never encompassed a broad range of styles and periods, mainly because Laos has a much more modest history in terms of power and because it has only existed as a political entity for a short period. Furthermore, since Laos was intermittently dominated by its neighbours, much of the art that was produced was either destroyed or, as in the case of the Emerald Buddha (p95), carted off by conquering armies.

Article 9 of the current Lao constitution forbids all religious proselytising, and the distribution of religious materials outside churches, temples or mosques, is illegal. Foreigners caught distributing religious materials may be arrested and expelled from the country.

BĄASĬI (BACI)

The *bąasǐi* ceremony is a peculiarly Lao ritual in which guardian spirits are bound to the guest of honour by white or orange strings tied around the wrists. Among Lao it's more commonly called *su khwǎn*, meaning 'calling of the soul'.

Lao believe everyone has 32 spirits, known as *khwǎn*, each of which acts as a guardian over a specific organ or faculty – mental and physical. *Khwǎn* occasionally wander away from their owner, which is really only a problem when that person is about to embark on a new project or journey away from home, or when they're very ill. Then it's best to perform the *bąasǐi* to ensure that all the *khwǎn* are present, thus restoring the equilibrium. In practice, *bąasǐi* are also performed at festivals, weddings, and when special guests arrive – hence villagers often hold a *bąasǐi* when trekkers arrive during a community-based trek.

The *bąasǐi* ceremony is performed seated around a *pha khwǎn*, a conical shaped arrangement of banana leaves, flowers and fruit from which hang cotton threads. A village elder, known as the *mǎw phon,* calls in the wandering *khwǎn* during a long Buddhist mantra while he, and the honoured guests, lean in to touch the *pha khwǎn*. When the chanting is finished villagers take the thread from the *pha khwǎn* and begin tying it around the wrists of the guests.

At this point the ceremony becomes a lot of fun. Villagers move around the room, stopping at guests to tie thread around their wrists. They'll often start by waving the thread across your hand, three times outwards accompanied by 'out with the bad, out with the bad, out with the bad', or something similar, and three times in with 'in with the good.' As they tie they'll also wish you a safe journey and good health, with the more comedic calling for beautiful wives, many children.

After the ceremony everyone shares a meal. You're supposed to keep the threads on your wrists for three days and then untie, not cut, them.

Laos's relatively small and poor population, combined with a turbulent recent history, also goes some way toward explaining the absence of any strong tradition of contemporary art. This is slowly changing, and in Vientiane and Luang Prabang modern art in a variety of media is finding its way into galleries and stores.

Weaving (p58) is the one art form that is found almost everywhere and has distinct styles that vary by place and tribal group. It's also the single most accessible art the traveller can buy, often from the artist herself – weavers are almost always women.

Architecture

The Laos Cultural Profile (www.culturalprofiles .net/Laos) is a new website established by Visiting Arts and the Ministry of Information and Culture of Laos covering a broad range of cultural aspects, from architecture to music. It's an easy entry point to Lao culture.

As with all other artistic endeavour, for centuries the best architects in the land have focussed their attention on Buddhist temples (see Temple Architecture, opposite). The results are most impressive in Luang Prabang.

However, it's not only in temples that Laos has its own peculiar architectural traditions. The *that* (stupa) found in Laos are different to those found anywhere else in the Buddhist world. Stupas are essentially monuments built on top of a reliquary which itself was built to hold a relic of the Buddha – commonly a hair or fragment of bone. Across Asia they come in varying shapes and sizes, ranging from the multi-level tapered pagodas found in Vietnam to the buxom brick monoliths of Sri Lanka. Laos has its own unique style combining hard edges and comely curves. The most famous of all Lao stupas is the golden Pha That Luang (p91) in Vientiane, the national symbol.

Traditional housing in Laos, whether in the river valleys or in the mountains, consists of simple wooden or bamboo-thatch structures with leaf or grass roofing. Among lowland Lao, houses are raised on stilts to avoid flooding during the monsoons and allow room to store rice underneath, while the highlanders typically build directly on the ground. The most attractive lowland Lao houses often have a starburst pattern in the architraves, though these are increasingly difficult to find.

Colonial architecture in urban Laos combined the classic French provincial style – thick-walled buildings with shuttered windows and pitched tile roofs – with balconies and ventilation to promote air circulation in the stifling Southeast Asian climate. Although many of these structures were torn down or allowed to decay following independence from France, today they are much in demand, especially by foreigners. Luang Prabang and Vientiane both boast several lovingly restored buildings from this era. By contrast, in the Mekong River towns of Tha Khaek, Savannakhet and Pakse French-era buildings are decaying at a disturbing rate.

L'Art du Laos (1954), by Henri Parmentier, is a thick, hard-to-find folio containing rare photographs of early Lao architecture and sculpture.

Buildings erected in post-Revolution Laos followed the socialist realism school that was enforced in the Soviet Union, Vietnam and China. Straight lines, sharp angles and an almost total lack of ornamentation were the norm. More recently, a trend towards integrating classic Lao architectural motifs with modern functions has taken hold. Prime examples of this include Vientiane's National Assembly and the Luang Prabang airport, both of which were designed by Havana- and Moscow-trained architect Hongkad Souvannavong. Other design characteristics, such as those represented by the Siam Commercial Bank on Th Lan Xang in Vientiane, seek to gracefully reincorporate French colonial features ignored for the last half-century.

Sculpture

Of all the traditional Lao arts, perhaps most impressive is the Buddhist sculpture of the period from the 16th to 18th centuries, the heyday of the kingdom of Lan Xang. Sculptural media usually included bronze, stone or wood and the subject was invariably the Lord Buddha or figures associated

TEMPLE ARCHITECTURE: A TALE OF THREE CITIES

The *uposatha* (Lao *sĭm*; ordination hall) is always the most important structure in any Theravada Buddhist wat. The high-peaked roofs are layered to represent several levels (usually three, five, seven or occasionally nine), which correspond to various Buddhist doctrines. The edges of the roofs almost always feature a repeated flame motif, with long, fingerlike hooks at the corners called *chaw fâa* (sky clusters). Umbrella-like spires along the central roof-ridge of a *sĭm*, called *nyâwt chaw fâa* or 'topmost *chaw fâa*', sometimes bear small pavilions (*nagas* – mythical water serpents) in a double-stepped arrangement representation of Mt Meru, the mythical centre of the Hindu-Buddhist cosmos.

There are basically three architectural styles for such buildings – the Vientiane, Luang Prabang and Xieng Khuang styles.

The front of a *sĭm* in the Vientiane style usually features a large veranda with heavy columns which support an ornamented, overhanging roof. Some will also have a less-ornamented rear veranda, while those that have a surrounding terrace are Bangkok-influenced.

In Luang Prabang, the temple style is akin to that of the northern Siamese or Lanna style, hardly surprising as for several centuries Laos and northern Thailand were part of the same kingdoms. Luang Prabang temple roofs sweep very low, almost reaching the ground in some instances. The overall effect is quite dramatic, as if the *sĭm* were about to take flight. The Lao are fond of saying that the roof line resembles the wings of a mother hen guarding her chicks.

Little remains of the Xieng Khuang style of *sĭm* architecture because the province was so heavily bombed during the Second Indochina War. Pretty much the only surviving examples are in Luang Prabang and to look at them you see aspects of both Vientiane and Luang Prabang style. The *sĭm* raised on a multilevel platform is reminiscent of Vientiane temples, while wide sweeping roofs that reach especially low are similar to the Luang Prabang style, though they're not usually tiered. Cantilevered roof supports play a much more prominent role in the building's overall aesthetics, giving the *sĭm*'s front profile a pentagonal shape. The pediment is curved, adding a grace beyond that of the typical Luang Prabang and Vientiane pediments.

A fourth, less common style of temple architecture in Laos has been supplied by the Thai Lü, whose temples are typified by thick, whitewashed stucco walls with small windows, two- or three-tiered roofs, curved pediments and *naga* lintels over the doors and steps. Although there are examples of Thai Lü influence in a few Luang Prabang and Muang Sing temples, their main location is in Sainyabuli Province.

with the Jataka (*sáa-dók*; stories of the Buddha's past lives). Like other Buddhist sculptors, the Lao artisans emphasised the features thought to be peculiar to the historical Buddha, including a beaklike nose, extended earlobes and tightly curled hair.

Two types of standing Buddha image are distinctive to Laos. The first is the 'Calling for Rain' posture, which depicts the Buddha standing with hands held rigidly at his side, fingers pointing towards the ground. This posture is rarely seen in other Southeast Asian Buddhist art traditions. The slightly rounded, 'boneless' look of the image recalls Thailand's Sukhothai style, and the way the lower robe is sculpted over the hips looks vaguely Khmer. But the flat, slablike earlobes, arched eyebrows and aquiline nose are uniquely Lao. The bottom of the figure's robe curls upward on both sides in a perfectly symmetrical fashion that is also unique and innovative.

The other original Lao image type is the 'Contemplating the Bodhi Tree' Buddha. The Bodhi tree ('Tree of Enlightenment'), refers to the large banyan tree that the historical Buddha purportedly was sitting beneath when he attained enlightenment in Bodhgaya, India, in the 6th century BC. In this image the Buddha is standing in much the same way as in the 'Calling for Rain' pose, except that his hands are crossed at the wrists in front of his body.

TEXTILES

Laos boasts over a dozen weaving styles across four regions. Southern weavers, who often use foot looms rather than frame looms, are known for the best silk weaving and for intricate *mat-mii* (*ikat* or tie-dye) designs that include Khmer-influenced temple and elephant motifs. In these provinces, beadwork is sometimes added to the embroidery. One-piece *phàa nung* (sarongs) are more common than those sewn from separate pieces.

In northeastern Laos, tribal Thai produce weft brocade *(yìap kǫ)* using raw silk, cotton yarn and natural dyes, sometimes with the addition of *mat-mii* techniques. Large diamond patterns are common.

In central Laos, typical weavings include indigo-dyed cotton *mat-mii* and minimal weft brocade *(jók* and *khit)*, along with mixed techniques brought by migrants to Vientiane.

Gold and silver brocade is typical of traditional Luang Prabang patterns, along with intricate patterns and imported Thai Lü designs. Northerners generally use frame looms; the waist, body and narrow *sín* (bottom border) of a *phàa nung* are often sewn together from separately woven pieces.

Natural sources for Lao dyes include ebony (both seeds and wood), tamarind (seeds and wood), red lacquer extracted from the *Coccus iacca* (a tree-boring insect), turmeric (from a root) and indigo. A basic palette of five natural colours – black, orange, red, yellow and blue – can be combined to create an endless variety of other colours. Other unblended, but more subtle, hues include khaki (from the bark of the Indian trumpet tree), pink (sappanwood) and gold (jackfruit and breadfruit woods).

The finest examples of Lao sculpture are found in Vientiane's Haw Pha Kaeo (p95) and Wat Si Saket (p94), and in Luang Prabang's Royal Palace Museum (p139).

Handicrafts

Lao Textiles and Traditions (1997), by Mary F Connors, is useful to visitors interested in Lao weaving; it's the best overall introduction to the subject.

Mats and baskets woven of various kinds of straw, rattan and reed are common and are becoming a small but important export. You'll still see minority groups actually wearing some of these baskets, affirming that until recently most Lao handicrafts were useful as well as ornamental. In villages it's possible to buy direct from the weaver, though you might need to commission your basket in advance and allow at least a day for the job to be finished. Or you could weave it yourself, under instruction from the experts for a small fee. Among the best baskets and mats are those woven by the Htin (Lao Thoeng).

Among the Hmong and Mien hill tribes, silversmithing plays an important role in 'portable wealth' and inheritances. In years past the main source of silver was French coins, which were either melted down or fitted straight into the jewellery of choice. In northern villages it's not unusual to see newer coins worn in elaborate head dress.

In Sekong and Attapeu, handwoven textiles often contain cryptic-looking symbols, including helicopter and aeroplane motifs that suggest the beginnings of a possible postwar cargo cult.

The lowland Lao also have a long tradition of silversmithing and goldsmithing. While these arts have been in decline for quite a while now, you can still see plenty of jewellers working over flames in markets around the country. If you're after something special head to Luang Prabang, where Thithpeng Maniphone (p155) has gone from crafting silverware for Luang Prabang royalty to filling commissions for the Thai royal family.

Paper handcrafted from *sǎa* (the bark of a mulberry tree) is common in northwestern Laos, and is available in Vientiane and Luang Prabang. Environmentally friendly *sǎa* is a renewable paper resource that needs little processing compared with wood pulp.

See Shopping p312 for more on handicrafts in Laos.

Music & Dance

Lao classical music was originally developed as court music for royal ceremonies and classical dance-drama during the 19th-century reign of Vientiane's Chao Anou, who had been educated in the Siamese court in Bangkok. The standard ensemble for this genre is the *sep nyai* and consists of *khâwng wóng* (a set of tuned gongs), the *ranyâat* (a xylophone-like instrument), the *khui* (bamboo flute) and the *pii* (a double-reed wind instrument similar to the oboe).

The practice of classical Lao music and drama has been in decline for some time – 40 years of intermittent war and revolution has simply made this kind of entertainment a low priority among most Lao. Generally, the only time you'll hear this type of music is during the occasional public performance of the *Pha Lak Pha Lam,* a dance-drama based on the Hindu Ramayana epic (see Literature, below).

Not so with Lao folk and pop, which have always stayed close to the people. The principal instrument in folk, and to a lesser extent in pop, is the *kháen* (common French spelling: *khene*), a wind instrument that is devised of a double row of bamboo-like reeds fitted into a hardwood soundbox and made air-tight with beeswax. The rows can be as few as four or as many as eight courses (for a total of 16 pipes), and the instrument can vary in length from around 80cm to about 2m. An adept player can produce a churning, calliope-like dance music.

When the *kháen* is playing you'll often see people dancing the *lám wóng* (circle performance), easily the most popular folk dance in Laos. Put simply, in the *lám wóng* couples dance circles around one another until there are three circles in all: a circle danced by the individual, a circle danced by the couple, and one danced by the whole crowd. Watch for a few minutes and you'll soon get the hang of it.

MĂW LÁM

The Lao folk idiom also has its own musical theatre, based on the *mǎw lám* tradition. *Mǎw lám* is difficult to translate but roughly means 'master of verse'. Led by one or more vocalists, performances always feature a witty, topical combination of talking and singing that ranges across themes as diverse as politics and sex. Very colloquial, even bawdy, language is employed. This is one art form that has always bypassed government censors and it continues to provide an important outlet for grass-roots expression.

Diverse other instruments, including electric guitar, electric bass and drums, may supplement the basic *kháen*/vocalist ensemble. Versions that appear on Lao national television are usually much watered down to suit 'national development'.

There are several different types of *mǎw lám,* depending on the number of singers and the region the style hails from. *Mǎw lám khuu* (couple *mǎw lám*), for example, features a man and woman who engage in flirtation and verbal repartee. *Mǎw lám jót* (duelling *mǎw lám*) has two performers of the same gender who 'duel' by answering questions or finishing an incomplete story issued as a challenge – not unlike free-style rap.

Northern Lao *kháen*-based folk music is usually referred to as *kháp* rather than *lám.* Authentic live *mǎw lám* can be heard at temple fairs and on Lao radio. CDs can be purchased in larger towns and cities.

North Illinois University has pages of information on Lao culture, language, history, folklore and music at www.seasite .niu.edu/lao/- including recordings of the *kháen.*

Literature

Of all classical Lao literature, *Pha Lak Pha Lam,* the Lao version of the Indian epic the Ramayana, is the most pervasive and influential in the culture. The Indian source first came to Laos with the Hindu Khmer as

LAO POP

Up until 2003 performing 'modern' music was virtually outlawed in Laos. The government had decided it just wasn't the Lao thing, and bands such as local heavy metal outfit Sapphire who chose to play anyway were effectively shut down. Instead the youth listened to pirated Thai and Western music, while Lao-language pop was limited to the *lûuk thûng*, syrupy arrangements combining cha-cha and bolero rhythms with Lao-Thai melodies.

Then the government decided that if Lao youth were going to listen to modern pop, it might as well be home-grown. The first 'star' was Thidavanh Bounxouay, a Lao-Bulgarian singer more popularly known as Alexandra. Her brand of pop wasn't exactly radical, but it was decidedly upbeat compared with what went before. In the last couple of years other groups have followed: the three guys and girl in Overdance wear matching outfits and produce expectedly poppy tunes. Girl-band Princess and pop-rock group Awake are also popular, while Aluna is evolving from a Kylie Minogue model to something less poppy. Pushing the boundaries a bit more is hard rock band Cells, which has a hardcore following of moshing teen boys. They perform mostly original songs and their singer also writes for other local artists.

But it's rap group L.O.G. which has been most successful, including a chart-topping hit in Thailand in 2006. Ironically, L.O.G. is one of the bands for whom success has been much more rewarding in Thailand, where they've played big and relatively lucrative gigs in Bangkok, than Laos, where they're encouraged in competition with Thai music.

This is an exciting new era for Lao music, but it's not as revolutionary as it might seem. Original, non-pirated CDs sell for just US$1.50 to US$2, so most musicians must work a day job. Indeed, Aluna might be a celebrity in Laos, but you'll still find her working behind reception in her family's Vang Vieng guesthouse. And the government's stance could best be described as pragmatic. Before recording all songs must be vetted by government censors, who can and do change both lyrics and video clips. Even after an album has been passed, some songs might not be approved for broadcast on radio. Needless to say, controversial social comment is at a premium.

These bands sometimes play venues in Vientiane (see p111), though you're more likely to see them at outdoor gigs to celebrate major holidays.

stone reliefs at Wat Phu Champasak and other Angkor-period temples. Oral and written versions may also have been available; eventually, though, the Lao developed their own version of the epic, which differs greatly both from the original and from Thailand's *Ramakian*.

Traditional Music of the Lao (1985), by Terry Miller, although mainly focused on northeast Thailand, is the only book-length work yet to appear on Lao music, and is very informative.

Of the 547 Jataka tales in the *Pali Tipitaka* (tripartite Buddhist canon) – each chronicling a different past life of the Buddha – most appear in Laos almost word-for-word as they were first written down in Sri Lanka. A group of 50 'extra' or apocryphal stories – based on Lao-Thai folk tales of the time – were added by Pali scholars in Luang Prabang between 300 and 400 years ago. Laos's most popular Jataka is an old Pali original known as the Mahajati or Mahavessandara (Lao: Pha Wet), the story of the Buddha's penultimate life. Interior murals in the *sĭm* of many Lao wat typically depict this Jataka as well as others.

Contemporary literature has been hampered by decades of war and communist rule. Only in 1999 was the first collection of contemporary Lao fiction, Ounthine Bounyavong's *Mother's Beloved: Stories from Laos*, published in a bilingual Lao and English edition.

SPORT

Like most poor countries, you won't read much about Laos when the Olympic circus sets up its tent. Laos has never won an Olympic medal, or much else in the international sporting arena, but that doesn't mean it's a complete sporting black hole.

Laos has a few traditional sports and these are as often an excuse for betting as they are a means of exercise. *Kátâw* and *múay láo* (Lao boxing, p62) certainly do involve exercise – and these are taken increasingly seriously as international competition raises their profiles. Cockfighting, however, does not. Cockfights follow the usual rules except that in Laos the cocks are not fitted with blades so often survive the bout. If you want to watch (or not), keep your eyes and ears open, particularly on Sundays and public holidays.

In ethnic Thai areas you might find the more off-beat 'sport' of beetle fighting. These bouts involve notoriously fractious rhinoceros beetles squaring off while a crowd, usually more vociferous after liberal helpings of *lào-láo*, bets on the result. The beetles hiss and attack, lifting each other with their horns, until one decides it no longer wants to be part of this 'entertainment' and runs. If you bet on the runner, you lose. Beetle bouts are limited to the wet season.

Kids in Laos are likely to be seen chasing around a football (or at least something that resembles a football). Opportunities for pursuing football professionally are few, limited by an almost complete lack of quality coaching, pitches, and youth leagues where players can get experience of proper competition. Laos does, however, compete in various regional tournaments, and on occasion you can see inter-provincial matches at the National Stadium in Vientiane or in modest stadia in provincial capitals.

In early 2007 Laos was ranked 151st by FIFA, above neighbours Cambodia and Vietnam.

Kátâw

Kátâw, a contest in which a woven rattan or plastic ball about 12cm in diameter is kicked around, is almost as popular in Laos as it is in Thailand and Malaysia.

Traditional *kátâw* involved players standing in a circle (the size of the circle depending on the number of players) and trying to keep the ball airborne by kicking it soccer-style. Points were scored for style, difficulty and variety of kicking manoeuvres.

A modern variation on *kátâw* – the one used in local or international competitions – is played with a volleyball net, using all the same rules as in volleyball except that only the feet and head are permitted to touch the ball. It's amazing to see the players perform aerial pirouettes, spiking the ball over the net with their feet. You're most likely to see *kátâw* in school yards, wats and public spaces, usually in the afternoon.

PETANG

While you'll see plenty of *kátâw* and football, the sport you'll most likely be able to actually play is *petang*. Introduced by the French, *petang* is obviously a local corruption of pétanque. All over Laos you'll see small courts made of packed dirt or gravel. There's usually a certain level of improvisation with the 'playing arena'; the backboard might be a length of coconut trunk, and the throwing circle is usually a bike tyre.

While it's been around for decades, on this trip we noticed many more courts than in previous years. It turns out that Lao involvement in international competition – presumably televised – has sparked a renewed interest in the game. In the 2005 Southeast Asian Games Laos won gold in the mens singles and silver in the mens doubles, quite an achievement for success-starved Laos.

As you travel around you'll see games are usually played in the afternoon and the players are usually men. If the game doesn't look like a life-and-death battle it's fine to ask to join in. The aim of the game is to get your *boule* (steel ball) as close to the *cochonnet* (piglet) as possible. *Petang* is supposed to be played between teams of two or three, though in practice it depends on how many *boules* and bodies are available. For technique, just watch and learn – and be careful not to injure any passing child or chicken.

Múay Láo (Lao Boxing)

The Lao seem to have an almost insatiable appetite for televised kickboxing, whether the pictures are coming from Thailand (múay Thai) or are of a local fight, known as *múay láo* (Lao kickboxing). *Múay láo* is not nearly as developed a sport in Laos as its counterpart in Thailand, and is mostly confined to amateur fights at upcountry festivals, but on most weekends you'll see the bigger fights broadcast on television.

All surfaces of the body are considered fair targets and any part of the body except the head may be used to strike an opponent. Common blows include high kicks to the neck, elbow thrusts to the face and head, knee hooks to the ribs and low crescent kicks to the calf. A contestant may even grasp an opponent's head between his hands and pull it down to meet an upward knee thrust.

International boxing *(múay sǎakǫn)* is gaining popularity in Laos and is encouraged by the government in spite of the obvious Lao preference for the bang-up Southeast Asian version.

Environment

In a part of the world where trees haven't done too well in recent decades, Laos is notable for its remarkably intact biodiversity. It's an aspect of the country that is being recognised by some as a potentially lucrative natural resource. In 2006, tourism was one of the Lao PDR's largest foreign income earners, and estimates suggest that about half of that money is from visitors who came in large part to experience this natural beauty (see Ecotourism in Laos, p72).

However, it's not all sweetness and light. The environment in Laos has long benefited from the country's small population, which has exerted relatively little pressure on the ecosystem. But with a growing population of poor, for whom wildlife equates to protein, those pressures are rising quickly. Add to that the ongoing problems of illegal logging and a renewed desire to sell its rivers to foreign hydropower developers, and Laos might yet miss the rare opportunity it has with such an intact environment. We can only hope not.

THE LAND

Covering an area slightly larger than Great Britain, landlocked Laos shares borders with China, Myanmar, Thailand, Cambodia and Vietnam. Rivers and mountains dominate, folding the country into a series of often-spectacular ridges and valleys, rivers and mountain passes, extending westward from the Lao-Vietnamese border.

Mountains and plateaus cover well over 70% of the country. Running about half the length of Laos, parallel to the course of the Mekong River, is the Annamite Chain, a rugged mountain range with peaks averaging between 1500m and 2500m in height. Roughly in the centre of the range is the Khammuan Plateau, a world of dramatic limestone grottoes and gorges where vertical walls rise hundreds of metres from jungle-clad valleys (see p230). At the southern end of the Annamite Chain, covering 10,000 sq km, the Bolaven Plateau (see p282) is an important area for the cultivation of high-yield mountain rice, coffee, tea and other crops that flourish in the cooler climes found at these higher altitudes.

The larger, northern half of Laos is made up almost entirely of broken, steep-sloped mountain ranges. The highest mountains are found in Xieng Khuang Province (p164), including Phu Bia, the country's highest peak at 2820m, though this remains off-limits to travellers for now. Just north of Phu Bia stands the Xieng Khuang plateau, the country's largest mountain plateau, which rises 1200m above sea level. The most famous part of the plateau is the Plain of Jars (p169), an area somewhat reminiscent of the rolling hills of Ireland – except for the thousands of bomb craters. It's named for the huge prehistoric stone jars that dot the area, as if the local giants have pub-crawled across this neighbourhood and left their empty beer mugs behind.

Much of the rest of Laos is covered by forest (see Plants, below), most of which is mixed deciduous forest. This forest enjoys a complex relationship with the Mekong and its tributaries, acting as a sponge for the monsoon rains and then slowly releasing the water into both streams and the atmosphere during the long dry season.

THE MEKONG & OTHER RIVERS

Springing forth over 4000km from the sea, high up on the Tibetan Plateau, the Mekong River so dominates Lao topography that, to a large extent, the entire country parallels its course. Although half of the Mekong's length

ROCK STARS

Odd-shaped rocks are venerated across Laos. Even in what appears to be the middle of nowhere, you'll see saffron robes draped over rocks that look vaguely like turtles, fishing baskets, stupas etc. Local legends explain how the rocks came to be or what they were used for, and some are famous around the country.

The Mekong River is known as Lancang Jiang (Turbulent River) in China; Mae Nam Khong in Thailand, Myanmar and Laos; Tonle Thom (Great Water) in Cambodia and Cuu Long (Nine Dragons) in Vietnam.

Marco Polo was probably the first European to cross the Mekong, in the 13th century, and was followed by a group of Portuguese emissaries in the 16th century. Dutch merchant Gerrit van Wuysthoff arrived by boat in the 17th century. In 1893 the French and Siamese signed the Treaty of Bangkok, designating the Mekong as the border between Siam and French Indochina.

runs through China, more of the river courses through Laos than through any other Southeast Asian country. At its widest, near Si Phan Don in the south, the river can expand to 14km across during the rainy season; spreading around thousands of islands and islets on its inevitable course south.

The Mekong's middle reach is navigable year-round, from Heuan Hin (north of the Khemmarat Rapids in Savannakhet Province) to Kok Phong in Luang Prabang. However these rapids, and the brutal falls at Khon Phapeng (p282) in Si Phan Don, have prevented the Mekong from becoming the sort of regional highway other great rivers have.

The fertile Mekong River flood plain, running from Sainyabuli to Champasak, forms the flattest and most tropical part of Laos. Virtually all of the domestic rice consumed in Laos is grown here, and if our experience seeing rice packaged up as 'Produce of Thailand' is any indication, then a fair bit is exported via Thailand, too. Most other large-scale farming takes place here as well. The Mekong and, just as importantly, its tributaries are also an important source of fish, a vital part of the diet for most people living in Laos. The Mekong valley is at its largest around Vientiane and Savannakhet, which, not surprisingly, are two of the major population centres.

Major tributaries of the great river include the Nam Ou (Ou River) and the Nam Tha (Tha River), both of which flow through deep, narrow limestone valleys from the north, and the Nam Ngum (Ngum River), which flows into the Mekong across a broad plain in Vientiane Province. The Nam Ngum is the site of one of Laos's oldest hydroelectric plants, which provides power for Vientiane area towns and Thailand. The Se Kong (Kong River) flows through much of southern Laos before eventually reaching the Mekong in Cambodia, and the rivers Nam Kading (Kading River) and Nam Theun (Theun River) are equally important in central Laos.

All the rivers and tributaries west of the Annamite Chain drain into the Mekong, while waterways east of the Annamites (in Hua Phan and Xieng Khuang Provinces only) flow into the Gulf of Tonkin off the coast of Vietnam.

WILDLIFE

Laos boasts one of the least disturbed ecosystems in Asia due to its overall lack of development and low population density. Least disturbed, however, does not mean undisturbed, and for many species the future remains uncertain.

Animals

The mountains, forests and river networks of Laos are home to a range of animals both endemic to the country and shared with its Southeast Asian neighbours. Nearly half of the animal species native to Thailand are shared by Laos, with the higher forest cover and fewer hunters meaning that numbers are often greater in Laos. Almost all wild animals however are threatened to some extent by hunting and habitat loss; see Environmental Issues, p69.

In spite of this Laos has seen several new species discovered in recent years, while others thought to be extinct have turned up in remote forests. Given their rarity, these newly discovered species are on the endangered list (see p66).

As in Cambodia, Vietnam, Myanmar and much of Thailand, most of the fauna in Laos belong to the Indochinese zoogeographic realm (as opposed to the Sundaic domain found south of the Isthmus of Kra in southern Thailand or the Palaearctic to the north in China).

Notable mammals endemic to Laos include the lesser panda, raccoon dog, Lao marmoset rat, Owston's civet and the pygmy slow loris. Other important exotic species found elsewhere in the region include the Malayan and Chinese pangolins, 10 species of civet, marbled cat, Javan and crab-eating

The Mekong: Turbulent Past, Uncertain Future (2000), by Milton Osborne, is a fascinating cultural history of the Mekong that spans 2000 years of exploration, mapping and war.

DEVELOPING THE MEKONG: RELIEVING POVERTY OR DAM CRAZY?

For millennia the Mekong River has been the lifeblood of Laos. As the region's primary artery, about 50 million people depend on resources from the river and its tributaries. The Mekong is the world's 12th-longest river and 10th-largest in terms of volume. But unlike other major rivers, a series of rapids have prevented it from developing into a major transport and cargo thoroughfare, or as a base for large industrial cities.

Except in China, the Mekong itself is not dammed. However the greater river system has long been seen as a potentially lucrative source of hydroelectricity. And with the regional demand for power rising rapidly, plans to turn Laos into the 'battery of Southeast Asia' have been revived after a decade of stagnation.

For a country as poor as Laos there are definite benefits. Selling electricity to Thailand, Vietnam, Cambodia and China will bring much-needed foreign exchange to the economy. In theory, this windfall can be spent on developing the country while at the same time reducing its reliance on foreign aid and loans. It's an attractive proposition, and one that the Laos government and several international agencies seem happy to pursue.

The first, and biggest, cab off the rank will be the Nam Theun 2 dam in Khammuan Province, due to be finished in 2010. This controversial hydropower project was 10 years in the planning, and as such is probably one of the most studied dam projects in history. Dozens of research projects were carried out because the dam needed World Bank approval before investors would commit, and the World Bank was under sustained pressure to reduce the negative impacts as much as possible.

However, not all projects are as big or get as much publicity as Nam Theun 2. When the World Bank finally approved the project in 2005, it was the equivalent of opening hydropower's Pandora's Box. In the ensuing period a flurry of agreements have been signed between the Laos government and private developers, all looking for a slice of the hydropower pie. At the time of writing more than 20 hydropower projects were either being built or were in the advanced stages of planning in Laos, raising the question of whether the government has gone 'dam' crazy.

For critics, including the International Rivers Network (IRN), the answer is a resounding yes. They claim that these lower profile dams have potentially far greater environmental and social impacts because there is no transparency and they are much harder to monitor. Although the government requires full environmental impact assessments for all hydropower schemes, if they have been carried out, few have been released to the public.

The negative impacts associated with dams include both the obvious and more difficult to see. Obvious effects include displacement of local communities, flooding upstream areas, reduced sediment flows and increased erosion downstream with resulting issues for fish stocks and the fisherman who work the rivers. Less immediately visible, but with a potentially much greater influence in the long term, are the changes these dams will have on the Mekong's flood pulse, which is critical to the fish spawning cycle, and thus the food source of millions of people.

All up this is a hugely complex issue. For more information, visit these websites:

Asian Development Bank (www.adb.org)
International Rivers Network (www.irn.org)
Laos Energy lobby (www.poweringprogress.org)
Mekong River Commission (www.mrc.org)
WWF (www.panda.org)

mongoose, the serow (sometimes called Asian mountain goat) and goral (another type of goat-antelope), and cat species including the leopard cat and Asian golden cat.

Among the most notable of Laos's wildlife are the primates. Several smaller species are known, including the Phayre's leaf monkey, François' langur, Douc langur and several macaques. Two other primates that are endemic to Laos are the concolour gibbon and snub-nosed langur. But it's the five species of gibbon that attract most attention. Sadly, the black-cheeked crested gibbon is endangered, being hunted both for its meat and to be sold as pets in Thailand. Several projects, including one treetop affair that would rather keep a low profile, are working to educate local communities to set aside safe areas for the gibbons.

ELEPHANTS

Laos might once have been known as the land of a million elephants, but these days only about 2000 remain. For an animal as threatened as the Asiatic elephant, this population is one of the largest in the region. Exact figures are hard to come by, but it's generally believed that there are about 800 wild elephants, roaming in open-canopy forest areas predominantly in Sainyabuli Province west of Vientiane, Bolikhamsai Province in the Phu Khao Khuay NPA (p118), and along the Nakai Plateau in central eastern Laos.

Hunting and habitat loss are their main threats. In areas such as the Nakai Plateau, Vietnamese poachers kill elephants for their meat and hides, while the Nam Theun 2 hydropower project will soon swallow up a large chunk of habitat. The Wildlife Conservation Society (WCS) has an ongoing project in this area, with a long-term aim of establishing a 'demonstration site that will serve as a model for reducing human-elephant conflict nationwide.'

Working or domesticated elephants are also found in most provinces, totalling between 1100 and 1350 countrywide. They have traditionally been used for the heavy labour involved in logging and agriculture, but modern machinery is rapidly putting them out of work. As a result, the mahouts (elephant keepers and/or drivers) in some elephant villages are working with NGOs to find alternative income through tourism. Projects in Kiet Ngong (p270) in Champasak Province, and Hongsa (p224) in Sainyabuli Province offer elephant trekking, and the elephant *baasii* (p224) is growing in popularity as a tourist event. Working elephants are most visible in Sainyabuli, Udomxai, Champasak and Attapeu Provinces.

Despite these problems, Laos is in the rare position of having the raw materials – enough elephants and habitat – to ensure the jumbos have a long and healthy future. What is missing is money and, perhaps, sufficient political will.

ENDANGERED SPECIES

The giant Mekong catfish may grow up to 3m long and weigh as much as 300kg. Due to Chinese blasting of shoals in the Upper Mekong, it now faces extinction in the wild.

To a certain extent, all wild animals in Laos are endangered due to widespread hunting and gradual but persistent habitat loss. Laos ratified the UN Convention on International Trade in Endangered Species of Wild Flora and Fauna (Cites) in 2004, which, combined with other legal measures, has made it easier to prosecute people trading species endangered as a direct result of international trade. But in reality you won't need 20/20 vision to pick out the endangered species – both dead and alive – on sale in markets around the country. Border markets, in particular, tend to attract the most valuable species, with Thais buying species such as gibbons as pets, and Vietnamese shopping for exotic food and medicines.

Of the hundreds of species of mammals known in Laos, several dozen are endangered according to the IUCN's Redlist (www.iucnredlist.org). These range from bears, including the Asiatic black bear and Malayan sun bear, through the less glamorous wild cattle such as the gaur and banteng, to high-profile cats like the tiger, leopard and clouded leopard. Exactly how endangered they are is difficult to say. Camera-trapping projects (setting up cameras in the forest to take photos of anything that goes past) are being carried out by various NGOs and, in the case of the Nakai Nam Theun NPA, by the Nam Theun 2 dam operators themselves.

The Nakai Nam Theun research is part of a deal brokered by the World Bank that ensures US$1 million a year is set aside for environmental study and protection in the dam's catchment area. Results of camera trapping in the Nakai Nam Theun NPA have been both encouraging and depressing. The cameras returned photos of limited numbers of several species, but also a hunter posing proudly with his kill – not quite the shots they were hoping for.

The WCS is focussing its conservation activities on species including the Asian elephant (see p66), Siamese crocodile, tiger, western black crested gibbon and Eld's deer, one of several endangered deer species including barking deer and sambar. For more details, see www.wcs.org.

Some endangered species are so rare they were unknown until very recently. Among these is the spindlehorn (*Pseudoryx nghethingensis;* known as the *saola* in Vietnam, *nyang* in Laos), a horned mammal found in the Annamite Chain along the Lao-Vietnamese border in 1992. The spindlehorn, which was described in 14th-century Chinese journals, was long thought not to exist, and when discovered it became one of only three land mammals to earn its own genus in the 20th century. Unfortunately, horns taken from spindlehorn are a favoured trophy among certain groups on both sides of the Lao-Vietnamese border.

In 2005 WCS scientists visiting a local market in Khammuan Province discovered a 'Laotian rock rat' laid out for sale. But, what was being sold as meat turned out to be a genetically distinct species named the *Laonastes aenigmamus*. Further research revealed it to be the sole survivor of a prehistoric group of rodents that died out about 11 million years ago. If you're very lucky you might see one on the cliffs near the caves off Rte 12 in Khammuan Province.

Among the most seriously endangered of all mammals is the Irrawaddy dolphin (see the boxed text, Dolphins Endangered, p279).

Birds

Those new to Laos often ask: 'Why can't I hear more birds?' The short answer is 'cheap protein' (p73). If you can get far enough away from people, you'll find the forests and mountains of Laos do in fact harbour a rich selection of resident and migrating bird species. Surveys carried out by a British team of ornithologists in the 1990s recorded 437 species, including eight globally threatened and 21 globally near-threatened species. Some other counts rise as high as 650 species.

Notable among these are the Siamese fireback pheasant, green peafowl, red-collared woodpecker, brown hornbill, tawny fish-owl, Sarus crane, giant ibis and the Asian golden weaver. Hunting keeps urban bird populations noticeably thin. Up until a few years ago, it wasn't uncommon to see men pointing long-barrelled muskets at upper tree branches in cities as large as Savannakhet and Vientiane. Those days are now gone, but around almost every village you'll hear hunters doing their business most afternoons.

Plants

According to the IUCN, natural unmanaged vegetation covers more than 75% of Laos and about half the country bears natural forest cover. Of these woodlands about half can be classified as primary forest – a very high proportion in this day and age – while another 30% or so represents secondary growth. Laos ranks 11th worldwide in terms of natural forest cover and in Southeast Asia only Cambodia boasts more, though rampant illegal logging there could soon reverse those positions.

SPECIES DECEASES

The World Conservation Union (www.iucn.org) believes wildlife in Laos has a much better change of surviving than in neighbouring Vietnam. Lending weight to this is the Vietnam warty pig *(Sus bucclentus)*, a species found in Laos but last recorded in Vietnam in 1892 and until recently considered extinct.

RESPONSIBLE TRAVEL IN LAOS – WILDLIFE CONSERVATION

Throughout your travels in Laos the opportunity to buy or consume wildlife is likely to come about. In the interests of wildlife conservation, the Wildlife Conservation Society – Lao PDR strongly urges you not to partake in the wildlife trade. While it's true that subsistence hunting is permitted by the Government of Lao PDR for local rural villagers, the sale and purchase of *any* wildlife is illegal in Laos. The wildlife trade is damaging to biodiversity and to local livelihoods.

While strolling through rural and city markets you'll come across wild animals for sale as meat or live pets. In a misguided attempt to do the right thing travellers have been known to buy these live animals in order to release them. While it might feel like this is a positive step towards thwarting the wildlife trade it actually has the opposite effect with vendors, unaware of the buyer's motivation, interpreting the sale as increased demand.

Be prepared for some bizarre and disturbing items on restaurant menus and in food markets in Laos. While it may be tempting to experience the unusual it's strongly recommended that the following animals be avoided: soft shelled turtles, rat snakes, mouse deer, sambar deer, squirrel, bamboo rat, muntjac deer, and pangolins. Many of these species are endangered or are a source of prey for endangered species.

Thinking of purchasing a stuffed wild animal? A bag or wallet made from animal skin? Or perhaps an insect in a framed box? Think again. The money made in the sale of these peculiar trinkets goes directly towards supporting the illegal wildlife trade. Also to be avoided are the rings and necklaces made from animal teeth (sellers may tell you that this is buffalo bone, but it's just as likely that it's bear or wild pig bone) and the bottles of alcohol with snakes, birds, or insects inside. Though widely sold, this trade is illegal in Laos, and you'll most likely find your new libido-enhancing snake oil confiscated by customs in your home country anyway. Keep an eye out for products with a CITES-certified label, these are legal to buy in Laos and take home.

For many species of wildlife in Laos populations are at critically low levels. The WCS Lao PDR programme (http://www.wcs.org/international/Asia/laos) is collaborating with the Vientiane Capital City government to monitor and control wildlife trade. If you observe wildlife trading please contact the local authorities.

By the Wildlife Conservation Society, Lao PDR (www.wcs.org/international/Asia/laos)

While opium has been cultivated and used in Laos for centuries, the country didn't become a major producer until the passing of the 1971 Anti-Narcotics Law, a move that helped drive up regional prices steeply.

Most indigenous vegetation in Laos is associated with monsoon forests, a common trait in areas of tropical mainland Southeast Asia that experience dry seasons lasting three months or longer. In such mixed deciduous forests many trees shed their leaves during the dry season to conserve water. Rainforests – which are typically evergreen – don't exist in Laos, although nonindigenous rainforest species such as the coconut palm are commonly seen in the lower Mekong River valley. There are undoubtedly some big trees in Laos, but don't expect the sort of towering forests found in some other parts of Southeast Asia – the conditions do not, and never have, allowed these sort of giants to grow here.

Instead the monsoon forests of Laos typically grow in three canopies. Dipterocarps – tall, pale-barked, single-trunked trees that can grow beyond 30m high – dominate the top canopy of the forest, while a middle canopy consists of an ever-dwindling population of prized hardwoods, including teak, padauk (sometimes called 'Asian rosewood') and mahogany. Underneath there's a variety of smaller trees, shrubs, grasses and – along river habitats – bamboo. In certain plateau areas of the south, there are dry dipterocarp forests in which the forest canopies are more open, with less of a middle layer and more of a grass-and-bamboo undergrowth. Parts of the Annamite Chain that receive rain from both the southwestern monsoon as well as the South China Sea are covered by tropical montane evergreen forest, while tropical pine forests can be found on the Nakai Plateau and Sekong area to the south.

In addition to the glamour hardwoods, the country's flora includes a toothsome array of fruit trees, bamboo (more species than any country outside Thailand and China) and an abundance of flowering species such as the orchid. However, in some parts of the country orchids are being stripped out of forests (often in protected areas) for sale to Thai tourists; look for the markets near the waterfalls of the Bolaven Plateau (see p283) to see them. In the high plateaus of the Annamite Chain, extensive grasslands or savanna are common.

NATIONAL PROTECTED AREAS (NPAS)

Laos boasts one of the youngest and most comprehensive protected area systems in the world. In 1993 the government set up 18 National Biodiversity Conservation Areas, comprising a total of 24,600 sq km, or just over 10% of the country's land mass. Most significantly, it did this following sound scientific consultation rather than creating areas on an ad hoc basis (as most other countries have done). Two more were added in 1995, for a total of 20 protected areas covering 14% of Laos. A further 4% of Laos is reserved as Provincial Protected Areas, making Laos one of the most protected countries on earth.

The areas were renamed National Protected Areas (NPAs) a few years ago. And while the naming semantics might seem trivial, they do reflect some important differences. The main one is that an NPA has local communities living within its boundaries, unlike a national park, where only rangers and those working in the park are allowed to live and where traditional activities such as hunting and logging are banned. Indeed, forests in NPAs are divided into production forests for timber, protection forests for watershed and conservation forests for pure conservation.

The largest protected areas are in southern Laos, which, contrary to popular myth, bears a higher percentage of natural forest cover than the north. The largest of the NPAs, Nakai-Nam Theun, covers 3710 sq km and is home to the recently discovered spindlehorn (see p66) as well as several other species unknown to the scientific world a decade ago.

While several NPAs remain difficult to access without mounting a full-scale expedition, several others have become much easier to reach in recent years. The best way in is usually by foot; for a list of the trekking possibilities see the boxed text, Where to Trek, p70.

The wildlife in these areas – from rare birds to wild elephants – is relatively abundant. The best time to view wildlife in most of the country is just after the monsoon in November. However, even at these times you'll be lucky to see very much. There are several reasons for this, the most important of which is that ongoing hunting mean numbers of wild animals are reduced and those living are instinctively scared of humans. It's also difficult to see animals in forest cover at the best of times, and many animals are nocturnal.

ENVIRONMENTAL ISSUES

Flying over Laos it's easy to think that the great majority of the country is blanketed with vast tracts of untouched wilderness. And while Laos does indeed have one of the most pristine ecologies in Asia, first impressions can be deceiving. What that lumpy carpet of green conceals is an environment facing several interrelated threats.

For the most part they're issues of the bottom line. Hunting endangers all sorts of creatures of the forest but it persists because the hunters can't afford to buy meat from the market. Forests are logged at unsustainable rates because the timber found in Laos is valuable and loggers see more profit in cutting than not. And hydropower projects affect river systems

For fuller descriptions of all Laos's National Protected Areas, see the comprehensive website www.ecotourismlaos.com

E TO TREK

The best way to get into the wilderness is on a trek into one of Laos's National Protected Areas (NPAs). Most treks have both a cultural and environmental focus, with trekkers sleeping in village homestays (p48) and your money going directly into some of the poorest communities in the country.

These treks are mostly run by provincial tourism authorities and have English-speaking guides. They can be organised once you arrive or in advance by phone, and are the cheapest trekking options available. Some companies, most notably Green Discovery (www.greendiscoverylaos.com), offer more elaborate trekking, often combining walking with mountain biking, kayaking and/or rafting. Guides will likely be more experienced but the trips are also more expensive.

To help you get an idea of the options, we've listed the areas where organised trekking is possible, from north to south. Each of these areas is covered in detail in this book. For more information, see p301 and the boxed text, Responsible Trekking on p204.

Phongsali (p210) From Phongsali. One to five-day treks in remote hills, overnighting in Akha and Up Noi villages. Treks are moderately easy and the emphasis is on culture.

Nam Ha NPA (p198) From Luang Nam Tha. One to four-day treks into this wild and wonderful area. Over 10 treks offered, the most popular including homestays in hilltop Akha villages. This is a true eco-experience.

Muang Sing (p203) From Muang Sing. One to three-day treks exploring the diverse ethnic villages in the area. There are seven different treks and each includes authentic homestays. Some delve slightly into Nam Ha NPA.

Vieng Phoukha (p202) From Vieng Phoukha. One to three-day treks in some of Northern Laos' most spectacular and culturally-rich landscape. Most encompass homestays in Akha, Khamu and Lahu villages and explore the south of Nam Ha NPA.

Phu Khao Khuay NPA (p118) From Vientiane. Two and three-day treks, the most popular of which include a stay in an elephant tower and a rare chance (not a guarantee) at seeing wild Asian elephants.

Phu Hin Bun NPA (p230) From Tha Khaek or Ban Khoun Kham (Ban Na Hin). For beauty, it's hard to beat these trekking and boating trips through the monolithic limestone karsts. Two and three-day options available, or four days with Green Discovery.

Dong Natad Provincial Protected Area (PPA) (p247) From Savannakhet. One and two-day trips to the provincial protected area near Savannakhet are cheap and popular for their homestay and explanations of how villagers use the sacred forest.

Dong Phu Vieng NPA (p249) From Savannakhet. This three-day trek (with a fair bit of road time at either end) takes you to two Katang villages where animist beliefs come with a host of taboos. It's a real head-bending cultural experience, but the transport makes prices a bit steep.

Phu Xieng Thong NPA (p261) From Pakse. A three-day trek and river trip along the Mekong. The village homestay isn't the most exciting, but visiting the hermit nun in the NPA is fascinating.

Se Pian NPA (p271) From Pakse or Attapeu. Taking in the elephants of Kiet Ngong (p270), this trek through forest, stream and rice field brings you to the remote Laven village of Ta Ong before returning by boat or over a hill with stunning views of the protected area. Two and three-day treks available.

Dong Ampham NPA (p297) From Attapeu. As far as we know fewer than five groups have ever done this trek into the most distant and well-preserved reaches of the country. The goal of the five day trip is the beautiful crater lake of Nong Fa – one of the holy grails of adventure travel in Laos. Not cheap.

and their dependent ecologies – including the forests – because Laos needs the money hydroelectricity can bring, and it's relatively cheap and easy for energy companies to develop in Laos.

Laws do exist to protect wildlife and, as mentioned, plenty of Laos is protected as NPAs. But most Laotians are completely unaware of world conservation issues and there is little will and less money to pay for conservation projects, such as organised park rangers, or to prosecute offenders. Lack of communication between national and local governments and poor definitions of authority in conservation areas just add to the issues.

One of the biggest obstacles facing environmental protection in Laos is corruption among those in charge of enforcing conservation regulations.

Illegal timber felling, poaching and the smuggling of exotic wildlife species would decrease sharply if corruption among officials was properly tackled.

However, there is some good news. With the support of several dedicated individuals and NGOs, ecotourism (see Ecotourism in Laos, p72) is growing to the point where some local communities are beginning to understand – and buying into – the idea that an intact environment can be worth money. Added to that, the government has mainly avoided giving contracts to companies wanting to develop large-scale resorts; though the same can't be said for many non-tourism projects. Air pollution and carbon emissions are about as low as you'll find anywhere in the region because most Lao still live at or just above a subsistence level and there is little heavy industry. Laos has one of the lowest per capita energy-consumption rates in the world.

One long-standing environmental problem has been the unexploded ordnance (UXO) contaminating parts of eastern Laos where the Ho Chi Minh Trail ran during the Second Indochina War. Bombs are being found and defused at a painstakingly slow rate, but progress is being made.

Thus the major challenges facing Laos's environment are the internal pressures of economic growth and external pressures from the country's more populated and affluent neighbours – particularly China, Vietnam and Thailand – who would like to exploit Laos's abundant resources as much as possible.

Hydropower Projects

At the time of writing the electricity industry lobby in Laos was proudly reporting on its website (www.poweringprogress.org) that since 2000 four hydroelectric dams had begun operation and construction was proceeding on four more. The Lao government was also at varying stages of contracting to award construction rights to foreign companies for a further 34 hydropower schemes. And, to top it all off, another 19 sites were being studied, and only six – including four huge proposals to dam the Mekong itself – had been declared 'not open to development'.

Hydropower is a relatively clean source of energy and to a certain extent dams in Laos are inevitable (see Developing the Mekong: Relieving Poverty or Dam Crazy, p65). But these are truly staggering numbers, with a potentially serious impact on the ecology of almost every major river system in the country.

Aside from displacing tens of thousands of people, dam projects inundate large swathes of forest (rarely agricultural land), permanently change the water flows, block or change fish migrations, thus affecting the fisheries local people have been relying on for centuries, and alter the ecosystems that support forests and the species that live in them. These forests are also the source of myriad non-timber products that contribute to local livelihoods, and the effects on these are often severe.

Like solar and wind power, hydropower is a potential source of sustainable and renewable energy when coupled with responsible land/resource planning and development. The question is, does Laos – and the companies looking to cash in on the resource – have the latter?

Habitat Loss

Deforestation is another major environmental issue in Laos. Although the official export of timber is tightly controlled, no-one really knows how much teak and other hardwoods are being smuggled into Vietnam, Thailand and especially China. The policy in northern Laos has been to allow the Chinese to take as much timber as they want in return for building roads. The Lao army is still removing huge chunks of forest in Khammuan

Several non-government organisations are working in Laos to help preserve, promote and protect the environment. See what they're doing at:

Elefant Asia
(www.elefantasia.org)

Traffic East Asia
(www.traffic.org)

Wildlife Conservation Society
(www.wcs.org)

World Conservation Union
(IUCN; www.iucnlao.org)

World Wildlife Fund
(www.wwf.org or www.panda.org)

ECOTOURISM IN LAOS *Steven Schipani*

With forests covering about half of the country, 20 National Protected Areas, 49 ethnic groups, over 650 bird species and hundreds of mammals, it's no mystery why Laos is known as having Southeast Asia's healthiest ecosystems and is a haven for travellers looking to get off the beaten path. Nowadays there are many tour companies and local tour guides offering forest trekking, cave exploration, village homestays and special river journeys to where the roads don't go. These types of activities are very popular in Laos and their availability has exploded over the past five years. Following the success of the Nam Ha Ecotourism Project in Luang Nam Tha Province, which began in 1999, the ecotourism industry has grown from the bottom up and today the Lao Government is actively promoting ecotourism as one way to help reduce poverty and support the protection of the environment and local culture. It is estimated that culture and nature based tourism generates more than half of the country's US$150 million in annual tourism revenue.

The Lao National Tourism Administration defines ecotourism as: 'Tourism activity in rural and protected areas that minimizes negative impacts and is directed towards the conservation of natural and cultural resources, rural socio-economic development and visitor understanding of, and appreciation for, the places they are visiting.' A few Lao tour operators and guesthouses have taken this definition to heart and operate their businesses in a way that uphold the principles of Lao ecotourism.

In Luang Nam Tha in the north the Boatlanding Guesthouse (www.theboatlanding.com) is Laos's first eco-lodge and winner of several international awards. Visit one of the National Protected Areas (NPAs) with Green Discovery Laos (www.greendiscoverylaos.com), which has offices in Luang Nam Tha, Tha Khaek, Vientiane, Pakse and Vang Vieng. In Luang Prabang, Tiger Trails Resort (www.laos-adventures.com) has partnered with local communities to offer treks, elephant rides and boat trips in the Nam Khan Valley. In the south, high quality eco-accommodation can be found in Champasak Province's Kingfisher Eco-Lodge (www.kingfisherecolodge.com), nestled inside the Se Pian NPA. For a chance to see wild elephants, don't miss the village-operated Elephant Tower at Ban Na (www.trekkingcentrallaos.com), about an hour from Vientiane. There are also locally run eco-guide services attached to the Provincial Tourist Information Centres in Luang Nam Tha, Luang Prabang, Savannakhet and Champasak Provinces offering one to four day trips at fair prices. These can be booked on a walk-in basis – see Where to Trek (p70) and www.ecotourismlaos.com for details.

Unfortunately, some uninformed companies label everything as "ecotourism" therefore it is important to determine who is actually upholding the principles of Lao ecotourism, and who is simply greening their pockets. Some questions to ask to ensure you are on the right track are:

- Does my trip financially benefit local people, help to protect biodiversity and support the continuation of traditional culture?
- What will I learn on this trip, and what opportunities will local people have to learn from me?
- Are facilities designed in local style, use local, natural construction materials, and conserve energy and water? Is there local food on the menu?
- Will I be led by a local guide who is from the area visited?
- Is there a permit, entrance fee or other fee included in the price of the trip that is directed towards conservation activities?
- Are there sensible limits in place concerning group size and frequency of departures to minimize negative impacts?

Supporting businesses that can give clear, positive and believable answers to these questions will most likely result in an enjoyable, educational experience, where you make more than a few local friends along the way. It also raises the profile of sustainable business operators, hopefully encouraging others to follow their example.

www.ecotourismlaos.com

Province and from remote areas in the country's far south, near the Se Pian and Dong Hua Sao NPAs, much of it going to Vietnam. The national electricity-generating company also profits from the timber sales each time it links a Lao town or village with the national power grid, clear-cutting a wider-than-necessary swathe along Lao highways.

Essentially, the Lao authorities express a seemingly sincere desire to conserve the nation's forests – but not at the cost of rural livelihoods. In most rural areas 70% of non-rice foods come from the forest. Thus forest destruction, whether as a result of logging or dam-building, will lead to increased poverty and reduced local livelihoods.

Other pressures on the forest cover come from swidden (slash-and-burn) methods of cultivation, in which small plots of forest are cleared, burnt for nitrogenation of the soil, and farmed intensively for two or three years, after which they are infertile and unfarmable for between eight and 10 years. Considering the sparse population, swidden cultivation is probably not as great an environmental threat as logging. But neither is it an efficient use of resources.

Forestry per se is not all bad, and effective management could maintain Laos's forests as a source of income for a long time to come. Creating NPAs has been a good start, but examples of forest regeneration and even planting high-value trees for future harvest are rare. All too often the name of the game is short-term gain.

> Around 85% of Laos is mountainous terrain, and less than 4% is considered arable.

Hunting & Overfishing

The majority of Lao citizens derive most of their protein from food culled from nature, not from farms or ranches. How threatening traditional hunting habits are to species survival in Laos is debatable given the nation's extremely sparse population. But, combined with habitat loss, hunting for food is placing increasing pressure on wildlife numbers.

The cross-border trade in wildlife is also potentially serious. Much of the poaching that takes place in Laos's NPAs is allegedly carried out by Vietnamese hunters who have crossed into central Laos illegally to round up species such as pangolins, civets, barking deer, goral and raccoon dogs to sell back home. These animals are highly valued for both food and medicinal purposes in Vietnam, Thailand and China, and as the demand in those countries grows in line with increasing wealth, so too do the prices buyers are prepared to pay.

Foreign NGOs run grass roots education campaigns across Laos in an effort to raise awareness of endangered species and the effects of hunting on local ecosystems. But as usual, money is the key to breaking the cycle. And while hunters remain dirt poor, the problem seems here to stay.

In more densely populated areas such as Savannakhet and Champasak provinces, the overfishing of lakes and rivers poses a danger to certain fish species. Projects to educate fishermen about exactly where their catch comes from, and how to protect that source, have been successful in changing some unsustainable practices. One area given particular attention is fishing using explosives. This practice, whereby fishermen throw explosives into the water and wait for the dead fish to float to the surface, is incredibly destructive. Most fishermen don't realise that for every dead fish they collect from the surface, another two or three lie dead on the river bed. The practice is illegal in Laos, and anecdotal evidence suggests education and the law have reduced the problem.

> *Wildlife Trade in Laos: The End of the Game* (2001), by Hanneke Nooren & Gordon Claridge, is a frightening description of animal poaching in Laos.

Food & Drink

Lao food doesn't have the variety and depth of the more famous cuisines of neighbouring China, Thailand and Vietnam, but you can eat well in Laos if you take the time to learn a little about the cuisine while you're there. While few people travel to this country with food as their prime objective, a little experimentation can take you a long way towards appreciating the cuisine and can be very rewarding.

It's little surprise that Lao food is similar to Thai cuisine, given the long interwoven history the two countries share. But while dishes such as *làap* (meat salad) and *tạm màak-hung* (som tam; papaya salad) will be familiar to anyone with even a basic knowledge of Thai food, there are some aspects of Lao cuisine that are unmistakably Lao. The most obvious of these is *khào nǐaw* (sticky rice), which is classed by scholars as being one of the main identifiers of Lao culture.

In the Mekong River valley areas, where Lao culture is strongest, sticky rice is ever-present. During five days of trekking through villages in Champasak Province we ate sticky rice with every meal. That might sound a bit repetitive, but the *khào nǐaw* was only part of these meals, and each one was complemented with at least two different and tasty Lao dishes.

Sticky rice isn't so popular in mountainous areas – the Hmong don't eat it at all – and the culinary variety can be pretty limited, too. The limits come from a lack of money and difficult growing conditions.

Ant Egg Soup (2004), by Natacha du Pont de Bie, is a well-written account of the author's encounters with food while travelling through Laos, garnished with recipes and line drawings.

STAPLES & SPECIALITIES

Travellers already hip to Thai cuisine will experience *déjà vu* in the Lao emphasis on simple, fresh ingredients coarsely blended into rustic dishes. Herbs like basil, mint, coriander and lemongrass lend bright tones to the mix, balanced by the spicy bitterness of roots and rhizomes (the thick, underground stem of certain plants), the tang of lime juice and Kaffir lime leaves, the pungent salt of fish sauce or shrimp paste and the fire of fresh chillies.

Staple ingredients include locally raised *phák* (vegetables), *pạa* (fish), *kai* (chicken), *pét* (duck), *mǔu* (pork) and *sìin ngúa* (beef) or *sìin khwái* (water buffalo). Because of Laos's distance from the sea, freshwater fish is more common than saltwater fish or shellfish. When meats are used, Lao cooks prefer to emphasise savoury tones imparted by grilling, roasting or mixing with cooked ingredients that are inherently savoury, such as roasted rice.

To salt the food, various fermented fish concoctions are used, most commonly *nâm pạa*, which is a thin sauce of fermented anchovies, and *pạa dàek*, a coarser, native Lao preparation that includes chunks of fermented freshwater fish, rice husks and rice 'dust'. *Nâm pạa dàek* is the sauce poured from *pạa dàek*. See the Health chapter (p336) for warnings on eating *pạa dàek*. *Phǒng súu lot – ajinomoto* (MSG) – is also a common seasoning, and in Laos you may even see it served as a table condiment in noodle restaurants.

Fresh *nâm màak náo* (lime juice), *sìi-khái* (lemongrass), *bại sálanae* (mint leaf) and *phák hǎwm* (coriander leaf) are added to give the food its characteristic tang. Other common seasonings include *khaa* (galingale), *màak phét* (hot chillies), *nâm màak khǎam* (tamarind juice), *khǐng* (ginger) and *nâm màak phâo* or *nâm káthí* (coconut milk). Chillies are sometimes served on the side in hot pepper sauces called *jạew*. In Luang Prabang, *nǎng khwái hàeng* (dried skin of water buffalo) is quite a popular ingredient.

One of the most common Lao dishes is *làap,* which is a Lao-style salad of minced meat, fowl or fish tossed with lime juice, garlic, *khào khûa* (roasted,

---

STREET FOOD

Laos is blessed with a rich variety of food cooked, served and eaten on the street. Among the most common is *tąm màak-hung* (generally known as *tąm sòm* in Vientiane), a spicy, tangy salad made by pounding shredded green papaya, lime juice, chillies, garlic, *pąa dàek*, *nǎm phàk-kàat* (a paste of boiled, fermented lettuce leaves) and various other ingredients together in a large mortar. This is a favourite market and street-vendor food – customers typically inspect the array of possible *tąm màak-hung* ingredients the vendor has spread out next to the mortar, then order a custom mix. For something different, ask the pounder to throw in a few *màak kàwk*, a sour, olive-shaped fruit.

The Lao love a good *pîng* (grill), and you'll find all manner of meats and offals grilling over makeshift barbecues. *Pîng kai* (grilled chicken) is a favourite, and involves the cook taking chickens (whole or dissected) and rubbing them with a marinade of garlic, coriander root, black pepper and salt or fish sauce before cooking them slowly over hot coals. But our favourite is definitely *pîng pąa* (grilled fish). *Pîng pąa* is prepared by scaling a fish, rubbing it with a thick layer of salt and stuffing a handful of lemongrass stems down its throat before slowly grilling it. Other ingredients can be added, but it's the lemongrass and the fact the fish retains most of its moisture that we love. Delicious.

---

powdered sticky rice), green onions, mint leaves and chillies. It can be very hot or rather mild, depending on the cook. Meats mixed into *làap* are sometimes raw *(díp)* rather than cooked *(súk)*. *Làap* is typically served with a large plate of lettuce, mint, steamed mango leaves and various other fresh herbs depending on season and availability. Using your fingers you wrap a little *làap* in the lettuce and herbs and eat it with balls of sticky rice which you roll by hand.

Many Lao dishes are quite spicy because of the Lao penchant for *màak phét*. But the Lao also eat a lot of Chinese and Vietnamese food, which is generally less spicy. *Fŏe* (rice noodle soup) is popular as a snack and for breakfast, and is almost always served with a plate of fresh lettuce, mint, basil, coriander, mung bean sprouts and lime wedges to add to the soup as desired. Especially in the south, people mix their own *fŏe* sauce of lime, crushed fresh chilli, *kápí* (shrimp paste) and sugar at the table using a little saucer provided for the purpose. In Luang Prabang, some *fŏe* shops may add *jąew ngáa*, a sesame paste.

Another common noodle dish, especially in the morning, is *khào pįak sèn*, a soft, round rice noodle served in a broth with pieces of chicken or occasionally pork, and often eaten with crushed fresh ginger. Many *khào pįak sèn* vendors also sell *khào-nŏm khuu*, small deep-fried, doughnut-like Chinese pastries. Some vendors even leave a pair of scissors on each table so that you can cut the pastries up and mix them into your soup. It may sound strange, but it's very tasty.

Khào pûn, flour noodles topped with a sweet and spicy *nâm káthí* (coconut sauce), is another popular noodle dish. These noodles are also eaten cold with various Vietnamese foods popular in urban Laos, particularly *nǎem néuang* (barbecued pork meatballs) and *yáw* (spring rolls).

Rice is the foundation for all Lao meals (as opposed to snacks), as with elsewhere in Southeast Asia. Although the Lao generally eat *khào nǐaw* (sticky or glutinous rice), *khào jâo* (ordinary white rice) is also common in the major towns.

In Vientiane, Savannakhet, Pakse and Luang Prabang, French bread *(khào jîi)* is popular for breakfast. Sometimes it's eaten plain with *kąa-féh nóm hâwn* (hot milk coffee), sometimes it's eaten with *khai* (eggs) or in a baguette sandwich that contains Lao-style pâté, and vegetables. Or you can order them *sai*

YOUR TASTEBUDS

...en't really been to Laos if you haven't dabbled in:

- Beerlao – the national beverage
- *khai phụn* – dried, seasoned river moss, a Luang Prabang speciality
- *làap pqa* – finely minced fish blended with herbs, dried chilli flakes and roasted ground sticky rice
- *lào hǎi* – fermented rice wine served in a large clay jar with long reed straws
- *nǎem khào* – balls of cooked rice mixed with sour pork sausage and fried whole, then broken into a saladlike dish eaten with fresh leaves and herbs; a Vientiane speciality
- *sìin sawǎn* – thin sheets of dried, spiced beef
- *tạm kûay* – green bananas pounded whole – skin and all – with chillies, lime juice, fish sauce and more.

nâm nóm: sliced in half lengthwise and drizzled with sweetened condensed milk. Fresh Lao baguettes can be superb. Croissants and other French-style pastries are also available in the bakeries of Vientiane and Luang Prabang.

DRINKS
Nonalcoholic Drinks
WATER
Water purified for drinking purposes is simply called *nâm deum* (drinking water), whether it is boiled or filtered. *All* water offered to customers in restaurants or hotels will be purified, so don't fret about the safety of taking a sip. In restaurants you can ask for *nâm pao* (plain water, which is always either boiled or taken from a purified source) served by the glass at no charge, or order plain or carbonated water by the bottle. In remote villages you'll often be served water with a distinct colour – usually yellow or red – and a smoky taste. This water is safe to drink and the colour comes from a root which is boiled with the water, the specific root differing depending on where you are.

COFFEE & TEA
Lao-grown coffee is regarded as among the world's best (see *Kạa-féh Láo*, p285). Traditionally, pure Lao coffee is roasted by wholesalers, ground by vendors and filtered through a sock-like cloth bag just before serving. The result is thick, black, strong and delicious. Increasingly, however, restaurants and hotels in particular are serving Nescafé or similar instant coffee to foreigners. To make sure you get real Lao coffee ask for *kạa-féh láo* (Lao coffee) or *kạa-féh bọh-láan* (old-fashioned coffee).

Brewed coffee is usually served in small glasses and mixed with sugar and a startling amount of sweetened condensed milk. Once you've mixed it all up it's delicious, but if you don't want either be sure to specify *kạa-féh dạm* (black coffee) followed with *baw sai nâm-tạan* (without sugar). An almost addictive variation is *òh-lîang* (iced coffee with condensed milk and sugar). Only in better hotels and restaurants will you find real milk.

In central and southern Laos coffee is almost always served with a chaser of hot *nâm sáa* (weak and often lukewarm Chinese tea), while in the north it's typically served with a glass of plain hot water.

Both Indian-style (black) and Chinese-style (green or semicured) teas are served in Laos, some of the latter now being grown on the Bolaven Plateau and elsewhere. An order of *sáa hâwn* (hot tea) usually results in a cup (or

Fish and Fish Dishes of Laos (2003), by Alan Davidson, is a thorough description of Laos's diverse freshwater fish cookery. The late Davidson was British ambassador to Laos in the 1970s and author of the esteemed *Oxford Companion to Food*.

glass) of black tea with sugar and condensed milk. As with coffee you must specify beforehand if you want black tea without milk and/or sugar. Ask for *sáa hâwn* followed by *baw sai nóm* (without milk) and/or *baw sai nâm-taan* (without sugar). Chinese tea is traditionally served in restaurants for free. For stronger fresh Chinese tea, request *sáa jiin*.

Alcoholic Drinks

BEER

It's hard to overestimate how important Beerlao is to the people of Laos – and not just as a means of getting drunk. In a country with so few exports and virtually zero in the way of international recognition, the constant approval of their national brew is a source of great pride. The success of the Lao Brewery Co (LBC), the government-controlled brewer based in Vientiane, is widely reported in official media. And when Carlsberg increased its stake to 50% of the business in 2006 it was yet further proof that Laos is doing something very right.

Until recently Beerlao had 99% of the domestic beer market. The distinctive yellow crates can be seen in all but the most remote parts of the country and despite competition from Carlsberg, Heineken and Tiger (all of which cost more), most people still opt for the local brew.

Beerlao comes in the ubiquitous 630ml bottles (US$1 in most bars) but is also available in 330ml cans. A draught version (*bia sót*: fresh beer) is tastier yet, but it has a limited distribution. Beerlao contains 5% alcohol. Bottles of Beerlao Dark (a dark ale with 6.5% alcohol) and Beerlao Light (2.9% alcohol) can also be found in larger cities and towns.

DISTILLED SPIRITS

Beerlao might be the source of much national pride but rice whisky, known as *lào-láo*, is responsible for many more sore heads. This is partly because it's so much cheaper than beer and partly because the lowland Lao, in particular, just like it. Chances are you'll be invited to partake in festivities with a neat shot of *lào-láo* at some point; see the Spirit of Spirits (below) for more on drinking customs.

The best *lào-láo* is said to come from Phongsali and Don Khong, the northern and southern extremes of the country, but it's available virtually everywhere, usually for between US$0.20 and US$0.50 per 750ml bottle.

Tourist hotel bars in the larger cities carry the standard variety of liquors.

WINE

Decent French and Italian wines are abundantly available in Vientiane at restaurants, shops specialising in imported foods and in some shops which sell nothing but wine. Some restaurants and hotels in Luang Prabang, Savannakhet and Pakse also stock wine. New World wines are more scarce, though we saw quite a few Australian wines around. Whatever the origin, wine is

> The teapots commonly seen on tables in Chinese and Vietnamese restaurants are filled with *nâm sáa* (weak Chinese tea); ask for a *jàwk pao* (glass) and you can drink as much as you'd like at no charge.

THE SPIRIT OF SPIRITS

In a Lao home the pouring and drinking of *lào-láo* at the evening meal takes on ritual characteristics. Usually towards the end of the meal, but occasionally beforehand, the hosts bring out a bottle of the stuff to treat their guests. The usual procedure is for the host to pour one jigger of *lào-láo* onto the floor or a used dinner plate first, to appease the house spirits. The host then pours another jigger and downs it in one gulp. Jiggers for each guest are poured in turn; guests must take at least one offered drink or risk offending the house spirits.

much cheaper than it is in Thailand because the import tax is lower, so it's worth stocking up if you're heading across the border.

Luang Prabang is famous for a type of light rice wine called *khào kam,* a red-tinted, somewhat sweet beverage made from sticky rice. It can be quite tasty when properly prepared and stored, but rather mouldy-tasting if not.

In rural provinces, a rice wine known as *lào-hǎi* (jar liquor) is fermented by households or villages. *Lào-hǎi* is usually drunk from a communal jar using long reed straws.

Mon-Khmer tribal villages on the Bolaven Plateau periodically hold special ceremonies where water buffalo are sacrificed to appease local spirits. Once the rituals have been performed, the villagers share the buffalo meat, washed down with copious moonshine.

CELEBRATIONS

Temple festivals *(bun wat)* make good opportunities to taste real home-cooked Lao food as temple regulars often bring dishes from home to share with other temple visitors. Chances are vendors will also set up food-stalls offering everything from *khûa fǒe* (fried rice noodles) to *pîng kai* (grilled chicken).

The annual boat races (p307) usually held in October in towns along the Mekong River, is another great chance to graze at long lines of vendor booths; *nǎem khào* is particularly popular at these events.

During *tut jiin* (Chinese New Year), also known by its Vietnamese name Tet, Laos's Chinese population celebrates with a week of house-cleaning, lion dances, fireworks and feasting. The most impressive festivities take place in Vientiane's Chinatown (at the north end of Th Chao Anou) and 'mooncakes' – thick, circular pastries filled with sweet bean paste or salted pork – are on sale all over town.

WHERE TO EAT & DRINK

Aside from eating on the street (see Street Food, p75), the cheapest most dependable places to eat are *hâan fǒe* (noodle shops) and *talàat sǎo* (morning markets). Most towns and villages have at least one morning market (which often lasts all day despite the name) and several *hâan fǒe*. The next step up is the Lao-style café (*hâan kheuang deum;* drink shop) or *hâan kǐn deum* (eat-drink shop), where a more varied selection of dishes is usually served. Most expensive is the *hâan qahǎan* (food shop), where the menu is usually posted on the wall or on a blackboard (in Lao).

You'll see turkeys free-ranging their way around most villages in Laos, but you'll rarely see them on the table, as they are reserved for ceremonial occasions such as weddings. They were introduced in the early 1960s by US-government aid organisation USAID, to bring much-needed protein to rural communities.

Many *hâan qahǎan* serve mostly Chinese or Vietnamese food. The ones serving real Lao food usually have a large pan of water on a stool – or a modern lavatory – somewhere near the entrance for washing the hands before eating (Lao food is traditionally eaten with the hands).

Many restaurants or food stalls, especially outside Vientiane, don't have menus and fewer still have menus in English. In these parts it's worth memorising the names of a few standard dishes. Most provinces also have their own local specialities and if you have an adventurous palate it's well worth asking for *qahǎan phisèht* (special food), allowing the proprietors to choose for you.

Especially in the larger cities along the Mekong River, the number of Western-style restaurants is growing fast. Vientiane and Luang Prabang, in particular, boast dozens of restaurants serving a wide variety of cuisine, from Japanese and North Korean to fine French fare, all at very reasonable prices.

VEGETARIANS & VEGANS

Almost all Lao dishes contain animal products of one kind or another. Two principal seasonings, for example, are fish sauce and shrimp paste. Some dishes also contain lard or pork fat.

A TASTE FOR THE WILD *Andrew Burke*

Driving through southern Laos with a Lao friend a few years ago we came across a snake slowly slithering its way across the road. We stopped for a look and a moment later a group of villagers walked over the hill about 150m in front of us, and a man on a bike pedalled over the crest about 200m behind us. Then they saw the snake…

Immediately several members of the group dropped what they were carrying and started bolting towards the snake. But this race was always going to be won by the guy pedalling frantically down the slope. A few seconds later he glided past and ran over the snake before calmly dismounting and strolling up to the stunned serpent. He grabbed it by the tail and swung it into the road, and a second later it was dead. The family ahead stopped running with a groan of disappointment and the guy stood holding up the snake, grinning with self-satisfaction. 'This is very special food,' he said, before heading home to grill it for lunch with his cousin.

Back in the car my friend, who was a little disappointed it wasn't him heading off to the grill, explained that most snakes were delicious (you guessed it, they taste a bit like chicken). 'Yes, and there are lots of wild animals in these forests that the villagers like to eat,' he added. While the number of rural people who can afford to buy domestically raised meat is rising, many still depend on wildlife they catch themselves for protein. And when you get off the main routes you'll see people selling and eating deer, wild pigs, squirrels, civets, monitor lizards, jungle fowl/pheasants, dhole (wild dogs), rats and just about any bird they can bring down with a slingshot or catch in a net.

In part this practice is due to the expense involved in animal husbandry, and partly due to the Lao preference for the taste of wild game. Either way, the eating of endangered species causes much consternation among wildlife conservationists (see p68) – and anyone who's walked through a virtually silent forest and wondered what happened to all the game.

Vegetarian or vegan restaurants are virtually nonexistent, but menus at tourist-oriented restaurants in larger towns and cities will often have vegetarian dishes available.

Outside of tourist areas, vegetarians and vegans will have to make an effort to speak enough Lao to convey their culinary needs. The best all-around phrase to memorise is 'I eat only vegetables' *(khàwy kịn tae phák)*. If you eat eggs you can add *sai khai dâi* (it's OK to add egg) to your food vocabulary. Dairy products such as cheese won't be much of a concern since they're rarely served in Lao restaurants.

HABITS & CUSTOMS

Eating in Laos is nearly always a social event and the Lao avoid eating alone whenever possible. Except for the 'rice plates' and the noodle dishes, Lao meals are typically ordered 'family style', which is to say that two or more people order together, sharing different dishes. Traditionally, the party orders one of each kind of dish, for example, one chicken, one fish, one soup. One dish is generally large enough for two people.

Most Lao consider eating alone to be rather unusual; but then as a *falang* (Westerner) you are an exception anyway. In Chinese or Thai restaurants a cheaper alternative is to order dishes *làat khào* (over rice).

Most Lao dishes are eaten with *khào nǐaw* (glutinous or sticky rice). *Khào nǐaw* is served up in lidded baskets called *típ khào* and eaten with the hands. The general practice is to grab a small fistful of rice from the *típ khào*, then roll it into a rough ball that you then use to dip into the various dishes. As always, watching others is the best way to learn.

If *khào jâo* (normal steamed rice) is served with the meal, then it is eaten with a fork and spoon. The spoon, held in the right hand, is used to scoop up the rice and accompanying dishes and placing it in the mouth. The fork, held in the left hand, is merely used to prod food onto the spoon.

Chopsticks *(mâi thuu)* are reserved for dining in Chinese restaurants (where rice is served in small Chinese bowls rather than flat plates) or for eating Chinese noodle dishes. Noodle soups are eaten with a spoon in the left hand (for spooning up the broth) and chopsticks in the right (for grasping the noodles and other solid ingredients).

Dishes are typically served all at once rather than in courses. If the host or restaurant staff can't bring them all to the table because of a shortage of help or because the food is being cooked sequentially from the same set of pots and pans, then the diners typically wait until all the platters are on the table before digging in.

The Lao don't concern themselves with whether dishes are served piping hot, so no one minds if the dishes sit in the kitchen or on the table for 15 minutes or so before anyone digs in. Furthermore it's considered somewhat impolite to take a spoonful of food that's steaming hot as it implies you're so ravenous or uncivilised that you can't wait to gorge yourself.

COOKING COURSES

Cooking courses are available in both Luang Prabang (p147) and Vientiane (p101).

EAT YOUR WORDS

Want to know *làap* from *lào- láo*? *Khào kam* from *khào nìaw*? Get behind the cuisine by getting to know the language. For pronunciation guidelines see p345.

Useful Phrases

What do you have that's special?	*mìi nyǎng phi-sèt baw*	ມີຫຍັງພິເສດບໍ່
Do you have ...?	*mìi ... baw*	ມີ ... ບໍ່
I didn't order this.	*khàwy baw dâi sang náew nîi*	ຂ້ອຍບໍ່ໄດ້ສັ່ງແບວນີ້
I eat only vegetables.	*khàwy kjn tae phák*	ຂ້ອຍກິນແຕ່ຜັກ
(I) don't like it hot and spicy.	*baw mak phét*	ບໍ່ມັກເຜັດ
(I) like it hot and spicy.	*mak phét*	ມັກເຜັດ
I'd like to try that.	*khàwy yàak láwng kjn boeng*	ຂ້ອຍຢາກລອງກິນເບິ່ງ
Please bring (a) ...	*khǎw ... dae*	ຂໍ ... ແດ່
menu	*láai-kqan qa-hǎan*	ລາຍການ ອາຫານ
plate	*jqa*	ຈານ
bowl	*thùay*	ຖ້ວຍ
glass	*jàwk*	ຈອກ
spoon	*buang*	ບ່ວງ
fork	*sâwm*	ສ້ອມ
chopsticks	*mâi thuu*	ໄມ້ທູ່
knife	*mìit*	ມີດ
bill	*saek*	ແຊັກ

After eating *khào nìaw* (sticky rice) don't forget to replace the lid on top of the *típ khào*, the small basket the sticky rice is served in. Not doing this is considered both rude to your host and bad luck.

Simple Laotian Cooking (2003), by Penn Hong-thong, is a collection of nearly 200 recipes along with straightforward expositions on the tools and techniques required to closely approximate Lao cuisine.

THE RIGHT TOOL FOR THE JOB

If you're not offered chopsticks, don't ask for them. When *falang* (Westerners) ask for chopsticks to eat Lao food, it only puzzles the restaurant proprietors. An even more embarrassing act is trying to eat sticky rice with chopsticks. Use your right hand instead. For ordinary white rice, use the fork and spoon provided (fork in the left hand, spoon in the right, or the reverse for left-handers).

Menu Decoder

DRINKS

water	*nâm*	ນ້ຳ
drinking water	*nâm deum*	ນ້ຳຕົ້ມ
boiled water	*nâm tôm*	ນ້ຳຕົ້ມ
hot water	*nâm hâwn*	ນ້ຳຮ້ອນ
cold water	*nâm yén*	ນ້ຳເຢັນ
soda water	*nâm sòh-dqa*	ນ້ຳໂສດາ
orange juice/soda	*nâm màak kîang*	ນ້ຳໝາກກ້ຽງ
plain milk	*nâm nóm*	ນ້ຳນົມ
ice	*nâm kâwn*	ນ້ຳກ້ອນ
glass	*jàwk*	ຈອກ
bottle	*kâew*	ແກ້ວ
hot Lao coffee with milk & sugar	*kqa-féh nóm hâwn*	ກາເຟນົມຮ້ອນ
hot Lao coffee with sugar, no milk	*kqa-féh dqm*	ກາເຟດຳ
iced Lao coffee with sugar, no milk	*kqa-féh nóm yén*	ກາເຟນົມເຢັນ
iced Lao coffee with milk & sugar	*òh-lîang*	ໂອລ້ຽງ
hot tea with sugar	*sáa hâwn*	ຊາຮ້ອນ
hot tea with milk & sugar	*sáa nóm hâwn*	ຊານົມຮ້ອນ
iced tea with sugar	*sáa wǎan yén*	ຊາຫວານເຢັນ
iced tea with milk & sugar	*sáa nóm yén*	ຊານົມເຢັນ
Ovaltine	*oh-wantin*	ໂອວັນຕິນ
beer	*bja*	ເບຍ
draught beer	*bja sót*	ເບຍສົດ
rice whisky	*lào láo*	ເຫຼົ້າລາວ

EGG DISHES

fried egg	*khai dqo*	ໄຂ່ດາວ
hard-boiled egg	*khai tôm*	ໄຂ່ຕົ້ມ
plain omelette	*jęun khai*	ຈືນໄຂ່
scrambled egg	*khai khùa*	ໄຂ່ຂົ້ວ

FISH & SEAFOOD

crisp-fried fish	*jęun pqa*	ຈືນປາ
fried prawns	*jęun kûng*	ຈືນກຸ້ງ
grilled prawns	*pîing kûng*	ປີ້ງກຸ້ງ

steamed fish	*nèung pqa*	ໜຶ້ງປາ
grilled fish	*pǐing pqa*	ປີ້ງປາ
sweet & sour fish	*pqa sòm-wǎan*	ປາສົ້ມຫວານ
catfish	*pqa dúk*	ປາດຸກ

MEAT SALADS (LÀAP)

beef laap	*làap sìin*	ລາບຊີ້ນ
chicken laap	*làap kai*	ລາບໄກ່
fish laap	*làap pqa*	ລາບປາ
pork laap	*làap mǔu*	ລາບໝູ

RICE DISHES

steamed white rice	*khào nèung*	ເຂົ້າໜຶ້ງ
sticky rice	*khào nǐaw*	ເຂົ້າໜຽວ
curry over rice	*khào làat kqeng*	ເຂົ້າລາດແກງ
'red' pork (char siu) with rice	*khào mǔu dqeng*	ເຂົ້າໝູແດງ
roast duck over rice	*khào nàa pét*	ເຂົ້າໜ້າເປັດ
fried rice with ...	*khào phát (khào khùa) ...*	ເຂົ້າຜັດ (ເຂົ້າຂົ້ວ) ...
chicken	*kai*	ໄກ່
pork	*mǔu*	ໝູ
shrimp/prawns	*kûng*	ກຸ້ງ
crab	*pqu*	ປູ

SNACKS

fried peanuts	*thua dịn jẹun*	ຖົ່ວດິນຈືນ
fried potatoes	*mán fa-lang jẹun*	ມັນຝລັ່ງຈືນ
fresh spring rolls	*yáw díp*	ຍໍດິບ
fried spring rolls	*yáw jẹun*	ຍໍຈືນ
grilled chicken	*pǐng kai*	ປີ້ງໄກ່
shrimp chips	*khào khìap kûng*	ເຂົ້າຂຽບກຸ້ງ
spicy green papaya salad	*tqm màak-hung*	ຕໍາໝາກຫຸ່ງ

NOODLE DISHES

rice noodle soup with vegetables & meat	*fǒe*	ເຝີ
rice noodles with vegetables & meat, no broth	*fǒe hàeng*	ເຝີແຫ້ງ
rice noodles with gravy	*làat nàa*	ລາດໜ້າ
fried rice noodles with meat & vegetables	*fǒe khùa*	ເຝີຂົ້ວ
fried rice noodles with soy sauce	*phát sá-yìu*	ຜັດສະອິ້ວ
yellow wheat noodles in broth, with vegetables & meat	*mii nâm*	ໝີ່ນໍ້າ
yellow wheat noodles with vegetables & meat	*mii hàeng*	ໝີ່ແຫ້ງ
white flour noodles served with sweet-spicy sauce	*khào pûn*	ເຂົ້າປຸ້ນ

SOUP

mild soup with vegetables & pork	kąeng jèut	ແກງຈິດ
mild soup with vegetables, pork & bean curd	kąeng jèut tâo-hûu	ແກງຈິດເຕົາຮູ້
fish & lemongrass soup with mushrooms	tôm yám pǫa	ຕົ້ມຍຳປາ
rice soup with ...	khào pìak ...	ເຂົ້າປຽກ ...
chicken	kai	ໄກ່
fish	pǫa	ປາ
pork	mǔu	ໝູ

STIR-FRIED DISHES

chicken with ginger	kai phát khǐing	ໄກ່ຜັດຂີງ
sweet & sour pork	mǔu sòm-wǎan	ໝູສົ້ມຫວານ
beef in oyster sauce	ngúa phàt nâm-mán hǎwy	ງົວຜັດນ້ຳມັນຫອຍ
stir-fried mixed vegetables	phát phák	ຜັດຜັກ

Food Glossary
BREAD & PASTRIES

plain bread (usually French-style)	khào jìi	ເຂົ້າຈີ່
baguette sandwich	khào jìi páa-tê	ເຂົ້າຈີ່ປາເຕ
croissants	khúa-sawng	ຄົວຊ່ອງ
'Chinese doughnuts' (*youtiao* in Mandarin)	pá-thawng-kó (khào-nǒm khuu)	ປະທ່ອງໂກະ (ເຂົ້າໜົມຄູ່)

CONDIMENTS, HERBS & SPICES

chilli	màak phét	ໝາກເຜັດ
dipping sauces	jaew	ແຈ່ວ
fish sauce	nâm pǫa	ນ້ຳປາ
ginger	khǐing	ຂີງ
lemongrass	hǔa sǐng khái	ຫົວສິງໄຄ
lime juice	nâm màak náo	ນ້ຳໝາກນາວ
salt	kęua	ເກືອ
soy sauce	nâm sá-ìu	ນ້ຳສະອິ້ວ
sugar	nâm-tąan	ນ້ຳຕານ
sweet basil	bąi hǒh-la-pháa	ໃບໂຫລະພາ
tamarind	màak khǎam	ໝາກຂາມ
vinegar	nâm sòm	ນ້ຳສົ້ມ

FOOD TYPES

beef	sìin ngúa	ຊີ້ນງົວ
butter	bǫe	ເບີ
chicken	kai	ໄກ່
egg	khai	ໄຂ່

fish	*pqa*	ປາ
pork	*sìin mǔu*	ຊີ້ນໝູ
rice	*khào*	ເຂົ້າ
seafood	*qa-hǎan tha-léh*	ອາຫານທະເລ
shrimp/prawns	*kùng*	ກຸ້ງ
vegetables	*phak*	ຜັກ
yogurt	*nóm sòm*	ນົມສົ້ມ

FRUITS

banana	*màak kûay*	ໝາກກ້ວຍ
coconut	*màak phǎo*	ໝາກພ້າວ
guava (year-round)	*màak sǐi-dqa*	ໝາກສິດາ
jackfruit	*màak mǐi*	ໝາກມີ້
lime	*màak náo*	ໝາກນາວ
longan (dragon's eyes)	*màak nyám nyái*	ໝາກຍ້າໃຍ
lychee	*màak lìn-jii*	ໝາກລິ້ນຈີ່
mandarin orange	*màak kîang*	ໝາກກ້ຽງ
mango	*màak muang*	ໝາກມ່ວງ
pineapple	*màak nat*	ໝາກນັດ
papaya	*màak hung*	ໝາກຫຸ່ງ
rambutan	*màak ngaw*	ໝາກເງາະ
sugarcane	*âwy*	ອ້ອຍ
watermelon	*màak móh*	ໝາກໂມ

VEGETABLES

bamboo shoots	*naw mâi*	ໜໍ່ໄມ້
beans	*thua*	ຖົ່ວ
bean sprouts	*thua ngâwk*	ຖົ່ວງອກ
cabbage	*ká-lam pji*	ກະລ່ຳປີ
cauliflower	*ká-lam pji dàwk*	ກະລ່ຳປີດອກ
Chinese radish (daikon)	*phák kàat hǔa*	ຜັກກາດຫົວ
cucumber	*màak tqeng*	ໝາກແຕງ
eggplant	*màak khěua*	ໝາກເຂືອ
garlic	*hǔa phák thíam*	ຫົວຜັກທຽມ
lettuce	*phák sá-lat*	ຜັກສະລັດ
long green beans	*thua nyáo*	ຖົ່ວຍາວ
onion (bulb)	*hǔa phák bua*	ຫົວຜັກບົ່ວ
onion (green 'scallions')	*tôn phák bua*	ຕົ້ນຜັກບົ່ວ
peanuts (groundnuts)	*màak thua djn*	ໝາກຖົ່ວດິນ
potato	*mán fa-lang*	ມັນຝລັ່ງ
tomato	*màak len*	ໝາກເລັ່ນ

Vientiane & Around

The capital of Laos is booming. Driven by rising foreign investment, plenty of foreign aid workers and a more urbane youth, change is coming as quickly as in any city in Asia. However, even with all this dynamism you won't see words like 'hustle' and 'bustle' being used to describe Vientiane, which can still mount a strong argument for being the most relaxed capital city on earth.

Vientiane means 'Sandalwood City', and is actually pronounced Viang Chan (Viang means 'city' or 'place with walls' in Lao; Chan means sandalwood); the French are responsible for the modern transliteration. The combination of tree-lined boulevards and dozens of temples impart an atmosphere of timelessness, while the kaleidoscopic architectural styles reflect it's historic influences, from classic Lao through Thai, Chinese, French, US and Soviet.

As Laos continues to open itself to the world, Vientiane is where the struggle between a communist past and inevitably more capitalist future is most dramatically played out. Lao bands sing lyrics censored by the government to dancing youths who'd look at home in any Western bar. The Lao National Museum still has displays glorifying the victory over capitalist foreign imperialists, but across the road another slick restaurant opens in what is becoming one of the best-value dining cities on earth. The contrasts are fascinating.

Of course, Vientiane is not only about witnessing change. The 6400 Buddhas at Wat Si Saket, the religious art of Haw Pha Kaeo, and the lotus-inspired lines of Laos's gilded national symbol, Pha That Luang, speak of the historical importance of the city. Patuxai and the surreal Xieng Khuan (Buddha Park) may have less artistic merit, but like the city itself, they're not short of appeal.

HIGHLIGHTS

- Gaze up at the tapered golden stupa of **Pha That Luang** (p91), the symbol of Lao nationhood
- Check out the concrete folly that is **Xieng Khuan** (p98), the bizarre park full of dozens of giant Buddhist and Hindu sculptures
- Treat yourself to a traditional herbal sauna and massage at Vientiane's **Wat Sok Pa Luang** (p96)
- Enjoy a night out, Lao-style, at **On the Rock Pub** (p111) and **Marina** (p111)
- Tube, climb, raft, kayak, cycle or walk through the rivers and imposing limestone karst terrain around **Vang Vieng** (p121)
- Catch a glimpse of wild elephants from the elephant observation tower at the **Phu Khao Khuay NPA** (p118)

Vang
Vieng
★

Phu Khao
Khuay NPA
★

On the   Pha That
Rock Pub;   ★ Luang
Marina ★★

Wat Sok   ★ Xieng
Pa Luang   Khuan

VIENTIANE

ວຽງຈັນ

☎ 021 / pop 234,000

HISTORY

Set on a bend in the Mekong River, Vientiane was first settled around the 9th century AD and formed part of one of the early Lao valley *meuang* (city-states) that were consolidated around the 10th century. The Lao who settled here did so because the surrounding alluvial plains were so fertile and initially the Vientiane *meuang* prospered and enjoyed a fragile sovereignty.

In the ensuing 10 or so centuries of its history, Vientiane's fortunes have been mixed. At various times it has been a major regional centre, at other times, it has been controlled by the Vietnamese, Burmese and Siamese.

The height of Vientiane's success was probably in the years after it became the Lan Xang capital in the mid-16th century. (King Setthathirat moved the capital of the Lan Xang kingdom from the city now known as Luang Prabang.) Several of Vientiane's wats were built following this shift and the city became a major centre of Buddhist learning.

It didn't last. Periodic invasions by the Burmese, Siamese and Chinese, and the eventual division of the Lan Xang kingdom took their toll on the city.

It wasn't until the Siamese installed Chao Anou (a Lao prince who had been educated in Bangkok) on the throne in 1805 that the city received an overdue makeover. Chao Anou's public works included Wat Si Saket (p94), built in 1815.

Unfortunately, Chao Anou's attempts to assert Lao independence over the Siamese (see p31) resulted in the most violent and destructive episode in Vientiane's history.

In 1828 the Siamese defeated Chao Anou's armies and wasted no time in razing the city and carting off much of the population. Wat Si Saket was the only major building to survive, and the city was abandoned.

In 1867, French explorers arrived but it wasn't until late in the century, after Vientiane had been made capital of the French protectorate, that serious reconstruction began. A simple grid plan was laid out for the city and a sprinkling of colonial-style mansions and administrative buildings emerged. However, Vientiane was always low in the French order of Indochinese priorities, as the modest building program testifies.

In 1928 the 'city' was home to just 9000 inhabitants – many of them Vietnamese administrators brought in by the French – and it wasn't until the end of WWII that Vientiane's population began to grow with any vigour. It was a growth fed primarily by Cold War dollars, with first French and later American advisors arriving in a variety of guises.

After a couple of coups d'état in the politically fluid 1960s, Vientiane had by the early '70s become a city where almost anything went. Its few bars were peopled by an almost surreal mix of spooks and correspondents, and the women who served them.

Not surprisingly, things changed with the arrival of the Pathet Lao (PL) in 1975. Nightclubs filled with spies were the first to go and Vientiane settled into a slumber punctuated by occasional unenthusiastic concessions to communism, including low level collectivisation and an initial crackdown on Buddhism. These days the most noticeable leftovers from the period are some less-than-inspired Soviet-style buildings. Things picked up in the 1990s and in recent years Vientiane has seen a relative explosion of construction, road redevelopment and vehicular traffic.

ORIENTATION

Vientiane curves along the Mekong River following a meandering northwest-southeast axis, with the central district of Muang Chanthabuli at the centre of the bend. Most of the government offices, hotels, restaurants and historic temples are located in Chanthabuli, near the river. Some old French colonial buildings and Vietnamese-Chinese shophouses remain, set alongside newer structures built according to the rather boxy social realist school of architecture.

Wattay International Airport (Map pp88–9) is around 4km northwest of the centre. The Northern Bus Station (Map pp88–9), where long-distance services to points north begin and end, is about 2km northwest of the centre. The Southern Bus Station deals with most services heading south and is 8km northeast of the centre on Rte 13. The border with Thailand at the Thai-Lao Friendship Bridge (Map p117) is 19km southeast of the city.

Street signs are limited to major roads and the central, more touristy part of town. Where they do exist, the English and French designations vary (eg route, *rue*, road and avenue) but the Lao script always reads *thanŏn* (Th). Therefore, when asking directions it's always best to just use *thanŏn*.

The parallel Th Setthathirat (which is home to several famous temples) and Th Samsenthai are the main streets in central Vientiane. Heading northwest they both eventually lead to Th Luang Prabang and Rte 13 north. In the other direction they run perpendicular to and eventually cross Th Lan Xang, a major boulevard leading from the presidential palace past Talat Sao (Morning Market) to Patuxai (Victory Gate) and, after turning into Th Phon Kheng, to Rte 13 south and the Southern Bus Station.

The *meuang* of Vientiane are broken up into *bâan* (Ban), which are neighbourhoods or villages associated with local wats. Wattay International Airport, for example, is in Ban Wat Tai – the area in which Wat Tai is located.

Maps
After years in which Vientiane seemed to be the world centre of 'advertising maps' – at one stage there were nine different 3D-style maps, all with a relaxed approach to details like scale and perspective – the excellent *Hobo Maps Vientiane* (US$2) has arrived. It's big and unwieldy but has all the main sights, hotels and restaurants marked, though the north point is way off; get it at bookshops and Phimphone Markets (see p109).

INFORMATION
Bookshops
Vientiane has Monument Books selling pricey new books and several other shops that stock mainly secondhand novels in English and French, travel guides, maps and years-old reports by development organisations.

Kosila Bookshop 1 (Map p92; ☎ 020-2240964; Th Chanta Khumman; ⏰ 9am-5pm)

Monument Books (Map p92; ☎ 243708; 124 Th Nokeo Khumman; ⏰ 9am-8pm Mon-Fri, 9am-6pm Sat & Sun) Big range of books on Asia, plus maps, magazines and postcards.

Vientiane Book Center (Map p92; ☎ 212031; laobook@hotmail.com; Th Pangkham; ⏰ 8.30am-5.30pm Mon-Fri, 9am-4.30pm Sat)

Cultural Centres
Centre Culturel et de Coopération Linguistique (Map p92; ☎ 215764; www.ambafrance-laos.org; Th Lan Xang; ⏰ 9.30am-6.30pm Mon-Fri & 9.30am-noon Sat) The French Centre, as it's known, has a busy schedule of movies, musical and theatrical performances, a library and French and Lao language classes.

Emergency
Ambulance (☎ 195)
Fire (☎ 190)
Police (☎ 191)
Tourist Police (Map p92; ☎ 251128; Lan Xang Ave)

VIENTIANE IN...

Two Days
Start with Lao coffee and the *Vientiane Times* before making your way to **Patuxai** (p97) to begin the **Monument to Mekong Walking Tour** (p100). This will take you through most of Vientiane's main sights, including **Wat Si Saket** (p94), **Haw Pha Kaeo p95**) and **Talat Sao** (p113). On day two check out the myriad concrete Buddhas and Hindu deities at **Xieng Khuan** (p98). On the way back stop at **Pha That Luang** (p91) for great afternoon photos. Enjoy a fine French meal at **Le Côte D'Azur Restaurant** (p107) and finish it off with drinks at **Chicago** (p110) and/or the **Spirit House** (p110).

Four Days
Start day three at the **Lao National Museum** (p97) then hire a bike and pedal out to **Bunmala Restaurant** (p106) for an authentic Lao lunch. Keep on to **Wat Sok Pa Luang** (p96) for a herbal sauna and massage. Enjoy sunset at **Sala Sunset Khounta** (p110) before adjourning to **On The Rock Pub** (p111) for rock, Lao style. On day four just take it easy in the morning before unleashing yourself on the **handicraft and textile shops** (p112) of Th Nokeo Khumman.

VIENTIANE

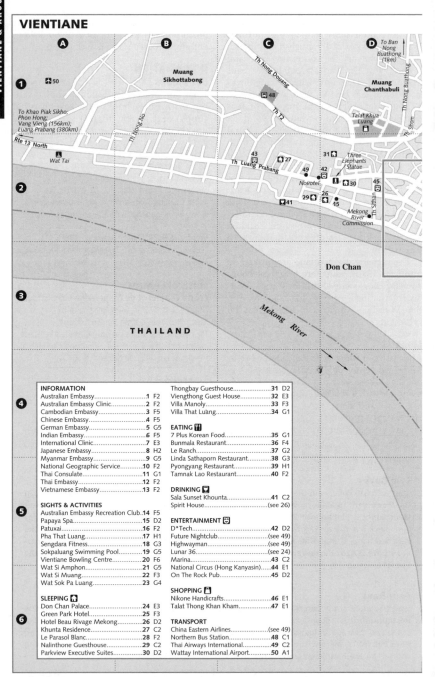

Muang
Sikhottabong

To Ban
Nong
Buathong
(1km)

Muang
Chanthabuli

To Khao Piak Sikho;
Phon Hong;
Vang Vieng (156km);
Luang Prabang (380km)

Rte 13 North

Wat Tai

Th Nong Bua

Th Luang Prabang

Three
Elephants
Statue

Novotel

Mekong
River
Commission

Don Chan

Mekong River

THAILAND

INFORMATION
Australian Embassy	1	F2
Australian Embassy Clinic	2	F2
Cambodian Embassy	3	F5
Chinese Embassy	4	F5
German Embassy	5	G5
Indian Embassy	6	F5
International Clinic	7	E3
Japanese Embassy	8	H2
Myanmar Embassy	9	G5
National Geographic Service	10	F2
Thai Consulate	11	G1
Thai Embassy	12	F2
Vietnamese Embassy	13	F2

SIGHTS & ACTIVITIES
Australian Embassy Recreation Club	14	F5
Papaya Spa	15	D2
Patuxai	16	F2
Pha That Luang	17	H1
Sengdara Fitness	18	G3
Sokpaluang Swimming Pool	19	G5
Vientiane Bowling Centre	20	F6
Wat Si Amphon	21	G5
Wat Si Muang	22	F3
Wat Sok Pa Luang	23	G4

SLEEPING
Don Chan Palace	24	E3
Green Park Hotel	25	F3
Hotel Beau Rivage Mekong	26	D2
Khunta Residence	27	C2
Le Parasol Blanc	28	F2
Nalinthone Guesthouse	29	C2
Parkview Executive Suites	30	D2

Thongbay Guesthouse	31	D2
Viengthong Guest House	32	E3
Villa Manoly	33	F3
Villa That Luang	34	G1

EATING
7 Plus Korean Food	35	G1
Bunmala Restaurant	36	F4
Le Ranch	37	G2
Linda Sathaporn Restaurant	38	G3
Pyongyang Restaurant	39	H1
Tamnak Lao Restaurant	40	F2

DRINKING
Sala Sunset Khounta	41	C2
Spirit House	(see 26)	

ENTERTAINMENT
D*Tech	42	D2
Future Nightclub	(see 49)	
Highwayman	(see 49)	
Lunar 36	(see 24)	
Marina	43	C2
National Circus (Hong Kanyasin)	44	E1
On The Rock Pub	45	D2

SHOPPING
Nikone Handicrafts	46	E1
Talat Thong Khan Kham	47	E1

TRANSPORT
China Eastern Airlines	(see 49)	
Northern Bus Station	48	C1
Thai Airways International	49	C2
Wattay International Airport	50	A1

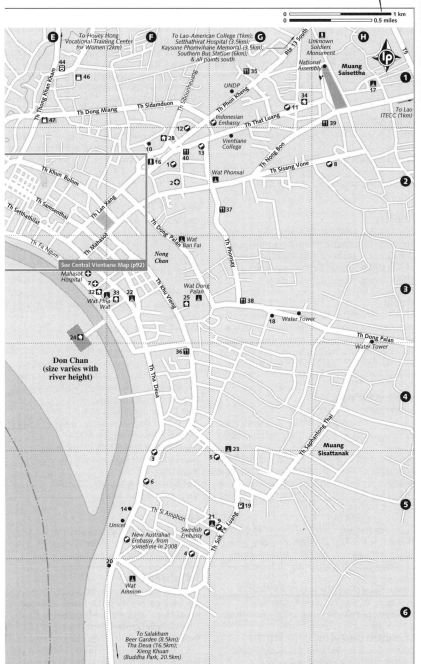

Internet Access

There are several places on Th Setthathirat between Nam Phu (Phu River) and Th Nokeo Khumman, and on Th Nokeo Khumman itself. Rates range from US$0.60 to US$1.20 an hour. Most have international telephone facilities for about US$0.20 a minute.

A1 Computer (Map p92; Th Setthathirat; ◷ 8.30am-11.30pm)

PlaNet Online (Map p92; Th Setthathirat; ◷ 8.30am-11pm) Sells prepaid internet cards for dial-up access, US$5/10/20.

Society Internet (Map p92; Th Samsenthai; ◷ 9am-9pm)

Star-Net Internet (Map p92; Th Nokeo Khumman; ◷ 7.30am-11pm)

Laundry

Most hotels and guesthouses offer laundry services. Otherwise, several laundries and dry-cleaners are on Th Samsenthai just east of Th Chao Anou. Typical rates are about US$1 per kg.

Media

Laos's only English-language newspaper is the government-run *Vientiane Times* (US$0.40), which carries the occasional critical piece in its six editions a week. The What's On page and bus-fare table are handy. French-speakers should look for *Le Rénovateur*.

Medical Services

HOSPITALS

Vientiane's medical facilities can leave a lot to be desired, so for anything serious make a break for the border and the much more sophisticated hospitals in Thailand. **Aek Udon International Hospital** (☎ 0066-4234 2555; www.aekudon.com) can dispatch an ambulance to take you to Udon Thani. Less serious ailments can be dealt with in Vientiane.

In Vientiane, try:

Australian Embassy Clinic (Map pp88–9; ☎ 413603; ◷ 9am-5pm Mon-Fri) For nationals of Australia, Britain, Canada, PNG and NZ only, this clinic's Australian doctor treats minor problems by appointment; it doesn't have emergency facilities.

International Clinic (Map pp88–9; ☎ 214021–2; Th Fa Ngum; ◷ 24hr) Part of the Mahasot Hospital, probably the best place for not-too-complex emergencies. Some English-speaking doctors.

Setthathirat Hospital (☎ 450197, 413720) A Japanese-funded overhaul means this hospital, located northeast of the city, is relatively well equipped.

PHARMACIES

Vientiane's better pharmacies are on Th Nong Bon near Talat Sao.

Pharmacie Kamsaat (Map p92; ☎ 212940; Th Nong Bon; ◷ 8.30am-5.30pm) English and French spoken.

Pharmacie Sengthong Osoth (Map p92; ☎ 213732; Th Nong Bon; ◷ 8am-8pm) English, French, Chinese, Vietnamese and Thai spoken.

Money

For cash, licensed moneychanging booths can be found in Talat Sao and a few other locations around town. You can also change at various shops, hotels or markets for no commission but at poor rates. The unofficial moneychangers hanging out near Talat Sao have particularly good rates but count your money carefully. See p310 for more information.

Banks listed here change cash and travellers cheques and issue cash advances against Visa and MasterCard. A couple also have ATMs that work with foreign cards, but it's often cheaper to get a cash advance manually; see p309 for the low-down. All are open 8.30am to 3.30pm Monday to Friday unless otherwise stated.

Bank of Ayudhya (Map p92; ☎ 214575; 79/6 Th Lan Xang)

Banque pour le Commerce Extérieur Lao (BCEL; Map p92; ☎ 213200; cnr Th Pangkham & Th Fa Ngum; ◷ 8.30am-7pm Mon-Fri, to 3pm Sat & Sun) Best rates. Longest hours. Exchange booth on Th Fa Ngum and ATM attached to the main building.

Joint Development Bank (Map p92; ☎ 213535; 75/1-5 Th Lan Xang) Usually charges the lowest commission on cash advances. Also has an ATM.

Lao-Viet Bank (Map p92; ☎ 214377; Th Lan Xang)

Siam Commercial Bank (Map p92; ☎ 227306; 117 Th Lan Xang)

Thai Military Bank (Map p92; ☎ 216486; cnr Th Samsenthai & Th Khun Bulom)

Post

Post, Telephone & Telegraph (PTT; Map p92; cnr Th Lan Xang & Th Khu Vieng; ◷ 8am-5pm Mon-Fri, to noon Sat & Sun) Come here for post restante.

Telephone & Fax

International calls can be made from most internet cafés (see left). Local calls can be made from any hotel lobby, often for free.

Lao Telecom Numphu Centre (Map p92; ☎ 214470; Th Setthathirat; ◷ 9am-7pm) Has fax and international-call facilities. Competition from internet cafés has seen rates slashed to US$0.20 a minute, or

US$0.10 for domestic calls. When we went staff suggested the office might soon be closed on weekends due to lack of interest.

Tourist Information
Between Talat Sao and Patuxai, the ground-floor office of the **Lao National Tourism Administration** (LNTA; Map p92; ☎ 212251; www.tourismlaos .gov.la, www.ecotourismlaos.com; Th Lan Xang; ☼ 8.30am-4.30pm) has finally become a place that is really worth a visit. The disorganised chaos of the past has been replaced by an attractive, easy-to-use room with descriptions of each province and what you'll find there. When we visited staff spoke English and were able to answer most of our questions. You can pick up brochures and some regional maps (US$1, though not always in stock), and staff can arrange trips to Phu Khao Khuay NPA for you (no charge).

Travel Agencies
For a list of reputable agencies able to organise tours, see p330. Central Vientiane has plenty of agencies that can book air tickets and in some cases Thai train tickets, including the following:

A-Rasa Tours (Map p92; ☎ 213633; www.laos-info .com; Th Setthathirat; ☼ 8.30am-5pm Mon-Sat) Happy to answer questions, runs some tours. Beside Lao Travellers Café.

Green Discovery (Map p92; ☎ 251564, 223022; www.greendiscoverylaos.com; Th Setthathirat) Large range of tours offered as well as normal travel agent services. Good reputation.

DANGERS & ANNOYANCES
By international standards Vientiane has a very low crime rate, but readers' reports and local anecdotes suggest there's an increasing risk of getting mugged. Be especially careful around the BCEL Bank on the riverfront where bag-snatchers, usually a two-man team with a motorbike, have been known to strike; common sense should be an adequate defence. Violent crime against visitors is extremely rare.

The repaving of most streets in the centre of town has improved the situation, but manhole covers seem to be given less importance here than you might be used to and at the time of writing there were still more than enough stormwater drains and open sewers big enough to swallow you – a thoroughly shitty end to any day.

All businesses in Vientiane are supposed to close by 11.30pm, though some stay open an extra hour or so. It's not dangerous to be out beyond midnight but you could be annoyed by military types if you're away from central Vientiane in an area where *falang* (Westerners) are seldom seen. If you are somewhere you shouldn't be (around the airport, for example) you might be escorted back to your hotel.

SIGHTS
With urban sprawl a fairly recent phenomenon in Vientiane it's no surprise that the bulk of sights are concentrated in a small area in the centre of the city. Except for Xieng Khuan (Buddha Park), all sights are easily reached by bicycle and, in most cases, on foot. Most wats welcome visitors after the monks have collected alms in the morning until about 6pm.

Pha That Luang
ພະທາດຫລວງ
The most important national monument in Laos, **Pha That Luang** (Great Sacred Reliquary or Great Stupa; Map pp88-9; admission US$0.20; ☼ 8am-noon & 1-4pm Tue-Sun) is a symbol of both the Buddhist religion and Lao sovereignty. Its full official name, Pha Chedi Lokajulamani, means World-Precious Sacred Stupa, and an image of the main stupa appears on the national seal and in countless other places. Legend has it that Ashokan missionaries from India erected a *thâat* or reliquary stupa here to enclose a piece of the Buddha's breastbone as early as the 3rd century BC. Excavations have found no trace of this, but did find suggestion of a Khmer monastery that might have been built near here between the 11th and 13th centuries AD.

When King Setthathirat moved the Lan Xang capital from Luang Prabang to Vientiane in the mid-16th century, he ordered the construction of Pha That Luang in its current form on the site of the Khmer temple. Construction began in AD 1566 and in succeeding years four wats were built around the stupa, one on each side. Only two remain today, **Wat That Luang Neua** to the north and **Wat That Luang Tai** to the south. Wat That Luang Neua is the residence of the Supreme Patriarch (Pha Sangkhalat) of Lao Buddhism. The main building is a reconstruction from the early 20th century.

The monument looks almost like a gilded missile cluster from a distance. Surrounding it is a high-walled cloister with tiny windows, added by King Anouvong in the early 19th century as a defence against invaders. Even more aggressive-looking than the thick walls

CENTRAL VIENTIANE

INFORMATION
A-Rasa Tours...........................(see 60)
A1 Computer................................1 C3
Bank of Ayudhya.........................2 E2
Banque pour le Commerce
  Extérieur Lao (BCEL)...............3 C3
Centre Culturel et de Coopération
  Linguistique............................4 E2
French Embassy............................5 E4
Green Discovery...........................6 C3
Immigration Office (Visa
  Extensions)..............................7 E2
Joint Development Bank...............8 E2
Kosila Bookshop 1........................9 D2
Lao National Tourism
  Administration.........................10 E2
Lao Telecom Numphu Centre...11 D3
Lao-Viet Bank.............................12 F2
Monument Books.......................13 C2
Pharmacie Kamsaat....................14 F3
Pharmacie Sengthong Osoth.....15 F3
PlaNet Online.............................16 C3
Post, Telephone & Telegraph.....17 E3
Siam Commercial Bank..............18 D3
Society Internet..........................19 C2
Star-Net Internet........................20 C2
Thai Military Bank......................21 B1
Tourist Police.......................(see 10)
US Embassy................................22 D3
Vientiane Book Center..............23 C3

SIGHTS & ACTIVITIES
Haw Pha Kaeo.........................24 D4
Jamé Mosque...........................25 D3
Lao Bowling Centre..................26 D1
Lao National Culture Hall.........27 C2
Lao National Museum...............28 C2
Shooting Range........................29 C2
That Dam.................................30 D2
Vientiane Swimming Pool........31 D2
Wat Chanthabuli......................32 B3
Wat Hai Sok.............................33 B2
Wat In Paeng...........................34 A2
Wat Mixai................................35 B2
Wat Ong Teu Mahawihan........36 B2
Wat Si Saket............................37 D3
White Lotus Massage & Beauty..38 C2

SLEEPING
Asian Pavilion Hotel.................39 D2
Chaleunxay Hotel.....................40 E2
Chanta Guest House.................41 B3
Chanthapanya Hotel................42 C2
Day Inn Hotel...........................43 D2
Douang Deuane Hotel..............44 B3
Dragon Lodge..........................45 C2
Hotel Lao.................................46 B1

Intercity Hotel.........................47 A3
Joe Guest House.......................48 B3
Lane Xang Hotel.......................49 C3
Lani I Guest House....................50 B2
Lao Orchid Hotel......................51 A3
Lao Plaza Hotel........................52 C2
Mali Namphu Guest House.....(see 56)
Mimi Guesthouse......................53 B3
Mixay Guesthouse....................54 B3
Mixok Guest House..............(see 41)
Orchid Guesthouse...................55 B3
Phonepaseuth Guesthouse........56 C2
Phorntip Guesthouse................57 A3
Praseuth Guest House...............58 C2
RD Guesthouse....................(see 54)
Riverside Hotel.........................59 B3
Sabaidy Guest House................60 C2
Saysouly Guest House...............61 C3
Settha Palace Hotel..................62 D1
Soukchaleun Guest House.....(see 41)
Soukxana Guesthouse...............63 D2
Syri 1 Guest House....................64 C1
Tai-Pan Hotel...........................65 B3
Vayakorn Guest House.............66 C2

EATING
Addy.....................................(see 84)
Ban Anou Night Market............67 B1
Ban Vilaylac Restaurant............68 B3
Croissant d'Or.....................(see 103)
Delight House of Fruit
  Shakes.............................(see 107)
Douang Deuane Restaurant &
  Wine Bar............................69 B3
Fathima Restaurant...................70 B1
Fujiwara Restaurant..................71 A2
Full Moon Café...................(see 95)
Guangdong Restaurant.............72 B2
JoMa Bakery Café.....................73 C3
Just for Fun..............................74 C3
Khop Chai Deu....................(see 6)
Khouadin Vegetarian................75 F3
La Cave de Chateaux................76 C3
La Gondola.............................77 B2
Le Belle Epoque..................(see 62)
Le Côte d'Azur Restaurant........78 B3
Le Silapa..................................79 A2
Le Vendôme.............................80 A2
L'Opera Italian Restaurant........81 C3
Makphet...................................82 B2
Mekong Riverside Restaurant...83 C4
Nok Noy Restaurant.................84 B3
Phikun.....................................85 A2
Phimphone Market...................86 C3
Phimphone Market 2................87 D3
PVO..88 C3
Rashmi's Indian Fusion.............89 C2

Restaurant Le Provençal...........90 C2
Restaurant-Bar Namphu...........91 C3
Riverfront Food & Drink Vendors 92 A3
Saovaly Restaurant...................93 B3
Scandinavian Bakery.............(see 90)
Sokhith Restaurant................(see 84)
Soukvemarn Lao Food..............94 D2
Sticky Fingers Café & Bar.........95 B3
Swedish Pizza & Baking House.96 B1
Taj Mahal Restaurant...............97 C2
Tum Zaap.................................98 A2
Vieng Sawan.............................99 B1
YuLaLa...................................100 C2

DRINKING
Blue Sky.................................101 B2
Bor Pen Nyang.......................102 A3
Chicago Bar...........................103 B3
Jazzy Brick.............................104 C3
Maison du Café......................105 C2
ParadIce.............................(see 4)
Samlo Pub..............................106 B2
Vins de France.......................107 D2

ENTERTAINMENT
Anou Cabaret.........................108 B2
Lao Traditional Show..............109 C3
Music House...........................110 B3
Wind West..............................111 A2

SHOPPING
Bari Jewellery.....................(see 107)
Camacrafts (Mulberries).........112 B3
Carol Cassidy Lao Textiles......113 C2
Carterie du Laos.....................114 B2
Couleur d'Asie.......................115 A2
Handicraft Products of Ethnic
  Groups...............................116 E3
Kanchana Boutique.................117 D3
Khampan Lao Handicraft........118 B3
KPP Handicraft Promotion
  Enterprise of Sekong Province.....119 B2
Mixay Boutique......................120 B3
Saigon Bijoux.........................121 D2
Satri Lao.................................122 C3
Talat Khua Din.......................123 F3
Talat Sao................................124 E3
True Colour.......................(see 41)
T'Shop Lai Galerie..................125 B2

TRANSPORT
Asia Vehicle Rental................126 D3
Lao Airlines...........................127 C3
PVO Motorbike Rentals.......(see 88)
Talat Sao Bus Station.............128 E3
Thai-Lao International Bus..(see 128)
Vietnam Airlines.................(see 52)

are the pointed stupas themselves, which are built in three levels (see Viewing Pha That Luang, p94).

In 1641 Gerrit van Wuysthoff, an envoy of the Dutch East India Company, visited Vientiane and was received by King Suriya Vongsa in a reportedly magnificent ceremony at Pha That Luang. The Lan Xang kingdom was at its peak at this time and van Wuysthoff was deeply impressed by the 'enormous pyramid, the top of which was covered with gold leaf weighing about a thousand pounds'.

Unfortunately, the glory of Lan Xang and Pha That Luang was only to last another 60 years or so. Repeated damaging assaults were carried out during the 18th century by invading Burmese and Siamese armies. Then, in

VIEWING PHA THAT LUANG

Each level of Pha That Luang has different architectural features in which Buddhist doctrine is encoded; visitors are supposed to contemplate the meaning of these features as they walk around. The first level is an approximately square base measuring 68m by 69m that supports 323 *siimáa* (ordination stones). It represents the material world, and also features four arched *hǎw wái* (prayer halls), one on each side, with short stairways leading to them and beyond to the second level.

The second level is 48m by 48m and is surrounded by 120 lotus petals. There are 288 *siimáa* on this level, as well as 30 small stupas symbolising the 30 Buddhist perfections (*páalamíi sǎamsíp thâat*), beginning with alms-giving and ending with equanimity.

Arched gates again lead to the next level, a 30m by 30m square. The tall central stupa, which has a brick core that has been stuccoed over, is supported here by a bowl-shaped base reminiscent of India's first Buddhist stupa at Sanchi. At the top of this mound the superstructure, surrounded by lotus petals, begins.

The curvilinear, four-sided spire resembles an elongated lotus bud and is said to symbolise the growth of a lotus from a seed in a muddy lake bottom to a bloom over the lake's surface, a metaphor for human advancement from ignorance to enlightenment in Buddhism. The entire *thâat* was regilded in 1995 to celebrate the Lao PDR's 20th anniversary, and is crowned by a stylised banana flower and parasol. From ground to pinnacle, Pha That Luang is 45m tall.

1828, a Siamese invasion ransacked and depopulated Vientiane to such an extent that Pha That Luang remained abandoned, and eventually dismantled by treasure seekers, until it was (badly) restored by the French in 1900.

That restoration left the stupa looking a bit too chunky and none too attractive, at least that's what the locals thought. In a victory of town planning over history, the orientation was changed so that the main entrance faced south, rather than east. This meant the wide new Th That Luang ran straight up to the stupa, but didn't fit with traditional Buddhist doctrine, which has most temples and religious monuments facing east.

In fairness to the French, they did try to fix it. Changing the orientation back was clearly too hard, but between 1931 and 1935 a French university department dismantled the stupa and rebuilt it in the original Lao-style lotus-bud shape. For guidance they used the drawings of French explorer and architect Louis Delaporte, who had stumbled on the abandoned and overgrown Pha That Luang in 1867 and made a number of detailed sketches of the monument.

Pha That Luang is about 4km northeast of the centre of Vientiane at the end of Th That Luang. Facing the compound is a statue of King Setthathiraṭ. The temple is the site of a major festival, held in early November (see p101).

Wat Si Saket

ວັດສີສະເກດ

Built between 1819 and 1824 by Chao Anou, **Wat Si Saket** (Wat Sisaketsata Sahatsaham; Map p92; cnr Th Lan Xang & Th Setthathirat; admission US$0.50; 8am-noon & 1-4pm) is believed to be Vientiane's oldest surviving temple. And it shows; this beautiful temple-cum-national museum is in dire need of a face-lift.

Chao Anou, who was educated in the Bangkok court and was more or less a vassal of the Siamese state, had Wat Si Saket constructed in the early Bangkok style but surrounded it with a thick-walled cloister similar to – but much smaller than – the one that surrounds Pha That Luang (p91). The stylistic similarity to their own wats might have motivated the Siamese to spare this monastery when they crushed Chao Anou's rebellion (p31), even as they razed many others. The French restored the temple in 1924 and again in 1930.

In spite of the Siamese influence, Wat Si Saket has several unique features. The interior walls of the cloister are riddled with small niches that contain over 2000 silver and ceramic Buddha images. Over 300 seated and standing Buddhas of varying sizes and materials (wood, stone, silver and bronze) rest on long shelves below the niches, most of them sculpted or cast in the characteristic Lao style. Most of the images are from 16th- to 19th-century Vientiane but a few hail from 15th- to 16th-century Luang Prabang.

Along the western side of the cloister is a pile of Buddhas that were damaged during the 1828 Siamese-Lao war. And in the *sim* (ordination hall) a slightly damaged Khmer-style Naga Buddha – which depicts the Buddha seated on a coiled cobra deity (*naga*), sheltered by the *naga*'s multiheaded hood – is also on display just in front of the main seated Buddha; it is believed to date from the 13th century and was brought from a nearby Khmer site.

The *sim* is surrounded by a colonnaded terrace in the Bangkok style and topped by a five-tiered roof. The interior walls bear hundreds of Buddha niches similar to those in the cloister, as well as beautiful – but decaying – Jataka murals depicting stories of the Buddha's past lives. Portions of the Bangkok-style murals are unrestored 1820s originals, while others are a 1913 restoration.

The flowered ceiling was inspired by Siamese temples in Ayuthaya, which were in turn inspired by floral designs from Versailles. At the rear interior of the *sim* is an altar with several more Buddha images, bringing the total number of Buddhas at Wat Si Saket to about 7000 – though we didn't count them ourselves. The standing Buddha to the left on the upper altar is said to have been cast to the same physical proportions as Chao Anou. The large, gilt wood candle stand in front of the altar is thought to be an original, carved in 1819.

On the veranda at the rear of the *sim* is a 5m-long wooden trough carved to resemble a *naga*. This is the *háang song nâm pha* (image-watering rail), which is used during Lao New Year to pour water over Buddha images for ceremonial cleansing.

To the far left of the entrance to the cloister, facing Th Lan Xang, is a raised *hăw tại* (Tripitaka library) with a Burmese-style roof. The scriptures once contained here are now in Bangkok.

Haw Pha Kaeo

ຫໍພະແກ້ວ

Once a royal temple built specifically to house the famed Emerald Buddha, **Haw Pha Kaeo** (Map p92; Th Setthathirat; admission US$0.50; ☾ 8am-noon & 1-4pm) is today a national museum of religious art. It is about 100m southeast of Wat Si Saket.

According to the Lao, the temple was originally built in 1565 by command of King Set-thathirat, who on inheriting the Lan Xang throne moved the capital from Luang Prabang to Vientiane and brought with him the so-called Emerald Buddha (Pha Kaeo in Lao, which means 'Jewel Buddha Image' – the image is actually made of a type of jade). Wat Pha Kaeo also served as Setthathirat's personal place of worship. Following a skirmish with the Lao in 1779, the Siamese stole the Emerald Buddha and installed it in Bangkok's Wat Phra Kaew. Later, during the Siamese-Lao war of 1828, Vientiane's Wat Pha Kaeo was razed.

The temple was finally rebuilt with French help between 1936 and 1942, supposedly following the original plan exactly. However, the 'original' 16th-century plan looks nothing like its contemporaries, instead bearing an uncanny resemblance to 19th-century Bangkok-style *sim*. The floor and the main wooden door at the southern end – with its angels carved in high relief that are reminiscent of Angkorean apsaras – are notable survivors of the original remains.

These aside, today's Haw Pha Kaeo is impressive mainly for its size. The rococo ornamentation that runs up and down every door, window and base looks unfinished. But some of the best examples of Buddhist sculpture found in Laos are kept here, with a dozen or so prominent sculptures displayed along the surrounding terrace. These include Dvaravati-style stone Buddha from between the 6th and 9th centuries; several bronze standing and sitting Lao-style Buddhas – including the 'Calling for Rain' (standing with hands at his sides), 'Offering Protection' (palms stretched out in front) and 'Contemplating the Tree of Enlightenment' (hands crossed at the wrist in front) poses; and a collection of inscribed Lao and Mon stelae. Most of the Lao bronzes are missing their *usnisa* (flame finial).

Inside the *sim* are more Buddhist sculptures (including a wooden copy of the Pha Bang), some Khmer stelae, various wooden carvings, palm-leaf manuscripts and a bronze frog drum. A 17th-century bronze 'Calling for Rain' Buddha, tall and lithe, is particularly beautiful; also unique is a 17th-century Vientiane-style bronze Buddha in the 'European pose' – with the legs hanging down as if seated on a chair. Attendants will point you to the most interesting pieces.

The *sim* is surrounded by a landscaped garden, which is also home to a single stone jar from the Plain of Jars.

Wat Ong Teu Mahawihan

ວັດອົງຕື້ມະຫາວິຫານ

This **temple** (Temple of the Heavy Buddha; Map p92; Th Setthathirat) is one of the most important in Laos. It was originally built in the mid-16th century by King Setthathirat and is believed to occupy a site first used for religious purposes as far back as the 3rd century. But like almost every other temple in Vientiane it was destroyed in later wars with the Siamese, then rebuilt in the early 20th century. The Hawng Sangkhalat (Deputy Patriarch) of the Lao monastic order has his official residence here and presides over the Buddhist Institute, a school for monks who come from all over the country to study *dhamma* (the Buddha's teachings).

The temple's namesake is a 16th-century bronze Buddha, measuring 5.8m tall and weighing several tonnes, that sits in the rear of the *sǐm*, flanked by two standing Buddhas. This *sǐm* is famous for the wooden façade over the front terrace, a masterpiece of Lao carving.

Wat Si Muang

ວັດສີເມືອງ

The most frequently used grounds in Vientiane are those of **Wat Si Muang** (Map p92; cnr of Th Setthathirat, Th Samsenthai & Th Tha Deua; ☺ 6am-7pm daily, until 10pm on special days), the site of the *lák meuang* (city pillar/phallus), which is considered the home of the guardian spirit of Vientiane (see No Sacrifice Too Great, below).

The *sǐm* (destroyed in 1828 and rebuilt in 1915) was constructed around the *lák meuang*, which now forms the centre of the altar. The pillar itself is believed to date from the Khmer period, indicating the site

has been used for religious purposes for more than 1000 years. Today it is wrapped in sacred cloth, and in front of it is a carved wooden stele with a seated Buddha in relief.

Several other Buddha images surround the pillar, including one partially damaged image that sits on a cushion. This rather melted-looking seated stone Buddha survived the 1828 inferno and locals believe it has the power to grant wishes or answer troubling questions. The practice is to lift it off the pillow three times while mentally phrasing a question or request. If your request is granted, then you are supposed to return later with an offering of bananas, green coconuts, flowers, incense and candles (usually two of each). This is why so many platters of fruit, flowers and incense sit around the *sǐm*.

Behind the *sǐm* is a crumbling laterite *jęhdii* (stupa), almost certainly of Khmer origin. Devotees deposit broken deity images and pottery around the stupa's base so the spirits of the stupa will 'heal' the bad luck created by the breaking of these items. In front of the *sǐm* is a little public park with a statue of King Sisavang Vong (1904–59).

Wat Sok Pa Luang

ວັດໂສກປ່າຫລວງ

In a shaded, almost semirural setting that is entirely in keeping with its name (*wat paa* means 'forest temple'), **Wat Sok Pa Luang** (Wat Mahaphutthawongsa Pa Luang Pa Yai; Map pp88-9; Th Sok Pa Luang) is famous for its herbal saunas and expert massage. The masseurs are usually lay people who reside at the temple. After a relaxing sauna, you can take herbal tea on the

---

NO SACRIFICE TOO GREAT

Legend has it that a group of sages selected the site for Wat Si Muang in 1563, when King Setthathirat moved his capital to Vientiane. Once the spot was chosen, a large hole was dug to receive the heavy stone pillar (probably taken from an ancient Khmer site nearby) that would become the *lák meuang* (city pillar). When the pillar arrived it was suspended over the hole with ropes. Drums and gongs were sounded to summon the townspeople to the area and everyone waited for a volunteer to jump in the hole as a sacrifice to the spirit.

Depending on who's relating it, the legend has several conclusions. What is common to all of them is that a pregnant woman named Sao Si leaps in and the ropes are released, killing her and in the process establishing the town guardianship. Variations include her leaping in upon a horse, and/or with a diminutive monk.

However, Lao scholars think that if there is any truth to this story it is likely to have occurred much earlier than Setthathirat's time, in the pre-Buddhist Mon or Khmer periods when human sacrifice was ritually practised…and that Sao Si's legendary leap might not have been her choice at all.

veranda, then opt for a massage. You're not supposed to wash away your accumulated perspiration for two or three hours afterwards to allow the herbs to soak into your pores. A few women have commented that some masseurs may cover more territory than is comfortable. The sauna (US$1) and massage (US$2) operate from 1pm to 7pm daily. Nearby **Wat Si Amphon** (Map pp88-9; Th Si Amphon) also does herbal saunas.

Wat Sok Pa Luang is also known for its course of instruction in *vipassana* (Lao *vipatsanáa*), a type of Buddhist meditation that involves careful mind-body analysis. See p101 for details.

Taxi, jumbo (motorcycle taxi) and tuk-tuk drivers all know how to get to Wat Sok Pa Luang. If you're travelling by car or bicycle, take Th Khu Vieng south past Talat Sao for about 2.5km until you come to a fairly major road on the left (this is Th Sok Pa Luang, but it's unmarked). Turn left here; the ornamented entrance to the wat is about 500m on the left. For Wat Si Amphon, go a few hundred metres further and turn right on Th Si Amphon.

Patuxai
ປະຕູໄຊ

Reminiscent of the Arc de Triomphe in Paris, the **Patuxai** (Map pp88-9; Th Lan Xang; admission US$0.30; 8am-4.30pm Mon-Fri, to 5pm Sat-Sun) is Vientiane's most prominent monument. The name is approximately equivalent to Arch (*pátuu*, also translated as 'door' or 'gate') of Triumph (*xái*, from the Sanskrit *jaya* or 'victory'), but unlike its Parisian namesake the Patuxai boasts four, rather than two, archways. It was built in the 1960s with US-purchased cement that was supposed to have been used for the construction of a new airport. Hence it's sometimes called 'the vertical runway'.

From a distance, Patuxai looks much like its French source of inspiration. Up close, however, the Lao design is revealed. The bas-relief on the sides and the temple-like ornamentation along the top and cornices are typically Lao, though the execution is at times shoddy. Don't miss the painted description on the southwest corner, which in a few lines reflects both Laos's endearing honesty and naivety to 'First World' preoccupations like marketing. One sentence reads: 'From a closer distance, it appears even less impressive, like a monster of concrete'; talk about brutal honesty.

A stairway leads through two levels stuffed with souvenir T-shirts (seriously, there are thousands) to the top levels, from where the views are grand. Photography is supposed to be banned from the top.

Patuxai is within walking distance of the town centre and work in recent years has transformed the surrounding field into the most popular park in Vientiane. It's a good place to soak up the atmosphere of modern Laos, with the Chinese-donated musical fountain a big hit in the late afternoon.

That Dam
ທາດດຳ

Sitting at the centre of a quiet roundabout near the centre of Vientiane, legend has it that the stupa now known as **That Dam** (Black Stupa; Map p92; Th Bartholomie) was once coated in a layer of gold. The gold is said to have been carted off by the Siamese during their pillaging of 1828, after which the stupa took the 'black' sobriquet in memory of the dastardly act. However, another myth is slightly at odds with this. It says That Dam is the abode of a dormant seven-headed dragon that came to life during the 1828 Siamese–Lao war and protected local citizens, though apparently not the stupa's gold…

Either way, the stupa appears to date from the Lanna or early Lan Xang period and is very similar to stupas in Chiang Saen, Thailand.

Lao National Museum
ຫໍພິພິທະພັນປະຫວັດສາດແຫ່ງຊາດລາວ

With a limited collection of historical and revolutionary exhibits, the **Lao National Museum** (Map p92; 212461; Th Samsenthai; admission US$1; 8am-noon & 1-4pm) will never be confused with the Louvre. But it does serve to sum up the country's ongoing struggle to come to grips with its own identity, so it's worth a look.

The museum is housed in a large administrative building originally built as the colonial police commissioner's office in the 1920s. It became a museum in the 1990s and until recently it was known as the 'Lao Revolutionary Museum'. And while the museum is being slowly overhauled room by room, much of the collection retains an unmistakable revolutionary zeal. There are many artefacts and photos from the Pathet Lao's lengthy struggle for power, as well as enough historic weaponry to arm all the extras in a Rambo film. Among the more notable exhibits are a chest expander once used by the founding father of communist Laos, Kaysone Phomvihane; mundane items like rice baskets, spoons and even dried herbs used by prominent revolutionaries during the resistance; and a modest collection of industrial items produced by Laos during the '90s, such as a few generic pharmaceuticals.

While these things might not have you panting with expectation – and let's face it, individually they are as unexciting as they sound – the real value in visiting the museum is to compare these older rooms to those upgraded more recently. These emphasise cultural influences, traditional musical instruments, Khmer sandstone sculptures that illustrate the Khmer influence on Laos, and rooms that deal with other historical periods that have nothing to do with the communist victory. Whether consciously or not, it appears to reflect a slow move away from the hardline socialist ideals that the Pathet Lao fought for, and which dominated domestic policy in the 15 to 20 years after 1975, towards a more broad-based, nationalist view of history and national identity. Most exhibits are labelled with at least some English.

Lao National Culture Hall
ຫໍວັດທະນະທຳແຫ່ງຊາດ

Opposite the Lao National Museum, and dwarfing it, is the monumentally proportioned **Lao National Culture Hall** (Map p92; Th Samsenthai). The outsized and ugly hall was built by the Chinese government in the late 1990s as a 'gift to the people of Laos'. It hosts occasional cultural events as varied as French cinema, Lao classical dance and even beauty pageants, but with no publicly available schedule of events you'll need to keep a close eye on the *Vientiane Times* for an announcement.

Kaysone Phomvihane Memorial
ຫໍພິພິດທະພັນແລະອະນຸສາວະລີໄກສອນພົມວິຫານ

Opened in 1995 to celebrate the late president's 75th birthday, the **Kaysone Phomvihane Memorial** (☯ 8am-noon & 1-4pm Tue-Sun), near Km 6 on Rte 13 south, serves as a tribute to Indochina's most pragmatic communist leader. The memorial is actually two jarringly different sites. Kaysone's old house is a model of modesty suggesting he might have lived in less luxury than any other world leader. In contrast the museum is a vast Vietnamese-style celebration of the cult of Kaysone, a cult he never encouraged. Visit the house first.

The relatively modest, American-built single-storey ranch house where Kaysone lived after the revolution is fascinating both because

of its history and that it remains virtually untouched since the great man died in 1992. The house is inside the former USAID/CIA compound, a self-contained headquarters known as 'Six Klicks City' because of its location 6km from central Vientiane. It once featured bars, restaurants, tennis courts, swimming pools, a commissary and assorted offices from where the Secret War (p38) was orchestrated. During the 1975 takeover of Vientiane, Pathet Lao forces ejected the Americans and occupied the compound. Kaysone lived here until his death.

A Lao People's Revolutionary Party (LPRP) guide will show you through the house, with Kaysone's half-empty bottles of Scotch, tacky souvenirs from the Eastern Bloc, white running shoes, notepads and original Kelvinator air-conditioners. Even the winter coats he wore on visits to Moscow remain neatly hanging in the wardrobe.

While the house is hard to find, the museum is impossible to miss, with its mega-sized bronze statue of Kaysone out front flanked by large sculptures in the Heroes of Socialism style, complete with members of various ethnic groups and a sportsman looking like a super-serious Superman. The building is a stark contrast, too, and is filled with a remarkably complete collection of memorabilia of both Kaysone and the Party. These include a mock-up of Kaysone's childhood home in Savannakhet, his desk from the French school he attended at Ban Tai and a model of a portion of 'Kaysone Cave' in Hua Phan Province, complete with revolver, binoculars, radio and other personal effects.

It's easy to cycle here or take any transport on Rte 13 south. For Kaysone's house, turn left just before the museum on Rte 13, turn left again just before the military entrance and follow the road another 800m or so, bending right, and stopping at a boom gate on the right. A shared tuk-tuk (US$0.25) from Talat Sao will drop you outside the main memorial.

Xieng Khuan (Buddha Park)
ພຣະຍຂວັນ

In a field by the Mekong River about 24km south of central Vientiane, **Xieng Khuan** (Buddha Park or Suan Phut; admission person US$0.50, camera US$0.50; ☯ 8am-4.30pm, sometimes longer) is a park full of Buddhist and Hindu sculpture that is a monument to one eccentric man's quite bizarre ambition.

Xieng Khuan was designed and built in 1958 by Luang Pu (Venerable Grandfather) Bunleua Sulilat, a yogi-priest-shaman who merged Hindu and Buddhist philosophy, mythology and iconography into a cryptic whole. Originally, Bunleua is supposed to have studied under a Hindu *rishi* (sage) who lived in Vietnam. Legend has it that their meeting was fortunate, to say the least, as while Bunleua was walking in the mountains he fell through a sinkhole and landed in the *rishi*'s lap. As you do. Bunleua developed a large following in Laos and northeastern Thailand, and moved to Thailand around the time of the 1975 Revolution. In 1978 he established the similarly inspired Wat Khaek in Nong Khai, Thailand. He died in 1996.

The concrete sculptures at Xieng Khuan (which means 'Spirit City') are bizarre but compelling in their naive confidence. They include statues of Shiva, Vishnu, Arjuna, Avalokiteshvara, Buddha and numerous other deities, all supposedly cast by untrained artists under Luang Pu's direction.

The large pumpkin-shaped concrete monument in the grounds has three levels joined by interior stairways. The levels are said to represent hell, earth and heaven, and lead to the roof and panoramic views of the park.

A few food vendors offer fresh coconuts, soft drinks, beer, *pîng kai* (grilled chicken) and *tạm màak-hung* (spicy green papaya salad).

Xieng Khuan is a definite favourite among kids.

GETTING THERE & AWAY

Bus 14 (US$0.40, 24km, one hour) leaves the Talat Sao terminal every 15 or 20 minutes throughout the day and goes all the way to Xieng Khuan. Alternatively, charter a tuk-tuk (about US$10 return, depending on your bargaining skills) or hop on a shared jumbo (US$0.30) as far as the old ferry pier at Tha Deua and walk or take a *sǎam-lâaw* (three-wheeled taxi) the final 4km to the park. Going by motorbike is popular.

ACTIVITIES
Bowling

Vientiane's bowling alleys are a fun diversion popular among travellers and locals alike. Watching some of the local form is certainly entertaining, but we've also heard an evening's bowling rationalised as a chance to drink plenty of Beerlao while 'working it off with a bit of exercise'. 'Exercise'? You be the judge.

Lao Bowling Centre (Map p92; ☎ 218661; Th Khun Bulom; per frame US$1/1.20 before/after 7pm; ☉ 9am-midnight) A short stroll from town. Book ahead on weekends.

Vientiane Bowling Centre (Map pp88-9; ☎ 313823; 58/1 Th Tha Deua; per frame US$0.40/0.60 before/after 8pm; ☉ 1-11pm)

Gyms & Aerobics

There is a free aerobics session on the riverfront just east of Haw Kang most weekend afternoons at about 5pm. Failing that, try:

Sengdara Fitness (Map pp88-9; ☎ 414061; 5/77 Th Dong Palan; ☉ 6am-10pm) Vientiane's first Western-style mega-gym, with stacks of machines, sauna, pool, massage, aerobics and yoga classes, and a juice bar and restaurant. Visitors can buy a US$6 day pass, which includes use of everything plus a one-hour massage – a very good deal.

Tai-Pan Hotel (Map p92; ☎ 216906; 22/3 Th François Nginn; per visit US$4) Small fitness room and sauna; central location.

Hash House Harriers

The **Vientiane Hash House Harriers** (www.laohash .com) welcome runners to their two weekly hashes. The Saturday hash is the more challenging run and starts at 3.45pm from Nam Phu. It's followed by food and no shortage of Beerlao. Monday's easier run starts at 5pm from varying locations – look for maps at the Scandinavian Bakery (p105) or Asia Vehicle Rentals (p328), where owner **Joe Rumble** (☎ 020-5511293) is more than happy to help out.

Massage/Sauna

Good massage comes cheap in this town.

Papaya Spa (Map pp88-9; ☎ 216550; www.papayaspa .com; ☉ 9am-9pm) In an old French villa west of town (follow the many signs), this is one of the classiest massage operations in town. Services include Lao massage (US$6), Swedish oil massage (US$12), facials, waxing, body scrubs, reflexology and sauna.

Wat Sok Pa Luang (Th Sok Pa Luang) The traditional Lao experience; see p96.

White Lotus Massage & Beauty (Map p92; ☎ 217492; Th Pangkham; ☉ 10am-10pm) Just north of Nam Phu; foot massage (US$4), aromatherapy body massage (US$10).

Shooting

At the southeast corner of the National Stadium a nondescript door leads into a **shooting** range (Map p92;Th Ki Huang; ☽ 9am-5pm), where you can take aim at a paper target with a range of handguns and rifles. Prices start at US$1.20 for five rounds with a 0.22 calibre handgun.

Swimming

There are several places in Vientiane where you can work on your strokes or simply take a cooling dip. The **Vientiane Swimming Pool** (Map p92; ☎ 020-5521002; Th Ki Huang; admission US$1; ☽ 8am-7pm) is central and usually fine for swimming laps. Further afield, the 25m-long **Sokpaluang Swimming Pool** (Map pp88-9; ☎ 350491; Th Sok Pa Luang; adult/child US$0.90/$0.60; ☽ 8am-8pm Tue-Sun) in southeastern Vientiane also has a children's pool and changing rooms; while the pool at the **Australian Embassy Recreation Club** (AERC; Map pp88-9; ☎ 314921; Km 3 Th Tha Deua; ☽ 9am-8pm) is probably the best in town. Several hotels welcome nonguests, including the **Settha Palace Hotel** (Map p92; ☎ 217581; Th Pangkham; US$6) with its decadent pool and surrounding bar.

MONUMENT TO MEKONG WALKING TOUR

This walking tour can be done on foot or bicycle. It covers about 6km and will take between four and six hours, depending on how often you stop, eat, drink and shop. When deciding how long to spend in Talat Sao and where to stop, remember Wat Si Saket and Haw Pha Kaeo close between noon and 1pm.

To start, take a jumbo to **Patuxai (1**; p97) and climb this concrete edifice for unbeatable views of the city. From here, head back into town along Th Lan Xang, a street sometimes (very) generously described as the 'Champs Elysées of the East'. Use this chance to stop in the **Lao National Tourism Administration (LNTA) office (2**; p91), pick up maps, brochures and perhaps even book a walk in the Phu Khao Khuay National Protected Area (NPA), before continuing to Vientiane's biggest market, **Talat Sao (3**; p113). Wander among textiles, TVs and pirated Thai pop to the **goldsmiths (4**), who craft their precious metal over a long line of fiery work benches at the southeast edge of the market. You could eat here at the fringes of the market, or head across to **Khouadin Vegetarian (5**; p109), on the northern side of the labyrinthine **Talat Khua Din (6**; p113), for some cheap but tasty fare before cutting through the market back to Th Khu Vieng.

Cross Th Lan Xang and walk past the high walls of the **US Embassy (7; p306)** to **That Dam (8**; p97), one of Vientiane's oldest Buddhist stupas. If you manage to pass here without being swallowed by the giant *naga* that lurks beneath, turn left (southwest) on Th Chanta Khumman and head for the Mekong. Turn left (east) down shaded Th Setthathirat and walk past the **Presidential Palace (9)**, a vast beaux-arts–style chateau originally built to house the French colonial governor. After independence King Sisavang Vong (and later his son Sisavang Vatthana) of Luang Prabang used it as a residence when visiting Vientiane; these days it is used mainly on ceremonial occasions.

Diagonally opposite the palace is the ochre-painted **Wat Si Saket (10**; p94), with its

MONUMENT TO MEKONG WALKING TOUR

thousands of Buddha figures, and across the street is the striking **Haw Pha Kaeo** (**11**; p95), the national museum for religious objects.

Turn down Th Mahasot and cross Th Fa Ngum to reach a modest, brick-paved riverside promenade that has benches for the weary or the romantic and, during the rainy season, views of the river. As you head northwest you'll pass under more than 25 tall, wide-girthed teak trees, each of them at least 200 years old, and two very old banyan trees. As the riverfront opens out you'll come across **PVO** (**12**; p106), famous for serving Vientiane's best *khào jīi páa-tê* (French baguette stuffed with Lao-style pâté, vegetables and dressings); and with a better riverfront view the **Mekong Riverside Restaurant** (**13**; p106), which serves decent Lao food and cold beer.

You could finish up here but if time permits kick on along Th Fa Ngum, passing several other eateries on the way, and turn up Th Nokeo Khumman, one of Vientiane's best shopping streets. Step left into **Wat Mixai** (**14**), with its Bangkok-style *sǐm* and heavy gates, flanked by two *nyak* (guardian giants). Walk through the wat and further along Th Setthathirat to **Wat Ong Teu Mahawihan** (**15**; p96). On the opposite side of the road is **Wat Hai Sok (16)** and its impressive five-tiered roof (nine if you count the lower terrace roofs), which is topped by an elaborate set of *nyâwt saw fâa* (roof-ridge spires).

Finally, Vientiane's temple district closes out with **Wat In Paeng (17)**, which is famed for the artistry displayed in the *sǐm*'s stucco relief. Finish the day by heading down Th Khun Bulom to the Mekong, find a seat at one of the **riverside food and drink vendors** (**18**; p106) and watch the sun set with as much Beerlao and *pîng kai* as you dare.

COURSES

Language Courses

For details on Vientiane language schools that teach Lao see p303.

Cooking

As well as being a good place to stay (p102), **Thongbay Guesthouse** (Map pp88-9; ☎/fax 242292; www .thongbay-guesthouses.com; US$10) offers cooking courses at 10am by appointment, involving a trip to the market, kitchen work and sampling your creation.

Weaving & Dyeing

You can learn how to dye textiles using natural pigments and then weave them on a traditional loom at the **Houey Hong Vocational Training Center for Women** (☎ 560006; hhtw@laotel .com; Ban Houey Hong; ⏲ 8.30am-4.30pm Mon-Sat). The NGO group, run by a Lao-Japanese woman, established this centre north of Vientiane to train disadvantaged rural women in the dying art of natural dyeing and traditional silk-weaving practices. Visitors can look for free or partake in the dyeing process (US$12, two hours, two stoles) or weaving (US$15, whole day). You keep the fruits of your labour. One American woman spent a whole month learning to weave.

To get there, you can take the 33 bus from Talat Sao, getting off at the first gasoline stand past the Houey Hong market, then following a small road 200m west. Much simpler is calling the centre, which will collect and return you for US$1. The centre's store in Vientiane is **True Colour** (Map p92; ☎ 214410; Th Setthathirat).

Vipassana Meditation

Every Saturday from 4pm to 5.30pm monks lead a session of sitting and walking meditation at **Wat Sok Pa Luang** (Th Sok Pa Luang); see p96. Both Lao and foreigners are welcome and there's no charge. There's usually a translator for the question period held after the meditation.

FESTIVALS & EVENTS

You can rest assured that whatever the festival, celebrations in Vientiane will be as vigorous as anywhere in the country.

Bun Pha That Luang (That Luang Festival), usually in early November, is the largest temple fair in Laos. Apart from the religious fervour, the festival features a trade show and a number of carnival games. The festivities begin with a *wíen thíen* (circumambulation) around Wat Si Muang, followed by a procession to Pha That Luang, which is illuminated all night for a week. The festival climaxes on the morning of the full moon with the *ták bàat* ceremony, in which several thousand monks from across the country receive alms food. That evening there's a final *wíen thíen* around Pha That Luang, with devotees carrying *pǎasàat* (miniature temples made from banana stems and decorated with flowers and other offerings).

Fireworks cap off the evening and everyone makes merit or merry until dawn.

Another huge annual event is **Bun Nam** (River Festival) at the end of *phansǎa* (the Buddhist rains retreat) in October, during which boat races are held on the Mekong River. Rowing teams from all over the country, as well as from Thailand, China and Myanmar, compete, and the riverbank is lined with food stalls, temporary discos, carnival games and beer gardens for three days and nights. Vientiane is jam-packed during Bun Nam, and given how far away the boat racing is and how difficult it is to find a vantage point, we think smaller towns like Vang Vieng and Muang Khong are better bets, though Muang Khong doesn't usually hold its festival until early December, around National Day.

SLEEPING

Vientiane's dozens of guesthouses and hotels range from US$3-a-night cells to opulent colonial-era affairs where no luxury is spared. Most rooms, particularly those at the cheaper end, suffer from capital-city syndrome – meaning they cost more than they would elsewhere.

Most accommodation is walking distance to the centre of town and comparing options is easy enough on foot. Some midrange and top-end places are a little further away, but it's usually only a couple of kilometres. Accommodation is listed by price, from cheapest up, and divided into budget (up to US$15), midrange (US$16 to US$50) and top end (more than US$50).

Budget

Mixay Guesthouse (Map p92; ☎ 262210; 39 Th Nokeo Khumman; dm US$2, r US$3-5) This is one of Vientiane's cheapest guesthouses. The rooms are clean, but very basic, and the atmosphere is very laid-back. It's popular with backpackers, particularly Japanese. Some rooms have hot-water bathrooms (US$5), many others have no windows – check a few.

RD Guesthouse (Map p92; ☎ 262112) This place, next door to Mixay, was being renovated when we passed but should be open when you read this. Expect a range of clean rooms at budget prices, and a good dorm.

Joe Guest House (Map p92; ☎ /fax 241936; 112 Th Fa Ngum; r US$5-13) In a prime position on the riverfront, this place has simple but clean rooms, some with shared bathrooms, on top of an open-fronted coffee shop. It's comfortable enough but the atmosphere can be a bit flat.

Soukchaleun Guest House (Map p92; ☎ 218723; soukchaleun_gh@yahoo.com; 121 Th Setthathirat; r US$5-13; ✷) Popular Soukchaleun has simple, clean rooms with TV and fan or air-con. The atmosphere is pretty friendly, and the location great – front rooms have views over Wat Mixai.

Saysouly Guest House (Map p92; ☎ 218384; saysouly@hotmail.com; 23 Th Manthatulat; r US$5-15; ✷) Two minutes' walk from Nam Phu, this three-storey place offers spacious, clean and quiet rooms with bathrooms (single/double US$10/12) and fan rooms with shared bathrooms (US$5/7). The atmosphere is relaxed and the balconies can be a good place to meet other travellers.

Syri 1 Guest House (Map p92; ☎ 212682; Th Saigon; r US$6-10; ✷) The vintage Mercedes limo that has been parked in the garage for years somehow captures the essence of this laid-back, welcoming guesthouse in a quiet old house near the National Stadium – ageing comfort that's seen better days. Rooms range from an enormous studio to compact doubles, some without windows or bathroom. Don't confuse it with the Syri 2.

Chanta Guest House (Map p92; ☎ 243204; Th Setthathirat; r US$6-15; ✷) The friendly Chanta has eight rooms, all different, in a converted French-era shophouse. The pick are the two with bathrooms and balconies (US$8) overlooking Wat Mixai, though these can be frightfully noisy in the mornings. All rooms have satellite TV and are cleaned daily.

Soukxana Guesthouse (Map p92; ☎ 264114; soukxana_guest_house@yahoo.com; 13 Th Pangkham; r US$8-15; ✷) Mr Si Mon has overhauled this place, a five-minute walk north of the centre, and given it a relaxed character. Rooms are clean and prices depend on the number of people in the room and whether rooms have air-con or an overhead fan. Recommended.

Orchid Guesthouse (Map p92; ☎ 252825; Th Fa Ngum; r US$10-15; ✷) In the heart of the action along the riverfront, the Orchid's rooms are simple and clean but those without bathroom or air-conditioning (tw US$10) are a bit pricey. It's welcoming.

Thongbay Guesthouse (Map pp88-9; ☎ /fax 242292; www.thongbay-guesthouses.com; r US$10-15; ✷) About 1.5km west of town, the Thongbay is a large traditional house on a quiet, leafy block. The large, cool rooms have low beds and modern bathrooms. Fan-rooms and rooms without bathrooms are also available. The English-speaking owners are passionate about Lao food and can organise cooking classes. Bikes and motorbikes can be hired.

Phonepaseuth Guest House (Map p92; ☎ 212263; www.phonepaseuth-gh.com; Th Pangkham; r US$10-16; ❄) Centrally located near Nam Phu, this guesthouse has a range of rooms, some windowless, so look at several (Room 841 is the best at US$16). The staff are a bit variable but its location keeps it popular. Rooms US$15 and over come with breakfast for two.

Vayakorn Guest House (Map p92; ☎ 241911; vayakone@laotel.com; 91 Th Nokeo Khumman; s/d US$12/15; ❄) Two blocks west of Nam Phu, Vayakorn's stylish and spacious rooms are a bargain. All have polished floors, satellite television and spotless bathrooms, though the singles are pretty small. Service is friendly and professional, and rooms are cleaned daily.

Douang Deuane Hotel (Map p92; ☎ 222301; DD_hotel@hotmail.com; Th Nokeo Khumman; s/tw/tr incl breakfast US$12/15/23; ❄) The Douang Deuane is a soulless four-storey place but the combination of location, price, and simple but clean, medium-sized rooms with fridge, phone and satellite TV make it good value.

Also recommended:

Phorntip Guesthouse (Map p92; ☎ 217239; Th In Paeng; r US$8-12; ❄) Quiet, family-run place with range of rooms – look at a few.

Praseuth Guest House (Map p92; ☎ 217932; 312 Th Samsenthai; r US$5-6; ❄) Beside Xayoh Café, rooms are ultrabasic but clean and the management helpful. Upstairs shared bathroom is best.

Sabaidy Guest House (Map p92; ☎ 213929; sabaidy_gh@hotmail.com; Th Setthathirat; dm/d US$2/4), and **Mixok Guest House** (Map p92; ☎ 251606; Th Setthathirat; s/d/tr US$3.50/4.50/5.40) are nearby and the cheapest places in town, though the price is the only reason you'd stay. **Mimi Guesthouse** (Map p92; ☎ 250773; 9 Th François Nginn; r US$3-7) is another cheap but bearable option, and has a better atmosphere.

Midrange

Many midrange hotels accept Visa and MasterCard, but guesthouses probably won't.

GUESTHOUSES

ourpick **Mali Namphu Guest House** (Map p92; ☎ 215093; 114 Th Pangkham; r incl breakfast US$11-17; ❄) A few metres north of Nam Phu, this attractive 40-room place is built around a pleasant courtyard. The rooms vary in size and are not huge, but they are spotless, and the staff are both efficient and eager to please.

Dragon Lodge (Map p92; ☎ 250112; dragonlodge2002@yahoo.com; Th Samsenthai; r US$12-30; ❄) Rooms here are spotless, comfortable and well kitted out, if a bit dark. Readers have written with mixed reviews, usually saying the chilled-out bar downstairs (which also has handy travel information) creates a fun atmosphere. However, others have reported nocturnal activities can get a bit noisy.

Viengthong Guest House (Map pp88-9; ☎ 212095; viengthongguesthouse@hotmail.com; 8 Th Fa Ngum; s/tw US$13/16; ❄) In a quiet *soi* (street) along the northwest side of Wat Phia Wat, the Viengthong mixes laid-back service (ie slow but smiling) with good-value rooms, a quiet location and some trippy wat-style murals. The rooms in the newer building are actually minisuites and are excellent value at US$16.

Villa That Luang (Map pp88-9; ☎ 413370; ecolodge@laotel.com; 307 Th That Luang; s/d incl breakfast US$15/18; ❄ 🖳) Not far from Pha That Luang, the attractive and well-equipped rooms in this clean, comfortable guesthouse give it a real homely feel. The staff are wonderfully obliging and speak English, French and Japanese. Huge discounts are available for long stays and there's a free daily laundry service.

Nalinthone Guesthouse (Map pp88-9; ☎ 243659, 020-7720220; namrinnvte@yahoo.com; r US$15-20; ❄) This family-run, modern place on the river lacks a little in atmosphere but the clean and comfortable rooms are great value considering the position – the doubles with river views (US$15) are the pick.

Lani I Guest House (Map p92; ☎ 214919; www.lanigh.laotel.com; 281 Th Setthathirat; s/d US$25/35; ❄) Down a quiet lane just north of Wat Hai Sok in the centre of town, this colonial-era mansion has a tranquil, historic feel. High ceilings, antiques, Lao handicrafts and no TVs in the 12 rooms all contribute to the atmosphere. And it's that – the ambience – you're paying for here, not luxury; you can get much better equipped rooms for less elsewhere.

Villa Manoly (Map pp88-9; ☎ /fax 218907; manoly20@hotmail.com; r US$25-40; ❄ 🖳) In a quiet street off Th Fa Ngum between Wat Si Muang and the Mekong, the Manoly is a large French-era villa (plus a newer building) fronted by a large garden with a pool. The house is all hardwood and terrazzo floors, high ceilings and tasteful furnishings (look for the collection of antique typewriters). Renovations at the time of writing should add to the polish of the place.

HOTELS

Riverside Hotel (Map p92; ☎ 244390; Th Nokeo Khumman; r US$15-16; 🐱) At the cheap end of midrange, this new place offers a good location and well-equipped rooms, even if it's not going to win prizes for its charisma. Rooms here do vary a bit – some are quite dark – so ask to see a few, starting with the even numbered rooms on the 4th and 5th floors, which have Mekong views. VIP rooms are well worth the extra dollar if you're prepared to walk up all those stairs.

Asian Pavilion Hotel (Map p92; ☎ 213430; asianlao@loxinfo.co.th; 379 Th Samsenthai; s/d/ste US$25/27/35; 🐱) While its claim to 'boutique' status might be overblown, the Asian Pavilion's ageing but comfortable rooms with satellite TV and minibar are decent value, especially when the routine hefty discount is thrown in. However, the history is more of a draw than the rooms. In its pre-Revolutionary incarnation, this was the Hotel Constellation (immortalised in John Le Carré's *The Honourable Schoolboy*) and was frequented by all sorts of secret-agent types during the '60s and '70s.

Day Inn Hotel (Map p92; ☎ 222985; dayinn@laopdr .com; 59/3 Th Pangkham; s/d/tw/tr incl breakfast US$27/32/37/42; 🐱) The centrally located Day Inn is two renovated buildings with large, airy rooms with attractive rattan furnishings, TV, minibar and, in most rooms, large bathrooms with bathtubs. Try for a room in the smaller building (out the back) as some in the main building have outside bathrooms but are the same price. Price includes airport pick-up.

Chanthapanya Hotel (Map p92; ☎ 241541; www .chantapanyahotel.com; 138 Th Nokeo Khumman; r incl breakfast US$30-45; 🐱 🖳) Centrally located right opposite the Lao National Culture Hall, the Chanthapanya is a new, 31-room hotel that feels a lot like a modern midrange Thai hotel. And that's not a bad thing. The service is efficient and the rooms feel like Asia, though some are a bit cramped. In-room internet is free if you BYO laptop.

our pick Intercity Hotel (Map p92; ☎ 242843–4; www.laointerhotel.com; 24-25 Th Fa Ngum; r incl breakfast US$30-70; 🐱 🖳) The Intercity's years-long makeover is complete and the rooms and atmosphere make this a great choice. Most rooms are huge, with high ceilings, polished wood floors, big windows and tasteful Asian furnishings and antique decorations. All front rooms have wonderful views of the Mekong. Suite 888 (US$70) is the standout. Rear rooms are cheaper ($30).

Lane Xang Hotel (Map p92; ☎ 214102; www .lanexanghotel.com; Th Fa Ngum; s/d incl breakfast US$30/33, ste incl breakfast $50-60; 🐱 🖳) Built in the 1960s on the site of a prominent Lan Xang–era wat, this hotel facing the Mekong was once the classiest place in town. It has long been popular with Lao government and military types and retains a certain socialist-era feel, something that is almost extinct elsewhere in Southeast Asia. All rooms have satellite TV and minibar, and other amenities include a bar, fitness centre, baby cots, sauna and the sort of nightclub that would have Karl Marx turning in his grave. However, even with the buffet breakfast the rooms are probably a touch overpriced.

our pick Hotel Beau Rivage Mekong (Map pp88-9; ☎ 243375; www.hbrm.com; s US$34, d & tw incl breakfast US$43-55; 🐱 🖳) Don't be put off by the preponderance of pink; this Australian-owned boutiqueish hotel on the banks of the Mekong is excellent value. All of the 16 rooms are stylishly laid out and furnished with a pink, blue or green theme, and those with Mekong views (US$55), terrazzo baths and small balconies are best.

Lao Orchid Hotel (Map p92; ☎ 264134; www.lao -orchid.com; Th Chao Anou; d/ste incl breakfast US$35-55; 🐱) Opened in mid-2006, the Lao Orchid is one of a new breed of tastefully designed hotels beginning to pop up in Vientiane. The 33 well-equipped rooms are fitted out with an emphasis on wood and silk, and the service is a step up from the standard. All rooms have a balcony, but ask for one at the front to take in the Mekong views. Good value.

Also recommended:

Chaleunxay Hotel (Map p92; ☎ 223407; Th Khu Vieng; r US$10-18; 🐱) 60-room Vietnamese-run place where rooms get cheaper as you climb the five storeys. Fair value.

Hotel Lao (Map p92; ☎ 219280; hotellao@laotel .com; 43 Th Heng Boun; s/d US$20/25; 🐱) In the heart of Chinatown; rooms have two beds, TV, fridge and some have balconies. Welcoming atmosphere.

Le Parasol Blanc (Map pp88-9; ☎ 215090; Th Sibounheuang; r incl breakfast US$35; 🐱 🖳) Ageing but comfortable and quiet rooms set around a pool, near Patuxai. Popular with NGO workers. Cable TV and good service.

Top End

All Vientiane's top-end establishments are hotels, and all of these have business centres, pool and at least one restaurant. Major credit cards are accepted.

Tai-Pan Hotel (Map p92; ☎ 216906; www.travelao .com; 22/3 Th François Nginn; r incl breakfast US$58-150; ⌗ 🖳 🗷) Near the riverfront, the Tai-Pan is very reliable with good service and has become popular with people on business. The best rooms have balconies, so it's worth requesting one. Prices drop out of season.

Lao Plaza Hotel (Map p92; ☎ 218800, in Bangkok 0066-2653 9972; www.laoplazahotel.com; 63 Th Samsenthai; r US$100-140, ste US$250-450; ⌗ 🖳 🗷) This busy 142-room complex, occupying an entire block east of the Lao National Museum, boasts four-star rooms with views across the city. Discounts are available if you book online and it pays to ask about breakfast when you book – they'll often included it.

Green Park Hotel (Map pp88-9; ☎ 264297; www .greenparkvientiane.com; Th Khu Vieng; r US$115-380; ⌗ 🖳 🗷) The Green Park doesn't have the spectacular location of the Don Chan Palace, but it's infinitely more classy. Set around a courtyard pool, the 34 rooms are attractive and details like wi-fi and bathtubs put it a cut above the rest. Good choice if you can afford it, though do book ahead.

Settha Palace Hotel (Map p92; ☎ 217581; www .setthapalace.com; 6 Th Pangkham; standard/deluxe r US$143/155; ⌗ 🖳 🗷) The Settha Palace is Vientiane's classic colonial hotel, and is probably the best hotel in town. It has been beautifully restored, with custom-made rosewood furniture, plank floors and landscaped gardens. The 29 tastefully appointed rooms have wi-fi (US$6 per hour) and black-and-white Venetian marble bathrooms (the deluxe rooms with bathtubs), but don't expect acres of space. Drinking a cocktail from the poolside bar is a delight, as is the food from Le Belle Epoque restaurant (p107).

Don Chan Palace (Map pp88–9; ☎ 244288; www .donchanpalacelaopdr.com; off Th Fa Ngum; r US$150-300; ⌗ 🖳 🗷) On an island in the Mekong believed to be home to a powerful *naga*, this gargantuan monstrosity was built for the Asean conference in 2004, somehow managing to bypass Vientiane's seven-storey height limit. It's certainly luxurious and the views are great, but classy it is not.

APARTMENTS

If you're going to be here for a while check out these luxury apartment complexes: **Parkview Executive Suites** (Map pp88-9; ☎ 250888; www.laos-hotels.com; Th Luang Prabang; ⌗ 🖳 🗷) and the French-run **Khunta Residence** (Map pp88-9; ☎ 251199; www.ahlao.com; ⌗ 🖳 🗷).

EATING

When we arrived in Vientiane this time and heard an expat describe the city's eating as 'dollar for dollar the best in the world', we thought he'd had one too many happy pizzas. But the more we ate the more we thought that actually, he might be right. The ever-growing number of cafés, street vendors, beer gardens and restaurants now embrace much of the world's cuisine, and we can't think of anywhere with this range for so little money – it's hard to argue with US$4 or $5 for a meal that would probably cost five times as much at home.

Countless simple eateries serving fresh and tasty Lao dishes are complemented by establishments offering food as diverse as French provençale, sushi, Indian fusion and North Korean (with rock 'n' roll waitresses direct from Pyongyang!).

Bakeries & Delis

Scandinavian Bakery (Map p92; ☎ 215199; Nam Phu; pastries US$0.80-1.50; ⏰ breakfast, lunch & dinner; ⌗) This long-running favourite on Nam Phu sells fresh bread, pies, sandwiches (US$2), real Scandinavian-style pastries, cakes and ice cream. It has indoor and outdoor seating, and the upstairs room has satellite TV tuned to BBC or CNN.

BREAKING THE FAST

Most hotels (but not guesthouses) offer set 'American' breakfasts (known as ABF; two eggs, toast and ham or bacon) usually for between US$1 and US$4. Or you could get out on the streets and eat where the locals do. One popular breakfast is *khào jìi páa-tê*, a split French baguette stuffed with Lao-style pâté (which is more like English or American luncheon meat than French pâté) and various dressings. These vendors also sell plain baguettes (*khào jìi*) – there are several regular bread vendors around town, but especially on Th Heng Boun between Th Chao Anou and Th Khun Bulom.

Croissant d'Or (Map p92; ☎ 223741; 96 Th Nokeo Khumman; meals US$2-3; ✪) The coffee, sandwiches and fine pastries make this petit French-run café a long-time favourite.

JoMa Bakery Café (Map p92; ☎ 215265; Th Setthathirat; meals US$2-5; ☯ breakfast, lunch & dinner Mon-Sat; ✪) JoMa is the first-choice lunch stop for many expatriate workers in Vientiane, partly because the large and stylish café is a good place for meetings but mainly because it does a brisk trade in delicious pastries, sandwiches, quiche, muesli, fruit, shakes and coffee. Wi-fi is available for US$2.50 an hour.

Swedish Pizza & Baking House (Map p92; ☎ 215705; Th Chao Anou; pizzas US$3-5) More pizza place than bakery, with some pastries and arguably the best pizzas in Vientiane. Delivery available.

Noodles, Chinese & Vietnamese

Noodles of all kinds are popular in Vientiane, especially in the unofficial Chinatown area bounded by Th Heng Boun, Th Chao Anou, Th Khun Bulom and the western end of Th Samsenthai. The basic choice is *fŏe* (a rice noodle that's popular throughout mainland Southeast Asia), *mii* (traditional Chinese egg noodle) and *khào pûn* (very thin wheat noodles with a spicy Lao sauce). *Fŏe* and *mii* can be ordered as soup (eg *fŏe nâm*), fried (eg *khùa fŏe*) or dry-mixed in a bowl (eg *fŏe hàeng*), among other variations.

PVO (Map p92; ☎ 214444; Th Fa Ngum; meals US$0.70-1.50; ☯ breakfast, lunch & dinner) After years selling the best *khào jîi páa-tê* (Vietnamese-style paté baguettes) in town (US$0.70/1.40 half/whole baguette) from their garage-style restaurant on Th Samsenthai, PVO has moved to the riverfront, opposite the BCEL. The food is as good and cheap as ever, with the spring rolls also a favourite. Motorbikes can be hired here, see p116.

ourpick **Vieng Sawan** (Map p92; ☎ 213990; Th Heng Boun; meals US$1.50-3.50; ☯ lunch & dinner) In the middle of Chinatown, Vieng Sawan is a bustling open-sided restaurant that is a real Lao eating experience. It specialises in *năem néuang* (barbecued pork meatballs) and many varieties of *yáw* (spring rolls), usually sold in 'sets' *(sut)* with *khào pûn*, fresh lettuce leaves, mint, basil, various sauces for dipping, sliced starfruit and green plantain. You can also order *sîin ja* here, thinly sliced pieces of raw beef which customers boil in small cauldrons of coconut juice and eat with dipping sauces, or some of the many varieties of spring rolls.

Guangdong Restaurant (Map p92; ☎ 217364; 91-93 Th Chao Anou; meals US$2-4; ☯ lunch & dinner; ✪) The menu here resembles a small phone book of mainly southern Chinese dishes.

On the riverfront just east of Th Nokeo Khumman are three little shophouse restaurants (Map p92) – Addy, Nok Noy Restaurant and Sokhith Restaurant – that have become a firm favourite among backpackers, or anyone seeking a cheap, tasty feed. There is little difference between the three: all serve a mix of reliable Asian dishes mostly for less than US$2 and are open for breakfast, lunch and dinner.

Lao

ourpick **Riverfront food and drink vendors** (Map p92; ☯ dinner) The long stretch of vendors that convenes along the levee beside the Mekong River is a great place to watch the sunset eating *pîng ka* (grilled chicken), *tàm màak-hung* or *năem* (minced sausage mixed with rice, herbs and roasted chillies with a plate of greens on the side) and cheap Beerlao.

ourpick **Ban Anou night market** (Map p92; ☯ dinner) This night market sets up in a small street off the north end of Th Chao Anou every afternoon. It's an encyclopaedia of street food, all fresh and freshly prepared – the locals love it.

Mekong Riverside Restaurant (Map p92; ☎ 241375; Th Fa Ngum; meals US$1.50-3; ☯ lunch & dinner) On the river, tucked just behind PVO, this comparatively formal riverfront eatery offers a small menu of tasty Lao staples supplemented by snacks you won't find at home; deep-fried underground *singer* (cricket; US$2.50) with your Beerlao, anyone?

Ban Vilaylac Restaurant (Map p92; ☎ 222 049; meals US$2-3.50; ☯ 8am-10.30pm) Hidden between Wat Ong Teu Mahawihan and Wat Chanthabuli, this romantic little place serves tasty Lao and Thai food.

ourpick **Bunmala Restaurant** (Map pp88-9; ☎ 313 249; Th Khu Vieng; meals US$2-4; ☯ lunch & dinner) It's a little out of town, but this open-sided, timber-floored restaurant is about as archetypal Lao as you can find – and the food is great, too. There are all manner of Lao favourites, including *pîng pét* (roast duck), *pîng pạa* (grilled fish), *pîng lîn* (roast cow tongue) and *pîng kai* made from particularly plump chickens. For a classic Lao meal, order the (very hot) *tạm màa-hung* (papaya salad), *kạeng naw mâi* (soupy bamboo-shoot salad), sticky rice and draught beer. Delicious. It's best to come in the evening when the full range of *ping* is on offer and the draught beer is US$0.50.

Soukvemarn Lao Food (Map p92; ☎ 214441; www .laofoods.com; 89/12 Ban Sisaket; meals US$2.50-3.50; ☺ lunch & dinner) Don't be put off by the location down a dirt alley from That Dam – the Lao food at Soukvemarn is very good. Specialities include *kǫeng pǫa khai mot* (fish soup with ant larvae – in season) and *làap pǫa* (spicy minced fish salad), among many others. The family who manage it make good conversation, too.

Douang Deuane Restaurant & Wine Bar (Map p92; ☎ 241154; Th François Nginn; meals US$2.50-5; ☺ breakfast, lunch & dinner Mon-Sat) The tasty Lao, Thai and Vietnamese favourites here are complemented by an attractive traditional setting and a welcoming French host. We always have a good time when eating here, it's that kind of place. The upstairs balcony has a good table for couples.

Tum Zaap (Map p92; ☎ 252368; Th Khun Bulom; meals US$3-5; ☺ lunch & dinner Mon-Sat) This new hole-in-the-wall is a reflection of the growing sophistication of Lao youth and their palate, serving Lao cuisine with a modern twist.

Makphet (Map p92; ☎ 260587; Th Setthathirat; meals US$3-6; ☺ lunch Mon-Sat) Run by Friends International (www.friends-international .org), this small restaurant trains homeless youths to cook and wait tables. The modern Lao cuisine is both interesting and tasty. A shop upstairs sells handicrafts made by underprivileged families.

Tamnak Lao Restaurant (Map pp88-9; ☎ 413562; Th That Luang; meals US$5-10; ☺ breakfast, lunch & dinner Mon-Sat; ☒) If you mention Tamnak Lao to locals, they will be impressed. It has a well-earned reputation for excellent Lao and Thai food. You can sit inside or in the manicured garden, and there is a traditional dancing show most nights.

French & Italian

It is no surprise that this former French colony should boast so many French restaurants, but their overall high quality is surprising. When you consider that this fine dining experience will cost a fraction of what you'd pay at home, it gets even better.

Saovaly Restaurant (Map p92; ☎ 214940; Th Manthatulat; meals US$2.50-6; ☺ lunch & dinner Mon-Sat) The French and Lao food here is wonderful, with subtle flavours and artistic presentation complemented by attentive but not harassing service. And all for very reasonable prices. It's just a pity the atmosphere is so, well, living room – when we ate here it was to the dulcet tones of Martin Tyler on a Man U TV re-run.

Le Vendôme (Map p92; ☎ 216402; Th In Paeng; meals US$3-7; ☺ lunch Mon-Fri, dinner daily; ☒) Tucked away in an old house in a quiet street behind Wat In Paeng, Le Vendôme's intimate, romantic ambience and mix of salads, French cuisine, wood-fired pizza and pasta make it a good choice.

Le Côte D'Azur Restaurant (Map p92; ☎ 217 252; 62-63 Th Fa Ngum; meals US$3-8; ☺ lunch Mon-Sat, dinner daily; ☒) Long-running Le Côte D'Azur is popular with French expats, and when your food arrives you'll understand why. The delicious Provençal cuisine and understated service make this a top choice. Also on offer are pastas, salads and pizzas (order anything with fresh herbs).

La Gondola (Map p92; ☎ 264057; 39 Th Chao Anou; meals US$5-8; ☺ lunch & dinner Tue-Sun) Reasonably good Italian fare is served up by the Italian owner in unpretentious surrounds. Warm atmosphere.

our pick Le Silapa (Map p92; ☎ 219689; 17/1 Th Sihom; meals US$5-12; ☺ lunch & dinner Mon-Sat; ☒) Le Silapa has been serving some of the best French cuisine in Vientiane for years, complemented by refined surrounds and discrete service. The menu changes frequently and consists of classic as well as improvised dishes. If you order a bottle of wine the restaurant contributes to a medical fund for economically disadvantaged children…what better excuse? The lunch set menu is good value.

Le Belle Epoque (Map p92; ☎ 217581; 6 Th Pangkham; ☺ breakfast, lunch & dinner; US$8-13; ☒) For a taste of colonial-era luxury it's hard to beat this restaurant in the Settha Palace Hotel. The menu is mainly French but also has a Lao component; dishes include braised lamb shank with organic mash potato (US$13.50) and the delicious flat noodles with grilled eggplant and cream sauce (US$5.50).

L'Opera Italian Restaurant (Map p92; ☎ 215099; Nam Phu; meals US$8-16; ☺ 11.30am-2pm & 6-10pm; ☒) L'Opera has become something of a Vientiane institution, but that doesn't make it either overly welcoming or great value. The food, however, is pretty good, with pasta (US$6.50 to US$7.50) being the standout.

The French influence is most noticeable around Nam Phu, where you'll find three small, atmospheric eateries each serving

Gallic cuisine. On the east side is the intimate **Restaurant-Bar Namphu** (Map p92; ☎ 216248; Nam Phu; meals US$4-10; ☼ lunch & dinner; ☒), where the menu offers a mix of French and Asian fare combined with sophisticated service and an extensive wine cellar – the lunchtime set menus are great value. Next door is the mercifully not-so-grotto-like **La Cave des Chateaux** (Map p92; ☎ 212192; Nam Phu; meals US$5-9; ☼ lunch & dinner Mon-Fri, dinner only Sat & Sun; ☒), which specialises in French cheeses (grilled to perfection) and wines; while on the other side of the circle the cosy **Restaurant Le Provençal** (Map p92; ☎ 219685; Nam Phu; meals US$3-10; ☼ lunch & dinner; ☒) serves rustic southern-French-style dishes, though its pastas and oven-baked pizzas are at least as good.

International

More expats and travellers means a demand for a greater variety of cuisines, one that Vientiane seems to be meeting fairly well. There are also plenty of eateries offering a combination of cuisines. And while you should justifiably be wary of any kitchen purporting to know *làap* as well as lasagne, there are a few here that manage to do their multicultural menus justice.

Khop Chai Deu (Map p92; ☎ 251564; 54 Th Setthathirat; meals US$2.50-8; ☼ lunch & dinner; ☒) In a remodelled colonial-era villa near Nam Phu, Khop Chai Deu has been a traveller's favourite for years because of its range of well-prepared Lao, Thai, Indian and assorted Western fare, and lively ambience. There's live music most days.

Full Moon Café (Map p92; ☎ 243373; Th François Nginn; meals US$3-6.50; ☼ breakfast, lunch & dinner; ☒) The relaxed-but-hip look of the Full Moon might lure you in, and once there the Asian fusion food won't disappoint. The tapas and ever-changing set menus are worth considering.

ourpick **Sticky Fingers Café & Bar** (Map p92; ☎ 215972; 10/3 Th François Nginn; meals US$3.50-6; ☼ breakfast, lunch & dinner Tue-Sun; ☒) It has the atmosphere of a Sydney café, but Sticky Fingers is actually one of the best places to eat in Vientiane. The cuisine could be described as 'modern international', with delicious dishes cooked up by Mr Cho and his team – Mr Cho's crispy fish (US$4.90) was subtle and delicious. And the hangover special (US$4, an extra 10c for paracetamol) works wonders.

Le Ranch (Map pp88-9; ☎ 413700; Th Phonsay; meals US$4-6; ☼ breakfast, lunch & dinner Thu-Tue) Oddly, for a place run by a French-Lao couple, this big, breezy restaurant northeast of the centre pays homage to the American southwest. The heavy wooden furniture and buffalo horns set the scene, and the steaks (US$4.50) and woodfired pizzas (US$4.50 to US$6) are worth the trip.

Thai

Considering Thailand is just over the Mekong, there are surprisingly few dedicated Thai restaurants in Vientiane. This, though, is partly because Thai dishes also appear on the menus of many Lao restaurants.

Phikun (Map pp88-9; ☎ 222340; Th Sihom; meals US$1-1.50; ☼ breakfast, lunch & dinner) It's none too inspiring to look at but give it a chance and you'll find Phikun's Thai food is both good and very cheap. Dishes vary, but the dozen or so preprepared dishes might include the delicious *kai phàt bai kàphrao* (chicken fried in holy basil). They're served with rice – about US$1 for two dishes, an extra 20c for each extra. The English sign reads 'Thai Food'.

Linda Sathaporn Restaurant (Map pp88-9; ☎ 415355; cnr Th Dong Palan & Th Phonsay; meals US$3-6; ☼ breakfast, lunch & dinner; ☒) Linda Sathaporn's three (yes, three) plastic folders filled with pictures of their varied tasty Thai dishes make it worth the trip. It's very popular with Thais, and with smart service and large portions it's easy to see why. Seating is inside or in the more pleasant shaded courtyard out back.

Indian

Fathima Restaurant (Map p92; ☎ 219097; Th Fa Ngum; meals US$1-2.50; ☼ breakfast, lunch & dinner) Indians like this place, and for good reason– the food is cheap and many times better than the décor. Vegetarian dishes (US$1) are a big draw, and the chicken and meat curries (about US$2) are also delicious. Real ice cream is sold outside.

Taj Mahal Restaurant (Map p92; ☎ 020-5611003; meals US$2-4; ☼ breakfast, lunch & dinner Mon-Sat, dinner Sun) It looks like a garage, but the Taj Mahal serves what we think is the best Indian food in Vientiane (and yes, we researched the lot). Prices are very reasonable and there are plenty of vegetarian dishes. Recommended.

Rashmi's Indian Fusion (Map p92; ☎ 251513; cnr Th Samsenthai & Th Pangkham; meals US$3-6; ☼ lunch & dinner) It was only a matter of time before fusion cuisine arrived in Vientiane, but a mix of Indian and Chinese isn't quite what we expected. It's actually better than it sounds, and if fusion doesn't appeal there are more traditional Indian offerings too. Letting Rashmi explain the menu is recommended.

Japanese & Korean

7 Plus Korean Food (Map pp88-9; ☎ 415343; meals US$2-5; ✆ breakfast, lunch & dinner) The Korean food here isn't bad but coming here is mainly about having a night out Lao style. The beer-garden-type place is huge, and with lots of young Lao and US$0.70 Beerlao the atmosphere is always 'up'.

YuLaLa (Map p92; ☎ 215214; Th Heng Boun; meals US$2.50-4; ✆ lunch & dinner Tue-Sun, closed last Sun of month; ✆) Run by a young Japanese couple, YuLaLa serves tasty, cheap Japanese fusion cuisine in a cool atmosphere – think music by Bob Dylan. Note there is no sushi or sashimi here.

Pyongyang Restaurant (Map pp88-9; ☎ 263118; Th Nong Bon; meals US$5-25; ✆ lunch & dinner) Owned by the same people as the Phnom Penh restaurant of the same name, this Pyongyang is even more surreal. Waitresses direct from North Korea, trained to sing and dance since childhood, will take your order one minute and step up to the microphone the next to perform perfectly choreographed dance routines and/or play electric guitar and drums (it starts about 7.30pm). It's a complete trip. Don't, however, let them order for you, as you'll be served only the most expensive dishes on what is a relatively pricey menu. There is no obvious sign; look for 'Korean Restaurant' on the window.

Fujiwara Restaurant (Map p92; ☎ 222210; Th Luang Prabang; meals US$6-10; ✆ breakfast & lunch Mon-Sat, dinner daily; ✆) Just west of Wat In Paeng, Fujiwara has an epic menu including all the Japanese favourites and several set meals. Sushi is the specialty and it's good, but not cheap.

Vegetarian

While you can find vegetarian dishes on almost every menu (particularly the Indian restaurants), only a couple of places market themselves directly to vegetarian diners.

Just for Fun (Map p92; ☎ 213642; 51/2 Th Pangkham; meals US$1-3; ✆ breakfast, lunch & dinner Mon-Sat) Just for Fun has been serving its small but mainly vegetarian menu for years, with offerings inspired by Thai and Lao cui-

sine. It also serves Lao coffee and lots of herbal teas.

Khouadin Vegetarian (Map p92; ☎ 215615; buffet US$1.30; ✆ breakfast & lunch) Hidden away behind Talat Sao, this simple restaurant serves precooked but thoroughly recommended vegetarian dishes. Great for a fast, tasty lunch.

Self-Catering

For the largest selection of fresh groceries and the best prices, you should stick to the markets. But if there's something 'Western' you're yearning for, or a bottle of wine, check out the following minimarkets and wine cellar.

Phimphone Market (Map p92; ☎ 94/6 Th Setthathirat; ✆ 7.30am-9pm) The mother of all Phimphones, this store near Nam Phu has a wide selection of imported goods, including canned and frozen foods, magazines, personal hygiene and women's products such as tampons. There's more wine upstairs.

Phimphone Market 2 (Map p92; ☎ 214609; cnr Th Samsenthai & Th Chanta Khumman; ✆ 8am-8.30pm) This is a smaller branch of the Phimphone market.

DRINKING

Vientiane is no longer the illicit pleasure palace it was when Paul Theroux described it, in his 1975 book *The Great Railway Bazaar*, as a place in which 'the brothels are cleaner than the hotels, marijuana is cheaper than pipe tobacco and opium easier to find than a cold glass of beer'. Nowadays, brothels are strictly prohibited, Talat Sao's marijuana stands have been removed from prominent display and cold Beerlao has definitely replaced opium as the nightly drug of choice. Most of the bars, restaurants and discos close by 11.30pm or midnight.

Vins de France (Map p92; ☎ 217700; 354 Th Samsenthai; ✆ 8.30am-8pm Mon-Sat) Vins de France is one of the best French wine cellars in Southeast Asia. Even if you don't like wine, it's worth popping in for a look at a place so completely out of character with its surrounds. If you do like wine, the US$6.90 degustation might be a wise investment.

Cafés

A growing number of cafés serve food and shakes along with a range of Lao and foreign coffees. Several more are listed under Bakeries & Delis in the Eating section (p105).

Maison du Café (Map p92; ☎ 214781; 70 Th Pangkham; ✆ 7am-6pm) A few metres north of Nam Phu, this welcoming place brews up a dizzying array of coffees (US$1 to US$2) and serves them with fresh sandwiches or baguettes (US$1.50), plus great shakes. There's plenty of reading matter around and the owner offers a range of tourist services.

Paradice (Map p92; ☎ 312836; Th Lan Xang; ⏰ 8am-8.30pm Mon-Sat) In the grounds of the Centre Culturel et de Coopération Linguistique, this airy, comfortable bar and café is, understandably, popular with Francophone expats and serves cheap coffee (from US$0.30), sandwiches and simple meals.

Delight House of Fruit Shakes (Map p92; ☎ 212200; Th Samsenthai; ⏰ 7am-9pm) One of two places here that make incredible fruit shakes. Understandably popular.

Beer Gardens

As the sun goes down, the banks of the Mekong River become one long beer garden, with tables and chairs set out under the stars and the 'Full Taste of Happiness' (Beerlao) flowing freely – it's a great way to finish a day. There's plenty of choice, from the more impromptu vendors lined along the river between PVO and Th Khun Bulom, where it's more beer than garden, to the more established structures overhanging the water as far west as the original of the species, Sala Sunset Khounta.

Several restaurants, such as 7 Plus Korean Food (p109), are also wildly popular local beer gardens. They tend to be found down non-descript side streets and typically involve a big *sala* (open-sided shelter), lots of staff and large groups of Vientiane youngsters.

Sala Sunset Khounta (Map pp88-9; ☎ 251079; snacks US$0.50-1.50; ⏰ 11am-11pm) At the west end of the dirt road along the riverfront, the 'Sunset Bar' is a Vientiane institution. The rustic wooden platform made of old boat timbers has been serving Beerlao at sunset for years, and was the only such bar to survive the government's riverfront-bar demolition a few years ago. The friendly and enterprising proprietors also offer local food and interesting snacks.

Bars

Bars open and close at a remarkable rate in Vientiane, though the recent trend has been leaning more heavily on the opening side. If you're looking for something cheaper and more local than the expat bars, look for nondescript *bia sót* (draught beer) bars with plastic jugs of beer on the tables.

Bor Pen Nyang (Map p92; ☎ 020-7873965; Th Fa Ngum; ⏰ 10am-midnight) The rooftop bar in this four-storey building was the place to be when we were researching. And it was easy to see why. With expansive views over the Mekong, a reliable range of music (if a little Aussie-centric), decent food and a generally 'up' atmosphere, it was a lot of fun. If you want to avoid backpackers, however, go elsewhere.

Chicago Bar (Map p92; ☎ 020-5526452; Th Nokeo Khumman; ⏰ 7pm-late; 🖥) The Chicago Bar is a sort of cocktail-cum-lounge bar with a leaning towards jazz and blues. It's fun, especially as it tends to stay open later than most Vientiane bars. Upstairs is a gallery/cinema with regular events. Tip though: avoid the mojitos.

Spirit House (Map pp88-9; ☎ 262530; 105 Th Fa Ngum; ⏰ 7am-midnight) Popular with expats, this classy place in a quiet position opposite the river specialises in cocktails, but also serves tasty tapas and burgers.

Jazzy Brick (Map p92; ☎ 020-2449307; www.jazzybrick.com; Th Setthathirat; ⏰ 11am-midnight) Run by a Lao who studied in Australia, the Jazzy Brick is a cut above most of its competitors on the style front. It's ostensibly a cocktail bar, and the cocktails are well mixed, but the prices (US$4 to US$5, or US$2.50 for a small Beerlao) are difficult to justify in a town as cheap as Vientiane. It's often open later than midnight.

Blue Sky (Map p92; ☎ 216368; cnr Th Setthathirat & Th Chao Anou; ⏰ 8am-10pm) Blue Sky is a four-storey backpacker bar with the seemingly obligatory Hollywood movies on screen. Better is the rooftop bar, which is ideal for sundowners – when it's open.

Samlo Pub (Map p92; ☎ 222308; Th Setthathirat; ⏰ 4-11.30pm) This dark, smokey dive is good for live sport.

ENTERTAINMENT

Like everything else, Vientiane's entertainment scene is picking up as money and politics allows, though the range remains fairly limited. You could make your way through all of Vientiane's live music venues and nightclubs in a couple of big nights out, though this is better than the couple of hours it would have taken a few years ago. Bowling and cinema are also gaining popularity. By law entertainment venues must close by 11.30pm, though most push it to about midnight.

Cinema

Lao cinemas died out in the video shop tidal wave of the 1990s.

Centre Culturel et de Coopération Linguistique (Map p92; ☎ 215764; www.ambafrance-laos .org/centre; Th Lan Xang; movies US$1; screenings 7.30pm Tue & Thu, 3.30pm Sat) The French Centre screens French films (usually subtitled in English); check the *Vientiane Times* or call the centre for information.

Lao ITECC (☎ 416374; Th T4) This centre includes a cinema that shows a mix of cinematic fare at hard-to-pin-down times.

Circus

National Circus (Hong Kanyasin; Map pp88-9; Th Thong Khan Kham) The old 'Russian Circus' established in the 1980s is now known as Hong Kanyasin. It performs from time to time in the National Circus venue, in the north of town. Check for dates in the *Vientiane Times*.

Traditional Music & Dancing

Laos Traditional Show (Map p92; ☎ 242978; Th Manthatulat; child/adult US$4/7, still/video camera charge US$1/3) The Lao National Theatre has a performance of traditional music and dancing aimed directly at the tourist market, and it's quite good. It plays nightly, though only during the tourist season (from November to March). At other times it can be seen in the Lane Xang Hotel (p104).

Live Music

On The Rock Pub (Map pp88-9; Th Luang Prabang; ☯ 7.30pm-midnight) Down a lane off Th Luang Prabang, On The Rock isn't quite what is was in its intimate old location, but has still been known to put on a good show. The live music is usually rock, or some variation of. Well worth a look.

Music House (Map p92; Th Fa Ngum; ☯ 8pm-midnight) This tiny venue was On The Rock until the owners, and the house band, had a dose of 'artistic differences'. It's still worth a look, though, with the band crammed into the corner and the mainly Lao patrons inches away, it's good fun.

Wind West (Map p92; ☎ 020-2000777; Th Luang Prabang; ☯ 5-11pm) A Western-US–style bar and restaurant, Wind West (yes, Wind, that's not a typo) has live Lao and Western rock

music most nights – the music usually starts about 10pm. Depending on the night it can be heaving, or completely dead.

Nightclubs

Vientiane's few nightclubs are split between big, independent affairs and those attached to a top-end hotel. Music is diverse, with DJs or sometimes live bands playing everything from electrified Lao folk (for *lám wóng* circular dancing) to quasi-Western pop, but is usually dominated by the latest Thai hits. Clubbers tend to be younger Lao, though not exclusively so. There is generally no charge to enter, but the Beerlao is more expensive than elsewhere. All up, good Lao-style fun.

Conveniently, three of the better clubs are within walking distance of each other on the way to the airport. First up is **Future Nightclub** (Map pp88-9; Th Luang Prabang; ☯ 8pm-1am), not far past the Novotel, where the music can make stepping into the Future seem more like leaping into the past. Fun though. Nearby is **Highwayman** (Map pp88-9; Th Luang Prabang; ☯ 8pm-midnight), which has occasional live acts but mainly DJs. A few hundred meters on is **Marina** (Map pp88-9; ☎ 216978; Th Luang Prabang; ☯ 8pm-1am), probably the biggest and most ostentatious of the lot. And if you get sick of dancing you can bowl instead!

HOTEL CLUBS

Lunar 36 (Map pp88-9; Don Chan Palace Hotel, off Th Fa Ngum; ☯ 6pm-3am Wed, Fri & Sat) This was the hottest nightclub in town when we passed, partly because two nearby clubs that had been popular were mysteriously forced to close after the Palace opened. In fairness, it is fun, though only on the prescribed nights – at other times it's just karaoke in private rooms.

D*Tech (Map pp88-9; ☎ 213570; Th Samsenthai) At the Novotel, this place often has a Philippine cover-band sharing space with its DJ.

Anou Cabaret (Map p92; ☎ 213630; cnr Th Heng Boun & Th Chao Anou) On the ground floor of the Anou Hotel, the cabaret has been swinging along for years. It's a funny place, with booths and old crooners that feel very 1960s.

Recreation Clubs

Australian Embassy Recreation Club (Australian Club; Map pp88-9; ☎ 314921; Km 3 Th Tha Deua; ☯ 6am-8.30pm) About 3km out of town on the way to the Thai-Lao Friendship Bridge, the AERC is universally known as the 'Australian Club'. It's

VIENTIANE & AROUND

probably best known for its brilliant salt-water pool, right next to the Mekong River, though the barbecues held every second and last Friday of the month (except in June and July) are also popular. There is also an air-con squash court (open from 6am to 8.30pm). Short-term memberships can be arranged for US$10/20 per single/family per day, or you could go as the guest of a member (US$2).

SHOPPING

Just about anything made in Laos is available for purchase in Vientiane, including hill-tribe crafts, jewellery, traditional textiles and carvings. The main shopping areas in town are Talat Sao (Morning Market), the eastern end of Th Samsenthai (near the Asian Pavilion Hotel), Th Pangkham and along Th Nokeo Khumman.

Handicrafts, Antiques & Art

Several shops along Th Samsenthai, Th Pangkham and Th Setthathirat sell Lao and Thai tribal and hill-tribe crafts. The Lao goods are increasingly complemented by products from Vietnam and Thailand, such as lacquer work and Buddha images. Many of the places listed under Textiles and Clothing (right) also carry handicrafts and antiques.

Handicraft Products of Ethnic Groups (Map p92; Th Khu Vieng) Beside the PTT office and opposite Talat Sao, this market-style place sells handicrafts from around Laos. The quality is variable, but at the least this is a good place to get an idea what is out there and how much it costs.

T'Shop Lai Galerie (Map p92; ☎ 223178; Th In Paeng; ☽ 8.30am-6pm Mon-Sat) This beautiful shop is well worth a look if you're interested in modern and traditional art in a range of media, furniture and interesting handicrafts. The owner is committed to promoting fair trade products.

Carterie du Laos (Map p92; ☎ 241401; 118/2 Th Setthathirat) This shop has a wide range of postcards, cards, posters and books, and a few small souvenirs.

Kanchana Boutique (Map p92; ☎ 213467; 102 Th Chanta Khumman; ☽ 8am-9pm Mon-Sat) Kanchana carries an extensive selection of Lao silk (the best is out the back) and can arrange visits to their Lao Textile Museum (open 10am to 4pm).

Satri Lao (Map p92; ☎ 244384; Th Setthathirat; ☽ 9am-8pm Mon-Sat, 10am-7pm Sun) This tastefully presented three-storey shop has an eclectic range of local and imported handicrafts and

clothes – from miniskirts and bikinis made from Hmong weavings to lacquer portraits of Ho Chi Minh.

Jewellery

Most of the jewellery shops are along Th Samsenthai and trade primarily in gold and silver. Among the better options are **Saigon Bijoux** (Map p92; ☎ 214783; Th Samsenthai), which also repairs jewellery, and **Bari Jewellery** (Map p92; ☎ 212680; Th Samsenthai), which deals in precious stones as well.

Talat Sao (opposite) has plenty of gold and silversmiths, though many are more artisan than artist.

Textiles & Clothing

Downtown Vientiane is littered with stores selling textiles to tourists. Th Nokeo Khumman is the epicentre; Talat Sao is also a good place to buy fabrics. You'll find antique as well as modern fabrics, plus utilitarian items such as shoulder bags (some artfully constructed around squares of antique fabric), cushions and pillows.

To see Lao weaving in action, seek out the weaving district of Ban Nong Buathong, northeast of the town centre in Muang Chanthabuli. About 20 families (many originally from Sam Neua in Hua Phan Province) live and work here, including a couple of households that sell textiles directly to the public; the **Phaeng Mai Gallery** (☎ 217341; 117 Th Nong Buathong; ☽ 10am-6pm), in a white, two-storey house, is among the best. It's out past the National Circus – most tuk-tuk drivers know it and will charge about US$2 one way.

Carol Cassidy Lao Textiles (Map p92; ☎ 212123; www.laotextiles.com; 84-86 Th Nokeo Khumman; ☽ 8am-noon & 2-5pm Mon-Fri, 8am-noon Sat, or by appointment) Lao Textiles sells high-end contemporary, original-design fabrics inspired by older Lao weaving patterns, motifs and techniques. The American designer, Carol Cassidy, employs Lao weavers who work out the back of the attractive old French-Lao house. They are internationally known, with prices to match.

Couleur d'Asie (Map p92; ☎ 223008; Nam Phu) The owner, a French-Vietnamese dress designer with Paris fashion-school experience, manages to fuse Lao and Western styles into some attractive designs at reasonable prices.

KPP Handicraft Promotion Enterprise of Sekong Province (Map p92; ☎ 241421; pholsana@laotel.com; cnr Th Setthathirath & Th Chao Anou; ☽ 9am-8pm) This modest-looking place sells fair-trade textiles from the Bolaven Plateau province of Sekong.

Nikone Handicrafts (Map pp88-9; ☎ 212191; nikone@hotmail.com; ☻ 9am-5pm Mon-Sat) Located out near the National Circus, this is another good place to see weaving and dyeing in action.

True Colour (Map p92; ☎ 214410; Th Setthathirat; ☻ 9am-8pm Mon-Sat) This store sells textiles and clothes made in the Houey Hong Vocational Training Center for Women (p101).

Other stores on Th Nokeo Khumman worth a look include **Khampan Lao Handicraft** (Map p92; ☎ 222000; ☻ 8am-9pm), with textiles from the Sam Neua area at very reasonable prices; upmarket **Mixay Boutique** (Map p92; ☎ 216592; ☻ 9am-8pm); and **Camacrafts** (Mulberries; Map p92; ☎ 241217; www.mulberries.org; ☻ 10am-6pm Mon-Sat), which stocks silk clothes and weavings from Xieng Khuang Province, plus some bed and cushion covers in striking Hmong-inspired designs.

Markets

Talat Sao (Map p92; Th Lan Xang; ☻ 7am-4pm) Vientiane's biggest market is a sprawling collection of stalls offering fabrics, ready-made clothes, jewellery, cutlery, toiletries, bedding, hardware and watches, as well as electronic goods and just about anything else imaginable. In the centre of the area is a large building that houses the Vientiane Department Store. Most of the existing structure was built in the 1960s, but like so much else in Laos Talat Sao is in a period of change. A huge new Malaysian-backed market should have opened next door by the time you arrive, bringing 'modernity' and homogenisation to Vientiane in equal measure. Exactly how this affects the existing market remains to be seen.

Talat Khua Din (Map p92; Th Khua Vieng) East of Talat Sao and beyond the bus terminal, this rustic market offers fresh produce and meats, as well as flowers, tobacco and assorted other goods.

Talat Thong Khan Kham (Map pp88-9; cnr Th Khan Kham & Th Dong Miang) This market north of the centre in Ban Khan Kham is open all day, but is best in the morning. It's one of the biggest in Vientiane and has virtually everything, including good food. Nearby are basket and pottery vendors.

GETTING THERE & AWAY
Air

Departures from Vientiane are perfectly straightforward. The Domestic Terminal is in the older, white building east of the impressive International Terminal. There is an (often unmanned) information counter in the arrivals hall, and food can be found upstairs in the International Terminal.

See p319 for details on air transport to Laos, p323 for information on flights within Laos.

AIRLINE OFFICES
See also Travel Agencies, p91.

China Eastern Airlines (Map pp88–9; ☎ 212300; www.chinaeastern.com; Th Luang Prabang) Same building as Thai Airways.

Lao Airlines (www.laoairlines.com) Airport Office (☎ 512028; ☻ 7.30am-noon & 1-4.30pm); Head Office (Map p92; ☎ 212051–4; 2 Th Pangkham; ☻ 8am-4.30pm Mon-Sat) Handles domestic and international ticketing.

Thai Airways International (Map pp88–9; ☎ 222527; Th Luang Prabang; 8am-5pm Mon-Fri, to noon Sat)

Vietnam Airlines (Map p92; ☎ 217562; www.vietnamairlines.com; 1st fl, Lao Plaza Hotel, Th Samsenthai; ☻ 8am-noon & 1.30-4.30pm Mon-Fri, 8am-noon Sat)

Boat

Passenger boat services between Vientiane and Luang Prabang have become almost extinct as most people now take the bus, which is both faster and cheaper.

Occasional six-passenger *héua wái* (speedboats) do run from Vientiane to Pak Lai, 115km away, and if you have the cash will go all the way to Luang Prabang – a full day's trip for at least US$240 for the boat. To charter a speedboat head out to Tha Heua Kao Liaw (Kao Liaw Boat Landing), which is 7.7km west of the Novotel (3.5km west of the fork in the road where Rte 13 heads north) in Ban Kao Liaw. It's best to go the day before you plan to travel.

If you get very lucky you might chance upon a rare cargo boat running to Luang Prabang, three to five days upriver. It would be an amazing trip, but you'll need patience to arrange it.

Bus

Our table (p114) gives timetable information. Buses use three different stations in Vientiane, all with some English-speaking staff, and food and drink stands. The **Northern Bus Station** (Map pp88-9; ☎ 260255; Th T2), about 2km northwest of the centre, serves all points north of Vang Vieng, including China, and

LEAVING VIENTIANE BY BUS

All services depart daily except where noted, though times do change so use this as a guide only. The bus to Huay Xai might not run in the wet season. Note that in Laos buses break down, so it might take longer than advertised. For buses to China, contact the **Tong Li Bus Company** (☎ 242657) at the Northern Bus Station. For Vietnam, buses leave daily for Hanoi (US$20, 24 hours) via Vinh (US$16, 16 hours), and less often for Hue (US$17), Danang (US$20) and even Ho Chi Minh City (US$45, up to 48 hours) – they all start at or go past the Southern Bus Station.

Destination	Fare normal/ air-con/VIP (US$)	Distance (km)	Duration (hr)	Departures
Northern Bus Station				
Huay Xai	20	869	30-35	5.30pm
Luang Nam Tha	14	676	19	8.30am
Luang Prabang	9/10/11.50	384	11/11/9-10	6.30am (air-con), 7.30am, 8am (VIP), 9am (air-con), 11am, 1.30am, 4pm, 6pm, 7.30pm (air-con)
Phongsali	15	811	26	7.15am (doesn't leave every day)
Phonsavan	9/10	374	9-11	6.30am, 7.30am (air-con), 3.30pm, 7pm (air-con)
Sainyabuli	10/11.50	485	14-16	4.30pm, 6.30pm
Sam Neua via Phonsavan	15	612	15-17	7am, 9.30am, 12.30pm (7am bus goes via Luang Prabang, takes up to 30 hours)
Udomxai	11/12	578	14-17	6.45am, 1.45pm, 4pm (air-con)
Southern Bus Station				
Attapeu	11	812	22-24	9.30am, 5pm
Don Khong	11	788	16-19	10.30am
Lak Sao	6	334	7-9	5am, 6am, 7am
Paksan	2.50	143	3-4	Take any bus going south, roughly every 30 mins from 4.30am to 5pm.
Pakse	8.5/11/13	677	14-16/9½ (VIP)	Normal buses every 30 mins 9.30am-5pm; air-con buses at 7pm, 7pm & 8pm; four VIP buses leave at 8.30pm
Salavan	10	774	15-20	4.30pm, 7.30pm
Savannakhet	5.50/7	457	8-10	Every 30 mins 6am-9am; air-con at 8.30pm; or any normal or air-con bus to Pakse.
Tha Khaek	4/5	337	6/4½	5am, 6am, noon, or any bus to Savannakhet or Pakse
Voen Kham	11	818	17-20	11am
Talat Sao Bus Station				
Vang Vieng	1.50	153	3½	7am, 9.30am, 10.30am, 11.30am, 1.30pm, 2pm

---

CROSSING THE THAI BORDER AT THE THAI-LAO FRIENDSHIP BRIDGE

The Thai-Lao Friendship Bridge (Saphan Mittaphap Thai-Lao) spans the Mekong River between Nong Khai in Thailand and Tha Na Leng in Laos, 19km southeast of Vientiane. The border is open between 6am and 10pm and the easiest and cheapest way to cross is on the comfortable Thai-Lao International Bus (US$1.50, 90 minutes), which leaves Vientiane's Talat Sao (Morning Market) Bus Station at 7.30am, 9.30am, 12.40pm, 2.30pm, 3.30pm and 6pm and stops at the Nong Khai bus station. From Nong Khai, it leaves at the same times and costs 55B. The Thai-Lao International Bus also runs to Udon Thani bus station (US$2.20, two hours) at 8am, 10.30am, 11.30am, 2pm, 4pm and 6pm, though the times do tend to change. A tuk-tuk from the bus station to Udon Thani airport should cost about 100B.

The border itself is easy; visas are issued on arrival in both countries (p315). Don't be tempted to use a tuk-tuk driver to get your Lao visa, no matter what they tell you – it will take far longer than doing it yourself, and you'll have to pay for the 'service'. Insist they take you straight to the border.

Alternative means of transport between Vientiane and the bridge include taxi or jumbo (US$5 to US$7 – bargain hard) or the regular public bus from Talat Sao (US$0.40) between 6.30am and 5pm. At the bridge, regular shuttle buses (15B or 20B on weekends) ferry passengers between immigration posts. On the Thai side you'll need to take a tuk-tuk between the bridge and bus or train stations (about 30B per person). For details on trains between Nong Khai and Bangkok see p322.

---

some buses to Vietnam. Destinations and the latest ticket prices are listed in English.

The **Southern Bus Station** (Map pp88-9; ☎ 740521; Rte 13 South), commonly known as Dong Dok Bus Station or just *khíw lot lák káo* (Km 9 Bus Station), is 9km out of town and serves everywhere south. Buses to Vietnam will usually stop here.

The final departure point is the **Talat Sao bus station** (Map p92; ☎ 216507), from where desperately slow local buses run to destinations within Vientiane Province, including Vang Vieng, and some more distant destinations, though for these you're better going to the Northern or Southern stations. The Thai-Lao International Bus also uses this station for its trips to Nong Kai and Udon Thani; see above for details.

Train

See p322 for information on Thai trains to the Lao–Thai border.

GETTING AROUND

Central Vientiane is entirely accessible on foot. For exploring neighbouring districts, however, you'll need transport.

To/From the Airport

Wattay International Airport is about 4km northwest of the city centre, which makes the US$5 flat fare for a taxi more than a little steep. The fare is set by the government and the US$5 takes you anywhere in Vientiane (to the Thai-Lao Friendship Bridge is US$9). Only official taxis can pick up at the airport, and even the drivers think the fare is too high because it costs them business.

Many passengers simply walk out of the terminal, across the car park and on for 500m to the airport gate, where jumbos and tuk-tuks loiter. These guys ask upwards of US$3 for the trip, but you might be able to bargain them down to US$2. Alternatively, walk a few metres further to Th Luang Prabang and hail a shared jumbo (US$0.30 per person), or even a bus (US$0.20). Prices on shared transport will rise if you're going further than the centre.

From the centre of town to the airport costs should be the same, though tuk-tuk and jumbo drivers will typically ask for twice as much. The Phon Hong bus from Talat Sao makes the journey for US$0.20.

Bicycle

Cycling is a cheap, easy and recommended way of getting around mostly flat Vientiane. Loads of guesthouses and several shops hire out bikes for between US$0.50 and US$2 a day; you won't need a map to find them.

Bus

There is a city bus system, but it's oriented more towards the distant suburbs than the central Chanthabuli district. Most buses leave from Talat Sao bus station; to the Thai-Lao Friendship Bridge costs US$0.40.

Car & Motorcycle

Small motorbikes are a popular means of getting around Vientiane and can be hired from several places. The cheapest are from outside the **Douang Deuane Hotel** (Map p92; Th Nokeo Khumman) where 110cc bikes cost US$5.50 a day, but we can tell you from experience that they're notoriously unreliable (we took back four in one day!). Much better Japanese bikes are available from **PVO** (Map p92; ☎ 214444; Th Fa Ngum; per day US$7). They also hire the best 250cc bikes, usually Honda Bajas, for US$20 a day, less for longer hire. Recommended.

For car hire and drivers, see p328.

Jumbo & Tuk-Tuk

Drivers of jumbos and tuk-tuks will take passengers on journeys as short as 500m or as far as 20km. Understanding the various types of tuk-tuk is important (see below) if you don't want to be overcharged. Tourist tuk-tuks are the most expensive; share jumbos that run regular routes around town (eg Th Luang Prabang to Th Setthathirat or Th Lan Xang to That Luang) are much cheaper – usually US$0.20 to US$0.40 per person.

Taxi

Car taxis of varying shapes, sizes and vintages can often be found stationed in front of the larger hotels or at the airport. Some of these (usually the newer models) are fitted with air-con and meters and wear a 'Taxi Meter' sign. The meters, however, are ornamental only – you'll still have to negotiate the fare, which will be higher than in a naturally cooled jumbo. To call a taxi, try **Lavi Taxi Company** (☎ 350000).

A car and driver costs about US$30 to US$40 per day as long as the vehicle doesn't leave town. If you want to go further afield, eg to Ang Nam Ngum or Vang Vieng, expect to pay more.

AROUND VIENTIANE

There are several places worth seeing within an easy trip of Vientiane. Some make good day trips while others could detain you much longer.

BAN PAKO

ບ້ານປະໃກ

Situated on a lushly forested bend of the Nam Ngum (Ngum River) about 55km from Vientiane, **Ban Pako** (☎ 030-525 7937; in Vientiane

---

AN IDIOT'S GUIDE TO TUK-TUKS & JUMBOS

Three different types of tuk-tuk/jumbo operate in Vientiane and if you know the difference it can save you money and a lot of argument.

Tourist tuk-tuks

You'll find these loitering in queues outside popular tourist spots, such as at Nam Phu. In theory, chartering a tuk-tuk should be no more than US$0.60 for distances of 1km or less, plus about US$0.20 for each kilometre beyond 2km. But these guys will usually show you a laminated card with a list of fares at least double what a Lao person would pay and never less than US$1. Bargaining is essential but probably won't get you far because there is an agreement within the queue that tuk-tuks won't leave without a minimum fare, which while lower than the outrageous printed fare is still significantly more than locals would pay.

Wandering tuk-tuks

These tuk-tuks will pick you up anywhere and negotiate a fare to anywhere – prices are lower than tourist tuk-tuks and rise as you head further away from main roads. It's best not to hail a wandering tuk-tuk near a queue of tourist tuk-tuks as he'll likely be harassed by drivers in the queue.

Fixed route share jumbos

The cheapest tuk-tuks are more like buses, starting at tuk-tuk stations and operating along set routes for fixed fares. The biggest station is near Talat Sao and one very useful route runs to the Friendship Bridge (US$0.40, compared with about US$6 for a charter). Just turn up and tell them where you want to go.

AROUND VIENTIANE

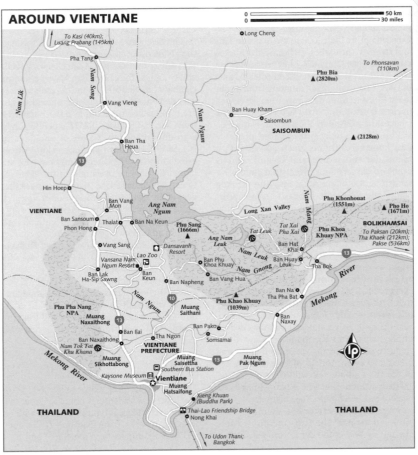

021-451841; www.banpako.com; d US$5, r US$25-50) is an ecolodge that has, over the years, been instrumental in creating a 40-hectare forest preserve and protecting the surrounding environs. The rustic bamboo and thatch 'village' is in a secluded spot that was first settled about 2000 years ago – archaeological excavations nearby have unearthed artefacts that shed light on village life around 2000 years ago. Activities include swimming, boating and hiking to nearby villages, a wat and waterfalls. Or just sit around sweating in the herbal sauna in the forest.

A change of management has seen standards rise dramatically but so too have prices, which seem a little steep at the top end. Lodgings are built of native materials

and include rooms with bathrooms and river views or jungle views, and dorms with share bathroom. Food is served on a picturesque riverside terrace. Power comes from solar cells.

Getting There & Away

The best way to reach Ban Pako is to drive or take the bus along Rte 13 south, turn left (north) after 24km, follow the signs to Somsamai and take a boat (US$1.50 per person one way, 30 minutes) to the lodge. Buses run between Talat Sao and Somsamai (US$0.50 one way, 90 minutes) six times daily between 6.30am and 5.30pm. With your own vehicle you can follow the road another few kilometres to Ban Pako itself.

PHU KHAO KHUAY NPA

ສວນອຸດທິຍານແຫ່ງຊາດພູເຂາຄວາຍ

Covering more than 2000 sq km of mountains and rivers to the east of Vientiane, the under-rated **Phu Khao Khuay NPA** (www.trekkingcentrallaos .com) is the most easily accessed protected area in Laos. Treks ranging in duration from a couple of hours to three days have been developed in close consultation with two villages on the edge of the NPA, Ban Na and Ban Hat Khai.

Phu Khao Khuay (pronounced poo cow kwai) means 'Buffalo Horn Mountain', a name derived from local legend, and is home to three major rivers that flow off a sandstone mountain range and into the Ang Nam Leuk Reservoir. It boasts an extraordinary array of endangered wildlife, including wild elephants, gibbons, Asiatic black bear, clouded leopard, Siamese fireback pheasant and green peafowl. About 88% of the NPA is forested, though only 32% has been classified as dense, mature forest. Depending on elevation, visitors may encounter dry evergreen dipterocarp (a Southeast Asian tree with two-winged fruit), mixed deciduous forest, conifer forest or grassy uplands. Several impressive waterfalls are accessible on day trips from Vientiane.

But while all of this is undoubtedly impressive – even more so if you actually get to see the endangered wildlife – by far the greatest attraction at Phu Khao Khuay is its herd of wild elephants (see below).

Several tour operators in Vientiane (see p91) can arrange the trips mentioned following, or you could do it yourself. Don't, however, just turn up unannounced (except at the waterfalls).

The best way to organise a trek is through the LNTA office in Vientiane (p91). It doesn't take any commission and can check on availability and, in the case of Ban Na, whether the elephants have been around recently. Prices vary depending on the number of trekkers but are reasonable; for example, a three-day trek from Ban Hat Khai is US$37/23 per person in a group of two/eight people. A one-day trip is US$18/13. From Ban Na trekking prices are slightly lower as there is no boat trip, but higher if you stay overnight in the elephant tower, which has a US$10 per person fee that goes to the Elephant Conservation & Research Fund. The prices do not include transport from Vientiane and are not negotiable. All monies go to the village and NPA. To contact Ban Na directly, call Lao-speaking **Mr Boun-thanom** (☎ 020-2208286). Or, get anyone else who speaks Lao to call for you.

There are additional small charges if you opt for 'luxury' items such as tents and hammocks with built-in mosquito nets. In addition trekkers need to buy a yellow trekking permit (US$4 per trip), which can be arranged in the village.

Ban Na

ບ້ານນາ

The lowland farming village of Ban Na, 82km northeast of Vientiane, is home to about 600 people. The village is typical Lao, with women weaving baskets from bamboo (skills they will happily impart for a small fee) and men

---

THE SWEET-TOOTHED ELEPHANTS OF BAN NA

The farmers of Ban Na grow rice and vegetables, but a few years ago they began planting sugar cane after being encouraged by a local sugar company. What they didn't count on was the collective sweet tooth of the elephants in the nearby mountains. It wasn't long before these jumbos had sniffed out the delights in the field below and were happily eating the sugarcane, pineapples and bananas planted around Ban Na. Not surprisingly, the farmers weren't happy. They decided the only way to get rid of the elephants was to rip up the sugarcane and go back to planting boring (and less lucrative) vegetables.

It was hoped the 30-odd elephants would take the hint and return to the mountains, but they didn't. Instead, they have made the lowland forests, bamboo belt and fields around Ban Na their home. The destruction they cause is significant, affecting both the environment and finances of Ban Na. The only way the villagers can continue to live with the elephants (ie not shoot them) is by making them pay their way. The result is elephant ecotourism. So far it's working and the number of elephants has actually grown to about 40. Though how long the peace can hold is anyone's guess if plans to build a sugar refinery nearby – with the resulting demand for locally produced sugarcane – come to fruition.

tending the fields. But it's the local herd of elephants that is most interesting to visitors (see the boxed text opposite).

Village guides lead one-, two- and three-day treks from Ban Na, including through elephant territory to Keng Khani (three to four hours one way), through deep forest to the waterfall of **Tat Fa** (four to five hours) and to the elephant observation tower at **Pung Xay** (4km). The trek to this tower is not the most spectacular in Laos, but if you're lucky your overnight stay will be. The tower overlooks the elephants' favourite salt lick, which they visit at dusk or later. Trekkers sleep in the tower, on the floor, with guides who cook a local dinner. We've met people who have had a fantastic time, seen 10 elephants and raved about this larger-than-life taste of the Laos wilderness. Others, however, have seen nothing and come away disappointed. So it's important to remember these pachyderms are wild and there's only about a 50/50 chance (perhaps less) they'll turn up. If you go, take a torch and a flash if you want photos, and/or go when the moon is full.

En route to Ban Na it's worth stopping briefly at **Wat Pha Baht Phonsan**, which sits on a rocky outcrop at Tha Pha Baht, beside Rte 13 about 2km south of Ban Na. The wat is revered for its large *pha bàat* (Buddha footprint) shrine, monastery and substantial reclining Buddha figure. You'll know it by the large and well-ornamented 1933-vintage stupa.

Ban Hat Khai
ບ້ານຫາດໄຂ່

Along with Ban Na, the village of Ban Hat Khai is a launch point for treks into Phu Khao Khuay NPA. Destinations include the huge cliff, views and beautiful landscape of **Pha Luang** (three to four hours one way), and the forested areas around **Huay Khi Ling** (two to three hours one way). A trek taking in both these areas takes two or three days, depending on the season; you sleep in the forest. Boats can be arranged here to take you upriver to **Pha Xai**. The villagers are also happy to have homestays (p48).

Waterfalls

Phu Khao Khuay's three most impressive waterfalls are accessed from the road running north from Rte 13, just before Ban Tha Bok. **Tat Xai** cascades down seven steps, and 800m downstream **Pha Xai** plunges over a 40m-high cataract. There's a pool that's good for swimming, though it can get dangerous during the wet season.

Tat Leuk is much smaller but makes a beautiful place to camp for the night. You can swim above the falls if the water isn't flowing too fast, and the Visitor Centre has some information about the area, including a detailed guide to the 1.5km-long **Huay Bon Nature Trail**. The guy who looks after the Visitor Centre can arrange local treks for about US$7 to US$10, and rents quality four-man tents for US$4, plus hammocks, mattresses, mosquito nets and sleeping bags for US$1 each.

Getting There & Away

Buses from Talat Sao in Vientiane leave regularly for Ban Tha Bok and Paksan. For Wat Pha Baht Phonsan and Ban Na get off near the Km 79 stone; the shrine is right on Rte 13 and Ban Na is about 2km north – follow the signs.

For Ban Hat Khai, keep on the bus until a turn-off left (north) at Km 92, just before Ban Tha Bok, or all the way into Tha Bok (a further 2km). From Tha Bok or the turn-off take a *sǎwngthǎew* or any transport the 5km to Ban Huay Leuk. Ban Hat Khai is 2km further, but the road beyond tends to get washed out in the rainy season, meaning you might have to take a boat (40 minutes, 12km), then walk another hour to Tat Xai.

From Ban Huay Leuk, continue 1km, cross an iron bridge and follow this laterite road a further 7km to the well-marked turn-off left to Tat Leuk – it's about 4km from here. For Tat Xai, follow the signs from Ban Huay Leuk (much more detailed instructions are available at www.trekkingcentrallaos.com or at the LNTA office in Vientiane, p91).

If you need a bed en route there are two decent guesthouses in Tha Bok. Note that as you come from Vientiane there are three signed entrances to Phu Khao Khuay, the second leads to Ban Na and the third to Ban Hat Khai and the waterfalls.

VIENTIANE TO ANG NAM NGUM

On the way to Ang Nam Ngum (Nam Ngum Reservoir) are a few interesting stopover possibilities. The **Nam Tok Tat Khu Khana** waterfall (also called Hin Khana) is easy to reach via a 10km dirt road, leading west from Rte 13 near the village of Ban Naxaithong, near Km 17.

At Km 52 on Rte 13 is **Ban Lak Ha-Sip Sawng** (Km 52 Village). As more established Hmong centres have been moved or depopulated, this town has evolved into the focal point for Hmong people for miles around. At the heart of town is a large daily market with plenty of stores selling 'traditional-style' Hmong dress. It's 'traditional style' because much of it is actually imported from China. You're unlikely to find locally made dress here because many Hmong have sold their locally made clothing to foreigners and Hmong in the USA, who onsell it for a tidy profit. There's plenty of good food available here, and it's cheap, and a couple of budget guesthouses.

At **Vang Sang**, 65km north of Vientiane via Rte 13, a cluster of 10 high-relief Buddha sculptures on cliffs is thought to date from the 16th century. Two of the Buddhas are over 3m tall. The name means 'Elephant Palace', a reference to an elephant graveyard once found nearby. To reach Vang Sang, follow the sign to the **Vang Xang Resort** (☎ 021-211526; r US$6), near the Km 62 marker, then take the laterite road around a small lake, up the hill and right until you reach the shaded forest at the end. Keep an eye out for lazy sunbathing snakes on this road; we met two and neither was especially hasty in slithering out of the way.

A bit further north is the prosperous town of **Phon Hong** at the turn-off for Thalat and Ang Nam Ngum; Rte 13 continues north from here to Vang Vieng. Phon Hong is another good place to stop for food, and like Ban Lak Ha-Sip Sawng it has a couple of cheap guesthouses.

ANG NAM NGUM
ອ່າງນ້ຳງຶມ

Ang Nam Ngum is the vast artificial lake created when the Nam Ngum was dammed. It's a popular destination for day-trippers from Vientiane, though doesn't attract too many foreign travellers.

The highest peaks of the former river valley became forested islands after the valley was inundated in 1971. Following the 1975 PL conquest of Vientiane, an estimated 3000 prostitutes, petty criminals and drug addicts were rounded up from the capital and banished to two of these islands; one each for men and women. Today the Nam Ngum hydroelectric plant generates most of the electricity used in the Vientiane area and sells power to Thailand.

About 250 sq km of forest were flooded when the river was dammed, submerging a mass of valuable timber. In the 1990s Thai timber companies decided all those submerged teak trees were worth the cost of buying and operating hydraulic underwater saws, and the trees are slowly being extracted. A few towns and villages on or near the shores of the lake, such as **Ban Tha Heua** at the northern end, specialise in crafting furniture from the salvaged teak.

Fishing is also an important local industry, and one that attracted thousands of people to the area during the '80s and '90s. Too many, perhaps. In recent years fishers have reported a drastic fall in their catch and many have been forced to find other work.

Ang Nam Ngum is dotted with picturesque little islands and it is well worth arranging a cruise. Boats holding up to 20 people can be hired from Ban Na Kheun, or any other lakeside village, for about US$10 to US$12 an hour if you bargain hard.

A short drive from the lake is **Thalat**, between Phon Hong and Ang Nam Ngum, which is known for its environmentally incorrect market (Thalat means 'market') selling all kinds of forest creatures – deer, spiny anteaters, rats and so on – for the dinner plate.

Sleeping & Eating

Since most people day-trip to Ang Nam Ngum from Vientiane the few guesthouses are often empty and it can be difficult to find anyone with a key. You should, eventually, find somewhere to sleep in either Ban Kheun, Ban Na Kheun or Ban Tha Heua, usually for less than US$10.

In villages around the lake, floating restaurants keep fish tethered beneath the deck and, when there's an order, the cook lifts a grate and yanks a flapping fish directly into the galley. They're famous for tasty *kâwy pąa* (tart and spicy minced fish salad), *kąeng pąa* (fish soup) and *neung pąa* (steamed fish with fresh herbs).

Vansana Nam Ngum Resort (☎ 023-241162; www
.vansanahotel-group.com; Ban Kheun; r US$30-40; 🖳 🖳)
More comfortable than the guesthouses, Vasana is actually on the banks of the Nam Ngum a few kilometres downstream from the dam at Ban Kheun. It's mainly aimed at families from Vientiane.

Dansavanh Nam Ngum Resort (☎ 021-217595; www.dansavanh.com; packages from US$30; ❌ 🏊) Opened in 1999, this US$200 million lakeside resort – 75% owned by a Malaysian company and 25% owned by the Lao military – is part of a planned mega-development centred around one of only two legal casinos in Laos. It's 10 minutes by boat from the landing at Na Nam, although most visitors and guests arrive on free shuttle buses from Vientiane or Nong Khai.

Getting There & Away

From Vientiane's Talat Sao Bus Station you can catch a 7am service all the way to Kheun Nam Ngum (Nam Ngum Dam; US$0.90, about three hours), near Ban Na Kheun. This trip goes along Rte 13 through Thalat. If you don't make the 7am bus, buses leave semi-frequently from Talat Sao to Thalat (US$0.80, 2½ hours, 87km); take a pick-up or jumbo to the lake.

Taxis in Vientiane usually charge from US$35 to US$50 return to the lake. Ask the driver to take the more scenic Rte 10 through Ban Kheun for the return trip.

VANG VIENG

ວັງວຽງ

☎ 023 / pop 30,000

Nestled beside the Nam Song (Song River) amid stunningly beautiful limestone karst terrain, Vang Vieng provokes a mix of responses. In the last edition we wrote that people either love or hate it, but that was probably a little unfair. It's more of a love *and* hate relationship – which parts you love depend on who you are.

The area's main attraction has always been the dramatic landscape surrounding Vang Vieng. Honeycombed with unexplored tunnels and caverns, the limestone cliffs are a spelunker's heaven. Several caves are named and play roles in local mythology – all are said to be inhabited by spirits. These caves and cliffs have also earned a reputation for some of the best rock-climbing in the region.

The Nam Song, meanwhile, plays host to kayakers and travellers floating along on tractor inner tubes – a pastime so thoroughly enjoyable and popular that it has become one of the rites of passage of the Indochina backpacking circuit. Other activities include rafting, trekking and bicycle and motorbike

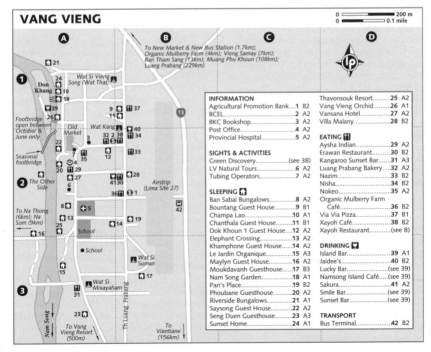

VANG VIENG

0 ————— 200 m
0 ————— 0.1 mile

To New Market & New Bus Station (1.7km);
Organic Mulberry Farm (4km); Vieng Samay (7km);
Ban Tham Sang (13km); Muang Phu Khoun (108km);
Luang Prabang (229km)

Wat Si Vieng Song (Wat That)

Don Khang

Footbridge open between October & June only

Old Market

Wat Kang

Seasonal footbridge

The Other Side

To Na Thong (6km); Na Som (9km)

Airstrip (Lima Site 27)

School

School

Wat Si Suman

Wat Si Mixayaham

Nam Song

To Vang Vieng Resort (500m)

Th Luang Prabang

To Vientiane (156km)

INFORMATION		
Agricultural Promotion Bank...1	B2	
BCEL...2	A2	
BKC Bookshop...3	A2	
Post Office...4	A2	
Provincial Hospital...5	A2	

SIGHTS & ACTIVITIES		
Green Discovery...(see 38)		
LV Natural Tours...6	A2	
Tubing Operators...7	A2	

SLEEPING 🛏		
Ban Sabai Bungalows...8	A2	
Bountang Guest House...9	B1	
Champa Lao...10	A1	
Chanthala Guest House...11	B1	
Dok Khoun 1 Guest House...12	A2	
Elephant Crossing...13	A2	
Khamphone Guest House...14	A2	
Le Jardin Organique...15	A3	
Maylyn Guest House...16	A2	
Moukdavanh Guesthouse...17	B3	
Nam Song Garden...18	A1	
Pan's Place...19	B2	
Phoubane Guesthouse...20	A2	
Riverside Bungalows...21	A1	
Saysong Guest House...22	A2	
Seng Duen Guesthouse...23	A3	
Sunset Home...24	A1	

Thavonsouk Resort...25	A2	
Vang Vieng Orchid...26	A1	
Vansana Hotel...27	A2	
Villa Malany...28	B2	

EATING 🍴		
Aysha Indian...29	A2	
Erawan Restaurant...30	B2	
Kangaroo Sunset Bar...31	A3	
Luang Prabang Bakery...32	A2	
Nazim...33	B2	
Nisha...34	B2	
Nokeo...35	A2	
Organic Mulberry Farm Café...36	B2	
Via Via Pizza...37	B1	
Xayoh Café...38	B2	
Xayoh Restaurant...(see 8)		

DRINKING 🍸		
Bar...39	A1	
Jaidee's...40	B2	
Lucky Bar...(see 39)		
Namsong Island Café...(see 39)		
Sakura...41	A2	
Smile Bar...(see 39)		
Sunset Bar...(see 39)		

TRANSPORT		
Bus Terminal...42	B2	

trips. Or you could just find a riverside seat for one of the regular postcard sunsets when, if you're lucky, you might see thousands of bats pouring forth from the karst like an oil slick flooding the skyline.

So what's to dislike, you might ask. The most common complaint is that in earning its stripes as a fully paid-up member of backpacker world, Vang Vieng has lost its soul. It's probably not as bad as that, but the growth of Vang Vieng has taken its toll. Inevitably, the profile of the town has changed and the reason travellers first came here – to experience small-town Laos in a stunning setting – has been replaced by multistorey guesthouses. Even the local market has moved to a big, soulless slab of concrete north of town.

But if we accept that most visitors are going to enjoy the scenery and at least some of the activities, if not the misfit Greco-Laotian architecture of the guesthouses, then it's the 'TV bars' and their 'happy' menus that provoke the real love and hate. For some travellers, sitting on an axe pillow, sucking down a shake laced with marijuana/mushrooms/opium/*yaba* (methamphetamine) and tripping through endless reruns of *Friends* is heaven on earth. For others, it's a nightmare.

If you're in the latter camp then take heart because it's easy enough to escape this scene by staying a bit away from the centre. It's also reassuring that the locals seem to have accepted this influx of *falang* without losing their sense of humour. And as Vang Vieng continues to evolve, its accommodation options have too. There are still plenty of cheap guesthouses where you can sleep off a hangover between long nights in the island bars, but there are now also more luxurious offerings.

No matter what you think of the Khao San Rd side of Vang Vieng's personality, you can't deny that this is a beautiful part of the world. So even if you're not a fan of *Friends*, it's worth stopping for at least a day or two.

Information

Internet cafés have popped up almost as fast as the mushrooms in Vang Vieng, most charging 300 kip per minute. New lines should reduce this price in coming years.

Agricultural Promotion Bank (Th Luang Prabang) Exchanges cash only.

BCEL (☎ 511434; ⏰ 8.30am-3.30pm Mon-Sun) Exchanges cash, travellers cheques and handles cash advances on Visa, MasterCard and JCB.

BKC Bookshop (⏰ 7am-7pm) Second-hand novels plus guidebooks and maps.

Post office (☎ 511009) Beside the old market.

Provincial Hospital (☎ 511604) The flash new hospital is a reflection of the money coming into Vang Vieng. It now has x-ray facilities and is fine for broken bones, cuts, malaria and most noninternal injuries.

Dangers & Annoyances

Most visitors leave Vang Vieng with nothing more serious than a hangover, but this tranquil setting is also the most dangerous place in Laos for travellers. At least five people have died around here in recent years from river accidents, drug misadventures and while caving. Theft can also be a problem, with fellow travellers often the culprits. Take the usual precautions and don't leave valuables outside caves.

ON THE RIVER

Whether tubing or kayaking down the Nam Song or rafting in more turbulent waters, rivers can be dangerous. Wearing a life jacket is a must when rafting any rapids and is advisable even on the normally tranquil Nam Song, especially during the wet season when waters flow up to four times faster than normal. Tubing/rafting/kayaking companies should provide one.

When tubing, it's worth asking how long the trip should take (durations vary depending on the time of year) and allowing plenty of time to get back to Vang Vieng before dark – it's black by about 6pm in winter. If you stop for the rope swing be a little careful, as one woman drowned here when something went wrong.

Finally, don't forget that while tubing the Nam Song might be more fun when you're off your head, it's also more dangerous.

DRUGS

With so many drugs washing around Vang Vieng it's no surprise that the local police are particularly adept at sniffing out spliffs, especially late at night, and if you're caught with a stash of marijuana (or anything else) it can be expensive. The normal practice is for police to take your passport and fine you US$500. If you don't have much cash on you, you might be able to negotiate the fine downwards. But ultimately you have broken the law and will have to pay something. Don't expect a receipt, and don't bother calling your embassy.

If you must use opium, don't mix it with too much else and certainly not with lime juice. We haven't tested this theory (our dedication to research doesn't go quite that far), but several Vang Vieng residents told us that at least one traveller has died after using opium and having an innocuous-sounding glass of lime juice! Sounds unlikely, but apparently/allegedly this mix has long been used by hill-tribe women who suicide as an ultimate act of protest against a bad husband.

CAVING
The caves around Vang Vieng are often spectacular, but being caves they come with certain hazards – they're dark, slippery and disorienting. It's easy to get lost, especially if you're torch batteries die. It's well worth hiring a guide at the cave (see below).

Sights & Activities
Vang Vieng has evolved into Laos's number-one adventure destination, with kayaking, rafting, caving, trail- and mountain-biking and world-class rock climbing all available. These activities tend to be more popular than the sights, which are mainly monasteries dating from the 16th and 17th centuries. Among these, **Wat Si Vieng Song** (Wat That), **Wat Kang** and **Wat Si Suman** are the most notable. Over the river are a couple of villages to which Hmong have been relocated, which are accessible by bicycle or motorbike (see p125).

CAVES
Following, we've described several of the most accessible *thàm* (caves). Most are signed in English as well as Lao, and an admission fee ranging from US$0.10 to US$1 is collected at the entrance to each cave. A guide (often a young village boy) will lead you through the cave for a small fee; bring water and a torch (flashlight), and be sure your batteries aren't about to die.

For more extensive multicave tours, most guesthouses can arrange a guide. Trips including river tubing and cave tours cost around US$8/13 for a half/full day.

Tham Jang (Tham Chang)
ຖ້ຳຈັງ
The most famous of the caves, **Tham Jang** (Tham Chang; Map p124; admission US$1; ☽ 8am-11.30am & 1-

4.30pm), was used as a bunker in defence against marauding *jjin háw* (Yunnanese Chinese) in the early 19th century (*jàng* means 'steadfast'). Stairs lead up to the main cavern entrance.

The main cave chamber isn't the most impressive, but it does afford magnificent views over the river valley through an opening in the limestone wall. A cool spring at the foot of the cave feeds into the river and you can swim up here about 80m into the cave. Inside are electric lights, which the caretakers turn on once you've paid the admission fee. You can swim outside the cave for free; not a bad option.

To get there, walk south to the Vang Vieng Resort where you must pay a US$0.20 fee to cross the grounds, plus US$0.20 for a bike. The cave is signed on the far side of the bridge.

Tham Phu Kham
ຖ້ຳພູຄຳ
Vast **Tham Phu Kham** (Blue Lagoon; Map p124; admission US$0.50) is considered sacred by Lao and is popular largely due to the lagoon in the cave. The beautiful green-blue waters are perfect for a dip after the stiff climb. The main cave chamber contains a Thai bronze reclining Buddha, and from here deeper galleries branch off into the mountain. To get there, cross the bridge and walk or pedal 6km along a scenic but unpaved road to the village of Ban Na Thong. From Ban Na Thong follow the signs towards the cliff and a stiff 200m climb through scrub forest.

Tham Sang Triangle
A popular half-day trip that's easy to do on your own takes in Tham Sang plus three other caves within a short walk. Begin this caving odyssey by riding a bike or taking a jumbo 13km north along Rte 13, turning left a few hundred metres beyond the barely readable Km 169 stone. A rough road leads to the river, where a boatman will ferry you across to Ban Tham Sang (US$0.50 return). Tham Sang itself is right here, as is a small restaurant.

Tham Sang (Tham Xang; admission US$0.20), meaning 'Elephant Cave', is a small cavern containing a few Buddha images and a Buddha 'footprint', plus the (vaguely) elephant-shaped stalactite that gives the cave its name. It's best visited in the morning when light enters the cave.

From Tham Sang a signed path takes you 1km northwest through rice fields to the entrances of **Tham Loup** and **Tham Hoi** (admission

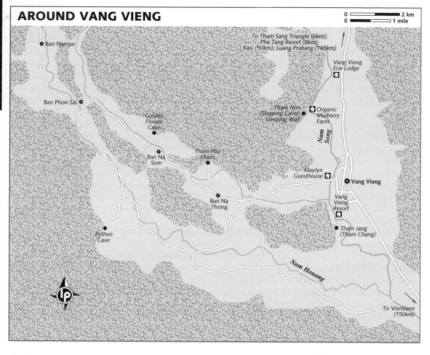

AROUND VANG VIENG

for both US$0.50). The entrance to Tham Hoi is guarded by a large Buddha figure; reportedly the cave continues about 3km into the limestone and an underground lake. Tham Loup is a large and delightfully untouched cavern with some impressive stalactites.

About 400m south of Tham Hoi, along a well-used path, is the highlight of this trip, **Tham Nam** (admission US$0.50). The cave is about 500m long and a tributary of the Nam Song flows out of its low entrance. In the dry season you can wade into the cave, but when the water is higher you need to take a tube from the friendly woman near the entrance; the tube and headlamp are included in the entrance fee. Dragging yourself through the tunnel on the fixed rope is fun.

From Tham Nam an easy 1km walk brings you back to Ban Tham Sang. This loop is usually included in the kayaking/ trekking/tubing combo trip run by most Vang Vieng tour operators.

KAYAKING

Kayaking is almost (but not quite) as popular as tubing and trips typically include visits to caves and villages and traverse a few rapids, the danger of which depends on the speed of the water. There are loads of operators and prices are about US$8/12 per person for a half/whole day. Kayaking trips to Vientiane involve a lot of paddling and part of the trip is by road.

Not all guides are as well trained as they could be. Before using a cheap operator, check the equipment and the guides' credentials, and ask other travellers.

RAFTING

The brutal Grade 4 and 5 rapids along the magical Nam Ngum are easily the most thrilling river ride around Vang Vieng. Two-day expeditions begin with a drive into the previously off-limits area formerly known as the Saisombun Special Zone (see p129) to put in on the Nam Ngum. A day's paddling takes you to Ang Nam Ngum, where you sleep on an island in the lake and finish with a ride to Vientiane.

Choosing a company with experienced guides is the best way to maximise safety. Guides, of course, come and go, but those at Green Discovery and Xplore-Asia are generally pretty good; ask around before you sign

WEST VANG VIENG LOOP

To get right into the heart of the limestone karsts rising out of the rice paddies oppo
Vieng, consider this loop by motorbike or bicycle (see Map p124). The scenery is stunning but
the roads are not, so give yourself plenty of time. The whole circuit, including the road to Nampe
and diversions to see caves, took us about six hours and was 43km. Not going to Nampe shaves
off about 10km. It's best done on a trail bike, though possible on smaller motos or mountain
bikes. It's much more difficult, if not impossible, in the wet season.

Starting from the road running past Maylyn Guest House, head west for about 4km and keep
right when the road splits. You'll pass through the Lao Loum village of **Ban Na Thong** and after
2km come to another fork and a sign pointing right to **Tham Phu Kham** (Blue Lagoon; p123),
about 700m along a track.

Back on the main track, continue west and you'll soon be in **Na Som**, a village of Hmong
who have been resettled here. Around here the vegetation on the karsts is scarred by slash-
and-burn farming. Just beyond Na Som are signs to **Golden Flower Cave**. Reaching it involves
walking through rice fields, climbing a fence and following two white arrows for a few minutes.
The cave is about 50m up the hill – look into the undergrowth for the vague stairs. It's barely
worth the effort.

Continuing west a beautiful stretch of track hugs the edge of the karsts and crosses a couple
of streams, that could be difficult in the wet, and eventually comes to **Ban Phon Sai**. Here the
track joins with a better dirt road, but first you need to cross the Nam Houang (Houang River),
which is tricky in the wet season.

You have a choice now: continue 5km west through more dramatic scenery to **Ban Nampe**, a
pretty village but nothing more, or start heading back east along the southern route. About 6km
southeast of Ban Phon Sai, over another couple of creeks, signs point across a small bridge to a
track to **Python Cave**, about 800m away. Once you've seen this, it's plain sailing back to Vang
Vieng. Keep along the road, then go left at the junction (follow the power poles), immediately
cross a stream and soon you'll be back on the main track, loop complete.

up. Rafting is best and safest between October
and March.

ROCK CLIMBING

In just a few years the limestone walls around
Vang Vieng have gained a reputation as some
of the best climbing in Southeast Asia. One
experienced climber we met had spent a week
in world-renowned Krabi in Thailand, then a
week climbing in Vang Vieng. He promptly
reported that he'd had a much better time
climbing the routes in Vang Vieng.

More than 100 routes have been identified by several well-regarded international
teams and most have been bolted. The
routes are rated between 4 and 8b, with the
majority being in or near a cave and less
than 20m high. The most popular climbing spots are at **Tham Non (Sleeping Cave)**,
with more than 20 routes, and the tougher
Sleeping Wall nearby, where some routes have
difficult overhangs.

The climbing season usually runs between October and May, with routes too
wet at other times. **Green Discovery** (☎ 511440;

www.greendiscoverylaos.com) runs a highly professional operation with experienced guides
and equipment. It also sells a handy guide
to the various climbs, with basic maps, and
conducts three-day beginners' courses.

TUBING

Virtually everyone who comes to Vang Vieng
goes tubing down the Nam Song in an in-
flated tractor-tyre tube. The 3.5km trip from
near the Organic Mulberry Farm, north of
Vang Vieng, has become such a popular rite
of passage on the Southeast Asia backpacker
circuit that 'bars' have been set up on islands
and beaches along the route, selling Beerlao
and food, among other things. The tubing
operators have formed a cartel so all tubing
is organised from a small building where
the old market once was. Prices are fixed at
US$3.50 and include your trip to the launch
point. There is, however, a catch.

There's a contract that, among other
things, says you must return the tube or
pay a US$7 fine. This is fair enough, but it
gets dodgy when you've finished the trip,

have planted yourself at one of the island bars and a kid offers to take your tube back for you. What a good idea, you might think. If you do think that, you'll have someone knocking on your door the next morning asking for US$7. The other thing you should remember is to take something – a sarong, perhaps – to put on when you finish the trip and have to walk through town. The locals don't appreciate people walking around in bikinis as much as you might think.

In times of high water, rapids along the Nam Song can be quite daunting; see Dangers & Annoyances p122.

Tours

Several companies operate so-called adventure tours out of Vang Vieng. Prices and standards vary, though the following have good reputations:

Green Discovery (☎ 511440; www.greendiscoverylaos .com; Th Luang Prabang) Green Discovery is the biggest and most reliable operator, offering trekking, kayaking, rafting, rock climbing and caving. Recommended.

LV Natural Tours (☎ 020-5208283; lavone_thips ady@yahoo.com) Good-value kayaking and trekking. Vone (a guide) gets good feedback.

Xplore-Asia (☎ 030-520 0746, 020-2255176; www .xplore-asia.com; Th Luang Prabang) Good for kayaking.

Sleeping

Vang Vieng has some of the best-value rooms in Laos, and prices often fall even further in low season. Prices in Vang Vieng haven't changed much in several years.

BUDGET

Pan's Place (☎ 511484; www.pansplace.net; r US$2-6) Pan's has had a makeover but you'll probably find the atmosphere more appealing than the basic but clean rooms. The 'backyard' has everything the backpacker could want – a TV *sala* with big screen, bar, restaurant and kiddie pool – but not a single Lao the night we drank there.

Maylyn Guest House (☎ 020-5604095; jophus_foley@hotmail.com; r US$3-6) On the far side of the Nam Song, the Maylyn's 15 rooms are set in a lush, butterfly-filled garden beside a stream. The mix of bungalows and rooms with and without bathrooms aren't luxurious, but they're clean and the atmosphere is good. Owner Joe can advise on various hikes in the surrounding peaks, the West Vang Vieng Loop (p125) and rents trail bikes and a range

of bicycles. Food is served at reasonable prices, the barbecued fish is a highlight.

Dok Khoun 1 Guest House (☎ 511032; r US$3-7; 🖵) Right in the centre of town, the Dok Khoun 1 has long been popular for its clean rooms and fair prices. A solid choice.

Saysong Guest House (☎ 511130; saysong1@yahoo .com; r US$4-15) This family-run place has a good atmosphere, popular communal balconies and a mix of rooms, some overlooking the island and river, others without a bathroom.

Le Jardin Organique (☎ 020-5474643; r US$4-15) These 26 bungalows and rooms are in a fantastic riverside position and the atmosphere here is upbeat but low-hassle. Price varies depending on facilities and proximity to the river.

Khamphone Guest House (☎ 511062; r US$5-10; 🖵) Khamphone's three buildings on the southern edge of town offer good-value rooms; the US$10 options with TV, air-con and fridge are best.

Villa Malany (☎ 511083; malany-guesthouse@hotmail .com; Th Luang Prabang; r US$5-12; 🖵) This four-storey Greco-Laotian style place has clean but unremarkable rooms in the centre of town.

Vang Vieng Orchid (☎ 020-2202259; r US$6-10; 🖵) On the banks of the Nam Song north of the old market, this three-storey place has 20 clean, spacious rooms, 12 of which have balconies and wonderful views over Don Khang and the karst peaks beyond. Rooms 101–4, 201–4 and 301–4 have the views, though noise from revellers on Don Khang (see p128) can make it hard to sleep.

Also recommended:

Bountang Guest House (☎ 511328; dm/tw US$1/3) Small, simple fan rooms and Vang Vieng's cheapest dorm; but one bathroom for 12 beds…

Chanthala Guest House (☎ 511146; r US$2-8) Psychedelic sheets in some of the cheapest rooms in town.

Moukdavanh Guesthouse (☎ 020-5812913; bungalows US$4) Several bungalows with double beds, fans and hot-water bathrooms around a well-kept garden.

Phoubane Guesthouse (☎ 511037; s/tw US$4/6) Tranquil riverside setting but still crawling distance to town. Simple bungalows, some on very edge of the river.

Seng Duen Guesthouse (☎ 511138; r US$3-10; 🖵 🏊) A mix of rooms, a bit out of town. The big draw is the pool.

Riverside Bungalows (☎ 511035; r US$4-12; 🖵) Good riverside location, but less character and value than some.

At the north end of town are three small, new places not far from the river that have a refreshing amount of soul. First up is the **Nam Song Garden** (☎ 511544; arnelao@hotmail.com; r US$5), with just five rooms but an atmosphere as serene as owner Arné. A little further is **Champa Lao** (☎ 020-5018501; www.thelongwander.com; r US$2-3), a real old-style Lao guesthouse in a wooden house with simple rooms, a communal *sala* and a good feel. Finally the **Sunset Home** (☎ 020-5623297; r US$4-6) has bungalows with hot-water bathrooms.

There are a couple of cheap places to stay on Don Khang, but given it's usually very loud very late, it's only recommend for insomniacs or those expecting to be too numb to care.

MIDRANGE

These places all have prime riverfront locations between the old market and the bridge.

Thavonsouk Resort (☎ 511096; www.thavonsouk .com; r US$18-75; ❄) Thavonsouk was one of the first Vang Vieng lodgings, and it's come a long way. There are now 39 rooms crammed onto the property representing different eras and price ranges. Look at a few.

our pick **Elephant Crossing** (☎ 511232; d incl breakfast US$25-30, f incl breakfast US$45; ❄) With almost every room boasting a balcony overlooking the Nam Song and out to the dramatic karsts, it's hard to beat this place. That the rooms are comfortable, relatively stylish and fair value doesn't hurt, either. Prices fall US$5 in low season.

Ban Sabai Bungalows (Xayoh Riverside Bungalows; ☎ 511088; r US$25-30; ❄) These modern bungalows in a serene riverside setting are a good choice. Some rooms have a bathtub and there are two romantic 'singles' with a double bed and balcony over a pond. There is a riverside bar-restaurant.

Vansana Hotel (☎ 511598; www.vansanahotel-group .com; r incl breakfast US$30-50; ❄ ❄) The 38 rooms here are comfortable if not desperately stylish, though quite a few don't have a view. It does, however, have a very nice pool.

OUT OF TOWN

If Vang Vieng town isn't your bag, head out of town for a quieter location.

Organic Mulberry Farm (☎ 511220; www.laofarm .org; r US$3-5) Known locally as *sǔran máwn phúu dịn dạeng* (Phoudindaeng Mulberry Farm), this organic farm 4km north of Vang Vieng raises mulberry trees for silk and tea production. It also grows organic produce and plays a vital role in the surrounding community. Accommodation is in rooms with shared bathroom, or in a dorm with spectacular views. Volunteer workers can no longer get free board. The attached restaurant, open for breakfast, lunch and dinner, makes great vegetarian food, or drink a delicious mulberry shake before beginning your tubing trip.

Vang Vieng Resort (☎ 511050; r US$5-10) Slightly south of town but near the river and opposite Tham Jang, Vang Vieng Resort is quiet and the cottages are comfortable, if ageing a bit.

Vang Vieng Eco-Lodge (☎ 020-2247323; r US$5.50, bungalows US$20-25) About 7km north of town (look for the sign after the Km 162 stone), calling this an 'eco-lodge' might be overstating it but the scenic location and attractive bungalows are still a good option away from the crowds. Lao food is served and it rents motorbikes (US$5.50 a day). Prices fall from May to September.

Pha Tang Resort (☎ 020-5319573; Rte 13; r US$7-10) It's a full 17km north of Vang Vieng, but the setting here is as dramatic as it gets. The rooms and bungalows sit on the Nam Song and the karst cliff of Phu Pha Tang rises almost on top of you. Rooms are simple but attractive and comfortable, and the riverside restaurant (meals US$1 to US$2.50) is a good place for lunch even if you're not staying. We like it.

Eating

You know by the time you sit down for your third meal that something is amiss in the Vang Vieng restaurant scene. 'This looks a lot like the menu at that other place,' is commonly heard. Usually followed by something like: 'Hang on, it *is* the same!' The sad truth is that several restaurants, particularly those TV bars on the main street, do serve virtually identical fare aimed squarely at perceived Western tastes. And as with most places offering such a varied selection of cuisines (usually including Lao, Thai, Chinese, Italian, American, French and with a Rasta option), none of it is done particularly well.

There are, however, a few decent eateries – which even have their own menus. Most restaurants are open from about 7am or 8am until about 11pm, though in the low season hours can be shorter. Note that this is just a small selection of restaurants we know to be reliable. You don't need a guidebook to find the others, just look around.

HAPPINESS IS A STATE OF MIND

'Don't worry, be happy' could be the national motto for Laos, but in some backpacker centres the term 'happy' has taken on a wholly different connotation. In the TV bars of Vang Vieng and the riverside bungalows of Si Phan Don (p272) seeing the word 'happy' in front of 'shake', 'pizza' or anything else does not, as one traveller was told, mean it comes with extra pineapple. The extra is usually marijuana, added in whatever quantity the shake-maker deems fit. However, it could also be mushrooms, *yaba* (methamphetamine) or opium, and these usually cost more, so orders must be specific.

For many travellers 'happy' is a well-understood alias, but there are others who innocently quaff down their shake or pizza only to spend the next 24 hours somewhere near the outer reaches of the galaxy paranoia, with no idea why. So if you'd prefer not to be nine miles high for your tubing trip, then avoid the 'happy' meals and steer well clear of anything described as 'ecstatic'. If you do fancy floating down both literally and figuratively, then at least consider wearing a life jacket.

ourpick Nokeo (meals US$1-3; ☼ 8am-8pm) Nokeo is one of the last remnants of the old Vang Vieng. There are no bells or whistles, but it's been around for years because it serves consistently good Lao food at prices low enough that locals can afford to eat here. The succulent *ping paa* is excellent, as are the various *làap* and curries. It's the most Lao place to eat in Vang Vieng.

ourpick Organic Mulberry Farm Café (☎ 511174; Th Luang Prabang; meals US$1-3.50) The ever-growing and innovative menu here is one of the best in Vang Vieng, especially for vegetarians. The mulberry shakes (US$0.80) and pancakes (US$1.30) are famous and everything is fairly priced. You can also eat at the organic farm itself (p127).

Luang Prabang Bakery (☎ 511145; meals US$1.50-7) This long-running bakery serves good breakfasts, pastries and strong coffee, but the pizzas (US$5.50 to US$6.50) and other meals can be a bit pricey.

Xayoh Restaurant (☎ 511088; meals US$2-4) The typically international menu has a heavy Italian influence; pizzas (US$2.50) and pastas (US$1.20) mix with burgers (US$1.80) and a pretty good caramel flan (US$0.80). The riverside patio is quite romantic by night and also has several sun loungers. The same menu is available at Xayoh Café, located on Th Luang Prabang.

Kangaroo Sunset Bar (☎ 020-7714291; meals US$2-4.50) This Australian-run place is a decent sunset and evening drinking hole (it does have the coldest Beerlao in town), and the Lao, Thai and fusion-ish food is very edible indeed. The garlic bread and prawn rolls are delicious.

Erawan Restaurant (☎ 511093; Th Luang Prabang; meals US$2-5) The good Asian and European food, lovely owner and chilled ambience refreshingly free of TVs makes Erawan a perennial favourite. Recommended.

Via Via Pizza (☎ 511543; Th Luang Prabang; pizzas US$4-6) Probably the best pizzas in Vang Vieng.

The Indian restaurants are predictably popular, especially with vegetarians. Tiny **Nisha** (☎ 511579; Th Luang Prabang; meals US$2-4) lacks atmosphere but the food is reliable. A few metres south is another branch of the empire **Nazim** (☎ 511214; Th Luang Prabang; meals US$2-5); while **Aysha Indian** (☎ 511369; meals US$1-3) offers something a bit different with its riverside balcony location and mix of Pakistani, Indian and Lao dishes.

Drinking

You can drink in every guesthouse and restaurant in town and you won't need a guidebook to track down the most happening places. In general, they're split into the open-air, anything-goes bars on Don Khang (aka 'the island'), and more familiar-looking places on or just off Th Luang Prabang.

On Don Khang, the **Island Bar** (☎ 020-539 9954), Namsong Island Café, Lucky Bar, Smile Bar and Sunset Bar are all competing for your business. We trust you to sniff out the best party.

In town, **Jaidee's** (Th Luang Prabang; ☼ 8am-1am) has consistently good music and Supermao (ask him) Jaidee maintains an upbeat vibe. **Sakura** (☼ 5-11.30pm) has regular DJs and is the best place to dance, though few people seem to bother.

Getting There & Away

Buses, pick-ups and *săwngthăew* continue to depart from a simple **bus terminal** (☎ 511341; Rte 13) on the eastern side of the airstrip, a few minutes' walk from town. This is mildly surprising given a new bus station has been built 2km north of town, opposite the New Market. No-one we met seemed to know if or when transport would move to the new station, but wherever you end up jumbo drivers will be there trying to talk you into taking a ride into town.

Minibuses and air-con buses catering especially to *falang* often leave from one of the guesthouses in town, but don't expect any extra leg room. Tickets are available almost everywhere, though buses do fill fast in peak season. Anyone who suffers motion sickness should take necessary precautions before the trip to Luang Prabang.

VIENTIANE

For buses from Vientiane see p114.

Heading south from Vang Vieng, regular buses leave for Vientiane (US$2.50, 3½ to 4½ hours, 156km) at 5.30am, 7am, 12.30pm and 1.30pm. Alternatively, pick-ups (US$2.50, 3½ to 4½ hours) leave about every 20 minutes from 5am until 4pm and as they're often not full can be quite enjoyable.

A minibus (US$7, three hours) leaves at 9am and air-con buses (US$5.50, three hours) at 10am and 1pm. You might also be able to jump on buses coming through from Luang Prabang at about 1pm.

LUANG PRABANG

Buses for Luang Prabang (US$7, seven to 11 hours, 168km) stop for about five minutes en route from Vientiane about every hour between 11am and 8pm. Minibuses (US$9.50, six to eight hours) and air-con buses (US$9.50) leave between 9am and 10am, the number varying depending on demand. All these services stop at Kasi and Muang Phu Khoun (for Phonsavan), though you might need to pay the full Luang Prabang fare on some.

For transport from Luang Prabang, see p155.

PHONSAVAN

There's one bus to Phonsavan (US$7.50, six to seven hours, 219km) which leaves between about 9am and 9.30am.

Getting Around

Vang Vieng is easily negotiated on foot. Renting a bicycle (about US$1 a day) is also popular; they're available almost everywhere. For cave sites out of town you can charter *săwngthăew* near the old market site – expect to pay around US$10 per trip up to 20km north or south of town.

VANG VIENG TO LUANG PRABANG

The road between Vang Vieng and Luang Prabang winds its way up over some stunningly beautiful mountains and back down to the Mekong at Luang Prabang. If you suffer from motion sickness, take precautions before you begin. In the middle of a fertile valley filled with rice fields, **Kasi**, 56km north of Vang Vieng, is a lunch stop for bus passengers and truck drivers travelling on this route. The surrounding area is full of interesting minority villages, but few people bother to stop as there isn't much in the way of tourist infrastructure. There are, however, a couple of simple guesthouses.

About 40km north of Kasi, at the T-junction between Rte 13 and Rte 7 east to Phonsavan, lies **Muang Phu Khoun**, site of a former French garrison. Surrounded by jagged, mist-shrouded mountain peaks, Muang Phu Khoun lies near the heart of Hmong country and it was only in the 1920s, when the French extended Rte 13 this far, that it became linked to the rest of French Indochina. During the Second Indochina War the RLA and PL constantly fought for control of the town (then known as Sala Phu Khun) because of its strategic location on the road to the Plain of Jars battlefields. Other than a market, a few shops and a single guesthouse, there is little to see.

As you go further north towards Luang Prabang, you'll start getting views (to the east starting at about Km 228) of Phu Phra, a craggy limestone peak considered holy to animist hill tribes and Buddhists alike.

(FORMER) SAISOMBUN SPECIAL ZONE

ເຂດພິເສດໄຊສົມບຸນ

After 30 years as a no-go zone, off-limits due to an armed insurgency by Hmong rebels that has persisted since 1975, the Lao government has finally decided the Saisombun Special Zone is no longer required. The zone was actually a 4506-sq-km area of rugged mountains and plateaus at the northeast corner of Vientiane Province, stretching into Xieng Khuang

GOING TO LONG CHENG: THE CIA'S SECRET CITY *Andrew Burke*

Long Cheng, the CIA's 'secret city' in its long war in Laos, had been somewhere I'd wanted to visit for years. Finally, it seemed, with the Saisombun Special Zone (p129) disbanded, getting there would be possible. So with rented dirt bikes, sunglasses and full tanks of gas, my friend Wil and I set off from Vang Vieng. First, though, a little background....

From the early 1960s until May 1975, Long Cheng (also spelt Long Tien) was the heart and soul of the American war against communism in Laos. Long Cheng means 'clear valley' and it was the relatively open space, combined with a population of Hmong who opposed the Pathet Lao–North Vietnamese push, that appealed to the CIA when they chose it as a base for training Hmong guerrillas (see p38).

As the fighting intensified on the Plain of Jars, just 60km north, so Long Cheng grew. By 1964 a 1260m-long runway had been built and sealed. Storage facilities, a communications centre and housing were constructed. The charismatic Hmong General Vang Pao, who was even then the most important man in Laos as far as the US was concerned, coordinated his fighters from Long Cheng. By 1966 it was one of the largest US installations on foreign soil; by 1969 Long Cheng had become one of the busiest airports on earth, with a takeoff or landing roughly every minute.

The planes were mainly a mix of small, propeller-driven T-28 attack planes flown by Hmong, Lao and Thai pilots, and tiny Cessnas flown by American Forward Air Controllers (FACs). These guys were known as Ravens and lived an almost comic-book superhero existence: plucked out of the regular military in Vietnam and signed up to the 'Steve Canyon Program', they seemingly disappeared into a world of secrecy when they arrived in Laos, even flying in civilian clothes because the US was, as far as everyone else was concerned, not actually fighting in Laos.

Long Cheng wasn't defeated until after the US left. By that time, in May 1975, there were almost 50,000 Hmong fighters and refugees living in the valley. In the chaotic US evacuation thousands were airlifted out, but tens of thousands more were left behind. Many of those chose to continue the struggle, and even today the insurgency has a few diehard adherents. It's little wonder, then, that Long Cheng has been off limits for decades...

The road leading up to Huay Kham, where the enormous Australian-run Phu Bia copper mine cuts a colossal red scar across the earth, wasn't too bad. But soon after we turned north the sign announcing the 'Long Cheng track' was ominous. Fortunately, the track with all its washouts and precipitous drops was at least as spectacular as it was dangerous. It was like

Province. It was established because the area is home to a large population of Hmong, and was the Hmong/CIA headquarters during the Second Indochina War. Saisombun means 'bountiful victory', and while the government has controlled the towns and places like Long Cheng since 1975, the irony is that the Hmong insurgents have had enough control over the rest of the area (or at least had the Lao army worried enough) that the authorities felt it too dangerous to open up to just anyone. The victory, it seemed, was in name only.

Despite a reported confrontation north of Vang Vieng in early 2007, the government has decided to disband the zone, close its administrative offices in Saisombun town and open it up to all comers (in theory, at least). This change was motivated by several factors, including the lack of insurgent attacks in the

area and the rapid development of foreign-run mining operations. But the main factor has been a series of surrenders by Hmong groups that have been pursued mercilessly by Lao and Vietnamese troops for most of the last 30 years. These people have been living in the forests of this area since 1975 and many have lived their entire lives on the run in the most primitive circumstances. Some Hmong have fled to Thailand and eventually been re-settled in the United States. The fate of many who have surrendered remains unknown.

Rafting trips out of Vang Vieng start in the zone, and it's possible to take infrequent buses from Ban Tha Heua, on Rte 13 at the north end of Ang Nam Ngum, to Ban Huay Kham (where there's a guesthouse) and the vast and already controversial Phu Bia mine site, run by Pan Australian Mining. Road conditions are rugged, to put it mildly. In your own transport riding through a traditional Chinese painting; jagged peaks and steep-sided valleys, surrounded by hills either forested or cleared for planting. We passed through only a few villages, some little more than military garrisons, before eventually stopping at an advanced base of Phu Bia Mining where a serious North American was cleaning a decades-old mortar with a toothbrush. He was assessing the amount of unexploded ordnance (UXO) lying around; his initial appraisal was that back here about 10km south of Long Cheng it wasn't too bad, but around Long Cheng itself the ordnance was 'everywhere'.

It turned out we couldn't make it in a day. The wiring for my headlight had broken and with mists washing into the valleys as the shadows grew long, it was too far back to the nearest guesthouse – in Huay Kham. Instead we stopped in a Hmong village where the headman reluctantly agreed to put us up. In Laos, and particularly among the Hmong, this reluctance seemed unusual. Later we learned Westerners are not allowed to stay in Hmong villages in this part of Laos. The lodgings were simple but as generous as they could offer. Dinner, a mix of rice and pot noodles, was prepared over a fire contained in a cluster bomb casing. Conversation was too interesting to safely report here.

Our bikes were wheeled into our room, whether out of fear they'd be stolen or fear they'd be seen by the military, we weren't sure. What was certain was the village was constantly under surveillance. When we asked about the lights on the hill across the valley the answer was simple: 'Soldiers'.

The village woke early and it was cold when we set off through the morning mists. After another hour of long, steep climbs and shorter but equally steep descents we rounded a bend to see a boom gate ahead, and several surprised Lao soldiers. This was Long Cheng, at 1000m elevation, and the runway was above us to the right. Beyond the valley stretched off to some menacing-looking peaks.

Unfortunately, our stay was brief. A colonel soon appeared and his reception wasn't warm. No, we couldn't come in for a look around, he told us, this is still a military base. We tried several different angles and reasons but each was promptly rejected. Finally, the colonel laughed, turned on his heel and said: 'Come back in five years' as he strode off.

For more on Long Cheng read: *The Sky is Falling: An Oral History of the CIA's Evacuation of the Hmong from Laos* by Gayle Morrison, and *The Ravens: Pilots of the Secret War of Laos* by Christopher Robbins. See also 'Secret Army and the Hmong', p38, for further details about Hmong involvement with the CIA.

(preferably a dirt bike or 4WD) it's also possible to reach Ban Huay Kham and Saisombun town via a mining road from near Tha Bok, on Rte 13 south. In theory, if you make it to Ban Huay Kham or Saisombun town you should be able to continue on to Phonsavan via an eastward loop. However, we haven't tried this so ask around before you set off.

Long Cheng, the 'secret city' from where the Hmong and CIA operated during the Second Indochina War (see opposite), is reachable but remains off limits to visitors.

thern Laos

Northern Laos' majestic curves rise in steep green folds from the earth and layer the terrain with cliffs, mountains and high plateaus. Their formidable bulk hinders modernity and access, and preserves much of the mystique that attracts visitors to Laos in the first place. Villages along the mighty Mekong and the subdued Nam Ou and Nam Tha waterways still cling to river transport and the pockets of unexplored territory are vast. This striking natural heritage has greatly influenced the country's human history. While lowland Lao migrants favoured the flatter, rice-friendly river plains of central and southern Laos, hill-tribe cultures from the more rugged territories of Tibet and southwestern China found the mountainous north suitable for small-scale farming of corn and opium, and the raising of domestic animals.

If you're a fugitive from routine, northern Laos provides ample hiding spots. Isolation is thick in this part of Southeast Asia and the rich ethnic diversity of the region thrives as a result. The opportunities to acquaint yourself with homestays, hilltop tribes and traditional village life are profuse. Big ticket attractions include exquisite Luang Prabang, the archaeological Plain of Jars and inspiring ecotrekking in Luang Nam Tha, which has received support from the UN and accolades from around the world. As more of the area opens itself to tourism, less-visited gems like village exploration in remote Phongsali, and the haunting Vieng Xai caves of Hua Phan gain great attention. Throughout northern Laos cycling tours and rafting excursions (without the 'happy' pit stops) present themselves and for every organised activity there is an avenue to cater to DIY junkies.

HIGHLIGHTS

- Ecotrekking in the Luang Nam Tha's wonderful **Nam Ha NPA** (p198)
- Wat-hopping and market-shopping in regal **Luang Prabang** (p134)
- Navigating the Nam Ou on a slow boat north from **Nong Khiaw** (p160)
- Exploring Hua Phan's stunning landscape and haunting **Vieng Xai** caves (p187)
- Visiting tribal villages in remote **Phongsali** (p210)
- Taking an archaeological amble through Xieng Khuang's **Plain of Jars** (p169)
- Taking the river less-travelled and slow-boating through **Sainyabuli** down to Vientiane (p220)

Climate

Because mountainous northern Laos has higher overall elevations than the rest of the country, and sits at higher latitudes as well, it generally boasts the coolest temperatures. In the short cool season – roughly late November through to mid-February – temperatures can easily fall into the single digits at night. During the hot season – March through to May – the more mountainous provinces (particularly Luang Nam Tha, Phongsali, Xieng Khuang and Hua Phan) are a good choice if you want to avoid the stifling heat of the Mekong River plains.

The annual southwest monsoon season generally runs a bit shorter in the north, so that while in Si Phan Don (southern Laos)

it may still be raining in October, in Luang Nam Tha and Udomxai the rainy season may be finished. The northeastern provinces of Hua Phan and Phongsali, on the other hand, often receive rain from Vietnam and China during the northeastern monsoon (from November to February) while the rest of the north is dry.

Getting There & Around

Many visitors enter northern Laos via Thailand at Huay Xai (p214), then make their way southeastward to Luang Prabang and Vientiane from here. Others come northwestward by bus from Vientiane (p86), and yet others fly to Luang Prabang (see p134) from Bangkok or Chiang Mai in Thailand. You

NORTHERN LAOS

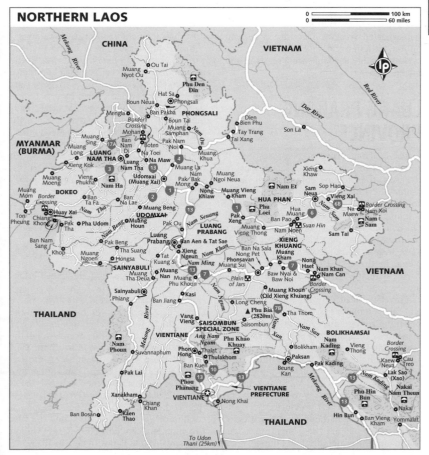

can also fly to some northern cities – namely Luang Prabang, Phonsavan, Udomxai, Luang Nam Tha and Sam Neua – from Vientiane.

Boat travel along the Mekong River is a popular way of moving between Huay Xai and Luang Prabang, and less so between Luang Prabang and Phongsali. The most common means of interprovincial transport in the north is public bus. Bus trips around the north can be quite slow due to the steep and winding nature of the roadways as well as the conditions of the roads themselves.

Săwngthăew (pick-up trucks fitted with benches in the back for passengers) do the job in less populated areas. These can often be chartered for between 10 and 15 times the individual passenger fare.

Some people travel the north by bicycle or motorcycle now that the government has loosened restrictions on the hire of two-wheeled vehicles. Car hire is also an option, although the only cities where hire cars are readily available are Vientiane and Luang Prabang.

LUANG PRABANG PROVINCE

Luang Prabang Province possesses one of Northern Laos' most diverse landscapes. In the west, the Mekong cuts through dense jungle and lines it with sandy banks. The south is dominated by awesome massifs climbing north from Vientiane and the Nam Ou (Ou River) voyages north from the city of Luang Prabang, humbled by sheer cliffs of karst around Nong Khiaw and Muang Ngoi Neua. In the east, Rte 7 ambles towards Xieng Khuang Province and the scenery gives way to soft hills of tawny brown.

Travellers head here for a few days and end up spending a few weeks exploring the beguiling topography. Access through the province is comparatively easy and all roads lead to and from Luang Prabang city, one of Laos' highlights. With Rte 13 almost fully sealed, putting the province within a day's drive of China as well as Vientiane, Luang Prabang is well on its way to becoming one of the country's richest provinces.

Luang Prabang harbours 12 ethnicities, of whom nearly half are Lao Thoeng, 40% Lao Loum and the remainder Lao Soung.

LUANG PRABANG

ຫລວງພະບາງ

☎ 071 / pop 26,000

Colour is the first of Luang Prabang's virtues to greet travellers. Pearly frangipanis with their heady perfume, banks of overgrown trees peppered with scarlet flowers, the burnt sienna robes of hundreds of monks and their novices, and resplendent gold and claret wats. The scent of fresh coffee, river activity, produce markets and spicy food soon follows. And then the broader aesthetics begin to unfold. Encircled by mountains, and set 700m above sea level at the confluence of the Nam Khan (Khan River) and the Mekong River, Luang Prabang is now Laos' foremost tourist showpiece. The brew of gleaming temple roofs, crumbling French provincial architecture and multiethnic inhabitants captivates even the most jaded travellers, and the quiet benevolence of the city's residents lulls them into a somnambulant bliss.

Sealed highways linking Luang Prabang with Thailand and China have turned the city into an important relay point for commerce between the three countries. City governors have wisely provided a road bypass system that gives the city centre a wide berth. Thus the sense of calm antiquity that first brought visitors to the city when Laos opened to tourism in 1989 has been well preserved. Moreover, the city is Unesco Heritage listed, which means a blessed ban on buses and trucks. Most road activity consists of bicycles or motorcycles, but an even score simply go by foot. Although the city teems with travellers, it is not a party destination, and the 11.30pm curfew silences the city by midnight and maintains its traditional disposition.

History

Early Thai-Lao *meuang* (city-states) established themselves in the high river valleys along the Mekong River and its major tributaries, the Nam Khan, the Nam Ou and the Nam Seuang, sometime between the 8th and 13th centuries. During the ascendance of the Chenla kingdom, centred in southern Laos and northern Cambodia between the 6th and 8th centuries, Luang Prabang became known as Muang Sawa, the Lao rendering of 'Java'. It is likely this name referred to Javanese sponsorship in Chenla. The Khmer-supported conqueror Fa Ngum consolidated the first Lao kingdom, Lan Xang Hom Khao (Million Elephants, White Parasol), here in 1353.

Four years later the name was changed to Xiang Dong Xiang Thong (City of Gold), and under Fa Ngum's son, King Samsenthai, the kingdom flourished. In 1512 his successor, King Visoun, accepted a celebrated Buddha image – the Pha Bang – as a gift from the Khmer monarchy, and the city-state became known as Luang (Great or Royal) Phabang (Prabang). Luang Prabang remained the capital of Lan Xang until King Phothisarat moved the administrative seat to Vientiane in 1545.

Even after the capital moved to Vientiane, Luang Prabang remained the main source of monarchical power throughout the Lan Xang period. When Lan Xang broke up following the death of King Suriya Vongsa in 1694, one of Suriya's grandsons set up an independent kingdom in Luang Prabang, which competed with kingdoms in Vientiane and Champasak.

From then on, the Luang Prabang monarchy was so weak that it was forced to pay tribute at various times to the Siamese, Burmese and Vietnamese. After a destructive attack by the Black Flag wing of the Chinese Haw in 1887, the Luang Prabang kingdom chose to accept French protection, and a French commissariat was established in the royal capital.

The French allowed Laos to retain the Luang Prabang monarchy and imported Vietnamese workers to erect the brick-and-stucco offices and villas that give the city its faded colonial atmosphere. Luang Prabang quickly became a favourite post for French colonials seeking a refuge as far away from Paris as possible – even during French Indochina's last years, prior to WWII, a river trip from Saigon to Luang Prabang took longer than a steamship voyage from Saigon to France.

The Japanese invasion of Southeast Asia during WWII weakened France's grip on Luang Prabang, and in 1945 Laos declared its independence from France. France, for its part, stubbornly insisted that Laos remained part of the French Union, and they did until the 1954 Vietnamese triumph over the French at Dien Bien Phu, Vietnam.

When the penultimate Luang Prabang king, Sisavang Vong, died in 1959, his son Crown Prince Sisavang Vatthana was scheduled to ascend the throne. According to official Pathet Lao (PL) history, the 1975 revolution prevented the prince's actual coronation, though many Lao and foreign diplomats insist he was crowned before the PL deposed him. At any rate, after two years as 'Supreme Adviser to

the President', King (or Crown Prince?) Sisavang Vatthana and his wife were exiled to Hua Phan Province, where they were imprisoned and died, one by one, from lack of adequate food and medical care between 1977 and 1981. The Lao PDR government has yet to issue a full report on the royal family's whereabouts following the Revolution.

By the time Laos finally reopened to tourism in 1989, after the fall of the USSR and Soviet bloc governments, Luang Prabang had become a ghost of its former self due to collectivisation of the economy and the resulting exodus of nearly 100,000 businesspeople, aristocracy and intelligentsia. Over the next decade, however, as the Lao government legalised private enterprise, long-closed shops reopened and dilapidated villas were converted into hotels and guesthouses. Restaurants, handicraft shops and art galleries sprang up on practically every corner of the formerly comatose city.

The placing of the city on Unesco's World Heritage list in 1995 has played a major role in preserving and enhancing historic architecture, and in raising the city's international profile.

Orientation

Most of the longer roadways through Luang Prabang parallel the river. Shorter roads – once mere footpaths – bisect the larger roads and lead to the riverbanks, serving as dividing lines between different villages. Each village is named for its local wat, eg Ban Khili for Wat Khili, Ban Ho Xiang for Wat Ho Xiang. On the west side of the river, opposite the royal city, is a village called Ban Xieng Maen (not to be confused with the similarly named Ban Xieng Muan on the east side).

A large hill called Phu Si (sometimes spelt Phousi or Phousy) dominates the town skyline, standing towards the middle of the peninsula formed by the confluence of the two rivers. Since it is visible from any point in town, Phu Si serves as a very helpful 'beacon' for orientating yourself. Most of the historic temples are located between Phu Si and the Mekong, while the trading district lies to the south of the hill. Virtually the whole town can be seen on foot in a day or two, though many visitors extend their stay in order to soak up the atmosphere.

The official street names in Luang Prabang have changed at least three times over the

Ban Aphay

NORTHERN LAOS

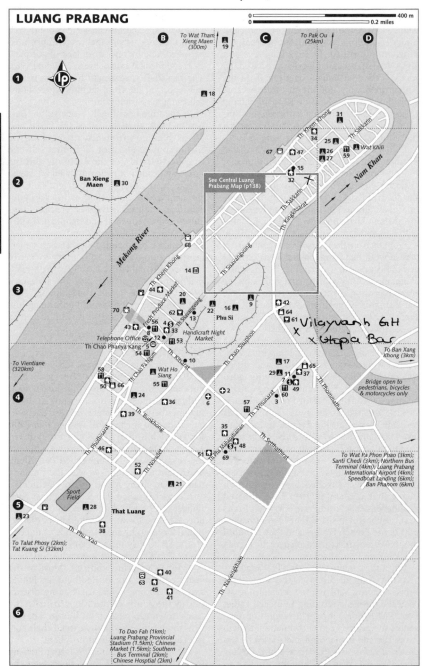

LUANG PRABANG

0 ————————————— 400 m
0 ————————————— 0.2 miles

To Wat Tham
Xieng Maen
(300m)
19

To Pak Ou
(25km)

18

31
34

Ban Xieng
Maen
30

67   47
25
26   Wat Khili
27   59

See Central Luang
Prabang Map (p138)

15

32

Th Sakkarin

Nam Khan

Th Kingkitsarat

68

Mekong River

Th Khem Khong

14

Th Sisavangvong

44

20

42

70

62
13

22   16
Phu Si

9

64
61   Vilayvanh GH

Fresh Produce Market

56

43   12

Handicraft Night
Market:

33

Utopia Bar

Telephone Office

5

53

To Ban Xang
Khong (3km)

Th Chao Phanya Kang

54

Th Chao Fa Ngum

10

Th Chao Siphom

17

Bridge open to
pedestrians, bicycles
& motorcycles only

To Vientiane
(320km)

58

Wat Ho
Siang

55

2

29   11
7
64   49
37

Th Kitsarat

50   66

6

60

57

3

24

36

Th Phommathat

39

Th Bunkhong

Th Wisunarat

Th Setthathirat

46

35

To Wat Pa Phon Phao (3km);
Santi Chedi (3km); Northern Bus
Terminal (4km); Luang Prabang
International Airport (4km);
Speedboat Landing (6km);
Ban Phanom (6km)

Th Phothisarat

51

48
69

Th Pha Mahapatsaman

52

Th Noradet

21

Sport
Field

28

That Luang

23

38

Th Phu Vao

To Talat Phosy (2km);
Tat Kuang Si (32km)

Th Nakiengkham

40

63

45

41

To Dao Fah (1km);
Luang Prabang Provincial
Stadium (1.5km); Chinese
Market (1.5km); Southern
Bus Terminal (2km);
Chinese Hosptial (2km)

INFORMATION
Banque pour le Commerce Extérieur
  Lao...**1** C4
Chinese Hospital........................**2** C4
Immigration & Foreigners
  Management..........................**3** C4
Lao Development Bank..............**4** B3
Post Office.................................**5** B4
Provincial Hospital.....................**6** B4
Provincial Tourism Department...**7** C4

SIGHTS & ACTIVITIES
Action Max Laos.........................**8** B3
Cave Shrine (Wat Tham Phu Si)..**9** C3
Children's Cultural Centre.........**10** B4
Lao Red Cross...........................**11** C4
Lao Youth Travel......................**12** B3
Phousi Massage.......................**13** B3
Royal Palace Museum...............**14** B3
Spa Garden.............................**15** C2
That Chomsi............................**16** C3
Tum Tum Cheng Restaurant...(see 59)
Wat Aham...............................**17** C4
Wat Chom Phet........................**18** B1
Wat Long Khun........................**19** C1
Wat Mai Suwannaphumaham...**20** B3
Wat Manolom..........................**21** B5
Wat Pa Huak...........................**22** B3
Wat Pha Baht Tai.....................**23** A5
Wat Pha Mahathat (Wat That)..**24** B4
Wat Si Bun Heuang..................**25** D2

Wat Sirimungkhun...................**26** D2
Wat Sop...................................**27** D2
Wat That Luang.......................**28** A5
Wat Wisunarat (Wat Visoun)...**29** C4
Wat Xieng Kang.....................(see 21)
Wat Xieng Maen.....................**30** B2
Wat Xieng Thong.....................**31** D1

SLEEPING
Ammata Guest House...............**32** C2
Ancient Luang Prabang Hotel...**33** B3
Auberge Le Calao.....................**34** C2
Jaliya Guest House....................**35** C4
Koun Savan Guest House..........**36** B4
Lane Xang Guest House.............**37** C4
Le Parasol Blanc Hotel..............**38** A5
Maison Souvannaphoum...........**39** B4
Maniphone Guest House...........**40** B6
Manoluck Hotel.......................**41** B6
Merry Lao Swiss Hotel..............**42** C3
Oudomphone Guest House......**43** B3
Pakam Guest House..................**44** B3
Sanakeo Guest House...............**45** B6
Satri House.............................**46** A4
Sayo River Guest House............**47** C2
Thavisouk Guest House............**48** C4
Thony II Guest House................**49** C4
Vanvisa Guest House................**50** A4
Villa Kiengkham......................**51** B5
Villa Suan Maak......................**52** B5

EATING
Baguette Stalls.........................**53** B3
JoMa Bakery Cafe....................**54** B4
Mr Hong's Coffeeshop &
  Restaurant...........................**55** B4
Night Stalls.............................**56** B3
Paradise Restaurant.................**57** C4
Somchanh Restaurant..............**58** A4
Tum Tum Cheng Restaurant.....**59** D2
Visoun Restaurant....................**60** C4

DRINKING
Martin's Pub............................**61** C3
Nao's Place.............................**62** B3

ENTERTAINMENT
Muangsua Hotel......................**63** B6
Royal Theatre.........................(see 14)

SHOPPING
Kopnoi...................................**64** C3
Pathana Boupha Antique
  House..................................**65** C4
Thithpeng Maniphone.............**66** B4

TRANSPORT
Charter Boat Pier.....................**67** C2
Ferry Boat Pier.........................**68** B3
Lao Airlines.............................**69** C5
Long-Distance Ferries..............**70** B3

NORTHERN LAOS

last decade, so you'll find that naming varies widely on city maps and address cards.

Currently the main street heading northeast up the peninsula is called Th Phothisarat (Phothisalat according to the modern Lao spelling) at its southwestern end, Th Sisavangvong in its middle reach and Th Sakkarin towards the northeastern end. Th Sakkarin (Sakkalin) is also sometimes known as Th Xieng Thong. The road that runs along the Mekong waterfront is variously known as Souvannakhamphong, Oun Kham and Suvannabanlang, although most locals call it Th Khem Khong. When giving directions, the locals fortunately almost never quote street names, using landmarks instead.

The airport, speedboat landing and northern bus terminal are all northeast of the city, while the southern bus terminal is to the southwest.

Information
BOOKSHOPS
L'Etranger Books & Tea (Map p138; booksinlaos@yahoo.com; Th Kingkitsarat; 8am-10pm Mon-Sat, 10am-10pm Sun) New and used books about Laos and Southeast Asia, plus book rental and books bought for cash or trade credit. Art is showcased on the 2nd floor, which doubles as a tea lounge.

EMERGENCY
Ambulance (195)
Fire (190)
Police (191, 212158)

IMMIGRATION
Numerous travel agents in town can arrange visa extensions for US$4 per day. You need to organise this before your visa has expired. **Immigration & Foreigners Management** (Map p136; 212435; Th Wisunarat; 8.30am-4.30pm Mon-Fri) Staff here can deal with any immigration problems you might have.

INTERNET ACCESS
There are internet cafés scattered along Th Sisavangvong in the historic district, all of which charge 300 kip per minute. Le Café Ban Vat Sene (p152) has wireless access if you've got your own laptop.

Good broadband access can be found at:
Internet Shop (Map p138; Th Sakkarin; 8am-11pm)
Treasure Travel Laos (Map p138; 245403; Th Sisavangvong; 7am-11pm)

MEDICAL SERVICES
Visitors with serious injuries or illnesses are almost always flown to Vientiane for emergency transit to hospitals in northeastern Thailand, or

put on direct flights to Chiang Mai or Bangkok. There are some services in the area:

Boua Phanh Pharmacie (Map p138; ☎ 252252; Th Sakkarin) One of the better pharmacies in town.

Chinese Hospital (Map p136; ☎ 254026; Ban Phu Mok) Modern medical equipment and supplies, but sometimes short of trained personnel.

Provincial Hospital (Map p136; ☎ 252049, 212123; Th Setthathirat) Neither this hospital nor the Chinese hospital receive high marks from foreign medical observers.

MONEY

Several tour companies on Th Sisavangvong offer cash advances from a Visa or Master-Card. The exchange rates usually match those of the banks and the commission is around 3%.

Banque pour le Commerce Extérior Lao Central Luang Prabang (BCEL; Map p138; Th Sisavangvong; ☒ 8.30am-3.30pm Mon-Sat); Luang Prabang (BCEL; Map p136; Th Pha Mahapatsaman; ☒ 8.30am-3.30pm Mon-Sat) Will exchange Thai baht, US, Australian and Canadian dollars, euros and UK pounds – cash or travellers cheques – for kip. The bank normally won't change in the other direction because of a claimed shortage of these currencies. BCEL also offers cash advances, in kip only, for Visa and MasterCard.

Lao Development Bank (Map p136; 65 Th Sisavangvong; ☒ 8.30am-3.30pm Mon-Sat) Foreign exchange services; does not accept credit cards.

POST

Post office (Map p136; cnr Th Chao Fa Ngum & Th Kitsarat; ☒ 8.30am-3.30pm Mon-Fri, to noon Sat)

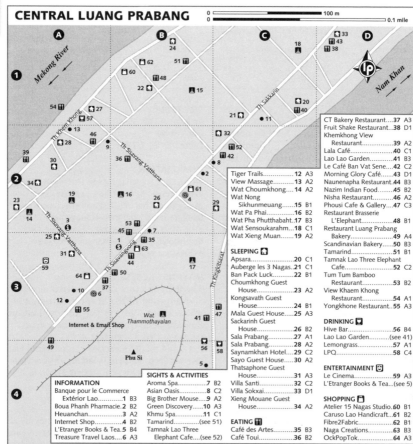

CENTRAL LUANG PRABANG

0 ———— 100 m
0 ———— 0.1 mile

Tiger Trails................**12** A3		
View Massage...........**13** A2		
Wat Choumkhong......**14** A2		
Wat Nong		
Sikhunmeuang........**15** B1		
Wat Pa Phai...............**16** B2		
Wat Pha Phutthabaht.**17** B3		
Wat Sensoukarahm...**18** C1		
Wat Xieng Muan.......**19** A2		

SLEEPING 🏠
Apsara.......................**20** C1
Auberge les 3 Nagas..**21** C1
Ban Pack Luck............**22** B1
Choumkhong Guest
  House.......................**23** A2
Kongsavath Guest
  House.......................**24** B1
Mala Guest House.......**25** A3
Sackarinh Guest
  House.......................**26** B2
Sala Prabang..............**27** A1
Sala Prabang..............**28** A2
Saynamkhan Hotel.....**29** C2
Sayo Guest House.......**30** A2
Thatsaphone Guest
  House.......................**31** A3
Villa Santi..................**32** C2
Villa Sokxai................**33** D1
Xieng Mouane Guest
  House.......................**34** A2

EATING 🍴
Café des Artes............**35** B3
Café Toui....................**36** B2

CT Bakery Restaurant....**37** A3
Fruit Shake Restaurant...**38** D1
Khemkhong View
  Restaurant.................**39** A2
Lala Café.....................**40** C1
Lao Lao Garden.............**41** B3
Le Café Ban Vat Sene....**42** C2
Morning Glory Café.......**43** D1
Naunenapha Restaurant.**44** B3
Nazim Indian Food........**45** B2
Nisha Restaurant..........**46** A2
Phousi Cafe & Gallery....**47** C3
Restaurant Brasserie
  L'Elephant................**48** B1
Restaurant Luang Prabang
  Bakery.....................**49** A4
Scandinavian Bakery.....**50** B3
Tamarind.....................**51** B1
Tamnak Lao Three Elephant
  Cafe..........................**52** C2
Tum Tum Bamboo
  Restaurant................**53** B2
View Khaem Khong
  Restaurant................**54** A1
Yongkhone Restaurant..**55** A3

DRINKING 🍷
Hive Bar.......................**56** B4
Lao Lao Garden...........(see 41)
Lemongrass..................**57** A1
LPQ.............................**58** C4

ENTERTAINMENT 🎬
Le Cinema....................**59** A3
L'Etranger Books & Tea...(see 5)

SHOPPING 🛍
Atelier 15 Nagas Studio.**60** B1
Caruso Lao Handicraft....**61** B2
Fibre2Fabric..................**62** B1
Naga Creations.............**63** B3
OckPopTok...................**64** A3

SIGHTS & ACTIVITIES
Aroma Spa..................**7** B2
Asian Oasis................**8** C2
Big Brother Mouse....**9** A2
Green Discovery.......**10** A3
Khmu Spa.................**11** C1
Tamarind.............(see 51)
Tamnak Lao Three
  Elephant Cafe....(see 52)

INFORMATION
Banque pour le Commerce
  Extérior Lao.............**1** B3
Boua Phanh Pharmacie.**2** B2
Heuanchan...............**3** A2
Internet Shop............**4** B2
L'Etranger Books & Tea.**5** B4
Treasure Travel Laos...**6** A3

TELEPHONE

Most internet cafés in town have Skype and MSN Messenger on their computers, which enable you to make cheap or free international internet phone calls if you have an account. Alternatively, they offer international phone calls for 2000 kip per minute.

Domestic and international phone calls can be made at a window inside the post office (opposite), down a corridor, to the right inside the entrance, and at a phonecard booth at the front of the post office. Cards may be purchased inside the post office or at sundries shops around town.

TOURIST INFORMATION

Provincial Tourism Department (Map p136; ☎ 212487; Th Wisunarat) This office, opposite Wat Wisunarat, stocks a few brochures but in general is of limited use to most visitors. Opening hours are unposted and erratic.

UNESCO WORLD HERITAGE INFORMATION

Heuanchan (Villa Xiengmouane, Ban Xieng Mouane; Map p138; ✆ 9am-6pm) The Heritage Information Centre of Luang Prabang contains posted public information on the Unesco project being conducted in Luang Prabang.

Dangers & Annoyances

During the late dry season – roughly from February to May – the air over Luang Prabang can become very smoky due to slash-and-burn agriculture in the hills and mountains around the city. It becomes so bad in March and April that even local residents will complain of red, watery eyes and breathing difficulties. Landscape photography is hopeless, except on the rare day when a strong breeze flushes out the smoke from the valley. With the arrival of rain in late May or June, the air clears and generally stays that way until the following year. One hopes the authorities will get a handle on the situation before all the surrounding forests are gone, and extensive erosion and flooding result.

Sights

ROYAL PALACE MUSEUM (HO KHAM)

ຫໍພິພິດທະພັນພະລາດສະວັງ(ຫໍຄຳ)

Start your tour of Luang Prabang with a visit to this quaint museum to get a sense of local history. You need to be appropriately dressed to enter, which means having your shoulders covered and no shorts. The **Royal Palace Museum** (Haw Kham or Golden Hall; Map p136; ☎ 212470; Th Sisavangvong; admission US\$2; ✆ 8-11am & 1.30-4pm) was

built in 1904 during the early French colonial era as a residence for King Sisavang Vong and his family. The site for the palace was chosen so that official visitors to Luang Prabang could disembark from their river journeys directly below the palace and be received there.

Architecturally, the building features a blend of traditional Lao motifs and French beaux-arts styles, and has been laid out in a double-cruciform shape with the entrance on one side of the lower crossbar. The steps leading to the entrance are Italian marble. Most of the private chambers of the royal family have been preserved since the day the Pathet Lao forced the royals into exile. Many locals believe the palace to be haunted by the spirits of the royal family, and few Lao will venture into the building after dark.

The large entry hall displays royal religious objects, including the dais of the former Supreme Patriarch of Lao Buddhism; an ancient Buddha head presented to the king as a gift from India; a reclining Buddha with the unusual added feature of sculpted mourners at his side; an equally uncommon seated Buddha with a begging bowl (the bowl is usually only depicted with a standing figure); and a Luang Prabang–style standing Buddha sculpted of marble in a 'Contemplating the Bodhi Tree' pose.

To the right of the entry hall is the king's reception room, where busts of the Lao monarchy are displayed along with two large, gilded and lacquered Ramayana screens crafted by local artisan Thit Tanh. The walls of the room are covered with murals that depict scenes from traditional Lao life. French artist Alix de Fautereau painted these in 1930, intending that each wall be viewed at a different time of day – according to the light that enters the windows on one side of the room – to correspond with the time of day depicted.

The front right corner room of the palace, open to the outside, contains a collection of the museum's most prized art, including the Pha Bang. Cast of a gold, silver and bronze alloy, this Buddha stands 83cm tall and is said to weigh 53.4kg. Legend has it the image was cast around the 1st century AD in Sri Lanka and later presented to Khmer King Phaya Sirichantha, who in turn gave it to King Fa Ngum in 1359 (other accounts have it that his successor, King Visoun, received it in 1512) as a Buddhist legitimiser of Lao sovereignty. Since stylistically it's obviously

NORTHERN LAOS

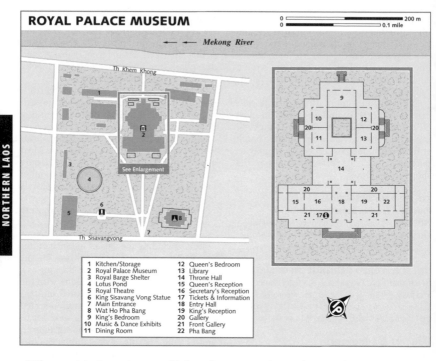

ROYAL PALACE MUSEUM

0 — 200 m
0 — 0.1 mile

← — Mekong River

Th Khem Khong

See Enlargement

Th Sisavangvong

1	Kitchen/Storage	12	Queen's Bedroom
2	Royal Palace Museum	13	Library
3	Royal Barge Shelter	14	Throne Hall
4	Lotus Pond	15	Queen's Reception
5	Royal Theatre	16	Secretary's Reception
6	King Sisavang Vong Statue	17	Tickets & Information
7	Main Entrance	18	Entry Hall
8	Wat Ho Pha Bang	19	King's Reception
9	King's Bedroom	20	Gallery
10	Music & Dance Exhibits	21	Front Gallery
11	Dining Room	22	Pha Bang

of Khmer origin, its casting most likely took place nearer to the latter date. The Siamese twice carried the image off to Thailand (in 1779 and 1827) but it was finally restored to Lao hands by King Mongkut (Rama IV) in 1867. Persistent rumours claim that the actual image on display is a copy and that the original is stored in a vault either in Vientiane or Moscow. The 'real' one supposedly features a bit of gold leaf over the eyes and a hole drilled through one ankle.

Also in this room are large elephant tusks engraved with Buddhas, including Khmer-crafted sitting Buddhas and Luang Pra-bang–style standing Buddhas; an excellent Lao frieze taken from a local temple; and three beautiful *saew mâi khán* (embroidered silk screens with religious imagery) that were crafted by the queen.

To the left of the entry hall, the secretary's reception room is filled with paintings, silver and china that have been presented to Laos as diplomatic gifts from Myanmar, Cambodia, Thailand, Poland, Hungary, Russia, Japan, Vietnam, China, Nepal, the USA, Canada and Australia. The objects are grouped according to whether they're from 'socialist' or 'capitalist' countries.

The next room to the left was once the queen's reception room. Large royal por-traits of King Sisavang Vatthana, Queen Kham Phouy and Crown Prince Vong Savang, painted by the Russian artist Ilya Glazunov in 1967, are hung on the walls. Also on display in this room are friendship flags from China and Vietnam, and repli-cas of sculpture from New Delhi's Indian National Museum.

Behind the entry hall is the throne hall where royal vestments, gold and silver sa-bres, and the king's elephant chair (or saddle) are exhibited. Glass cases hold a collection of small Buddhas made of crystal and gold that were found inside the That Makmo (Makmo Stupa). Intricate wall mo-saics, placed on a deep red background, took eight craftsmen 3½ years to complete and are a highlight of the palace's art.

Beyond the throne room are the halls or galleries that lead to the royal family's resi-dential quarters. The royal bedrooms have been preserved as they were when the king departed, as have the dining hall and a room that contains royal seals and medals. One of the more interesting displays in the museum is a room in the residential section that now contains Lao classical musical instruments and masks for the performance of Ramayana dance-drama – just about the only place in the country where you see these kinds of objects on display.

Towards the southeastern corner of the compound stands a large, unlabelled bronze statue of King Sisavang Vong. Behind the statue is a palace building now designated as the **Royal Theatre**. See p154 for more information.

Wat Ho Pha Bang

A project planned before the monarchy was abolished in 1975, construction on this highly ornate pavilion began in 1993. Upon completion the highly revered Pha Bang will be moved from palace museum to an altar in the centre of the pavilion.

WAT XIENG THONG

ວັດຊຽງທອງ

Near the northern tip of the peninsula formed by the Mekong River and the Nam Khan is Luang Prabang's most magnificent temple, **Wat Xieng Thong** (Map p136; admission US$1; 8am-5pm). King Setthathirat ordered the construction of Wat Xieng Thong's *sim* (ordination hall) in 1560, and the compound remained under royal patronage until 1975. Like the royal palace, Wat Xieng Thong was placed within easy reach of the Mekong. The *hăw tại* (Tripitaka library) was added in 1828, and the *haw kạwng* (drum tower) in 1961.

Along with Wat Mai Suwannaphumaham, this was the only Luang Prabang wat spared by the 1887 Black Flag Haw sacking of the city. The Black Flag's leader, Deo Van Tri (a Thai Khao or White Thai from the north Vietnam province of Lai Chau), had studied here as a monk earlier in his life, and he used the desecrated, if not destroyed, temple as his headquarters during the invasion.

NORTHERN LAOS

BUN PI MAI LAO (LAO NEW YEAR)

In the middle of April the three-day Songkan (Water Festival) celebrates the start of Lao New Year. Songkan, from the Sanskrit *samkranta* (fully passed over), signifies the passage of the sun from the zodiac sign of Pisces into Aries. All of Laos observes this festival, but it is particularly well celebrated in Luang Prabang, where many people dress in traditional clothes for the major events and stretch the event out to a full seven days.

On a spiritual level, the Lao traditionally believe that during this period the old Songkan spirit departs and the new one arrives. On the first day of the festival, when the old spirit departs, people give their homes a thorough cleaning. At Hat Muang Khoun, a Mekong River island beach near Ban Xieng Maen, locals gather to build and decorate miniature sand stupas for good luck, amid much playful throwing of river water. On the second day, civic groups mount a colourful, costumed parade down Luang Prabang's main avenue from Wat Pha Mahathat to Wat Xieng Thong. The third day is a 'rest day', when all parading stops and the devout take time to wash Buddha images at their local wat.

In the early morning of the fourth day, people climb Phu Si to make offerings of sticky rice at the summit stupa. Then in the afternoon they participate in *bạasǐi* (sacred string-tying) ceremonies with family and friends. On the fifth day the Pha Bang (the Khmer-style standing Buddha figure) leaves the Royal Palace Museum, where it's kept, and is taken to Wat Mai Suwannaphumaham (Wat Mai) in a solemn procession, while on the sixth day the new spirit arrives. This day is considered especially crucial, and cleansing rituals extend to the bathing of Buddhist holy images – particularly the Pha Bang, in a temporary pavilion erected in front of Wat Mai – by pouring water onto them through wooden sluice pipes shaped like *naga* (mythical water serpents). Senior monks receive a similar treatment, and younger Lao will also pour water over the hands (palms held together) of their elderly relatives in a gesture of respect. On the last day, a final procession carries the Pha Bang from Wat Mai back to the museum.

Although the true meaning of the festival is kept alive by ceremonies such as these, nowadays it's mainly a festival of fun. As in Thailand and Myanmar, this is the height of the hot, dry season, and the locals revel in being able to douse one another with cold water to cool off. Foreigners are not exempt from the soaking, so watch out!

The *sim* represents what is considered classic Luang Prabang temple architecture, with roofs that sweep low to the ground. The rear wall of the *sim* features an impressive 'tree of life' mosaic set in a red background. Inside, the elaborately decorated wooden columns support a ceiling stencilled in gold with *dhammachakka* (dharma wheels). Other gold-stencilled designs on the interior walls depict the exploits of legendary King Chanthaphanit, about whom there exists no verifiable written history.

To one side of the *sim*, towards the east, stand several *haw* (small halls) and stupas containing Buddha images of the period. The *hǎw tại pha sai-nyàat* (reclining Buddha sanctuary; dubbed La Chapelle Rouge – Red Chapel – by the French) contains an especially rare reclining Buddha that dates from the construction of the temple. This one-of-a-kind figure is exquisitely proportioned in classic Lao style (most Lao recliners imitate Thai or Lanna styles), with the monastic robes curling outward at the ankle like rocket fumes. Instead of merely supporting the head, the unique right-hand position extends away from the head in a simple but graceful gesture. In 1931 this image was taken to Paris and displayed at the Paris Exhibition, after which it was kept in Vientiane until its return to Luang Prabang in 1964.

Gold-leaf votives line the upper walls of the sanctuary on either side of the reclining image. In front of the image are several seated bronze Buddhas of different styles and ages, and on either side of the altar are small embroidered tapestries depicting a stupa and a standing Buddha. A mosaic on the back exterior wall of this chapel was done in the late 1950s in commemoration of the 2500th anniversary of the Buddha's attainment of *parinibbana* (final nirvana, or passing away). The mosaic is unique in that it relates the exploits of Siaw Sawat, a hero from a famous Lao novel, along with scenes of local village life, rather than a religious scene.

Near the compound's eastern gate stands the *hóhng kép mîen* (royal funerary carriage house). Inside is an impressive funeral carriage (crafted by local artisan Thit Tanh), standing 12m high, and various funeral urns for the members of the royal family. (The ashes of King Sisavang Vong, the queen and the king's brother, however, are not interred here but at Wat That Luang at the southern end of Luang Prabang.) Glass cabinets hold royal puppets that were once used for performances of *la-kháwn lek* (traditional small puppet show). Gilt panels on the exterior of the chapel depict semierotic episodes from the Ramayana epic.

WAT WISUNARAT (WAT VISOUN)
ວັດວິຊຸນນະລາດ

Originally built in 1513 during the reign of Chao Wisunarat (King Visoun), **Wat Wisunarat** (Map p136; Th Wisunarat; admission US$1; ☉ 8am-5pm) is the oldest operating temple in Luang Prabang. It was rebuilt between 1896 and 1898 following an 1887 fire set by Black Flag Haw raiders. The original was wooden, and in the brick and stucco restoration the builders tried to make the balustraded windows of the *sim* appear to be fashioned of lathed wood (an old South Indian and Khmer contrivance that is uncommon in Lao architecture). The front roof that slopes sideways over the terrace is another unique feature. Inside the high-ceilinged *sim* is a collection of gilded wooden 'Calling for Rain' Buddhas and 15th- to 16th-century Luang Prabang *siimáa* (ordination-precinct stones). These were placed here by Prince Phetsarat after the Haw invasion. The Pha Bang was kept here from 1507 to 1715 and from 1867 to 1894.

Standing well in front of the *sim* – instead of in the usual spot for a large stupa, immediately behind the *sim* – stands the 34.5m That Pathum (Lotus Stupa). Locally the stupa is more commonly known as That Makmo (Watermelon Stupa) because of its semispherical

WAT XIENG THONG

0 ——————— 50 m

Th Khem Khong

Drum Tower
Stupa
Golden Stupa
Stupa
Stupa
Funerary Carriage House
City Entrance
River Entrance
Wihaan
Sim
Kuti (Monks Quarters)
Elephant Pillars
Th Sakkarin
Boat Shelter
Tripitaka Library
Reclining Buddha Sanctuary (Red Chapel)
Stupa
Stupa
Stupa
Octagonal Stupa
Stupa
That Kraduk
Stupa
Stupa

NORTHERN LAOS

shape. Work on the stupa began in 1503 by order of Nang Phantin Xieng, wife of King Visoun, and was completed 19 months later. Workmen filled the interior of the stupa with small Buddha images made of precious materials and other sacred items. Many of these were stolen when the Haw destroyed the temple, while those recovered can be seen on display in the Royal Palace Museum. The stupa underwent reconstruction in 1895 and again in 1932 after a partial collapse due to rain.

WAT AHAM
ວັດອາຮາມ

Between Wat Wisunarat and the Nam Khan stands **Wat Aham** (Map p136; admission US$1; 8am-5pm), formerly the residence of the Sangkharat (Supreme Patriarch of Lao Buddhism). Two large banyan trees grace the grounds, which are semideserted except for the occasional devotee who comes to make offerings to the town's most important spirit shrine at the base of the trees.

WAT MAI SUWANNAPHUMAHAM
ວັດໃໝ່ສຸວັນນະພູມອາຮາມ

Inaugurated in 1821 (some sources claim 1797), **Wat Mai** (Map p136; Th Sisavangvong; admission US$0.50; 8am-5pm) succeeded Wat Aham as the residence of the Sangkharat until that position moved to Pha That Luang in Vientiane. The five-tiered roof of the wooden *sim* follows the standard Luang Prabang style, but the roofed front veranda, with its gables angled towards the sides of the chapel rather than towards the front, is an anomaly. This unusual plan may have been influenced by local vernacular architecture, as exemplified in the old wooden house just across the street from Wat Mai. The front veranda is also remarkable for its decorated columns and the sumptuous gold relief walls that recount the tale of Vessantara (Pha Wet in Lao), the Buddha's penultimate birth, as well as scenes from the Ramayana and village life.

Behind the main *sim* stands an open-sided shelter housing two long racing boats. These slender, graceful craft are brought out during Bun Pi Mai Lao (Lao New Year) in April and again in October during Bun Nam (Water Festival). Heavily decorated with flower garlands, each boat will hold up to 50 rowers, plus a coxswain.

Wat Mai was spared destruction by the Chinese Haw, who reportedly found the *sim* too beautiful to harm. Most of the other 20 or so buildings are newer.

The Pha Bang, which is normally housed in the Royal Palace Museum, is brought here and put on public display in a temporary pavilion in front of the *sim* at Wat Mai during the Bun Pi Mai Lao celebrations.

WAT THAT LUANG
ວັດທາດຫລວງ

Legend has it that **Wat That Luang** (Map p136; Th Phu Vao) was originally established by Ashokan missionaries from India in the 3rd century BC. However, there is no evidence whatsoever to confirm this, and the current *sim* was built in 1818 under the reign of King Manthaturat. The ashes of King Sisavang Vong and his brother are interred inside the large central stupa, which was erected in 1910. A smaller *thâat* (stupa) in front of the *sim* dates back to 1820. Inside the huge *sim* are a few Luang Prabang Buddha images and other artefacts.

WAT MANOLOM
ວັດມະໂນລົມ

Although its outer appearance isn't very impressive, **Wat Manolom** (Wat Mano; Map p136; Th Pha Mahapatsaman) stands just outside the barely visible city walls and occupies possibly the oldest temple site in Luang Prabang. City annals say it was founded in 1375 on the site of a smaller temple established by King Fa Ngum. The decaying *sim* held the Pha Bang from 1502 to 1513 and still contains a sitting bronze Buddha cast in 1372. This image is about 6m high and weighs an estimated two tonnes – some parts of the bronze are 15mm thick. An important city talisman, the image would probably be moved to another temple if anyone could figure out how!

The Buddha's arms reportedly came off during a battle between French and Thai armies in the late 19th century. After the battle the colonialists allegedly made off with most of the appendages, except for a portion of one forearm, now placed beside one of the feet. The Lao later reconstructed the missing arms with cement. Near the *sim* are the scant remains of an older temple, **Wat Xieng Kang** (Map p136), allegedly constructed in 1363.

PHU SI
ພູສີ

The temples on the upper slopes of 100m-high **Phu Si** (Map p136 & p138; Th Sisavangvong; admission US$1;

NORTHERN LAOS

A TRAVELLER'S TALE *Katie Horner*

Wandering Luang Prabang's cracked pavements, sweat making me resemble a fried tomato, I spy a wat, not unusual in itself. I look it up in my trusty guide book and find it is Wat Manolom. It looks rather shabby from the outside, but upon approaching it and pausing in the shade of the entrance I am greeted with a hearty *sabqi-dii* from a couple of friendly monks leaving. Intrigued by this open welcome I ask if it's OK to wander around? Yes they nod in unison, and usher me in.

As I enter the grounds and turn a corner of one of the buildings, a youngish monk of 12 or 13 calls to me in Lao. I indicate I can't understand him and in excellent English he asks if I can speak Lao. I bashfully reel out a few words I have picked up and he smiles encouragingly. He asks where I am from and when I tell him Australia, I get another grin and the word 'kangaroo'. He has a book in his hand and explains that he is studying.

'On the weekend?' I inquire with raised eyebrows. He nods somewhat reluctantly and explains he has to study on the weekends because he has to go to school the other days. He needs a holiday, he states without a hint of irony.

I ask if it's OK to join him in the shade. We chat about where I have been and at the mention of Nong Khiaw he points to his chest, swathed in orange, and says that's where he's from! 'It's a beautiful place' I say and he tells me that his parents come down to visit him sometimes. I ask if I can see the book is studying from. Not only is he very good at speaking English but it, seems, quite proficient at writing it as well. I am impressed and tell him so.

However, I don't want to keep him (well, I do, but he may get into trouble and I am boiling hot) so I walk around the wat, with more *sabqi-diis* from the young monk and his friends following me out. What a refreshing end to my visit to Luang Prabang. If only I had asked him his name.

⏰ 8am-6pm) were recently constructed, but it is likely there were once other temples located on this important hill site. There is an excellent view of town from the top of the hill.

On the lower slopes of the hill are two of the oldest (and now abandoned) temples in Luang Prabang. The decaying *sĭm* at **Wat Pa Huak** (Map p136) – on the lower northern slope near the Royal Palace Museum – has a splendid carved wood and mosaic façade showing Buddha riding Airavata, the three-headed elephant of Hindu mythology (in which he is usually depicted as Lord Indra's mount). The gilded and carved front doors are often locked, but during the day there's usually an attendant nearby who will open the doors for a tip of a couple of hundred kip. Inside, the original 19th-century murals have excellent colour, considering the lack of any restoration. The murals show historic scenes along the Mekong River, including visits by Chinese diplomats and warriors arriving by river and horse caravans. Three large seated Buddhas and several smaller standing and seated images date from the same time as the murals or possibly earlier.

Around on the northeastern flank of the hill are the ruins of **Wat Pha Phutthabaht** (Map p138), originally constructed in 1395 during the reign of Phaya Samsenthai on the site of a 'Buddha footprint'. The ruins are of mixed style but are said to show a definite Lanna or Chiang Mai influence, as well as some later Vietnamese augmentation.

The fee to climb to the summit of the hill is collected at the northern entrance near Wat Pa Huak (you don't have to pay the fee to reach Wat Pa Huak, however).

The 24m-high **That Chomsi** (Map p136), erected in 1804 and restored in 1914, stands at the summit, clearly visible from most ground-level points in the city. This stupa is the starting point for a colourful Lao New Year procession in mid-April. If you continue over the summit and start down the path on the other side, you'll come to a small **cave shrine** (Map p136; sometimes called Wat Tham Phu Si, although without monks it's not officially a wat). Plopped down in the middle of the cave is a large, fat Buddha image – called Pha Kasai in Lao – and a sheltered area for worshippers. On a nearby crest is a Russian anti-aircraft cannon that children use as a makeshift merry-go-round.

WAT XIENG MUAN
ວັດຊຽງມ່ວນ

The *sĭm* at **Wat Xieng Muan** (Map p138) dates back to 1879, though no doubt the monastery site is much older. The sculpture inside is better than average and the ceiling is painted with gold *naga*, an uncommon motif in this position – possibly a Thai Lü influence. Also notable is the elaborate *háang thíen* (candle rail) with *naga* at either end.

With backing from Unesco and New Zealand, Wat Xieng Muan has restored the monks' quarters as a classroom to train young monks in the artistic skills needed to maintain and preserve Luang Prabang's temples. Among these skills are woodcarving, painting and Buddha-casting, all of which came to a virtual halt after 1975. If you step into the grounds of Wat Xieng Muan during the day you'll see the monastic residents learning or teaching these arts.

OTHER TEMPLES

In the northeastern corner of town near the meeting of the Nam Khan and the Mekong River is a string of historic, still active temples. Facing Th Sakkarin is **Wat Sensoukarahm** (Map p138), a Thai-style wat built in 1718 and restored in 1932 and 1957. The name reportedly refers to its founding on an initial 100,000 kip donation. It has one of the most dazzling façades of all of Luang Prabang's temples; rich ruby red with intricate gold overlay. Behind Villa Santi near the river road, the simple **Wat Nong Sikhunmeuang** (Map p138) was built in 1729, burned in 1774 and rebuilt in 1804.

Southwest of Villa Santi and set back off the street is **Wat Pa Phai** (Map p138), whose classic Tai-Lao fresco over the gilded and carved wooden façade is at least 100 years old; the picture depicts scenes from everyday Lao life from the era in which it was painted.

Wat Pha Mahathat (Wat That; Map p136), the third wat southwest of the Phousi Hotel, is named for a venerable Lanna-style *thâat* erected in 1548. The *sǐm* in front, built in 1910, is quite ornate, with carved wooden windows and portico, rosette-gilded pillars, exterior Jataka (stories of the Buddha's past lives) reliefs and a roof in the Luang Prabang style lined with temple bells. The massive *naga* along the steps, also Lanna in style, resemble those at Wat Phra That Doi Suthep in Chiang Mai, Thailand.

An easy 3km walk or bicycle ride northeast of town is **Wat Pa Phon Phao**, a forest meditation wat famous for the teachings of the late abbot, Ajahn Saisamut. Saisamut's funeral in 1992 was the largest and most well attended

monk's funeral Laos had seen in decades. The monastery's **Phra That Khong Santi Chedi** (Peace Pagoda; donation expected; ☽ 8-10am & 2-4pm Mon-Fri), built in 1988, has become a favourite Lao tourist attraction. This large yellow stupa contains three floors inside and an outside terrace near the top with a view of the surrounding plains. The inside walls are painted with all manner of Buddhist stories and moral admonitions.

On the Mekong River near the north-western end of Th Phu Vao is a modern Vietnamese-Lao temple, **Wat Pha Baht Tai** (Map p136). The temple itself is rather garish but behind the temple is a shady terrace overlooking the Mekong; on a hot afternoon this is a good place to cool off and watch the sunset.

Almost next door to Wat Xieng Muan, **Wat Choumkhong** (Map p138) is a small but very pretty temple with one of the loveliest gardens in town. In November and December it's awash with colour courtesy of poinsettia trees.

ACROSS THE MEKONG RIVER

Across from central Luang Prabang there are several notable temples in Ban Xieng Maen. Ban Xieng Maen itself played an important role as the terminus of the historic road between Luang Prabang and various northern Thai kingdoms, eg Nan and Phayao.

Wat Long Khun (admission US$0.50; ☽ 8am-5pm), almost directly across the Mekong River from Wat Xieng Thong, is the best place to disembark by boat for Xieng Maen explorations if you're chartering a boat. This wat features a nicely decorated portico, vintage 1937, plus older sections from the 18th century and a few fading Jataka murals. When the coronation of a Luang Prabang king was pending, it was customary for him to spend three days in retreat at Wat Long Khun before ascending the throne. A restoration project, completed in 1995 by the Department of Museums and Archaeology, with the assistance of the Ecole Française d'Extrême Orient, has brought new life and beauty to the monastery buildings.

Founded in 1889 and since abandoned, **Wat Tham Xieng Maen** (admission US$0.50; ☽ 8am-5pm) is in a 100m-deep limestone cave called Tham Sakkarin Savannakuha, a little northwest of Wat Long Khun. Many Buddha images from temples that have been torched or otherwise fallen into decay are kept here; during Bun Pi Mai Lao many local worshippers come to Wat Tham to pay homage and cleanse the images.

The large stone-block entrance built around the mouth of the cave displays good relief work on stair pedestals, and is flanked by two large ruined spirit houses and a couple of plumeria (frangipani) trees. An iron gate across the cave mouth is usually locked; inquire at Wat Long Khun and someone will come and unlock the gate and guide you through the cave. It's very long and dark, and parts of the cave floor are slippery, so it's a good idea to go with a guide; bring a torch (flashlight). There are several other caves nearby that are easily found and explored with local help, although none are quite as extensive as Tham Sakkarin Savannakuha.

At the top of a hill above Wat Long Khun and Wat Tham is peaceful **Wat Chom Phet** (Map p136; admission US$0.50), built by the Thai army in 1888 and offering an undisturbed view of the town and river. A small *thâat* here contains the bones of Chao Thong Di (wife of King Sakkarin), who died in 1929.

Southwest of Wat Chom Phet in the village of Xieng Maen, **Wat Xieng Maen** (Map p136) was founded in 1592 by Chao Naw Kaewkumman, son of Setthathirat, but it fell into ruin and had to be rebuilt in 1927. The newer *sǐm* contains a few artefacts dating from the original temple, including the original doors. This spot is especially sacred to Xieng Maen residents because it once housed the Pha Bang for seven days and seven nights on its way back to Luang Prabang in 1867 following a lengthy stay in Vientiane.

Ban Xieng Maen itself is worth a wander since, like Luang Prabang, it's maintained its original urban plan, possibly dating back to the 14th century. Unlike Luang Prabang though, most of the main roads (paralleling the river) and byways (leading to the river) haven't been paved over, so the plan is technically more intact.

Getting There & Away

You can charter boats from Luang Prabang's charter boat pier to Wat Long Khun or Ban Xieng Maen for US$3 return, or you can wait for the infrequent ferry boats at the ferry boat pier further south, which charge around US$0.25 per passenger.

HERITAGE HOUSE
ເຮືອນມໍລະດົກ

A Unesco-sponsored exhibit and information centre called **Heritage House** (La Maison de Patrimoine; ✆ 8.30am-4pm Mon-Fri) occupies an old wooden Lao house on teak pillars in Ban Xieng Muan. Other than the very impressive wood and *colombage* (bamboo lattice daubed with natural mortar) house itself, there is little to take in here. Occasional weaving demonstrations are held in the house.

Activities
CYCLING

Luang Prabang is far bigger than the inner grid many people stick to and exploring the surrounding bans and wats on a bicycle is a beautiful way to enjoy the city. Bikes can

---

GOODWILL ACTIVITIES

Get in touch with the local community by making the most of some commendable enterprises in Luang Prabang. Pop into **Big Brother Mouse** (Map p138; ✆ 5377486; www.laobooks.com; Ban Xieng Mouane; ✆ 9am-6pm) and pick up some books to distribute to local children. Books cost 15,000 kip each and the idea behind the programme is to encourage visitors to hand out something more beneficial than candy, while promoting literacy. Run by a retired American publisher, the staff is made up of Laotian college and high-school students, all of whom contribute to the content, illustrations, and admin of the office. You can also purchase books at the night market or make a donation to support the production of new material, and the office gladly accepts volunteers when the need arises.

Rather than trashing your used water bottles, cans and other recyclable waste, donate it to the **Children's Cultural Centre** (Map p136; Th Kitsarat; ✆ 9am-3pm), which on-sells the waste to other dealers and uses the funds to provide after-school activities for kids.

If you've bought up big at the night markets and need to lighten your pack, you can donate used, washed clothing to the **Lao Red Cross** (Map p136; ✆ 252856; Th Wisunarat). You can also donate money, and, if you're feeling particularly perky, you can even donate blood; a precious commodity in Laos.

be rented from guesthouses, tour companies and shops around Th Sisavangvong for US$1 to US$3 per day depending on the state and style of the bike. The old quarter can be easily covered in half a day, taking in temples and other sights. It doesn't take much effort to get out of town either: head south past Talat Phousy (Phousy Market) and into the hills, but watch out for punctures on rocky roads.

MASSAGE & SAUNA

Luang Prabang is one of the best places in Southeast Asia to indulge in a herbal sauna or Swedish, Lao or Khamu massage. Prices are generally 30,000 kip for an hour-long body or foot massage, 40,000 kip for an oil massage, and 10,000 kip for a sauna. Options are abundant, but the following are recommended based on the tireless and selfless research by the author:

Aroma Spa (☎ 020-761 1255; Th Sisavangvong; ◷ 10am-10pm) Facials, body scrubs and indulgent combination packages ranging from US$30 to US$50.

Khmu Spa (Map p138; ☎ 212092; Th Sakkarin; ◷ 10am-10pm) Excellent traditional Lao and Khamu massages.

Lao Red Cross (Map p136; ☎ 252856; Th Wisunarat; ◷ massage 9am-9pm, sauna 5-9pm) Housed in a nicely preserved Lao-French building with half-timbered walls. Proceeds go towards the Lao Red Cross so really any visit here is an act of pure selflessness. Take your own towel or sarong.

Phousi Massage (Map p136; Th Sisavangvong; ◷ 10am-10pm) Friendly and attentive.

Spa Garden (Map p136; ☎ 212325) In a quiet pocket near Wat Nong Sikhunmeuang, this spot offers the same indulgent treatments as Aroma (above).

View Massage (Map p138; ☎ 212271; Th Khem Khong; ◷ 10am-11pm) Tranquil setting and particularly good oil massages.

Courses
COOKING

Tamarind (Map p138; ☎ 020-7770484; www.tamarind laos.com; Ban Wat Nong) Excellent cooking classes for truly authentic Laotian food, including market tours for fresh ingredients, jungle picnics where you can actually catch your own fish, and more.

Tamnak Lao Three Elephant Cafe (Map p138; ☎ 252525; www.laocookingcourse.com; Th Sakkarin; per person US$25) Full-day cooking classes including market shopping and a Lao lunch and dinner.

Tum Tum Cheng Restaurant (Map p136; ☎ 253224; tumtumcheng@yahoo.com; 29/2 Th Sakkarin; 1/2/3 days

per person US$25/45/60) Well-regarded classes including market shopping and drinks.

WEAVING

OckPopTok (Map p138; ☎ 212597; www.ockpoptok .com; classes per half/full day US$30/40) has a weaving and cultural centre where you can witness the silk- and cotton- weaving process from scratch. The skill and patience required to master these looms is quite remarkable and the 15 weavers here are true masters. Fortunately you can try your own hand at the art by taking a small-group class in dyeing and weaving. A Lao lunch is included and you take home your handiwork. Make bookings at its gallery.

Walking Tour

> ### WALK FACTS
>
> This walk starts in the heart of town, near the western bank of the Mekong, loops around the highlights of the central area, and ends in the main strip of Th Sisavangvong. The entire walk is about 3.5km and will take four to six hours, depending on how long you stop at some of the sights.

Start your walking tour with a visit to **Big Brother Mouse** (**1**; opposite), just off Th Sisavangvong, where you can purchase books to distribute to kids during your exploration. Heading south along this back street you'll come across **Wat Xieng Muan** (**2**; p144), home to an arts' school for monks. Almost next door is petite **Wat Choumkhong** (**3**; p145) with its exquisite garden. If you continue south along this back street you'll hit a T-junction and the northeastern wall of the **Royal Palace Museum** (**4**; p139). Turn left and then right onto Th Sisavangvong to access the front gates. Potter here for an hour or so and then continue south along Th Sisavangvong, turning right at the Palace's southwestern wall. **Wat Mai Suwannaphumaham** (**5**; p143), noted for its exterior gilded relief, will be on your left. If you follow this street towards the Mekong, you'll stumble across some gorgeous **Lao-French colonial houses** (**6**) and the first left will land you in the colourful **fresh produce market** (**7**; p155). Walk the length of the market and turn right onto Th Kitsarat so you can hit the waterfront.

Follow Th Khem Khong north. This stretch provides a good range of Luang Prabang's architectural diversity, including beautifully preserved colonial villas, traditional Lao abodes and shop fronts, old and new.

Finish your river walk at **Wat Xieng Thong** (**8**; p141), where you'll need to stop for an hour or so. Exit the temple grounds at Th Sakkarin, and head right, past **Wat Si Bun Heuang (9)**, **Wat Sirimungkhun (10)**, **Wat Sop (11)**, and **Wat Sensoukarahm (12**; p145). Turn right where Auberge les 3 Nagas sits regally on the corner and then left at the next T-junction. Just around the corner is **Tamarind (13**; p153), the perfect spot for a refreshing cooler, or even better, lunch.

After your pit stop make your way to Th Sisavang Vatthana and head left until you hit the eastern bank of Luang Prabang's peninsula. Some stairs leading down to the water on the opposite side of the road provide a good vantage point for photos. Walk south along Th Kingkitsarat and turn right at Th Wisunarat, so you can gander at **Wat Wisunarat (14**; p142), one of the city's oldest temples. At the eastern end of the temple's compound is the bulbous That Makmo – the Watermelon Stupa.

Continue southwest along Th Wisunarat and take your next main right, onto Th Kitsarat. A block up you'll find the **Children's Cultural Centre (15**; p146), where you can discard any empty water bottles for a good cause.

Turning right onto Th Sisavangvong you'll find yourself back on the main drag, and ultimately at steps to **Phu Si (16**; p143). The ascent is worthwhile – sunset vistas from the western side of the hill next to the 19th-century **That Chomsi (17**; p143) can be superb, except in the late dry season when even the sun's intensity is strongly muted.

If you've got the energy and your timing's right you can top the day off with a wander through the ambient **Handicraft night market (18**; p155).

Tours

Luang Prabang has an abundance of travel agents vying for your patronage for half- to multiday tours. Tours to the waterfalls and the Pak Ou Caves (p158) are particularly popular. Many also book domestic and international flights. Tour prices are competitive but it still pays to shop around. Most operators line Th Sisavangvong, but the following are recommended for good trekking, rafting and cycling excursions:

Action Max Laos (Map p136; ☎ 252417; actionmaxasie@yahoo.fr; Ounheuan & Th Khem Khong) Elephant treks and comfortable, small group tours to surrounding area. Prices around US$30 per person per day.

Asian Oasis (Map p138; ☎ 252553; fax 252304; www .asian-oasis.com; Ban Vat Sene) Operates the luxury *Luang Say* boat from Luang Prabang to Huay Xau, three days weekly in each direction (two weekly May to September). See also p218.

Green Discovery (Map p138; ☎ 212093; www.green discoverylaos.com; Th Sisavangvong) Kayaking, trekking, mountain biking, motorcycling and multiday trips north including motorcycle tours.

Lao Youth Travel (Map p136; ☎ 253340; www .laoyouthtravel.com; 72 Th Sisavangvong) Highly recommended for its focus on community-based ecotourism. One- and two-day tours between Vientiane, Vang Vieng and Luang Prabang, and rewarding multiday trips to minority villages in the far north. Prices around US$35 to US$50 per day, all inclusive.

Tiger Trails (Map p138; ☎ 252655; www.laos-ad ventures.com; Th Sisavangvong) Single- and multi-day trips involving trekking, rafting and cycling around Luang Prabang. Longer trips to Muang Ngoi or Muang Khua and

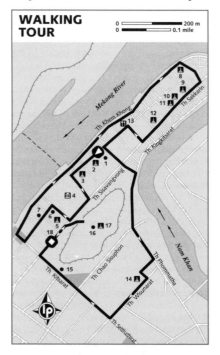

WALKING TOUR

0 —— 200 m
0 —— 0.1 mile

accommodation homestays. Tiger Trails also has an elephant camp about 15km outside of Luang Prabang on the banks of the Nam Khan, where it offers elephant treks and mahout (elephant trainer) courses. This company places a strong emphasis on conservation and community support. Prices range from US$29 to US$40 per day.

Treasure Travel Laos (Map p138; ☎ 254403; www .treasureTravelLaos.com; Sisavangvong Rd) Organised and customised tours throughout Laos. Prices depend on duration and group size.

Festivals & Events

The two most important annual events in Luang Prabang are **Bun Pi Mai Lao** (Lao New Year) in April (see Bun Pi Mai Lao, p141) and the **boat races** during Bun Awk Phansa (the End of the Rains Retreat) in October. Both events draw large numbers of both Lao and foreigners to the city, so be sure to book a room in advance if you're coming to town then.

Sleeping

BUDGET

Near the Mekong

The old silversmithing district near the Mekong, a neighbourhood known as Ban Wat That (named for nearby Wat Pha Mahathat, or 'Wat That' for short), and the adjacent Ban Ho Xiang, have become a centre for a cluster of modest guesthouses.

Oudomphone Guest House (Map p136; ☎ 252419; s/d US$5/6, shared bathroom US$4/5) Spick-and-span rooms with spring mattresses, fans and small windows greet the weary traveller at this homely guesthouse. Hidden in a residential block, it's perfect for those looking to escape the tourist glut for a quiet night's sleep.

Pakam Guest House (Map p136; ☎ 253436; Ban Pakam; s/d US$8/10) Tucked away in a pretty, provincial side street, this small guesthouse has modest rooms with dark wood furnishings, wall fans, comfortable beds, writing desks and never-fail hot water in the gleaming bathrooms. There is only a handful of rooms so the young and friendly staff (who will happily practise their French and Lao with you) will treat you like a member of the family early on. Upstairs there is a small balcony with lovely residential views.

Vanvisa Guest House (Map p136; ☎ 212925; vandara1@hotmail.com; 42/2 Ban Wat That; s/d US$8/15) Vanvisa Guest House features six rooms at the back of a shop that sells textiles, antiques and handicrafts. The owner, a cultured Lao lady, sometimes makes breakfasts and family-style dinners for guests and can even arrange an informal cooking workshop.

Historic Temple District

On and off Th Sisavangvong/Th Sakkarin is the most concentrated area of colonial architecture and historic monasteries. It's scenic and central.

Choumkhong Guest House (Map p138; ☎ 252690; Ban Xieng Mouane; r US$5) Just across the road from Wat Choumkhong, this friendly guesthouse has small alabaster rooms with good beds, tiled floors, crisp linen and ceiling fans. The bathrooms are shared but they're the cleanest in town.

Sackarinh Guest House (Map p138; ☎ 254512; off Th Sisavangvong; r $15; ✷) Signposted from the main street, this solid guesthouse has a handful of slightly clinical, but clean and spacious rooms with satellite TV and good bathrooms. We like the koala motif rugs and comfy beds. It's excellent value, but can be noisy.

Also available:

Mala Guest House (Map p138; ☎ 212800; Ban Xieng Mouane; r $5) Basic, friendly and good value.

Thatsaphone Guest House (Map p138; ☎ 020-5671888; Ban Xieng Mouane; r $8-10) Gorgeous location with airy rooms.

Elsewhere

Koun Savan Guest House (Map p136; ☎ 212297; off Th Kitsarat; r shared bathroom US$4-6, with bath US$12; ✷) This guesthouse sits in a quiet street and is spread around a lush, colourful garden. Tight and simple rooms have outside bathrooms, and slightly larger and more expensive rooms have nicer shared amenities. The doubles with air-con and private bathrooms are spotless, and the owners are lovely.

Maniphone Guest House (Map p136; ☎ 212636; Th Phu Vao; r $15; ✷) This personable, single-storey guesthouse is set back from the main road, providing a decent buffer of space from the traffic. The compact rooms have pristine linen, small TVs, minibars, wardrobes and clean bathrooms. It's one of the friendliest spots in town.

Th Pha Mahapatsaman

This area is quieter and less inspiring than other pockets of town, but you'll find good-value accommodation here as a result.

Thavisouk Guest House (Map p136; ☎ 252022; Th Pha Mahapatsaman; r US$4; ✷) The friendly Thavisouk features fatter-than-usual mattresses in

NORTHERN LAOS

clean, sunny rooms with fans and blue-tiled bathrooms. Owners are warm and laid-back and the entrance houses an internet cafe and a fridge full of Beerlao.

Thony II Guest House (Map p136; ☎ 254779; off Th Wisunarat; r $5) A far cry from your average budget bunker options, Thony II has airy, unadorned rooms with attached bathrooms, fans and crisp linen. Owners are young and helpful and there's a common TV room out the front.

Jaliya Guest House (Map p136; ☎ 252154; Th Pha Mahapatsaman; r US$6-12; 🕸) The ever-popular Jaliya has a range of rooms including spartan, fan-cooled versions with shared bathroom, all the way up to those with cable TV and air-con. All are appealing and well priced. Motorbikes and bicycles are available for hire.

MIDRANGE
Historic Temple District

Ammata Guest House (Map p136; ☎ 212175; pphila souk@yahoo.com; Ban Wat Nong; r $15; 🕸) One of the best deals in town, this small, popular guesthouse has a low-key ambience, spotless and spacious rooms with polished wood interiors, and renovated bathrooms. It's midrange quality at small-pocket prices. Most rooms are upstairs, running off a shared and shaded balcony.

Villa Sokxai (Map p138; ☎ 254309; sokxaigh@yahoo .com; Th Sakkarin; r US$25; 🕸) A reliable midrange option in a pleasant pocket with cool and spotless rooms and cable TV. The friendly owners speak a little English and although rooms are small, they're very comfortable.

Sayo Guest House (Map p138; ☎ 252614; http:// sayoguesthouse.free.fr/cms; Ban Xieng Mouane; r US$25-50, f US$50-60; 🕸) The Sayo is a popular fixture on midrange itineraries and for good reason. Set in a French colonial mansion, it offers rooms with high ceilings, louvred windows, four-poster beds, TVs and lovely tiled bathrooms. Upstairs two capacious family rooms come with a mezzanine level for kids or itinerant spouses and sizable bathrooms with tubs. Out the back are the less-expensive former servants' quarters.

Xieng Mouane Guest House (Map p138; ☎ /fax 252152; 86/6 Ban Xieng Mouane; r/f US$30/40; 🕸) The rooms in this white two-storey colonial house are snug, but stylish. Muted colours, quilted beds, low lighting and high ceilings are matched by ample bathrooms. Many are set in a quadrangle around a flourishing

garden at the back, and family rooms have a connecting twin.

Sayo River Guest House (Map p136; ☎ 212484; http:// sayoguesthouse.free.fr/cms; Th Khem Khong; r incl breakfast US$30-50; 🕸) This new and stylish sibling of the longstanding Sayo has sizeable rooms, all tastefully decorated with contemporary Lao wooden furniture and woven bedspreads. The cheapest rooms are ground floor with compact bathrooms; pricier versions have glossy bathrooms with tubs and/or balconies with lovely river views.

Ancient Luang Prabang Hotel (Map p136; ☎ 212264; www.ancientluangprabang.com; Th Sisavangvong; s/d/tr incl breakfast US$40/45/50; 🕸) Push past the Ancient Luang Prabang's grandiose entrance and you'll be rewarded with boutique-style studio rooms. Features including cable TV and mini-bars play an aesthetic second to polished teak, local handicrafts and divine timber-clad bathrooms. Some rooms also have street views, but triples are a tight squeeze.

Also available:

Saynamkhan Hotel (Map p138; ☎ 212976; saynam khane-lp@hotmail.com; Th Kingkitsarat; r US$20-35; 🕸) Two-storey colonial building with rustic rooms and river views.

Ban Pack Luck (Map p138; ☎ 253373, 020-5516517; packluck@hotmail.com; Ban Wat Nong; r $30-35; 🕸) Intimate villa with small but classy rooms.

Near the Mekong

Kongsavath Guest House (Map p138; ☎ 212994; khongsavath@hotmail.com; Th Khem Khong; r/ste US$20/30; 🕸) Perched on the northern bank of the Mekong, Kongsavath is a cosy, homely guesthouse with quality rooms. All have large beds, Lao lamps, gleaming bathrooms and shuttered windows. Suites are considerably larger than the standard rooms.

Merry Lao Swiss Hotel (Map p136; ☎ 260211; www .freewebs.com\merrylao_swiss; Th Kingkitsarat; r US$30-50, f US$80; 🕸) Wide, low-slung beds, silk textiles, splashes of polished teak, couches, satellite TV and generous bathrooms are standards at this very comfortable hotel. The pricier rooms are upstairs and are larger, and one interconnecting room up top suits families.

Elsewhere

Villa Suan Maak (Map p136; ☎ 252775; www.villa-suan -maak-laos.com; Th Noradet; r incl breakfast $20-35; 🕸) Formerly known as Noixdarec, this gorgeous villa is set behind a handsome garden. The house itself is beautifully maintained and contains sweet rooms with local handicrafts, spreads and cushions. Owners are endearing and breakfast is served alfresco.

Lane Xang Guest House (Map p136; ☎ 212794; villalanexang@yahoo.com; Th Wisunarat; r incl breakfast US$26-40; ☒) This supremely tasteful villa has just seven capacious and cool rooms with lofty ceilings, hand-woven textiles and oversized tubs. It's a wonderfully sophisticated blend of colonial and traditional Lao beauty and highly recommended.

Villa Kiengkham (Map p136; ☎ /fax 212219; Th Wisunarat; r $25; ☒) The ideal spot for fussy folk who don't want to break the bank. This quiet hotel has high ceilings, timber flourishes and clinically clean rooms with satellite TV. Breakfast (not included) is served on a serene patio overlooking a pond.

Le Parasol Blanc Hotel (Map p136; ☎ 252124; www.hotelinlaos-vicogroup.com; Th Phu Vao; r incl breakfast from US$55; ☒) This quaint little hotel overlooks a small man-made pond in a tranquil setting. Generous rooms have polished floorboards, large TVs and private balconies with leafy green views. There's a free shuttle to town or the airport.

Also recommended:

Sanakeo Hotel (Map p136; ☎ 252992; sanakeohotel@yahoo.com; Th Phu Vao; r US$35-70; ☒) Kitschy hotel with good facilities capturing the Chinese tour bus market.

Manoluck Hotel (Map p136; ☎ 212250; manoluck@laotel.com; 121/3 Th Phu Vao; r incl breakfast US$45; ☒) Comfy, clean and snug if a little charmless.

TOP END
Historic Temple District

Apsara (Map p138; ☎ 212420; www.theapsara.com; Th Kingkitsarat; r incl breakfast US$55-85; ☒) Commonly tagged Luang Prabang's most chic hotel, the Apsara fills its rooms with contemporary Asian décor in bold and vivacious colours. The cheaper standard rooms are much more minimalist than the opulent superior rooms, but all have huge beds and excellent facilities.

Sala Prabang (Map p138; ☎ 252460; http://salaprabang.salalao.com; 102/6 Th Khem Khong; r incl breakfast US$60-75; ☒) This artistically refurbished, century-old mansion facing the river is joined by a newer wing a few doors up, built in similar style, all painted in earth tones. Boutique and beautiful, rooms come with flowers on the pillows, tiled interiors, gracious French doors and plush sheets and towels. Service is exceptional.

Auberge les 3 Nagas (Map p138; ☎ 253888; www.3nagas.com; Th Sakkarin; r US$105, ste US$140-180; ☒) Straddling both sides of Th Sakkarin in two gloriously restored villas, this hotel has boutique rooms in discrete east-meets-west panache. Cool interiors swim in teak scents, silk spreads adorn the king-size beds, and chrome fittings bounce of the polished wood bathrooms. All the suites have private courtyards or balconies. Internet access is available if you have your own laptop.

Villa Santi (Map p138; ☎ 252157; www.villasantihotel.com; Th Sakkarin; s/d/ste US$150/170/250; ☒) This 120-year-old residence was once home to King Sisavang Vong's wife. Steeped in history and classic French-Lao architecture, the rooms feature Lao art, antiques and mod cons. There is a herbal sauna and traditional massage on site.

Auberge Le Calao (Map p136; ☎ 212100; www.calaoinn.laopdr.com; Th Khem Khong; s/d incl breakfast US$65/70; ☒) Hopeless romantics will adore this vintage Sino-Portuguese–style mansion facing the Mekong. The five capacious and delicate rooms have tiled floors, private balconies with river views, crisp, white embroidered linen and positively regal bathrooms.

Ban Wat That

Satri House (Map p136; ☎ 253491; www.satrihouse.com; 057 Th Phothisarat; r incl breakfast US$100; ☒ ☒) Built at the turn of the last century as a royal villa, the seven rooms here are furnished with Southeast Asian antiques. The décor is colourful and unique and tubs in the bathrooms sit beneath louvred windows. In the private garden timber sun lounges surround the swimming pool.

Maison Souvannaphoum (Map p136; ☎ 212200; www.coloursofangsana.com; Th Phothisarat; r US$200-400; ☒) Once the official residence of Prince Souvanna Phouma (suite 214 was his bedroom), the glorious Souvannaphoum is now part of the Thailand-based Angsana Resorts Hotel group. The aromatherapy-scented rooms are opulent but subtle, with elegant stone-floored showers, huge beds and couches. There is an open-air restaurant and spa on site, and the service is flawless.

Eating
BAKERIES

Strong Lao coffee and sweet European pastries tempt foreign visitors at several bakeries along Th Sisavangvong and Th Chao Fa

Ngum. The pastry selection is generally better during the high season when consumption is at its peak, and supplies are fresh.

Scandinavian Bakery (Map p138; Th Sisavangvong; meals US$0.80-3; ☺ breakfast, lunch & dinner) A *falang*-fave, this branch of the Vientiane bakery serves delicious cakes, pastries and cookies, as well as large breakfasts and fabulous baguettes. It's small and pricey but you can enjoy air-con and yesterday's *Bangkok Times* with your meal.

JoMa Bakery Café (Map p136; ☎ 252292; Th Chao Fa Ngum; meals US$1-2; ☺ breakfast, lunch & dinner) Arguably the best bakery in town, JoMa has alfresco tables along the street or in a spacious air-con dining room. A great menu of sandwiches, soups and salads joins the large bread and pastry selection, and the coffee is excellent.

CT Bakery Restaurant (Map p138; Th Sisavangvong; meals US$1-3; ☺ breakfast & lunch) Although it lacks a decadent array of chocolate treats and pastries, this bakery serves outstanding 'breakfast baguettes' stuffed with delicious meats and cheeses. It also has an extensive Thai, Lao and European menu at reasonable prices and a secondhand bookshop.

CAFÉS

Phousi Cafe & Gallery (Map p138; Th Kingkitsarat; meals US$2-2.50; ☺ breakfast, lunch & dinner) In a leafy bamboo courtyard, this quiet café serves set Western breakfasts, salads, sandwiches and a host of quasi-Lao and Thai stir-fries. It's deliberately tranquil with bubbling water features, stylish timber slab tables, and local art on the walls.

Morning Glory Café (Map p138; ☎ 020-7774122; Th Sakkarin; meals US$2-3.50; ☺ breakfast & lunch, closed Tue) This smart and cosy café dishes up some of the tastiest breakfasts in town: smoked ham omelettes, fresh muesli, rice soup, and fabulous coffee. For lunch tuck into esto chicken pasta or a fragrant Thai curry. Comfy chairs sit on the pavement and jazz bubbles in the background.

Restaurant Luang Prabang Bakery (Map p138; ☎ 252499; Th Sisavangvong; meals US$3-5; ☺ breakfast, lunch & dinner) This swish restaurant treats timid palates to excellent burgers, pizzas, pastas, steaks and salads, and fairly generic 'Lao food'. The beautiful timber seating is worth a visit, as is the French and Australian wine, superb coffee and gluttony-inducing cakes.

Café des Artes (Map p138; Th Sisavangvong; meals US$3-10; ☺ breakfast, lunch & dinner) The scrummy

selection of deli goods on this menu satiates chorizo, salami, *saucisson*, pâté and cheese cravings. It also boasts French fare, soups, *tartines*, burgers, brochettes and set menus, plus some fusions like duck pizza.

Le Café Ban Vat Sene (Map p138; Th Sakkarin; meals US$3.50-5; ☺ breakfast, lunch & dinner) In a restored colonial building decorated with antiques, this fine café serves tapenades and tapas, smoked chicken and feta salads, and roast pork and tarragon-filled baguettes. The tarts and cakes are delicious. It's quietly chic, and the service is excellent.

EUROPEAN

Café Toui (Map p138; ☎ 253397; Th Sisavang Vatthana; meals US$3-5; ☺ breakfast, lunch & dinner) This little cosmopolitan oasis serves delicious breakfast bagels and mostly European mains such as grilled buffalo with red wine and tomato sauce. The setting is terracotta and tasteful and the wine list is French.

Lala Café (Map p138; Th Kingkitsarat; meals US$3.50-6; ☺ breakfast, lunch & dinner) A refreshing variation from the ubiquitous burger-and-pizza selection greets diners at this trendy little spot. Gracing the menu are Greek dishes, massaman curries and a kicking spicy catfish and mango salad. Dine in the intimate café or at the tables on the riverbank across the road.

Restaurant Brasserie L'Elephant (Map p138; ☎ 252482; Ban Wat Nong; meals US$8-16; ☺ lunch & dinner) One of Luang Prabang's most elegant eateries features wooden floors, subdued lighting and Lao antiques. The menu is mostly French but you'll find other treats such as New Zealand rib eye with gorgonzola cheese sauce, and delectable seafood.

INDIAN

Nisha Restaurant (Map p138; Ban Xieng Mouane; meals US$1-2; ☺ breakfast, lunch & dinner) Smaller than Nazim and tucked on a quieter street, this place serves Indian specialities, Western breakfasts and Lao dishes, both veg and nonveg.

Nazim Indian Food (Map p138; ☎ 253493; Th Sisavangvong; meals US$1.50-2.50; ☺ lunch & dinner) This vacuous Indian diner has a huge menu of north and south Indian food. The curries come as spicy as you like and the vegetarian selection is extensive. The Indian deities and faux tandoori chickens adorning the walls are more appealing after several bottles of Kingfisher.

LAO, THAI & VIETNAMESE

Fruit Shake Restaurant (Map p138; ☎ 5672376; Th Sakkarin; meals US$1; ☺ breakfast, lunch & dinner) The effort they didn't spend on the moniker has all gone into the fine Lao food at this local restaurant. Fried dried beef, Luang Prabang–style, fresh chilli pastes and wild deer with basil are up for grabs as well as three-course set menus for US$3.

Paradise Restaurant (Map p136; ☎ 253200; Th Pha Mahapatsaman; meals US$1.50-2; ☺ breakfast, lunch & dinner) This ambient spot resides in a quiet neck of the woods and serves great Lao and Luang Prabang specialties like sweet and sour Mekong squid, or *áw lám* – stewed meat with green beans and eggplant. Diners sit at picnic benches in a leafy courtyard.

Khemkhong View Restaurant (Map p138; Th Khem Khong; meals US$1.50-2; ☺ breakfast, lunch & dinner) One of the many riverside restaurants lining the Mekong, the split-level Khemkhong View has an extensive menu with choices such as spicy prawn and coconut soup, squid *láap* (salad) or intestine *láap* for the more adventurous) or steamed, fermented fish.

Naunenapha Restaurant (Map p138; ☎ 252998; Th Sisavangvong; meals US$2; ☺ breakfast, lunch & dinner) The no-nonsense Naunenapha has a pleasant tumble of tables edging onto the street and a wide variety of Thai, Lao and Western dishes. There are ample vegetarian options and the hot soupy curries are particularly delicious.

Mr Hong's Coffeeshop & Restaurant (Map p136; 71/6 Ban Thongchaleun; meals US$2-2.50; ☺ breakfast, lunch & dinner) Mr Hong draws a steady clientele with his long menu of reasonably priced Lao dishes like *jeow* eggplant, and *láap pet* (duck salad). The cocktails are potent and the conversation easy.

Tamarind (Map p138; ☎ 020-7770484; www.tamarindlaos.com; Ban Wat Nong; meals US$2.50-4; ☺ breakfast & lunch) Chic little Tamarind injects a great deal of style into the Luang Prabang dining scene, inventing its very own make of 'Mod-Lao' cuisine. The à la carte menu boasts delicious sampling platters with bamboo dip, stuffed lemongrass and *meuyang* – DIY parcels of noodles, herbs, fish and chilli pastes, and vegetables. With a day's notice they also serve banquets (per person US$6 to US$8) with variations like a Lao Celebration Feast (Pun Pa), and the degustation-style Adventurous Lao Gourmet. Dishes include whole fish, marinated in local herbs, stuffed with lemongrass and barbecued in banana leaves, traditional

eggplant and meat stew, or Lao-style barbequed pork. Meals are enhanced considerably by the owners' detailed explanation of the ingredients and how they're eaten. The fruit coolers are divine on a hot day and the *khai pene* (seaweed), chilli pastes and teas (which you can buy) are wholesaled to restaurants around the world.

View Kheam Kong Restaurant (Map p138; ☎ 212726; Th Khem Khong; meals US$2.50-3; ☺ breakfast, lunch & dinner) Alongside *falang* fare and generic stir-fries, this riverside restaurant serves a good Luang Prabang sausage salad, fried green chilli with duck, and Luang Prabang–style stewed fish. Seating is on a large balcony with fairy lights.

Lao Lao Garden (Map p138; Th Kingkitsarat; meals US$3-5; ☺ lunch & dinner) Superlative Thai, Lao and Western fare graces the long menu at this hip, alfresco restaurant, where tables tumble into a hilly, candlelit garden. The Lao barbecue here is a must – diners are served a basket of raw meat and vegetables, which they cook at their own leisure on a round hotplate in the centre of the table. It's about as much fun as dinner gets.

Tum Tum Cheng Restaurant (Map p136; ☎ 252019; Th Sakkarin; meals US$3-5; ☺ lunch & dinner) Years of experience have made this one of the best restaurants in town, and the Lao chef here prepares an interesting menu of Lao and Lao-European fusion. As he lived in Hungary for some years, some of the dishes display a European touch.

Also recommended:

Visoun Restaurant (Map p136; ☎ 212268; Th Wisunarat; meals US$2-3; ☺ breakfast, lunch & dinner) Good selection of Lao and Chinese dishes.

Tum Tum Bamboo Restaurant (Map p138; Th Sisavangvong; meals US$2.50-4; ☺ breakfast, lunch & dinner) Authentic flavours in an ambient setting.

Tamnak Lao Three Elephant Cafe (Map p138; ☎ 252525; Th Sakkarin; meals US$2.50-6; ☺ lunch & dinner) Lao, Luang Prabang and Thai food.

LUANG PRABANG

Luang Prabang has a unique cuisine all its own. One of the local specialities is *jąew bąwng*, a jamlike condiment made with chillies and dried buffalo skin. A soup called *áw lám*, made with dried meat, mushrooms, eggplant and a special bitter-spicy root, is also a typical Luang Prabang dish (roots and herbs with bitter-hot effects are a force in Luang Prabang cuisine). Other local delicacies include *phák nâm,* a delicious watercress that's rarely found outside the Luang Prabang area, and *khái pâen*, dried river moss fried in seasoned oil, topped with sesame seeds and served with *jąew bąwng*. *Khào kam*, a local red, sweet, slightly fizzy wine made from sticky rice, is abundantly and inexpensively available by the bottle in Luang Prabang. It can be good or bad depending on the brand.

Somchanh Restaurant (Map p136; ☎ 252021; Th Suvannabanlang; meals US$1-3; ☼ breakfast, lunch & dinner) This simple but pleasant outdoor place near the cluster of guesthouses in Ban Wat That serves a large selection of Lao and Luang Prabang dishes, including the best choice of vegetarian Lao food in town. Dining areas are divided between tables on a slight bluff near the kitchen and seating across the road on the riverbank.

QUICK EATS

You can get a huge chicken, mayo and salad baguette for around US$1 from the baguette stalls (Map p136) at the corner of Th Sisavangvong and Th Kitsarat. There are also fruit stalls across the road.

Some of the cheapest and tastiest dishes in town can be found at the night stalls (Map p136) that emerge at dusk on streets running off Th Sisavangvong where the night market takes place. The main congregation is one street north of Th Kitsarat, where you can dine on a whole barbequed pig's head, superb vegetarian dishes and noodles, and just about everything in between. There's even a 'vegan' stall. All-you-can-fit bowls cost around US$0.50.

SELF-CATERING

If you've got the will or facilities you can pick up fresh fruit, vegetables, meat (in more versions than you can imagine) and other goods at the Talat Phosy or the fresh produce market in Ban Pakam (see Markets, opposite).

Drinking

Most of Luang Prabang is sound asleep, or at least nodding off behind a bottle of *khào kam*, by 10pm, but there are a few bars around. Closing time, by law, is 11.30pm.

LPQ (Map p138; Th Kingkitsarat) Numerous name changes in recent years hasn't changed the sexual orientation of this chichi bar, which remains gay-friendly. A hint of the South Pacific permeates the interior and the atmosphere is subdued until the after-dinner

crowd creates a relaxed and happy buzz. Women and couples are welcome.

Hive Bar (Map p138; Th Kingkitsarat) This sultry den has a honeycomb of brick-lined, candle-lit rooms and corridors, plus a cluster of alfresco tables out the front. The debaucherous mood is offset a tad by the blaring soundtrack, which travels from old-school Pixies to Thai pop. *Lào-láo* (rice whiskey) cocktails are the house specialty.

Lemongrass (Map p138; Th Khem Khong) This sleek and sophisticated bar serves classic cocktails and good wine in a chic setting. Unfortunately it's mostly for the benefit of gay travellers (women might find they are presented with this fact in hushed tones if they attempt to enter).

Martin's Pub (Map p136; Th Vatmou-Enna) This relaxed drinking hole is an English pub à la Laos. It's got the obligatory curved wooden bar with stools but the décor is distinctly local. There's a good range of booze and burgers on the menu and '70s, '80s and '90s classics in the background. Movies are screened nightly at 6pm and you can buy and sell sci-fi books.

More drinking holes:

Nao's Place (Map p136; Th Sisavangvong) Central spot with international sports on a big screen.

Lao Lao Garden (Map p138; Th Kingkitsarat) Two-for-one cocktails, Beerlao and shooters once the dining's done.

Entertainment
NIGHTCLUBS

Luang Prabang thus far has only two places where dancing is permitted. Both close at 11.30pm sharp.

Dao Fah (☼ 9-11.30pm) A young Lao crowd packs this cavernous club, located off the road to the southern bus terminal. Live bands playing Lao and Thai pop alternate with DJs who spin rap and hip-hop. The bar serves Beerlao as well as mixers for patrons bringing their own liquor.

Muangsua Hotel (Map p136; ☎ 212263; Th Phu Vao; ☼ 9-11.30pm) In a low-ceilinged room behind the hotel, a Lao band plays the usual mix of Lao and Thai pop. Only Beerlao is sold.

THEATRE

Royal Theatre (Map p136; Th Sisavangvong; admission US$6-15; ☼ shows 6pm) Inside the Royal Palace Museum compound, local performers put on a show that includes a *bąasii* ceremony, traditional dance and folk music. There are traditional dances of Lao ethnic minorities such as the Phoo Noi and Hmong people.

CINEMA

There are several places in town where you can catch a flick.

Le Cinema (Map p138; Ban Xieng Mouane; tickets US$3; 6pm-midnight) In a laneway opposite the eastern wing of the Royal Palace, this ingenious spot enables you to hire a room and recent release DVD for the night. It's fun and cosy.

L'Etranger Books & Tea (Map p138; booksinlaos@yahoo .com; Th Kingkitsarat; 7pm) Screens nightly films ranging from new blockbusters to old art house.

Martin's Pub (Map p136; Th Vatmou-Enna; 6pm) Also screens recent releases every night.

Shopping

HANDICRAFTS, ART, TEXTILES & ANTIQUES

Fibre2Fabric (Map p138; ☎ 254761; 71 Ban Wat Nong) This nonprofit gallery curates three exhibitions annually and promotes textiles from the diverse ethnic minorities of Laos. The quality is superb and the products are an education in Lao culture in themselves.

Kopnoi (Map p136; Th Vatmou-Enna) This shop targets the discerning shopper with east-meets-west clothing in natural fabrics and dyes, designer jewellery, homewares and handicrafts, books on Lao cuisine, architecture and crafts, packaged spices and teas and local art.

Naga Creations (Map p138; ☎ 020-7775005; Th Sisavangvong) Specialising in jewellery, Naga Creations produces individual masterpieces using a variety of precious stones and silver. All items are hand crafted and you can see the jewellers at work in the store. Suits all budgets.

OckPopTok (Map p138; ☎ 254406; Th Sisavangvong) This unique textile company offers naturally dyed, house-woven Lao silk and cotton, from which you can order custom-tailored clothing, as well as household decorative items. Lengths of fabric can also be purchased. OckPopTok also offers weaving classes (see Courses, p147.

Pathana Boupha Antique House (Map p136; ☎ 212262; 29/4 Ban Visoun) In an impressive old French mansion, Pathana Boupha carries antique statuary, jewellery, silverwork, Royal Lao government currency and old photos, mostly from the Lao owners' private collection. It also sells high-quality textiles from various ethnic groups. The late patriarch designed many of the costumes and ornaments used in the former Royal Palace.

Thithpeng Maniphone (Map p136; Ban Wat That) Thithpeng crafted silverware for Luang Prabang royalty before 1975 (Thailand's royal family are now some of his best customers). He has 15 apprentice silversmiths but still does the most delicate work himself. To get here follow the signs opposite the Maison Souvannaphoum.

Also available:

Atelier 15 Nagas Studio (Map p138; ☎ 567216; The Khem Khong) Contemporary Lao paintings.

Caruso Lao Handicraft (Map p138; ☎ 254574; Th Sakkarin) Beautiful homewares, photo frames, linen and silk.

MARKETS

Handicraft night market (cnr Th Sisavangvong & Th Kitsarat; 5-11pm) Every evening this market assembles along Th Sisavangvong from the Royal Palace Museum to Th Kitsarat, closing this section of the street off to motor vehicles. It's one of Luang Prabang's biggest tourist lures. Low-lit and quiet, it's devoid of hard selling and is possibly the most tranquil market in Asia. Tens of dozens of traders sell silk scarves and wall hangings, plus Hmong appliqué blankets, T-shirts, clothing, shoes, paper, silver, bags, ceramics, bamboo lamps and more. It's incredibly cheap and because you're injecting currency directly into the local economy you *have* to feel good about spending dosh here.

Fresh produce market (5.30am-4pm Sat-Mon) A colourful market that fills the street between Th Sisavangvong and the Mekong in Ban Pakam. You can watch locals stock up on leafy greens, eggs, dried shrimp and live frogs. It's very photogenic and best in the early morning.

Talat Phosy is a huge warehouselike structure built by the Chinese, encompassing the biggest market for fresh produce, meats, herbs and just about any other basic requisite of Lao life.

There's also a Chinese market, opposite the Luang Prabang Provincial Stadium on the outskirts of town, selling dry goods, textiles and hardware.

Getting There & Away

AIR

Lao Airlines (Map p136; ☎ 212172; Th Pha Mahapatsaman) operates at least three daily flights between Luang Prabang and Vientiane (one way/return US$62/118, 40 minutes), plus flights to Pakse (one way/return US$135/258,

Monday and Thursday) and Phonsavan (one way/return US$40/70, Wednesday, Friday and Saturday).

It's wise to confirm your flight the day before departure. Lao Airlines in Luang Prabang accepts credit cards and can book flights on THAI (between Laos and Thailand only). Most travel agents also book domestic and international flights; see p139 for details.

For information on international flights to Luang Prabang from Asia see p319. Don't forget that you'll need to pay US$1/10 for domestic/international flights at the airport. It's an airport tax that isn't included in your ticket.

When flying into Luang Prabang, try to get a window seat – as the plane descends over the mountains in preparation for landing the view of the town is excellent.

The **Luang Prabang International Airport** (☎ 212173), 4km from the city centre, has a restaurant, **Lao Airlines** (☎ 212173) and **Bangkok Air** (☎ 253 253) offices, phonecard telephone, post office, exchange booth, a branch of Lao Development Bank, and an air-conditioned departure lounge.

BOAT

Ferries are a major form of transport between Luang Prabang and Huay Xai on the Thai border to the northwest. The main landing for long-distance Mekong River boats, at the northwestern end of Th Chao Phanya Kang, is called Tha Heua Meh (literally 'mail boat pier'; ferry boat pier on our map). A blackboard at the Navigation Office announces long-distance boat departures, but it's all in Lao. A second pier near the Royal Palace Museum is sometimes used when the river level is too low for the main pier.

Speedboats use a landing (Map p136; Charter Boat Pier) at Ban Don, 6km north of Luang Prabang. For charters, speedboat pilots usually ask for the equivalent of six passenger fares, but they'll go if you pay for four spaces – often they have paid cargo to carry, too. If you want to share the cost of hiring a speedboat with other passengers it's best to show up at the speedboat pier in Ban Don the day before you want to leave and see what your prospects are. Then show up again around 6am on the morning of your intended departure to queue. Speedboat fares are often quoted in Thai baht, though either kip or US dollars are acceptable payment. Travel agents in town also arrange speedboats.

Speedboat passengers are required to wear life vests and helmets but the helmets are very often substandard. Helmets or no, speedboat travel is ridiculously dangerous – see p304 for warnings on travelling by speedboat.

Tha Suang, Pak Beng & Huay Xai

This is the most popular way for visitors to travel between Huay Xai at the Thai border and Luang Prabang. The Lao border crossing at Huay Xai in Bokeo Province, across the Mekong River from Chiang Khong, Thailand, grants visas on arrival to most nationalities.

See p217 for details on Mekong River boat travel between Huay Xai, Pak Beng and Luang Prabang.

If you're heading to Hongsa in northern Sainyabuli Province, coming from Luang Prabang, take the slow boat from the ferry pier as far as Tha Suang (US$8, half day), where you can continue on to Hongsa by jumbo. You can also disembark at Pak Beng (US$10) and head north to Udomxai and Luang Nam Tha.

Smaller, faster speedboats from the pier in Ban Don pound up the Mekong to Tha Suang (US$15, two hours), Pak Beng (US$20, three hours) and Huay Xai (US$30, six hours) in double the time.

Nong Khiaw & Muang Khua

Most passengers and cargo going to Nong Khiaw travel by road nowadays as it's much quicker than by boat. Slow boats still head up the Nam Ou to Nong Khiaw (US$12, four or five hours) from the ferry pier, but less frequently than they used to. Dates are posted on a chalkboard in front of the Navigation Office in Luang Prabang about a week in advance of the departures. You can also book this through any number of tour operators in town. The Nong Khiaw landing is sometimes referred to as Muang Ngoi, or as Nam Bak, a larger village to the west.

The same situation applies to Muang Khua, further up the Nam Ou – it's more quickly reached by road than by slow boat. Slow boats do travel to Muang Khua (US$20, eight to nine hours) when there are sufficient passengers, or on posted dates.

When there are sufficient passengers, speedboats travel from Luang Prabang to Nong Khiaw (US$16, two hours) and Muang Khua (US$30, four hours).

Be sure to inquire thoroughly as to river conditions before embarking on a Nam Ou trip; from mid-February on it's not unusual for speedboat pilots to get stranded in Nong Khiaw, unable to bring their boats back until the rains arrive in May or June.

Tha Deua, Pak Lai & Vientiane
Once in a blue moon slow cargo boats travel between Luang· Prabang and Vientiane (US$40, around three days) via Tha Deua (US$8, six hours). Passenger travel on these boats, except for merchants accompanying fragile cargo, is rare now that Rte 13 is sealed and fast. The fare depends on the size of your group, how much space is in the boat and your bargaining skills, but expect to pay around US$40 to Vientiane, or about US$8 to Tha Deua. Bear in mind that these boats are not kitted out with passenger seats like those travelling between Huay Xai and Luang Prabang. They are basically large floating trucks, and it actually makes for a brilliant experience.

When there are sufficient passengers, or they're chartered, speedboats travel downriver to Vientiane (US$40, eight or nine hours) via Tha Deua (US$15, one hour) and Pak Lai (US$25, four to five hours).

BUS & TRUCK
Interprovincial buses and trucks – large *săwngthăew* – operate out of two bus terminals in Luang Prabang. In general, vehicles going to destinations north of Luang Prabang leave from the northern bus terminal (on Rte 13 about 4km north of the town centre, past the turn-off for Luang Prabang International Airport) while those going south leave from the southern bus terminal (several kilometres south of the town centre near the Luang Prabang Provincial Stadium). There are a few exceptions to this, due to the fact that different transport companies operate in each terminal, and on certain routes they compete.

The following travel times are only estimates – in Laos such factors as number of passengers, number of stops, the weather and road conditions affect travel times. Departure times may also change so check for updates when you're in town.

Vientiane
From Luang Prabang public buses go to Vientiane (ordinary, $9, 11 hours, five to eight daily; air-con, $10, 11 hours, two daily) leave from the southern bus terminal. The same buses stop in Vang Vieng (ordinary, US$7.50,

six to seven hours; air-con, US$8.50, six to seven hours). The air-con buses leave between 6.30am and 9am in the morning.

For quicker and more comfortable transport, try the travel agents in town who can also arrange minivan transport (US$18, eight hours, four daily) and VIP bus (US$12, 10 hours, two daily) to Vientiane. The VIP buses aren't exactly modern, but they have air-con and once every seat is taken, they are full (as opposed to public buses which use the 'never full' approach).

Anyone who suffers motion sickness should take necessary precautions before the trip to Vang Vieng. See p113 for details on buses from Vientiane to Luang Prabang.

Udomxai, Luang Nam Tha & Phongsali
Luang Prabang is linked with Udomxai and Luang Nam Tha Province via paved roads. However, the road from Udomxai to Phonsavan is mostly unpaved. From the northern bus terminal, daily passenger trucks and buses go to Udomxai (US$4.50, five hours, 8am), Luang Nam Tha (US$7, eight hours, 9am and 4.30pm) and to Phongsali (US$10, 15 hours, 4pm).

For further details on transport to and from these places, see the Getting There & Away sections for Udomxai (p192) and Luang Nam Tha (p200).

Nong Khiaw & Sam Neua
From the northern terminal, *săwngthăew* and buses head north to Nong Khiaw (US$3.20, four hours, two to five daily), and Sam Neua (US$10, 16 hours, 4pm).

Xieng Khuang, Sainyabuli & Huay Xai
From the southern bus terminal there are daily buses to Phonsavan (US$8.50, 10 hours, 8.30am), Sainyabuli (US$4, five hours, 9am) and Huay Xai (US$14, eight to 11 hours, 5pm), although in the rainy season it's best to take a boat up the Mekong River to reach Huay Xai due to the road conditions.

Getting Around
TO/FROM THE AIRPORT
From the airport into town, jumbos (motorised three-wheeled taxis) or minitrucks charge a uniform US$5.50 per vehicle, and up to six can share the ride. In the reverse direction you can usually charter an entire jumbo for US$2 to US$4.

NORTHERN LAOS

TO/FROM THE SPEEDBOAT LANDING

A shared jumbo into town from the speedboat landing in Ban Don costs around US$1 per person depending on your bargaining skills. To charter one, figure on US$4 to US$6.

LOCAL TRANSPORT

Most of the town is accessible on foot. Jumbos charge US$0.40 per kilometre in town, although they usually just ask foreigners for US$1 a ride.

Motorcycles can be hired from several shops in the town centre for US$5 a day. Bicycles are available from many of the same shops, as well as from guesthouses, for between US$1 and US$3 a day depending on the condition of the bike.

AROUND LUANG PRABANG
Pak Ou Caves

ถ้ำปากอู

About 25km by boat from Luang Prabang along the Mekong River, at the mouth of the Nam Ou, are the famous **Pak Ou caves** (admission US$1). Two caves in the lower part of a limestone cliff facing the river are crammed with Buddha images of all styles and sizes (but mostly classic Luang Prabang standing Buddhas). The lower cave, known as Tham Ting, is entered from the river by a series of steps and can easily be seen in daylight. Stairs to the left of Tham Ting lead around to the upper cave, Tham Phum, which is deeper and requires artificial light for viewing – be sure to bring a torch (flashlight) if you want to see both caves.

On the way to Pak Ou, most people have the boat stop at small villages on the banks of the Mekong. Opposite the caves at the mouth of the Nam Ou, in front of an impressive limestone cliff called Pha Hen, is a favourite spot for local fishers.

VILLAGES NEAR PAK OU

The most common village stop on the way to the caves is **Ban Xang Hai**. The name means 'Jar-Maker Village' because at one time that was the cottage industry here. Nowadays the jars come from elsewhere, and the community of around 70 fills them with *lào-láo* made in the village. Australian archaeologists have excavated pots beneath the village that may be 2000 or more years old.

At **Ban Thin Hong**, opposite the jar village and close to Pak Ou, a cave excavated in early 2000 has yielded artefacts dating back 8000 years, including stone, bronze and metal tools, pottery, fabrics and skeletons.

During the late dry season (from January to April) villagers paddle out to sand bars in the middle of the Mekong and pan for gold using large wooden platters.

GETTING THERE & AWAY

You can hire boats to Pak Ou from Luang Prabang's charter boat landing on the Mekong River. A longtail boat costs US$15 for one to three people and US$20 for four to five people, including petrol. The trip takes two hours upriver, and one hour down, not including optional stops at villages. Speedboats from Ban Don (US$15, 30 minutes upriver and 20 to 25 minutes down) can carry up to six passengers and take up to two hours for the total trip.

Travel agencies and guesthouses around town advertise tours for US$5 per person.

You can also get to Pak Ou by jumbo. To the village of Ban Pak Ou it costs US$7 for one or two people, US$10 for three to four, or US$12 for up to eight. From here, you then take a ferry (US$1.50) to the caves.

Ban Xang Khong

This comely village sits on the banks of the Mekong River, about 3km east of the town centre, and is home to numerous weaving and textile houses. The work is very fine quality and cheaper than comparable products sold in town. Often you'll be buying directly from the artist, and you can watch some of the weavers in action. There are also two excellent cheap paper galleries and some craft shops. All the houses are scattered along the one dirt road that runs parallel to the Mekong. It's a pleasant walk or bike ride from the town centre (around 40 to 60 minutes). Alternatively a *săwngthăew* there and back should cost about US$4.

Among the best houses:

Lao Textile Natural Dyes (☎ 252803) Owned by the same family that runs OckPopTok (p155), with work of the same high standard.

Miss Bouekham Silk (☎ 253988) Silk and cotton textiles.

Miss Bouvane Syodomphan Lao Silk Shop (☎ 253863) Brightly coloured, very distinctive pieces.

Ms Boualay Douang Dara (☎ 253771) Less chance of finding individual pieces, but the quantity on offer keeps prices very cheap.

Nalong Kone Paper & Souvenir Shop Elephant-dung paper impregnated with flowers and colour is made into lanterns, photo albums, wall prints, gift cards and all manner of gifts.

Ban Phanom & Mouhot's Tomb

ບ້ານພະນົມ/ສຸສານມູໂຫ

This Thai Lü village, 6km east of Luang Prabang, is also well known for cotton and silk hand-weaving. You can wander around the village and watch the weavers in action on their hand looms, or stop in at the textile centre to view a variety of potential purchases. For a while Ban Phanom prices were higher than in Luang Prabang, but these days Luang Prabang has gone much more upmarket and Ban Phanom textiles can be a good bargain.

Beyond Ban Phanom near the river stands the tomb of the French explorer Henri Mouhot, best known as the person who 'discovered' Angkor Wat. Mouhot perished of malaria in Luang Prabang on 10 November 1861, and the French erected a tomb over his grave six years later. The last entry in his journal was 'Have pity on me, O my God' and his engraved tomb was neglected until found by foreign aid staff in 1990. Mouhot's simple monument is about 4km along the Nam Khan from Ban Phanom; follow the road along the river until you see a sign on the left, descend a track towards the river, then walk about 300m along a path (upriver from the sign) to reach the whitewashed tomb.

GETTING THERE & AWAY

Many visitors ride hired bikes or motorbikes to Ban Phanom and Mouhot's tomb. If you're pedalling, note that the terrain is hilly, so don't forget to bring a bottle of drinking water. By motorbike it takes only around 40 minutes.

Săwngthăew from Luang Prabang to Ban Phanom leave from Talat Dala several times a day for US$0.70 per person.

Tat Kuang Si

ຕາດກວາງຊີ

This beautiful spot 32km south of town has a wide, many-tiered waterfall tumbling over limestone formations into a series of cool, turquoise pools. With thick banks of green and florid vegetation on either side, the setting is impossibly picturesque and photogenic. The lower level of the falls has been turned into a well-maintained **public park** (parking US$0.25, admission US$2) with shelters and picnic tables;

some of the trees near the waterfall have been labelled. Just past the entrance are two enclosures, one housing sun bears and the other a tiger. All have been confiscated from poachers and are kept here in preference to releasing them to the same certain fate.

A trail ascends through the forest along the left side of the falls to a second tier that is more private (most visitors stay below) and has a pool large enough for swimming and splashing around. A cave behind the falls here goes back 10m. For a view of the stream that feeds into the falls you can continue along a more slippery extension of the trail to the top of the falls. The best time to visit is between the end of the monsoon in November and the peak of the dry season in April.

On the way to Kuang Si you'll pass Ban Tat Paen, a scenic Khamu village with a cool stream, rustic dam and several miniature waterfalls. **Vanvisa 2 Guest House** (per person incl breakfast & dinner US$20) is a simple Lao-style wooden guesthouse in this village, operated by the owner of the Vanvisa Guest House in Luang Prabang. With advance notice, they can arrange cooking classes for US$15 per person.

GETTING THERE & AWAY

Freelance guides in Luang Prabang offer trips by jumbo for US$5 per person for two people, US$4 per person for three to five people, or US$3 for six to eight. An alternative to going by jumbo all the way would be to take a boat an hour (25km) down the Mekong and a shorter jumbo ride over to the falls. Freelancers can arrange the latter trip for about the same cost as a straight jumbo trip.

Many visitors make their way to Tat Kuang Si by hired bicycle or motorcycle, stopping in scenic villages along the way. If you opt to cycle be warned that it's a dirt, rocky road, and the climb in the midday sun can be taxing so take plenty of water.

Tat Sae

ນໍ້າຕົກຕາດແຊ່

Found at a conjunction of the Huay Sae and the Nam Khan, the falls at Tat Sae feature multilevel limestone formations similar to those at Kuang Si except that the resulting pools are more numerous, the falls are shorter in height, and the site is much closer to Luang Prabang. Popular with local picnickers on weekends, this place is almost empty during the week.

A 35-minute, 15km jumbo ride south of town will take you to the turn-off from Rte 13, then it's 2km to the pristine Lao village of Ban Aen on the Nam Khan. Jumbo drivers will travel to Ban Aen for US$6.75 for one to two persons, US$8 for three to four, or US$9 for up to eight persons, including waiting time in the village while you visit the falls for a few hours. You could also easily reach Ban Aen by bicycle – there's a sign reading 'Tat Se' at the Rte 13 turn-off.

From the riverbanks at Ban Aen you can hire a boat to the falls – only five minutes upstream – for US$1 return.

The falls are best visited from August to November when there is still an abundance of water in the pools.

NONG KHIAW

ໜອງຂຽວ

☎ 071

Nong Khiaw is a sleepy market village with a humbling backdrop in northern Luang Prabang Province. It dozes on the west bank of the Nam Ou, which cuts a languid swathe between close mountains, soaring in a haphazard tumble of slate and green. Arriving at the town's dry and dusty bus stop isn't the best introduction and many travellers breeze through in favour of longer stays at Muang Ngoi Neua. But once you venture out, particularly if you cross the striking bridge to Ban Sop Houn, where the Nam Ou meets the Nam Houn, the surrounding scenery rears in dramatic form.

Locals sometimes refer to Nong Khiaw as Muang Ngoi (the name of the surrounding district). As a result many visitors confuse this Muang Ngoi with the Muang Ngoi Neua – a town found about an hour north of Nong Khiaw by boat.

In addition to Tham Pha Thok (see below), there are other caves in the vicinity of Nong Khiaw, and also a few Hmong villages within easy trekking distance.

Nong Khiaw and Ban Sop Houn have electricity from 6pm to 10pm.

SIGHTS & ACTIVITIES

Fine **trekking** opportunities present themselves in the range of wooded karst around Nong Khiaw. A 40-minute walk will take you to **Tham Pha Thok**, a limestone cave where villagers lived during the Second Indochina War, and to a nearby waterfall. To find the cave, walk 2.5km east of the bridge along Rte 1, then look for a clearly visible cave mouth in a limestone cliff to your right, about 100m from the road. Descend along a path from the road to reach the cave.

Longer treks to Hmong and Khamu villages are arranged by the Sunset Guest House (opposite) for around US$10 per day. You can also try your hand at traditional river fishing with nets in the wide rocky shallows of the Nam Ou. Ask at Bamboo Paradise (opposite) for more info.

The **GreenHeart Foundation** (www.wowlao.com) based at Chan-a-Mar Guest House is a twofold operation: GreenHeart Gallery – at the front of the property, selling Lao and Bhutan textiles – and GreenHeart Tours. The latter offers small-group tours to the region with an emphasis on traditional Lao culture and cuisine and a commitment to cultural preservation. GreenHeart also supports a bomb-removal program and takes on administrative volunteers occasionally, for those looking to inject more than currency into the local community.

Sleeping & Eating

Near the bridge and river landing there are a number of rustic but charming and cheap guesthouses. Most have restaurants attached.

NONG KHIAW

Manypoon Guest House (r US$2) The friendly Manypoon offers rooms with mosquito nets and shared bathroom downstairs. Its restaurant boasts one of the better local guesthouse kitchens.

Phayboun Guest House (r US$2-6) Phayboun consists of a few rooms in a two-storey wooden house that's in better condition than most of the others in town. Rooms have private bathrooms and screened windows to keep the mosquito at bay.

Sengdao Guest House (r US$8, without bathroom US$3) With the best views from the Nong Khiaw side of the river, this guesthouse has simple huts or pleasant bamboo bungalows with clean en suites. All rooms have mosquito nets and fans. There's also a fairy-lit restaurant (meals US$1 to US$2), open for breakfast, lunch and dinner, overlooking the river.

Bouavieng Restaurant (meals US$0.50-2; ☯ breakfast, lunch & dinner) This simple restaurant serves a variety of fairly good Lao rice and noodle dishes.

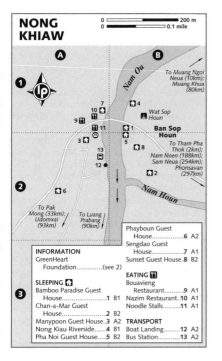

NONG KHIAW

INFORMATION	
GreenHeart	
Foundation..............(see 2)	
SLEEPING	
Bamboo Paradise Guest	
House......................**1** B1	
Chan-a-Mar Guest	
House......................**2** B2	
Manypoon Guest House..**3** A2	
Nong Kiau Riverside......**4** B1	
Pha Noi Guest House......**5** B2	

Phayboun Guest	
House................**6** A2	
Sengdao Guest	
House................**7** A1	
Sunset Guest House..**8** B2	
EATING	
Bouavieng	
Restaurant..........**9** A1	
Nazim Restaurant...**10** A1	
Noodle Stalls........**11** A1	
TRANSPORT	
Boat Landing.........**12** A2	
Bus Station............**13** A2	

To Muang Ngoi
Neua (10km);
Muang Khua
(80km)

Wat Sop
Houn

**Ban Sop
Houn**

To Tham Pha
Thok (2km);
Nam Noen (188km);
Sam Neua (254km);
Phonsavan
(297km)

To Pak
Mong (33km);
Udomxai
(93km)

To Luang
Prabang
(90km)

Nazim Restaurant (meals US$2-3; ☺ lunch & dinner) Good subcontinent curries are to be had at this open-walled restaurant, which also advertises itself as (not-so-Indian) Deen's Restaurant.

There are also noodle stalls selling tasty *fŏe* (US$0.50 to US$1) near the bridge.

BAN SOP HOUN

The best views of the Nam Ou are from this side of the river and most guesthouses take advantage of them with balconies.

Bamboo Paradise Guest House (r US$2) The friendly owners make this spot a good choice. The decent bungalows have floor mattresses, visitors are encouraged to brush up on their Lao language skills, and owners can organise guides for trekking.

Sunset Guest House (r US$12, s/d without bathroom US$2.50/5) This Lao-style guesthouse on stilts has simple rooms with floor mattresses, fans and mosquito nets in a rickety bamboo-thatch house. There are also much more comfortable bungalows with en suites and private balconies overlooking the river. A common sitting area with floor cushions

provides great sunset views. Good Lao and Thai food is available.

Pha Noi Guest House (r US$3) Right next to the bridge, this spot has five rickety but pleasant bamboo bungalows with small balconies and basic bathrooms attached. They have a fine view of the river.

Nong Kiau Riverside (☎ 254770; www.nongkiau .com; s/d incl breakfast US$12/16) Every now and then you stumble across a delightful bargain that makes you feel like royalty – this fits the bill perfectly. This quiet resort has huge bungalows with timber floors, bamboo walls, stone bathrooms and wide balconies. The four-poster beds have high-slung mosquito nets and there are ceiling fans and writing desks in every room. There's also a good restaurant (meals US$1.50 to US$3), open for breakfast, lunch and dinner, serving tasty Lao food, and the setting is gorgeous.

Chan-a-Mar Guest House (www.wowlao.com; r US$100) Exclusive in that it's small and pricey, this spot has a modest number of bamboo bungalows with lovely open-air bathrooms overlooking the surrounding foliage. Each bungalow has comfortable beds, mosquito nets, fans and sleeps up to three people. Rates include a large breakfast along with evening cocktails and appetisers. The bungalows are pleasant but a stretch for the price, although your money also supports the GreenHeart Foundation based here (see opposite).

Getting There & Away

Rte 1 crosses the river here via a steel bridge. Rte 13 north from Luang Prabang meets Rte 1 about 33km west of town at Pak Mong.

BOAT

Boat travel along the Nam Ou south of Nong Khiaw has largely been eclipsed by travel along the improved Rte 13, but it's still possible. See p156 for information on boat travel from Luang Prabang. In high season boats heading to Muang Ngoi Neua (US$1.80, one hour) leave regularly until about 3pm. In low season they're less regular, but boats usually tout for business between noon and 2pm, when buses arrive from Luang Prabang. Tickets are bought at an office at the bus station. These boats infrequently continue on to Muang Khua (US$10, seven hours).

BUS & SĂWNGTHĂEW

Săwngthăew going to Udomxai (US$2.50, three hours, three daily) leave from the west end of the bridge. You can also take one of the more frequent *săwngthăew* southwest to Pak Mong (US$1.80, two hours), then change to another *săwngthăew* to Udomxai (US$2, two to three hours from Pak Mong). *Săwngthăew* and buses to Luang Prabang (US$3.20, four hours, two daily) depart between 8am and 11am; the earliest is usually a public bus.

If you're heading east towards Hua Phan or Xieng Khuang, you can get a bus to Sam Neua (US$7, 12 hours, one daily).

MUANG NGOI NEUA

ເມືອງງອຍເໜືອ

The tourist trail has well and truly found this idyllic village, tucked away on a peninsula on the Nam Ou, but unless you're here in peak season the locals still outweigh the *falang*. Flanked by shadowy, majestic mountains on all sides, it's a pretty spot to hang the boots for a few days, or rather give them a workout on some picturesque trekking. Because it's cut off from regular roadways by that steep mountain range, Muang Ngoi Neua remains isolated and small (perhaps that's why the rooster cacophony seems louder here), and the narrow dirt footpaths lined with coconut palms that act as roads are trafficked only by unhurried pedestrians or two-wheeled transport.

Like most river villages in Laos, Muang Ngoi Neua's basic layout parallels the river on which the village once depended for its traditional livelihoods, fishing and farming. Tourism, however, has now become the main source of income and every second building seems to be a guesthouse or restaurant in need of business.

Information

Generators provide electricity from 6pm to 10pm. There's no internet or telephone facilities, so it's wise to let anxious loved ones know you may be out of range (some travellers come for a couple of days, but stay a couple of weeks). You can exchange US dollars at several guesthouses, but for rather unexceptional rates, and a couple of pharmacies sell basic medicines.

Sights & Activities

You'll find a sea of signs advertising guides for fishing trips, tubing, kayaking and trekking in town. Some guides speak decent English, which is imperative if you want to enjoy the cultural aspect of any activity. Treks cost US$5 to US$10 per day, depending on the destination, and tubing costs around US$1.50 per day.

Recommended, English-speaking guides include **Sang Tours** (🕐 8am-9pm), not far from the boat landing on the main 'street', and **Lao Youth Travel** (www.laoyouthtravel.com; 🕐 7.30-10.30am & 1.30-6pm), to the left of the boat landing. Run by a former village school teacher, **Muang Ngoi Tour Office** (🕐 7-8am & 6-7pm) is located behind the main street 300m south of the boat landing – look for the signs directing you. From here you can organise small-group treks to Hmong and Khamu villages for around US$8 per day including food, and fishing trips.

CAVES

Behind the village and its rice fields sits a curtain of cliffs riddled with caves, streams and forest. Two of these caves can easily be visited in under an hour's walk. At the southern end of the village, turn left (east) in front of Kaikeo Restaurant, and follow the path through a large rural schoolyard and into an area of brush and secondary forest. Just past the schoolyard there is a shelter where village volunteers collect an admission fee of US$1 per person.

After a pleasant 5km walk you'll come to a crystal-clear stream running into **Tham Kang** (Middle Cave), a large limestone cavern entrance on your left. You can either wade into the cave via the stream – which can become rather deep in spots during the rainy season – or climb a limestone bank along the left side of the stream. The roof of this cave is at least 30m high for some distance, after which the floor descends into darkness.

About an additional five minutes' walk along the same trail is **Tham Pha Kaeo** (Holy Image Cave), with a much smaller entry and a small stone Buddha image to one side. According to Speleo Nederland, a Dutch caving group that has explored both caves, Tham Kang and Tham Pha Kaeo are connected via a subterranean passageway.

Beyond the caves you can easily walk to mixed Lao and Khamu villages of **Huay Bo** (3km), **Huay Sen** (4km) and **Ban Na** (another 1km from Huay Sen). If you fancy a village stay, try the **Konsavan Guest House** (US$1) in Huay Bo.

NORTHERN LAOS

TAT MOK

Twenty minutes downriver by boat is a trail that leads to a series of falls called Tat Mok. The walk from the landing to the falls takes about an hour. The third in the series reaches 40m tall, and you'll find pools for a cool dip at all three.

TEMPLES

Muang Ngoi, which may date back to the 15th century, once had three Buddhist monasteries: **Wat Neua** at the northern end of town, **Wat Kang** in the middle and **Wat Tai** in the south. All three were destroyed during the Second Indochina War, but among the remains of Wat Tai you can still see the main pediment for the original *sĭm*, as well as a pedestal for an old Buddha that once sat at one end of the *sĭm*. That image has long disappeared, to be replaced by a cement Buddha and a few smaller wooden Buddhas beneath a little tin-roof shelter at one end of the pediment. The original brick-and-stucco entry stairway to the slightly elevated wat grounds is also still standing.

Of Wat Kang there appears to be virtually no trace.

Wat Neua, at the northern end of the village not far from the main boat landing, has been rebuilt. As at Wat Tai, the ground supporting the monastery was artificially raised to protect the facilities from flooding. Here again you can see the original steps ascending the raised earth. It appears the current *sĭm* may have been rebuilt atop the original brick-and-stucco pediment. Now the only functioning wat in the village, it has been renamed Wat Okat Muang Ngoi. The Wat's drum often resounds at 4am, providing an early but resonant wake-up call.

Sleeping

Most guesthouses here are strung out along the main footpath that leads from the landing, down through the centre of the village. Most consist of either bamboo-thatch huts or bamboo rooms in a longhouse, with shared bathroom. Many have attached restaurants. Be warned that rats can be a problem in Muang Ngoi Neua.

Saylom Guest House (r US$2) This guesthouse is on the right-hand side of the boat ramp as you walk into town, and has clean bungalows with decent beds, mosquito nets and hammocks outside. All have shared bath-

rooms. The owners are friendly and the restaurant has good river views.

Sunset Guest House & Talee 2 (r US$2) At the southern end of the village, this guesthouse is tucked away from the sounds of generators at night. Hastily built bamboo bungalows stand side-by-side along the river, all with mattresses on the floor, mosquito nets, river views and hammocks.

Ning Ning (r US$2) The handful of simple bungalows here have mosquito nets, hammocks and wee balconies. The deck restaurant here has a lovely outlook.

Phetdavanh Guest House (r US$2) This sturdy two-storey building on the main strip is clean and secure. Rooms are rat-free and have crisp sheets and tidy bathrooms, but the structure is devoid of hammocks and river views.

Lattanavongsa Guest House (r US$5) A step up from the bamboo bungalow brigade, this friendly place to the left of the boat landing has a solid concrete structure (although the walls are bamboo), where rooms have clean, tiled private bathrooms but no fans. The beds are monastically firm but the whole place sits around a grassy lawn with a statue fashioned from (spent) UXO (unexploded ordnance).

Aloune Mai Guest House (r US$5) Off the path and away from the river, this is a good spot for a quiet night's sleep. The relatively recent structure contains solid timber and bamboo rooms with private bathrooms. It's signposted off the main path through town.

More options:

Kham's Place Bungalows & Restaurant (r US$1) Simple bungalows and cold beer.

Shanti Guest House (r US$1) Small and simple.

Eating

Sengdala Bakery (meals US$0.50-1.50; ☻ breakfast, lunch & dinner) This bakery–restaurant serves good rice, noodles, curries, soups and salads, but also distinguishes itself with great pancakes and baguettes. Water-bottle refills cost US$0.10 per litre.

Nang Phone Keo Restaurant (meals US$0.50-1.50; ☻ breakfast, lunch & dinner) The '*falang* roll' of peanut butter, sticky rice and vegies lure ravenous travellers to the open-air deck of this restaurant on the main street. Also whips up good *fŏe*.

Lattanavongsa Guest House (meals US$1-2; ☻ breakfast, lunch & dinner) The restaurant at this guesthouse cooks outstanding spring rolls and a hearty noodle soup. The open-air deck is large and ambient.

Basic Lao and Western food including omelettes, soups and fried rice can be found at **Sky** (meals US$0.80-1.50) and **Shanti** (meals US$0.80-1.50).

Getting There & Away

Regular boats ply between Nong Khiaw and Muang Ngoi Neua (US$1.80, one hour). Departures are most frequent in the morning, with the last boat leaving Nong Khiaw at around 3pm or 4pm. Boats also run far less frequently to Muang Khua (US$8, five hours). If you have the opportunity to take this trip, do! This section of the Nam Ou is isolated and the river cuts a khaki ribbon through an endless verdant spread.

NAM BAK & PAK MONG

ບ້ານບາກ/ປາກມອງ

These two towns, respectively 23km and 33km west of Nong Khiaw, are little more than supply depots along Rte 1 between the Nam Ou and Udomxai. Pak Mong, at the junction of Rtes 1 and 13, has eclipsed Nam Bak since the sealing of Rte 13 north from Luang Prabang. Both towns have post offices, guesthouses (one in Pak Mong, two in Nam Bak) and noodle shops, but Pak Mong is the place to make bus connections: west to Udomxai (US$2, two to three hours) and Luang Nam Tha (US$3.50, six hours); east to Hua Phan and Xieng Khuang Provinces; and south to Luang Prabang (US$2.30, two hours).

XIENG KHUANG PROVINCE

Xieng Khuang Province is marked by contrasts, cultural and geographical. In the centre, broad ochre hills, laid bare from logging and slash and burn agriculture, coat the semiflat terrain. Orderly farms intersperse the brown hues, and the eucalypts and pine plantations invoke antipodeans impressions. As the province stretches north it finds the base of Hua Phan's mountainous ascent. Flying in from the south, one is struck by the beauty of high green mountains, rugged karst formations and verdant valleys. But as the plane begins to descend, you notice how much of the province is pockmarked with bomb craters in which little or no vegetation grows. Xieng Khuang was one of the most devastated provinces of the war. Virtually every town and village in the province was bombed at some point between 1964 and 1973.

The province has a total population of around 230,000 people, mostly comprised of lowland Lao, Vietnamese, Thai Dam, Hmong and Phuan. The original capital, Xieng Khuang, was almost totally bombed out, so the capital was moved to Phonsavan (often spelt Phonsavanh) after the 1975 change of government. Near Phonsavan is the mysterious Thong Hai Hin (Plain of Jars).

The altitude (average 1200m) in central Xieng Khuang creates an excellent climate – not too hot in the hot season, not too cold in the cool season and not too wet in the rainy season. The coldest months are December and January, when visitors should come with sweaters or pullovers, plus a light jacket for nights and early mornings.

History

Although briefly a part of the Lan Xang kingdom in the 16th century, Xieng Khuang has more often than not been an independent principality or a vassal state of Vietnam under the name of Tran Ninh. From the early 19th century until 1975, central Xieng Khuang – including the Plain of Jars – was a recurring battle zone. In 1832 the Vietnamese captured the Phuan king of Xieng Khuang, publicly executed him in Hué and made the kingdom a prefecture of Annam, forcing people to adopt Vietnamese dress and customs. Chinese Haw also ravaged Xieng Khuang in the late 19th century, which is one of the reasons Xieng Khuang accepted Siamese and French protection later that century.

Major skirmishes between the Free Lao and the Viet Minh took place from 1945 to 1946, and as soon as the French left Indochina the North Vietnamese commenced a build-up of troops to protect Hanoi's rear flank. By 1964 the North Vietnamese and Pathet Lao had at least 16 anti-aircraft emplacements on the Plain of Jars, along with a vast underground arsenal. By the end of the 1960s, this major battlefield was undergoing almost daily bombing by American planes, as well as ground combat between the US-trained and supplied Hmong army and the forces of the North Vietnamese and Pathet Lao.

A single 1969 air campaign – part of the secret war waged in Laos by the US Air Force and the CIA – annihilated at least 1500 buildings in the town of Xieng Khuang, along with some 2000 more on the Plain of Jars, permanently erasing many small towns and villages off the map. Continuous saturation bombing forced virtually the entire population to live in caves; 'The bombs fell like a man sowing seed' according to one surviving villager.

North Vietnamese troops did their share of damage on the ground as well, destroying nearby Muang Sui, a city famous for its temples, and virtually all towns or villages held by the Royal Lao Army (RLA) in the west of the province.

Now that eastern Xieng Khuang is peaceful, village life has returned to a semblance of normality, although the enormous amount of war debris and UXO spread across the central and eastern areas of the province are a deadly legacy that will remain here for generations to come.

PHONSAVAN
ໂພນສະຫວັນ
☎ 061 / pop 60,000

It may not be the prettiest of Laos' provincial capitals, but urban charm isn't what brings tourists to Xieng Khuang's largest city. They arrive in droves to visit the Plain of Jars and other sights in the area. Most congregate in the central crisscross of streets, peppered with none-too-appealing buildings and a hodgepodge of new and old guesthouses. But Phonsavan sprawls itself over a much larger distance, and the human milieu of tourists and locals, combined with the undulating backdrop, holds a bucolic charm.

Traditionally, the area surrounding Phonsavan and the former capital of Xieng Khuang has been a centre of Phuan language and culture (part of the Thai-Kadai family, like Lao, Siamese and Thai tribal). The local Vietnamese presence continues to increase and you'll hear the Vietnamese language in the streets almost as frequently as Lao and Phuan.

Outside the province most Lao (including Lao Airlines) still call the capital 'Xieng Khuang'.

Information

EMERGENCY
Ambulance (☎ 195)
Fire (☎ 190)
Police (☎ 191, 312449)
Mines Advisory Group (MAG; ⏰ 4-8pm) Office for the British organisation involved in clearing UXO in the province; see p167.

INTERNET ACCESS
Hot Net (Rte 7; per hr US$3; ⏰ 8am-10pm) Slow internet connections.
Phoukham Guest House (⏰ 312121; per hr US$3; ⏰ 8am-10pm) Similarly slow internet access.

MEDICAL SERVICES
Lao-Mongolian Friendship Hospital (☎ 312166) Good for minor needs, but medical emergencies will need to be taken to Vientiane.

MONEY
Travel agents in town also offer currency exchange.
Lao Development Bank (☎ 312188) Currency exchange; has two branches.

POST
Post office (☎ 312005; ⏰ 8am-4pm Mon-Fri, to noon Sat) Has a domestic phone service.

TOURIST INFORMATION
Provincial Tourist Office (☎ 312217) Useful for simple information if you can find any staff. Private travel agencies are a better option.

TRAVEL AGENCIES
Tours to the Plain of Jars can be booked through guesthouses and a number of travel agents for US$10 to US$12 per person in a mini-van of around eight passengers. The following also offer tours further afield and transport bookings.
Diethelm Tours (☎ 213200, 020-5561116) Plain of Jars and Muang Khoun tours plus kayaking on the Nam Nguen from May to September.
Indochina Travel (☎ 312121, 020-5975556)
Sousath Travel (☎ 312031; www.malyht.laotel.com; Maly Hotel) A reader fave. Trips further afield include Tham Piu, Muang Sui, Sam Neua and Long Cheng (former site of the CIA's infamous mountain base during the Second Indochina War).

Dangers & Annoyances
Take care when walking in the fields around Phonsavan as UXO are common. Muddy

NORTHERN LAOS

NORTHERN LAOS

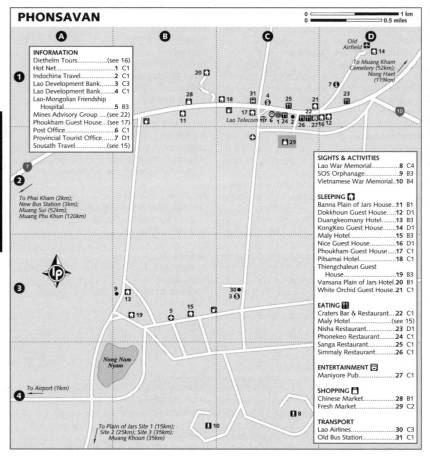

PHONSAVAN

INFORMATION
Diethelm Tours................(see 16)
Hot Net...............................1 C1
Indochina Travel.................2 C1
Lao Development Bank........3 C3
Lao Development Bank........4 C1
Lao-Mongolian Friendship
  Hospital..........................5 B3
Mines Advisory Group ....(see 22)
Phoukham Guest House....(see 17)
Post Office...........................6 C1
Provincial Tourist Office.......7 D1
Sousath Travel................(see 15)

To Phai Kham (2km);
New Bus Station (3km);
Muang Sui (52km);
Muang Phu Khun (120km)

Old Airfield

To Muang Kham
Cemetery (52km);
Nong Haet
(119km)

Lao Telecom

Nong Nam Nyam

To Airport (1km)

To Plain of Jars Site 1 (15km);
Site 2 (25km); Site 3 (35km);
Muang Khoun (35km)

SIGHTS & ACTIVITIES
Lao War Memorial...............8 C4
SOS Orphanage....................9 B3
Vietnamese War Memorial..10 B4

SLEEPING
Banna Plain of Jars House..11 B1
Dokkhoun Guest House.......12 D1
Duangkeomany Hotel.........13 B3
KongKeo Guest House.......14 D1
Maly Hotel.........................15 B3
Nice Guest House...............16 D1
Phoukham Guest House......17 C1
Pitsamai Hotel....................18 C1
Thiengchaleun Guest
  House.............................19 B3
Vansana Plain of Jars Hotel.20 B1
White Orchid Guest House.21 C1

EATING
Craters Bar & Restaurant....22 C1
Maly Hotel.....................(see 15)
Nisha Restaurant................23 D1
Phonekeo Restaurant.........24 C1
Sanga Restaurant...............25 C1
Simmaly Restaurant..........26 C1

ENTERTAINMENT
Maniyore Pub....................27 C1

SHOPPING
Chinese Market...................28 B1
Fresh Market......................29 C2

TRANSPORT
Lao Airlines........................30 C3
Old Bus Station.................31 C1

---

areas are sometimes dotted with 'bomblets' – fist-sized explosives that are left over from cluster bombs dropped in the 1970s.

Sights

Just south of town are two major war memorials, each standing on a different hill-top about 1km apart. One is Lao and the other Vietnamese, both in the shape of Lao-style stupas. The hill-top with the **Lao War Memorial** (☼ sunrise-sunset) affords sweeping views of Phonsavan. Built in 1998, the monument is inscribed with the slogan 'The nation remembers your sacrifice'. Large, polished granite slabs standing nearby bear the inscribed names of PL soldiers who died in the area. The stupa-like monument allegedly

contains the bones of 4500 who died during the war.

At the **Vietnamese War Memorial** (☼ sunrise-sunset), the faux stupa contains the bones of Vietnamese soldiers who died in battle in northeastern Laos, and is emblazoned with the inscription 'Lao-Vietnamese solidarity and generosity forever'. If the gates are locked, wait for a caretaker to come along and unlock them.

East of town is the large **Muang Khan Cemetery** – unique because it mixes together Thai Dam animist tombs, Catholic headstones and Lao *thâat kádụuk* (Buddhist reliquary).

There's a German-funded **SOS Orphanage** just west of the main crux of town. You can visit students on weekdays during school hours and on Saturday mornings; the visitor book here indicates that it's a positive experience on both sides. When you arrive, ask the nearest staff member what the best method of involvement is – it may be joining teachers in a classroom or something as simple as playing football with the kids.

Sleeping
BUDGET

KongKeo Guest House (☎ 211354; www.kongkeojar.com; r US$4-5) Hidden off the main street, the popular KongKeo has four spartan rooms with shared bathroom, or there's a scattering of great en-suite bungalows with cool interiors. The industrious owner can organise tours.

Dokkhoun Guest House (☎ 312189; r US$5-8) In two multistorey blocks, the ever-popular Dokkhoun has spartan rooms with mosquito nets and good mattresses. The more expensive rooms have private showers and TVs although they're a tad dark and dank.

Nice Guest House (r US$6) If the grouting holds up in this new guesthouse then it will indeed remain very nice. Clean and generous rooms contain firm beds, warm covers, ceiling fans

and petite, pretty bathrooms with hot water. Rooms upstairs share a balcony.

Banna Plain of Jars House (☎ 212484; www.bannagroup.com; r US$10) This polished guesthouse has unadorned but neat rooms upstairs with tiled floors and comfy beds. Some have small TVs and some lack sunlight so ask to see a few before you settle. A small and cheery restaurant downstairs serves breakfast.

Pitsamai Hotel (☎ 211678; r US$10) This small and personable hotel has wee but welcoming rooms with immaculate tiled floors, frilly floral décor, small TVs and compact bathrooms. They're fan-cooled and have big sunny windows.

Thiengchaleun Guest House (☎ 211774; r US$10-15) This isolated and pleasant guesthouse has sunny rooms with pastel hues, large Western-style bathrooms, small TVs and ceiling fans. The pricier rooms are bigger and have small lounge settings.

Phoukham Guest House (☎ 312121; r US$4-5) Opposite the bus station, the rooms in this shophouse-style building are cheap and compact, with warm-water bathrooms and lumpy beds. The price includes 20 minutes

---

UXO IN XIENG KHUANG

Unexploded munitions, mortar shells, white phosphorous canisters (used to mark bomb targets), land mines and cluster bombs of French, Chinese, American, Russian and Vietnamese manufacture left behind from nearly 100 years of warfare have affected up to half of the population in terms of land deprivation and accidental injury or death. A distressing profusion of UXO are still imbedded in rice fields, beneath schools, houses and playgrounds, and even in the branches of bamboo trees, where they lodged themselves when the trees were seedlings. Many of the reported unexploded ordnance (UXO) accidents that have occurred in Xieng Khuang happened during the first five years immediately following the end of the war, when many villagers returned to areas of the province they had evacuated years earlier. Today about 40% of the estimated 30–60 casualties per year are children, who continue to play with found UXO – especially the harmless-looking, ball-shaped 'bomb light units' (BLUs, or bombies) left behind by cluster bombs – in spite of public warnings.

Hunters also open or attempt to open UXO to extract gunpowder and steel pellets for their long-barrelled muskets – a risky ploy that has claimed many casualties. Several groups are working steadily to clear the province of UXO, including the Lao National UXO Programme (UXO Lao), financed by a UN trust fund that has significantly increased the availability of multilateral aid for this purpose.

Tourists can play a role in reducing the number of UXO and their casualties by visiting the **Mines Advisory Group** (MAG; 4-8pm) office in Phonsavan. MAG is a British organisation that has been clearing UXO in conjunction with UXO Lao since 1994. The office has an information display and sells T-shirts and DVDs to fund its operations. Buying a US$10 T-shirt will not only contribute to the organisation's efforts, but will also raise awareness simply by being on your back. The DVDs are distressing but important in that they show the full scale of the trauma, from footage of US bombers in action to the ongoing casualties of this horrific legacy.

of internet use and the staff can be very helpful with travel info.

MIDRANGE & TOP END

Maly Hotel (☎ 312031, www.malyht.laotel.com; r US$8-50; ✷) The well-run Maly offers 30 comfortable rooms in a variety of standards. Rates vary according to the size of the room and whether they have a TV and/or balcony, but the best value are the US$15 rooms. A cosy restaurant downstairs has some of the best Lao and Western cooking in town, especially if you order in advance. The owner speaks good English, German and French, and Sousath Travel is located here (p165).

White Orchid Guest House (☎ 312403; r US$10-40) A commendable option in the midrange bracket, this hotel has a range of rooms from small, dark and cheap, to bright and clean with private bathrooms. The top floor and top-priced rooms have oceans of room and lacquered tables settings. All rooms have TV and a modicum of Lao textiles and décor.

Duangkeomany Hotel (☎ 020-5516553; r US$25) The best value in town for fussy travellers, this hotel has large carpeted halls off which spring capacious rooms with bright interiors, crisp bedding, TVs, wardrobes and gleaming bathrooms with tubs. Excellent value.

Vansana Plain of Jars Hotel (☎ 213170; vphotel@laotel.com; s/d/ste US$30/40/50) Opulent by Phonsavan standards, this grand hotel occupies its own summit at the top of a gravel road. The commodious rooms have plush carpeting, large TVs, minibars, tasteful décor and big tubs in the bathroom. Each also has a small balcony with great views over town. The VIP suites are huge. Popular with tours.

Eating

Phonekeo Restaurant (meals US$1; ✷ breakfast, lunch & dinner) This friendly noodle shop serves the best *fŏe* in town.

Simmaly Restaurant (☎ 211013; meals US$1-1.50; ✷ breakfast, lunch & dinner) Simmaly's menu may be simple, but what it whips up it does well. Fried spicy meats, rice dishes and good noodle soups. Service is friendly and speedy and it's popular with both tourists and locals.

Sanga Restaurant (Sa-Nga; ☎ 312318; meals $1-4; ✷ lunch & dinner) The clean and well-run Sanga, near the market and post office, offers an ex-

tensive menu of Chinese, Thai and Lao food, including good *yám* (a tart, spicy Thai-style salad), *tôm yám* (spicy lemon grass–based soup), *khào khùa* (fried rice) and *fŏe*, plus a few Western food items.

Maly Hotel (meals US$1-5) This hotel has a great selection of Lao and Western food. It's especially good during the rainy season when *hét wâi* (wild matsutake mushrooms) are plentiful.

Nisha Restaurant (meals US$1-4; ✷ breakfast, lunch & dinner) Tuck into delicious aloo ghobi, dosas, tikka masalas and rogan josh at this spacious Indian diner. The list of vegetarian options is long and you can down a whole tandoori chicken for US$4.

Craters Bar & Restaurant (☎ 020-7805775; meals US$2-4; ✷ breakfast, lunch & dinner) This very cosmopolitan eatery has a mostly *falang* menu of club sandwiches, pizzas and even an Australian T-bone. There are also Thai and Lao dishes tamed to Western palates. Two shell cartridges mark the entrance so you can't miss it. You can also exchange money here and book bus and air tickets.

Entertainment

Maniyore Pub on the main street serves as a dimly lit nightclub and drinking den. It's well-patronised by locals and backpackers and can be quite busy on weekends.

Shopping

The fresh market behind the post office stocks exotic fruits you won't typically see elsewhere in Laos, such as Chinese pear. Other local delicacies include *nok ạen dạwng* (swallows stored whole in jars until they ferment), and *hét wâi*, which grow wild around Xieng Khuang and fetch high prices in Japan.

West of the main strip, the **chinese market** (✷ 8am-6pm) is over two storeys tall and sells plenty of plastic tack and souvenirs, although you can also get some decent gold and silver.

Getting There & Away

AIR

Lao Airlines (☎ 212027), located next to the Lao Development Bank, flies to/from Vientiane (one way/return US$53/101, daily except Tuesday and Thursday) and to/from Luang Prabang (one way/return US$40/77, Wednesday, Friday and Saturday).

BUS
Most buses now leave from the new bus station, which is about 4km west of town. The relocation from the old bus station has been slow, but there's a good chance that everything will have moved by the time you read this.

Most long-distance buses depart between 7.30am and 8am.

Sam Neua
Daily buses run between Phonsavan and Sam Neua (US$7, eight to 10 hours, two daily) along Rte 7 and Rte 6.

Vientiane & Luang Prabang
Buses head daily to Vientiane (ordinary, US$9, 11 hours, 9.30am and 4pm; VIP, US$10, 11 hours, 7.30am), Vang Vieng (ordinary, US$7.50, six hours, 7.15am; VIP US$10, six hours, 7.30am) and Luang Prabang (ordinary, US$8.50, 10 hours, 8.30am; VIP US$9.50, 10 hours, 8.30am).

Paksan
Phonsavan is linked with Paksan in Bolikhamsai Province by a road in deplorable condition – especially south of Tha Thom (102km from Phonsavan). There is, however, a daily bus to Paksan (US$8, 8am).

Within Xieng Khuang Province & to Vietnam
There are public buses and *săwngthăew* to Muang Kham (US$2, two hours, four daily), Muang Sui (US$2, one hour, three daily) and Nong Haet (US$2, four hours, four daily).

Other destinations include Lat Khai (Plain of Jars site 3; US$1, 30 minutes, one daily) and Muang Khoun (US$2, 30 minutes, six daily).

Buses also go all the way through to Vinh in Vietnam (US$11, 11 hours, 6.30am Tuesday, Thursday and Sunday).

Getting Around
Jumbos are the main form of public transport in town. The price anywhere within a 3km radius is US$0.50 to US$1 per person. A ride to the airport will cost US$1.50 per person.

Cars and 4WDs can also be hired through the guide services at Sousath Travel at the Maly Hotel or through just about any guesthouse or hotel for jaunts outside of town.

You could easily visit all three Plain of Jars sites by bike or motorcycle. Guesthouses can help you find motorcycle hire (per day

US$15), and Craters Bar & Restaurant (see opposite) has two bicycles for rent (US$3 per day).

PLAIN OF JARS
ທົ່ງໄຫຫິນ

The Plain of Jars is a large area extending around Phonsavan from the southwest to the northeast, where huge jars of unknown origin are scattered about in over a dozen groupings. Despite local myth (see the Plain of Jars boxed text, p170), the jars have been fashioned from solid stone, most from a tertiary conglomerate known as molasse (akin to sandstone), and a few from granite. 'Quarries' (actually boulder fields) west of Muang Sui have been discovered containing half-finished jars. Apparently the jars were carved from solid boulders of varying sizes, which goes a long way to explain the many different sizes and shapes.

Many of the smaller jars have been taken away by various collectors, but there are still several hundred or so on the plain in the five major sites (out of the 20 or so known to exist) that are worth visiting.

Site 1 (Thong Hai Hin; admission US$0.70), the biggest and most accessible site, is 15km southwest of Phonsavan and features 250 jars, most weighing 600kg to one tonne each. The largest jar weighs as much as six tonnes and is said to have been the victory cup of mythical King Jeuam and so is called Hai Jeuam. The site has two pavilions and

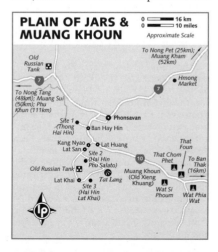

PLAIN OF JARS & MUANG KHOUN

NORTHERN LAOS

A POTTED HISTORY

Among the most enigmatic sights in Laos are several meadowlike areas close to Phonsavan littered with large stone jars. Quite a few theories have been advanced as to the functions of the jars – that they were used as sarcophagi, or as wine fermenters, or for rice storage – but there is no evidence confirming one theory over the other. Lying around are the stone lids for a few of the jars. White quartzite rocks have also been found lying next to some of the jars, along with vases that may have contained human remains.

Madeleine Colani, a noted French archaeologist who spent three years studying the Plain of Jars in the 1930s, found a human-shaped bronze figure in one of the jars at Site 1, as well as tiny stone beads. The current whereabouts of these cultural artefacts and other Colani discoveries – photographs of which exist in her 1935 *Megalithes du Haut Laos (Megaliths of Highland Laos)* – are unknown. You can see the relief of a human figure carved onto jar No 217 at Site 1 – a feature Colani missed. Aerial photographic evidence suggests that a thin 'track' of jars may link the various jar sites in Xieng Khuang.

The jars are commonly said to be 2000 years old, but in the absence of any organic material associated with the jars – eg bones or food remains – there is no reliable way to date them. The jars may be associated with the equally mysterious stone megaliths ('menhirs' in Colani's words) found off Rte 6 on the way north to Sam Neua, and/or with large Dongson drum-shaped stone objects discovered in Luang Prabang Province. Archaeological investigation has been slowed by years of war and by the presence of unexploded ordnance (UXO).

Meanwhile, local legend says that in the 6th century a cruel chieftain named Chao Angka ruled the area as part of Muang Pakan. Sensitive to the plight of Pakan villagers, the Tai-Lao hero Khun Jeuam supposedly came down from southern China and deposed Angka. To celebrate his victory, Khun Jeuam had the jars constructed for the fermentation of rice wine. According to this version, the jars were cast from a type of cement that was made from buffalo skin, sand, water and sugar cane, and fired in a nearby cave kiln. A limestone cave on the Plain of Jars that has smoke holes in the top is said to have been this kiln (the Pathet Lao used this same cave as a shelter during the war).

---

restrooms that were built for a visit by Thailand's crown prince.

Two other jar sites are readily accessible by road from Phonsavan. **Site 2** (Hai Hin Phu Salato; admission US$0.70), about 25km south of town, features 90 jars spread out across two adjacent hillsides. Vehicles can reach the base of the hills, so it's only a short if steep walk to the jars.

More impressive is 150-jar **Site 3** (Hai Hin Lat Khai; admission US$0.70). It's about 10km south of Site 2 (or 35km from Phonsavan) on a scenic hill-top near Lat Khai, southeast of Phonsavan. Ban Xieng Di contains a small monastery where the remains of Buddha images that were damaged in the war have been displayed. The villagers, who live in unusually large houses compared with those of the average lowland Lao, grow rice, sugar cane, avocado and banana. Villagers can lead you on a short hike to a local waterfall called **Tat Lang** (admission US$0.50). To reach the jar site you must hike around 2km along rice paddy dykes and up the hill.

Many smaller sites can also be seen in Muang Kham district, but none of them contain more than 40 or so jars. Only Sites 1, 2 and 3 are considered to be reasonably free of UXO. Even at these sites you should take care to stay within the jar areas and stick to worn footpaths.

Getting There & Away

The easiest way to see the jars is on a tour from Phonsavan – see p165. Options include hiring a jeep and driver, which costs US$14 per person for four passengers, or taking a minivan tour, which costs US$10 to US$12 for eight passengers. These tours generally include the three main sites, the wreck of a Russian tank which was bombed during the war, and a pit stop for *lào-láo* at a village. Optional extras for a higher price include Viet Cong bunkers and Muang Khoun.

You can also visit the sites independently by bicycle or motorcycle; see p169. Alternatively, charter a jumbo from Phonsavan to Site 1, 15km from the Phonsavan market, for US$5 return including waiting time, for up to six people. For Sites 2 and 3 your best bet is to arrange a 4WD and driver through one of the guesthouses or hotels. There is a bus from Phonsavan to Site 3 (Hai Hin Lat Khai; US$1, 30 minutes, one daily).

PHONSAVAN TO NONG HAET

Rte 7 heads east from Phonsavan to north Vietnam via Muang Kham and Nong Haet (see Map p166).

About 30km east of Phonsavan en route to Muang Kham (northern side of the road) is **Nong Pet**, a Hmong village with a picturesque spring surrounded by rice fields; it's said to be the source of the Nam Ngum. A sizable **Hmong market** (7am-7pm Sun) is held here every Sunday. Between Muang Kham and Nong Haet you may notice Thai Dam funerary shrines along the way – large white tombs with prayer flags, offerings of food and a pile of the departed's worldly possessions.

Muang Kham is little more than a rustic highway trading post, but there are several jar sites in the vicinity. Further east along Rte 7, 119km from Phonsavan, is the market town of **Nong Haet**, situated only 13km short of the Vietnamese border.

See p169 for information on bus and *săwngthăew* to this area.

Mineral Springs
ບໍ່ນ້ຳຮ້ອນ

Two hot mineral springs can be visited near Muang Kham. **Baw Nyai** (admission US$0.50; 9am-7pm) is the larger of the two and lies 18km east of Muang Kham, 51km from Phonsavan. The spring source is in a heavily wooded area where several bamboo pipes have been rigged so that you can bathe nearby, although the experience is a little disappointing owing to the muddy texture of the water. A much nicer way to experience the spring water is to overnight here at the very comfortable bungalows of **Nam Horn Resort** (US$10). These timber structures with mosquito nets and fans have lovely baths which you can fill with spring water. Alternatively **Sonebot Guest House** (US$10) has more modern rooms, but again, baths you can fill with spring water.

Baw Noi (Little Spring) feeds into a stream just a few hundred metres off Rte 7, a couple of kilometres before Baw Nyai on the way from Muang Kham. You can sit in the stream where the hot spring water mixes with the cool stream water and 'adjust' the temperature by moving from one area to another.

The easiest way to get to the springs is by hiring a *săwngthăew* or tuk-tuk from Muang Kham for around US$5.

Tham Piu
ຖ້ຳປິວ

At this cave near the former village of Ban Na Meun, an estimated 200 to 400 people were killed when a fighter plane fired a single rocket into the cave during the Second Indochina War. A plaque identifies the date as 24 November 1968, but other accounts claim the incident occurred in December 1969. The floor of the large cave, in the side of a limestone cliff, is littered with rubble from the partial cave-in caused by the rocket, as well as with minor debris left from the two-storey shelter built into the cave. Government propaganda says many of those who died in the bombing were Lao women and children, but another version of events says that it was a makeshift Vietnamese hospital where troop casualties were treated. Adding credence to the latter story is the fact that Vietnamese officials visited the cave in the 1980s, removed virtually all of the human remains and artefacts, and took them back to Vietnam.

Although Tham Piu is certainly a moving sight, the journey to the cave is the main attraction, since it passes several Hmong and Thai Dam villages and involves a bit of hiking in the forest. From the cave mouth is a view of the forest and the plains below. A stream and small irrigation dam at the base of the cliff is picturesque. Another cave known as **Tham Piu Song** (Tham Piu 2) can be found a little higher up on the same cliff. This one has a small entrance that opens up into a large cavern; since it wasn't bombed, the cave formations can be seen in their original state. Don't forget your torch (flashlight).

Tham Piu is just a few kilometres east of Muang Kham off Rte 7.

GETTING THERE & AWAY
You can hire a 4WD and driver in Phonsavan for around US$30 a day for trips to Tham Piu and back.

To get to Tham Piu by public transport, you'd have to take a Nong Haet bus and ask to be let out at the turn-off for Tham Piu. From the turn-off, walk towards the limestone

CROSSING THE VIETNAMESE BORDER AT NAM KHAN & NAM CAN

The Nam Khan–Nam Can crossing became an official international border crossing in 2003, but so far few people aside from Lao and Vietnamese seem to use it. Coming up to Nam Can (200km north of Vinh) from the Vietnamese side is quite a journey, with winding mountain roads as you approach the lip of the Plain of Jars. After exiting Vietnam, you'll enter Laos at Nam Khan, 13km east of Nong Haet via Rte 7. Tourist visas are available on arrival for US$30. From Nong Haet you can reach Phonsavan by bus (US$2, three to four hours, four daily). Between bus departures you may be able to charter a private car for between US$30 and US$40.

It's also possible to catch a bus directly between Phonsavan and Vinh in Vietnam (US$11, 11 hours, Tuesday, Thursday and Sunday), with an immigration pit stop at the border.

cliff north of the road until you're within a kilometre of the cliff. At this point you have to plunge into the woods and follow a honeycomb of trails to the bottom of the cliff and then mount a steep, narrow trail that leads up to the mouth of the cave. It would be best to ask for directions from villagers along the way or you're liable to get lost; live ordnance is another danger. Better still, find someone in Phonsavan who knows the way and invite them to come along for the hike.

MUANG KHOUN (OLD XIENG KHUANG)

ຊຽງຂວາງເກົ່າ(ເມືອງຄູນ)

pop 14,000

Muang Khoun's ancient capital was so heavily bombarded during the Second Indochina War (and ravaged in the 19th century by Chinese and Vietnamese invaders) that it was almost completely abandoned by 1975. More than 20 years after war's end the old capital is once again flourishing. Officially the town has been renamed Muang Khoun. Many of the residents are Thai Phuan, Thai Dam or Thai Neua, along with a smattering of lowland Lao and Vietnamese.

Only one French colonial building still stands: the former commissariat, now used as a social centre. The former palace of a Thai Phuan prince is in ruins. For the most part the town consists of nondescript wooden buildings with corrugated roofs, although outside of town you'll also see original Phuan-style stilted longhouses made of thick timber.

Several Buddhist temples built between the 16th and 19th centuries lie in ruins. The foundation and columns of **Wat Phia Wat** are still standing at the east end of town, along with a large seated Buddha. Sadly, the only intact Xieng Khuang–style temples left in Laos today – characterised by striking pentagonal silhouettes when viewed from the front – are in Luang Prabang. More modern **Wat Si Phoum** is the town's most active Buddhist temple.

That Foun (also called That Chomsi), a tall 25m to 30m jęhdii (Buddhist stupa) constructed in the Lan Xang/Lanna style, towers over the town. You can climb right through the foliage-covered stupa via a large cavity that Chinese Ho marauders tunnelled into the brick stupa over century ago to loot valuable Buddha images enshrined in the dome. Take a glance upwards once you're inside, and you can see the perfectly formed outline of a smaller, much older stupa that was 'entombed' by the larger one. From here you can also see historic **That Chom Phet** (reputedly built by the Cham) standing atop a nearby hill.

Ban Na Si, near Wat Phia Wat, is a sizable Thai Dam village. Around 16km further east along Rte 7B, the Thai Phuan village of **Ban Thak** is worth a visit to see its terraced rice fields and stately Phuan-style homes.

There are no sleeping options in Muang Khoun, and it's best visited as a day trip from Phonsavan. Opposite the market in the centre of town there is a row of noodle shops with basic Lao fare.

Shopping

If you ask around you may be able to buy Thai tribal textiles (especially Phuan, Thai Dam or Thai Neua) in town, although forget about buying antique Xieng Khuang styles – these were picked over long ago by collectors from Vientiane and abroad.

Getting There & Away

Several buses a day travel to/from Phonsavan (US$2, 30 minutes, six daily) from the market in the centre of town.

(Continued on page 181)

JOHN BANAGAN

Grounds of Wat Si Muang (p96), home of the guardian spirit of Vientiane

Reclining Buddha at eccentric Xieng Khuan (Buddha Park; p98)

CHRISTOPHER GROENHOUT

RICHARD I'ANSON

Famed Emerald Buddha housed in Haw Pha Kaeo (p95), Vientiane

Ceiling detail inside Patuxai (p97), Vientiane's 'vertical runway'

CHRISTOPHER GROENHOUT

Climb up to Tham Jang (p123) and take a dip in the cave's spring

Tubing down the Nam Song (p125), one of Vang Vieng's most popular activities

Bronze reclining Buddha inside the sacred Tham Phu Kham (Blue Lagoon; p123)

Crossing the Nam Song, Vang Vieng (p121)

JANE SWEENEY

'Tree of Life' mosaic set in classic Luang Prabang temple architecture at Wat Xieng Thong (p141)

KRAIG LIEB

Muang Sing (p203), a trade
centre for the Thai Dam people

Take the trip from Huay Xai to Luang Prabang along the
mighty Mekong (p218)

LAWRENCE WORCESTER

Buddha images inside Tham Ting, Pak Ou caves (p158)

Splash out on a Nam Tha river trip (p201)

Ritual bathing of the sacred Pha Bang, in the Royal Palace Museum (p139), Luang Prabang

Worth the climb – view of Luang Prabang from Phu Si (p143)

JOE CUMMINGS

Interior of Tham Pha Pa (p239), recently discovered cave with 229 bronze Buddha images

BILL WASSMAN

Buddha is believed to have stopped to rest at the site of That Ing Hang (p247)

Traditional Thai Lü architecture, Muang Sing (p203)

KRAIG LIEB

French colonial architecture, Savannakhet (p242)

Pha That Sikhottabong (p238), the site of a major festival each February

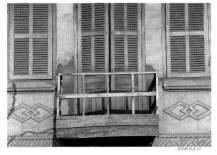

French era shophouses, Tha Khaek (p234)

Wat Luang (p256), Pakse, home to a monastic school featuring ornate pillars, carved wooden doors and murals

ANDERS BLOMQVIST

Ancient Khmer-style ruins, Wat Phu Champasak (p265)

BETHUNE CARMICHAEL

Spectacular Tat Fan plunges out of dense forest at the edge of Dong Hua Sao NPA (p283)

Take a longtail boat (p292) along the scenic Se Kong to Attapeu, the 'wild east' of Laos

JOHN ELK III

ANDREW BURKE

See silk weaved into stunning creations on Don Kho (p260)

Fisherman's cottage in laid-back Si Phan Don (Four Thousand Islands; p272)

ANTHONY PLUMMER

Rock and roll – Khon Phapheng Falls (p282)

VALERI

(Continued from page 172)

MUANG SUI

ເມືອງສຸຍ

pop 20,200

Once a city of antique Buddhist temples and quaint provincial architecture, Muang Sui became the headquarters of the Neutralist faction and 'Lima Site 108' (a landing site used by US planes) during the Second Indochina War. The North Vietnamese Army (NVA) totally razed Muang Sui late in the war after running the Royal Lao Army out of Xieng Khuang Province.

Like Muang Khoun (Old Xieng Khuang), the town is still rebuilding and is part of a new district called Muang Phu Kut. On some government maps the town is labelled Ban Nong Tang.

Visiting Muang Sui is best done as a day trip from Phonsavan.

Sights

Although the devastation wrought upon Muang Sui by the NVA seriously damaged every temple in the district, the ruins of several older temples can be seen. **Wat Ban Phong**, which still has resident monks, once contained a beautiful bronze Xieng Khuang–style Buddha called Pha Ong, said to hail from the 14th century. Lao communists reportedly transferred the image to Sam Neua in Hua Phan Province, although no one there seems to know anything about it.

Towards the eastern end of the district, a large picturesque natural lake called **Nong Tang**, flanked by high limestone cliffs, is a favourite local picnicking site. Five caves in the cliffs to the northeast of the lake can easily be visited by following posted signs, or you may be able to hire a local guide from one of the noodle stalls near the lake. Also near the lake is a semiruined 15th-century Xieng Khuang–style stupa called **That Banmang**.

Further afield are two more limestone caves that are well worth visiting. **Tham Pha** is a large network of caverns in which hundreds of small Buddha figures were stashed away to protect them from Haw invasions a couple of centuries ago. In the main entry cavern stands a very large sitting Buddha. The cave continues deep into the hillside, with ample passageways linking one cavern with another. The NVA reportedly used the cave as a hospital during the Second Indochina War. The local Lao have rigged electric lights in Tham Pha so that visitors can easily tour most of the accessible caverns, and will turn them on for a small donation. Near there is a second large cave, **Tham That**, which contains an old stupa ruin.

In the same general vicinity, but less accessible, is a **coffin cave** high up in a limestone cliff. To reach this one you'll have to do a little rock climbing and a lot of boulder scrambling. Inside the relatively small cave are the remains of large prehistoric wooden coffins, carved from single tree trunks. They've all already been opened and raided, but human skeletal remains and potsherds are still spread over the cave floor.

Around 32km east of Muang Sui, south of Rte 7, is a **boulder field** where you can see half-carved stone jars like those from the famous jar sites near Phonsavan.

Keep in mind that there are still a lot of UXO around Muang Sui. It's best to visit the area around Tham Pha, Tham That and the coffin cave with a guide who knows the terrain. Travel agents in Phonsavan (p165) can provide a 4WD vehicle (necessary to reach the coffin cave), driver and guide for up to

NORTHERN LAOS

THE LAST OF THE HMONG RESISTANCE

In the mountains of Xieng Khuang Province, pockets of Hmong resistance lived on nearly 30 years after the US defeat in Laos. These rebels reportedly financed their survival and armaments through the sale of agarwood (*mâi kítsanáa* in Lao, less commonly known as 'eaglewood' in English), a highly aromatic wood that fetches high prices in Arab countries where it's used for incense.

In early 2003 around 700 Hmong rebels in Xieng Khuang Province and neighbouring Luang Prabang Province surrendered to Lao authorities and were resettled in more populated areas of these provinces. Further surrenders of 170 in 2005 and more than 400 (mostly children) in 2006 have reduced the remaining rebels to just a handful. Poor living conditions have been the main impetus for surrender, although fear of persecution and human rights abuse has kept many in deplorable states of existence for decades.

WAR JUNK

War scraps have become an important part of the local architecture and economy in Xieng Khuang. Torpedo-shaped bomb casings are collected, stored, refashioned into items of everyday use or sold as scrap metal. Among the most valuable are the 1.5m-long casings from US-made cluster bomb units (CBUs), which split lengthways when released and scattered 600 to 700 tennis-ball-size bomblets (each containing around 250 steel pellets) over 5000-sq-metre areas.

Turned on its side, a CBU casing becomes a pot for plants; upright the casings are used as fence posts or as substitutes for the traditional wooden stilts used to support rice barns and thatched houses. Hundreds of casings like this can be seen in Xieng Khuang villages along Rte 7, which stretches northeast all the way from Phonsavan to Hanoi, or in villages in the vicinity of the old capital. Aluminium spoons sold in local markets are said to be fashioned from the remains of downed American aircraft.

Farmers from around the province keep piles of French, Russian, Chinese and American war junk – including Soviet tanks and pieces of US planes shot down during the war – beneath their stilt houses or in unused corners of their fields. They use bits and pieces as needed around the farm or sell pieces to itinerant scrap dealers who drive their trucks from village to village. These trucks bring the scrap to warehouses in Phonsavan, where it is sold to larger dealers from Vientiane. Eventually the scrap is melted down in Vientiane or across the Mekong River in Thailand as a source of cheap metal.

In Laos it is illegal to trade in leftover war weaponry – bombs, bullets, arms – of any kind. According to National Law Chapters 71 and 72, the illegal purchase, sale, or theft of these can result in a prison term of between six months and five years.

four people for an all-day journey to sites around Muang Sui, for US$80.

Getting There & Away

Rte 7 to Muang Sui from Phonsavan is in good condition and it takes less than an hour to drive the 52km distance. Buses leave Phonsavan (US$0.70, two daily) at approximately 7am and 1pm.

HUA PHAN PROVINCE

Steeped in florid beauty, and separated from surrounding provinces by long, bumpy bus rides, Hua Phan in Laos' emerald northeast retains a great degree of mystique. It's so far from Laos' tourist trail that the few travellers who do explore the region generally come in from Vietnam. But for anyone with a yen for the unspoilt it's a must. It's so mountainous that as the roads descend south from Sam Neua, the provincial capital, they curl down into seas of cloud trapped in cleaved valleys. The most inspiring time to visit is after the rains from April to October, when the bucolic *bâan* (villages) and their vast rice fields are lush.

For much of the last 500 years Hua Phan has been either an independent Thai Neua kingdom or part of an Annamese vassal state known as Ai Lao. It only became a Lao entity under French colonial rule, and the French commissariat at Sam Neua gave the Thai Neua chiefs and village headmen a great deal of autonomy. By the end of the Second Indochina War, all traces of the French presence had been erased.

A fifth of the province's modest population live in Sam Neua ('Northern Sam', a reference to its position towards the northern end of the Nam Sam). Twenty-two ethnic groups make the province their home, predominantly Thai Khao, Thai Daeng, Thai Meuay, Thai Neua, Phu Noi, Hmong, Khamu, Yunnanese and Vietnamese. The Vietnamese influence is very strong here as Sam Neua is closer to (and more accessible from) Hanoi than Vientiane.

As a tourist attraction, the province's main claim to fame is that Vieng Xai served as the headquarters for the Pathet Lao throughout most of the war years. But the small tourist industry here is finding its feet and planting them firmly in community-based adventures. Textiles in the 'Sam Neua' style – of tribal Thai origins – are another drawcard. The best textiles are said to come from the areas around Muang Son and Sop Hao.

SAM NEUA (XAM NEUA)

ບ້ອງເຫຼືອ(ສ່ຳເຫຼືອ)

☎ 064 / pop 46,800

Tucked away in a narrow valley formed by the Nam Sam at about 1200m above sea level, Sam Neua remains one of the country's least visited provincial capitals. Swimming in the milieu of history, eye-widening produce markets (and less appealing Chinese goods) and ethnic diversity, it possesses the tang ardently sought by inquisitive travellers. The town and its surrounds shift through great contrasts of climate and colour. From April to October the landscape is lush and warm from the rains. As the cooler dry sets in, flowers speckle the streets until the wet begin again in December. Sam Neua makes an excellent base to explore the rest of the province, which is slowly but surely opening up. Residents are mostly Lao, Vietnamese and Hmong, along with some Thai Dam, Thai Daeng and Thai Lü.

Information

Internet Shop (per hr US$1.20; 🕑 4-9pm Mon-Fri) Operates out of a private house in the evenings only.

Lao Development Bank (☎ 312171) Exchanges Thai baht or US dollars at the same rate as in Vientiane.

Lao Telecom (🕑 8.30-11.30am & 1-4pm Mon-Fri) IDD phone service available.

Post office Opposite the bus terminal.

Provincial Tourist Office (☎ 312567; 🕑 8am-noon & 1.30-4pm Mon-Fri) An excellent tourist office with English-speaking staff eager to help with information.

Sights

Sam Neua boasts one of the most colourful **markets** in the region. Products from China and Vietnam line up beside fresh produce and domestic goods. Sam Neua–style textiles can be found inside the main market building; prices can be very good, although quality is generally not up to the standard of markets in Vientiane. Local Hmong, Thai Dam, Thai Daeng and Thai Lü frequent this market. Connoisseurs agree that the Thai Daeng weave the most attractive textiles. Along with textiles you'll find field rats (live or skinned), banana leaves stuffed with squirming insects, and forks and spoons made with aluminium salvaged from war debris.

A 1978 **independence monument** mounted by a red star sits on a hill at the northwest edge of town; it's an easy climb, worthwhile for the modest view from the top. From this hill you can continue walking on to **Wat PhoXaysanalam**, about 2km from the market. The only monastery in town, with just five monks in residence (the minimum needed for holding the monastic ordination ceremonies), the wat features a small *sim* that was destroyed during

NORTHERN LAOS

SAMANA (RE-EDUCATION CAMPS)

Hua Phan is infamous for the *samana* (re-education camps) established around the eastern half of the province immediately following the 1975 Revolution. Inspired by Vietnamese examples (several in Hua Phan were actually designed and constructed by Vietnamese architects and labourers), these camps mixed forced labour with political indoctrination to 'rehabilitate' thousands of civil servants from the old regime. Many Royal Lao Government officials were lured to the camps with the promise of a two-week 'job training' session, only to find themselves captives of the Pathet Lao for many years.

Although almost all of the camps were closed by 1989, it is alleged that Re-education Camp No 7 somewhere near Sam Neua still held political prisoners into this century. According to Amnesty International (AI), three political prisoners (all former senior officials in the Lao People's Democratic Republic – PDR – government) were sentenced to 14 years' imprisonment in Hua Phan for peacefully advocating a multiparty political system in 1992. There were no defence lawyers at their trial. All three subsequently became very ill and one of the prisoners, 59-year-old Thongsouk Saysangkhi (former deputy minister of science and technology), died of alleged maltreatment in February 1998. Three more political prisoners received life sentences in 1992 after having been held without trial for 17 years.

The harsh conditions in these camps fell well short of international minimum standards, and prisoners were denied medical treatment, visits and all access to reading or writing material.

Although as many as 30,000 people were thought to have been interned by 1979 – the *samana* numeric peak – the Lao government has never issued a statement either confirming or denying the existence of the camps. It is unknown whether any remain active today.

NORTHERN LAOS

the war and rebuilt in 1983. The backdrop of misty green hills seems to remove the wat from its urban setting entirely. The two small *thâat* you'll see on the way to the independence monument are the last remnants of local prewar temples.

There are some weaving houses near the wat where you can watch weavers master their craft. You'll need guidance from the Tourist Office to visit, however, mostly because it's rude to just wander in. Sadly the best textiles produced here are shipped directly to Japan and Singapore where they fetch high prices.

Chasing the riverbank north, Sam Neua has its very own **promenade**, which begins at the northern end of the market and follows the Nam Sam for kilometre or so. A walk here reveals backyards and residential vegetable plots. In June and July you'll also see people planting rice, and in November, harvesting. Two suspension bridges join the promenade to the opposite side of the river, so you can continue your exploration further afield.

Sleeping

Phootong Guest House (☎ 312271; r US$3.50) Simple, cheap and central, this small guesthouse behind a shopfront has basic rooms with ceiling fans and mosquito nets. They're a little bit tired but decent value and the owners are extremely gracious. The attached bathrooms are petite and have cold water only.

Bounhome Guest House (☎ 312223; r US$4-6) Plenty of sunlight fills the fine little rooms upstairs in this guesthouse. Their neat interiors contain small dressers and firm, low-set beds. They're fan-cooled and clean.

Paeng Pane Guest House (☎ 312006; r US$5) A short walk from the centre of town, this big, airy structure contains bright rooms with wallpapered floors. The narrow, attached bathrooms have hot water. Open sporadically, there's a simple restaurant next door serving noodle soups (meals US$0.50 to US$1).

Shuliyo Guest House (☎ 312462; r US$5-6) Tucked into an alley near the market, Shuliyo has rudimentary but welcoming rooms with decent bathrooms, hot water, ceiling fans and aged beds. There's a lovely central sitting area with free tea and coffee.

Kheamxam Guest House (☎ 312111; r US$5-7) This pastel-hued, corner hotel is the best value in town. It offers a range of rooms from neat and simple affairs with spotless, shared bathrooms, to large corner rooms with satel-

lite TV, attached hot-water bathrooms and street views.

Eating

For cheap *fŏe*, samosas, spring rolls and fried sweet potato, the **market** (6am-6pm) is the place to go.

Dan Nao Restaurant (☎ 314126; meals US$1-1.50; breakfast, lunch & dinner) This neat, petite restaurant has a spotless interior and serves a limited but tasty array of noodles, grilled chicken and beef, and fried dishes with plenty of ginger, chilli and garlic. The menu is in English so there's no guesswork.

Sokdee Restaurant (☎ 312380; meals US$1-1.50; breakfast, lunch & dinner) A good spot for the adventurous gastronome, Sokdee serves authentic Lao food a-la intestine and meats that diverge from chicken, beef and pork. Not ideal for vegetarians, but it's extremely popular with the locals.

Chittavanh Restaurant (meals US$1.20-2; breakfast, lunch & dinner) Extremely popular with local diners, Chittavanh serves fabulous *fŏe* as well as good *tôm yám*, Cantonese stir-fries, and the usual roster of noodle and rice dishes.

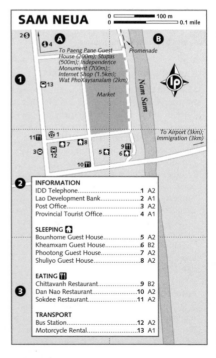

SAM NEUA

0 — 100 m
0 — 0.1 mile

To Paeng Pane Guest House (200m); Stupas (500m); Independence Monument (700m); Internet Shop (1.5km); Wat PhoXaysanalam (2km)

Promenade

Nam Sam

Market

To Airport (3km); Immigration (3km)

INFORMATION
IDD Telephone..1 A2
Lao Development Bank.........................2 A1
Post Office..3 A2
Provincial Tourist Office.....................4 A1

SLEEPING
Bounhome Guest House.......................5 A2
Kheamxam Guest House......................6 B2
Phootong Guest House........................7 A2
Shuliyo Guest House.............................8 A2

EATING
Chittavanh Restaurant.........................9 B2
Dan Nao Restaurant...........................10 A2
Sokdee Restaurant..............................11 A2

TRANSPORT
Bus Station...12 A2
Motorcycle Rental...............................13 A1

The décor is dominated by demure calendar girls, the smells are great and the table condiments will knock your socks off.

Getting There & Away

AIR

Lao Airlines (☎ 312023; airport) currently flies between Vientiane and Sam Neua three times a week (one way/return US$75/143, Monday, Wednesday and Saturday). The airport lies around 3km from the main area of town. A motorcycle taxi from the airport to any lodging in town costs around US$1, but you'll need to flag one down as they don't hang around waiting for fares. From the market, however, it's easy to hire jumbos or *săwngthăew* to the airport.

BUS

Sam Neua can be reached by road from both Xieng Khuang and Udomxai Provinces. From Phonsavan the journey travels along the good, flat Rte 7 to Muang Kham. From Muang Kham Rte 6 is decent by Lao standards to Nam Noen, a small truck stop near the junction of Rtes 6 and 1 just north of the Hua Phan Province border. Between Nam Noen and Sam Neua it's a steep, winding and rough – but highly scenic – dirt road that passes through numerous Lao, Hmong and Khamu villages.

There are two buses a day from Sam Neua to Phonsavan (US$7, eight to 10 hours, 9am and noon); the bus then continues on to Vientiane (from Sam Neua US$13, 20 to 24 hours).

A daily bus heads southwest along Rte 6 and then Rte 1 to Nong Khiaw (US$7, 12 hours, 8am) in Luang Prabang Province, and continues on to Luang Prabang (from Sam Neua US$8, 16 hours). Alternatively you can stop at Nong Khiaw and continue to Udomxai. The Nong Khiaw to Nam Noen leg runs along winding roads and brilliant scenery, passing many Blue Hmong villages along the way and an international narcotics control project in the district of Muang Vieng Thong (also known as Muang Hiam).

MOTORCYCLE

You can rent a motorcycle for day trips from a shop between the Provincial Tourist Office and the bus station. The owner doesn't speak English, but you can ask for linguistic assistance from the Tourist Office. The cost of rental is about US$6, plus a US$500 deposit or your passport. All bikes need to be returned to the shop by 6pm.

AROUND SAM NEUA

A dirt road on the right-hand side of Wat Pho Xaysanalam winds its way out of Sam Neua and into surrounding villages. If you follow it for 11km you'll stumble onto the **Ban Tham Buddha cave**. The journey out here is stunning – an anarchy of tumbling landscape interrupted by ordered rice fields and tidy *bâan*. The cave is just before Ban Tham; if you reach the only school in the district you've gone 100m too far.

You can easily walk to Ban Tham but only if you're prepared to walk back. Alternatively you can hire a motorbike, catch the daily *săwngthăew* from Sam Neua (US$0.50, 40 minutes, noon) in one or both directions, or charter a *săwngthăew* (about US$12 whether it's one way or return).

A 580-sq-km area of forested hills along the Nam Sam near Sam Thai in the southeastern section of the province was declared the **Nam Sam National Protected Area** (Nam Sam NPA) in 1993. Nam Sam NPA is thought to be a habitat for wild elephant, various gibbons, gaur, banteng, tiger, clouded leopard, Asiatic black bear and Malayan sun bear. Despite the NPA designation – and even though the area can only be reached by a 4WD track from Vieng Xai – shifting cultivation by hill tribes and cedar logging by Chinese companies threatens the forests.

Sam Tai itself is famous for producing magnificent textiles. If you feel like getting off the beaten track you can head out here on a daily *săwngthăew* from Sam Neua (US$3.40, six hours, 6.50am) and spend the night at **Syphanh Guest House** (☎ 314449; US$2) or the more comfortable **Sengkeo Guest House** (☎ 314416; r US$3-5).

Tat Saloei (also known as Phonesai Waterfall), about 35km south of Sam Neua off the road to Nam Noen, is a waterfall said to be very beautiful just after the rainy season. Reaching a height of 100m, it's a popular picnic spot for locals. To get here catch a *săwngthăew* travelling to Nam Noen and tell the driver where you want to stop. It should cost around US$1.20.

NORTHERN LAOS

The road northeast from Sam Neua to Sop Hao on the Vietnamese border passes by several Hmong and Yao villages, which make for fascinating day trips or more. There's a daily *săwngthăew* from Sam Neua (US$1.60, two hours, 6.30am). The border at Pahang is open to Vietnamese and Lao citizens only. If you want to extend your stay in the area, there are several guesthouses in Sop Hao, including **Sop Hao Guest House** (☎ 314375; US$3) and **PhouBao Guest House** (☎ 314387; US$3). Both have basic rooms with fans, mosquito nets and share bathrooms.

Officials in the area can be very touchy about foreigners owing to speculation that the last of Laos' *samana* camps may still operate here. It's believed that the Royal Family were transported to a *samana* camp near Sop Hao in 1977 in order to prevent them becoming a symbol of resistance against the Pathet Lao. The conditions they faced were harsh and it is alleged that the Crown Prince Say Vong Savang died in May 1978, followed 11 days later by his father King Savang Vatthana from starvation. Queen Khmaboui died in December 1981. Eyewitness have said they were all were buried in unmarked graves outside the camp's perimeter.

Hintang Archaeological Park (Suan Hin)
ສວນຫີນ

This 'stone garden' *(suan hin)*, far more interesting than its name makes it sound, is better known locally as Hintang Archaeological Park, although it's also known locally as Sao Hin Tang (Standing Stone Pillars). Often likened to Britain's Stonehenge because of its rough-hewn, 2m stone uprights, Suan Hin is as much of a mystery as the Plain of Jars – indeed they may be historically related. The stone chosen for the megaliths coincides with that used to fashion the jars; beneath some of the pillars are tunnel-like ditches whose purpose is as enigmatic as the pillars and jars themselves – current speculation suggests a funerary function and that these graves are around 2000 years old. The park has been nominated as a World Heritage site.

Large stone discs about a metre in diameter can also be seen lying among the menhirs. Local animist lore says the discs once sat atop the megaliths to form dining and drinking tables for a sky spirit named Jahn Hahn. The meaning of the discs is as lost to the world as that of the pillars.

The pillars are a 5.4km hike off Rte 6 via a road beginning at a point 55km southwest of Sam Neua. This road passes the village of Ban Pakha on the way.

To get here by public transport is a bit of a hassle because once you get off and make the hike, it could be several hours before another bus comes by. However, if you're up for it you can catch the daily *săwngthăew* from Sam Neua to Nam Noen and get off at Ban Pao (also known as Ban Natok, US$1.70, 2½ hours, 6.20am). From here it's a 6km walk to the park, which is signposted.

Alternatively you can inquire at the Tourist Office in Sam Neua about hiring transport out to Suan Hin – a private *săwngthăew* should cost around US$45 for the day. Sousath Travel (p165) in Phonsavan can also provide transport and guidance to Suan Hin.

SAM NEUA TO VIENG XAI
Whether or not you visit the famous Pathet Lao caves, Vieng Xai district is worth wandering about for its scenic beauty. Between Kms 11 and 12, coming from Sam Neua, is a fairly big Hmong Lai (Striped Hmong) village called **Ban Hua Khang**. After Km 13 you'll start seeing karst formations, many with cave entrances, along with pretty little valleys terraced in rice. At Km 20 there is an intersection; the right fork reaches Vieng Xai after 9km, then continues to Na Maew on the Vietnamese border (87km from Sam Neua), while the other road goes to Sop Hao.

Six kilometres before the Vieng Xai turn-off, coming from Sam Neua, is the 80m-high **Tat Nam Neua**. You can walk to the top of the falls straight from a bridge where the road crosses the Nam Neua just after the road forks towards Vieng Xai. For an all-in-one view from the bottom, take the left fork and proceed for 2km until you see some terraced rice fields on the right-hand side of the road. A trail winds for 1km or so through the fields, along and across a stream and through bamboo thickets before reaching the bottom. You may have to ask locally for directions as the trail isn't particularly obvious. Be sure to apply insect repellent to your feet and ankles in order to keep leeches at bay. As you'd expect, the falls are most beautiful just after the rainy season, when you can swim in the lower pools.

VIENG XAI

ວຽງໄຊ

☎ 064 / pop 32,800

The former Pathet Lao (PL) revolutionary headquarters of Vieng Xai sit in a striking valley of fertile hills and limestone cliffs riddled with caves, several of which were used to shelter PL officers during the Second Indochina War. The town is famous for the caves in which the stoic officers and some 23,000 people found shelter, but Vieng Xai itself is unbearably pretty. Manmade lakes spot the landscape and wildflowers explode in crimson and yellow to join the emerald and karst backdrop. The beauty of the terrain somehow underscores the decimation it suffered during the American bombing campaign.

Caves

According to the guides, there are approximately 400 caves in the district, 100 near Vieng Xai, and around a dozen with war history. Only a few years ago local authorities treated them as if they were a military secret, even while the National Tourist Authority of Laos (NTAL) in Vientiane promoted the caves as tourist attractions. Today, six of the caves are open to the public as revolutionary memorials and tourist attractions. Inside are former meeting rooms, government offices, markets, temples, printing presses, hospitals, army barracks and more.

The setting of the caves – inside a narrow and precipitous limestone-walled valley – is quite impressive. The PL leadership first started using them in 1964 because the caverns are virtually unassailable by land or air. Today the caves considered the most historically important are named after the figures who once occupied them. Their respective residences now stand defiantly, surrounded by vivid gardens, and some of the houses are used as holiday homes. The caves are within easy walking distance of town.

High in the side of a limestone cliff, **Tham Than Souphanouvong** (called Tham Pha Bong before the war) was deemed fit for royalty, and housed Prince Souphanouvong, the so-called 'Red Prince', who was allegedly killed by Hmong guerrillas at the age of 28, just 4km away. There is a memorial stupa for the Prince on site. Wooden walls and floors, as well as natural cave formations, divided the cavern into bedrooms, meeting rooms, artillery and weapons storage areas and various

other spaces. Souphanouvong eventually built a house in front of the cave entrance and today the house is treated with the same mix of fear and respect as the cave.

Tham Than Kaysone, the office and residence of the PL chief – who served as prime minister and president from 1975 until his death in 1992 – extends 140m into a cliff that was scaled by rope before steps were added. A bust of Kaysone sits inside the entry, and images of Lenin and Che Guevara – gifts from Russia and Cuba – adorn the political party centre. The cave's other rooms include a reception room, bedroom, recreation room, meeting room, library, and an emergency room containing an oxygen generator in case gas was ever dropped in the area (it wasn't). Meals were prepared in the kitchen here with gas donated by Russia, and local villagers provided the food. The rear of the cave opens onto a clearing that was used as an outdoor meeting place and kitchen. Kaysone's handsome two-storey house sits out the front.

Tham Than Khamtay, named after the current president Khamtay Siphandone, is an artificial cave dug out of a limestone cliff, similarly divided into various rooms, with a Franco-Chinese–style house in front of it. Frangipani trees fill the landscaped garden. Below the artificial cave is a natural cave that was used as barracks for up to 300 soldiers (some estimates are higher). This site is also home to the 'Theatre Cave', where visiting artists from Russia, China and Vietnam performed during the war. It was also used for weddings and the occasional volleyball match between soldiers.

Tham Than Nouhak, named for Nouhak Phoumsavang, who served as Lao PDR president from 1992 to 1998, is the most recent to open to the public. Like his PL comrades, Nouhak had a house built for himself in front of the cave.

One of the deepest caves (200m) is **Tham Xieng Muang**, which was used for hospital facilities. Other caves housed weaving mills, printing presses and other facilities needed by the PL to remain self-sufficient.

VISITING THE CAVES

Before entering any of the caves, visitors must report to the **Kaysone Phomvihane Memorial Cave Tour Office** (tour US$3, video camera US$1, still camera US$0.50; ☼ 8am-11.30am & 1-4.30pm) to pay the

CROSSING THE VIETNAMESE BORDER AT NAM XOI & NAMEO

The border crossing between Nam Xoi in Hua Phan Province, Laos and Nameo in Thanh Hoa Province, Vietnam has been open to foreigners for several years, but is used sparingly owing to the difficulty of the terrain on the Vietnamese side.

Travelling to Nam Xoi from within Laos, there's a daily *săwngthăew* from Sam Neua (US$2.30, four hours, 6.30am), or several from Vieng Xai (US$1.50, two hours, 8am to11am). The border is open from 7.30am to 11.30am and 1.30pm to 4.30pm. If you're arriving in Laos from Vietnam, the above *săwngthăew* return to their respective destinations about half an hour after arriving at the border.

Regardless of which direction you're travelling in, you must have organised a visa beforehand; there was no visa on arrival available at the time of writing. This may change so check ahead. It's also likely that you'll need to pay an additional US$1 fee when you pass through Lao immigration from Vietnam (but not the other way round).

In Vietnam you can negotiate a motorbike to Thanh Hoa or to Ba Thuoc. Both options can be pricey and are unfortunately monopolised by unscrupulous drivers. If you get stuck at the border there are a couple of guesthouses on the Vietnamese side where you can bed down for US$5 to US$8. If you get stuck in Nam Xoi the immigration officials may help you arrange a room with a local family.

necessary fees. Guided tours are mandatory and are conducted by guides from the office at 9am and 1pm. They take in three to four caves, and last for about two hours. Two of the guides speak English, and one was a resident of the caves for a short while during the war. If you want to see the caves outside of these official tour times you will need to pay an additional fee of US$5 per tour to cover staff costs.

Sleeping & Eating

Naxay Guest House (☎ 314336; r US$2-4) Rooms here are housed in a separate structure at the back of a green property. There are five cute twins with mosquito nets that share a homely living room. Rudimentary bathrooms are out the back, although there's also a private bungalow with its own bathroom attached.

Kamnome Guest House (☎ 020-5665026; r US$2.50-3) This simple guesthouse has seven basic rooms with small, scoop-water bathrooms and squat toilets. Rooms have mosquito nets and there's a small restaurant on site serving simple fare (meals US$1 to US$2) that's open for breakfast, lunch and dinner.

Thavisay Hotel (☎ 020-5712392; r US$4-6) Currently being renovated, this two-storey hotel promises to be the best place to stay in town. All rooms have private hot-water bathrooms and two double beds with mosquito nets. It's simple but the setting is lovely and the owners are very friendly. There's also a restaurant (meals US$2 to US$3), open breakfast, lunch and dinner, overlooking a man-made lake.

The menu is fairly generic (fried rice etc), but the food is hot and tasty and there are a handful of huts for secluded dinners.

Xailam Guest House (r US$4-6) This large timber guesthouse sits on stilts overlooking a small lake. Most of the eight rooms have cold-water showers, large TVs, fans and mosquito nets. Although they have shared bathrooms, the cheaper rooms are actually larger and more airy.

Several *főe* shops in the market serve rice and noodle dishes.

Getting There & Away

Săwngthăew run regularly between Sam Neua and Vieng Xai (US$0.80, 50 minutes, 29km, 6.20am to 5.20pm), with departures more frequent in the morning.

The Provincial Tourist Office (p183) in Sam Neua can arrange half-day tours to Vieng Xai for US$35 per group. You could also charter a pick-up truck to take you and up to eight other passengers from Sam Neua to Vieng Xai and back for about US$20, for a half day.

NAM NOEN
ນ້ຳເນີນ

Anyone travelling by road between Nong Khiaw and Phonsavan or between Sam Neua and Phonsavan will pass through this settlement, 7km south of the junction of Rtes 6 and 1. Once upon a time you needed to overnight here, but direct buses have negated the need. As a destination it doesn't have much to offer, but if you find yourself here for a night you can stay at **Nam Noen Guest House** (dm US$2), which offers beds with mosquito nets in dormlike rooms, while **Nang Lam Phon** (meals US$0.50-1.50; ☉ lunch & dinner) provides sticky rice and instant noodles. There are a couple of other noodle shops as well.

There's a daily *săwngthăew* to/from Sam Neua (US$2.30, 3½ hours, 6.20am) and one or two daily to Nong Khiaw (US$6, six hours). If you're looking to leave Nam Noen your best bet is in the morning.

NAM NOEN TO NONG KHIAW

Rte 1 between Nong Khiaw and Nam Noen passes through stretches of beautiful scenery with lots of green mountains – even in the dry months when everywhere looks brown – rivers, fern-covered cliffs and villages of Striped and Blue Hmong. The districts of **Muang Vieng Kham** and **Muang Vieng Thong** are populated with Blue Hmong and other ethnicities. Vieng Kham, about 50km east of Muang Ngoi, is a fairly substantial village with a couple of wats and a couple of places to eat. **Ban Wang Wai**, the next town west after Vieng Kham, is more prosperous than many others along the road and a little bigger than Vieng Kham itself. Besides Hmong, you'll see plenty of lowland Lao here, many of whom keep looms beneath their stilted houses.

Hugging 1465 sq km of forest in the north of Hua Phan and Luang Prabang Provinces is the **Nam Et/Phu Loei National Protected Area**. Species in the park are thought to include clouded leopard and tiger. To date there are no organised tours or guides to access the park. However if you stop in Vieng Thong (below) you can pop into the **Wildlife Conservation Society Office** and ask them about their tiger monitoring work and other developments in the park.

Muang Vieng Thong

ວຽງທອງ

More than a few travellers who have found themselves stuck in Muang Vieng Thong – also known by its pre-1975 name of Muang Hiam – have opted to stay an extra night or two. This village, inhabited by a collection of hill tribes (particularly Hmong) and lowland Lao, has a very pleasant mountain setting alongside the Nam Khao.

A **hot spring**, roughly 1km north of town on the road to Ban San Tai, makes an excellent bathing alternative in the cold season.

Further down the same road you'll find a few Lao Soung villages between the Nam Et and Phu Loei NPAs.

The road ends after 64km at **Ban San Tai** (San Teu in local dialect), a village that brings together lowland Lao, Thai tribals and Hmong-Mien groups. Several *săwngthăew* ply this route daily from Vieng Thong. **Souksavan Guest House** (☎ 314478; r US$2-3) and **Dok Champa Guest House** (☎ 314469; r US$3-4) both have rooms with fans, mosquito nets and attached bathrooms.

Several modest, friendly restaurants in the centre of the village offer basic Lao fare.

GETTING THERE & AWAY

A daily *săwngthăew* travels to Vieng Thong from Sam Neua (US$3.10, six hours, 6.30am), returning in the afternoon. *Săwngthăew* also ply between here and Nong Khiaw (US$2.60, three hours, four daily) and buses pass through from Luang Prabang (US$4, seven hours, one daily). You will also see buses and trucks that originated elsewhere passing through Vieng Thong, and can flag these down anywhere on the road.

UDOMXAI PROVINCE

This rugged province is wedged between Luang Prabang to the east, Phongsali to the northeast, Luang Nam Tha to the northwest and Sainyabuli to the south, with a small northern section that shares a border with China's Yunnan Province. Most of the provincial population of 265,000 is a mixture of some 23 ethnic minorities, mostly Hmong, Akha, Mien, Phu Thai, Thai Dam, Thai Khao, Thai Lü, Thai Neua, Phuan, Khamu, Lamet, Lao Huay and Yunnanese Chinese (Haw).

The Yunnanese presence continues to intensify with the influx of Chinese skilled labourers working in construction and cash crops, as well as traders from Kunming. In the 1960s and early 1970s the Chinese were appreciated in Udomxai because they donated a network of two-lane paved roads, vital in moving Pathet Lao and NVA troops and supplies around the north during the war. Following the 1979 ideological split over Cambodia (China sided with the Khmer Rouge, Laos with Vietnam), the Chinese withdrew all support until the early 1990s.

The new Chinese influx is regarded by many Udomxai inhabitants as economic infiltration, since the construction and road building is no longer foreign aid but paid work for hire, using plenty of imported Chinese materials and labour.

Because Udomxai has a road system of sorts (it has deteriorated considerably since the 1970s but is still the best in the north), this province is the most accessible of the country's far northern provinces.

To cross the border to China from Udomxai Province, you need to travel east to the Boten border crossing (p201) in Luam Nam Tha Province.

UDOMXAI (MUANG XAI)

ອຸດົມໄຊ (ເມືອງໄຊ)

☎ 081 / pop 80,000

Udomxai is a booming Laos-China trade centre riding on imported Chinese wealth. Although few people visit Udomxai as a tourist destination, it's an important northern crossroads where Rtes 1, 2 and 4 intersect. Thus it's difficult to avoid if you're travelling to Luang Nam Tha or Phongsali from points south.

After roughing it through some beautiful countryside along the Mekong River and along Rte 2 from Pak Beng (or from the east via Nong Khiaw and the Nam Ou), the town seems fairly bland. Modest in size, it features tidy asphalt strips lined with modern buildings and some very comely houses. More traditional thatched houses are spread across the rim of the valley towards the base of the surrounding mountain range. If you get off the main street you can find some very picturesque villagelike sections.

The town is roughly 60% Lao Thoeng and Lao Soung, 25% Chinese and 15% Lao Loum. Thousands of Chinese workers may be in the area at any one time, and the Yunnanese dialect is often heard more than Lao in the cafés and hotels.

Information

INTERNET ACCESS

Internet Kiosk (Bus station; per hr US$1.60; ⏰ 8am-5pm) Slow but not a bad way to kill time.

Lithavixay Guest House (Rte 1; per hr US$2; ⏰ 7am-9pm) Has three temperamental terminals.

Udomxai Internet (Rte 1; per hr US$1.80; ⏰ 8am-7pm) Speedy and reliable internet access.

MONEY

You can spend yuan, US dollars, Thai baht or kip in Udomxai, but travellers cheques are not accepted, so bring cash.

BCEL (☎ 211260; Rte 1) Changes US dollars, Thai baht or Chinese yuan into kip.

Lao Development Bank (☎ 312059; Rte 4) Changes US dollars, Thai baht or Chinese yuan into kip.

POST

Post office (⏰ 8am-4pm Mon-Fri, to noon Sat) Also houses Lao Telecom.

TELEPHONE

Lao Telecom (Post office; ⏰ 8-11.30am, 2-4.30pm & 6.30-9pm) Phonecards are available here for use in the international and domestic phone booth out the front.

TOURIST INFORMATION

Oudomxay Provincial Tourism Office (☎ 211797; ⏰ 8am-noon & 1.30-4pm Oct-Mar, 7.30-11.30am & 1.30-6pm Apr-Sep) Information about onward travel, accommodation and so forth. Also ecotourism tours.

Oudomxay Travel (☎ 212020; laos@laotel.com; Rte 1) Car hire, air travel and tours.

Sights & Activities

Samlaan Cycling (☎ 020-5609790; Rte 1) organises excellent one-day cycling tours and two- to five-day combination cycling and trekking tours in and around Udomxai Province. Some of these reach Luang Prabang or go as far north as Muang Sing. Prices vary depending on group size and tour duration. Bicycle rental is also available (US$3 per day) if you just want to do your own thing.

The **Lao Red Cross** (☎ 312391; steam US$1, massage per hr US$3; ⏰ 3-7pm) offers Lao-Swedish style massage as well as herbal steam baths.

The Oudomxay Provincial Tourism Office (above) arranges one-day trekking tours (US$3.50 to US$5 per person) to some of the sights around Udomxai, including Tat Lack Sip-Et and Muang La. It also has a three-day trek to Khamu villages including homestays (US$28 to US$50 per person).

Sleeping

Many of the guesthouses in Udomxai cater to Chinese workers and either won't accept other nationalities or will ask double the Chinese price. We've not listed any that we know are guilty of two-tier pricing.

Vilavong Guest House (☎ 212503; r US$4) This spotless little guesthouse has polished rooms with warm bed covers and soft beds. All have shared bathrooms, which are spacious and clean and have hot water showers. The industrious owners take pride in their property.

Linda Guest House (☎ 312147; r US$4) Linda Guest House has 14 simple but slightly stuffy rooms with ceiling fans, lovely clean sheets and towels, and large bathrooms. Some rooms are smaller to accommodate singles, although the price doesn't change. It's a decent option but there's not much to buffer the TV noise.

Linda Guest House II (r US$4) Once you get past the hodgepodge ground floor, where you may find kilometres of raw sausage and boxes of electrical goods, you'll find reasonable rooms. They're upstairs and are bright and basic with three single beds and a cold shower and squat toilet bathroom attached.

Vivanh Guest House (☎ 212219; r US$5) This wee establishment only has a handful of rooms but they're tiled and sparkling clean, and have comfortable double beds, fans TV and private bathrooms. The owners are very gracious, and it's excellent value.

Lithavixay Guest House (☎ /fax 212175; r US$7-15; ✕ ⌨) At one of the most accommodating guesthouses in town, all rooms come with private hot-water shower. The more expensive rooms are larger and include breakfast, satellite TV and air-con. Internet access is available downstairs.

Surinphone Hotel (☎ 212789; srphone@laotel .com; r US$15; ✕) This flashy number accommodates the comfort-needy with bright and positively glistening rooms containing TV, generous bathrooms (with bath) and dining tables. The beds are new and the atmosphere welcoming.

Also available:

Vongprachit Guest House (☎ 312455; r US$4) Weary but central.

Phouxay Hotel (Phuxai; ☎ 312140; r US$5, without bathroom US$4) Decent rooms with TV and bathrooms, or gloomy rooms with shared bathroom.

Eating

The Lao food on local menus often tastes more Chinese than Lao, so you're usually better off ordering Chinese. The restaurants at the guesthouses are good but you generally need to order in advance.

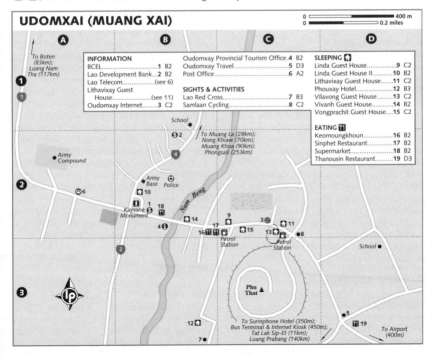

UDOMXAI (MUANG XAI)

INFORMATION	
BCEL	1 B2
Lao Development Bank	2 B2
Lao Telecom	(see 6)
Lithavixay Guest House	(see 11)
Oudomxay Internet	3 C2
Oudomxay Provincial Tourism Office	4 B2
Oudomxay Travel	5 D3
Post Office	6 A2

SIGHTS & ACTIVITIES	
Lao Red Cross	7 B3
Samlaan Cycling	8 C2

SLEEPING	
Linda Guest House	9 C2
Linda Guest House II	10 B2
Lithavixay Guest House	11 C2
Phouxay Hotel	12 B3
Vilavong Guest House	13 C2
Vivanh Guest House	14 B2
Vongprachit Guest House	15 C2

EATING	
Keomoungkhoun	16 B2
Sinphet Restaurant	17 B2
Supermarket	18 B2
Thanousin Restaurant	19 D3

Sinphet Restaurant (meals US$0.50-1.50; ⊙ breakfast, lunch & dinner) At the base of a basic guesthouse, this restaurant whips up good Chinese-Lao fusion dishes and a few Western faves such as pancakes and scrambled eggs. The menu boasts plenty of chicken, fish, pork and beef and the owners are bubbly.

Thanousin Restaurant (meals US$0.50-2) This restaurant is conveniently located near the junction of Rtes 1 and 2 and thus receives a lot of business from drivers passing through. It has the most Lao menu in town, although not everything on the menu is on hand all the time.

Keomoungkhoun (meals US$1-3) This restaurant has a large dining room and serves extensive Chinese and Lao fare. The fruit shakes are also good, but the owners are often glued to the TV.

There's a supermarket on the main north–south road; there's also a vibrant fresh fruit and vegetable market out front.

Getting There & Away

AIR

Lao Airlines (☎ 312047; airport) flies to/from Vientiane (one way/return US$75/143) every Tuesday, Thursday and Saturday.

BUS & SĂWNGTHĂEW

The Chinese-built bitumen roads that radiate from Udomxai are in fair condition (except for the road to Pak Beng on the Mekong River) and the city is the largest land transport hub in the north.

The **bus terminal** (☎ 212218) is at the southwestern edge of town. Buses head to Luang Prabang (ordinary US$4, five hours, three daily; VIP US$5, three hours, two daily), Nong Khiaw (US$3.10, three to five hours, four daily), Pak Beng (US$3.30, five hours, two daily), Luang Nam Tha (US$3.20, four hours, three daily), Muang Khua (US$2.80, four hours, three daily), Boten (US$3, four hours, two daily), Phongsali (US$6, eight to 12 hours, one daily) and Vientiane (ordinary US$11, 16 hours, two daily; VIP US$12.10, 16 hours, two daily).

AROUND UDOMXAI

North and south of town there is a string of Hmong villages where the tribespeople have come down from higher elevations – either because of mountaintop deforestation due to swidden agriculture, or because they have

been pressured by the government to integrate into lowland society.

East of town off Rte 1 at Km 11 is **Tat Lak Sip-Et** (Km 11 Waterfall; admission US$0.50), a slender cataract that cascades over a limestone cliff into a Nam Beng tributary. Look for a small blue-and-white sign (in Lao only) on the northern side of the road.

Baw nâm hâwn (hot springs) can be found 28km from Udomxai near Muang La, off the road to Phongsali near the banks of the Nam Pak.

TO LUANG PRABANG VIA PAK BENG

The river-and-road trip from Huay Xai or Luang Prabang to Udomxai is an experience in itself. Three hours by speedboat, or a day's travel by river ferry, the Mekong River journey to Pak Beng (jumping-off point for the road to Udomxai) passes craggy stone cliffs, sandy shores, undulating mountains, fishing villages, and expanses of both primary and secondary forest.

Pak Beng itself (see below) is worth an overnight stay if time allows, then it's on to Udomxai via Rte 2, an old Chinese-built road that runs parallel to the Nam Beng most of the way. The mostly sealed road is very rough in spots but is supposed to be resealed soon. Along the way you'll pass Phu Thai, Thai Lü, Hmong, Thai Dam, Lao and Khamu villages, plus primary monsoon forest alternating with secondary growth and slash-and-burn plots.

At Km 90 (about one-third of the way to Udomxai) is **Muang Houn** (52km from Pak Beng), the largest village between Pak Beng and Udomxai and a convenient rest stop. Muang Houn has a few basic guesthouses including **Bounnam Guest House** (☎ 212289; r US$2-3). There are also a few places to eat, or stock up on food supplies. Around Km 18 to Km 21 (counting south from Udomxai) are at least a dozen Hmong villages.

There are a couple of scenic waterfalls not far from the main road. **Tat Yong** is said to be the largest and is a 12km hike from Km 87.

PAK BENG
ปากแบ่ง

This rustic town at the junction of the Mekong River and the smaller Nam Beng (Pak Beng means Mouth of the Beng) lies about halfway between Luang Prabang and Huay Xai (Bokeo Province). Pak Beng's mostly wooden houses sit along a steep hillside. Close to the ferry and speedboat piers is a collection of makeshift shops and cafés that get more interesting the further away from the river you go. Hmong and tribal Thais are frequently seen on the main street. A few vendors along the street sell local textiles and handicrafts. Sip espresso and peruse new and used books at the **Khok Khor Café & Bookshop**.

Most guesthouses and restaurants in Pak Beng have generators to provide electricity between 6pm and 10pm.

Dangers & Annoyances

In peak season there's a general fear that the number of guests arriving en masse from Huay Xai or Luang Prabang will outnumber the beds in town. This is likely to be a thing of the past as touts often meet the boat lobbying for your business now.

We've also heard about a local scam where groups of young local boys offer to carry your luggage up the hill from the boat, then when you reach your guesthouse they

demand US$4 for the service. If you decide to enlist the assistance of the boys, consider setting an exact tip beforehand.

Lastly, drugs are fairly abundant in Pak Beng and you can expect to be offered some (particularly if you're male) soon after you arrive. Purchasing is not a good idea for obvious reasons, but the dealers can also be aggressive and you may end parting with more worldly possessions than just a few kip.

Sights & Activities

Two wats of mild interest can be visited in town, both of which are off the left side of the road north, overlooking the Nam Beng. **Wat Khok Kho** is the newer of the two, with a *sim* of rather recent construction and wooden monks' quarters.

Further up the road, a series of stairs on the right-hand side lead past a small school to **Wat Sin Jong Jaeng**, an older temple that dates back to the early French colonial period or possibly earlier. On the front exterior wall of the small but classic Lao *sim* is a mural that includes figures with moustaches and big noses – presumably early Dutch or French visitors. Inside there are a number of Buddha images of varying ages. The Lao-style *tháat* on the premises was constructed in 1991; it's gilded at the top, and the base is said to contain a cache of *sák-sìt* (sacred) material (probably small Buddha images of crystal or silver, prayer cloths and rosaries from revered monks).

There's a **Traditional Massage & Sauna** (sauna US$1, massage US$3; sauna 4-10pm, massage 8am-noon & 2.30-11.30pm) near Bounmee Guest House, where you can work any kinks out embedded from your boat trip.

Sleeping
BUDGET

Most guesthouses in Pak Beng offer small rooms with hard-mattress beds, mosquito nets, and shared facilities around the back or downstairs.

Monsavan Guest House (5771935; r US$2-5) This big guesthouse on the main strip has an alabaster front and polished wood doors, but the rooms inside are a simpler affair with bamboo walls and shared bathrooms. It's clean and tidy though and in a good position.

Villa Salika (212306; r US$5-7) A good option if you want a step up from basic and budget, the Salika has spacious rooms with twin beds

NORTHERN LAOS

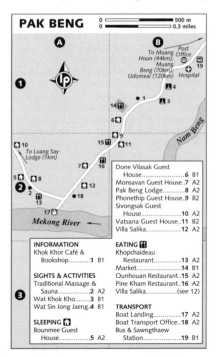

PAK BENG   0 — 500 m   0 — 0.3 miles

Done Vilasak Guest House	6	B1
Monsavan Guest House	7	A2
Pak Beng Lodge	8	A2
Phonethip Guest House	9	B2
Sivongsak Guest House	10	A2
Vatsana Guest House	11	B2
Villa Salika	12	A2

INFORMATION
Khok Khor Café & Bookshop	1	B1

SIGHTS & ACTIVITIES
Traditional Massage & Sauna	2	A2
Wat Khok Kho	3	B1
Wat Sin Jong Jaeng	4	B1

SLEEPING
Bounmee Guest House	5	A2

EATING
Khopchaideau Restaurant	13	A2
Market	14	B1
Ounhouan Restaurant	15	A2
Pine Kham Restaurant	16	A2
Villa Salika	(see 12)	

TRANSPORT
Boat Landing	17	A2
Boat Transport Office	18	A2
Bus & Sawngthaew Station	19	B1

and private bathrooms. Giant thermoses in the rooms provide hot water for your shower or tea, depending on which need is more urgent. There's no buffer between windows and the street so it can be noisy at night.

Bounmee Guest House (r US$5-7) To find this one, walk a short distance down a road that branches off the main street, not far from the boat landing. Since it's off the main drag, Bounmee offers a slightly quieter alternative, although the bamboo-and-wood rooms are very similar to those at most other guesthouses. All rooms have private hot-water bathrooms.

Other budget options:

Sivongsagk Guest House (r US$2) Simple rooms with cold water.

Done Vilasak Guest House (tw US$2.50) Two-storey wooden place with typical two-bed rooms and shared bathroom.

Vatsana Guest House (☎ 212302; r US$3) Ten rooms with fan, mosquito net and shared bathroom.

Phonethip Guest House (r US$3-4) Simple fan rooms, five with shared bathroom and three with private bathroom.

MIDRANGE & TOP END

Pak Beng Lodge (r US$30; 🖭) Rivalling Luang Say for the finest digs in town, this relatively recent addition to Pak Beng has indulgent (well for this neck of the woods) and spotless rooms with pretty interiors, Western-style bathrooms and minibars. The common balcony affords good views of the river.

Luang Say Lodge (☎ 212296; www.mekongcruises .com; r from US$60) If you continue along the road past Bounmee Guest House, you'll come to this ecolodge built mainly for the use of passengers cruising between Huay Xai and Luang Prabang aboard the *Luang Say* (see p218). Built in traditional Lao style of solid wood, the lodge encompasses 19 rooms divided among a dozen or so pavilions, all with fan and private hot-water shower. A terrace restaurant overlooks the Mekong.

Eating

Kopchaideau Restaurant (☎ meals US$1-2; 🕙 10am-11pm) This popular restaurant sits on a deck overlooking the Mekong and specialises in Indian; the vindaloo and naan are great. There's also a smattering of Lao and Thai on the menu and plenty of vegetarian options.

Pine Kham Restaurant (meals US$1-2) The kitchen here does justice to a wide range of Thai, Chinese and Lao dishes, plus Western breakfasts.

Villa Salika (☎ 212306; meals US$1-3; 🕙 breakfast, lunch & dinner) The restaurant here has nice river views and tourist-friendly food, although it's a tad overpriced. They can whip up sandwiches in the morning for your boat ride ahead.

Ouanhouan Restaurant (meals US$1.20-2; 🕙 breakfast, lunch & dinner) Elevated from the street, this small eatery does great Lao and Thai food along the lines of *láap* (salads) and creamy coconut curries. Service can be a little erratic and you may not end up with exactly what you ordered, but all the food's good so think of it as a lucky dip.

Market (🕙 6.30am-5pm) In the centre of town, this market has a few vendors with prepared Lao food.

There are several other simple restaurants along the street leading from the pier, most serving *fŏe* and a few basic Chinese and Lao dishes.

Getting There & Away

BOAT
See p217 for details on river travel between Pak Beng, Luang Prabang and Huay Xai.

SĂWNGTHĂEW
From the *săwngthăew* and bus station (1.5km from the boat landing), *săwngthăew* run along potholed Rte 2 between Pak Beng and Udomxai (US$3.30, five hours, two daily).

If you miss one of the direct *săwngthăew* to Pak Beng from Udomxai, you can catch one of the more frequent *săwngthăew* to Muang Houn (US$2.10, two hours, four to eight daily), 92km southwest of Udomxai on the way to Pak Beng. In Muang Houn it's easy to pick up another *săwngthăew* on to Pak Beng (US$2, two hours). The same is true in reverse; you can take a *săwngthăew* from Pak Beng to Muang Houn, then pick up a Udomxai-bound vehicle fairly easily. There are two or three basic guesthouses in Muang Houn if you get stuck.

LUANG NAM THA PROVINCE

Blessed with a mountainous tapestry, a vast protected area, and diverse ethnic villages, Luang Nam Tha is synonymous with culture, adventure and trekking for most travellers. Although much of the province is untamed wilderness, the infrastructure to explore it is some of the best in Laos. Guided explorations into the magnificent Nam Ha National Protected Area (p198), a 2224-sq-km area containing some of the most densely forested regions (96% primary forest cover) in Laos, can be complimented with independent travel to small villages surrounding Muang Sing, Luang Nam Tha and Vieng Phoukha.

The provincial population is 145,000, made up of 39 classified ethnicities (the largest number in the nation), including Hmong, Akha, Mien, Samtao, Thai Daeng, Thai Lü, Thai Neua, Thai Khao, Thai Kalom, Khamu, Lamet, Lao Loum, Shan and Yunnanese. As in Udomxai Province, the Chinese presence is increasing rapidly with the arrival of skilled labourers from Yunnan.

LUANG NAM THA

ຫລວງນ້ຳທາ

086 / pop 35,400

The capital of the province, Luang Nam Tha is a quiet, ordered town where a grid pattern of streets reveals ever-so-quietly humming businesses and residences. It's a lovely spot to chill out for a couple of days before or after a trek into the Nam Ha NPA (see p198). The town is surrounded by a patchwork of rich rice paddies and ethnically diverse villages, and exploring them would be a highlight of a trip to the area. It's also a transport hub for buses from all directions, including China, and consequently attracts a transient population of traders and travellers, all of whom add to the melting pot.

The original town, which was always prone to flooding, was virtually destroyed during the Second Indochina War, and the administrative centre was consequently moved 7km north in 1976. The newer town centre sits on higher ground, and is close to where the highways come in from Muang Sing, Boten and Udomxai. Most visitors spend their limited time around the main street of this northern district, but the older southern district is mostly residential and, in general, much more interesting. Locals often refer to the southern centre as *meuang* (city-state) and to the northern centre as *khwăeng* (province).

Information

INTERNET ACCESS

Internet Cafe (per hr US$1.80)

KNT Internet (5486086; per hr US$1.80; 8am-10pm) Fast and reliable.

MONEY

BCEL (8.30am-3.30pm Mon-Fri) Foreign exchange for US travellers cheques and US dollars, Thai baht and Chinese yuan; cash advances on credit cards.

Lao Development Bank (8.30am-noon & 2-3.30pm Mon-Fri) Exchanges US travellers cheques, US dollars, Thai baht and Chinese yuan.

POST

Post office (312007; 8am-noon & 1-4pm Mon-Fri)

TELEPHONE

Lao Telecom Long-distance phone services available.

TOURIST INFORMATION

Luang Nam Tha Provincial Tourism Office (211534, 312047; 8am-noon & 2-5pm) Excellent tourist office with English-speaking staff. See Activities (p197) for available guided tours.

Sights

At the time of research a **night market** was being constructed near the Provincial Tourism Office. When completed it will showcase a colourful array of textiles, clothing, basketry, paper and other handicrafts from the diverse ethnic groups in the area.

The **Luang Nam Tha Museum** (admission US$0.50; 8.30-11.30am & 1.30-3.30pm Mon-Thu, 8.30-11.30am Fri) contains a collection of local anthropological artefacts, such as ethnic clothing, Khamu bronze drums, and ceramics. There are also a number of Buddha images and the usual display chronicling the Revolution.

Near the airfield are two 50-year-old wats, **Wat Ban Vieng Tai** and **Wat Ban Luang Khon**, both of mild interest. **Ban Luang Khon** itself (the area around Wat Ban Luang Khon) is largely a Thai Kalom neighbourhood.

East across the Nam Tha from the boat landing are four or five Thai Dam villages; at **Ban Pa Sak** you can observe Thai Dam silk weaving in action.

Three kilometres west of the airfield atop a hill surrounded by rice fields stands **That Phum Phuk**, an impressively large stupa that shares stylistic similarities with That Ing Hang and other stupas more customarily found in Southern Laos. The brick-and-stucco stupa is said to have been erected in 1628, although it's likely that its current form dates to a more recent – possibly 19th century – renovation.

During the Second Indochina War a bomb explosion knocked the *jęhdii* on its side, where it remains undisturbed. Despite its semiruined

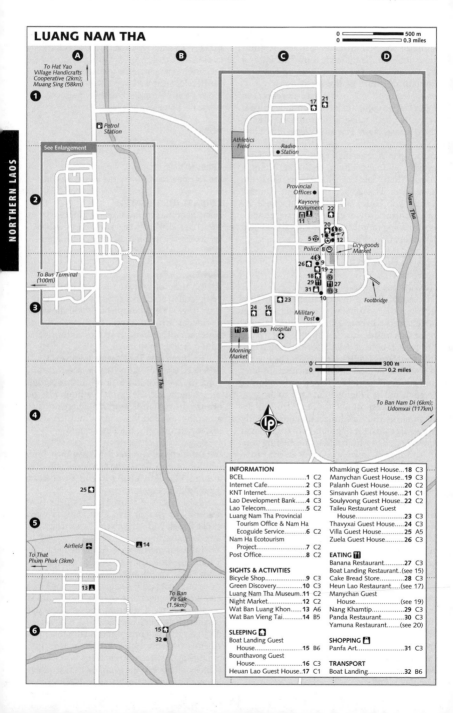

LUANG NAM THA

| 0 | 500 m |
| 0 | 0.3 miles |

To Hat Yao
Village Handicrafts
Cooperative (2km);
Muang Sing (58km)

Petrol
Station

See Enlargement

To Bus Terminal
(100m)

Nam Tha

Athletics
Field

Radio
Station

Provincial
Offices

Kaysone
Monument
11

Dry-goods
Market

Police 8

Footbridge

Military
Post

24 16

28 30 Hospital

Morning
Market

| 0 | 300 m |
| 0 | 0.2 miles |

To Ban Nam Di (6km);
Udomxai (117km)

Nam Tha

25

Airfield

14

To That
Phum Phuk (3km)

13

To Ban
Pa Sak
(1.5km)

15
32

INFORMATION
BCEL.....................................1 C2
Internet Cafe.........................2 C3
KNT Internet.........................3 C3
Lao Development Bank.......4 C3
Lao Telecom.........................5 C2
Luang Nam Tha Provincial
   Tourism Office & Nam Ha
   Ecoguide Service..............6 C2
Nam Ha Ecotourism
   Project.............................7 C2
Post Office............................8 C2

SIGHTS & ACTIVITIES
Bicycle Shop.........................9 C3
Green Discovery..................10 C3
Luang Nam Tha Museum...11 C2
Night Market.......................12 C3
Wat Ban Luang Khon.........13 A6
Wat Ban Vieng Tai.............14 B5

SLEEPING
Boat Landing Guest
   House...........................15 B6
Bounthavong Guest
   House...........................16 C3
Heuan Lao Guest House.....17 C1

Khamking Guest House...18 C3
Manychan Guest House..19 C3
Palanh Guest House........20 C2
Sinsavanh Guest House...21 C1
Soulyvong Guest House..22 C2
Taileu Restaurant Guest
   House.........................23 C3
Thavyxai Guest House....24 C3
Villa Guest House...........25 A5
Zuela Guest House.........26 C3

EATING
Banana Restaurant...........27 C3
Boat Landing Restaurant..(see 15)
Cake Bread Store.............28 C3
Heun Lao Restaurant.....(see 17)
Manychan Guest
   House.......................(see 19)
Nang Khamtip.................29 C3
Panda Restaurant.............30 C3
Yamuna Restaurant.......(see 20)

SHOPPING
Panfa Art.........................31 C3

TRANSPORT
Boat Landing..................32 B6

NORTHERN LAOS

state – a large fig tree is now growing out of the base, lending a 'lost-in-the-jungle' atmosphere – the stupa is well worth visiting if you have any interest in Lao religious architecture, as it's a masterful piece of work. Much of the original stucco ornamentation is still in place; not far from the base stands a *síláa jáaleuk* (stele) inscribed in old Lao script. A newer replica of the stupa was erected nearby in 2003.

You can hire a jumbo from the dry-goods market out to That Phum Phuk for US$5 return, including waiting time. If you decide to walk or bike, take the graded dirt road that runs west along the south side of the airport. After 700m this road ends at a T-junction. Make a right here and follow this road as it bends around to the northwest and passes rice fields. About 2.3km further on (3km total from the main paved road) you should see a hill to your right. Turn right on another dirt road just before the hill. After 100m on this road, look for a steep road on your left; this leads to the stupa at the top of the hill. Jumbos won't be able to climb this steep road, and you might not be able to pedal it either, especially when it's wet. On foot the climb takes between 10 and 15 minutes. Watch out for leeches in the rainy season.

About 6km northeast of the new town centre, off Rte 1, the Lao Huay (Lenten) village of **Ban Nam Di** is a good place to observe the process of bamboo papermaking. The villagers turn bamboo into pulp along the banks of the Nam Di adjacent to the village. They then spread the pulp into thin sheets over square cotton screens to fashion a rustic paper on which they record religious literature in a script based on Chinese characters. The paper is also much prized these days by the handicraft industry. Less than 1km away from Ban Nam Di is a waterfall that villagers will be glad to take you to for a small tip.

Activities

TREKKING, RAFTING, MOUNTAIN BIKING & KAYAKING

Luang Nam Tha is the main jumping-off point for trekking, rafting, mountain biking and kayaking trips in the magnificent Nam Ha NPA (see the boxed text, p198), and for boat trips down the Nam Tha to the Mekong River (see p201).

Many of the tours stop for at least a night in a village; largely Khamu and Lenten to the south and Akha to the north, west and east,

but there are also Yao, Thai Lü and Thai Dam villages nearby.

All the treks are rewarding, and follow the same sustainability guidelines, but they vary in duration and difficulty. The trails for multiday treks are narrow and steep in parts and involve a decent dose of huffing and puffing. In the wet season you also share the landscape with leeches, but guides are fully versed in extricating the little pests. These are minor inconveniences however, given the spectacular landscape you'll traverse.

At the time of writing, tours were offered by the **Nam Ha Ecoguide Service** (☎ 211534; ☺ 8am-9pm), a wing of the Provincial Tourism Office, and the privately owned **Green Discovery** (☎ 211484; www.greendiscoverylaos.com; ☺ 8am-9pm). Those offered by Green Discovery differ to those offered by the Tourism Office, in order to eliminate direct competition and increase the spread of proceeds.

CYCLING

Cycling is the ideal way to explore the wats, waterfalls, bans and landscape surrounding Luang Nam Tha. If you're not up for a multiday mountain-bike tour, you can head out at your own pace by renting a mountain bike or ubiquitous rabbit-ear bicycle for US$0.30/1 per hour/day from the **Bicycle Shop** (☺ 9am-6pm) on the main street. It also rents motorcycles for US$2 to US$3 per day.

Sleeping

Most lodging in Luang Nam Tha is in the newer, northern part of town. Rooms fill up fast during the December to March high season, so if you schedule a morning arrival you'll stand a better chance of getting a room.

BUDGET

Besides the places described here, there are a few less desirable Chinese guesthouses in town with overpriced rooms. We don't list them because we don't recommend them.

Sinsavanh Guest House (☎ 211141; r US$2-4) Sinsavanh occupies a brightly painted two-storey wooden house and offers basic rooms with mosquito nets and capacious shared bathrooms with squat toilets and cold-water showers. There's a pleasant sitting area on the upper terrace.

Khamking Guest House (r US$5) Glistening and new, the Khamking has plain but welcoming rooms with large, screened windows,

NAM HA NPA

Named for the river that flows through it, the Nam Ha National Protected Area (NPA) extends 2224 sq km, from riverine plains to 2000m peaks. Running to the Chinese border and contiguous with Yunnan's Shang Yong NPA, it represents one of the most important international wildlife corridors in the region. Dense evergreen and semi-evergreen submontane forests, and upland broadleaf woodlands harbour clouded leopard, tiger, elephants, gaur, muntjac and 288 bird species. Several different ethnic groups inhabit the Nam Ha NPA, including Lao Huay, Akha and Khamu.

The natural beauty and cultural experiences are reasons enough to visit the Nam Ha NPA, but it's also one of the few projects in Southeast Asia that truly achieves sustainable ecotourism. The collective interest of the Provincial Tourism Office, Unesco and New Zealand government-sponsored **Nam Ha Ecotourism Project** (www.unescobkk.org/culture; Luang Nam Tha), tour operators and villages is to provide a genuine experience to tourists with minimum impact to the local communities and environment. Tours are limited to small groups and each village receives visitors no more than twice a week.

The large pool of trained guides enables each to lead about one trek a month. This ensures an even distribution of proceeds, and more importantly, it prevents communities from becoming dependent on tourism. You'll find that your guides may be teachers, farmers or shop owners who are able to supplement their traditional income from a monthly trek. Provincial Tourism Offices and registered tour operators demonstrate how your tour fee is distributed, and the vast majority (over 50%) goes to the villages and guides.

Many of the trails are established via a Memorandum of Understanding (MOU) between the Provincial Tourism Office and villages in order to preserve the NPA. Rather than dictate what villages can and can't do, the MOU provides information about sustainable forestry and fishing practises, which in turn maintains the integrity of the villages own environments.

Guided tours into the Nam Ha NPA can be arranged from Luang Nam Tha, Muang Sing (p203) or Vieng Phoukha (p202). Those from Luang Nam Tha are true forest treks, while those from Muang Sing have more of a cultural bent because the area is more heavily populated by ethnic villages. The tours from Vieng Phoukha have been most recently established and see the least amount of tourist traffic. An even blend of village visits and trekking, they are an excellent opportunity for people looking to get off the beaten track.

Tourists also play a major role in the success of any sustainable tourism project, and bearing the following in mind will help to ensure the conservation of the Nam Ha NPA and its communities:

- Always use a registered guide. This prevents local 'entrepreneurs' from undercutting the villages and other guides, and from harming the fragile ecology of the protected area. It's also much safer – it quite literally is a jungle out there.

- If you want to give gifts, fruit and vegetable seeds or saplings are best because they continue to give after you've left. But always ask your guide first if it's appropriate to give anything and if so, only give directly to the chief. Giving gifts to children can encourage begging, which is belittling for people who have always been self-sufficient.

- Always ask permission before taking photos.

- As with all trekking, stick to the trails. See the Responsible Trekking boxed text on p204 for more information.

---

comfy beds, fans and snug but spotless tiled bathrooms with hot-water showers. You'll have to sit sideways for your ablutions if you're any bigger than a pygmy, but otherwise this is excellent value.

Zuela Guest House (☎ 312183; r US$5) Another newbie, Zeal is a glorious brick and timber two-storey house with spacious rooms devoid of even a speck of dirt. High ceilings and fans

keep things cool and the big, clean bathrooms have hot water. There are sitting areas upstairs and down, and a laundry service and mountain-bike rental.

Taileu Restaurant Guesthouse (☎ 211266; r US$5) Behind a restaurant that resembles a concrete bunker, this guesthouse has decent rooms with gloriously comfortable beds, fans, satellite TV and slightly dingy bathrooms with scoop toilets. The rooms are a tad bunker-like themselves but the restaurant closes at a reasonable hour so it's quiet.

Manychan Guest House (☎ 312209; r US$5) Central and exceedingly popular, this guesthouse has had a good makeover and contains pleasant, fan-cooled rooms with temperamental hot-water showers.

Huean Lao Guest House & Restaurant (☎ 211111; r US$6) The atmospheric rooms beneath this restaurant (see right) are cool and dark, with fans and Western-style bathrooms. The aesthetics are appealing, with a modicum of traditional textiles and handicrafts in each room.

Thavyxai Guest House (☎ 5110292; r US$6.50) A great choice close to the bus station, Thavyxai has immaculate rooms that verge on hotel standard. Dazzling white interiors contain fans, TVs, large beds and pristine, Western bathrooms. It's run by a friendly family and is a good spot for a quiet night's sleep.

Also available:

Soulyvong Guest House (☎ 312256; s/d US$3/5) Cheap, friendly and simple.

Bounthavong Guest House (☎ 312256; r US$3-5) Cool, clean rooms with thick floor mattresses and attached squat-toilet bathrooms.

Palanh Guest House (☎ 312439; r US$5) Worn but reliable.

MIDRANGE

Villa Guest House (☎ 312425; r incl breakfast US$20) Just south of town, this guesthouse is a notch up from most in town and offers light and spacious rooms with plenty of sunlight, large beds, spotless tiled bathrooms and TV. The décor is colourful, and there's an open-air restaurant (meals US$2 to US$4), open for dinner.

Boat Landing Guest House & Restaurant (☎ 312 398; www.theboatlanding.laopdr.com; r incl breakfast US$32-42) Located 6km south of the new town and about 150m off the main road, this quiet lodge close to the Nam Tha boat landing offers easy access to the Nam Tha river and several Thai Dam villages. Spacious, nicely designed wooden bungalows feature verandas overlooking the river, and private bathrooms with solar-heated showers. There's also an excellent restaurant on the premises. The staff can arrange rafting or tubing excursions on the Nam Tha, fishing trips, bird-watching, mountain biking and trekking to nearby villages or to the Nam

Ha NPA with English- and French-speaking guides. Bicycles are available for hire.

Eating

Banana Restaurant (☎ 5718026; meals US$1-1.50; ☯ breakfast, lunch & dinner) Underneath a shady thatched roof, this entrepreneurial little restaurant captivates the *falang* market with Western breakfasts (even cornflakes) plus a long menu of fried chicken, pork and vegetarian dishes (spicy and mild), plus curries, Thai dishes and salads. It's cheap and tasty food.

Panda Restaurant (☎ 5663122; meals US$1.50-2.50; ☯ breakfast, lunch & dinner) The huge menu at this modest, open-air restaurant encompasses everything from (divine) pancakes and eggs to fish on tomato chilli, beef with basil and tasty tofu fry-ups. The fruit shakes are also delicious and it's run by an affable family.

Huean Lao (☎ 211111; meals US$1.50-3; ☯ lunch & dinner) With its open-air, 2nd-floor dining room and polished wood floors, Heuan Lao easily has the nicest atmosphere of any eatery located in the northern part of town. The mostly Lao menu is authentic and tasty – try the dried pickled bamboo with pork or the tangy chicken with chilli.

Manychan Guest House (☎ 312209; meals US$1.50-2.50; ☯ breakfast, lunch & dinner) The most popular *falang* venue in town has an extensive menu boasting Lao, Thai and tame Chinese dishes. The chef's spell in Vientiane and Luang Prabang restaurants has served the kitchen well and the buzzing tourists manage to wolf down their meals while swapping trekking tales and glasses of Beerlao.

Yamuna Restaurant (meals US$1.50-2.50; ☯ breakfast, lunch & dinner) The inventive menu at this Indian restaurant satisfies subcontinent cravings with curries of all piquants as well as South Indian specialties like Masala dosai. The stock of tables are neatly ordered inside and out.

Boat Landing Guest House & Restaurant (☎ 312398; US$2-5) Although it's the most expensive place to eat in Nam Tha (but only by a small measure), the restaurant here serves the best and most authentic northern Lao cuisine you'll find in Nam Tha outside the market. The menu includes a good selection of vegetarian dishes. A *tuk-tuk* (round trip US$1) departs Green Discovery at 6.30pm every night, and returns at 8.45pm.

The large morning market next to the bus terminal contains a couple of very good *fŏe* places and several *khào sáwy* stands.

NORTHERN LAOS

NORTHERN LAOS

Also recommended:

Cake Bread Store (meals US$0.30-1; breakfast & lunch) Delicious tarts, rolls and baguettes.

Nang Khamtip (meals US$0.40-1; 7am-2pm) Some of the best *fŏe*, *khào pîak* (rice soup) and *khào sáwy* in Laos.

Shopping

Panfa Art (5698684) This small textiles shop on the main street sells some truly stunning scarves and wall hangings made from raw silk. It's all locally crafted and the workmanship of some of the pieces is quite bamboozling.

There's also a tiny, nameless textiles shop (well the front of someone's house really) opposite the Provincial Offices on the main street, which sells vivid silks, *sin* (traditional sarongs) and scarves at reasonable prices.

Getting There & Away

AIR

At the time of writing Luang Nam Tha's airport was under renovations in order to become an 'International' airport. The idea is to cater to flights from Thailand, although Chinese investment is likely to make more use of it. Once construction is completed **Lao Airlines** (312180) is likely to resume its flights to/from Luang Prabang (one way/return US$45/86) and Vientiane (one way/return US$84/160). Schedules are anyone's guess.

If you don't want to bus the whole way up here consider a flight to Udomxai (see p192) and then take a bus from there.

BOAT

See the Nam Tha River Trip (opposite) for details on boat transport between Luang Nam Tha and the Mekong River.

BUS & SĂWNGTHĂEW

The main **bus terminal** (312164) is just west of the morning market.

Luang Nam Tha can be reached via all-weather Rte 1 from Udomxai (US$3.20, four hours, three daily). A side road going north off Rte 1 about one-third of the way to Udomxai leads directly to Boten (US$2, two hours, four daily) on the Lao-Chinese border. At the intersection of Rte 1 and the road to Boten, the small town of Na Toei has one guesthouse (US$2), a market, health clinic and customs checkpoint.

A *săwngthăew* plies daily between Luang Nam Tha and Ban Na Lae (US$3.90, three hours, 9am), roughly halfway to Pak Tha alongside the Nam Tha.

One *săwngthăew* travels daily to Huay Xai (US$6.50, eight hours), stopping in Vieng Phoukha (US$2.50, four hours) on the way, and there are about six *săwngthăew* to Muang Sing daily (US$2, two hours). There is also one bus daily to Muang Long (see p209; US$3.60, five hours).

One bus a day also goes to/from Luang Prabang (US$7, eight hours, 8.30am). It's the same bus that goes to Vientiane (US$14, 19 hours) and because you can't buy tickets the day before, it's advisable to get the bus station early as it fills up fast.

Getting Around

From the bus terminal to the main street a jumbo costs US$0.50. Jumbos from the main street to the airport, 7km away, cost US$4. Shared pick-ups also ply this route several times daily for just US$0.30 per person.

To the Nam Tha boat landing, or the nearby Boat Landing Guest House & Restaurant, figure on US$5 to charter a jumbo from the bus terminal, or US$0.30 per person on a shared jumbo as far as the turn-off for the boat landing. From that intersection it's only around 150m to the boat landing or the guesthouse.

You can hire bikes and motorcycles from a shop in town; see p197.

BOTEN

ບໍ່ເຕນ

This village on the Chinese border in the northeastern corner of Luang Nam Tha Province is little more than a transit point for visitors travelling between Laos and China, since Boten is a legal border crossing for all nationalities. There's a branch of Lao Development Bank in Boten where US dollars, Thai baht and Chinese yuan may be exchanged for kip, but not vice versa. **Boua Vanh Guest House** (071-252606; r US$5) has basic rooms and shared bathrooms, and there are around 10 small restaurants and noodle shops serving simple dishes. However, much better facilities are available in Mengla on the Chinese side. Many Chinese visit Boten on day passes to buy imported Thai goods.

See Luang Nam Tha (left) and Udomxai (p192) for details on transport to/from Boten.

CROSSING THE CHINESE BORDER AT MOHAN & BOTEN

From Mohan in the Yunnan Province, China, you can legally enter Laos at Boten in the Luang Nam Tha Province, Laos. Thirty-day tourist visas for Laos are available from the Lao immigration post on arrival in Boten for US$30, plus any overtime fees the officials may like to charge. To cross in the opposite direction, into China, you will need to have arranged a Chinese visa in advance.

The Lao border crossing is open from 8am to 4pm, while the Chinese crossing is open from 8am to 5pm. The best time of day to cross into Laos from China is the early morning when public transport onward to Luang Nam Tha and Udomxai is most frequently available. Similarly, the best time to cross the border into China is early in the morning; this enables you to get transport to Mengla relatively easily.

From Boten it's a short bus hop to the provincial capital, Luang Nam Tha, but if you arrive in Boten too late to take a bus, there are a couple of cheap guesthouses (US$1 to US$2) in the border town.

NAM THA RIVER TRIP

When the water is high enough, open-topped, longtail passenger boats navigate the Nam Tha between Pak Tha (where the Nam Tha feeds into the Mekong River) and Luang Nam Tha. This is a beautiful two-day river trip and it can be expensive, but thoroughly worthwhile as it's one of the few authentic river journeys in the region.

Along the way you can stop off and visit **Tham Davadeung**, a cave complex containing a large Buddha and several caverns. The cave is a short hike from the village of Ban Mo on the western bank of the river, about a third of the way between Pak Tha and Luang Prabang. Ask in the village for a key to the cave and a local guide to lead the way. A tip is expected for this service. Near **Ban Peng**, a village further along towards Pak Tha, there are reportedly two waterfalls and two caves of interest.

Most travellers stop over in **Ban Na Lae**, a charming village, located more or less the halfway point between Pak Tha and Luang Nam Tha.

In Pak Tha itself, you can visit an old Buddhist temple and wander through the local market.

Sleeping & Eating

Whether you manage to charter a boat for the entire trip, or have to change boats in Ban Na Lae, you will have to spend at least one night along the way.

There are two **guesthouses** (r US$2) in Na Lae, one near the boat landing, the other at the local market, and a noodle shop.

In Pak Tha you can stay at the **Souphanee Guest House** (r US$2) or the basic **Anusone Guest House** (r US$5).

You may also stay at your boatman's home, depending on where he lives along the river. Figure on spending about US$4 for the night; this generally includes a dinner of instant noodles and the price is negotiated when you charter your boat.

Getting There & Away

Because so many foreigners enter Laos via Huay Xai in the north, more people take this trip upstream from Pak Tha (about 36km via the Mekong River from Huay Xai) to Luang Nam Tha rather than vice versa, although the reverse direction is faster and less expensive.

Whether upriver or downriver, there is no regular boat service all the way from one end to the other, so you need to charter a boat. Many boat pilots in Pak Tha will only go as far as Na Lae. Conversely, most boat pilots in Luang Nam Tha will also only take you to Na Lae. We've heard reports of boat pilots who say they will take you the whole way, but who then stop in Na Lae and refuse to go further. For this reason, you should not pay for the trip until you reach the agreed-upon destination.

Charter prices vary according to several factors, including size of the boat, amount of paid cargo, river level and current fuel costs. In the March to May dry season, boats don't run at all since the river is usually too low for navigation then.

FROM LUANG NAM THA

If you're heading downriver from Luang Nam Tha, it's a good idea to get accurate advice about the river conditions from the **Boat Landing Guest House & Restaurant** (☎ 312398) – see p199. You can charter a boat for four to 10 people from the **boat station** (☎ 312014), **Nam**

NORTHERN LAOS

Tha River Boatman's Association (☎ 211305) right next door, or book through **Green Discovery** (☎ 211484; www.greendiscoverylaos.com). The latter charges a small booking fee. At the time of research the *approximate* cost of a boat from Luang Nam Tha to Na Lae was US$100, to Pak Tha US$170 and all the way to Huay Xai US$180 to US$200. Initiatives were afoot to establish more economical rates for travellers so these may change. Also, if you manage to find a boat going with a lot of paid cargo, your charter price could come down.

FROM HUAY XAI

From Huay Xai the best way to charter a boat is to speak to the boatmen directly – you can find them to the left of the immigration boat landing. You'll need to speak Lao or acquire the services of an interpreter as most of the boatmen don't speak English. The alternative that most travellers are faced with is to organise the trip through one of the tour agencies in town, who take up to 50% of the fare. This leaves the boatmen understandably disgruntled as they're barely making any money off the trip. Additionally, most boatmen in Huay Xai are reluctant to go further than Na Lae due to their inexperience with the rapids beyond here. So you may need to charter a second boat from Na Lae. Charters from Huay Xai to Na Lae cost US$100 to US$120, and from Na Lae to Luang Nam Tha around US$85. If you can find someone to go all the way from Huay Xai to Luang Nam Tha a charter is around US$180 to US$200. BAP Guest House (p216) is a good place to get information about the boat trip, and to arrange boat travel down the Mekong to Pak Tha, where you can then arrange for a boat up the Nam Tha.

TOURS

Finally, a much pricier but easier alternative is to book a Nam Tha River tour with Green Discovery. Tours start in either Huay Xai or Luang Nam Tha and last for two days. Rates include dinner and an overnight stay in the boatman's home and the cost per person is US$424/222/154/121/100/87 for one/two/three/four/five/six people.

So far speedboats aren't allowed on the Nam Tha. This appears to be more a case of quashing competition than harbouring concerns about noise pollution or safety, but the absence of speedboats makes the Nam Tha trip all the more pleasant.

LUANG NAM THA TO HUAY XAI

Route 3 between Luang Nam Tha and Huay Xai passes through several different kinds of terrain, from river plain to high mountains. The road is gradually being improved, and most vehicles with high road-clearance can make the drive as long as it's not too wet.

Vieng Phoukha

Vieng Phoukha is a pleasant trading town largely populated by Khamu farmers and mine workers. Sitting 66km south of Luang Nam Tha on Rte 3 towards Huay Xai, it doesn't draw too much stopover traffic, but it offers some of the most spectacular trekking in Luang Nam Tha Province...and that's saying something for a province defined by its magnificent landscape. The **Vieng Phoukha Ecoguide Service** (☎ 212400, 020-5985289) has an office on Rte 3 in the village centre, and arranges four treks to the region, ranging from one to three days. These treks are an excellent balance of cultural and natural exploration; they visit Akha, Khamu and Lahu ethnic villages, as well as various local limestone caves, including the 5km-long **Tham Nam Eng**. These caves have some of the most complex natural underground formations of any in Laos. Guides can also lead you to see the ruins of **Wat Mahapot** and the **khúu wíeng** (city walls) of an abandoned city thought to be 400 years old. The three-day Akha Trail encompasses the southern section of the Nam Ha NPA (see boxed text, p198), which is the stomping grounds of the endangered Black Cheek Crested Gibbons. Accommodation for multiday treks is homestays in villages. These treks are some of the most authentic in northern Laos, simply because they don't see much tourist traffic.

Vieng Phoukha has four guesthouses, all of them simple thatched-bamboo or wooden affairs: **Phonsavath** (☎ 212397; r US$3-5), **Don Vieng** (☎ 212394; r US$3-5), **Vieng Phoukha** (☎ 212390; r US$3-5) and **Bo Kung** (r US$3-5). All cater mostly to passing truck drivers, and each has its own rustic karaoke bar. Of the lot, Bo Kung is the quietest as it's about a kilometre off the main road through town.

There are one or two *săwngthăew* daily to/from Huay Xai (US$4.50, five hours), Luang Nam Tha (US$2.50, three hours) and Udomxai (US$4.50, seven hours). They depart and arrive from the market in the village centre.

Chaloen Suk

This small Khamu village inside the Nam Ha NPA is about 32km south of Luang Nam Tha. It makes a lovely day trip from Luang Nam Tha by bicycle, but it's also worthwhile spending the night here. The Nam Ha Ecoguide Service (see p197) has established a homestay in the village, providing the community with a share of the tourist dollar and travellers with the opportunity to spend a night with the Khamu. A one-night tour costs US$6.50 per person and includes your accommodation, dinner, breakfast and a day's guided trekking through the forest. You can also incorporate a night here into a longer trek or just book the homestay and make your own way to the village.

MUANG SING

ເມືອງສິງ

☎ 081 / pop 29,307

Lying on the broad river plains of the Nam La northwest of Luang Nam Tha, Muang Sing is a small town that grows on you by the hour. Its main appeal is a confluence of cultures – a traditional Thai Lü and Thai Neua cultural nexus, it's also a trade centre for Thai Dam, Akha, Hmong, Mien, Lolo and Yunnanese. This makes for some colourful people scenery in town, and traditional garb is a mainstay here. It's a utopia for trigger-happy photographers, but gaining permission for all shots will ensure a much more rewarding visit.

Beyond the town limits lies a bucolic mantle of rice paddies and quiet *bâan*, framed by hilly monsoon forest to the south and rising mountains to the north. It's magical territory to explore, particularly for culture junkies.

One of the arms of the 'China Road' passes through Muang Sing on its way to Mengla in Yunnan Province, China, and the area has come under a lot of Chinese influence since the 1960s. Visiting Chinese soldiers can be seen strutting around the streets and even some local hill-tribe men wear olive-drab Mao hats. Most telling is the presence of Chinese tractors, often bearing Chinese licence tags and transporting goods and people back and forth from the Chinese border – sugar cane to China, garlic and onions to Muang Sing.

History

From at least the late 16th century until 1803 Muang Sing belonged to the Thai principality of Chiang Khong, after which it came under the control of the Nan Kingdom. In the early 19th century much of Muang Sing's population was transferred to Chiang Kham district in Nan (now part of Thailand). Both the Siamese and the British subsequently laid claim to the area, but in 1896 France took Muang Sing as part of French Indochina.

As soon as the French left Laos in 1954, the area fell into the conflict between the Royal Lao Government and the Vietnamese-backed Pathet Lao. From then until the Pathet Lao takeover of Vientiane in 1975, ancient Muang Sing served as a setting for a series of international intrigues involving the Chinese, Vietnamese, Americans and Lao. The famous American 'jungle doctor'

NORTHERN LAOS

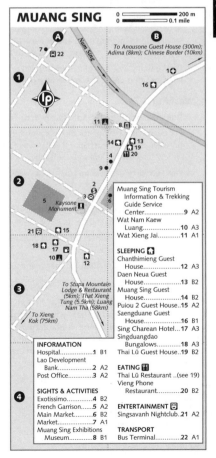

Muang Sing Tourism Information & Trekking Guide Service Center	9 A2
Wat Nam Kaew Luang	10 A3
Wat Xieng Jai	11 A1

SLEEPING

Chanthimieng Guest House	12 A3
Daen Neua Guest House	13 B2
Muang Sing Guest House	14 B2
Puiou 2 Guest House	15 A2
Saengduane Guest House	16 B1
Sing Charean Hotel	17 A3
Singduangdao Bungalows	18 A3
Thai Lü Guest House	19 B2

EATING

Thai Lü Restaurant	(see 19)
Vieng Phone Restaurant	20 B2

ENTERTAINMENT

Singsavanh Nightclub	21 A2

TRANSPORT

Bus Terminal	22 A1

INFORMATION

Hospital	1 B1
Lao Development Bank	2 A2
Post Office	3 A2

SIGHTS & ACTIVITIES

Exotissimo	4 B2
French Garrison	5 A2
Main Market	6 B2
Market	7 A1
Muang Sing Exhibitions Museum	8 B1

NORTHERN LAOS

RESPONSIBLE TREKKING

To help preserve the ecology and beauty of Laos, consider the following tips when trekking.

Rubbish

- Carry out all your rubbish. Don't overlook easily forgotten items, such as silver paper, orange peel, cigarette butts and plastic wrappers. Empty packaging should be stored in a dedicated rubbish bag. Make an effort to carry out rubbish left by others.

- Never bury your rubbish: digging disturbs soil and ground cover and encourages erosion. Buried rubbish will likely be dug up by animals, who may be injured or poisoned by it. It may also take years to decompose.

- Minimise waste by taking minimal packaging and no more food than you will need. Take reusable containers or stuff sacks.

- Sanitary napkins, tampons, condoms and toilet paper should be carried out despite the inconvenience. They burn and decompose poorly.

Human Waste Disposal

- Contamination of water sources by human faeces can lead to the transmission of all sorts of nasties. Where there is a toilet, please use it. Where there is none, bury your waste. Dig a small hole 15cm (6in) deep and at least 100m (320ft) from any watercourse. Cover the waste with soil and a rock. In snow, dig down to the soil.

- Ensure that these guidelines are applied to a portable toilet tent if one is being used by a large trekking party. Encourage all party members, including porters, to use the site.

Washing

- Don't use detergents or toothpaste in or near watercourses, even if they are biodegradable.

- For personal washing, use biodegradable soap and a water container (or even a lightweight, portable basin) at least 50m (160ft) away from the watercourse. Disperse the waste water widely to allow the soil to filter it fully.

- Wash cooking utensils 50m (160ft) from watercourses using a scourer or sand instead of detergent.

Erosion

- Hillsides and mountain slopes, especially at high altitudes, are prone to erosion. Stick to existing trails and avoid short cuts.

- If a well-used trail passes through a mud patch, walk through the mud so as not to increase the size of the patch.

- Avoid removing the plant life that keeps topsoil in place.

Tom Dooley, a pawn of the CIA in Laos from 1957 to 1961 and a man who courted Catholic sainthood until he was dismissed from the US Navy for his sexual orientation, founded a hospital in Muang Sing during this era. The town was virtually abandoned until after the 1975 revolution.

Information

Lao Development Bank (⏰ 8am-noon & 2-3.30pm Mon-Fri) Exchanges US dollars, Thai baht and Chinese yuan but at less than favourable rates.
Post office (⏰ 8am-4pm Mon-Fri)

Sights
ARCHITECTURE

Among the buildings in Muang Sing left standing from the French era is a 75-year-old brick and plaster **French garrison** that once housed Moroccan and Senegalese troops. It's now a Lao army outpost and some of the buildings have been restored; others stand in ruins.

Along the town's main street you'll also see hybrid Lao-French architecture where the ground-floor walls are brick and stucco and the upstairs walls are wooden. The top

Fires & Low-Impact Cooking

- Don't depend on open fires for cooking. The cutting of wood for fires in popular trekking areas can cause rapid deforestation. Cook on a lightweight kerosene, alcohol or Shellite (white gas) stove and avoid those powered by disposable butane gas canisters.

- If you are trekking with a guide and porters, supply stoves for the whole team. In alpine areas, ensure that all members are outfitted with enough clothing so that fires are not a necessity for warmth.

- If you patronise local accommodation, select those places that do not use wood fires to heat water or cook food.

- Fires may be acceptable below the tree line in areas that get very few visitors. If you light a fire, use an existing fireplace. Don't surround fires with rocks. Use only dead, fallen wood. Remember the adage 'the bigger the fool, the bigger the fire'. Use minimal wood, just what you need for cooking. In huts, leave wood for the next person.

- Ensure that you fully extinguish a fire after use. Spread the embers and flood them with water.

Wildlife Conservation

- Do not engage in or encourage hunting. It is illegal in all parks and reserves.

- Don't buy items made from endangered species.

- Don't attempt to exterminate animals in huts. In wild places, they are likely to be protected native animals.

- Discourage the presence of wildlife by not leaving food scraps behind you. Place gear out of reach and tie packs to rafters or trees.

- Do not feed the wildlife as this can lead to animals becoming dependent on hand-outs, to unbalanced populations and to diseases.

Camping & Walking on Private Property

- Always seek permission to camp from landowners.

- Public access to private property without permission is acceptable where public land is otherwise inaccessible, so long as safety and conservation regulations are observed.

Useful Websites

- **www.ecotourismlaos.com** This website, established by the Lao National Tourism Administration (LNTA), is a great resource for trekking, cultural activities and ecotourism throughout Laos.

NORTHERN LAOS

---

floor usually features a long wooden-railed veranda overlooking the street.

One of the better examples of the latter architectural style has been restored to contain the **Muang Sing Exhibitions Museum** (admission US$0.50; ☻ 8.30am-4pm Mon-Fri, 8-11am Sat), also known as the Tribal Museum. Inside is a collection of cultural artefacts from the area. On display are fishing utensils, looms, cooking utensils, old gongs, bells, pottery, musical instruments, Lao-style Buddha images, local ethnic costumes and a Buddha votive. The house containing the exhibition was once occupied by a local prince named Phanya Sekong. Note that the opening hours aren't always adhered to.

The two Buddhist temples in town show Thai Lü architectural influence. At **Wat Xieng Jai** on the main street, you can see this in the monastic quarters, with the massive steps and tiny windows, while in the less typical, rustic *wihǎan* (main Buddha sanctuary) you'll see classic Thai Lü–style *thóng* (long vertical prayer flags woven of colourful patterned cloth and bamboo). Red- and silver-lacquered pillars are also a Thai Lü temple design characteristic.

THE STORY OF O

Once upon a time, Muang Sing produced four to five tonnes of opium per year, about 3% of all opium produced in Laos. Some surveys estimate that over 45% of Akha villages were cultivating opium in 2000. This situation has changed drastically since the prime minister's decree of December 2000, ordering the elimination of opium in Lao PDR by 2006. Although the crop has not been entirely eradicated, the use of it as a commercial enterprise is now nonexistent.

Opium is still used in some villages as medicine, as food, in exchange for hired labour, for the hosting of guests and for spiritual ceremonies. A darker statistic estimates that there are still over a thousand opium addicts in Muang Sing, whose addiction rate as a district ranks fifth in all of Laos. As elsewhere in Southeast Asia the hill tribes appear to be most susceptible.

Opium is traditionally a condoned vice of the elderly, yet an increasing number of young people in the villages are now taking opium, heroin and amphetamines. In the town of Muang Sing, local Yunnanese and hill-tribe addicts sometimes peddle opium openly to *falang* visitors, thus setting a poor example for unaddicted local youth, and everyone knows where the local 'dens' are. If you're tempted to experiment with a little 'O', keep in mind the effect your behaviour may have on the local culture – you may smoke once and a few weeks later be hundreds of kilometres away, while the villagers continue to face the temptation every day.

Further south near the beginning of the road to Xieng Kok, **Wat Nam Kaew Luang** also has monastic quarters in the Thai Lü style, actually converted from a former *wihǎan*. Mudbrick antechambers before a wooden passageway leading to the *wihǎan* are unusual and may be a Yunnanese addition.

The northern end of town is the best place to see thatched Thai Lü and Thai Dam houses known as *héuan hǒng* (swan houses).

MARKETS

The **main market** at Muang Sing – *talàat nyai* in Lao, *kaat long* in Thai Lü – was once the biggest opium market in the Golden Triangle, a function officially sanctioned by the French. It was also one of the most colourful markets in northern Laos, selling textiles and wares from Thai Dam, Thai Lü, Hmong and Akha among other ethnic groups. But today it's largely a venue for fresh produce and Chinese-made, Western-style clothing.

Another **market** near the bus station in the town's northwest sells fresh produce and all manner of plastic goods and production-line clothing, which is great if you need to stock up on flip-flops or Tupperware.

VILLAGES

A number of Lao Thoeng and Lao Soung villages in the vicinity – particularly those of the Akha – can be visited on foot from Muang Sing. In general you'll find Hmong and Akha villages to the west and northwest of Muang Sing in the hills, repatriated Mien to the northeast, and Thai Neua and Thai Dam to the south. The Thai Dam are doing the best weaving in the district these days. One of the closest Thai Dam villages is Nong Bua.

Activities

The **Muang Sing Tourism Information & Trekking Guide Service Center** (☎ 020-2393534; 8-11am & 1.30-5pm Mon-Fri, 8-10am & 3-5pm Sat & Sun) has seven different treks to remote hill-tribe villages in the area, ranging from one- to three-day treks including homestays. Prices are US$35 per person per day for one person, but drop significantly the more people there are (as little as US$10 if there are seven people).

Exotissimo (www.exotissimo.com; 8am-noon & 1.30-5pm Mon-Fri) have a recently opened office right next door and offer day trips to eight different villages in the area. Its operation may have expanded to multiday trips by the time you read this.

If you're not up for a tour, you can experience Muang Sing's verdant surrounds by hiring a mountain bike (see Getting Around, p209) and riding north to within spitting distance of the Chinese border. The road passes by friendly *bâan* where people offer waves and *sabąi-diis*, and seamless rice paddies with hazy mountains rising in the background. Heading north the road is on a slight incline so making a start in the morning is a good idea, mostly so you can enjoy the free wheeling back in the hotter afternoon. Some guesthouses sell a sketch map with information about the various villages and how to find them for about US$0.75.

The Chinese–Lao border (crossings legal for Lao and Chinese citizens only) is only 10km from Muang Sing, with a checkpoint 1km before the border. Along the way the narrow, paved road (originally constructed by the French) passes through three villages, including one called **Ban Nakham** at Km 100 (about 4km or 5km from the Chinese border) whose mudbrick homes suggest a Yunnanese population.

Festivals & Events

During the full moon of the 12th lunar month, which usually occurs between late October and mid-November, all of Muang Sing and half of the province turns out for the **That Xieng Tung Festival**. Centred around a Thai Lü stupa (That Xieng Tung) on a sacred hill 5.5km south of town, the festival combines Theravada Buddhism and animistic elements of worship, and includes many of the ceremonies associated with the That Luang Festival in Vientiane (which occurs at the same time).

The *thâat* is around 10m high and is constructed in the Lanna–Lan Xang style, with a stepped, whitewashed octagonal base and gilded spire. A shrine building off to one side contains a row of Buddha images on a sarcophagus like Thai Lü altar.

The festival begins a few days before the official full moon day as merit-makers climb a broad winding path to the *thâat* grounds atop the hill and pay their respects by carrying offerings of candles, flowers and incense around the base of the stupa – a tradition called *wíen thíen*. On the morning of the full moon Buddhist monks from around the province gather at the stupa for *ták bàat*, the collection of alms and food. There are also traditional dance performances, carnival-style game booths, and plenty of food vendors selling *khào laam* (sweetened sticky rice baked in bamboo), noodles and other snacks. Many Chinese vendors cross over from Yunnan during the festival to sell cheap Chinese cigarettes, beer and apples. Festival activities spill over into town, where there are nightly outdoor Lao pop-music performances with lots of drinking and dancing. Food vendors line the main street at night with candlelit tables.

In spite of its Thai Lü origins, the That Xieng Tung Festival is celebrated by virtually all ethnic groups in the area (including festival-goers from as far away as Xishuangbanna, the original Thai Lü homeland in China's Yunnan Province), as much for its social and entertainment value as for anything else. This is the biggest event of the year here, and one of the best times to visit Muang Sing.

THE BATTLE FOR LUANG NAM THA'S FORESTS

Across Luang Nam Tha, vast tracts of forest are being cleared to fuel the increasing economic partnership between Lao and China. Cash crops such as banana, corn and sugar cane are replacing traditional agriculture at a rapid pace, as the appetite of the Chinese economy continues to swell. Although the crops have brought millions of dollars to Laos, the ultimate winner is corporate China, and the environmental impact, particularly in the case of rubber plantations, poses a devastating, long-term threat.

The forests of Luang Nam Tha, and in particular Nam Ha NPA, are some of the most biodiverse in Southeast Asia. So rich is the park in flora and fauna that it has been declared an Asean Natural Heritage Site. Unfortunately this has not prevented over 4,580 ha of degraded forest in the province being cleared for rubber plantations.

Replacing natural forest with a monocrop reduces biodiversity and erodes the soil, not only within its borders but in the surrounding area also. In July and August 2006, heavy rains in the Luang Nam Tha district that would once have been absorbed by the indigenous landscape resulted in flooding, killing at least two people and damaging countless hectares of farmland. Additionally this devastation reduces the land that can be used for ecotourism; an endeavour that reaps greater and more egalitarian financial rewards as well as social benefits. There is a push from the Unesco Nam Ha Ecotourism project to limit the future of rubber plantations in favour of expanded ecotourism. Although this decision is well and truly out of tourists' hands, they can contribute by taking a guided tour into the park, consequently fuelling the sustainable alternative to cash crops.

Sleeping

Thai Lü Guest House (☎ 212375; r US$3) The large and airy rooms with simple beds, mosquito nets and squat-toilet bathrooms at this atmospheric guesthouse run off a lovely timber balcony upstairs. It's all housed in a two-storey French-era wooden structure.

Chanthimieng Guest House (☎ 212351; r US$4-8) Just opened at the time of research, this guesthouse has fresh, wide-open rooms with less-than-comfy beds but decent bathrooms with Western toilets and cold showers. The location, off the main street, is idyllic, and the sweeping balcony upstairs makes the most of the oceanic rice paddies out back. The owners adopt all guests upon entry.

Anousone Guest House (r US$5) Just outside of town, this grand-looking guesthouse has fine rooms with polished floors and bathrooms, hot-water showers and ample space. It's not as interesting as some of the cheaper guesthouses but an extra US$2 buys you a good dose of clean comfort.

Singduangdao Bungalows (r US$5) Tucked behind a clutch of residences, this spread of bungalows is set on a spacious property. Some of the bungalows are brick but the nicest are the timber and bamboo versions with plenty of room, spotless interiors and hot water showers.

Saengduane Guest House (☎ 212376; r US$5-8) At the northern end of town is the large and well-run Saengduane. This concrete/plaster rectangular building has simple rooms out the back with acceptable cold-water showers, mosquito nets and wallpapered floors. There are also two thatched bungalows with hot-water bathrooms. With good views across to the mountains from the balcony, there are even better views from the accessible rooftop. There's also a restaurant out front.

Sing Charean Hotel (☎ 212347; r US$5-8) In a large alabaster building, this spot has clean but ageing and slightly clinical rooms. They're a huge step up from the very budget guesthouses though and the bright bathrooms have hot water. It's accommodating enough, just a little soulless.

Puiou 2 Guest House (☎ 212348; r US$9) Cornered around a grassy lawn, this series of quaint concrete and bamboo bungalows have gloriously tidy interiors, comfortable beds, fans and clean, tiled bathrooms with hot-water showers. They're a private alternative to the guesthouses and each has a wee veranda.

Stupa Mountain Lodge & Restaurant (☎ 020-5686555; stupamtn@laotel.com; r US$10) Sitting pretty on a hillside 5km south of 'town', this lodge has a handful of lovely wooden bungalows with hot-water bathrooms and private verandas. There's also a restaurant on site.

Also available:

Daen Neua Guest House (☎ 212369; r US$3) Basic rooms upstairs with grotty bathrooms.

Muang Sing Guest House (☎ 212375; s/d US$3/4) Snug but airy rooms and affable owners. Glorious views from the roof.

OUTSIDE MUANG SING

Adima (☎ 212372; r US$5-6) In a village 8km outside Muang Sing towards the Chinese border, the Adima's ethnic-style houses are set in the middle of rice paddies, and the guesthouse is within walking distance of several Mien and Akha villages. Adima offers ad-hoc transport to/from Muang Sing throughout the day (US$0.50).

Eating

Daen Neua Guest House Restaurant (☎ 212369; meals US$0.60-1.50; ☾ breakfast, lunch & dinner) The street-front restaurant beneath this guesthouse dishes up good, hot, filling Lao and Thai food, plus good fruit shakes.

Vieng Phone Restaurant (meals US$0.80-1.50; ☾ breakfast, lunch & dinner) This cavernous indoor restaurant could do with a splash of sunshine on the menu, but it's a decent spot to fill up on pad thai, fried rice, *láap* and roasts (including fish). Western breakfasts cater to those who aren't up for hot noodles first thing in the am.

Thai Lü Restaurant (☎ 212375; meals US$1-1.60; ☾ breakfast, lunch & dinner) Muang Sing's best spot for authentic Thai Lü fare such as *nam pik awng* – fermented soy bean paste, or *jeow* (local chilli paste), wafers. There are also Thai, Lao and Western dishes and the wide-open setting makes for a pleasant spot to enjoy it all.

Most of the guesthouses have small dining areas downstairs and the main street is peppered with simple *fǒe* shops selling tasty cheap fare. The large market next to the bus station sells a limited selection of fresh fruit and vegetables.

Entertainment

Singsavanh Nightclub (☼ 9-11.30pm) Most of Muang Sing is dead asleep by 9pm except at the Singsavanh, near the Sing Charean Hotel, where the locals get down to live Lao and Chinese pop.

Getting There & Away

Săwngthăew ply back and forth between Muang Sing and Luang Nam Tha (US$2, two hours, about six daily). The winding, partially sealed 58km road from Luang Nam Tha to Muang Sing parallels the Nam Tha, Nam Luang and Nam Sing, crossing them at various points along the way, and passes through strikingly beautiful monsoon forest and several hill-tribe villages. The deep trench you'll see alongside the road between Nam Tha and Muang Sing is part of a hydropower and irrigation project intended to serve the Muang Sing plain.

There are also about four *săwngthăew* a day to Xieng Kok (US$2, three to four hours).

In Muang Sing most passenger vehicles depart from the 'new' **bus terminal** in the northwest of town, near the Nam Sing.

CHINA

Although Muang Sing is only 10km from the Chinese border, you can't legally cross into China here without permission arranged through the Lao National Tourism Administration (LNTA) in Vientiane (see p91).

Getting Around

Bicycle hire is available from most guest houses and the Muang Sing Tourism Information & Trekking Guide Service Center (p206) for around US$2 per day. There are no jumbos or public transport within Muang Sing.

XIENG KOK

ບຊຽງກົກ

Roughly 72km from Muang Sing via a smooth, graded road that parallels the Nam Ma much of the way, this bustling river port on the Mekong River has little to attract the traveller aside from its semiremote location. Until as recently as the early 1990s, up to six refineries along the Mekong between Xieng Kok and Huay Xai refined opium for world markets. Today huge Chinese barges from Yunnan Province call at Xieng Kok frequently, and it's reported that Xieng Kok is a major smuggling conduit for opium, heroin and amphetamines in both directions, depending on market destination.

Perhaps the best time to schedule a Xieng Kok visit is on the 14th and 28th of each month, when traders from Myanmar, Thailand, China and Laos gather to buy and sell their wares. Many different hill tribes, particularly the Akha, descend on the town on these days.

Most visitors to Xieng Kok are more interested in taking a boat down the Mekong to Huay Xai. See below for more details.

Some travellers stop off at **Muang Long**, a heavily Akha district a little more than halfway to Xieng Kok from Muang Sing. There are some very good forest walks near Muang Long, especially along the Nam Long.

Sleeping & Eating

In Xieng Kok, the **Xieng Kok Resort** (r US$5) sits on a hill and boasts simple but comfortable wooden bungalows on stilts. Not far from the boat landing, **Kaemkhong Guest House** (r US$3) offers basic rattan-walled rooms with shared facilities. Two restaurants in Xieng Kok serve simple but remarkably good Lao food for the location.

In Muang Long, **Jony** (r US$3) has simple rooms with private squat toilet and coldwater bathrooms attached, **Ounseng** (r US$3-4) has rooms with and without private bathrooms, and **Thatsany** (r US$3) has similarly basic rooms with attached bathrooms.

Getting There & Away

BOAT

The journey from Muang Sing to Huay Xai via Xieng Kok is a chop-and-change affair that can be more trouble than it's worth. Transport from Muang Sing is straightforward (see *săwngthăew* below), but once in Xieng Kok you are largely limited to speedboat charter down to Huay Xai. Holding up to six passengers, these cost in the vicinity of US$150. The journey takes four hours and, like all speedboat travel in Laos, is risky (see the boxed text, p219).

The alternative is to hang around Xieng Kok for a few days in the hope of hitching a ride with a slow boat, or chartering one. Chinese traders operate them and if you can negotiate passage (be prepared to pay around US$100 for the eight- to 10-hour journey) it's a beautiful trip. Something to

NORTHERN LAOS

be aware of is that these boats often dock in Thailand, which would entail you entering Thailand without having passed through Laos immigration.

Via Muang Mom & Ton Pheung

You can get better rates by asking for a speedboat to Muang Mom rather than Huay Xai. Muang Mom, about two hours downriver, is a large speedboat depot near the point where the borders of Thailand, Myanmar and Laos meet. All boats must stop here anyway to allow Lao immigration and customs officers to check everyone's papers.

A speedboat from Xieng Kok to Muang Mom costs around US$15 per person (assuming there are six passengers), and another speedboat on to Huay Xai – just 1½ hours further downriver – will cost around US$6 per person.

Another way to reach Huay Xai is to catch a speedboat to Ton Pheung (US$10 per person or US$60 charter), the Lao town opposite Chiang Saen. From Ton Pheung you can catch a bus onward to Huay Xai (US$1.50), along a decent graded road.

SĂWNGTHĂEW

A graded, unsealed road extends 72km from Muang Sing to Xieng Kok (US$2, two hours, three daily).

PHONGSALI PROVINCE

Enclosed on three sides by China and Vietnam, Phongsali is a visual feast, kept pristine by arduous journeys and unwieldy terrain. The road north from Udomxai ribbons around infinite hills; their lush counterparts cascading into the distance beyond the line of sight. In parts the forest is so congested that vines and trees clamour on top of each other in competitive and glorious mayhem. Tiny *bâan* appear around random bends, tumbling down dusty slopes, and villagers are still a little flummoxed at the sight of foreigners. This will change if road conditions ever improve, but for now this neck of the country remains relatively remote to the tourist trail.

Phongsali's population density is just 9.4 per square kilometre, the lowest in the country after Sekong and Attapeu Provinces. Twenty-two ethnicities make up the prov-

ince's population of approximately 166,000, among them Kheu, Sila, Lolo, Hanyi, Hmong, Pala, Oma, Eupa, Loma, Pusang, Mien, Akha, Haw, Thai Dam, Thai Khao, Thai Lü, Phuan, Khamu, Phai, Vietnamese and Yunnanese. The Phu Noi (recognisable by their white leggings) are by far the most numerous, followed by the Thai Lü, Haw, Akha and Khamu. As in Udomxai and Luang Nam Tha, the Chinese presence has increased steeply with recent road and construction development. In fact Chinese-style tea continues to replace poppy farms as a significant cash crop.

Phongsali's Phu Den Din NPA covers 1310 sq km in the northeastern corner of the province along the Lao–Vietnamese border, adjacent to Vietnam's Muong Nhe Nature Reserve. Mountains in this area reach up to 1948m and bear 77% primary forest cover. Many threatened or endangered mammals live in the area, including elephant, tiger, clouded leopard, banteng, gaur and Asiatic black bear. Access to Phu Den Din remains difficult due to the lack of roads, and there are as yet no guided treks to the NPA.

The best areas for hill-tribe village exploration are found in the extreme northwest corner of the province, where there are also few roads. Reaching this area involves walking two or more days; guides are available in Phongsali.

PHONGSALI

ຜົ້ງສາລີ

☎ 088 / pop 25,000 / elevation 1400m

Sitting high on a mountainous platform on the steep slopes of Phou Fa (1626m), the provincial capital of the north is a petite town with one of the most colourful populations in the country. About 70% of the population is Phu Noi, but modernity has begun its steady trickle, and stoic Phu Noi women carrying ungainly loads on their backs totter alongside cell phone–clad Chinese and brand-new 4WDs. The town remains dormant until around 10am, when vendors open their wooden shutters and the streets suddenly teem with spirited schoolchildren keen to practise their English, or simply offer a shy *sabąi-dii*. It's an enchanting place to hang the boots for a while and observe.

Phongsali possesses a year-round cool climate that comes as a welcome relief during the hotter season (March to May). In fact, the climate is closer to what you find in northern Vietnam than in much of Laos. It can be quite cold during the cool season, with temperatures as low as 5°C at night and 10°C during the day. Fog and low clouds are common in the morning at any time of year. Rainfall can be intense and cold. Be sure to bring a pullover, jacket and waterproofs, even in March, April and May, just in case.

Information

Lao Development Bank Can change US dollars, Thai baht or Chinese yuan (but no travellers cheques) for kip.
Lao Telecom Office Cardphone available.
Post office Across the road from the Telecom Office.

Sights

The **Museum of Tribes** (admission US$0.20; ☒ 8-11.30am & 1.30-4.30pm Mon-Fri) displays locally curated exhibits on the Phongsali Province's diverse cultures.

If you wander through the town's backstreets and alleys you'll find some interesting old Phu Noi (similar to Tibetan) and Chinese brick-and-wood architecture.

The hike to the top of **Phou Fa** is glorious, if punishing, but the 400-odd stone steps are mercifully interrupted by shady rest areas. Towards the top is a grassy plateau with picnic tables and a carer's residence – you need to pay him US$0.30/0.50/1 per person/camera/video camera to climb the remaining steps to the summit. The dramatic views from the top show the town dissipating into a hazy, hilly film.

Activities

Trekking is a highligh. ... province, and the intre... with some of the least affe... villages in Indochina.

The **Provincial Tourism Off**. ... (☎ 210098; ☒ 9am-4pm Mon-Fri) is actu... ...mall room within the 'Organisation of People Prosecutor Provincial Phongsali' building. Staffed by exceptionally friendly staff with reasonable English, it arranges one- to five-day treks in the surrounding hills. Accommodation is in Akha and Up Noi villages, which receive about 50% of your fee. Like those in Luang Nam Tha, these tours have a heavy emphasis on ecological and cultural sensitivity, and the office equips trekkers with the information they need to tread lightly. The cost depends on the size of the group and duration of a trek, but for an indication, a one-day trek for one person costs US$25, and for the maximum size group of six it costs US$12 per person.

Sleeping

Yu Houa Guest House (210186; r US$3-5) This friendly Phu Noi–owned guesthouse near the bus terminal has plain but clean rooms. Those on the top floor have cold-water showers and Western toilets and those on the lower levels share squat toilet bathrooms.

Sengsaly Guest House (☎ 210165; r US$3-5) This small and simple guesthouse has rudimentary rooms with mosquito nets and attached bathrooms containing squat toilets

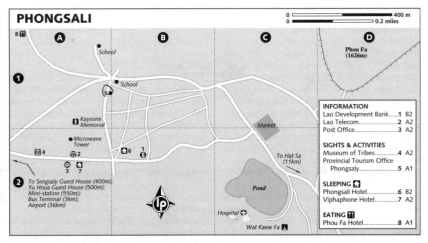

PHONGSALI

0 — 400 m
0 — 0.2 miles

School
School
Kaysone Memorial
Microwave Tower
Market
To Hat Sa (11km)
To Sengsaly Guest House (400m);
Yu Houa Guest House (500m);
Mini-station (550m);
Bus Terminal (3km);
Airport (36km)
Pond
Hospital
Wat Kaew Fa
Phou Fa (1626m)

INFORMATION
Lao Development Bank.....1 B2
Lao Telecom.....................2 A2
Post Office.......................3 A2

SIGHTS & ACTIVITIES
Museum of Tribes............4 A2
Provincial Tourism Office Phongsaly....................5 A1

SLEEPING ⌂
Phongsali Hotel................6 B2
Viphaphone Hotel............7 A2

EATING ⊞
Phou Fa Hotel..................8 A1

NORTHERN LAOS

...oop showers. Each room has complimentary Lao tea and the beds are dressed in warm covers.

Phongsali Hotel (☎ 412042; r with/without bathroom US$3/5) The Chinese-built Phongsali Hotel, in a centrally located four-storey building, has austere but bright rooms owing to large windows – the upper storey rooms afford decent views. Most rooms have three beds and the most expensive have hot water. The whole place could do with a scrubbing, but it's tidy. The staff are indifferent though.

Viphaphone Hotel (☎ 210111; r US$6) The three-storey Viphaphone offers good value with spacious sunny rooms packing Western-style bathrooms and glorious hot-water showers. They make a good stab at furnishing the rooms with coffee tables, wardrobes and even hat stands. Try to get a corner room for 180-degree views of the street below from the sizable windows.

HAT SA

If you get stuck in Hat Sa, a stopover for visitors heading to Phongsali via boat, **Wanna Guesthouse** (tr US$3) has three-bed rooms with floor mattresses and mosquito nets above a family home.

Eating

Yu Houa Guest House restaurant (☎ 210186; meals US$0.50-2; ☼ breakfast, lunch & dinner) The ground floor of this guesthouse is devoted to an airy restaurant serving filling and cheap fare. The menu has excellent Lao-Yunnan dishes and a modicum of stodgy Western fare.

Phongsali Hotel (☎ 412042; meals US$1-2.50; ☼ lunch & dinner) The restaurant here has a reasonable menu with ubiquitous *tôm yám* and stir-fries, plus a good selection of regional specialities like sweet sausage. You can choose between Beerlao and Beer China to wash it all down. It's a sunny space during the day, although you have to share the ambience with Chinese soap operas on the TV. At night it thuds out lurid pop and if you join the modest crowd you're sure to be the main event.

Phou Fa Hotel (☎ 412057; meals US$1.50-2.50; ☼ dinner) This reformed army barracks once moonlighted as a hotel but all that remains now is a concrete bunker of a bar and restaurant. The aesthetics are a little odd, but the fireplace keeps things cosy and the food is good. The menu offers stir fries for the tame and authentic Lao dishes for the adventurous.

There are several noodle shops on the main street through town towards the market. Chinese beer is cheap all over town, while Beerlao is relatively expensive. The local *lào-láo* is tinted green with herbs and is quite a smooth tipple. Good Chinese-style tea is also available.

Getting There & Away

AIR

Lao Airlines (☎ 210794; Boun Neua airport) operates a Y-12 to/from Vientiane (one way/return US$92/175, 1½ hours, Thursday and Sunday) to Boun Neua, about 36km west of Phongsali on Rte 1B (the main road). You then need to wait for the bus heading to Phongsali from Udomxai, which arrives anywhere between 4pm and 6pm and costs US$5. You may also find a *săwngthăew* to do the trip for a similar fare.

BOAT

Hat Sa can be reached by boat along the Nam Ou from Muang Khua. In Muang Khua you can choose between slow boats (US$10, six hours) and speedboats (US$13, three hours), departures depend on passenger demand). Either type of boat may be chartered from Muang Khua to Hat Sa for US$80 to US$100, carrying up to 15 passengers in a slow boat or six passengers in a speedboat. Bear in mind, however, that river traffic is sporadic and you may need to wait a day or two for passage. When the river level is low, particularly from March to May, the boat service may be cancelled altogether.

BUS & 4WD

There is one bus daily to/from Udomxai (US$6, eight to 12 hours, 8am). The Phongsali bus terminal is about 3km west of town; if you don't fancy walking you can catch a *săwngthăew* (US$0.30 to US$0.50 depending on the number of passengers and your bargaining skills) from a ministation about 50m west of Yu Houa Guest House (p211). Trucks to Hat Sa (US$7, one hour) also leave from this mini-station between 7am and 7.30am daily.

Hat Sa

From the boat landing at the small town of Hat Sa, passengers can share a 4WD vehicle (US$1.50 per person, US$15 charter) for the 20km journey along an unsealed road to Phongsali.

Mengla (China)

If the Yunnan–Phongsali border should open to foreign travellers in the future (it is currently open to Chinese and Lao nationals only), it will be easier to reach Phongsali from Mengla (in Yunnan), than from most points in Laos. From the Lao settlement of Ban Pakha (a village of Akha refugees who fled the communist takeover of China in the 1940s), near the Chinese border, to Phongsali you could take a bus to Bun Neua, where you would change to another bus for the final leg to Phongsali.

UDOMXAI TO PHONGSALI

Sixty-two kilometres northeast of Udomxai, Rte 2E reaches a three-way junction at the village of Pak Nam Noi. From Pak Nam Noi, Rte 3 continues east-northeast to Muang Khua and to the Vietnamese border, while route 1B proceeds north-northeast to Phongsali.

From Udomxai to Pak Nam Noi about two-thirds of the road is now sealed, and before long this entire stretch will no doubt be sealed. On the way to Pak Nam Noi you'll pass through scenic **Muang La** (25km from Udomxai), a tidy Thai Lü village with a classic Thai Lü temple and a couple of restaurants built alongside a river.

In Pak Nam Noi the **Pak Nam Noy Guest House** (r US$2), near the three-way junction, can provide a room if you miss a bus connection and become stranded here.

Roughly halfway between Udomxai and Phongsali, **Boun Tai** (60km from Udomxai) is a prospering Thai Lü town popular as a base for NGOs and as a rest-stop for people travelling to and from Phongsali. The **Khem Nam Lan** (r US$2-4), **Boun Tai** (r US$2-4) and **Hong Thong** (r US$2-4) guesthouses all offer decent accommodation. The Hong Thong prepares good Chinese food, while the slightly more elaborate River View Restaurant does Lao as well as Chinese.

Two- to three-day treks into the Nam Lan Conservation area and surrounding Thai Yang, Akha and Thai Lü villages can be organised through the District Tourism Office, which you can find at the top of the hill next to the district administration office. Trek highlights, aside from pristine jungle and homestays in the villages, include Thai Lü temples and hot springs.

Next comes **Ban Yo** (30km from Boun Tai), where a turn to the left leads directly to **Ban Pakha** (19km) on the Chinese border and a turn right goes to **Boun Neua** (21km) and Phongsali. Although Boun Neua is essentially a Thai Lü village, the abundance of Chinese signs and the presence of a Chinese-style guesthouse and restaurant demonstrates the close connection with China, only 40km away. The bus from Udomxai stops in Bou Neua for a wee break, but long enough for everyone to trundle off. Make sure you don't confuse this with Phongsali, as it's a hefty 36km hike to Phongsali if you let the bus leave without you. Alternatively there's a decent guesthouse right next to the bus station if you do get stuck.

At Boun Neua the road forks into one road leading northeast to Phongsali (41km) or another heading north to **Ou Tai** (93km). Ou Tai is known to be a centre for several Phongsali Province hill tribes.

MUANG KHUA

ເມືອງຂວາ

☎ 081 / pop 20,000

Muang Khua is a small but thriving trading town that climbs from the banks of the Nam Ou in a jumble of shacks and concrete. It sits at the junction of the Nam Ou and Rte 1A, which connects Udomxai and Phongsali Provinces with Dien Bien Phu in Vietnam. Many Vietnamese and Chinese people have migrated here to do business and it's growing steadily as a result.

Although Muang Khua is not much of a destination in itself, a quick walk around town will reveal a few older French colonial buildings amid the growing number of cement shophouses. A stroll across the old woodplank and steel-cable suspension bridge over the Nam Phak, a Nam Ou tributary, affords some good river and mountain views and leads to the Khamu village of Ban Na Tum.

The Lao Development Bank here can change US dollars, Thai baht and Chinese yuan (cash only) for kip. Electric power comes on nightly from 6.30pm to 10pm.

There have been rumours that the Lao–Vietnamese border, around 55km east of Muang Khua, will someday be open to international travellers. When it does, this route will surely become popular among those travelling to or from Dien Bien Phu in Vietnam. The border town on the Lao side is called Tai Xang; on the Vietnamese side it's Tay Trang. At present the only way to reach the Vietnamese border is by tug across the Nam Ou, although the influx of trade may result in a bridge spanning the relatively short divide.

Sleeping & Eating

Singsavanh Guest House (r US$3) In a convenient spot right outside the bus station, this simple property has rudimentary rooms with shared bathrooms.

Nam Ou Guest House & Restaurant (r US$5, without bathroom US$3/5) This rambling and homely guesthouse overlooks the boat landing and has pleasant, clean rooms upstairs, some with attached hot shower and squat toilets. There are also a few rooms downstairs although they're squalid in comparison. The restaurant (meals US$0.50 to US$1.50) has good river views and a basic menu. The friendly owner speaks French and English. You can reach the guesthouse from the town's main road or from the main boat landing.

Keophila Guest House (☎ 210907; r US$4) This central guesthouse on the main drag has fresh rooms with private bathrooms. Unfortunately the rigid beds are murder on the back, and it's often full. The bar next door serves a seemingly permanent crowd with a seemingly endless supply of Beerlao.

Sernnaly Hotel (☎ 212445; r US$10) This central, Chinese-built hotel is a huge leap from all other accommodation in town. Immaculate rooms have attached Western bathrooms, hospital-clean sheets on the beds and plenty of space. The downstairs restaurant (meals US$1 to US$3) serves Chinese, Vietnamese, Thai and Lao food, but you need to give advance notice.

Other than the restaurants at the Nam Ou Guest House and Sernnaly Hotel, you'll find the usual crop of noodle stands at the market near the bus terminal.

Getting There & Away
BOAT
When the river level is high enough, you can reach Muang Khua via boat on the Nam Ou. See Luang Prabang (p156), Nong Khiaw (p161) and Muang Ngoi Neua (p164). See Phongsali (p212) for details on boat travel from Muang Khua to Hat Sa, 20km north of Phongsali.

BUS
The bus terminal is 2km west of the city. Morning buses to/from Udomxai (US$4, four hours, two daily) and Luang Prabang (US$6, eight hours, two daily).

To get to Phongsali you need to catch a *săwngthăew* to Pak Nam Noi (US$2, one hour, 8am) and then wait for the bus that passes through from Udomxai at around 10am. The bus journey from Pak Nam Noi to Phongsali costs US$4.80 and takes seven to 10 hours including frequent stops.

BOKEO PROVINCE

Laos's smallest and second least populous province, wedged between the Mekong River border with Thailand and the border with Myanmar, has a population of just 145,000. The river defines much of Bokeo's character – bringing trade and tourists in from Thailand and China. Huay Xai gets the lion's share, but villages nearby hold archaeological and cultural gems, and are deserving of exploration. Moreover it's a good launching pad for journeys to Luang Nam Tha and Udomxai.

In earlier times Bokeo was known as Hua Khong (Head of the Mekong); its current name means 'Gem Mine', a reference to minor sapphire deposits in Huay Xai district. Despite its diminutive size, Bokeo harbours 34 ethnicities, the second-highest number of ethnic groups per province (after Luang Nam Tha) in the country. They include Lao Huay (Lenten), Khamu, Akha, Hmong, Mien, Kui, Phai, Lamet, Samtao, Tahoy, Shan, Phu Thai, Thai Dam, Thai Khao, Thai Daeng, Thai Lü, Phuan, Thai Nai, Ngo, Kalom, Phuvan, Musoe (Lahu) and Chinese people. Bokeo is the only Lao province with a significant population of Lahu, a hill tribe common in northern Myanmar and Thailand.

HUAY XAI
ຫ້ວຍຊາຍ
☎ 084 / pop 15,500
This bustling river port on the Mekong is in a slow and steady state of flux, encouraged by tourist dollars and Thai, Lao and Chinese trade. The crux of town only spans a few hundred metres and the main street is a strip of guesthouses, shops and tour op-

NORTHERN LAOS

erators. Once you head a kilometre or so in either direction, however, you'll find yourself in sleepy *bâan* populated by friendly residents. The rich green hills of Bokeo rise in the background and the mighty Mekong, intrinsic to the town's character, forms a natural border with Thailand. Most visitors head here solely for the opportunity to take a slow boat journey on the Mekong (see p218), or to head north, but Huay Xai has managed to remain relaxed and to avoid the hassle common to pit stops and border towns. This makes for some pleasant ambling. It's also a good base for trips into Bokeo Province itself.

For centuries Huay Xai was a disembarkation point for Yunnanese caravans led by the Hui (Chinese Muslims) on their way to Chiang Rai and Chiang Mai in ancient Siam; today Chinese barges from Yunnan are able to navigate this far, so there is still a brisk trade in Chinese goods.

Information

Lao Development Bank (🕔 8am-3.30pm Mon-Fri) Also has an exchange booth at the immigration and customs office near the ferry pier. US dollars, travellers cheques or cash in baht and Japanese yen can be changed for kip at either location, but not vice versa.

Khaenlao Tours (Th Saykhong) Travel agent selling boat tickets and tours around Bokeo.

Phoudoi Travel Co (Th Saykhong) Boat tickets and tours to Lanten and Khamu villages.

Post office (Th Saykhong) Also contains a telephone office open 8am to10pm.

Dangers & Annoyances

When arriving in Huay Xai from Thailand there's an official-looking desk at the boat landing. Men here will do their best to convince you that there's no bus to Luang Nam Tha (this is false) and try to sell you a ticket along the Mekong to Luang Prabang for the next day. They may also try to sell you an overpriced ticket along the Nam Tha, up to Luang Nam Tha. It pays to walk past them and find out your best options once you're in town.

Sights & Activities

A set of *naga* stairs ascends from a point not far from the ferry landing to **Wat Jom Khao**

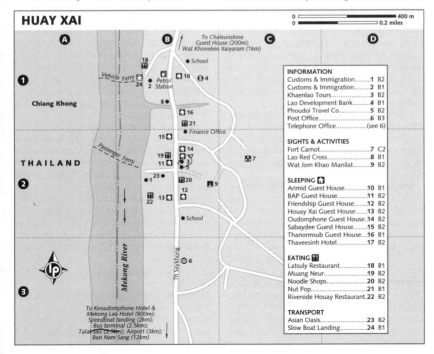

HUAY XAI

0 — 400 m
0 — 0.2 miles

To Chaleunshine Guest House (200m); Wat Khonekeo Xaiyaram (1km)

INFORMATION
Customs & Immigration........1 B2
Customs & Immigration........2 B1
Khaenlao Tours...................3 B2
Lao Development Bank.........4 B1
Phoudoi Travel Co...............5 B2
Post Office.........................6 B3
Telephone Office............(see 6)

SIGHTS & ACTIVITIES
Fort Carnot.........................7 C2
Lao Red Cross.....................8 B1
Wat Jom Khao Manilat........9 B2

SLEEPING 🛏
Arimid Guest House............10 B1
BAP Guest House................11 B2
Friendship Guest House.......12 B2
Houay Xai Guest House.......13 B2
Oudomphone Guest House..14 B2
Sabaydee Guest House........15 B2
Thanormsub Guest House....16 B1
Thaveesinh Hotel...............17 B2

EATING 🍴
Latsuly Restaurant..............18 B1
Muang Neur......................19 B2
Noodle Shops....................20 B2
Nut Pop...........................21 B1
Riverside Houay Restaurant.22 B2

TRANSPORT
Asian Oasis.......................23 B2
Slow Boat Landing..............24 B1

Chiang Khong

THAILAND

Vehicle Ferry
Petrol Station
Passenger Ferry
Finance Office
School
School

Mekong River
Th Saykhong

To Keoudomphone Hotel & Mekong Lao Hotel (800m); Speedboat landing (2km); Bus terminal (2.5km); Talat Sao (2.5km); Airport (3km); Ban Nam Sang (12km)

Manilat, a thriving temple that overlooks the town and river. Constructed in 1880, the teak Shan-style temple houses a 1458 stele donated by a former Chiang Khong prince. Many of the brightly coloured Jataka paintings that decorate the exterior of the *sĭm* were sponsored by Lao refugees who had been repatriated from the US.

It's worth walking the short distance north to **Wat Khonekeo Xaiyaram** in Ban Khone Keo. The lavish frontage has magnificent gold, green and red pillars and doors. It's also in a peaceful setting, with banks of green hills rising in the background.

French-built, high-walled **Fort Carnot**, atop an adjacent hill and clearly visible from the Thai side of the Mekong, is occupied by Lao troops and is off limits to visitors.

Huay Xai's main morning market, **Talat Sao** (Th Saykhong) attracts traders from numerous ethnic backgrounds and is situated at the southern end of town near the bus terminal.

You can take a traditional herbal sauna and/or Swedish-Lao massage at the **Lao Red Cross** (☎ 211264; Th Saykhong; sauna US$1, massage per hr US$3; ☺ 4-8.30pm).

Sleeping

Most hotels and guesthouses in Huay Xai quote their rates in Thai baht.

Houay Xai Guest House (Th Saykhong; r US$2.50-3) An older two-storey place with wooden floors and a nice little seating area that overlooks the river. The fan-cooled rooms are tight, tidy and accommodating.

Friendship Guest House (☎ 211219; Th Saykhong; sUS$3, d US$5-10) Friendship lives up to its name with friendly, efficient service. The small but neat rooms have slightly dank bathrooms but windows, wooden floors and a nice rooftop view compensate.

BAP Guest House (☎ 211083; Th Saykhong; s/d US$3/6) Turn left coming from the pier, and BAP is 50m up on the left. All rooms come with fan and hot-water shower. This friendly two-storey place is a good spot to find out about boats going to Luang Nam Tha via Pak Tha or Xieng Kok. There's also a good restaurant downstairs.

Thanormsub Guest House (☎ 211095; Th Saykhong; r US$5) One of the best deals in town, this single-storey guesthouse has fresh rooms with ceiling fans and hot-water showers attached. It's low-key, immaculate and extremely friendly.

Arimid Guest House (Alimit; ☎ 211040; fax 312006; Ban Huay Xai Neua; r US$5.50-13; ☒) This is a collection of thatched bamboo bungalows with attached hot-water showers. The most expensive versions also have air-con. The husband-and-wife owners speak French and English. The pier for slow boats going to Pak Beng and Luang Prabang is only about 200m away.

Oudomphone Guest House (r US$5) This guesthouse is a spotless option with fan-cooled rooms, clean sheets and surfaces and friendly owners. It's slightly tucked off the main street and good for a quiet night's sleep. There's a small café out the front serving good breakfasts (US$1).

Keoudomphone Hotel (☎ 211405; Th Saykhong; r US$5-10; ☒) The nicest hotel in town is a 15-minute walk from the main strip but it's well worth the effort for the spick, span and spacious rooms. Each has a TV, small couches and plenty of charm and sunlight. Pricier rooms have air-con.

Sabaydee Guest House (☎ 211751; Th Saykhong; r US$6) A good cut above the cheaper options in town, this immaculate guesthouse has pristine rooms with firm beds, large windows and commodious hot-water bathrooms. It's efficiently run and recommended.

Thaveesinh Hotel (☎ /fax 312039; Th Saykhong; r US$6.50-16; ☒) This grand pink structure contains an assortment of rooms ranging from cosy, fan-cooled versions to capacious suites with air-con. All have TV, hot water and garish bedspreads. It's not as clean as some of the guesthouses but you're paying for the amenities.

Mekong Lao Hotel (☎ 211277; r US$7.50; ☒) Opposite the Keoudomphone, this hotel has a promising exterior and although the rooms are large and comfy, they're pretty musty. They all have air-con and TVs though and are decent for the price.

Chaleunshine Guest House (☎ 212076; Th Saykhong; r US$10) Its short distance from town puts this lovely guesthouse in a more authentic *bâan* location. Rooms are breezy and bright, with spotless tiled floors and hot-water showers in the bathrooms.

Eating

Nut Pop (☎ 211037; Th Saykhong; meals US$1-3; ☺ lunch & dinner) On an atmospheric timber deck surrounded by foliage, this restaurant serves great Lao dishes like peppery hot pork, baked fish or chicken with chilli and lime.

PĄA BÉUK

The Mekong River stretch that passes Huay Xai was until recently an important fishing ground for the giant Mekong catfish (*pqa béuk* in Lao, *Pangasianodon gigas* to ichthyologists), probably the largest freshwater fish in the world. A *pqa béuk* takes at least six and possibly up to 12 years (no-one's really sure) to reach full size, when it will measure 2m to 3m in length and weigh up to 300kg. Locals say these fish swim all the way from Qinghai Province (where the Mekong originates) in northern China. In Thailand and Laos its flesh is considered a major delicacy; the texture is very meaty but it has a delicate flavour, similar to that of tuna or swordfish.

These fish are only taken between mid-April and May when the river depth is between 3m and 4m and the fish are swimming upriver to spawn in Lake Tali in Yunnan Province, China. Before netting them, Thai and Lao fishers hold a annual ceremony to propitiate Chao Mae Paa Beuk, a female deity thought to preside over the giant Mekong catfish. Among the rituals comprising the ceremony are chicken sacrifices performed aboard the fishing boats. After the ceremony is completed, fishing teams draw lots to see who casts the first net, and then they take turns casting.

The annual catch has dwindled to almost nothing in recent years, a situation thought due to Chinese blasting of Mekong River rapids to the north. The blasting is intended to make the Mekong more navigable but it has also destroyed the underwater caves that serve as natural nurseries for the giant catfish. When a catch is made, fisherfolk sell the meat on the spot for US$40 or more per kilogram (a single fish can bring up to US$5000 in Bangkok), most of which ends up in restaurants in Bangkok or Kunming, since local restaurants in Huay Xai and Chiang Khong can't afford such prices; transport to Vientiane is considered too costly.

Because of the danger of extinction, Thailand's Inland Fisheries Department has been taking protective measures since 1983, including a breed-and-release programme. Every time a female is caught, it's kept alive until a male is netted, then the eggs are removed (by massaging the female's ovaries) and put into a pan; the male is then milked for sperm and the eggs are fertilised in the pan. In this fashion over a million *pqa béuk* have been released into the Mekong since the experiment began. Although the results of releasing *pqa béuk* into the wild have been very mixed, the domestic farming of *pqa béuk* in central and northern Thailand has been very successful. This means that farms on both sides of the border may one day be able to breed the fish for local consumption for little more than the cost of feed.

Latsuly Restaurant (meals US$1.50-2; breakfast, lunch & dinner) Right next to the slow boat landing, this spot overlooking the Mekong serves an assortment of fried noodle and rice dishes, buffalo steaks, and a good basil pork. It can also whip up sandwiches for you to take on the boats.

Muang Neur (Th Saykhong; meals US$1.50-3; breakfast, lunch & dinner) There's plenty of fragrant Lao cuisine to be had at this humble little restaurant, like whole crisp fried fish stuffed with ginger and garlic, spicy seafood soup with lemongrass, and delicious *fŏe*. It also advertises itself as the Gecko Bar for those in need of *lào-láo*.

Riverside Houay Restaurant (off Th Saykhong; meals US$1.50-3; breakfast, lunch & dinner) The only thing broader than the Mekong view at this restaurant is the menu. A huge array of Thai and Lao is on offer with some good seafood dishes including fried prawn cakes. The *tôm yám* and curries come in all manner of meats, or you can just tuck into an omelette. It has a particularly ambient setting, although the cheesy Thai pop music detracts a little from it.

At night spontaneous noodle shops and barbeques spring up on Th Saykhong and you can dine for around US$1.

Getting There & Away

AIR

Huay Xai's airport of US construction lies a few kilometres south of town. **Lao Airlines** (☎ 211026, 211494) flies to/from Vientiane (one way/return US$84/160, Tuesday, Thursday and Saturday).

BOAT

Huay Xai is a major jumping-off point for visitors planning to travel downriver to Luang Prabang by boat. It's also possible to travel upriver to Xieng Kok (see p209), where a road leads to Muang Sing.

CROSSING THE THAI BORDER AT HUAY XAI & CHIANG KHONG

The small town of Chiang Khong, in Thailand's Chiang Rai Province, sits on the Mekong River opposite Huay Xai, Laos. The main boat landing for international crossing is Tha Bak, at the northern end of Chiang Khong. After you've legally exited Thailand via the small Thai **customs & immigration post** at the landing, you can board a longtail boat (one way US$1, five minutes, 8am to 6pm) to Huay Xai. On the Huay Xai side, the Lao immigration post is alongside the pedestrian ferry landing. Thirty-day tourist visas are available on arrival for US$30. There is an additional US$1 overtime charge from 4pm to 6pm weekdays and all weekend.

If you're crossing in your own car or truck, you'll use the huge vehicle ferry (US$50) that lands at the northern end of Huay Xai.

Plans to construct a bridge from Chiang Khong to Huay Xai by late 1997 were derailed by the economic crash but it's only a matter of time before a span makes the ferry crossing obsolete.

Slow Boats

Long-distance ferries – the *héua sáa* (slow boat) – travel down the Mekong from Huay Xai to Pak Beng (US$9.50, six to eight hours) and Luang Prabang (US$20, two days). Some travellers rave about this journey, others are disappointed. The river is indeed very beautiful, but your experience will depend largely on the condition of the boat and number of fellow passengers. The boats should hold around 70 people, but many captains pack in more than 100, and spending two days in an engine room like cattle isn't much to write home about. It's worth noting, however, that there is strength in numbers, and if passengers refuse, en masse, to travel in an overcrowded boat then captains have been known to relent and agree to two boats.

The journey generally requires an overnight stay in Pak Beng, unless you charter your own boat (US$500). If you can pull a crowd together this latter option is a good one as you'll have much more room. Departure times for slow boats depend largely on passenger demand, but they usually leave between 8am and 11am each morning. Be sure to carry a cushion if you have a sensitive bum, as the wooden seats can be uncomfortable and the boats are very crowded during the high season.

Several different kinds of slow boats make the journey from Huay Xai to Luang Prabang, and it's a good idea to have a look at the boat in advance. The photos of beautifully maintained vessels you'll be shown at the tour agencies in town don't bear any resemblance to the boats you'll end up on. Other boats have better seating, and so on. The situation is constantly changing, but BAP Guest House (p216) is a good source of info on how to select the better boats. Tour agencies and most guesthouses sell tickets but you can purchase them for a couple of bucks less from the **ticket office** (212012) at the slow boat landing, which is located north of the town centre.

You can also book a slow boat in advance, in Chiang Khong, before crossing to Huay Xai, for a surcharge of US$2.50. In the high season this is worth considering, as boats fill very fast.

You can also cruise to Pak Beng and Luang Prabang on the large, comfortably outfitted *Luang Say*, a 34m, 36-seat, steel-hulled boat operated by **Asian Oasis** (www.asian-oasis.com; per person May-Sep/Oct-Apr US$185/270) three days weekly in each direction (two weekly May to September). The two-day package includes meals, guides and a night at Luang Say Lodge in Pak Beng (see p194). The office is near immigration. Asian Oasis also has an office in Luang Prabang (see p148).

Phoudoi Travel Co (Th Saykhong) sells tickets for a comfortable, 34m boat with chairs, tables and food and drink on board. Tickets are US$60 and the boat takes one day to reach Luang Prabang. Departures are every Monday and Friday. You can also book this from Thailand; see www.chiangsaenriverhill.com for details.

Speedboats

Six-passenger *héua wái* (speedboats) to Pak Beng (US$14, three hours) and Luang Prabang (US$28, six hours) leave from a landing about 2km south of the town centre. You can hire a whole boat for four to six times the individual fare.

BAP Guest House (p216) can arrange speedboats to Xieng Kok for US$150 for up to four passengers. From Xieng Kok it's possible to travel by road to Muang Sing in Luang Nam Tha; see p209 for more information on this journey.

Bear in mind that although the speedboat is much quicker, it's a noisy, cramped and risky ride. See below for warnings on travelling by speedboat.

BUS & SĂWNGTHĂEW

The road northeast to Luang Nam Tha can be difficult because of its poor surface, but it is slowly being upgraded.

Buses and large *săwngthăew* ply the road northeast to Vieng Phoukha (US$4.50, five hours, three to four daily), Luang Nam Tha (US$6.50, eight hours, three daily) and Udomxai (US$10, 11 hours, one daily).

There are also daily buses to Luang Prabang (US$13, eight hours) and Vientiane (US$17, 18 hours).

These time estimates apply only during dry months; during the rainy season the road can be very slow, occasionally even impassable for a day or two. A bandanna is handy for dust protection in the dry season. When the upgrading project is done, the road will be traversable year-round and buses should be able to make the Huay Xai–Nam Tha trip in four to six hours.

The bus terminal is about 2.5km south of town, a tuk-tuk there costs US$1.

AROUND HUAY XAI

Various hill-tribe villages can be visited from Huay Xai, some of them within walking distance and others a short drive north or south of town. One that everyone seems to know about is the Lao Huay village of **Ban Nam Sang**. It's less than an hour east by *săwngthăew* – 17km to be exact – and you can either charter a pick-up truck from the morning market in Huay Xai for about US$6 each way, or catch the regular morning *săwngthăew* from the same market at around 8am or 8.30am for US$0.60 per person. If you go it's best to check in with the *phùu nyai bâan* (village headman) first.

A reminder: do not bring sweets, T-shirts, pharmaceuticals or any other such items to give away to the villagers as this 'generosity' threatens to interfere with their traditional way of life, and worse, threatens to foster a culture of dependency and turn Ban Nam Sang into a village of beggars. If you feel strongly about contributing to the community you might offer the headman a small monetary contribution to be used for the village school.

Phoudoi Travel Co and Khaenlao Tours in Huay Xai (see p215) can organise one-day tours to Lanten and Khamu villages along the Mekong for US$8 to US$30 per person, depending on group size. An increasingly popular tour is the car-and-boat trip to **Souvannakhomkham** in Ton Pheung. This ancient

---

DANGER, WILL ROBINSON

Will Robinson had an unhappy knack of finding danger, but the robot would have been screaming warnings if he'd seen the speedboats that ply this stretch of the Mekong and the Nam Ou in Luang Prabang Province. Known locally as *héua wái* (literally 'fast boat', usually translated 'speedboat' or 'jetboat' in English), these things are little more than surfboards with car engines on the back.

The comfort of passengers wasn't high on the list of design imperatives. The seats are numbingly uncomfortable and the motors run without modern luxuries like mufflers, so they are deafeningly loud. This noise not only makes the trip even less enjoyable, but it's disturbing to both animal and human life along the riverbanks.

Lack of comfort aside, speedboats are genuinely dangerous. Serious accidents, sometimes including fatalities, are alarmingly common. Usually they involve a boat striking a hidden rock or a tree limb, although occasionally contact with a standing wave is enough to capsize these light craft. Because they're going so fast a simple capsize may have serious consequences for the passengers.

Although reliable statistics are unavailable, our own observation is that the accident risk for this type of boat outweighs the potential savings in time they may represent over slower boat alternatives. So considering safety, comfort and aural disturbance, we recommend you avoid speedboat travel unless absolutely necessary.

LAO HUAY

Also known as Lene Tene, Lenten or Laen Taen (Dressed in Blue), the Lao Huay (Lao Stream) are classified by the government as Lao Soung despite the fact they do not – and never have – lived anywhere other than lower river valleys. Ethnolinguistically they fall within the Hmong-Mien family, most of whom live at higher elevations.

The Lao Huay build their homes – multifamily longhouses of palm and bamboo thatch – beside rivers or streams from which they irrigate rice fields using simple wooden hydraulic pumps. Unlike the closely related Mien, they do not cultivate the opium poppy for trade, only for smoking. Lao Huay women can be identified by the single large coin (usually an old Indochina piastre, sometimes accompanied by several smaller coins) suspended over the parting in their long, straight hair and by their lack of eyebrows, which are completely depilated at age 15 according to custom. Both sexes favour dark blue or black clothes – baggy shirts and trousers – trimmed in red.

The Lao Huay use Chinese characters to write their language, often on handmade bamboo paper. Their belief system encompasses a mix of Taoism, ancestor worship and animism, with spirits attached to the family, house, village, sky, forest, earth, water and birds. Around 5000 Lao Huay live in Laos; in Bokeo Province they're mostly concentrated in Nam Nyun district. This tribe isn't found in Myanmar or Thailand, though there are some Lao Huay villages in Yunnan (China) and northern Vietnam.

---

city, which successively became known as Nakha Nakhorn or Nakhorn Xieng Lao, Nakhorn Ngeun Nyuang (Ngeun Nyang) Hiranya Nakhorn, and Nakhorn Xieng Saen (ancient), has over 40 archaeological sites, including temples, stupas, and a 7.22m-high Buddha image seated in the meditation posture. Looting has left Souvannakhomkham a fraction of its former splendour, but it's still worth the journey. Tours (US$40 to US$140 depending on group size) also take in waterfalls and lunch at a river village.

There's some worthwhile monkey business to be had north of Huay Xai off Rte 3 towards Luang Nam Tha. You'll hear about it on the traveller grapevine, but out of respect for the operators it's not listed in this book.

SAINYABULI PROVINCE

This upside-down-L–shaped province lying between Thailand to the west and Vientiane and Luang Prabang Provinces to the east is one of the most remote provinces in Laos, despite its geographic proximity to the nation's capital. Mountains – several higher than 1000m and one as high as 2150m – define the northern half of the province, where roads are scarce, while the southern half flattens into river plains.

Tourists seldom find themselves here, which is a shame because the journey from Luang Prabang is a simple affair and the landscape is quite spectacular. Moreover, traversing Sainyabuli is a fascinating alternative to the well-trodden *falang*-route of Luang Prabang–Vang Vieng–Vientiane.

Sainyabuli (also spelt Xaignabouri, Xayaboury, Saiyabouli and Sayabouri) shares a 645km border with six different Thai provinces. The province was the site of a brief but heated border skirmish between the Thai and Lao in 1988. More than 100 Thai and Lao soldiers died in battle before an agreement was reached and a compromise border was fixed.

The light population includes Lao, Thai Dam, Thai Lü, Khamu, Htin, Phai, Kri, Akha and Mabri; many of these groups migrate between Sainyabuli and Thailand, since the border is fairly unpoliced.

A string of rocky limestone precipices known as **Pha Xang** (Elephant Cliffs, so named because from a distance the grey-white cliffs resemble walking elephants) parallels the Mekong River on the eastern side of the province. Along the western edge of the province is the inaccessible **Nam Phoun NPA**, a 1150-sq-km tract of rugged, forested hills thought to sustain elephant, Sumatran rhino, gaur, gibbon, dhole, Asiatic black bear, Malayan sun bear and tiger.

The southern part of the province harbours several scenic waterfalls, including 150m Nam Tok Na Kha (3km from Ban Nakha), 105m Nam Tok Ban Kum (5km from Ban Kum) and 35m Tat Heuang (40km from Ban Muang Phae). Unfortunately, none of these villages are easily accessible by road as yet, and this corner of the province is reputedly a hang-out for smugglers and possibly insurgents. It's probably best if travellers avoid the border area between Muang Ngoen (to the north) and Kaen Thao (to the south).

The 30m **Tat Jao**, a 1km walk northwest of the Mekong ferry crossing at Muang Tha Deua, is a popular local picnic spot.

Sainyabuli Province has more elephants than any other province in Laos. Two of the highest concentrations of working elephants can be found in Thong Mixai district about 40km northwest of Pak Lai at Hongsa, 85km north of the provincial capital.

SAINYABULI

ໄຊຍະບຸລີ

☎ 074 / pop 17,000

Sainyabuli is an unassuming town on the banks of the Nam Houng, a tributary of the Mekong River towards the northern end of Sainyabuli Province. Flanked by mountains and commonly shrouded in cloud in the

mornings, it has a handsome [...]
hanced no end by the lack of t [...]
Easy to explore on foot, Sainyabuli's lack of stereotypical attractions is precisely what makes it such a breath of fresh air. Very little English is spoken in Sainyabuli so be sure to pack your phrasebook.

Information

Lao Development Bank (☺ 8.30am- 4pm Mon-Fri) The bank accepts only cash (Thai baht or US dollars) at a lower rate than in Vientiane.

Lao Telecom (☺ 8am-10pm) You can buy international and domestic phonecards here or at the post office.

Post office (☺ 8-11am & 1-5pm Mon-Fri)

Sights

The grounds of **Wat Si Bun Huang**, south of town past the police station in an adjacent village, contain the brick foundations of Buddhist monuments rumoured to be over 500 years old. Nearby, **Wat Si Phan Don** contains an unusual diamond-shaped stupa with no known stylistic antecedents. In town, **Wat Sisavang Vong**, reportedly built by King Sisavang Vong on an older temple site, displays

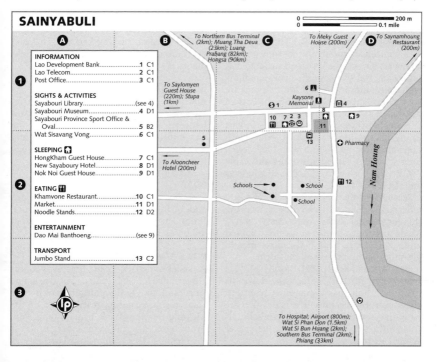

SAINYABULI

0 — 200 m
0 — 0.1 mile

INFORMATION
Lao Development Bank...................1 C1
Lao Telecom...................................2 C1
Post Office.....................................3 C1

SIGHTS & ACTIVITIES
Sayabouri Library.......................(see 4)
Sayabouri Museum.......................4 D1
Sayabouri Province Sport Office &
Oval...5 B2
Wat Sisavang Vong........................6 C1

SLEEPING
HongKham Guest House.................7 C1
New Sayaboury Hotel.....................8 D1
Nok Noi Guest House.....................9 D1

EATING
Khamvone Restaurant...................10 C1
Market...11 D1
Noodle Stands.............................12 D2

ENTERTAINMENT
Dao Mai Banthoeng.....................(see 9)

TRANSPORT
Jumbo Stand................................13 C2

To Northern Bus Terminal
(2km); Muang Tha Deua
(23km); Luang
Prabang (82km);
Hongsa (90km)

To Meky Guest
House (200m)

To Saynamhoung
Restaurant
(200m)

To Saylomyen
Guest House
(220m); Stupa
(1km)

Kaysone
Memorial

To Alooncheer
Hotel (200m)

Pharmacy

Nam Houng

Schools

School

School

To Hospital; Airport (800m);
Wat Si Phan Don (1.5km);
Wat Si Bun Huang (2km);
Southern Bus Terminal (2km);
Phiang (33km)

a colourful version of Buddhist hell on its front walls.

At the western edge of town a lone **stupa** sits atop a column of steps with sweeping views of the town.

The tiny **Sayabouri Museum** sidles up to the **Sayabouri Library** on the main east–west street in town. Opening hours are sporadic and entry is by donation. In fact, if you can get in let us know.

Other visual treats include a spontaneous football match at the **Sayabouri Province Sport Office & Oval**, the fording and bathing ritual in the Nam Houng that takes place every afternoon, or being the main spectacle at the market.

Sleeping

HongKham Guest House (☎ 211381; s/d US$5/10) Modest, spotless and very friendly, the Hong-Kham has simple rooms with attached bathrooms. The whole lot is housed in a stone and wood villa and the owners are lovely.

Nok Noi Guest House (☎ 211122; s/d US$5/10; ✹) A decent cheapie, the Nok Noi has weary beds and covers, but tidy rooms with small windows and hot-water showers. It shares a plot of earth with the Dao Mai Banthoeng nightclub though (right) so things may get noisy at night.

Saylomyen Guest House (☎ 211156; r US$6; ✹) This immaculate guesthouse has something of a ranch exterior – the L-shaped structure has pure white walls and polished wooden doors with a pleasant veranda out front. Rooms are cosy and clean, and although the beds are a tad thin, it's excellent value.

Mekee Guest House (☎ 2399388; r US$8; ✹) This lovely guesthouse is fabulous value, with hotel-sized rooms stocked with tiled floors, king-size beds, large bathrooms and cable TV. Rooms upstairs have screened windows and street views.

Alooncheer Hotel (☎ 213136; r US$8; ✹) In a quiet spot behind a fortress of security gates, this large hotel packs some classy punch. Moderately sized rooms are softly coloured and sunlit. Large beds, TVs, minibars and gleaming bathrooms are all the norm.

New Sayaboury Hotel (☎ 211116; r US$15-17; ✹) Not so new for quite some time now, this mammoth hotel has a grandiose front but close, overpriced rooms. The bedclothes are a bit drab and the bathrooms shambolic, although the tubs and air-con (in the pricier rooms) are pluses.

Eating

Khamvone Restaurant (☎ 211103; meals US$1-2; ⊙ breakfast, lunch & dinner) This casual restaurant has a sunny setting with wooden picnic tables outside or low-slung wicker settings in the shade. It's menuless so you'll need your phrasebook, or you can simply point. The *fŏe* is great here.

Saynamhoung Restaurant (☎ 412109; meals US$2.50-4; ⊙ lunch & dinner) This open-air, riverside spot has a nice atmosphere, good service and an extensive Lao, Thai and Chinese menu. You can test your culinary mettle on bowels or fried intestine...or steamed fish and prawn toast if you're not so game. Whatever you order the food is good and the Beerlao cold.

The cheapest and most interesting eats are to be had at the **market** (⊙ 8am-6.30pm), where you can pick up takeaway noodles; peanut, rice and spring onion packages in lettuce, samosas, barbecued sausage and a whole host of unidentifiable goodies. You can feast for US$0.50 to US$1 and vendors will let you try before you buy.

There are also cheap noodle stands on the road to the airport.

Entertainment

Dao Mai Banthoeng (⊙ 8-11.30pm) You might catch live bands playing Lao and Thai pop here during the week. Although slow on weeknights, it's very popular on weekends.

Getting There & Away

AIR

Lao Airlines (☎ 412059; airport) advertises fares between Sainyabuli and Vientiane (one way/return US$53/101), but this currently doesn't translate to actual flights. One day it might.

BOAT

Speedboats are available between Tha Deua and Luang Prabang (US$10, one hour). From Tha Deua you can hop on a shared jumbo or *săwngthăew* into Sainyabuli.

BUS & SĂWNGTHĂEW

A daily bus departs Luang Prabang's southern terminal for Sainyabuli (US$4, five hours, 9am) and travels the partially paved road southwest to a landing at Pak Khon, on the Mekong's eastern bank near Muang Nan. From here, tugs pull vehicle barges across the Mekong. This is all included in your bus fare and you don't even need to disembark. On the Sainyabuli side of the Mekong there is a passport inspection post where the bus may stop for five, or 30 minutes, depending on the number of foreigners. In general, however, it's not the overseas travellers they're most interested in. The bus then continues to Sainyabuli.

There is also a road running north to Sainyabuli from Kaen Thao, which is on the Nam Heuang opposite the Thai villages of Ban Pak Huay and Ban Nong Pheu – both are legal crossing points for Thai and Lao, but not for foreigners.

In Sainyabuli there are two bus terminals, one 2km southeast of town and one about the same distance northeast of town. Buses from Sainyabuli to Pak Lai leave from the southern terminal when there are enough passengers, usually between 7.30am and 10am (US$3.50, three to four hours). Buses from the northern terminal head to Luang Prabang (US$4, five hours, 9am and 3pm) and to Vientiane (US$10, 15 hours, 11.30am and 4pm). Tuk-tuks leave from the jumbo stand throughout the day; to either terminal it costs US$0.50.

AROUND SAINYABULI
Pak Lai
ปากลาย
☎ 074

This small riverside community of old French colonial buildings and traditional wooden Lao homes clustered around a village green, with the Pha Xang mountain range as a scenic backdrop, makes a pleasant stopover between Sainyabuli and Vientiane.

A branch of Lao Development Bank can change US dollars and Thai baht to kip.

SLEEPING & EATING
Ban Na Guest House (☎ 211995; r US$4) At this rather unusual three-storey guesthouse, where the bottom floor is cement, the middle one brick and the top one wood, the 17 rooms have screened windows and ceiling fans. Clean shower and toilet facilities are shared. Food can be ordered downstairs.

Lam Douan Guest House (r US$4) Run by a friendly lady who speaks Lao, Thai and a little French, the Lam Douan offers 10 basic but clean rooms with shared bucket bath and toilet. The upper floor has a balcony with a Mekong view.

Nang Noy Restaurant (meals US$0.50-1.50; ☼ breakfast, lunch & dinner) Between the boat landing and the market, Nang Noy specialises in simple rice and noodle dishes, and can do takeaway for the boat ride to Vientiane.

Right above the boat landing, a no-name restaurant in a clean, cement pavilion with tiled floors opens early in the morning to serve thick Lao coffee and *khào-nŏm khuu* (Chinese-style fried pastry). Later in the day good rice and noodle dishes are available – this is a good spot to take in a Mekong sunset. The eatery doubles as a snack shop for the boat passengers.

GETTING THERE & AWAY
Săwngthăew travel between Pak Lai and Sainyabuli (US$3.20, three hours, two daily). The *săwngthăew* drops passengers off at a spot about 3km outside Pak Lai where you must continue by shared jumbo for US$0.50 per person.

It's still possible to travel to Vientiane by slow boat along the Mekong (US$10, seven to eight hours). Unlike other slow boat journeys in Laos, this one is a beautifully local, uncomfortable

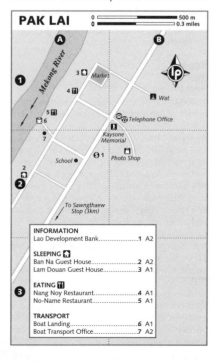

PAK LAI

0   500 m
0   0.3 miles

INFORMATION
Lao Development Bank....................1 A2

SLEEPING 🏠
Ban Na Guest House.......................2 A2
Lam Douan Guest House.................3 A1

EATING 🍴
Nang Noy Restaurant......................4 A1
No-Name Restaurant......................5 A1

TRANSPORT
Boat Landing..................................6 A1
Boat Transport Office.....................7 A2

NORTHERN LAOS

NORTHERN LAOS

THAI LÜ

Thai Lü dominate local culture and commerce in Hongsa district. Keen traders, they have been unusually successful in maintaining their traditions despite the pressures of outside Lao influence, while at the same time enjoying the relative prosperity that their district has developed as a Thailand-Laos trade centre.

The matrilineal Thai Lü practise a mix of Theravada Buddhism and animism; though traditionally endogamic (tending to marry within one's own clan) they've recently begun marrying outsiders – usually Thai Lü or Thai Neua from other districts. Women are said to enjoy greater political freedom and power than in most ethnic groups in Laos.

Typical Thai Lü villages are on the eastern bank of a stream or river, with at least one wat at the northern end and a cemetery at the west. An important folk tale says a swan deity flew down from heaven and showed the Thai Lü how to build their houses on stilts as protection from animals and flooding, and with long sloping roofs to shield the inhabitants from sun, wind and rain. Small shuttered windows known as *pong liem* allow residents to see out but restrict outsiders from seeing in. In reference to this bit of folklore, they call their traditional homes *héuan hông* (swan houses).

Their more distinctive customs include *suu khwăn khuwái* (string-tying ceremony for water buffaloes) and *suu khwăn sâang* (string-tying ceremony for elephants).

---

and decidedly Laotian experience. Boats leave the Pak Lai boat landing from 8am to 9am but they often fill up by 7.30am so it's a good idea to be at the ticket office, located at the Boat Transport Office, at 7am. There are no more slow boats north.

Speedboats from Pak Lai to Vientiane (US$30, four hours) leave when there are six passengers.

Hongsa

ຫົງສາ

☎ 074

This district, tucked away in the northwestern corner of Sainyabuli Province, roughly 85km northwest of the provincial capital, is a major centre for Thai Lü culture. Several villages in the area boast historic Thai Lü temples and strong local traditions. Travelling through this district, and even en route to Hongsa from Sainyabuli, you may see elephants walking along the road with their mahouts, as this part of Sainyabuli is a major centre for the logging of padauk and other timber. Elephants are also used for agricultural work in the area. So important are the pachyderms to daily life here that the Thai Lü perform yearly *bąasii* ceremonies (p55) on their behalf. Sadly elephant numbers have been on a steady decline due to their hefty workloads and a decreasing knowledge in the local community about how to care for them properly. However, in recent years **ElefantAsia** (www.elefantasia.org), a French organisation, has promoted education in the province regard-

ing elephant health and care, and an Elephant Festival has been established in mid-February in Hongsa to further the tourism revenue generated by them. This is good news for the elephants because it spells improvements to their general well-being. Elephant trekking is also possible here; see Sleeping (below) for more information.

In Hongsa itself the main temple is **Wat Simungkhun** (also known as Wat Yai), where a very old, whitewashed *wihăn* contains an oddly raised stone floor that allegedly covers a large hole that 'leads to the end of the world', according to locals. Women aren't allowed to enter the *wihăn*, but from the doorway you can see the impressive collection of Lao Buddha figures on the altar inside.

In nearby **Vieng Kaew** old houses built with padauk (*Pterocarpus indicus,* a reddish-orange tropical hardwood sometimes called 'Asian rosewood') abound.

SLEEPING & EATING

Jumbo House (Xang Luang; r US$8) This one-storey guesthouse offers five large rooms. Information on Vieng Kaew and Muang Ngoen is available here, and bicycles can be hired. Jumbo can also arrange elephant trekking with a few hours notice.

Sunflower Guest House (r US$5.50-7.50) Just around the corner from the Jumbo House, Sunflower boasts 10 rooms in a two-storey house next to a lotus pond and spacious garden with café.

Villa Sisouphanh (☎ 211791; r US$3) Found opposite the market, Sisouphanh is the better of a couple of older guesthouses in Hongsa, with adequate rooms.

Lotus Café (meals US$1-3) A pleasant new spot for a drink or a meal overlooking lotus ponds, the menu covers Lao, Italian and Korean barbecue.

In the market are several restaurant stalls. At the best, **Tui** (meals US$0.50-1.50), you can get *khào sáwy, khào píak, fŏe* and cold beer.

GETTING THERE & AWAY

You can reach Hongsa via a wild *sǎwngthǎew* ride over high mountain ridges and into deep valleys from Sainyabuli (US$10, six hours, one daily). Most of this road is unsealed and crosses several low bridges made from logs, so in the rainy season the usual six hours could easily stretch to eight or 10. During heavy rains the road may wash out entirely for several days.

Alternatively, catch a slow boat along the Mekong River from Luang Prabang (US$8, half-day) or Huay Xai (US$17.50, one and a half days). From Tha Suang you can hop on a shared jumbo to Hongsa (US$3.50, two to three hours).

Speedboats also connect Tha Suang to Luang Prabang (US$15, two hours).

Muang Ngoen
ເມືອງເງິນ

This Thai Lü village in the extreme northeast corner of the province, 3km from the Thai border, is worth a visit if you're in the area already or passing through from Thailand (once

the border opens, that is). There are still a few houses on stilts with high-pitched roofs sloping low to the ground (similar to those found in Muang Sing and in China's Xishuangbanna District), although many of these were destroyed when the Thai air force bombed Laos during the 1988 Thai–Lao border war.

Farming is the main activity, and one made more profitable by the open Thai–Lao border at nearby Ban Huay Kon – a crossing thus far permitted for Thai and Lao nationals only. There have been plans to open this crossing to all nationalities for several years. If this eventuates this will become the fastest land route between Luang Prabang and Thailand.

Muang Ngoen's **Wat Ban Khon**, a traditional Thai Lü–style temple where the monks still use palm leaves for the preservation of Buddhist texts, is notable for its natural-pigment, folk-art murals, which combine animal and floral motifs with tiny mirrors to unique effect.

Another old Thai Lü wat, **Wat Salibun Nyeun**, stands on a high bluff overlooking a town, with a lovely stream winding through the valley below. Pillars inside the main *wihǎan* are cut from huge padauk trunks.

Few foreign visitors choose to spend the night in Muang Ngoen, but if you feel like digging into local life, you can choose between the **Amphawan Guest House** (r US$1-3) and **Saijaloen Guest House** (r US$2-3).

The easiest way to reach Muang Ngoen is via a dirt road from the bank of the Mekong River opposite Pak Beng, a distance of roughly 35km. Ask in Pak Beng about transport to Muang Ngoen. Your best bet may be to hitch a ride with someone coming from here.

NORTHERN LAOS

Central Laos

The area at the waist of the country, between the Mekong River and Thailand in the west and the Annamite range bordering Vietnam in the east, has traditionally been skipped over by most travellers. But improved roads and several sustainable tourism initiatives, which give you a full-flavoured taste of the 'real Laos', mean central Laos is more open to exploration than ever. And it's not overrun yet.

Exploration is the key word. You might not be the first person to trek into the mediaeval limestone karsts that emerge with a menacing beauty from the Phu Hin Bun National Protected Area (NPA), but it will probably feel like it and there won't be a banana pancake or happy shake for miles.

Instead, you'll find a diverse mix of ecology, environment and ethnicity that is very different to the north – and as much tough and memorable travel as you like. The Mekong River towns of Tha Khaek and Savannakhet, with their lowland Lao communities, slowly crumbling French histories and lethargic lifestyles, will be your bases. This part of the country claims the most forest cover and the highest concentrations of wildlife, including some species that have disappeared elsewhere in Southeast Asia, and these protected areas will be your main destinations.

To find them, you could do 'The Loop' through Khammuan and Bolikhamsai Provinces by motorbike, detouring via the incredible 7km-long cave Tham Kong Lo in the process. Or trek into far-off Dong Phu Vieng NPA in Savannakhet Province to sleep with the spirits in a Katang village. Branches of the Ho Chi Minh Trail await the most intrepid, or just go forth and create your own trail….

HIGHLIGHTS

- Trek amid the gothic limestone karsts, subterranean caves and meandering rivers of the **Phu Hin Bun NPA** (p230)
- Do **The Loop** (p240) and experience upcountry Laos; good roads, bad roads, stunning scenery, a big dam site and unexpected challenges
- Climb up the cliff to **Tham Pha Pa** (p239), the recently discovered cave of 229 bronze Buddha images
- Stay in the remote villages of **Dong Phu Vieng NPA** (p249) and experience life in the spirit forests
- Schlep out to **Tham Kong Lo** (p231) for a boat trip through this astonishing 7km-long limestone cave

Phu Hin Bun NPA ★
Tham Kong Lo ★
Tham Pha Pa ★
Dong Phu Vieng NPA ★

Climate

The Mekong valley is always pretty warm and from March to May Savannakhet is positively steaming. It gets cooler as you head east toward the Annamite range and Lak Sao and the villages along Rte 8B can be close to freezing during winter nights. The southwestern monsoon brings bucket-loads of rain from June to October. Far-eastern areas around the Nakai Nam Theun NPA also receive rain from the South China Sea that lasts longer, thus supplying enough water to maintain the thicker vegetation.

National Protected Areas

Central Laos is the most protected part of the country with eight National Protected Areas (NPAs) accounting for vast swathes of the region. Access to Hin Namno, Nakai Nam Theun and Se Ban Nuan NPAs is limited to those with decent Lao language skills and plenty of time and money, but others are easy to get to.

In Khammuan the labyrinth of limestone karsts, caves and rivers in Phu Hin Bun NPA (p230) is accessible either on your own or on a community-based trek. Similar treks lead to the sacred forests and animist villages of Dong Phu Vieng (p249) in Savannakhet Province.

The Nam Kading NPA (p229) in Bolikhamsai Province doesn't have any organised treks, but you can take a boat upriver to the World Conservation Society's research centre.

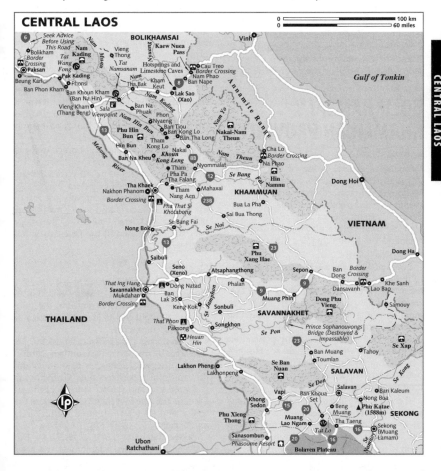

CENTRAL LAOS

Getting There & Around

Gone are the days when travelling anywhere south of Vientiane involved inordinately large amounts of time and incredible fortitude. These days Rte 13 is sealed and, somewhat surprisingly after seven years, still pretty smooth; congratulations to the road maintenance teams. Other roads have graduated from 'bone-jarring nightmare' status to 'smooth as silk', including Rte 9 from Savannakhet to the Vietnamese border at Lao Bao, and Rte 8 between Rte 13 and the Vietnamese border at Nam Phao. The eastern half of Rte 12 between Tha Khaek and the Vietnamese border is brand new and in late 2006 work was well advanced on the final 50km or so into Tha Khaek.

Apart from on the Nam Kading and Nam Hin Bun, arranging boat transport is more difficult and you'll need a fat wad of persuasion if you want a boatman to take you more than an hour or two in any direction.

BOLIKHAMSAI & KHAMMUAN PROVINCES

Bolikhamsai and Khammuan straddle the narrow, central 'waist' of the country. Physically the land climbs steadily from the Mekong valley towards the north and east, eventually reaching the Annamite range bordering Vietnam, via an area of moderately high but often spectacular mountains. Laidback and well-connected Tha Khaek (p234) is the logical base.

Lowland Lao, who speak a dialect peculiar to these two provinces, dominate the population and, with smaller groups of tribal Tais, are the people you're most likely to meet. In more remote areas the Mon-Khmer-speaking Makong people (commonly known as Bru) make up more than 10% of the population of Khammuan, while you might see Hmong, Kri, Katang, Maling, Atel, Phuan and Themarou in the markets and villages of the mountainous east.

It's worth keeping an eye out for *khanome parn*, a desert of soybean and sweetened sticky rice flour usually served in hollowed bamboo; markets and bus stations are a good place to look.

Much of the region is relatively sparsely populated and five large tracts of forest have been declared National Protected Areas (p227). These areas have turned into a major battleground between those wishing to exploit Laos's largely untapped hydroelectricity capacity and those wishing to preserve some of the most pristine wilderness areas in Asia. For now, the developers are winning.

PAKSAN

ປາກຊັນ

☎ 054 / pop 39,000

Located at the confluence of the Nam San (San River) and the Mekong River, Paksan (Pakxan or Pakxanh) is the capital of Bolikhamsai Province. Its position on Rte 13 between Vientiane and the nearest border with Vietnam makes it an increasingly busy highway town. This coupled with money coming from vaguely legitimate logging and plantation projects have prompted something of a building boom; look for the spectacularly tasteless four-storey wedding cake.

The local population has a large number of Phuan, a tribal Thai group, many of whom are also Christian – a combination that has traditionally made them doubly suspicious in the eyes of Lao authorities.

We'd like to say there's not much to see in Paksan, but that would be overstating it. It's possible to cross into Thailand from Paksan, though hardly anyone ever does.

There's a **Lao Development Bank** just east of the market, which is also where buses stop. It's a short walk from here east to the bridge over the Nam San and the first two hotels listed here.

Sleeping

When we first visited Paksan in 2001 the only lodgings were a couple of seedy guesthouses where rooms were mainly rented by the hour. The town's rapid growth means there are now several decent options.

BK Guesthouse (☎ 212638, 020-5612348; r US$5-8; ❀) This is Paksan's best budget choice. Rooms are pokey, but they're spotless and the atmosphere is welcoming. Mr Syhavong is a good guy and speaks some English and French. Take the first right (south) east of the bridge and it's a few hundred metres along on the right.

Paksan Hotel (☎ 791333; fax 791222; Rte 13; r US$10-15; ❀) This new Vietnamese-run hotel just east of the bridge is probably the closest you'll come to luxury, with the 32 rooms all kitted out the same but varying in price depending on size.

If the BK is full and you can't afford the Paksan Hotel, the **Vilaysack Hotel** (☎ 212311; Rte 4B; r US$3-7; ✪) and the **Hongxaykham Hotel** (☎ 212362; Rte 4B; r US$3-7; ✪) are several hundred metres west of the market and then 800m north on Rte 4B. Neither will have you writing home.

Eating

You won't have any trouble finding noodle and *fŏe* (rice noodles soup) options around Talat Sao (Morning Market) and there are a couple of Lao restaurants near the junction of the Mekong and the Nam San that are great at sunset.

Our favourite place to eat, however, is the **local restaurant** (meals US$1.40) about 50m along the street from the BK Guesthouse, which is known up and down Rte 13 for its top-notch Lao, Vietnamese and Thai food.

In town, the family-run **Saynamxan Restaurant** (☎ 212068; meals US$2-3.50; ✪ 7am-9.30pm), at the northwest end of the bridge crossing the Nam San, serves decent fish dishes. Best to avoid the roast turtle.

Getting There & Away

For buses from Vientiane see p114. From Paksan, buses leave from Rte 13 outside the Talat Sao for Vientiane (US$2.50, three to four hours, 143km) between 6.05am and 4.30pm, with most in the morning. *Sǎwngthǎew* (literally, 'two rows'; a passenger truck) also leave frequently from the market, or you could just hail anything going west.

If you're heading to Vietnam, *sǎwngthǎew* depart for Lak Sao (US$5, five to six hours, 189km) at 5am, 5.30am and 6.30am, or when they fill. After this take a *sǎwngthǎew* to Vieng

Kham, usually known as Thang Beng (US$2, 1½ to two hours), where Rte 13 joins Rte 8, then change for other transport along Rte 8 to Lak Sao (US$3, 3½ to five hours, 122km). For Pak Kading take anything going south.

All buses heading south from Vientiane pass through Paksan about two hours after they leave the capital – wait outside the Talat Sao.

PAKSAN TO LAK SAO

If the hellish 24-hour bus journey between Vientiane and Hanoi doesn't appeal, take local transport instead and stop to enjoy some of central Laos along the way.

Nam Kading NPA

ປ່າສະຫງວນແຫ່ງຊາດນ້ຳກະດິງ

Heading east along Rte 13 you'll come to the sleepy yet picturesque village of **Pak Kading**, 187km from Vientiane. Pak Kading sits just upstream from the junction of the Mekong River and the **Nam Kading**, one of the most pristine rivers in Laos – for now (see p65). Flowing through a forested valley surrounded by high hills and menacing-looking limestone formations, this broad, turquoise-tinted river winds its way into the **Nam Kading NPA**. The river is undoubtedly the best way into this wilderness, where confirmed animal rarities include the elephant, giant muntjac, pygmy slow loris, François' langur, Douc langur, gibbon, dhole, Asiatic black bear, tiger and many bird species. As usual in Laos you'll count yourself very lucky to catch anything more than a glimpse of any of these.

If you're interested, the **World Conservation Society** (WCS; www.wcs.org) has a research centre on the banks of the Nam Kading about 30 minutes upstream from Phonsi. It welcomes travellers, who can stay in the centre for the same price researchers pay. A stay is best combined with a trip to **Tat Wang Fong**, a small

CENTRAL LAOS

CROSSING THE THAI BORDER AT PAKSAN & BEUNG KAN

This rarely used crossing of the Mekong between Paksan and Beung Kan could almost be described as 'family run'. The customs officers invited us to play cards with them while their wives breastfed babies and small children played in the dust. Still, if you turn up at the at the **immigration office** (✪ 8am-noon & 1.30-4.30pm) they should process the paperwork without too much fuss, though they do not issue visas on arrival. The boat (60B, 20 minutes) leaves when five people show up or you charter it (300B). To get there, go west along Rte 13 from Paksan for about 1.5km and turn south – look for the 'Port' sign.

In Thailand buses leave Beung Kan for Udon Thani and Bangkok (infrequently).

ı a wonderfully picturesque setting
ninutes upstream.

ı∪ᵤ there, some travellers have reported
chartering boats on the Pak Kading side of the
Nam Kading, underneath the bridge. However, it's simpler to continue east about 15km
to the village of Ban Phon Kham, just past
Phonsi; follow a blue sign along a rough laterite
road until you reach the river and ask for a
boat to Tat Wang Fong. It should cost about
US$20 return, including waiting time while
you swim and picnic at the falls – bring food
and water as the falls are mercifully free of
salespeople. Boats just to the research centre
cost US$7/15 one-way/return.

Falls or no falls, Pak Kading is a good
place to stop for a meal at the **Bounxou
Restaurant** (☎ 055-320046; Rte 13; meals US$1-2.50;
🕑 8am-9pm), where the fish dishes are famous. If you have to stay there is one
simple guesthouse.

Ban Khoun Kham (Ban Na Hin)
The village of Ban Khoun Kham (also
known as Ban Na Hin) on Rte 8, 41km east
of Rte 13, sits at the northern tip of Khammuan Province in the lush Hin Boun valley.
Surrounded by tall karst peaks, the village
itself is notable for its position near the
Theun Hin Bun dam, which is recognisable
more by its blue-roofed Lao-European–style
bungalows and golf course than any large
dam wall.

Ban Khoun Kham is not without charm
but its main role is as a base from which to
visit the extraordinary **Tham Kong Lo** (opposite).
The other main attraction is the impressive
twin-cataract of **Tat Namsanam**, 3km north of
town. The falls are in a striking location surrounded by karst and the upper tier is quite
high. To get there from the market, cross Rte
8 and go through the archway and follow the
signs. Vehicles will need to stop after about
1km, and the ensuing 2km walk gets rocky
and slippery in the latter stages.

The Khammuan tourism office has built
a **Tourist Information Centre** (Rte 8) just south of
the Tat Namsanam entrance. While it wasn't
manned when we passed, the plan is to run
community-based treks from here into the
Phu Hin Bun NPA.

As you approach Ban Khoun Kham from
Rte 13, there is a **sala viewpoint** near Km 36.
Do not, whatever you do, miss the spectacu-
larly dramatic scenery here.

SLEEPING & EATING
Ban Khoun Kham has several sleeping options, with more expected to follow the new
road to Tham Kong Lo.

The standout favourite, both for its rooms
and meals, is **Mi Thuna Restaurant & Guesthouse**
(☎ 020-2240182; Rte 8; r US$5-9; 🕮 🖳). The new
rooms offer modern comforts such as hot
water, air-con and cable TV and owners Ralph
and Mon are a great source of local information (especially on getting to Tham Kong Lo)
and Western and Lao food – the big English
breakfast is the perfect way to start the long
trip to Kong Lo. They also provide packed
lunches. Other services include limited free
(if slow) internet for guests; mountain-bike
hire where the money goes to the local school
(US$1.50 per day); free laundry (a tip for the
washer is appreciated); and a 25m-long swimming pool expected to be finished in 2008. Mi
Thuna is about 800m south of the market on
Rte 8, past the Shell station.

Opposite the market **Seng Chen Guesthouse**
(☎ 051-214399; s/d US$4/6) has three clean rooms
with nets, fans and cold bathrooms. It's the
second-best option.

If these are full, try the simple **Xok Xai** (☎ 051-
233629; Rte 8; r US$4-6) on Rte 8 at the southern
edge of town or **SK Guesthouse** (☎ 051-250598;
r US$4-5), about 300m north of the market. For
food, Mi Thuna Restaurant is recommended
and the **DK Restaurant** (meals US$0.75-1.50), oppo-
site SK Guesthouse, serves tasty Lao food.

GETTING THERE & AWAY
All transport along Rte 8 stops at Ban Khoun
Kham. Buses for Vientiane (US$4) usually
stop about 7am, 8.30am and 9.30am, and
there are a couple that go all the way to Tha
Khaek (US$4, three hours, 143km) in the
morning. Beyond these you'll need to take
any of the semi regular *săwngthăew* to Vieng
Kham (Thang Beng) or Lak Sao and change.
For transport to Tham Kong Lo see p232.

Phu Hin Bun NPA
ປ່າສະຫງວນແຫ່ງຊາດພູຫິນປູນ
The Phu Hin Bun NPA is a huge (1580 sq km)
wilderness area of turquoise streams, monsoon forests and striking karst topography
across central Khammuan. It was made a protected area in 1993 and it's no overstatement
to say this is some of the most breathtaking
country in the region. Passing through on
foot or by boat it's hard not to feel awestruck

by the very scale of the limestone cliffs that rise almost vertically for hundreds of metres into the sky. Flora clings to the cracks in the cliff face, at once wonderfully isolated and desperately exposed.

Although much of the NPA is inaccessible by road, local people have reduced the numbers of key forest-dependent species through hunting and logging. Despite this, the area remains home to the endangered Douc langur, François' langur and several other primate species, as well as elephants, tigers and a variety of rare species of deer.

A trip out to **Tham Kong Lo** (see p232) will give you a taste of what the protected area has to offer. But there are two better ways to really get into this area of almost mythical gothic peaks and snaking streams.

Khammuan Province and Dutch NGO SNV have established two and three-day community-based treks (see p70) into the NPA at reasonable rates. The treks start in either Tha Khaek or Ban Khoun Kham (Ban Na Hin). From Tha Khaek, the two-day trip (US$86 for one person, US$46 each for two or three, US$33 for four or more) into the Phu Hin Bun is especially good. The route includes plenty of karst scenery, a walk through Tham Pa Chan, accommodation in a village and four different swimming locations, including the stunning **Khoun Kong Leng** (aka the Blue Lagoon; see p239).

There's also a three-day trek to and around Tham Kong Lo. This trek has a couple of variations, depending on where you start, the time of year and how keen you are to climb over a mountain (rather than boat through it). Including all food and transport, treks cost US$88 per person for one, U$77 for two or three and US$65 for four or more, a bit less starting in Ban Khoun Kham. There's an extra charge of US$50 per boat (maximum four people) between June and October. These treks were designed to bring tourist dollars into some of the poorest parts of Laos and they do; we highly recommend them. Bookings can be made through the Ecoguide Unit at the **Tourist Information Centre** (☎ 212512; Th Vientiane; 8am-4pm) in Tha Khaek (p236).

With a little more time and money **Green Discovery** (www.greendiscoverylaos.com) offers similar treks plus one very tempting four-day kayaking trip between spectacularly sheer cliffs, as the Nam Hin Boun follows a large anticlockwise arc towards the Mekong (US$138 per person, minimum four). Thai-based **North by North-East Tours** (www.thaitourism.com), also runs tours into the NPA. Alternatively, you might be able to arrange a similar trip yourself with a boatman, though it wouldn't be cheap.

Tham Kong Lo

ຖ້ຳລອດກອງລໍ

Imagine a river disappearing at the edge of a monolithic limestone mountain and running 7km through a pitch-black, winding cave and you'll start to get an idea of **Tham Kong Lo**, truly one of the natural wonders of Laos. Pronounced *thàm kạwng láw,* the cave-cum-tunnel is quite awesome – up to 100m wide in some places and almost as high. It takes a motorised canoe nearly an hour to pass through.

Boat pilots hired for the journey can lead visitors to natural *thâat* (stupas) that are actually groups of glittering stalagmites in a dry cavern branching off the main tunnel. Be sure to bring a torch (flashlight) and wear rubber sandals; the gravel in the riverbed is sharp and it's usually necessary to disembark and wade at several shallow points.

Besides snaking through the tunnel, the Nam Hin Bun meanders through some spectacular scenery – Gothic mountains and cliffs of jagged black karst. Amazingly, a fair amount of hardy trees have managed to take root on the cliffs. Keep an eye out for sago palms that have attained rare heights of more than 2m; in more accessible places these slow-growing trees have been dug up and sold to landscape gardeners in Thailand.

At the north end of the tunnel lies a scenic valley that once served as a refuge for lowland Lao fleeing Haw harassment during the 19th century. Temple ruins believed to date from that period can be seen in the valley.

SLEEPING & EATING

It's possible to visit Tham Kong Lo as a day trip from Ban Khoun Kham, using the accommodation there (opposite), but until the road is complete it will remain a very long day. More fun are the options closer to the cave.

At the edge of Phon Nyaeng on the banks of the Nam Hin Bun about 12km from Tham Kong Lo is **Sala Hin Boun** (☎ 020-561 4016; www.sala lao.com; r incl breakfast US$18-23). The 12 comfortable Lao-style rooms have hot-water bathrooms and balconies, those with river views being the biggest and most expensive. Cheaper rooms are s/d US$13/18, and all are US$5 cheaper in low season. Lounging in the wicker chairs overlooking the mountains and river is a great way to spend an afternoon. Lao and Western food is available for about US$3 to US$4 a meal, though you need to order in advance. Staff can arrange guided trips to Tham Kong Lo and other caves.

In Ban Tiou, about 6km closer to Ban Kong Lo, the same outfit runs the **Sala Kong Lor** (www .salalao.com; r US$4-12), a much simpler Lao-style place aimed at those who can't afford the Sala Hin Boun. In Ban Thone Ngeng, nearer again, is the **Guesthouse Saynamngeng** (r US$6-8) where the rooms are even simpler but have bathrooms; look for the yellow sign on the 'road' towards Ban Kong Lo.

For a real experience of Lào village life say the word **'homestay'** (US$5 per person, incl dinner & breakfast) when you reach Ban Kong Lo, about 1km downstream from the cave mouth, and you'll be hooked up with a family somewhere in the charming, mazelike village. We met one guy here who speaks English well, so it might not necessarily be so hard to communicate. For more on homestays, see p48.

GETTING THERE & AWAY

A 50km road from Ban Khoun Kham to Ban Kong Lo is being built and is scheduled to be complete before the wet season in 2008. This road will make getting to Kong Lo an easy one-hour motorbike ride or *săwngthăew* (US$3). In the meantime, however, there are two ways of getting to the cave; by land (note that we don't say 'road') or river.

As things are changing so quickly here, ask Ralph and Mon at Mi Thuna Guesthouse for the latest information.

By Land

When we rode it the first 30km of the new road was smoothly steamrolled laterite. Nice. It was so easy we were almost wishing it would get more interesting – until the road ended and was replaced by the track people have been using for decades.

Until the new road is finished, this track is only passable between about the end of October and June. It is, after all, just a bone-jarring series of rice paddies which have dried like concrete. And you know those buffalo you see lazing about in rivers and mud holes? During the dry season they are working in the fields and every hoof step leaves a big indentation. Dried hard, these and the countless dikes you need to haul your rattling Chinese 100cc bike across are like riding a jackhammer. The whole trip took us more than two hours, though this will get shorter as every new kilometre of road is built. If you do find yourself shuddering across the earth, with your wrists acting as shock absorbers (it rattled the pins right out of our watchband), then take some comfort in the knowledge that Mi Thuna Guesthouse can call in a masseuse to loosen out the knots when you get back to Ban Khoun Kham.

By River

For now, the only way to reach Tham Kong Lo during the wet is by river. If you're not riding a bike, take a *săwngthăew* or jumbo (three-wheeled taxi) from near the market in Ban Khoun Kham to the village of Ban Na Phuak (US$1 per person, 35 minutes, 14km); one service is guaranteed from Ban Na Phuak to Ban Khoun Kham at 9.30am, returning at 10.30am; after this you have to wait for it to fill.

From Ban Na Phuak boats follow the beautiful Nam Hin Bun for about 3½ hours to Ban Kong Lo, just downstream from the cave entrance. It's a stunning trip, with the walls of the valley slowly closing in as the river winds southward. It's also stunningly expensive at US$50 a boat for the return trip, with a maximum of four people. This is the price the local boatmen have agreed upon and given that they use at least 18L of fuel each way and probably only make a trip on average every few days, it's not as outrageous as it sounds.

Whatever the season, puttering up the river is undoubtedly the most enjoyable way of reaching Tham Kong Lo. In the dry season the river drops and boats might not be able to take four people.

Through the Cave

So you've arrived, one way or another, in Ban Kong Lo. You're only here for one reason, so everyone (kids, grannies, stray dogs…) will point you toward the river and a boatman. It costs US$10 per boat for the return trip (about 2½ hours, maximum four people) through the cave, including a short stop on the far side. Cave entrance costs US$0.20 and there's a US$0.50 motorbike parking fee.

CENTRAL LAOS

Tha Bak
ບ້ານທ່າບັກ

About 18km east of Ban Khoun Kham, Tha Bak sits near the confluence of the Nam Kading and Nam Theun rivers. The town itself is pretty, and pretty quiet, and the only real reason to stop is to take photos of the river or actually get out on the incredible **bomb boats**. The name is slightly misleading, as the boats are actually made out of huge missile-shaped drop tanks that carried fuel for jets operating overhead during the 1960s and '70s. Empty tanks were sometimes dropped and those that weren't too badly damaged when they hit the deck have been turned into boats.

We're not exactly sure which planes carried these tanks, though that's not for want of trying. After enquiring with veterans we found ourselves in an acronym-filled email discussion that bounced around the world, from retired USAF generals to ex-Ravens (see p130) and pilots of various other aircraft flying over Laos during that period. The villagers themselves usually attribute the tanks to the giant B-52 bombers; however, the pilots who flew them say no, it wasn't them. More likely they were dropped by F-4 Phantoms or F-105 Thunderchiefs flying from bases in Thailand.

If you fancy a spin in a bomb boat just head down to the riverbank at the east end of the bridge and negotiate a price.

LAK SAO
ຫລັກຊາວ

☎ 054 / pop 28,000

While the forest, mountain and karst scenery along the upper stretches of Rte 8 on the way to Lak Sao (Lak Xao; literally, Kilometre 20) is strikingly beautiful, the town itself is a disappointment. In the eastern reaches of Bolikhamsai Province near the Vietnam border, Lak Sao is a frontier boomtown that has grown rapidly as the headquarters for logging operations that continue to decimate surrounding forests. And while it's the nearest real town to the border, that border is still 32km away – raising some good questions about why it's called 'Kilometre 20'.

The wedding-cake-shaped market at Lak Sao was once known for its trade in wildlife and forest products, but these days there is little on offer, no doubt due to the destruction of nearby forests. Instead you'll find Vietnamese traders flogging basic consumer goods, some-times to families of White Hmong and Striped Hmong who come in to trade for provisions. The only real sights in the vicinity are some **limestone caves** (the most accessible, Tham Mangkhon, is 17km northwest of town on Rte 8) and **hot springs** (a further 1km); neither is a must-see. The vast majority of people pass straight on through and it's hard to blame them. If you're travelling to Hanoi, however, it's a good place to stop.

Information

Lao Development Bank (Rte 8B) Changes Thai baht, dollars, UK pounds and Vietnamese dong.

Post office (cnr Rte 8 & Rte 8B; 8am-noon & 1-5pm Mon-Fri, 8am-noon Sat)

Sleeping & Eating

You don't need 20/20 vision to see where this town made its money and it's nowhere more obvious than in the sleeping and eating establishments. There's enough high-quality timber in these places to keep a carpenter busy for several lifetimes. The hotels mentioned here have recently promoted themselves from guesthouse status, but neither the price nor

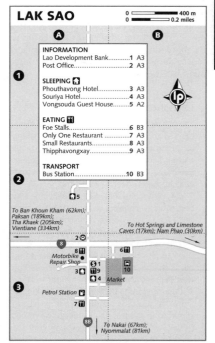

LAK SAO

0 — 400 m
0 — 0.2 miles

INFORMATION
Lao Development Bank............1 A3
Post Office.............................2 A3

SLEEPING
Phouthavong Hotel.................3 A3
Souriya Hotel.........................4 A3
Vongsouda Guest House........5 A2

EATING
Foe Stalls...............................6 B3
Only One Restaurant..............7 A3
Small Restaurants...................8 A3
Thipphavongxay.....................9 A3

TRANSPORT
Bus Station............................10 B3

To Ban Khoun Kham (62km);
Paksan (189km);
Tha Khaek (205km);
Vientiane (334km)

To Hot Springs and Limestone
Caves (17km); Nam Phao (30km)

Motorbike
Repair Shop

Market

Petrol Station

To Nakai (67km);
Nyommalat (81km)

the standards have changed much. Having said that, most are good value. These three have hot-water bathrooms, cable TV and air-con, though it's seldom hot enough to need it. All are a short walk to the market and bus station.

Souriya Hotel (☎ 341111; Rte 8B; r US$5-8; ❄) Opposite the Phouthavong, this three-storey place has 30 clean twin and double rooms with cable TV; those at the front (US$8) have expansive views of the town and mountain behind from the balcony. The friendly manager speaks some French and English; there's a good restaurant next door.

Phouthavong Hotel (☎ 341074; Rte 8B; r US$5.50-6.60; ❄) The ever-expanding Phouthavong now has 49 clean, spacious rooms with cable TV to complement the timber. Very good value. Fan rooms (US$5.50) are slightly smaller.

Vongsouda Guest House (☎ 341035, 020-5653251; r US$6; ❄) About 300m north of Rte 8 along a dirt road, this family-run place has decent, relatively large rooms and a cosy communal area with a fireplace, though you'll be lucky if anyone else is around.

Thipphavongxay (☎ 341038; Rte 8B; meals US$1.50-3.50; ❄ 6am-11pm) Next door to the Souriya Guest House, Thipphavongxay has a good range of *làap* (spicy meat salad) in its large menu of mostly Lao dishes. It's now the most reliable eating option in town. The manager speaks some English and is a good source of information.

Only One Restaurant (☎ 341034; Rte 8B; meals US$1.50-3.50; ❄ 6am-10pm) The Lao and Vietnamese dishes here aren't bad and it's encouraging that the local endangered species are found on preservation posters rather than on the menu – apart from the stuffed civet staring out from the counter.

Several **small restaurants** (❄ 6am-8pm) and *fŏe* stalls serve Lao and Vietnamese around the market.

Getting There & Away

Buses leave from east of the market for Vientiane (US$6, six to eight hours, 334km) daily at 5am, 6am and 8am. For services from Vientiane see p114. These buses stop at Vieng Kham (Thang Beng; US$3, 100km, 1½ to 2½ hours), where you can change for regular buses heading south, and Paksan (US$5, five to six hours, 189km). Other buses and *săwngthăew* head along Rte 8 to Thang Beng (between 8.30am and 5pm) and one bus to Tha Khaek (US$5, five to six hours, 202km) at 7.30am.

THA KHAEK

ທ່າແຂກ

☎ 051 / pop 70,000

Who'd have thought it? In a couple of years Tha Khaek, the archetypal somnolent Lao riverside town, has gone from a charming but relatively boring place to the base for an ever-growing range of adventure travel in central

---

CROSSING THE VIETNAM BORDER AT NAM PHAO & CAU TREO

The border at Nam Phao (Laos) and Cau Treo (Vietnam) through the Kaeo Neua Pass is 32km from Lak Sao and is open from 7am to 6pm, though lunch time often slows things down. *Săwngthăew* (US$1.50, 45 minutes) leave every hour or so from Lak Sao market and drop you at the typically relaxed Lao border post. There is an exchange booth on the Lao side, though the rates aren't generous. You'll need to have your Vietnamese visa arranged in advance. Laos issues 30-day visas at the border.

Once into Vietnam you'll be welcomed by an assortment of piranhas masquerading as transport to Vinh. Contrary to their claims, a minibus to Vinh doesn't cost US$20 per person – about US$5 for a seat is more reasonable, though you'll do very well to get that price. Hook up with as many other people as possible to improve your bargaining position.

You can hopefully avoid these guys by taking a bus direct from Lak Sao to Vinh (100,000d, three to four hours; pay in Vietnamese dong, dollars or kip); there are usually four buses leaving between about noon and 2pm. Once in Vinh you can take a bus or a sleeper on the **Reunification Express** (www.vr.com.vn) straight to Hanoi.

Coming from Vinh, buses leave for Tay Son (10,000d, 70km) regularly between 6am and 2pm. From Tay Son take a motorbike or minibus (both about 50,000d) for the spectacular last 26km climb up to the frontier. Expect to be ripped off on this route (p323). Jumbos and *săwngthăew* to Lak Sao leave the border when full or cost about US$10 to charter.

Laos. Idling attractively on the east bank of the Mekong River 332km south of Vientiane, Tha Khaek means 'guest landing', believed to be a reference to its earlier role as a boat landing for foreign traders. Appropriately, the capital of Khammuan Province is a place you can soon feel comfortable.

Particularly around the old town near the riverfront, the surviving Franco-Chinese architecture, mixed with newer structures, is similar to that found in Vientiane and Savannakhet, with tall trees shading quiet streets and no-one seeming in any particular hurry to do anything. The epicentre (if we can call it that) of the old town is the modest fountain square at the western end of Th Kuvoravong near the river. River-

side beer shops near here are a good place for sundowners.

It's busier around the markets, and traffic between Vietnam and Thailand is increasing. The population is mostly lowland Lao, Thai and Vietnamese.

History

Once an outpost of the Mon-Khmer Funan and Chenla empires, when it was known as Sri Gotapura (Sikhottabong in Lao) and was ruled by King Suryavarman (r AD 578–614), Tha Khaek traces its present-day roots to French colonial construction in 1911–12. Evidence of this period can be found in the slowly decaying buildings around Fountain Sq, few of which have so far been restored. The town

THA KHAEK

0   500 m
0   0.3 miles

CENTRAL LAOS

INFORMATION
BCEL..1 C1
Immigration..........................(see 29)
Lao Development Bank................2 C1
Lao Development Bank exchange
  service..............................(see 29)
Main Post Office........................3 B2
Police.....................................4 B2
Tha Kaek Hospital......................5 A3
Tourist Information Centre..........6 B1
Tourist Police...........................7 A2

SIGHTS & ACTIVITIES
Talat Lak Sawng........................8 D2

SLEEPING ⌂
Khamuane Inter Hotel................9 A2
Mekong Khammouane Hotel.....10 A2
Phoukhanna Guesthouse..........11 B1
Sooksomboon Hotel.................12 A2
Southida Guest House..............13 A2
Tha Khaek Travel Lodge...........14 D2
Thakhek Mai..........................15 B2
Thipphachanh Guesthouse........16 B2

EATING 🍴
Bakery...................................17 A2
Duc Restaurant.......................18 A2
Kaysone Restaurant & Ice Cream
  Parlour...............................19 A2

Latdavanh..............................20 D2
Local Food Place.....................21 A2
Minimart................................22 D2
Phavilai Restaurant..................23 A2
Smile Barge Restaurant............24 A2
Thakhek Restaurant.............(see 15)
Van Thiu Restaurant................25 A2

ENTERTAINMENT 🎭
Boua's Place...........................26 A2
Phudoi Disco..........................27 D1

TRANSPORT
Motorbike Shop......................28 A2
Passenger Ferry......................29 A2
Talat Lak Saam (Talat
  Sooksomboon)....................30 D2
Vehicle Ferry..........................31 A2

CENTRAL LAOS

served as a port, border post and administrative centre during the French period, when a large number of Vietnamese were bought in to serve as administrators. More arrived during the 1950s and '60s fleeing the Viet Minh movement in North Vietnam, and by the late '60s Vietnamese made up about 85% of Tha Khaek's population. Their numbers dropped drastically in the late 1970s as many fled another Communist regime.

In the '60s and early '70s the city also drew a large number of Thais, though these were mostly visiting on decadent daytrips to gamble. The fun stopped when the North Vietnamese Army and Pathet Lao cut the road to Vientiane. These days there's the usual border-town talk of a new casino, but no-one has started building yet.

Information

EMERGENCY
Police (cnr Th Kuvoravong & Th Unkham)
Tourist Police (☎ 250610; Fountain Sq) Know how to write insurance reports if you can track down an officer.
Tha Khaek Hospital (cnr Th Chou Anou & Th Champasak) Fine for minor ailments or commonly seen problems such as malaria or dengue. Anything more serious, head to Thailand.

INTERNET
At the time of writing the only place to get online was the **Tha Khaek Travel Lodge** (☎ 030-530 0145; travell@laotel.com; per hr US$3).

MONEY
BCEL (☎ 212686; Th Vientiane) Changes Thai baht, US dollars, euros, Vietnamese dong and travellers cheques. Cash advances made on Visa.
Lao Development Bank (☎ 212089; Th Kuvoravong) Changes cash, but doesn't offer cash advances. Another branch changes cash at the port immigration post.

POST & TELEPHONE
Main post office (Th Kuvoravong) Also offers pricey international phone calls.

TOURIST INFORMATION
The **Tourist Information Centre** (☎ 212512; Th Vientiane; 8am-4pm) is the place to get all the latest information on the various community-based trekking options, book yourself on a trip and meet your English-speaking guide. The centre has plenty of informative pamphlets and sells maps of the town and province (US$1). As trek prices vary depending on group size, it's worth calling Mr Somkied (☎ 020-5711797)

to coordinate with other travellers. The office is beside the rusting old Ferris wheel and should be open seven days, though you'd be lucky to find it open on weekend afternoons.

Sights & Activities
Tha Khaek's more about being than seeing and there's not much in the way of sights. One place in town worth checking out is the large **Talat Lak Sawng** (Km 2 Market; Th Kuvoravong), which purveys hardware, clothes, fresh produce and just about everything else the people of Tha Khaek use in daily life. In addition to the usual gold shops there are a large number of vendors selling work in silver.

Sleeping
Perhaps surprisingly, given it is the nearest big town to the vast Nam Theun 2 dam site, Tha Khaek has a pretty small range of rooms.

ourpick Tha Khaek Travel Lodge (☎ 030-530 0145; travell@laotel.com; dm US$2.50, r US$5-11;) It's not the cheapest place in town nor the nearest to the Mekong, but the Travel Lodge is the clear favourite with travellers for its easy atmosphere, decent food, 17 clean rooms and welcoming staff. Run by charming Pok, rooms range from a comfortable dormitory (US$2.50), through fan rooms with or without bathroom to the attractive air-con rooms with private bathroom (US$11). The internet, camp-style fire, decent food and coffee are other draws, topped off by the travellers' book, which has the latest feedback on The Loop (p240). They have a few motorbikes for hire (US$10 to US$15 per day).

Phoukhanna Guesthouse (☎ 212092; Th Vientiane; r US$3.50-8;) The English-speaking woman manager gives this place an easy-going atmosphere. Simple rooms without bathrooms are US$3.50, but the pick are those in the newer building out back, which are bigger, quieter and generally better. The restaurant (meals US$1.50 to $3.50; open from 7.30am to 11pm) serves a mix of Western and Asian food and gets good reviews.

Khamuane Inter Hotel (☎ 212171; Th Kuvoravong; r US$4-6;) Located in the centre of town in an appealing French-era building with Deco hints, rooms here are some of the cheapest in town, which makes up for the lack of any atmosphere and the dubious plumbing.

Thakhek Mai (☎ 212551; Th Vientiane; r US$8-10;) Privatisation of public assets in Laos has opened this former government guesthouse to everyone. If you like rooms with a strong green or blue influence, this might be a good thing. In fairness, the rooms are not bad and the attached restaurant is pretty good.

Southida Guest House (☎ 212568; Th Chao Anou; r US$8-11; 🈁) Not far from the riverfront and Fountain Sq, the family-run Southida has clean rooms with cable TV in a modern two-storey building. Most rooms have at least one balcony but size can vary considerably, so ask to see several. The downstairs restaurant (meals US$1.50 to US$4; open from 6.30am to 10pm) is reliable.

Sooksomboon Hotel (☎ 212225; Th Setthathirat; small/large rooms US$8/12; 🈁) In a colonial-era police station right on the Mekong, the exterior promises more than the slightly surreal faux–Art Deco interior delivers. Rooms in the main building are far superior and some have bathtubs to go with the peeling paint.

Mekong Khammouane Hotel (☎ 250777; Th Setthathirat; r US$11; 🈁) The bright blue exterior of this Vietnamese-run, four-storey hotel on the riverfront is impossible to miss. Staff wearing *ao dai* (Vietnamese national dress) and clean, well-equipped-if-a-bit-dim rooms will be familiar to anyone who's travelled in Vietnam. Fair value.

Other hotels include:

Samy Guesthouse (d US$3.50) Simple place at the bus station.

Thipphachanh Guesthouse (☎ 212762; r US$5-12; 🈁) Motel-style place with clean rooms and TV.

Eating

Most guesthouses and hotels also have restaurants, with the kitchens in the Southida Guest House and the Tha Khaek Travel Lodge both serving above average fare; the latter has a shrinking range of decent Western food and good Lao. Several *khào jîi* (baguette) vendors can be found on Fountain Sq in the morning, and if you're looking to stock up before doing The Loop the **minimart** (🈁 7am-8pm) at Talak Lak Săam is pretty well stocked.

Bakery (🈁 7am-5pm) For the best plain baguettes head for the Vietnamese bakery, a couple of blocks south of Fountain Sq.

Local food place (Th Chao Anou; meals about US$1) Head to the busy local food place, a block back from the river, if you fancy tasty Lao favourites such as *pîng kai* (grilled chicken), *làap* and sticky rice for next to no money.

Latdavanh (*fŏe* US$1; 🈁 6.30am-8pm) Nearer to the Tha Khaek Travel Lodge, Latdavanh

serves great *fŏe* and a few other basics; there's no English sign but it's the only place near that corner.

Phavilai Restaurant (Fountain Sq; meals US$1-2; 🈁 6am-9pm) Serves standard Lao-Chinese rice and noodle dishes.

Van Thiu Restaurant (☎ 212138; meals US$1-3.50; 🈁 lunch & dinner) This no-frills place, accessed through a shop, serves tasty Vietnamese dishes.

Duc Restaurant (meals US$1.50; 🈁 6am-10pm) On the riverfront, this place does a delicious *fŏe hàeng* (dry rice noodles served in a bowl with various herbs and seasonings but no broth).

Kaysone Restaurant & Ice Cream Parlour (☎ 212563; meals US$1.50-4; 🈁 9.30am-11.30pm) With dining on the rooftop or indoors, this is a popular place serving mainly Lao fare with a strong emphasis on seafood; the ice cream is also pretty good.

Thakhek Restaurant (Th Vientiane; meals US$1.50-4; 🈁 7.30am-10.30pm) Next door to the Thakhek Mai guesthouse, this big place has indoor and outdoor seating and a large menu of Lao and Thai dishes, fish being especially good.

Smile Barge Restaurant (☎ 212150; meals US$3-4.50; 🈁 noon-1am) One of several floating restaurants set up along the Mekong, the Smile Barge has been so successful it now has a landlubbing venue as well. It's hard to know whether the tasty food or the karaoke is more popular.

Entertainment

Tha Khaek is no London or New York, but there are a couple of options.

Boua's Place (Th Setthathirat; 🈁 3pm-10pm) On the river just south of Fountain Sq, wonderfully camp Boua used to cut hair by day and sell beer and good spirit by night. But the sundowners became so popular that the cutting has stopped. There's no food, just beer and atmosphere at tables overlooking the river; snacks can be ordered from nearby restaurants. Look for the tables.

Phudoi Disco (🈁 8pm-midnight) Behind the Phudoi Guest House, this place can be a fun Lao night out if you fancy getting down to lots of Thai pop, a bit of Lao pop and some cheesy Western classics with the local youth.

Getting There & Away
BUS

Tha Khaek's **bus station** (Rte 13) is about 3.5km from the centre of town and has a sizable market and basic guesthouses to complement

---

CROSSING THE THAI BORDER AT THA KHAEK & NAKHON PHANOM

Crossing the Mekong from Tha Khaek to Nakhon Phanom in Thailand is simple. The boat landing and **immigration office** (🕑 8am-6pm) are about 400m north of Fountain Sq and boats travel in both directions at least every hour; they usually leave when there are 10 people on board. From Laos, the ferry costs US$1.50 or 60B, while from Nakhon Phanom it's 50B. On weekends boats might be less frequent and you'll be asked for an extra US$1 on the Lao side, and an extra 10B in Thailand. After hours you can charter a boat for about 500B, but border formalities will be difficult.

In Tha Khaek, Lao immigration *usually* issues 30-day tourist visas on arrival and there's a **money exchange service** (🕑 8.30am-3pm) at the immigration office. In Thailand, it's a 30B share tuk-tuk ride to the bus station, from where buses leave Nakhon Phanom for Udon Thani (regular) and Bangkok (at 10am and in the evenings).

---

the regular services going north and south. For Vientiane (US$4, six hours, 332km), buses originate in Tha Khaek at 4.30am, 5.30am, 7am and 8.30am. From 9am to midnight buses stop en route from Pakse and Savannakhet every hour or so. Any bus going north stops at Vieng Kham (Thang Beng; US$2, 90 minutes, 102km), Pak Kading (US$2.50, three hours, 149km), or Paksan (US$3, three to four hours, 193km). For buses from Vientiane see p114.

Heading south, buses for Savannakhet (US$2, two to three hours, 125km) and Pakse (US$4.50, 368km, six to seven hours) are reasonably frequent between 10.30am and midnight. A 4pm bus goes all the way to Don Khong (US$6, about 15 hours, 452km) and Voen Kham (US$6, about 16 hours, 482km) on the Cambodian border, but you'd need to be in a hurry.

If you're heading to Vietnam, a bus for Hue (US$8) leaves daily at 8am, while for Danang (US$8) and Hanoi (US$16, 17 hours) the bus goes at 8pm.

SĂWNGTHĂEW

Săwngthăew depart when full from the **Talat Lak Săam Terminal** (Sooksomboon Bus Terminal) into the Khammuan Province interior. Along Rte 12, *săwngthăew* leave every hour or so between 7am and 3pm for Mahaxai (US$1.50, 1½ to 2½ hours, 50km), Nyommalat (US$2, two to three hours, 63km), Nakai (US$2.50, 2½ to 3½ hours, 80km) and Na Phao for the Vietnam border (US$3.50, five to seven hours, 142km). Rte 12 is being upgraded and the stretch between the Vietnam border and Nyommalat is finished. Depending on who you believe, the remainder will be completed in 2007 or 2010 (when the Nam Theun 2 dam is complete

and trucks will stop using this route). In the meantime prepare to chew plenty of dust on the unsealed sections.

There is allegedly a *săwngthăew* to Ban Kong Lo (US$4) every day at 7.30am, though this seems doubtful in the wet season when the village is not accessible by road.

Getting Around

It should cost about US$1.50 to hire a jumbo to the bus terminal, though you'll need to negotiate. Rides around town cost about US$0.50 per person or US$1 for the whole thing.

The Tha Khaek Travel Lodge (p236) rents Chinese 110cc bikes for US$10 per day for nearby attractions and US$15 for The Loop; and a small riverfront **motorbike shop** (Th Setthathirat) rents similar bikes for similar prices. The Tourist Information Centre (p236) can arrange bicycle hire.

AROUND THA KHAEK
Pha That Sikhottabong

About 6km south of town is the much-venerated **Pha That Sikhottabong** (Pha That Muang Ka; admission US$0.30; 🕑 8am-6pm) stupa which stands in the grounds of a 19th-century monastery of the same name. According to local lore the stupa was erected on the site of a 6th- to 10th-century *thâat* (Buddhist stupa or reliquary) built by King Nanthasen during a time when Tha Khaek was part of a principality called Si Khotabun. Considered one of the most important *thâat* in Laos, Sikhottabong was first renovated by King Setthathirat in the 16th century, when it assumed its current general form. It was again restored in the 1950s and later augmented in the 1970s. It's the site of a major festival each February.

A *wihǎan* (hall) on the temple grounds contains a large seated Buddha, constructed by the order of King Anouvong (Chao Anou).

Tham Pha Pa (Buddha Cave)

When Mr Bun Nong used a vine to scramble 15m up a sheer 200m-high cliff in April 2004, he was hoping to make a dinner of the bats he'd seen flying out of the rock face. Instead he discovered a narrow cave mouth and, stepping into the cavern beyond, was greeted by 229 bronze Buddha images. The Buddhas, ranging from 15cm to about 1m tall, were sitting as they had been for centuries facing the entrance of a cave of impressive limestone formations. It took him a week but Mr Bun Nong eventually told friends in the nearby village of Ban Na Kan Sarng and the cave was named **Tham Pha Pa** (Buddha Cave; entry US$0.20; ☺ 8am-noon & 1-4pm).

It's hard to say exactly how long the Buddha images have been there, but experts think they are more than 600 years old. Whatever their age, the cave has become a pilgrimage site for Buddhists from around Laos and Thailand.

Mr Bun Nong has become a hero in Ban Na Kan Sarng because the village is now living fat off the fruits of his discovery. Electricity has arrived and a market selling food, drinks and forest products to visitors is bringing much-needed income. And perhaps best of all the new laterite road linking the cave site to Rte 12 has made going anywhere that much easier for the locals. Tourism, it would seem, is a force for good in the case of Ban Na Kan Sarng…mostly. The concrete staircase leading to the cave is undoubtedly practical, but it's hideous too.

Tham Pha Pa is about 18km from Tha Khaek. The new road runs north from Rte 12 about 4km after you cross Rte 13; look for a blue sign pointing to Ban Tha Khe. After about 500m the road turns east along the old railway bed and after a few more kilometres bends north. Take the left fork and the cave is at the end of the road. The **railway line**, a French scheme aimed at connecting Thailand and Vietnam, was abandoned when money ran out in the early 1920s. On the Vietnamese side the line runs right to the border, but here only a couple of concrete bridges remain.

If you don't have your own transport, tuk-tuks will do the trip return for about US$12 to US$15 depending on your bargaining skills. Alternatively, you might be able to get on a *sǎwngthǎew* from Talat Lak Sǎam. The Buddha Cave day trek through Tha Khaek's Tourism Information Centre (US$30 for one, US$17 each for two or three people, US$13 for four to eight) also stops at a beautiful swimming cave, reached via a wet swampy walk.

Khoun Kong Leng

ຂຸນກອງແລງ

Nestled amid the limestone karsts of the southern reaches of the Phu Hin Bun NPA is the stunningly beautiful 'Evening Gong Lake'. The luminescent green waters spring from a subterranean river that filters through the limestone, making the water crystal clear. The lake is reputed to be 70m deep.

Khoun Kong Leng is named after a legend that describes a gong sounding on the full moon each month. Villagers from nearby Ban Na Kheu believe the lake is sacred and ask visitors to follow a few rules. First, you must ask at the village before swimming in the lake. Once you get the approval, only swim in the stream that flows from the lake, near the wooden footbridge, and not in the lake itself. Fishing is banned.

Khoun Kong Leng is only about 30km northeast of Tha Khaek as the crow flies, but given you're not a crow and the road is terrible, it's going to be quite a trip. Head north along Rte 13 and turn right (east) at Km 25 onto a dirt road. After 2km, turn right (south) again, and bump up over hills and through villages for 16km until you reach Ban Na Kheu. Once you've got approval for swimming, it's another 1km to the lake.

Khoun Kong Leng is one of the stops on the two-day trek run by the Tourism Information Centre (p236) into the Phu Hin Bun NPA; see p230.

East on Rte 12

Whether as a day trip or as part of The Loop (p240), the first 22km of Rte 12 east of Tha Khaek is an area with several caves, an abandoned railway line and a couple of swimming spots that are worth a look. This is part of the vast Khammuan Limestone area, which stretches roughly between Rtes 12 and 8 and east towards Rte 8B. There are thousands of caves, sheer cliffs and jagged karst peaks. Remember to check your odometer when you cross Rte 13 and record the number (write it on the back of your hand); with no kilometre stones and few signs, this will be useful when

THE LOOP

The Loop is an off-the-beaten-track circuit through some of the more remote parts of Khammuan and Bolikhamsai Provinces. The trip is possible by bicycle, but is best done on a motorbike. Fuel is available in most villages along the way. Give yourself at least three days, though four is better if you want to see Tham Kong Lo and have time to find yourself after being lost. Ultimately though, it's up to you…we met one guy who took five days; another did it in 24 hours.

As we discovered on The Loop this time, this part of central Laos is changing fast as the massive Nam Theun 2 dam (p65) project swings into high gear. By mid-2007 more than 11,000 people will be working on the site, and when the area is flooded in 2010 parts of the road will likely disappear and be replaced by new roads. For the latest information we recommend the travellers' book in the Tha Khaek Travel Lodge (p236).

Once you've got your wheels, spend day one heading **East on Rte 12** from Tha Khaek for visiting the caves and swimming spots on the way. It's possible to stay in pretty **Mahaxai** (about 45km), but the guesthouse (rooms US$6) isn't up to much. It's better to continue north through the dust/mud and endless annoying trucks along Rte 8B. After 16km you'll pass the sealed Rte 12 turn-off to Vietnam and the expansive **NT2 main camp** before coming to **Nyommalat** 5km further. The 10km stretch north of Nyommalat is as busy as an LA freeway, but when the dust settles you'll be passing the site of the **Nam Theun 2 power house** and heading up 6km of steep, winding and jarring road: this is no smooth ride. At the top of the hill the road splits at a busy village called **Ban Oudomsouk**; keep straight for 3km to **Nakai**, where there is a stable guesthouse (rooms US$3), and fuel. But travellers report the best place to stop is at **Ban Tha Long,** 17km further north, where the road crosses the Nam Theun via a new bridge. There's a small but attractive bamboo guesthouse (US$4) in a nice spot overlooking the river. From Mahaxai to Ban Tha Long took us about three hours.

After crossing the bridge at Ban Tha Long it's 50km to **Lak Sao** (p233) along a road that's pretty rocky in places. This stretch is stunning as you drive through the corridor between the Nakai Nam Theun and Phu Hin Bun NPAs. After 17km keep straight at the junction (the left fork will take you to the Nam Theun 2 dam site). In the dry season the 50km took us about two hours.

When you finally hit the tarmac at Lak Sao you (and your butt) will offer up thanks to whichever god you're into. This otherwise unremarkable town is also a good place if you need bike repairs (eg two new shocks and labour, US$10). Riding the 62km of smooth Rte 8 between Lak Sao and Ban Khoun Kham (Ban Na Hin) is like stepping into a video game – the road runs between walls of impregnable karst on one side, into winding hills of deep forest, and crosses the wide Nam Theun at **Tha Bak** (p233), where it's worth stopping for a look at the bomb boats.

Ban Khoun Kham (p230) is the base for trips into **Tham Kong Lo** – see p231 for all the teeth-chattering details. From Ban Khoun Kham it's about 145km back to Tha Khaek. Good luck!

looking for the various turnoffs. Of course, if you get lost just ask a local.

All these places can be reached by tuk-tuk, bicycle or hired motorcycle.

THAM XANG (THAM PHA BAN THAM)

ถ้ำช้าง (ถ้ำพะ บ้านถ้ำ)

The first cave is **Tham Xang** (Elephant Cave) also known as Tham Pha Ban Tham after the nearby village of Ban Tham. It's famous for its stalagmite 'elephant head', which is found along a small passage behind the large golden Buddha; take a torch (flashlight). This cave has an unusually lively recent history. Before 1956 it was home to a limestone formation believed to resemble an evil monster's head.

Various taboos were observed to avoid upsetting the monster's spirit, but when a wave of sickness hit the village in that year the locals decided the evil head had to go and promptly blew it to smithereens with dynamite. Soon after this the elephant's head miraculously appeared and village health improved. It's been revered ever since.

To find it, take the right fork about 2.5km east of the Rte 13 junction. You'll see the large cave mouth in the distance – just keep following the road. In the wet season you might need to cross a river by foot, or it might be too flooded to cross at all. In this case, try continuing along Rte 12 and turn right (south) onto a dirt road shortly after a bridge.

Back on Rte 12 you can continue east or turn north to the **old railway** and **Tham Pha Pa** (p239).

THA FALANG
ທ່າຟະລັ້ງ

At Km 13 (about 9km from Rte 13) a rough trail leads 2km north to the water-sculpted rocks at **Tha Falang** (French Landing) on the scenic Nam Don. Tha Falang features a wooded area on a stream where colonials used to picnic and, during the wet season, is a nice enough place for a swim. Tha Falang is much more easily accessed than Khoun Kong Leng (see p239) but is not nearly as attractive, especially in the dry season. In the wet season you'll probably need to hire a small boat from near the Xieng Liap bridge to get there.

THAM XIENG LIAP
ກ້ຳຊ្យງລ្យບ

A track heading south for about 400m at Km 14, near the bridge over the Huay Xieng Liap and the village of Ban Song-khone (about 10.5km from Rte 13) leads to the stunning limestone cave **Tham Xieng Liap**, the entrance of which is at the base of a dramatic 300m-high cliff. It's named for a legendary former novice monk (*xieng*) who was sneaking around (*liap*) in the cave looking for the beautiful daughter of a local hermit; he eventually tracked her down at Tham Nang Aen. The cave is about 200m long and, in the dry season, you can walk/wade through and swim in the picturesque valley on the far side. *Paa faa* (soft-shelled turtles) live in the cave, while the cliffs outside are said to be home to the recently discovered *khan you* (Laotian rock rat).

THAM SA PHA IN (THAM PHANYA INH)
ກ້ຳສະພາອິນ (ກ້ຳພະຍາອິນ)

With high cliffs either side, Rte 12 continues through a narrow pass (about 11.5km from Rte 13) and immediately beyond a track leads north to **Tham Sa Pha In** (Tham Phanya Inh). This rarely visited Buddhist holy cave is said to have magical healing powers; swimming is not allowed.

THAM NANG AEN
ກ້ຳນາງແອນ

The last cave along this stretch of Rte 12 is the touristy **Tham Nang Aen** (admission US$0.50), about 18km from Tha Khaek. Much concrete has been added to the limestone here though thankfully the large wooden *sala* (hall) that obstructed views of the front of the cave has recently been torn down. You certainly won't feel like you're the first person here, but at least you'll be able to see inside as it's pretty well lit.

The cave's name is also related to the legend of the sneaky novice monk of Tham Xieng Liap. He is believed to have tracked down his beautiful girl at the entrance to this cave before sitting (*nang*) with her and flirting (*aen kan*) – thus it's the Cave of Sitting and Flirting. When we visited there were plenty of people sitting and eating, but we didn't notice much flirting.

It's easy enough to find; look for two big signs in Lao pointing right (south) as you come around a left-hand bend 16km from the junction with Rte 13. The 700m-long track should be passable at all but the wettest times, when you'll need to park and wade across the stream. The pitiful 'zoo' near the entrance will appeal to people who don't like animals.

CENTRAL LAOS

CROSSING THE VIETNAM BORDER AT NA PHAO & CHA LO

Despite the road from Nyommalat to Na Phao now being almost perfect, for *falang* (Western-ers) this remains one of the least-used of all Laos's borders (open from 7am to 5pm). This is partly because transport on both sides is infrequent, though it's definitely possible to find some *săwngthăew* (literally, two rows: passenger truck) from Tha Khaek (US$3.50, five to seven hours, 142km) leave at least daily. The other problem is you can't get a Laos visa at the border, even though they are supposed to be issued there. This might change when the road from Tha Khaek to Nyommalat is completed, but check first. Leave early as there's no accommodation and you'll probably have to wait a while for transport.

On the Vietnam side the nearest sizable city is Dong Hoi. A bus does run directly between Tha Khaek and Dong Hoi (US$13, 10 to 14 hours), leaving Tha Khaek at 7am on Wednesdays and Sundays and returning from Dong Hoi at 6am on Mondays and Fridays.

THAM PHA CHAN & THE NAM DON RESURGENCE
ຖ້ຳພະຈັນ/ຂຸບນ້ຳໂດນ

Further afield is **Tham Pha Chan**, with an entrance 60m high and about 100m wide. A stream runs about 600m through a limestone karst and in the dry season it's possible to walk to the far side. At its western end there is a sandalwood Buddha image in a crevice about 15m above the ground, hence the cave's name means Sandalwood Buddha Cave.

Not far from Tham Pha Chan is the **Nam Don Resurgence**, a cave where the Nam Don (Don River) emerges from the ground. It's quite a physical marvel to see the water coming up and out from the cave, and the lagoon that sits at the bottom of the tall limestone karst is a beautiful swimming spot.

Unfortunately, getting to these sights isn't easy. They are accessed via a rough road that runs north from Km 14 (about 10km east of Rte 13) for about 9km. Go by motorbike, tuk-tuk or arrange an English-speaking guide through the **Tourist Information Centre** in Tha Khaek (p236). In the wet season this road deteriorates pretty badly.

SAVANNAKHET PROVINCE

Savannakhet is the country's most populous province and is home to about 15% of all Lao citizens. Stretching between the Mekong and Thailand in the west and the Annamite mountains and Vietnam in the east, it has in recent years become an increasingly important trade corridor between these two bigger neighbours. With the luxuriously smooth tarmac of Rte 9 now complemented by a new Thai-Lao Friendship Bridge, opened in December 2006, the province is gearing up for even more traffic.

The population of 826,000 includes lowland Lao, Thai Dam, several small Mon-Khmer groups (Chali, Bru, Kaleung, Katang, Lave, Mangkong, Pako and Suay), and long-established and growing communities of Vietnamese and Chinese. Particularly in the lowland farming lands east of the Mekong, the villages of Savannakhet are among the most typically Lao in the country.

There are three NPAs wholly or partly in the province, Dong Phu Vieng (p249) to

the south of Rte 9, Phu Xang Hae (p250) to the north and Xe Ban Nuan straddling the border with Salavan Province. Eastern Savannakhet is a good place to see remnants of the Ho Chi Minh Trail (p251), the primary supply route to South Vietnam for the North Vietnamese Army during the Second Indochina War. It is also a major gateway for visitors arriving from Vietnam via Lao Bao.

SAVANNAKHET (MUANG KHANTHABULI)
ສະຫວັນບະເຂດ

☎ 041 / pop 124,000

The slowly crumbling colonial-era buildings of Savannakhet serve as reminders of the importance the French attached to what was their largest trading and administrative centre south of Vientiane. These days the city's riverside centre retains a languid ambience, with tall trees shading French-era buildings that are unfailingly appealing despite their evermore forlorn appearance. Unfortunately many of these buildings will be lost in the coming years; the government is unsentimental about such colonial reminders and is unlikely to start spending money on their upkeep.

While central Savannakhet can seem a little like the land that time forgot, change is expected to come more quickly now that Laos's third bridge across the Mekong has been completed. The city's traditional role as a hub of trade between Vietnam and Thailand should grow, while the busy riverfront will likely become much slower. Which is a pity, because the trucks, customs office, overloaded merchants, labourers playing *petang* (Lao pétanque, see p61) between jobs, food and drink stalls and general hubbub of the border was one of the most attractive aspects of the city. That's progress.

Outside the centre, Savannakhet (officially known as Muang Khanthabuli but more commonly known simply as Savan) is growing fast. The large and lively **Talat Savan Xai** (Th Sisavangvong; ☾ 7am-5pm), north of the centre near the bus terminal, is the centre of much of the city's commerce.

Savannakhet is on a simple north–south grid and is pretty easy to navigate on foot.

Information
EMERGENCY
Police (☎ 212069; Th Ratsaphanith)
Provincial Hospital (☎ 212051; Th Khanthabuli)

CENTRAL LAOS

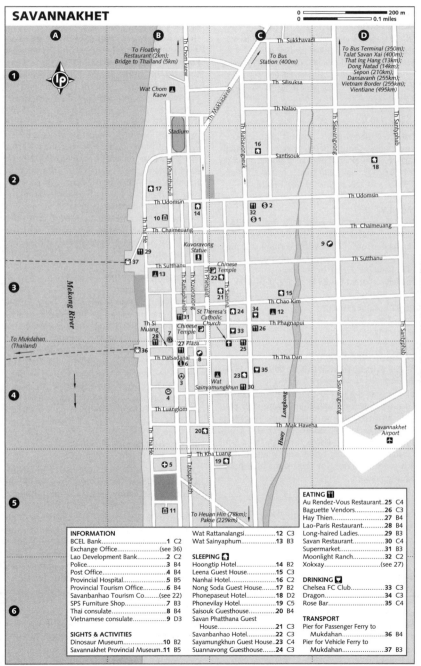

SAVANNAKHET

CENTRAL LAOS

INFORMATION
BCEL Bank.................................1 C2
Exchange Office......................(see 36)
Lao Development Bank...........2 C2
Police.......................................3 B4
Post Office..............................4 B4
Provincial Hospital.................5 B5
Provincial Tourism Office.......6 B4
Savanbanhao Tourism Co.......(see 22)
SPS Furniture Shop..................7 B3
Thai consulate.........................8 B4
Vietnamese consulate.............9 D3

SIGHTS & ACTIVITIES
Dinosaur Museum..................10 B2
Savannakhet Provincial Museum.11 B5

Wat Rattanalangsi.................12 C3
Wat Sainyaphum...................13 B3

SLEEPING
Hoongtip Hotel.....................14 B2
Leena Guest House................15 C3
Nanhai Hotel........................16 C2
Nong Soda Guest House.......17 B2
Phonepaseut Hotel...............18 D2
Phonevilay Hotel..................19 C5
Saisouk Guesthouse.............20 B4
Savan Phatthana Guest
   House................................21 C3
Savanbanhao Hotel..............22 C3
Sayamungkhun Guest House.23 C4
Suannavong Guesthouse.......24 C3

EATING
Au Rendez-Vous Restaurant..25 C4
Baguette Vendors................26 C3
Hay Thien............................27 B4
Lao-Paris Restaurant............28 B4
Long-haired Ladies...............29 B3
Savan Restaurant.................30 C4
Supermarket........................31 B3
Moonlight Ranch.................32 C2
Xokxay................................(see 27)

DRINKING
Chelsea FC Club...................33 C3
Dragon................................34 C3
Rose Bar..............................35 C4

TRANSPORT
Pier for Passenger Ferry to
   Mukdahan.........................36 B4
Pier for Vehicle Ferry to
   Mukdahan.........................37 B3

FOREIGN CONSULATES

Thai consulate (☎ 212373; Th Kuvoravong; ⌚ drop-off 8.30am-noon & collection 3-3.30pm Mon-Fri) Tourist and non-immigrant visas issued the same day.

Vietnamese consulate (☎ 212418; Th Sisavangvong; ⌚ 7.30-11am & 1.30-4.30pm Mon-Fri) One-month tourist visa costs US$45; bring one photo and allow three working days.

INTERNET ACCESS

Internet places are scattered around town and charge about US$0.60 per hour. Particularly good is **SPS Furniture Shop** (Th Khanthabuli; per hr US$0.60; ⌚ 10am-10pm) which burns CDs and DVDs and has plenty of fast machines.

MONEY

Both these banks change cash for a range of currencies and make cash advances on Visa or MasterCard. There's also a small exchange office at the river immigration post.

BCEL Bank (☎ 212261; Th Ratsavongseuk)

Lao Development Bank (☎ 212272; Th Udomsin)

POST & TELEPHONE

Post office (☎ 212205; Th Khanthabuli) For calls, use an internet café instead.

TOURIST INFORMATION

The **Provincial Tourism Office** (☎ 214203; Th Ratsaphanith; ⌚ 8am-11.30am & 1.30pm-4.30pm) is one of the best-organised tourism offices in the country. Several English-speaking staff provide information ranging from bookings for treks to Dong Natad (p247) and Dong Phu Vieng (p249) NPAs through their Eco-Guide Unit, to bus times and where to hire a motorbike. Look for the bright blue doors on the corner.

TRAVEL AGENCIES

Savanbanhao Tourism Co (☎ /fax 212944; Th Saenna) In the Savanbanhao Hotel, these guys can arrange tours to Sepon and the Ho Chi Minh Trail and Heuan Hin, and sell bus tickets to Vietnam.

Sights

Much of the charm of Savannakhet is in just wandering through the quiet streets in the centre of town, between the new and old buildings, the laughing children and, along Th Phetsalat near Wat Sainyamungkhun, among the slow-moving, *petang*-playing old men.

SAVANNAKHET PROVINCIAL MUSEUM

ພິພິດຕະພັນແຂວງສະຫວັນນະເຂດ

In a French-era mansion on expansive grounds is the mildly interesting **Savannakhet Provincial Museum** (admission US$0.50; ⌚ 8-11.30am & 1-4pm Mon-Fri). In the front yard are a few rusting artillery pieces aimed at Thailand and the barely recognisable remains of an American-built T-28, the main combat aircraft of the Royal Lao Army. Inside is more rusting ordnance, but otherwise this is a shrine to Kaysone Phomvihane, who was born nearby. There are hundreds of photos, most with basic English captions, and if you're interested in Kaysone or in the beatification of socialist heroes, then it's fascinating. The curator is rarely there at 8am so come later.

The American-built tank that sat in the grounds of the nearby School of Medicine has been replaced by a new building for trainee nurses.

DINOSAUR MUSEUM

ຫໍພິພິດຕະພັນໄດໂນເສົາ

It might come as some surprise to learn Savannakhet Province is an exciting place for palaeontologists. In a colonial-era building, this small but well-presented **museum** (☎ 212597; Th Khanthabuli; admission US$0.50; ⌚ 8am-noon & 1-4pm) displays some of the finds from the five sites where dinosaur bones or footprints have been found. The curators' unfailing enthusiasm is infectious and they're willing to use their limited English or French on you. It's good Lao-style fun.

WAT SAINYAPHUM

ວັດໄຊຍະພູມ

The oldest and largest monastery in Savan, with more than 100 novices and monks in residence, **Wat Sainyaphum** (Th Tha He) is thought to have first been built in 1542, though most of what you see today dates from the 20th century. It's a pleasant place to wander, and the monks may be willing to show you around and practise their English in the process. Look for the workshop near the river entrance – it's a veritable golden-Buddha production line.

WAT RATTANALANGSI

ວັດລັດຕະນະລັງສີ

Nearly as large as Wat Sainyaphum, **Wat Rattanalangsi** (Th Phangnapui) was built in 1951 and houses a monks' primary school. The *sim* (ordination hall) is unique in that it has glass windows (most windows in Lao temples are unglazed). Other structures include a rather gaudy Brahma shrine, a modern *săaláa lóng thám* (sermon hall) and a shelter containing a 15m reclining Buddha backed by Jataka (stories of the Buddha's past lives) paintings.

Sleeping

Savannakhet has a reasonable range of budget options but little to excite if you're looking for luxury. Most guesthouses are located in the attractive old town, and there are also a couple of basic guesthouses at the bus station.

BUDGET

Saisouk Guesthouse (☎ 212207; Th Phetsalat; r US$2.50-5; ☒) Just south of the centre of town, the atmosphere in this airy wooden house is almost invariably warm and welcoming. Rooms come in several shapes and sizes but are clean and some are quite big; ask to see a few. The husband-and-wife owners speak English. Recommended.

Phonevilay Hotel (☎ 212284; 172/173 Th Phetsalat; r US$3.50-7.50; ☒) In several buildings around a garden in the south of town, Phonevilay's air-con rooms with TV and fridge (US$5 rooms are best value) are decent enough, but the dingy US$3.50 fan rooms with cold water are not. Cleanliness could be better and some staff are totally indifferent.

Leena Guesthouse (☎ 212404 or 020-564 0697; Th Chaokeen; r US$4-8; ☒) While it's a little further from the river, the 26 smallish rooms here are clean and good value. All have attached bathroom, with hot water in the US$7 and US$8 rooms. This place also hires out bicycles (US$1.50 per day) and motorbikes (US$8 per day).

Savanbanhao Hotel (☎ 212202; sbtour@laotel.com; Th Saenna; r US$4.50-9.50; ☒) In four buildings set around a soulless concrete courtyard, rooms here aren't bad but there's not much on the atmosphere front. All rooms have hot water, air-con and English-language TV but differ by size and the age of the fittings; the cheapest ones have the noisiest air-con and aren't great. This is also the headquarters for Savanbanhao Tourism Co (opposite).

Sayamungkhun Guest House (☎ 212426; Th Ratsavongseuk; r US$5-8; ☒) The super-friendly Sayamungkhun has spacious, spotlessly clean rooms (some with fridge) and an inviting atmosphere in an appealing colonial-era building on the main road, which means front rooms are a bit noisy.

Nong Soda Guest House (☎ 212522; Th Tha He; r US$8; ☒) About 200m north of Wat Sainyaphum, this modernish house on the river's edge has great views from the elevated bar but not the rooms, which are comfortable if a bit dark. The owner hires out motorbikes for US$8 per day.

Other guesthouses include the following:

Savan Phattana Guesthouse (☎ 213955; Th Saenna; r US$3.50-7.50; ☒) Good value rooms if you don't mind peeling paint. VIP rooms are big, with three beds.

Suannavong Guesthouse (☎ 212600; Th Saenna; r US$4-8) In an old house, the four rooms are simple but clean, but a little overpriced. The manager may let you play his electric guitar. Hires out motorbikes for US$7 per day.

MIDRANGE & TOP END

There aren't a lot of midrange options in Savannakhet, and only one room worthy of being called 'top end'.

Nanhai Hotel (☎ 212371; fax 212380; Th Santisouk; s/d/ste with breakfast US$16/25/44; ☒) The ugly, six-storey Nanhai has semi-luxurious rooms with decent views, but has all the character of a Chinese business hotel – not much. The restaurant (meals US$2.50 to US$6; open from 10am to 2pm and 5pm to 10pm) serves good Chinese and fair Thai and French dishes. Sadly, the pool remains (years on) closed.

Hoongtip Hotel (☎ 212262; hoonghthip@hotmail .com; cnr Th Phetsalat & Th Udomsin; r with breakfast US$18-25; ☒) Rooms in the Hoongtip's two buildings have TV (English channels in the best rooms) and minibar but aren't as good as they could be. Those in the old building (US$18) are overpriced; and while those in the new building (US$25) are better, several have no window.

Phonepaseut Hotel (☎ 212158; fax 212916; Th Santisouk; r US$25-100; ☒) The Phonepaseut is a bit far from the Mekong but is easily the best hotel in town for rooms and service. Rooms are spotlessly clean and have English TV, minibar and (in some) bathtubs, while the 'luxury suite' (US$100) is a huge, wood-panelled affair with a flat-screen TV the size of a small cinema screen. Discounts might be possible in low season.

Eating

Savannakhet's culinary scene is slowly improving but couldn't yet be described as inspirational even if finding decent Lao, Thai and Vietnamese food is easy enough. Local specialities include *sìin sawǎn* (a slightly sweet, dried, roasted beef) and *jǎew pǎa-dàek* (a thick sauce of mashed chilli, onion, fish sauce and lotus bulb). There's also a handy small supermarket on Th Phagnaphui.

North of town are several floating restaurants popular with Lao and notable for their *khào pûn* (DIY rolls of spaghetti-style noodles with fish, lemongrass and herbs wrapped in lettuce and dipped in peanut sauce). You'll need a tuk-tuk to get there; ask for the *héuan pháe* (raft house).

Hay Thien (☎ 212754; Th Si Muang; all dishes US$1.50; ☯ 10am-8pm) This modest-looking restaurant in the centre of town specialises in freshly prepared, delicious and cheap Chinese dishes.

Xokxay (☎ 213122; meals US$1-2) A couple of doors up from Hay Thien, this place serves a similar menu.

Lao-Paris Restaurant (☎ 212792; Th Si Muang; meals US$1.50-4; ☯ 7am-10pm) In an old Chinese shophouse near the river the mostly reliable Lao, Vietnamese and French offerings here make this a travellers' favourite. Service is rarely enthusiastic, but the portions are big and prices reasonable.

Au Rendez-Vous Restaurant (☎ 213181; 179 Th Ratsavongseuk; meals US$1-3) A couple of blocks north of the Sayamungkhun Guest House, this small and clean restaurant serves a few decent Western dishes with its predominantly Asian menu, and has a good reputation for Western breakfasts.

Savan Restaurant (☎ 214488; Th Mak Havena; meals from US$2; ☯ 6-10pm) In an oddly romantic outdoor setting with private compartments, this place is all about *sìin daat* (Korean-style barbecue). There's no English menu but it's easy enough to just point and shoot.

Moonlight Ranch (☎ 030-531 5718; Th Ratsavongseuk; meals US$2-8; ☯ 10am-11pm) Run by a quirky Lao-Danish couple, this place has become popular with travellers and expats seeking comfort food. The hamburgers, in particular, aren't bad.

Several **baguette vendors** (cnr Th Ratsavongseuk & Th Phagnapui) along this strip sell *khào jìi páa-tê* (baguette sandwiches) all day and *khào jìi sai khai* (breakfast baguettes filled with scrambled eggs).

Opposite the Wat Sainyaphum the **riverside snack and drink vendors** (☯ afternoons & evenings) are great for sundowners. Beerlao and ice is the most common purchase but fresh *tàm màak-hung* (green papaya salad) and a range of grilled meats are usually on hand. Look for the friendly family of **long-haired ladies** who run one of these places; one who speaks English apologised to us this time for cutting her hair from calf-length to merely waist-length. *Baw pen nyǎng*, we say, it's still pretty impressive.

Drinking & Entertainment

Savannakhet is no party town but there are now a few more Western style places to drink, if not dance; they tend to come and go quickly so ask around. When we hit the town **Dragon** (Th Ratsavonseuk; 7-11pm) was the place of choice for young Savannakhet hipsters, though the deafeningly loud karaoke might not be so appealing to Western tastes. Just down the road the **Rose Bar** (Th Ratsavongseuk; ☯ 6-11pm) has occasional live music and a more spacious feel. You're unlikely to find Roman Abramovich partying at the **Chelsea FC Club** (Th Saenna; ☯ 6-11pm). On quiet nights it closes early.

Getting There & Away

Savannakhet's **bus terminal** (☎ 212143), usually called the *khíw lot*, is near the Talat Savan Xai at the northern edge of town. Buses leave here for Vientiane (US$5.50, eight to 11 hours, 457km) every half-hour from 6am to 10am, then about every hour until 10pm. They stop at Tha Khaek (US$2.50, 2½ to four hours, 125km). A VIP bus (US$7, six to seven hours) to Vientiane leaves at 9.30pm, or you could try to pick up a seat on one of the VIP buses coming through from Pakse. For buses from Vientiane, see p114.

Nine buses to Pakse (US$3, five to six hours, 230km) originate here, the first at 7.30am and the last one at 1.30am. Otherwise jump on one of the regular buses passing through from Vientiane.

Buses leave for Lao Bao (US$3, five to seven hours, 236km) at 6.30am, 9.30am and noon, stopping at Sepon (US$3, four to six hours). *Sǎwngthǎew* leave more frequently.

There are no longer any commercial flights to or from Savannakhet.

Getting Around

Savannakhet is just big enough that you might occasionally need a jumbo – or the Savannakhet equivalent, a *sakai-làep* ('Skylab'). Apparently someone thought a jumbo looked like the famed space station that fell to earth, though we suspect that whoever drew such a conclusion was probably on drugs at the time.

CROSSING THE THAI BORDER AT SAVANNAKHET/MUKDAHAN

The new Friendship Bridge linking Savannakhet and Mukdahan in Thailand means the days of regular ferries might be numbered. As in Vientiane and Pakse, a Thai-Lao International Bus is expected to connect the towns; check at the tourism office for details. Ferries will continue at a reduced level, at least for the short term.

On the Lao side, the boat pier is near the centre of town. Ferries (US$1.30 or 50B, 30 minutes) cross the Mekong at 9.10am, 10am, 11.10am, 1.30pm, 2.30pm and 4pm from Monday to Friday; on Saturday at 9.30am, 11.10am, 12.30pm and 4.30pm; and on Sunday at 9.30am, 11.10am and 3pm. For some reason, Lao boats only carry passengers *from* Laos, returning empty. The reverse is true of Thai boats, which run about every hour from 9am to 4.30pm Monday to Friday but less frequently on weekends.

When you're arriving in Laos, English-speaking immigration officers issue 30-day visas (p315). From Mukdahan, VIP (nine hours) and public (at least 11 hours) buses run to Bangkok, at 8am, 7pm and 9.30pm; just ask a tuk-tuk for the 'Bangkok bus'.

Sakai-làep tend to loiter outside the passenger ferry pier. Trips cost from US$0.50 for shorter trips to US$1 to the bus station, for the whole vehicle. Prices double after dark.

Several guesthouses and the Lao-Paris Restaurant hire out bicycles (between US$1 and US$2 per day) and motorcycles (US$7 to US$10 per day). When we passed, most were only willing to hire out motorbikes a day at a time, the Lao-Paris being the exception.

AROUND SAVANNAKHET
That Ing Hang
ທາດອິງຮັງ

Thought to have been built in the mid-16th century, this well-proportioned, 9m-high *thâat* is the second holiest religious edifice in southern Laos after Wat Phu Champasak. Built on or near the spot where Chao Fa Ngum's forces were based during the takeover of Muang Sawa in the mid-14th century, **That Ing Hang** (admission US$0.50; ⏱ 7am-6pm) may occupy an earlier site sacred to the Si Khotabun kingdom. The Buddha is believed to have stopped here when he was sick during his wanderings back in ancient times. He rested by leaning *(ing)* on a hang tree (thus Ing Hang). A relic of the Buddha's spine is reputed to be kept inside the *thâat*.

Not including the Mon-inspired cubical base, That Ing Hang was substantially rebuilt during the reign of King Setthathirat (1548–71) and now features three terraced bases topped by a traditional Lao stupa and a gold umbrella weighing 40 *baht* (450g). A hollow chamber in the lower section contains a fairly undistinguished collection of Buddha images; by religious custom, women are not permitted to enter the chamber. The French restored That Ing Hang in 1930.

The That In Hang Festival is held on the full moon of the first lunar month.

That Ing Hang is about 11.5km northeast of Savannakhet via Rte 9, then 3km east; the turn-off is clearly signed. Any northbound bus can stop here, or you could haggle with a *sakai-làep* driver and will do well to knock him down below US$8 return. Going by hired bicycle or motorbike makes more sense.

Dong Natad
ດົງນາທາດ

Dong Natad is a sacred, semievergreen forest within a provincial protected area 15km from Savannakhet. It's home to two villages that have been coexisting with the forest for about 400 years, gathering forest products such as mushrooms (in the rainy season), fruit, oils, honey (from March to May), resins and insects. If you visit, there's a good chance you'll encounter villagers collecting red ants, cicadas or some other critter, depending on the season; all are important parts of their diet and economy.

It's possible to visit Dong Natad on your own, by bicycle, motorbike or in a tuk-tuk (US$4 charter, one way; bargain hard) from Savannakhet. However, it will be something of a 'forest-lite' experience. It's better to engage one of Savannakhet's English-speaking guides through the Eco-Guide Unit at the **Provincial Tourism Office** (☎ 214203), for a day trip (US$20 per person for two or three people, US$15 each four to seven, and US$12 each eight or more) or an overnight stay (US$45/35/30 for the same numbers), sleeping in the village.

CENTRAL LAOS

SPIN THROUGH SAVANNAKHET

Muang Champhone (Champhone District) southeast of Savannakhet city is home to several sites that might not be fascinating individually, but together make a fun motorcycle day-trip through this archetypal Lao Loum area of scattered villages and rice paddies. This trip is only possible between about November and May; there are few signs and no kilometre stones. Before you set out, read Motorcycle Diaries (p328).

After checking the odometer (if it's working), head south from Savannakhet to Ban Lak 35, where you turn left (east) on the decent sealed road towards Keng Kok. After 8km turn left (north) onto a laterite road at Ban Khoum; look for a blue and white sign saying 'The tourism place of entry'. About 3km along turn right (east) at Ban Don Dok Mai; the turn is just before a wat. The first 'sight' is the **Sui Reservoir**, which you'll skirt for 3km until you'll come to an irrigation levee.

Beyond the levee (dry season only) follow the roller-coaster road a few kilometres and turn left (north) at a T-junction in Ban Sakhon Neua, then immediately right (east). Soon you'll be in Ban Dong Mouang (Ban Tha Thouang) where you turn left (north). About 400m along here you'll come to the **Monkey Forest**, in a shaded area opposite a bunch of small white *thâat* (stupas). If you've picked up some bananas along the way, get them out and start feeding. The hundreds of 'sacred' monkeys are quite used to being fed.

After monkeying around, go back about 50m and turn left along a trail winding into the beautiful sacred forest. Before long you'll be at the Se Champhone for the most challenging part of this ride. After walking across the river to check its depth (or following the tyre trails to see where the locals go), put the bike in first and hit the gas. If you stall, you'll have to get off and push. Alternatively, you could wait for the occasional *dok dok* (mini tractor) that crosses here.

Once across, follow the road about 2km to Ban Nong Lan Chanh where you take the left fork to **Wat Jan Tak Sa Po**. The wat is famous for its library, which is said to be more than 200 years old (though recent renovations make it look about two years old). Until recently, palm-leaf texts documenting centuries of district events and other tales were kept here. These manuscripts are one of the few records of Lao life not burnt in the 19th century Siamese invasion, and some now-common Lao folk songs are said to have survived thanks to these writings. The other wat buildings are also interesting; the wooden prayer hall actually does look 200 years old, and the old monks' quarters (the one on a decided lean) has some interesting wooden 'bells' hanging underneath.

From Ban Lan Chanh continue east about 1km and turn right (south). Follow this good laterite road about 30km to the four-way junction at Ban Taleo Mai (a good place for lunch) and 4km further to Ban Don Daeng. In the centre of the village is **Nong Luang** (Turtle Lake; admission US$0.30), where dozens of soft-shelled turtles have been living as long as anyone can remember. The oldest turtle (imaginatively known as 'Big One') is about 1m long and is thought to be more than 60 years old. These sacred turtles are quite a tourist attraction and local custom is to feed them unhealthy, radioactive-looking fried snacks. A healthier alternative (as recommended by the Wildlife Conservation Society) is to feed them small dried fish; buy them in the market in Savannakhet before you leave.

To get back to Savannakhet, ride back to Ban Taleo Mai and turn left (west). This road leads about 11km to Keng Kok, from where it is 19km of sealed road back to Ban Lak 35, and on to Savannakhet.

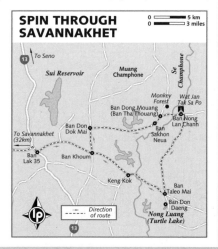

SPIN THROUGH SAVANNAKHET

0 — 5 km
0 — 3 miles

To Seno
Sui Reservoir
Muang Champhone
Se Champhone
Monkey Forest
Wat Jan Tak Sa Po
Ban Dong Mouang (Ban Tha Thouang)
Ban Nong Lan Chanh
Ban Don Dok Mai
To Savannakhet (32km)
Ban Sakhon Neua
Ban Khoum
Ban Lak 35
Keng Kok
Ban Taleo Mai
Ban Don Daeng
Nong Luang (Turtle Lake)

---- Direction of route

These community-based treks (see p70) have had plenty of positive feedback and the combination of English-speaking guide and village guide proves a great source of information about how the local people live. However, prices are relatively high compared with trekking elsewhere in Laos. Arrange trips at least a day ahead.

Heuan Hin
ເຮືອນຫີນ

On the Mekong River south of Savannakhet is this set of Cham or Khmer ruins (the name means Stone House), built between AD 553 and 700. Apart from a few walls, most of the stones of this pre-Angkorian site now lie in piles of laterite rubble. No carvings remain, the only known lintel having been carted off to Paris.

It's a long haul by public transport and you'd need to be a truly dedicated temple enthusiast to make the trip. Sǎwngthǎew (US$2, two to three hours, 78km) leave Talat Savan Xai when full, usually in the midmorning. With your own transport, head south along Rte 13 and turn west at Ban Nong Nokhian, near Km 490, from where it's a dusty 17km to the site. Guided tours are also available from Savannakhet.

DONG PHU VIENG NPA
ປ່າສະຫງວນແຫ່ງຊາດດົງພູວຽງ

One of the most fascinating treks in Laos is to Dong Phu Vieng NPA, which offers a rare chance to step into a rapidly disappearing world. The park, south of Muang Phin in the centre of Savannakhet Province, is home to a number of Katang villages, where you can stay if you behave yourself (see the boxed text below).

The trek involves a fair bit of walking through a mix of forests ranging from dense woodlands to bamboo forests and rocky areas with little cover. There's a boat trip on the third day. All food is included and eating local forest specialities is a highlight. A village guide leads trekkers through a sacred forest where you'll see Lak La'puep – clan posts placed in the jungle by village families. Animals regularly seen include the rare silver Langur leaf monkey and hornbill.

CENTRAL LAOS

SLEEPING WITH SPIRITS

The Katang villagers of Dong Phu Vieng live in a starkly different world to the Lao Loum of the Mekong River valley. They are not Buddhist, but instead believe strongly in the myriad spirits that surround them in the forest. One of the most important is the house spirit, one of which is believed to live in the home of every village family. Over the centuries a series of taboos have been developed in an effort to avoid disturbing this spirit and as a visitor it is vitally important you don't break the taboos. If the house spirit is seriously disturbed the village is obliged to call a meeting to work out how the spirit can be mollified. Usually a sacrifice must be made – ranging from a chicken all the way to a buffalo for the most serious indiscretions. As the villagers have little money, the unnecessary loss of a pig or buffalo can have a dire impact both socially and economically.

So, when you're in a Katang house:

■ never enter the owner's bedroom or touch the spirit place

■ do not sleep beside a person of the opposite sex, even if that person is your spouse: if you really can't be separated tell the Eco-Guide Unit and they can bring a tent for you

■ sleep with your head pointed toward the nearest outside wall; never point your feet at the outside wall or, spirits forbid, another person's head

■ do not bang on the walls of the house.

While clapping without first checking with the house spirit is also a no-no, the villagers decided this was no fun so they now clear it with the spirit as a matter of course before any trekking group arrives. It goes without saying that these villages are extremely sensitive to outside influence, which is why you can only visit them as part of the organised trek through the Eco-Guide Unit in Savannakhet. Guides have been trained, and the trek was established after extensive consultation with the villagers themselves.

The three-day trek uses local transport for the 180km to and from the NPA, and it's the long trip that goes some way towards explaining the high prices (US$150 each for two or three, US$110 for four to seven, and US$65 for eight to 10). Clearly getting a bigger group together makes sense, and if you're interested it pays to go straight to the **Provincial Tourism Office** (☎ 214203) and put your name on a list as soon as you arrive in Savannakhet. Better still, call ahead to see when a trip is departing.

Phu Xang Hae NPA

Named after Wild Elephant Mountain, Phu Xang Hae NPA is a long expanse of forest stretching east–west across the remote north of Savannakhet Province, and its hills are the source of several smaller rivers. The Phu Thai people who live here, like the Katang of Dong Phu Vieng NPA, observe a series of taboos (see p249).

Unfortunately, the diabolical state of the roads means getting into Phu Xang Hae is very difficult. In theory the Eco-Guide Unit (p244) in Savannakhet runs a five-day community-based trek staying in villages and in the jungle. However, when we passed no-one had done the trek for close to two years, due also to the high cost (US$300 per person for two or three people, less for more people) – it's just too expensive.

SEPON (XEPON) & THE HO CHI MINH TRAIL

ເຊໂປນ/ເສັ້ນທາງໂຮຈິມິນ

☎ 041 / pop 35,600

Like so many other towns that needed to be rebuilt following the Second Indochina War, Sepon (often spelt 'Xepon') today is fairly unremarkable. The main reason for coming here is to see parts of the Ho Chi Minh Trail and what's left of the old district capital, Sepon Kao, 5km to the east.

A trip to **Sepon Kao** (Old Sepon) is a sobering experience. On the banks of the Se Pon, Sepon Kao was bombed almost into the Stone Age during the war. All that remains is the bomb-scarred façade of the wat, inside which a new temple has been built; a large pile of bricks around a safe, which was once the bank; and broken bricks scattered everywhere. If you're on foot or bike, take the first right turn heading east from Sepon, then go another 2km on a bad road. On four wheels, take the second right, just after the 199km stone.

Ban Dong, 20km east of Sepon, was on one of the major thoroughfares of the Ho Chi Minh Trail and is the easiest place to see what little materiel is left from the war. Two American-built tanks used during Operation Lam Son 719 – a disastrous ARVN (Army of the Republic of Vietnam) assault on the Ho Chi Minh Trail in February 1971 – rust in the undergrowth a short walk from town. Despite support from US combat aircraft, the ARVN troops retreated across the border at

---

CROSSING THE VIETNAM BORDER AT DANSAVANH & LAO BAO

Crossing the border (open from 7am to 11am and from 1pm to 6pm, though you can usually cross during lunch for a fee) at Dansavanh (Laos) and Lao Bao (Vietnam) is a relative pleasure. From Savannakhet, buses (US$3, five to seven hours) leave at 6.30am, 9.30am and noon for the border. Alternatively, take a săwngthăew to Sepon (US$3, five to six hours, 190km), and another from there to the border (US$1.40, one hour, 45km). If you're passing this way it's worth breaking the journey for a night in Sepon as a base for seeing the Ho Chi Minh Trail.

It's a 500m walk between the border posts and formalities don't take long, assuming you've arranged your Vietnam visa in advance. Laos issues 30-day visas on arrival.

Once through, take a motorbike (10,000d) 2km to the Lao Bao bus terminal and transport to Dong Ha (20,000d, two hours, 80km) on Vietnam's main north–south highway and railway. Entering Laos, săwngthăew to Sepon leave fairly regularly. Simple accommodation is available on both sides of the border.

An alternative is to take the daily 10pm bus from Savannakhet to Dong Ha (US$12, about eight hours, 329km), Hué (US$11, 409km, about 12 hours) or Danang (US$14, 508km, about 14 hours). Savanbanhao Travel (see p244) also has a bus running to Dong Ha (US$12) on even dates and returning on odd dates. Note that no matter what you are told, you *will* have to change buses at the border.

HO CHI MINH TRAIL

The infamous Ho Chi Minh Trail is actually a complex network of dirt paths and gravel roads running parallel to the Laos–Vietnam border from Khammuan Province in the north to Cambodia in the south.

Although mostly associated with the 1963–74 Second Indochina War, the road network was originally used by the Viet Minh against the French in the 1950s as an infiltration route to the south. The trail's heaviest use occurred between 1966 and 1971 when more than 600,000 North Vietnamese Army (NVA) troops – along with masses of provisions and 500,000 tonnes of trucks, tanks, weapons and ordnance – passed along the route in direct violation of the 1962 Geneva accords (see p37). At any one time around 30,000 NVA troops guarded the trail, which was honeycombed with underground barracks, fuel and vehicle repair depots, hospitals and rest camps as well as ever more sophisticated anti-aircraft emplacements.

The North Vietnamese denied the existence of the trail throughout most of the war. The USA denied bombing it. In spite of 1.1 million tonnes of saturation bombing (begun in 1965 and reaching up to 900 sorties per day by 1969, including outings by B-52 behemoths), traffic along the route was never interrupted for more than a few days. Like a column of ants parted with a stick, the Vietnamese soldiers and supplies poured southward with only an estimated 15% to 20% of the cargo affected by the bombardment. One estimate says 300 bombs were dropped for every NVA casualty. The Yanks even tried bombing the trail with canned Budweiser beer (incapacitation through intoxication!), Calgonite dishwasher detergent (to make the trail too slippery for travel), and massive quantities of defoliants and herbicides.

Contrary to popular understanding, the trail was neither a single route nor a tiny footpath. Several NVA engineering battalions worked on building roads, bridges and defence installations and methods to hide the trails from the air were simple but ingenious. Bridges were built just below the water level and branches were tied together to hide what had become wide roads. As the war went on the various trails stretched deeper into Laos, and virtually all roads running north–south in the southeast of Laos were once part of the trail.

Today the most accessible points are at Ban Dong (opposite), east of Sepon, and the village of Pa-am (p296) in Attapeu Province, which sits almost right on the main thoroughfare. South of here the trail enters Cambodia, where (until March 1970 when a coup toppled Prince Sihanouk in Phnom Penh) it met up with the Sihanouk Trail, another Communist supply route running up from the Gulf of Thailand.

Seeing evidence of the trail, however, isn't easy. Except in the most remote and inaccessible areas, scrap-metal hunters have removed almost all of what was once a huge amount of war scrap. In Ban-Dong and Pa-am, a couple of tanks and a surface-to-air missile remain, protected by government order. Elsewhere you'll need to get way out into the sticks and get locals to guide you.

In eastern Savannakhet Province, Salavan, Sekong and Attapeu, joint Lao-American teams are still searching for the remains of American soldiers missing in action. Eighty percent of American servicemen still missing in Laos are thought to have gone down somewhere along the Ho Chi Minh Trail.

Lao Bao after being routed by seasoned North Vietnamese Army (NVA) troops at Ban Dong. The two tanks are all that is left of what locals say was once a graveyard of destroyed and abandoned equipment. The village headman has been instructed to prevent scrap collectors from dismantling these last two reminders of the NVA/Pathet Lao victory. To see them, head 200m south from Rte 9 on the road out of Ban Dong. One of the tanks is a 50m-walk off to the left (east). It's best to seek guidance from the local children, who will also take you a few hundred metres west to the second tank.

This north–south road was in fact one of the main branches of the **Ho Chi Minh Trail**. It is still used, and if you head another couple of kilometres south you'll come to a swing bridge built by the Vietnamese after the war ended.

Much unexploded ordinance (UXO) remains and the slow work to find and remove it continues, four decades on. During one visit here we met a team from UXO Lao that was detonating two American 1000-pound bombs found near a village. Once the villagers had been moved, the team took cover and triggered the explosion. Even at more than 800m away, the earth shook and the sound reverberated up the valley like some sort of awesome, deadly thunder. If you multiply that by a full bomb cargo in a B-52, you can imagine something of what it was like to live along the trail.

In **Muang Phin**, 155km east of Savannakhet and 34km west of Sepon, stands an imposing Vietnamese-built monument to Lao-Vietnamese cooperation during the Indochina wars. Done in the stark 'Heroes of Socialism' style, the monument depicts NVA and PL soldiers waving an AK-47 and Lao flag aloft.

Sleeping & Eating
Nang Toon Guest House (Rte 9; r US$3-5; 🗙) Located about 1.5km east of Sepon, the US$5 air-con rooms at the Nang Toon Guest House are small but clean, and the fan rooms with hot-water bathroom are the best value in town.

Vieng Xay Guesthouse (☎ 214895; Rte 9; r US$3-5; 🗙) In the centre of town, just past the market on the south side of Rte 9, has rooms with paper-thin walls with bathrooms (US$5) and without (US$3). Look for the ordnance in the front fence.

Pa Bouaphan (🕙 6am-8pm) The Lao food and breakfasts are recommended at this modest eatery at the west edge of the market.

Getting There & Away
A couple of buses leave from outside the market for Savannakhet (US$3, four to six hours, 196km) between about 7am and 10am. For Ban Dong (US$0.80) and the border at Dansavanh (US$1.40, one to two hours) take a *săwngthăew*.

Southern Laos

A contrasting combination of archetypal Mekong River life, the cooler climes of the Bolaven Plateau and three remote and little-visited eastern provinces make southern Laos a real mixed bag of tasty offerings. The whole area remains refreshingly raw, but as in the rest of Laos a series of community-based tourism projects have made getting inside Lao-style life easier than ever.

The obvious, almost unavoidable staging point is Pakse, the Mekong River–side capital of Champasak Province with an all-round good vibe. From here the Mekong flows south past the ancient Khmer religious complex at Wat Phu Champasak and Don Daeng, before spreading out in Si Phan Don, the 'four thousand islands' that straddle the Cambodian border. Among this stunningly beautiful maze of waterways are the palm-lined Don Khong, Don Det and Don Khon, where you can soak up the million-dollar sunsets from your hammock without being interrupted by endless reruns of *Friends* (for now, at least).

Going east from Pakse you climb to the cooler climes of the Bolaven Plateau, with its picturesque waterfalls and high-grade coffee. Keep going and you start getting well off the beaten track and into the little visited provinces of Salavan, Sekong and Attapeu where minority ethnic groups are still surprised to see *falang* visitors. More adventurous souls will love the Southern Swing motorbike loop or negotiating themselves a boat trip down the remote and untouched Se Kong (Kong River). So whether you're seeking an off-beat adventure or are happy just lazing in a riverside hammock, prepare to stay longer than you planned.

HIGHLIGHTS

- Get better acquainted with your hammock in the laidback Mekong islands of **Si Phan Don** (p272)

- Wake up early for a dramatic sunrise at the ancient Khmer temple complex at **Wat Phu Champasak** (p265)

- Walk and wade your way into the jungles and stay in a remote Lavae village in the **Se Pian NPA** (p271)

- Gaze in awe at 100m-high waterfalls and sip fair-trade coffee on the cool **Bolaven Plateau** (p282)

- Ride out to the wild east of **Attapeu** (p293) and back via **Nam Tok Katamtok** (p292) on the **Southern Swing** (p263)

National Protected Areas

Southern Laos has six National Protected Areas (NPAs) covering habitats as diverse as the riverine forest along the Mekong River in Phu Xieng Thong NPA to the remote mountains of Se Xap NPA. For now Phu Xieng Thong (p261) and Se Pian NPA (p271) are the easiest to get into, with village-based treks the best way to do it. Dong Hua Sao NPA at the edge of the Bolaven Plateau and the wilderness of Dong Amphan NPA can also be accessed with more time, money and organisation.

Climate

The Mekong Valley is hot most of the year but becomes hellishly so between March and May. Some relief comes from relatively

soothing river breezes, but not much. The Bolaven Plateau, on the other hand, is relatively cool all year, and from November to February it's cold after dark. The plateau also has its own mini weather system, which brings rain right into December.

Getting There & Around

There are three border crossings into Southern Laos – one each from Thailand, Cambodia and Vietnam. Once you're in, the main roads are smooth and well-serviced by buses and *săwngthăew* (passenger trucks). The exceptions are Rte 18 between Attapeu and Thang Beng in Champasak Province, and all the roads running north and east of Salavan. Cargo boats no longer work the Mekong.

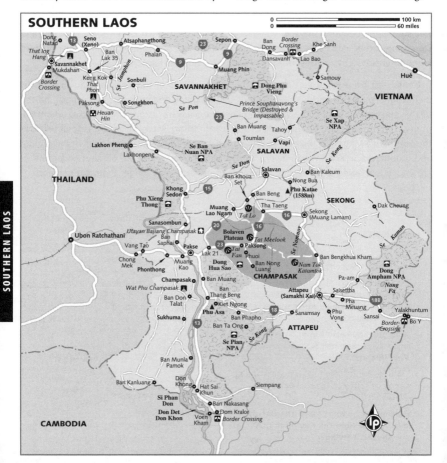

CHAMPASAK PROVINCE

Big ticket attractions including Wat Phu Champasak, the Mekong River islands of Si Phan Don and the Bolaven Plateau make Champasak one of the most visited provinces in Laos. Champasak has a long history that began with participation in the Funan and Chenla empires between the 1st and 9th centuries AD. Between the 10th and 13th centuries it became part of the Cambodian Angkor empire. Following the decline of Angkor between the 15th and late 17th centuries, it was enfolded into the Lan Xang kingdom but then broke away to become an independent Lao kingdom at the beginning of the 18th century. The short-lived Champasak kingdom had only three monarchs: Soi Sisamut (r 1713–37), who was the nephew of Suriya Vongsa, Sainyakuman (r 1737–91) and finally Fai Na (r 1791–1811).

Today Champasak Province has a population of more than 500,000 including lowland Lao (many of them Phu Thai), Khmers and a host of small Mon-Khmer groups, most of whom live in the Bolaven Plateau region.

PAKSE
ປາກເຊມ
☎ 031 / pop 66,000

Founded by the French in 1905 as an administrative outpost, Pakse sits at the confluence of the Mekong River and the Se Don (Don River) and is the capital of Champasak Province. The town has grown quickly since the Lao-Japanese Bridge across the Mekong was opened in 2002, facilitating brisk trade with Thailand. Its position on the way to Si Phan Don in the far south, the Bolaven Plateau and remote provinces to the east, and Thailand to the west means anyone choosing to travel in the south will almost certainly spend time in Pakse.

The centre of Pakse retains the sort of Mekong River–town lethargy found in Savannakhet and Tha Khaek further north. Fewer colonial-era buildings remain, though do look for the Franco-Chinese–style **Chinese Society building** on Th 10 in the centre of town.

The vast Talat Dao Heung (New Market) near the Lao-Japanese Bridge is one of the biggest in the country, famous for its selection of fresh produce and coffee from the fertile Bolaven Plateau. Short day trips from Pakse can be made to Ban Saphai and Don Kho (p260), weaving centres 15km north of town.

Information

EMERGENCY
Hospital (☎ 212018; Th 10 & Th 46)
Police (☎ 212145; Th 10)

INTERNET ACCESS & TELEPHONE
ADSL has arrived in Pakse and the main street, or nearby, has several options, including the following:
@d@m's Internet (Rte 13; per hr US$0.60; ⊙ 8am-10pm) Can download image files and burn CDs (US$1.50); international calls are about US$0.30 per minute.
Next Step Internet (Th 24; per hr US$0.60; ⊙ 8am-11pm) Burns CDs and DVDs for US$1.50 each.
SD Internet (Rte 13; per hr US$0.60; ⊙ 7am-8pm) Fast connections.

MONEY
BCEL (☎ 212770; Th 11; ⊙ 8.30am-3.30pm Mon-Fri, 8.30-10am Sat) South of Wat Luang, has best rates for cash and travellers cheques and makes cash advances on Visa and MasterCard.
Lao Development Bank (☎ 212168; Rte 13; ⊙ 8am-4pm Mon-Fri, 8am-3pm Sat & Sun) Changes cash and travellers cheques in the smaller exchange office; cash advances (Monday to Friday only) in the main building.
Lao Viet Bank (☎ 251470; Rte 13; ⊙ 9.30am-4pm Mon-Fri)

POST
Main post office (cnr Th 8 & Th 1) South of the town centre.

TOURIST INFORMATION
Provincial Tourism Office (☎ 212021; Th 11; ⊙ 8am-noon & 1.30-4pm Mon-Fri) On the Se Don (Don River) near the Lao Airlines office, the well-organised English-speaking staff here can book you onto community-based treks in Se Pian NPA and Phu Xieng Thong NPA, and into homestays on Don Kho and Don Daeng; there's no commission. They also should be armed with all the latest schedules for buses heading anywhere from Pakse.

TRAVEL AGENCIES & TOUR OPERATORS
Most hotels can arrange day trips to the Bolaven Plateau, Wat Phu Champasak and Si Phan Don. For longer and more adventurous trips, try these:
Green Discovery (☎ 252908; www.greendiscoverylaos.com; Rte 13) Operates rafting, kayaking (both US$27 per person for four or more), mountain biking and trekking trips. Well respected.

Lane Xang Travel (Xplore Asia; www.xplore-asia.com; Rte 13) Similar trips to Green Discovery, with more to Si Phan Don.

Vat Phou (www.asian-oasis.com; Th 11) Operates luxury cruises between Pakse and Don Khong.

Sights & Activities

Much more about being than seeing, Pakse's 'sights' are limited.

CHAMPASAK HISTORICAL HERITAGE MUSEUM

ພິພິດທະພັນມໍລິດົກປະຫວັດສາດຈຳປາສັກ

Near the Hotel Residence du Champa, the **Champasak Historical Heritage Museum** (Rte 13; admission US$0.50; 8.30-11.30am & 1.30-4pm) has a few artefacts and a lot of boring documents chronicling the history of the province. Once you get past the Lao and Communist hammer-and-sickle flags at the entrance you're in the best part of the museum – three very old Dong Son bronze drums and striking 7th-century sandstone lintels found at Uo Moung (Tomo Temple). The simple textile and jewellery collection from the Nyaheun, Suay and Laven groups is also interesting for its large iron ankle bracelets and ivory ear plugs since these are rarely worn nowadays.

Also on the ground floor are musical instruments, stelae in the Tham script dating from the 15th to 18th centuries, a water jar from the 11th or 12th century, a small lingam (Shiva phallus), plus a model of Wat Phu Champasak.

Once you head upstairs you'll be beginning your last five minutes in the museum. Apart a small collection of Buddha images and forlorn-looking American weaponry, it's all headshots of Party members.

WATS

There are about 20 wats in the city, of which Wat Luang and Wat Tham Fai (both founded in 1935) are the largest. A monastic school at **Wat Luang** features ornate concrete pillars, carved wooden doors and murals; the artist's whimsy departs from canonical art without losing the traditional effect. Behind the *sǐm* is a monks' school in an original wooden building. A *thâat* on the grounds contains the ashes of Khamtay Loun Sasothith, a former prime minister in the Royal Lao Government.

Wat Tham Fai, near the Champasak Palace Hotel, is undistinguished except for its spacious grounds, making it a prime site for tem-

ple festivals. It's also known as Wat Pha Baht because there is a small Buddha footprint shrine. The stupas and Pepsi billboard near Rte 13 make good photos in the afternoon.

GYM

The **Champasak Palace Hotel** (212777; www.champasak-palace-hotel.com; Rte 13; 2-10pm) gym is free for guests and a bargain US$0.70 for visitors to use the weight room. There's also massage, sauna, and Jacuzzi.

MASSAGE & SAUNA

The professional and popular massage and sauna **Clinic Keo Ou Done** (Traditional Medicine Hospice; 251895, 020-5431115; 4-9pm Mon-Fri, 10am-9pm Sat-Sun) has an air-con massage room and herbal sauna segregated by gender. A massage (highly recommended!), usually with medicated balms, costs US$2.50 per hour. Unlimited use of the herbal sauna costs US$0.80. To get there, take a jumbo east on Rte 13. About 100m before the Km 3 marker, turn right and follow the 'Massage Sauna' signs another 800m.

Sleeping
BUDGET

Sabaidy 2 Guesthouse (/fax 212992; www.sabaidy2laos.com; Th 24; dm US$1.90; r US$3.50-5.50;) If you want cheap-but-clean lodgings, good information and to be surrounded by other backpackers, this is the place for you. It's often so busy you'll need to book ahead to get a bed. Service, however, can be very relaxed and you might need to jump around waving your arms to get someone's attention. They also hire motorbikes (p260).

Phonsavanh Hotel (252912; cnr Th 12 & Rte 13; r US$3-4) Above Nazim Restaurant, which also runs the hotel, Phonsavanh has very basic fan rooms with or without cold-water bathroom.

Sedone River Guesthouse (212158; Th 11; tw US$4-6;) In a couple of old buildings right on the Se Don, this relaxed place has small twin rooms with cold-water bathrooms plus a couple of larger rooms with hot water and air-con. It's not crystal clean, but OK for the money. The shaded riverside sala (open-sided shelter) is ideal for sundowners.

Narine Thachalern Hotel (212927; Th 21; s/d US$4/8;) Rooms with fridge and TV are clean and quiet. Not all are the same, though, so ask the English-speaking man-

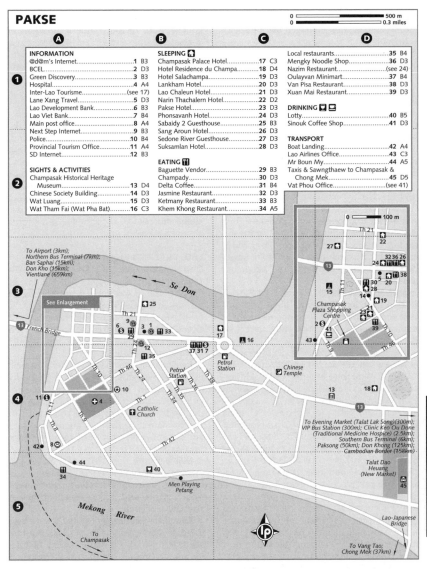

PAKSE

0 _____ 500 m
0 _____ 0.3 miles

INFORMATION		
@d@m's Internet.....................................**1** B3		
BCEL...**2** D3		
Green Discovery.....................................**3** B3		
Hospital...**4** A4		
Inter-Lao Tourisme.............................(see 17)		
Lane Xang Travel...................................**5** D3		
Lao Development Bank........................**6** B3		
Lao Viet Bank...**7** B4		
Main post office....................................**8** A4		
Next Step Internet...............................**9** B3		
Police...**10** B4		
Provincial Tourism Office.................**11** A4		
SD Internet..**12** B3		

SIGHTS & ACTIVITIES		
Champasak Historical Heritage		
Museum..**13** D4		
Chinese Society Building..................**14** D3		
Wat Luang..**15** D3		
Wat Tham Fai (Wat Pha Bat)...........**16** C3		

SLEEPING		
Champasak Palace Hotel....................**17** C3		
Hotel Residence du Champa.............**18** D4		
Hotel Salachampa.................................**19** D3		
Lankham Hotel......................................**20** D3		
Lao Chaleun Hotel...............................**21** D3		
Narin Thachalern Hotel......................**22** D2		
Pakse Hotel..**23** D3		
Phonsavanh Hotel................................**24** D3		
Sabaidy 2 Guesthouse.........................**25** B3		
Sang Aroun Hotel.................................**26** D3		
Sedone River Guesthouse..................**27** D3		
Suksamlan Hotel...................................**28** D3		

EATING		
Baguette Vendor...................................**29** B3		
Champady..**30** D3		
Delta Coffee...**31** B4		
Jasmine Restaurant..............................**32** B3		
Ketmany Restaurant.............................**33** B3		
Khem Khong Restaurant.....................**34** A5		

Local restaurants..................................**35** B4		
Mengky Noodle Shop..........................**36** D3		
Nazim Restaurant..............................(see 24)		
Oulayvan Minimart...............................**37** B4		
Van Pisa Restaurant.............................**38** D3		
Xuan Mai Restaurant............................**39** D3		

DRINKING		
Lotty..**40** B5		
Sinouk Coffee Shop.............................**41** D3		

TRANSPORT		
Boat Landing...**42** A4		
Lao Airlines Office...............................**43** C3		
Mr Boun My...**44** A5		
Taxis & Sawngthaew to Champasak &		
Chong Mek.......................................**45** D5		
Vat Phou Office..................................(see 41)		

SOUTHERN LAOS

ager to show you a couple. All up, not a bad option in the old part of town.

Lankham Hotel (☎ 213314; lanekhamhotel@yahoo .com; Rte 13; r US$5-10; 🖟) The Lankham is right in the centre of town and front-facing rooms (some of the few with windows that don't look onto a corridor) can be noisy. Rooms are small and smaller.

Lao Chaleun Hotel (☎ 251333; fax 251138; Th 10; s/d/tw US$5.40/10.80/12; 🖟) Both the rooms and service in this three-storey place are decent if uninspiring. Singles have fan and cold-water bathrooms. They also rent vehicles (p260).

Suksamlan Hotel (☎ 020-563 2077; Th 14; r US$5.50-6.50; 🖟) The central Suksamlan has 24 ageing but large and clean rooms with hot-water bathrooms. The building itself has a certain fading charm and manager Mr Bouphan is helpful.

MIDRANGE & TOP END

Pakse Hotel (☎ 212131; www.paksehotel.com; Th 5; r US$12-32; ✳) This well-run six-storey place in the centre of town is excellent value. Rooms all come with fridge and satellite TV; the cheapest have no windows, but the US$19 rooms have Mekong views. Service is the best in southern Laos and the cafeteria downstairs and rooftop restaurant-cum-bar are reasonably good.

Hotel Salachampa (☎ 212273; fax 212646; Th 14; r US$13-15; ✳) Just around the corner from the Pakse Hotel, this French-era villa has some wonderful big rooms with wooden floors (tiled downstairs), high ceilings and tasteful furnishings. Rooms in the villa (US$15) are much better value, as those in the newer building (US$13) are small and altogether less appealing.

Sang Aroun Hotel (☎ 252111; Rte 13; r US$17-20; ✳) This modern Thai-style hotel has compact but clean and well-equipped rooms if not much soul. For affordable comfort it's a good choice.

Champasak Palace Hotel (☎ 212777; www.champasak-palace-hotel.com; Rte 13; r incl breakfast US$20-150; ✳ 🖳 ✕) You can't miss the vast, wedding-cake style Champasak Palace, on Rte 13 about 1km east of the town centre. It was originally built as a palace for Chao Boun Oum na Champasak, the last prince of Champasak and the prime minister of the Kingdom of Laos between 1960 and 1962. Boun Oum started building the palace in 1968, fled to Paris in 1974 and died soon after. It was renovated, and in some places completed, by a Thai group during the 1990s, with government help; look at the architraves above the fourth floor for the tell-tale hammer and sickle stucco work. New management has taken it a step further, and the 115 comfortable rooms now offer excellent value, particularly the superior (US$40) and VIP suites (US$50), the latter of which have panoramic views. Rooms in a second building are not as good. All rooms superior and above have free broadband internet connections. The only downside is that service remains a bit raw and language can be a problem.

Hotel Residence du Champa (☎ 212120; champare@laotel.com; s/d incl breakfast US$25/30; ✳) This place in a small road off Rte 13 is a good option. In four modern buildings of concrete, marble and teak, all 45 rooms have satellite TV, minibar and IDD phone, and some have bathtubs. French and English are spoken and there's a decent restaurant.

Eating

Eating with the locals, especially at breakfast and lunch, is a fun Lao experience. The restaurant under the **Lankham Hotel** and, just across Rte 13, the **Mengky Noodle Shop** are safe and popular places for noodles and soup; Mengky is rightly famous for its duck *fŏe* breakfasts. Even better is the spread of **local restaurants** on Th 46, each one serving something slightly different; just wander along and take your pick. The restaurants are open all day.

LAO, THAI AND VIETNAMESE

Xuan Mai Restaurant (☎ 213245; Th 4; meals US$1-2.50; ✳ breakfast, lunch & dinner) On the corner opposite the Pakse Hotel, Xuan Mai serves top-notch *fŏe* (US$0.80; the chicken *fŏe* is best), *khào pûn* (white flour noodles with sweet-spicy sauce), fruit shakes and even garlic bread. Open until midnight, it's the best place for a late feed.

Ketmany Restaurant (☎ 212615; Rte 13; meals US$1.50-4; ✳ breakfast, lunch & dinner) Ketmany serves decent European food and very good Vietnamese dishes, though many are not on the English menu so you'll need to ask by name. It also has good ice cream and packed-with-processed-meat Western breakfasts (US$2).

Champady (☎ 020-513 0513; meals US$1.50-4.50; ✳ breakfast, lunch & dinner) In a French-era building, atmospheric Champady serves Thai cuisine and coffee in an attractive streetside location.

Khem Khong Restaurant (☎ 213240; Th 11; meals US$2-5; ✳ lunch & dinner) On the Mekong just south of town, this is one of several floating restaurants and has a well-earned reputation for excellent seafood. It's best in a group so you can share several dishes, especially the *pîng pąa* (grilled fish).

WESTERN & INDIAN

Delta Coffee (☎ 030-534 5895; Rte 13; meals US$1.50-5; ✳ breakfast, lunch & dinner) Delta serves a vast array of food, the best being the Italian and Thai dishes. The vegetarian lasagne and pizzas are particularly recommended, but not the gnocchi. Breakfasts are tasty and great value. Owners Alan and Siriporn serve probably the best coffee in town from their plantation near Paksong, and raise money to build schools for the children of plantation workers.

Van Pisa Restaurant (☎ 212982; Rte 13; pizzas US$3.50; ☯ breakfast, lunch & dinner) An Italian-run Italian restaurant where the pizzas are quite good and pastas are as tasty as the ingredients allow. They also serve delicious shakes and ice cream.

Travellers flock to two Indian restaurants in the centre of town. **Jasmine Restaurant** (☎ 251002; Rte 13; meals US$2-4; ☯ breakfast, lunch & dinner) is the original but now faces competition from a former partner running **Nazim Restaurant** (☎ 252912; Rte 13; meals US$1.50-3.50; ☯ breakfast, lunch & dinner). Both are cheap and the competition has drastically improved service. The food, including loads of vegetarian dishes, is invariably tasty if a little over-enthusiastic on the masala.

Just west of @d@m's Internet a **baguette vendor** (Rte 13) sells decent *khào jịi* in the morning and afternoon. Self-caterers should head to the market and **Oulayvan Minimart** (Rte 13; ☯ 7am-10pm).

Drinking & Entertainment

Sinouk Coffee Shop (☎ 212552; cnr Th 9 & Th 11; coffee US$0.60; ☯ 7am-8pm) In a renovated French shophouse this café is best-known for its coffee, sold both in the cup and by the bag (from US$2 for 250g). They also sell Beerlao and have a small menu of Western dishes.

The **Champasak Palace Hotel** (opposite) should have its top-floor bar and restaurant open by the time you arrive and it should be the classiest drinking spot in town. The rooftop bar at the **Pakse Hotel** (opposite) is also good for a sunset Beerlao or two.

For some Lao-style partying, check out **Lotty** (Th 11; ☯ 6-11pm), the current favourite nightclub among young Lao looking to drink and dance; downstairs is where the action is.

Getting There & Away

AIR
Lao Airlines flies between Pakse and Vientiane daily (US$95 one way, 70 minutes). There are also two flights per week to Luang Prabang (US$135, one hour 40 minutes), though these might not run all year.

International flights go to Phnom Penh (US$95, one way, 70 minutes) twice per week and three times per week to Siem Reap (US$85, 45 minutes), though these flights can be cancelled if there's no demand, and in the low season this is often the case. To be sure, check at the Pakse **Lao Airlines office** (☎ 212252; Th 11; ☯ 8-11.30am & 1.30-4.30pm Mon-Fri) the day before. Bangkok Airways and its subsidiary Siem Reap Airways should be flying a couple of services per week between Pakse and Bangkok (about US$100) and Pakse and Siem Reap by the time you read this.

The airport is 3km northwest of town and has a BCEL exchange office. A jumbo should cost about US$1.

BOAT
Like so many others (p325), the public boat from Pakse to Champasak and Don Khong has more-or-less stopped, unable to compete with soaring fuel prices and *săwngthăew* that do the trip in half the time for less money. At the time of writing occasional boats still ran as far as Champasak, but it was impossible to know whether it would go until it actually pulled out from the riverbank near the confluence of the Se Don and the Mekong.

If you don't have endless time to wait for one of these occasional boats and you have the money it's possible to rent a boat, though they don't really have the charm of boats packed with locals, farm animals, snakes, bags of rice and monks sitting on the roof. With some language skills you could charter a boat at the aforementioned confluence of the rivers. Alternatively, ask **Mr Boun My** (☎ 020-5631008; Th 11), who can be found nearby at the first barbecue pork stall opposite the Mekong as the road bends left. He rents boats to Champasak (US$50, one hour), to Um Tomo (US$60, 90 minutes) and Don Khong (US$140, four to five hours). These prices are for six people or less and rise with the number of passengers – for example, 25 people (the maximum) to Champasak costs US$80 for the boat.

BUS & SĂWNGTHĂEW
Pakse has several bus and *săwngthăew* terminals.

VIP Bus Station

The **VIP Bus Station** (☎ 212228; off Rte 13), also known as the Evening Market Bus Station or Km 2 Bus Station, is where most VIP buses to Vientiane (US$13, eight to 10 hours, 677km) originate, though they also usually stop in town, either at the Indian restaurants or near the bus offices beside the Se Don. It's possible to take these buses to Seno (for Savannakhet) and Tha Khaek, but the arrival times are pretty unfriendly and you have to pay the full fare. Tickets for the various VIP buses are available in guesthouses, restaurants and internet cafes all over town; just ask where you need to be when the bus is leaving.

The other service leaving here is the handy Thai-Lao International Bus; see opposite for details.

Dao Heung Market (Morning Market)

Buses and *săwngthăew* leave the *săwngthăew* farm at the edge of the **Dao Heung Market** for Champasak (US$1.30, one to two hours) and for Ban Saphai (US$0.50, about 40 minutes) regularly between about 6.30am and 3pm.

Northern Bus Terminal

At the **northern terminal** (☎ 251508), usually called *khíw lot lák jét* (Km 7 bus terminal), 7km north of town on Rte 13, you'll find a steady procession of agonisingly slow normal buses (without air-con) heading north. Every 50 minutes or so between 6.30am and 4.30pm a slow bus starts the long haul to Savannakhet (US$3, four to five hours, 277km), Tha Khaek (US$5.50, eight to nine hours), and, for those of you with plenty of time, no money and a wide masochistic streak, Vientiane (US$8.50, 16 to 18 hours). The durations of these journeys are very flexible and depend on how long the bus stops in Savannakhet – sometimes as long as two hours.

For buses from Vientiane see p113.

Southern Bus Terminal

For transport anywhere south or east, head to the **southern terminal** (*khíw lot lák pǫet* or 'Km 8 bus terminal'), south of town on Rte 13. The transport might be a bus, but it could just as easily be a *săwngthăew*. For Si Phan Don, there are several departures for Muang Khong (US$3.50 including ferry, three hours, 120km) between 10am and 3pm; while transport to Ban Nakasang for Don Det and Don Khon (US$3, three to four hours) leaves between 7.30am and 3pm. Transport going to Ban Nakasang stops at Hat Xai Khun or nearby on Rte 13, from where an 800m walk and a boat will have you at Don Khong. Some of these buses/*săwngthăew* go all the way to Voen Kham (US$4, 3½ to 4½ hours) on the Cambodian border. One *săwngthăew* runs to Kiet Ngong and Ban Phapho (US$1.50, two to three hours) leaving at 1pm.

Transport to the Bolaven Plateau leaves for Paksong (US$1.50, 90 minutes) five times between 9am and 1pm, stopping at Tat Fan if you ask. Transport to Salavan (US$2, three to four hours, 115km) leaves at 7.30am, 9.10am, 10.40am, 12.15pm and 2pm, most going via smooth Rte 20 and Tat Lo, if you ask. Buses to Sekong (US$2.50, 3½ to 4½ hours, 135km) leave at 7.30am, 9.30am and 2pm; and to Attapeu (US$3.50, 4½ to six hours, 212km) at 6.30am, 8am and 10.30am, and sometimes at 1pm. Transport for Attapeu also stops at Paksong, Tha Taeng and Sekong.

Getting Around

Using any of Pakse's local transport on a shared basis costs between US$0.25 and US$0.40; you might need to bargain a bit. A ride to either bus terminal costs about US$0.50. For charter, the standard fares to the bus stations are US$1.50 (*săam-lâaw*) or US$2 (jumbo or tuk-tuk).

Several shops and guesthouses rent bicycles, usually for US$1 per day. Motorbikes are also readily available, with the Sabaidy 2 Guesthouse (p256) having the cheapest bikes (US$8 per day, or US$7 for more than one day). The Lankham Hotel (p258) has better bikes, but their US$8 'a day' only buys you 12 hours. If you fancy tackling the Ho Chi Minh Trail, their Honda Baja 250cc trail bikes for US$20 per full day might interest. Discounts are possible for longer hire. The Lao Chaleun Hotel (p256) also hires out motos (US$10 per day), and cars and vans with driver (price depends on destination, but to Champasak return is about US$40).

AROUND PAKSE

You don't have to go far from Pakse for a fun day out.

Don Kho & Ban Saphai

ບ້ານສະພາຍ/ດອນໂຄ

About 15km north of Pakse, the Mekong island of Don Kho and the nearby village of Ban

---

CROSSING THE THAI BORDER AT VANG TAO & CHONG MEK

The crossing at Vang Tao (Laos) and Chong Mek (Thailand) is the busiest in southern Laos and is open from 5am to 6pm daily. From Pakse, săwngthăew (US$0.80, 75 minutes, 44km) and some of the most battered taxis (US$2 per person or US$10 for whole vehicle, 45 minutes) you're ever likely to see run between Talat Dao Heuang (New Market) and Vang Tao. When your transport stops, walk about 300m up to the green-roofed building, where you'll be stamped out. Immigration is also here, plus an exchange office offering criminally poor rates.

Walk through the throngs of traders and small-time smugglers loitering around the border, then another 100m or so to Thai immigration, who by the time you arrive should be in their startling new building that looks vaguely like a plate full of purple nachos minus the guacamole. They'll issue your visa in short order. Taxi drivers usually wait outside immigration and want about B700 to B900 for a whole air-con van to Ubon Ratchatani (one hour, 82km). The cheaper option is to walk to the end of the stall-lined street and find a săwngthăew (35B, one hour, 42km) to Phibun Mangsahan. It will drop you at a point where another săwngthăew will soon pick you up for the trip to Ubon (B35, one hour, 40km). For details on buses and trains between Ubon and Bangkok, see p322.

Much easier is the Thai-Lao International Bus (200B or equivalent, 2½ to 3 hours, 126km) direct between Pakse and Ubon. Buses leave Pakse at 7am, 8.30am, 2.30pm and 3.30pm, and run from Ubon's main bus station at 7.30am, 9.30am, 2.30pm and 3.30pm; check these times with the Provincial Tourism Office (p255).

Saphai are famous as silk weaving centres. Women can be seen working on large looms underneath their homes producing distinctive silk and cotton *phàa salóng*, long sarongs for men, and are happy to let you watch.

Like Don Daeng further south, there are no cars on Don Kho and despite the recent arrival of electricity it's easy to feel like you're stepping back to a more simple time. The 300 or so residents live in villages at either side of the 800m-wide island and farm rice in the centre. Believe it or not, Don Kho was briefly the capital of southern Laos following the French arrival in the 1890s, and it later served as a mooring point for boats steaming between Don Det and Savannakhet. These days, however, the only real sight is **Wat Don Kho**, which has some French-era buildings and an impressive drum tower. In the southeast corner of the grounds is a soaring tree that locals say is 500 years old, though 200 seems more realistic. These trees periodically have fires burned inside the trunks to extract a resin used to seal boats.

The villages of Don Kho are some of the best places to experience a homestay (see p48) in southern Laos. Just turn up on the island and say 'homestay' and the villagers will sort you out. A homestay will cost US$2 per bed, with a maximum two people per house. You'll eat with your host family (US$2 per meal or US$1.50 each for three people or more); in our experience the food was delicious.

If homestay doesn't sound like your thing there's a **community guesthouse** at the edge of the **sacred forest** on the far side of the island. Bed and meal rates are the same as a homestay, and villagers will help you make a small offering to the forest spirit to smooth your stay. Just say 'guesthouse' when you turn up and someone will lead you there (it's about a 700m walk). Alternatively, the guys in the new **tourist office** at the boat pier in Ban Saphai speak better English and can phone ahead for you.

A couple of villagers speak enough English to arrange the homestays, guided tours of the island (US$3 per guide, one to four people), Lao-style fishing trips (US$2.50) and even lessons in silk weaving (US$5 per day, plus materials) – we heard of one woman who spent four days 'homestaying' and learning to weave.

GETTING THERE & AWAY

Săwngthăew to Ban Saphai (US$0.60, 45 minutes) leave fairly regularly from Pakse's Dao Heung Market (Morning Market), or hire a tuk-tuk or *săam-lâaw* for about US$5 one way. From Ban Saphai to Don Kho boats cost US$1 for one to five people, or US$0.20 per person for more.

Phu Xieng Thong NPA

ປ່າສະຫງວນແຫ່ງຊາດພູຊຽງທອງ

Although the majority of the 1200 sq km **Phu Xieng Thong NPA** (www.ecotourismlaos.com) lies in

SOUTHERN LAOS

Salavan Province, its most accessible areas are about 50km upriver from Pakse. The area features scrub, mixed monsoon deciduous forest and exposed sandstone ridges and cave-like outcroppings, some of which contain pre-historic paintings. On the Thai side of the Mekong is Pha Taem National Park.

The Phu Xieng Thong NPA is home to a range of wildlife, including important concentrations of banteng, green peafowl and clouded leopard. Elephant, Douc langur, gibbon, Asiatic black bear and tiger might also pass through, but visitors will be very lucky to see any of these. If the season is right you're much more likely to see some striking wild orchids.

The best way into Phu Xieng Thong NPA is on a two- or three-day community-based trek beginning in the Mekong village of **Ban Singsamphan**. The trip involves river transport, a homestay in Ban Singsamphan and a trek over historically important **Phu Khong** (Khong Mountain). It's best to start the four to five-hour trek early, as it can get pretty warm. Parts of the trek cross exposed rock outcroppings that are home to mysterious archaeological ruins and afford amazing views. More enjoyable is the two-hour walk through beautiful forest, with the possibility of a lunch-stop with a hermit nun. The nun lives in a cave and has forsaken speaking and many foods for several years, in the name of world peace. Bizarre, yes, but her dedication is quite inspirational. The two-day trip finishes after the trek but we recommend the three-day version, which heads downriver to Don Kho (p260) for a homestay there.

Limited transport means it is possible but difficult to reach Ban Singsamphan independently – if you're interested get the low-down from the Provincial Tourism Office in Pakse (p255).

CHAMPASAK
จำปาสัก
☎ 031

It's hard to imagine Champasak as a seat of royalty, but until only 30 years ago it was just that. These days the town is serenely quiet, the fountain circle in the middle of the main street alluding to a grandeur long gone. The remaining French colonial-era buildings, including one that once belonged to Chao Boun Oum na Champasak and another to his father Chao Ratsadanai, share space with traditional

Lao wooden houses. The few vehicles that venture down the narrow main street share it with buffaloes and cows which seem relaxed even by Lao standards – it's easy to spend a couple of days here.

The Angkor-period ruins of Wat Phu Champasak (p265) lie 8km southwest of town and are the main attraction; Champasak has the only accommodation in the immediate vicinity of Wat Phu. The town also acts as a jumping off point for Don Daeng (see p268).

Just about everything in Champasak is spread along the one riverside street, either side of the fountain circle.

Information

The **Lao Development Bank** (⏱ 8.30am-3.30pm Mon-Fri) changes cash and travellers cheques – US$2 per cheque if you want dollars, no charge at all for kip.

The new **Champasak District Visitor Information Centre** (☎ 020-220 6215; ⏱ 8am-4.30pm Mon-Fri) should be your first point of call in Champasak. It has well-presented displays with information about the town, Wat Phu, Um Tomo and Don Daeng; and will arrange boats to Don Daeng and a bed in the guesthouse there. Local guides, some of whom speak English, lead day walks around Wat Phu and the ancient city, and to Um Tomo. Guides charge US$5/10 for a half/full day, irrespective of numbers.

Internet Nam Oly (per hr US$1.80; ⏱ 9am-7pm), about 150m south of the Vong Paseud Guest House, is the only place to get online.

Sights

Champasak has a couple of mildly interesting temples. On a dirt road parallel to the main north–south street, is the late 19th-century **Wat Nyutthitham**, more commonly known as Wat Thong. An old *sǐm* features an arched and colonnaded veranda, and has a washed pastel stucco relief on the front. This was the wat used by Champasak's royal family, and the *thâat kádyuk* here contain the ashes of King Nyutthitham (died 1885), Chao Ratsadanai (died 1946) and Chao Boun Oum (died 1975), among other royalty.

About 8km south of town on the Mekong stands the oldest active temple in Champasak, **Wat Phuthawanaram**, more popularly known as Wat Muang Kang. Like the *sǐm* at Wat Thong, the intriguing *hǎw tại* (Tripitaka library) at Wat Muang Kang combines elements of French-colonial and

THE SOUTHERN SWING

The Southern Swing is a motorbike or bicycle trip starting in Pakse and taking in the Bolaven Plateau and other southern provinces, see Map p254. By motorbike it can take anywhere from three days to as long as you like, depending on how fast you go and how often you stop. The route we've laid out here takes six days but this is only a guide – everything about it is as flexible as you like. On a bicycle doing it in reverse is a good idea. Distances are fairly accurate, if not exact (we didn't trust our bike's odometer). Most roads are sealed, and those that are not are in relatively good condition, meaning 110cc bikes are fine. Read Motorcycle Diaries (p328) before you go.

Day 1 – Pakse to Tat Lo

Head south out of Pakse and up toward the plateau, keeping straight at the bus station. After about 20km turn left (north) at the junction (labelled Lak 21) of routes 16 and 20 and go another 17km or so to **Utayan Bajiang Champasak** (Phasoume Resort, p285), which is good for lunch. Continue on Rte 20 towards **Tat Lo** (p286) and look for the **Katu village** with a textile market (on the right).

Day 2 – Tat Lo to Sekong

It's easy to spend two nights in Tat Lo, but if not then head about 28km up the road for a look around **Salavan** (p288). If that doesn't appeal, go just 4km to Ban Beng and turn right on the road to Tha Taeng. This 30km, bumpy road climbs up onto the **Bolaven Plateau** through **Katu** and **Alak villages**. Look carefully and you'll see coffins stacked beneath buildings, and perhaps traditional graves in small clearings in the forest. The dead are always buried in the forest, and usually with a significant possession; in one case we saw a child's bicycle atop a grave, in another a farmer's hoe. There are a couple of guesthouses in Tha Taeng or take 46km of sealed road to **Sekong** (p290).

Day 3 – Sekong to Attapeu

The smooth 77km road from Sekong to **Attapeu** (p293) goes past a couple of smaller waterfalls, though there are plenty of those later on. Instead, punch on through and spend the afternoon in or around pleasant Attapeu. If you're in a hurry, you could skip Attapeu and head straight up the mountain road to **Paksong** (see Day 5).

Day 4 – Around Attapeu

You could spend days exploring this province; check out the options on p296.

Day 5 – Attapeu to Paksong

We absolutely loved this ride, but would have loved it even more if we'd left Attapeu earlier. Do that (before 10am), and head 47km north on Rte 16 to Ban Bengkhua Kham. Top up your tank and check your odometer here before heading up the beautiful, shaded road through pristine jungle. You won't see many people, but the few Laven we saw included cheroot-sucking women in *sĭn*, and a couple of guys with unfeasibly long rifles slung over their shoulders with dead birds hanging from the end. After about 16km look for a waterfall in the distance to the north, and at 18km for the awesome but unsigned **Nam Tok Katamtok** (p292). Continue uphill and at about 27km you're on the **Bolaven Plateau**. Several villages dot this road towards Paksong, the last 15km of which is sealed but badly potholed. There is cheap accommodation in Paksong (p284) or smarter lodgings at Tat Fan (p284). The distance between Ban Bengkhua Kham and Paksong is 71km.

Day 6 – Paksong & around

Check out some of the **waterfalls** (p285), take a trek from **Tat Fan** and drink some decent coffee (p284). And that's it. Hang around here another day or head back to Pakse.

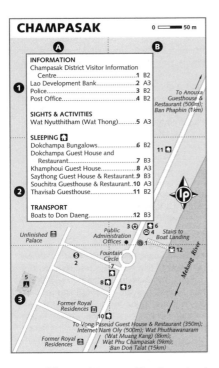

CHAMPASAK

INFORMATION
Champasak District Visitor Information
Centre...1 B2
Lao Development Bank.......................2 A3
Police..3 B2
Post Office..4 B2

SIGHTS & ACTIVITIES
Wat Nyutthitham (Wat Thong).........5 A3

SLEEPING
Dokchampa Bungalows.......................6 B2
Dokchampa Guest House and
Restaurant.......................................7 A3
Khamphoui Guest House....................8 A3
Saythong Guest House & Restaurant..9 B3
Souchitra Guesthouse & Restaurant..10 A3
Thavisab Guesthouse.......................11 B2

TRANSPORT
Boats to Don Daeng.........................12 B3

Lao Buddhist architecture. The three-tiered roofs of the *sĭm* and *hăw tại* have coloured mosaics at the corners, and a small box with coloured crystal windows at the centre of the top roof ridge – reminiscent of Burmese architecture.

Ostensibly these crystal-sided boxes hold Buddha images, but local legend ascribes a more magical purpose to the one atop the *hăw tại*. Supposedly at a certain moment in the annual lunar calendar (most say it's during the Wat Phu Festival), in the middle of the night, a mystic light beam comes from across the river, bounces through the *kâew* (crystal) and alights atop Sri Lingaparvata, the holy mountain above Wat Phu Champasak.

You can reach Wat Muang Kang by boat from Champasak, or come by bike on the narrow dirt road along the riverbank. You could combine a boat trip to Wat Muang Kang with a visit to Uo Moung (p270).

Sleeping & Eating

Finding a room in Champasak is easy enough except during the Wat Phu Champasak Fes-

tival (Magha Puja; usually in February, see p268), when you can sleep on the ground at Wat Phu Champasak. If you do this, ask at one of the food tents for a safe spot and take particular care of your valuables.

The restaurants in the following guesthouses are open for breakfast, lunch and dinner.

Saythong Guest House & Restaurant (☎ 030-534 6603; r US$2) English-speaking Mr Sing's restaurant (meals US$1 to US$2) is in one of the best locations in town, and while his rooms with cold-water bathrooms are pretty basic, they're good value.

Khamphoui Guest House (☎ 252700; r US$2-3) Just south of the circle, the simple rooms with hot-water bathrooms (in a concrete building) and overhead fans (US$3) are recommended, and the two particularly good bungalows (US$2) with cold-water bathrooms aren't bad either. Bike rental is also available. Good choice.

Vong Paseud Guest House (☎ 920038, 020-271 2402; r US$3-7) About 600m south of the fountain circle, the Vong Paseud is popular with backpackers because of the English- and French-speaking owners, social riverside restaurant and free tuk-tuk from the ferry. The original rooms feature bathrooms with dubious plumbing and paper-thin walls. Newer air-con rooms are more solid. The restaurant (meals US$1 to US$2) serves up better-than- average travellers' fare.

Souchitra Guesthouse (☎ 920059; r US$3-15; 🖳) These clean and relatively stylish double and twin rooms (some with fridge) are good value if you opt for a fan (US$5); the same room with air-con is overpriced at US$15. Simple rooms with cold-water bathrooms are US$3. The spacious common veranda, riverside hammocks and restaurant (meals US$1 to US$2.50) are all good places to hang out. Motorbikes can be hired for US$5/10 for a half/full day.

Anouxa Guesthouse (☎ 213272; d US$4-10, f US$15; 🖳) This welcoming place has several clean rooms with balconies overlooking the river. They are the best in town, though the location 1km north of the fountain circle is not. Fan rooms are US$6 and bamboo bungalows with cold-water bathrooms US$4. The attached riverside restaurant (meals US$1 to US$2) serves a mean fish soup (US$1.20).

Other options include the **Thavisab Guesthouse** (☎ 020-573 4517; r US$5-10; 🖳) where rates might be negotiable but there's no atmosphere to speak of; and the ultra-basic **Dok-champa Guest House and Restaurant** (r US$1.50-3). The Dokchampa has newer bungalows north of the circle but they're still not fantastic.

Getting There & Away

Buses and *săwngthăew* from Pakse leave between 6.30am and about 3pm; see p260.

Ferries (US$0.20 per person, US$0.50 for motorbikes) from Ban Muang on the eastern side of the Mekong to Ban Phaphin (1.8km north of Champasak) on the western side run regularly during daylight hours, and 24 hours during the Wat Phu Champasak Festival. Travel from Ban Phaphin to Champasak by any vehicle is US$0.20 per person; US$1 charter.

You can also charter a ferry – actually two canoes lashed together with a few planks to create a rustic catamaran – from Ban Muang straight across to the Champasak boat landing for US$0.20 per person or US$1.50 for the whole thing. Jump on anything going between Ban Lak 30 and the ferry landing.

Leaving Champasak, *săwngthăew* and buses depart for Pakse (US$1.30) until about 3.30pm, with early morning the busiest. Going south, get to Ban Lak 30 and hail anything going past.

Getting Around

Bicycles (US$1 to US$2 per day) and motorbikes (US$5/10 per half/full day) can be hired from several guesthouses.

WAT PHU CHAMPASAK

ວັດພູຈຳປາສັກ

The ancient Khmer religious complex of **Wat Phu** (admission US$3, children 8 & under free; ☉ 8am-4.30pm) is one of the highlights of any trip to Laos. Stretching 1400m up to the lower slopes of the Phu Pasak range (also known more colloquially as Phu Khuai or Mt Penis), Wat Phu is small compared with the monumental Angkor-era sites near Siem Reap in Cambodia. But the tumbledown pavilions, ornate Shiva-lingam sanctuary, enigmatic crocodile stone and tall trees that shroud much of the site in soothing shade give Wat Phu an almost mystical atmosphere. These, and a site layout that is unique in Khmer architecture, led to Unesco declaring the Wat Phu complex a World Heritage Site in 2001.

Sanskrit inscriptions and Chinese sources confirm the site has been worshipped since the mid 5th century. The temple complex was designed as a worldly imitation of heaven and fitted into a larger plan that evolved to include a network of roads, cities, settlement and other temples. What you see today is the product of centuries of building, rebuilding, alteration and addition, with the most recent structures dating from the late Angkorian period.

At its height the temple and nearby city formed the most important economic and political centre in the region. But despite its historic importance, the 84ha site remains in considerable danger from the elements. Detailed studies reveal that water erosion is pressuring the site and without a systematic

SOUTHERN LAOS

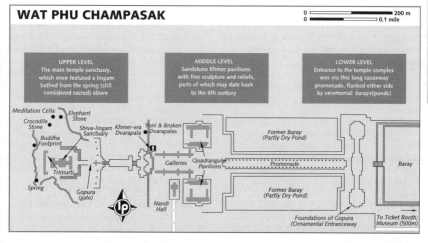

WAT PHU CHAMPASAK

0 ——— 200 m
0 ——— 0.1 mile

UPPER LEVEL
The main temple sanctuary, which once featured a lingam bathed from the spring (still considered sacred) above

MIDDLE LEVEL
Sandstone Khmer pavilions with fine sculpture and reliefs, parts of which may date back to the 6th century

LOWER LEVEL
Entrance to the temple complex was via this long causeway promenade, flanked either side by ceremonial *barays*(ponds)

Meditation Cella
Crocodile Stone
Elephant Stone
Shiva-lingam Sanctuary
Khmer-era Dvarapala
Yoni & Broken Dvarapalas
Buddha Footprint
Trimurti
Spring
Gopura (gate)
Galleries
Quadrangular Pavilions
Nandi Hall
Promenade
Former Baray (Partly Dry Pond)
Former Baray (Partly Dry Pond)
Baray
Foundations of Gopura (Ornamental Entranceway)
To Ticket Booth; Museum (500m)

water management plan the buildings will eventually collapse. Italian and Japanese-funded projects have helped stabilise the southern of two ancient canals built to channel water away from the central structures. However, the equally important northern canal has collapsed completely resulting in a slow but steady destruction of the northern side of the site. To see it, compare the relatively intact terraced steps and pavilions on the south of the site with those on the north. With about US$1 million needed to repair the northern canal and terraces, Wat Phu's future is by no means secure.

But it's not all doom and gloom. Years of work by the Italian Archaeological Mission and the inimitable Dr Patrizia Zolese, the leading expert on Wat Phu who has been working at the site since 1990, have resulted in the first detailed map on the site and surrounding 400 sq km, revealing much about the way the ancients lived. During the last two years the local and *falang* archaeologists have restored the ceremonial causeway, replacing slabs and re-erecting stone markers that had been scattered across the site. Restoration of the Nandi Hall is underway and is expected to be finished in 2009.

Don't miss the **museum** (admission with Wat Phu ticket; ⌚ 8am-4.30pm) beside the ticket office. Extensive cataloguing work has recently been completed on the dozens of lintels, *naga*s (mythical water serpents), Buddhas and other stone work from Wat Phu and its associated sites. Descriptions are in English.

The Archaeological Site

Wat Phu is situated at the junction of the Mekong plain and Phu Phasak, a mountain that was sacred to local peoples centuries before the construction of any of the ruins now visible. The original Austro-Asiatic tribes living in this area undoubtedly paid respect to animist spirits associated with the mountain and its rock shelter spring.

The archaeological site itself is divided into six terraces on three main levels joined by a long, stepped promenade flanked by statues of lions and *naga*s.

LOWER LEVEL

A modern sala built by Chao Boun Oum in the 1960s stood at the western side of the great *baray* (ceremonial pond; *nǎwng sá* in Lao) until it was dismantled recently,

revealing the sandstone base of the ancient main entrance. From here begins a causeway-style ceremonial promenade, sided by two *baray*. Parts of both the northern and southern *baray* still fill with water, lotus flowers and the odd buffalo during the wet season and the site looks better since the stone markers lining the promenade have been re-erected.

MIDDLE LEVEL

The middle section features two exquisitely carved, **quadrangular pavilions** built of sandstone and laterite. Believed to date from the mid 10th or early 11th century, the style resembles Koh Ker in Cambodia. Some people (but not the Unesco experts) suggest these pavilions were used for gender-segregated worship and they are sometimes called 'lady pavilion' and 'man pavilion'.

Wat Phu was converted into a Buddhist site in later centuries but much of the original Hindu sculpture remains in the lintels, which feature various forms of Vishnu and Shiva. Over the western pediment of the north pavilion is a relief of Shiva and Parvati sitting on Nandi, Shiva's bull mount. The building consists of four galleries and a central open courtyard, though entry is forbidden for safety reasons.

Just behind the southern pavilion stands a smaller building known as the **Nandi Hall** (dedicated to Shiva's mount) and two collapsed galleries flanking a set of laterite steps leading to the next level. From the Nandi Hall an ancient royal road once lead south for about 1.3km to Ho Nang Sida (see p268), and eventually to Angkor Wat in Cambodia. Six ruined brick shrines – only their bases remain – separate the lower two levels from the final and holiest level. Roots and mosses hold the bricks together in some places, and drive them apart in others.

An impressive **dvarapala** (sentinel figure) stands ramrod straight with sword held at the ready near what was once a *gopura* (ornate entranceway). If you step down off the walkway and onto the grassy area just north of here you'll come to the remains of a **yoni pedestal**, the cosmic vagina-womb symbol associated with Shaivism. Very near the yoni lie two unusually large, headless and armless **dvarapala statues** half-buried in the grass. These are the largest dvarapala found anywhere in the former Angkorian kingdom.

CHAMPASAK IN ANTIQUITY

Under the palm trees and rice paddies 4km south of Champasak town is the remains of a city that was, about 1500 years ago, the capital of the Mon-Khmer Chenla kingdom. The site is known today as Muang Kao (Old City), but scholars believe it was called Shrestapura.

Aerial photographs show the remains of a rectangular city measuring 2.3km by 1.8km, surrounded by double earthen walls on three sides and protected on the east by the Mekong River. Other traces of the old city include small *baray* (a Khmer word meaning 'pond', usually used for ritual purposes), the foundations for circular brick monuments, evidence of an advanced system of irrigation, various Hindu statuary and stone carvings (including a lintel in the style of 7th-century Sambor Prei Kuk), stone implements and ceramics. The sum of all this is an extremely rare example of an ancient urban settlement in Southeast Asia, one whose design reveals how important religious belief was in the workings of everyday life.

The origin of the city remained a mystery until Southeast Asia's oldest Sanskrit inscription was discovered here. The 5th-century stele stated the city was founded by King Devanika and was called Kuruksetra and also mentions the auspicious Sri Lingaparvata nearby, a clear reference to the mountain near Wat Phu Champasak. 'Honoured since antiquity', the mountain was believed to be the residence or the manifestation of the Hindu god Shiva, and even today local people honour the mountain as the place of Phi Intha (the soul or protecting spirit of the mountain).

By the end of the 5th century the city was thriving. It continued as a major regional centre until at least the 7th century, as showed by two Nandi pedestal (Shiva's bull mount) sculptures discovered in 1994-95 bearing inscriptions by King Citrasena-Mahendravarman, the 'conqueror' who later shifted the kingdom's capital to Sambor Prei Kuk in northeast Cambodia. Archaeological material suggests the city was inhabited until the 16th century.

Ongoing research by Dr Zolese (p265) and her team has revealed that a second city was built near Wat Phu after the 9th century. She believes the Nang Sida temple (p268) was at the centre of this city, which was probably Lingapura, a place mentioned in many ancient inscriptions but which has not been categorically identified by modern scholars.

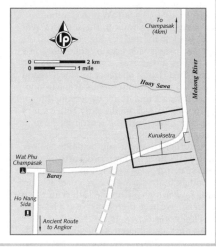

SOUTHERN LAOS

A steep *naga* stairway leads onwards to the sanctuary and probably dates from the 11th century. It is lined with *dàwk jạmpạa* (plumeria or frangipani), the Lao national tree.

UPPER LEVEL

On the uppermost level is the sanctuary itself, which once enclosed a Shiva lingam that was bathed – via a system of stone pipes – by waters from the sacred spring above and behind the complex. A lintel inside the southern entrance depicts the story of Krishnavatara in which Krishna kills his uncle Kamsa. The sanctuary now contains a set of unsophisticated-looking Buddha images on an altar. The brick rear section, which might have been built in the 9th century, is a *cella* (cell), where the holy linga was kept.

Sculpted into a large boulder behind the main sanctuary is a Khmer-style **Trimurti**, the Hindu holy trinity of Shiva, Vishnu and Brahma. Further back, beyond some terracing, is the cave from which the holy spring flowed into the sanctuary.

East of the sanctuary and a newer wat building a winding path leads north to the so-called **crocodile stone**, a boulder with a deep, highly stylised carving of a croc that is believed to date from the Angkor period. Crocodiles were semi-god figures in Khmer culture, but despite much speculation that the sculpture was used for human sacrifices its function, if there was one, remains unknown. Further along the same path is the **elephant stone**, a huge boulder bearing the likeness of an elephant thought to date from the 16th century. Nearby you can see remains of a stone **meditation cella**.

When you've seen everything here, just sitting and soaking up the wide-angle view of the *baray*, the plains and the Mekong is fantastic, especially in the morning before the hordes arrive.

Other Sites Associated with Wat Phu

South of Wat Phu are three smaller Angkor-era sites in very poor condition that will mainly interest die-hard fans of Khmer architecture. Each of the three stands beside the ancient road to Angkor Wat in Cambodia.

An easy 1.3km walk to the south of Wat Phu – stick to the trail heading south from the terraced promenade because there are some landmines in the area – stands **Ho Nang Sida** ('Lady Sida Hall', a reference to a local legend unrelated to the monument's original function). Its exact function is uncertain, though it probably dates from the early 10th century and might have been the central shrine for a second ancient city.

A further kilometre south stands another rubble pile, **Hong Tha Tao** (Lord Turtle Room). This structure, or what's left of it, resembles hospitals built during the reign of Khmer King Jayavarman VII in the 13th century, so it might have been there to serve as a hsopital for ill pilgrims.

Another few kilometres on, close to the village of Ban That, stand three Khmer *prasat* (square-based brick stupas) reminiscent of similar tripartite monuments in Thailand's Lopburi. No doubt symbolic of the Hindu Trimurti of Shiva, Brahma and Vishnu, the towers are believed to date from the 11th century and were likely never completed; they are in poor condition. A large, dried-up *baray* can be seen nearby. Ban That can be reached by jumbo from Champasak or Ban Thong Khop.

Festivals

The highlight of the year in Champasak is the three-day Bun Wat Phu Champasak (Wat Phu Champasak Festival), held as part of Magha Puja (Makha Busa) during the full moon of the third lunar month – usually in February.

The central ceremonies performed are Buddhist, culminating on the full-moon day with an early-morning file of monks receiving alms food from the faithful, followed that evening by a candle-lit *wíen thíen* (circumambulation) of the lower shrines.

Throughout the three days of the festival Lao visitors climb around the hillside, stopping to pray and leave offerings of flowers and incense. The festival is more commercial than it once was and for much of the time has an atmosphere somewhere between a kids carnival and music festival. Events include Thai boxing matches, cockfights, comedy shows, and plenty of music and dancing. Food is available from vendors who set up along the road from Ban Thong Khop, and after dark several areas are cordoned off for open-air nightclubs featuring bands from as far away as Vientiane. After dark the beer and *lào-láo* (rice whisky) flow freely and the atmosphere can become rather rowdy.

Getting There & Away

Wat Phu Champasak is 46km from Pakse, 12km from Ban Phaphin and 10km from Champasak. A shared jumbo from Champasak to Ban Thong Khop, the village opposite Wat Phu, should cost about US$0.50 per person. More likely you'll have to haggle with a *sǎamlâaw* or tuk-tuk driver who will do the return trip for about US$6 to US$8. Cycling is also popular, but there's not much shade so it pays to get going early.

DON DAENG

ດອນແດງ

Stretched out like an old croc sunning itself in the middle of the Mekong, Don Daeng is a little like an island that time forgot. It's classic middle Mekong, with eight villages scattered around its edge and rice fields in the middle. The small and mostly shaded track that runs around the edge of the 8km-long island is mercifully free of cars – bicycles, slow-moving motorbikes and the odd *dok dok* (mini tractor) are all the transport that's required.

The remains of a square-based brick **prasat** in the centre of the island and another, hiding under the *sǐm* at **Wat Ban Boung Kham,** suggest the island has been inhabited since Khmer times, at least. But the attraction of Don Daeng is more about just soaking up village life. Walking or cycling around you'll find people refreshingly welcoming.

While life on Don Daeng is much as it has been for decades, the introduction of tourism will threaten that somewhat. The village elders told us specifically that they don't want Don Daeng to go the way of Don Det (p276). That means they don't want *falang* openly smoking spliffs or getting overly amorous in public, and women are asked to wear sarongs when they bath, not bikinis; ditto for sunbathing. As you are a guest in their village, please respect these requests.

The village of **Hua Don Daeng**, at the northern tip of the island, is where the first tourist accommodation has been built. The simple **community guesthouse** (dm US$2), with two rooms and mattresses on the floor, makes the perfect base from which to visit Wat Phu Champasak and Uo Moung. There is a bathroom with bucket shower, but we recommend bathing in the Mekong. Delicious meals (US$2 per meal, US$1.50 for three people or more) are prepared by the villagers, who also rent out bikes. Village homestays (p48) are possible.

A more upmarket **lodge** (☎ 020-559 8719; r incl breakfast US$40; ❄), on the riverbank facing Wat Phu and complete with 24 attractive rooms and a pool, is set to open soon, when Don Daeng is connected to the electricity grid.

To get to Don Daeng take a small boat from Ban Muang or Champasak for US$2 between December and May, or US$3 from June to November (when the trip takes more

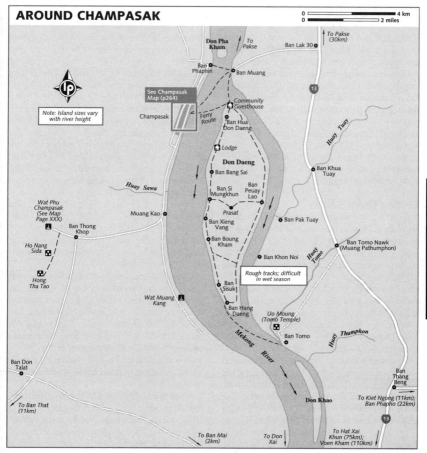

AROUND CHAMPASAK

0 — 4 km
0 — 2 miles

Note: Island sizes vary with river height

See Champasak Map (p264)

Don Pha Kham

To Pakse

Ban Lak 30

To Pakse (30km)

Ban Phaphin

Ban Muang

Champasak

Ferry Route

Community Guesthouse

Ban Hua Don Daeng

Huay Tuay

Lodge

Don Daeng

Ban Bang Sai

Ban Khua Tuay

Huay Sawa

Ban Si Mungkhun

Ban Peuay Lao

Wat Phu Champasak (See Map Page XXX)

Muang Kao

Prasat

Ban Xieng Vang

Ban Pak Tuay

Ban Thong Khop

Ban Boung Kham

Huay Tomo

Ban Tomo Nawk (Muang Pathumphon)

Ho Nang Sida

Ban Khon Noi

Hong Tha Tao

Rough tracks; difficult in wet season

Ban Sisuk

Wat Muang Kang

Ban Hang Daeng

Uo Moung (Tomo Temple)

Ban Tomo

Huay Thumphon

Mekong River

Ban Don Talat

Ban Thang Beng

To Ban That (11km)

Don Khao

To Kiet Ngong (11km); Ban Phapho (22km)

To Ban Mai (2km)

To Don Xai

To Hat Xai Khun (75km); Voen Kham (110km)

SOUTHERN LAOS

fuel). The **Champasak District Visitor Information Office** (p262) in Champasak can arrange boats and will let the villagers know you're coming, as will the **Provincial Tourism Office** in Pakse (p255).

UO MOUNG (TOMO TEMPLE)

ອຸໂມງ (ວັດໂຕະໂມະ)

The Khmer temple ruin of **Uo Moung** (Tomo Temple; admission US$1; 7.30am-4.30pm) is thought to have been built late in the 9th century during the reign of the Khmer King Yasovarman I. It's about 45km south of Pakse off Rte 13 in a wonderfully shaded forest beside a small tributary of the Mekong. The exact function of the temple is unknown, though its orientation towards the holy mountain Phu Pasak suggests its location was somehow related to Wat Phu.

The ruins include an entranceway bordered by distance markers (often mistaken for lingas) and two crumbling *gopura* (ornate entranceways). The more intact of the *gopura* contains an unusual lingam-style stone post on which two faces have been carved. It's unusual because a common *mukhalinga* has four faces (*mukha*), while most ordinary linga have no face at all. Several sandstone lintels are displayed on rocks beneath towering dipterocarp trees, but the best examples of lintels from this site are in the Champasak Historical Heritage Museum in Pakse (p256). The white building at the heart of the site houses a bronze Sukhothai-style Buddha.

Getting There & Away

The easiest way to get to Uo Muong is by boat from Don Daeng, Ban Muang (the village on the far side of the Mekong from Champasak) or Champasak. You can charter a boat to Ban Tomo (the riverbank village about 400m south of the ruins) for about US$12 return, including waiting time of an hour or so while you locate and tour the ruins. Prices fall as the boat distance gets shorter, so riding a bicycle to Ban Sisouk at the south end of Don Daeng and taking a boat from there is cheapest (US$4 return).

From Ban Tomo, climb the riverbank and walk north through the village, following the road right, then left. The temple is in a forest; if in doubt, ask the kids along the way. The ruins can also be reached by vehicle from Pakse by turning west just before Km 42.

By boat, you could combine a trip to Uo Muong with a stop at Wat Muang Kang on the west bank of the Mekong. Another option is to rent a bike on Don Daeng, take it by boat first to Uo Moung, then Wat Muang Kang, and ride the riverside path back to Champasak.

KIET NGONG & BAN PHAPHO

ບ້ານຜາໂຄງ/ກຸດຍໍ້ງ

At the edge of the Se Pian NPA, the mainly Lao Loum villagers of Kiet Ngong have had a centuries-long relationship with elephants. The elephants have traditionally worked moving logs or doing heavy work in the rice fields. Typically each elephant has a different owner and in many cases the relationship between owner and pachyderm has existed for the majority of both lives. But as elephants are expensive to keep and machines now do much of their traditional work, the village has turned to tourism to help pay their way.

Kiet Ngong is at the edge of a wetland 11km from Rte 13 and is also home to Kingfisher Eco-Lodge (see opposite), one of Laos's first real eco-lodges. The wetland is used by an unusually large herd of buffalo and more than 90 species of bird have been sighted.

Almost everyone who comes to Kiet Ngong takes the elephant ride to the summit of a hill called **Phu Asa**, named for a group of 19th-century nationalists who fought against the Siamese. The flat-topped hill is topped by an expansive archaeological site. Unmortared slate-brick columns, topped by larger slabs, stand about 2m high and enclose a rectangular space about 180m long and 50m wide. At the centre of the site is a crumbling and overgrown temple. At its far end a trail leads down to a Buddha footprint. The site has a Stone Henge feel to it but, contrary to what the locals will tell you, the columns are probably not 1000 years old.

From the top you can see across the wetlands and vast swathes of forest, though the 90-minute elephant trek (US$10 per elephant) follows a steep laterite road rather than a forest path. Talk of making a new and infinitely more attractive forest trail may have come to something by the time you arrive. Either way, you could hire a guide and walk up and back through the forest (US$4 per four people or less).

Guides can be found at the new **Visitor Information Centre** (030-534 6547) at the entrance to the village, built as part of the Asian Development Bank's pro-poor tourism initiative, designed to bring tourist dollars to some of

SOUTHERN LAOS

the poorest communities in the country. The centre arranges elephant rides and local accommodation (see below), and has information about the local area and Se Pian NPA. If telephoning for information ask a Lao speaker to call for you.

About 15km east of Kiet Ngong along a road devastated by logging trucks is the Suay village of **Ban Phapho** (22km east of Rte 13), a traditional breeding centre for working elephants. However, elephant breeding appears to be a dying art because the mahouts of Kiet Ngong and Ban Phapho won't let their female elephants mate for fear they will wind up with broken hips (not uncommon, apparently). The owners just can't risk the loss of income. Clearly this isn't a sustainable policy, but no-one seemed to have any alternative plan when we asked.

Ban Phapho itself is old and quite attractive. Mr Bounhome, who runs the only guesthouse (see below), arranges elephant rides (US$10) or can take you to watch the elephants working (US$7, in season). At either village it's worth arriving early or calling ahead as it takes a couple of hours to fetch and prepare the elephants.

Sleeping & Eating

Kiet Ngong might seem an unlikely place for one of Laos's first real eco-lodges, but that is exactly what opened there in 2006. Run by a Lao-Italian family, **Kingfisher Eco-Lodge** (☎ 030-534 5016; www.kingfisherecolodge.com; r US$16-48) is set on 7ha at the edge of a wetland, about 700m east of Kiet Ngong. It's a beautiful spot and sitting on the balcony at dawn, watching a herd of buffalo splash their way across the wetland while mahouts ride their elephants towards work is memorable.

Activities include various elephant rides, bird watching (November to January is best), mountain biking, trekking by foot and even a day-long course to learn how to become a mahout (US$50 for two people). It's also the best place to arrange the Ta Ong trek into Se Pian NPA (right) because they have the most-knowledgeable English-speaking guide. There are four classy bungalows (US$43/48 low/high season), and four eco-rooms (that's 'eco' for economy; US$13/16 low/high season), which are nice enough with spotless share bathrooms, but have paper-thin walls. Lights and hot water are solar powered. The highlight is the restaurant and bar, which could easily be in an East African safari lodge.

On the far side of the village, a 15-minute walk through rice fields, are five basic and rundown **community-run bungalows** (US$4). The location is fantastic, but the bungalows are not. Instead, get the villagers to set up your mattress and mosquito net on the sala overlooking the wetland. Homestays for US$2 per person are also possible. Arrange either at the Visitor Information Centre (opposite) – for bungalows say '*heuan pak*', for homestay say 'homestay'.

In Ban Phapho, the **Boun Home Guest House** (☎ 030-534 6293; per bed US$1.50) has small, ultra-simple rooms in an authentic wooden house. The bathroom is shared and there's no hot water, but Mr Bounhome and his family are welcoming and speak some English and French. Order meals of *làap* (US$2) and *khào nĭaw* in advance.

Getting There & Away

Kiet Ngong and Ban Phapho are off diabolical Rte 18A that runs east from Ban Thang Beng, 48km south of Pakse on Rte 13, to Attapeu. The turn-off for Kiet Ngong is about 8.5km east of Rte 13 and the village is 1.8km further south. For Ban Phapho, continue along Rte 18 and soon after the Kiet Ngong turn-off take the right fork; it's about 15km along this road. These roads are easily travelled on 110cc motorbikes and should be passable, if difficult, most of the year.

Cheaper are *săwngthăew* (US$2, 1½ to 2½ hours) that leave Kiet Ngong at about 8am. From Ban Phapho *săwngthăew* leave at 8am and 9am (sometimes only one runs). If you miss the 8am from Kiet Ngong, you should be able to jump on one of these when they pass on Rte 18. These same *săwngthăew* return from Pakse's southern bus terminal between about noon and 2pm; Kiet Ngong is often misunderstood so ask instead for 'Phu Asa'.

Alternatively, board anything going south on Rte 13, get off at Ban Thang Beng and wait for transport bumping its way east.

SE PIAN NPA

ປ່າສະຫງວນແຫ່ງຊາດເຊປຽນ

Se Pian NPA is one of the most important protected areas in Laos. Stretching between Rte 18 in the north, Rte 13 to the west and the Cambodian border in the south, the 2400 sq km is fed by three major rivers, the Se Pian, Se Khampho and Se Kong. It boasts globally

SOUTHERN LAOS

significant populations of tiger, banteng, Asiatic black bear, yellow-cheeked crested gibbon and gaur, among others. It's also home to many birds, including the rare sarus crane and vulture, and hornbill species.

The reason Se Pian's wildlife population is so significant (unlike most other NPAs) is that barely anyone lives here, so the wildlife hasn't been hunted to the verge of extinction. The most southern permanent settlement is the ethnic Lavae (commonly known as Brou) village of **Ta Ong**, and it's in this extremely poor village that you'll stay if you do the two-day Ta Ong trek. This is the hardest of the treks we've done in Laos, but it's the only way to get into this way-off-the-beaten-track part of Se Pian. Much of the five-hour first day involves barely visible trails and wading through streams.

The villagers' belief system is a mix of animism and Buddhism and, if our experience is anything to go by, they know how to have fun – especially the guy playing the *kaen*, a bamboo instrument that looks like a long pan-flute but sounds more like a piano accordion.

The second day starts with a fantastic dawn walk through the forest. If you're lucky you might hear the haunting call of rare yellow-cheeked crested gibbons. After breakfast you can choose an easy one-hour walk and boat trip, or a steamy three-hour bush bash via a spectacular natural viewpoint.

You can book the trek (dry season only) through either the Provincial Tourism Office in Pakse (p255) or Kingfisher Eco-lodge in Kiet Ngong (p271). The latter trek costs a little more but includes an excellent English-speaking guide. There's no electricity in Ta Ong so bring a torch (flashlight).

SI PHAN DON (FOUR THOUSAND ISLANDS)
ສີພັນດອນ

There must be some rule in Laos that says the further south you go the more relaxed it becomes, because just when you thought your blood pressure couldn't drop any more, you arrive in Si Phan Don… The name literally means 'Four Thousand Islands', and the few you are likely to visit on this scenic 50km-long stretch of the Mekong are so chilled you're liable to turn into a hammock-bound icicle.

During the rainy season this section of the Mekong fills out to a breadth of 14km, the river's widest reach along its 4350km journey from the Tibetan Plateau to the South China Sea. During the dry months between monsoons the river recedes and leaves behind hundreds (or thousands if you count every sand bar) of islands and islets. The largest of the permanent islands are inhabited year round and offer fascinating glimpses of tranquil river-oriented village life – 'more detached from time to time than from the riverbank' as one source described it. Communities tend to be self-sufficient, growing most of their own rice, sugar cane, coconut and vegetables, catching fish and weaving textiles as needed.

Island life is changing, however, and electricity and tourism are the big drivers. Don Khong attracts travellers looking for better lodgings while Don Det has become one of Southeast Asia's backpacker magnets, with all that entails; Don Khon falls somewhere in between. Power pylons are slowly being erected and Don Khong is on the grid, though Don Det and Don Khon will have to wait until at least 2008. In the meantime most homes are linked to one generator or another and at night you'll see extended families sitting glued to the new-found joy of Thai soap opera.

The villages of Si Phan Don are often named for their position at the upriver or downriver ends of their respective islands. The upriver end is called *hŭa* (head), the downriver end is called *hăang* (tail). Hence Ban Hua Khong is at the northern end of Don Khong, while Ban Hang Khong is at the southern end.

The French left behind a defunct short railway (the only railway ever actually completed in Laos), a couple of river piers, and a few colonial buildings. Other attractions include some impressive rapids and the Khon Phapheng (p282) waterfall, where the Mekong suddenly drops in elevation at the Cambodian border. The increasingly rare Irrawaddy dolphin (p279) also likes to hang out in the Mekong south of the falls.

Don Khong (Khong Island)
ດອນໂຂງ

☎ 031 / pop 13,000

Named for the surrounding river (using the Thai pronunciation *khæng* rather than the Lao *khăwng*), this large island measures 18km long by 8km at its widest point. Most of the islanders live in and around two villages, Muang Khong on the eastern shore and Muang Saen on the west; an 8km road links the two.

Even in Laos, where 'sleepy' seems an almost universal adjective where provincial

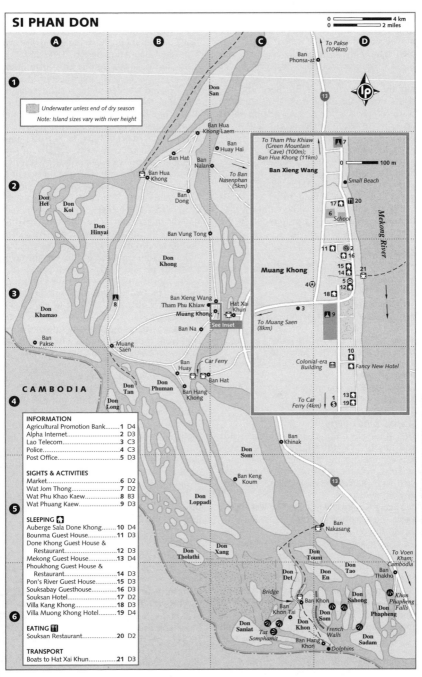

SI PHAN DON

0 — 4 km
0 — 2 miles

Underwater unless end of dry season
Note: Island sizes vary with river height

To Pakse (104km)

Ban Phonsa-at

Ban Hua Khong Laem

Don San

Ban Huay Hai

Ban Hat
Ban Nalan

Ban Hua Khong

Ban Dong

To Ban Nasenphan (5km)

Don Het
Don Koi

Don Hinyai

Ban Vung Tong

Don Khong

Don Khamao

Ban Xieng Wang
Tham Phu Khiaw
Muang Khong
Hat Xai Khun
See Inset

Don Pakse

Muang Saen

Ban Na

CAMBODIA

Don Tan
Don Long
Don Phuman

Ban Huay
Car Ferry
Ban Hat
Ban Hang Khong

Inset — Muang Khong:

To Tham Phu Khiaw (Green Mountain Cave) (100m); Ban Hua Khong (11km)

Ban Xieng Wang

0 — 100 m

Small Beach

School

Mekong River

Muang Khong

Colonial-era Building

Fancy New Hotel

To Muang Saen (8km)

To Car Ferry (4km)

Ban Khinak

Don Som

Ban Keng Koum

Don Loppadi

Don Tholathi

Don Xang

Don Toum

Ban Nakasang

To Voen Kham; Cambodia

Don Det
Don En
Don Tao
Ban Thakho

Bridge
Ban Khon
Don Sahong
Khon Phapheng
Don Falls
Don Phapheng

Don Saniat
Tat Somphamit
French Walls
Don Sadam

Ban Khon Tai
Don Khon
Don Som
Ban Hang Khon
Dolphins

INFORMATION
Agricultural Promotion Bank........1 D4
Alpha Internet.............................2 D3
Lao Telecom................................3 C3
Police..4 C3
Post Office...................................5 D3

SIGHTS & ACTIVITIES
Market..6 D2
Wat Jom Thong...........................7 D2
Wat Phu Khao Kaew....................8 B3
Wat Phuang Kaew.......................9 D3

SLEEPING
Auberge Sala Done Khong........10 D4
Bounma Guest House................11 D3
Done Khong Guest House &
    Restaurant............................12 D3
Mekong Guest House...............13 D4
Phoukhong Guest House &
    Restaurant............................14 D3
Pon's River Guest House...........15 D3
Souksabay Guesthouse.............16 D3
Souksan Hotel...........................17 D3
Villa Kang Khong......................18 D3
Villa Muong Khong Hotel..........19 D4

EATING
Souksan Restaurant..................20 D2

TRANSPORT
Boats to Hat Xai Khun..............21 D3

SOUTHERN LAOS

towns are concerned, **Muang Khong** is the very definition of the sleepy district capital. Life moves slowly here, like a boat being paddled against the flow on the Mekong, and you'll seldom be disturbed by a vehicle. It's no party town – keep going south for that – but the torpid pace of life here and the sights around the island make it an attractive place to spend a day or two, getting about on a bicycle or motorbike or just chilling by the river.

As his surname suggests, the postman who went on to become president of Laos, Khamtay Siphandone, was born in Si Phan Don in 1924 – in Ban Hua Khong at the north end of Don Khong, to be exact. His family are quite influential here though tales that he is seeing out his retirement on the island are apparently untrue.

INFORMATION

The police are a block back from the river in Muang Khong. If you get sick, head for Pakse or Thailand.

Agricultural Promotion Bank (9.30am-4pm Mon-Fri) South of town, this bank offers poor if not terrible rates for US dollars and Thai baht cash and travellers cheques, for which there is also a US$1 charge per cheque.

Alpha Internet (214117; per hr US$6; 8am-9pm) Also burns CDs and offers international phone calls at US$1 per minute.

Lao Telecom On the road to Muang Saen.

Post office Just south of the bridge.

SIGHTS & ACTIVITIES

Don Khong is quite scenic; with rice fields and low hills in the centre and vegetable gardens around the perimeter, punctuated by small villages, most of which have their own wats. Bicycle or motorbike is the best way to explore it.

Muang Khong is dominated by **Wat Phuang Kaew** and its towering modern 'naga protected' Buddha image facing east. The locals believe the abbot used supernatural powers gained in meditation to defeat government efforts to oust him after the Revolution. Elsewhere in Muang Khong, the **market** is fascinating between 4.30am and 6.30am, when people come from throughout the islands to buy and sell. Many come by boat and getting yourself down to the **small beach** at dawn to watch the boats unload their fish, fowl and other fare is a fantastic way to start the day. Take your camera and a tripod.

At Ban Xieng Wang, a neighbourhood at the northern end of Muang Khong, is **Wat Jom Thong** the oldest temple on the island. Dating from the Chao Anou period (1805–28), the main *sim* features a unique cruciform floor plan in crumbling brick and stucco with a tile roof. Carved wooden window shutters are a highlight, and an old wooden standing Buddha in one-handed *abhaya mudra* (offering protection) is notable. The sandy wat grounds are shaded by coconut and betel palms and mango trees.

A kilometre or so north of Muang Khong, in some hills more or less behind the mayor's office, a trail leads to **Tham Phu Khiaw** (Green Mountain Cave). The cave – actually more of an overhanging ledge – contains some old Buddha images and is the object of local pilgrimages during Lao New Year in April. To find it, head north from Muang Khong for 1.5km and take a track to the left, through a banana plantation. It's only a 15-minute walk (mostly uphill) to the cave entrance, marked by two tree trunks, but the track isn't always obvious – it's best to get a local to guide you.

Muang Saen, on the opposite side of the island from Muang Khong, is a bustling little town with boats servicing the islands to the west of Don Khong that have no road access whatsoever. **Wat Phu Khao Kaew**, on a low hill north of Muang Saen (about 5km from the junction of the north–south and east–west roads), was built on the site of some Khmer ruins. It is believed to be home to a *naga*, though the entrance to its lair is covered. Look for a stand of frangipani trees on the eastern side of the hill to locate the path to the temple, or hire a motorcycle taxi in Muang Saen for around US$2 return.

Two smaller villages at the southern tip of the island worth visiting for old wats are **Ban Huay** and **Ban Hang Khong**.

TOURS

The luxurious **Vat Phou** (www.asian-oasis.com), a 34m steel-hulled barge-cum-hotel has 12 wooden staterooms with single berths and western bathrooms. A three-day, two-night trip between Pakse and Don Khong takes in Wat Phu Champasak, Uo Moung and Khon Phapheng Falls. Fares vary, but are roughly US$414 per person from May to October (when there is only one trip per week), and US$538 at other times (three per week). For bookings, go to the website, or to the office in Pakse (p255).

FESTIVALS & EVENTS

A boat racing festival (Bun Suang Heua or Bun Nam) is held on Don Khong in early December around National Day – usually the first or second weekend. Four or five days of carnival-like activity culminate in races opposite Muang Khong, much closer to the shore than in larger towns.

SLEEPING

Muang Khong has the best range of accommodation anywhere in the islands and standards are significantly higher than those on Don Det or Don Khon. They are all on, or just back from, the riverbank along a 700m-stretch. Most rent bicycles for US$1 per day and have attached restaurants (see Eating, right).

Souksan Hotel (☎ 212071; r US$4-35; 😡 🖵) About 250m north of the bridge, Souksan has spotlessly clean rooms in a range of buildings jammed onto a block about 30m back from the river. The wooden fan-conditioned bungalows are good value at US$4 or US$5 each. The US$30 to US$35 rooms which include breakfast and air-con are grossly overpriced, if you go without these extras, the rate drops to just US$6! Unfortunately there's no real communal area.

Souksabay Guesthouse (☎ 214122; r US$5-10; 😡) Just back from the main road, the Souksabay's six rooms are clean and decent enough, if a little dark. But the welcoming owner and garden setting make up for that.

Villa Kang Khong (☎ 213539; r US$5-10; 😡) If being laid back was a palpable thing, you'd be able to feel it here. The traditional teak house is a favourite for its easy, convivial atmosphere, large and clean rooms and shaded communal balcony (that guests actually use) where you can enjoy breakfast. Fan rooms are US$5 to US$7 and most rooms are different, so ask to see a few. The owner speaks a little French.

Done Khong Guest House & Restaurant (☎ 214010; r US$6-12; 😡) In a prime position just south of the bridge, the upstairs fan-rooms open onto a balcony and are good value at US$6; but the downstairs rooms are a bit pricey.

Pon's River Guest House (☎ 214037, 020-2270037; r US$6-20; 😡) At this guesthouse just north of the bridge, English-speaking Mr Pon is full of useful information and can sell you transport to almost anywhere you like. His 18 clean rooms are fair value, particularly the US$6 fan rooms. The US$20 rooms have satellite TV. Good option.

Auberge Sala Done Khong (☎ /fax 212077; www .salalao.com; s/d incl breakfast US$23/28; 😡) About 250m south of the bridge and part of the Auberges Sala Lao chain, these two French-era teak mansions are atmospheric, but the rooms could be better; ask to see several. Prices drop US$5 from May to September.

Villa Muong Khong Hotel (☎ 213051; www.xbtravel -vlmkhotel.laopdr.com; r incl breakfast US$30/35; 😡 🖵) About 450m south of the bridge, this place is spread through four buildings all squeezed onto one riverfront site. The 40 rooms can differ much more significantly than the prices suggest, so it pays to look at a few – Block A is best. This hotel popular with tour groups, and French and English are spoken.

Other options include the **Mekong Guest House** (☎ /fax 213668; r US$4-15; 😡), which has simple fan-rooms and pricier air-con rooms; the **Bounma Guest House** (r US$3), about 50m down a lane north of Pon's, which is fair value if you can find someone to rent you a room; and the **Phoukhong Guesthouse & Restaurant** (☎ 213673; r US$3), just next to Pon's, which has small, clean rooms with cold-water bathrooms.

What promises to be the fanciest place in town was nearing completion when we passed. Just south of the Auberge Sala Done Khong, the location is great, the rooms are big and there was no shortage of style.

EATING

Apart from the odd place selling *fŏe* and Lao snacks, all the eating options are restaurants attached to the aforementioned accommodation. In them you can try Don Khong's famous *lào-láo* (rice whisky), which is often cited as the smoothest in the country.

Phoukhong Restaurant (meals US$1-3; 🕒 breakfast, lunch & dinner) This restaurant next to Pon's has a virtually identical menu of cheap and tasty local dishes, with an emphasis on fresh river fish. The riverside setting is popular.

Done Khong Guest House & Restaurant (meals US$1.50-3; 🕒 breakfast, lunch & dinner) In an appealing position by the river, this place serves tasty Lao dishes such as *làap* (US$1.50), the mysterious 'soup with chicken gallingly root' (US$1.50), and various rice dishes.

Pon's (meals US$1.50-3.50; 🕒 breakfast, lunch & dinner) Pon's fresh river fish are worth a shot;

the steamed fish in banana leaf is particularly good. A large menu that includes reasonable Lao, Thai and backpacker food, an attractive riverfront setting (and the nearby guesthouses) make this a travellers' favourite.

Souksan Restaurant (meals US$2-5; ⊙ 7am-10pm) In a building overhanging the river, Souksan serves a range of Chinese, Lao, Thai and comfort food including (allegedly) a Sunday roast lunch (US$5).

Villa Muong Khong Hotel (meals US$2-6; ⊙ breakfast, lunch & dinner) This airy restaurant has an intimate ambience and the Lao and Western dishes are among the best on the island. Worth the walk.

Auberge Sala Don Khong (meals US$2.50-7; ⊙ lunch & dinner) The Lao and European fare here is enjoyable and the setting romantic by Don Khong standards; the speciality is *mók pạa* (fish steamed with herbs in banana leaves, US$3.50) and it's worth trying. Non-guests should give an hour's notice.

GETTING THERE & AWAY
Boat
The slow boat to Pakse is dead. RIP. There was some talk that a semi-regular boat might start running during the tourist high season, but don't count on it. If it starts, Mr Pon will know the details.

There are regular boats between Hat Xai Khun and Don Khong; it's US$3 per boat for one to three people, or US$1.50 per person for more. Bargaining is futile. The boatman will take you as near as possible to your guesthouse of choice. The vehicle ferry between Ban Hat and Ban Na charges US$0.10 per pedestrian, US$0.50 per motorcycle and US$2.50 per car/van/pick-up.

Seven-seat boats (with roofs) can be hired to Don Det and Don Khon (US$15, 1½ hours), though getting to Don Khon in the dry season will require a smaller boat. Mr Pon also runs a daily service to Don Det and Don Khon (US$4 per person), leaving at 8.30am.

Bus, Săwngthăew & Minibus
Săwngthăew and buses head to Pakse (US$3.50 or US$4, 2½ to 3½ hours, 128km) at about 6am, 7am and 8am. After that, head over to Rte 13 and wait for anything going north.

To Voen Kham and the Cambodian border, get across to Rte 13 and wait for buses coming south from Pakse; they usually pass between 8.30am and 9am and cost US$2. Alternatively,

take a tuk-tuk all the way from Hat Xai Khun for about US$10 per vehicle.

Finally, Pon's River Guest House and the Souksan Hotel have air-con minibuses that run daily to Pakse for US$7, linking if you choose with a VIP bus to Vientiane (US$20). They can also be chartered to Pakse (US$60), the Thai border at Chong Mek (US$80) or Voen Kham.

GETTING AROUND
Bicycles (US$1 per day) and motorbikes (US$10 per day) can be hired from guesthouses and elsewhere along the main street. Alternatively, haggle with a jumbo driver.

Don Det & Don Khon
ດອນເດດ/ດອນຄອນ
Life on Don Det and Don Khon feels so laid back that you could imagine the islands just drifting downriver into Cambodia with barely anyone rolling out of their hammock in the process. Vang Vieng, the town most often compared with these two islands, feels like the Glastonbury Festival by comparison.

But in the few years since we first came here Don Det, in particular, has become a lot more rock'n'roll. From a couple of ultra-basic guesthouses and no electricity Ban Hua Det, at the north end of the island, has emerged as a sort of backpacker tractor beam. This market is serviced by generator-driven music and TV, pool tables and restaurant-bars where travellers make *anything* 'happy' – 'happy' mash potatoes, 'Happy' Lao coffee – for an extra US$0.50. We didn't notice any *Friends* but you get the feeling it's only a matter of time.

The islanders are mainly happy to have the income tourism brings, but they are aware enough of the potential changes to cite Vang Vieng as an example of what they *don't* want to become. Having a spliff is part of travelling and the locals we spoke with seemed to have accepted the arrival of marijuana in Ban Hua Det, but they'd prefer it was an incidental part of your visit rather than your sole reason for coming. They are not, however, that pleased about the arrival of harder drugs, worrying about the influence on their kids. Wherever you are it's polite to ask before you light up.

If this isn't your scene don't scratch the islands off your itinerary yet. Respite is only a short walk away and it's on Don Khon, or at the guesthouses along the southern bank of

Don Det, where things are much more serene. This is more what the islands were like when people were first drawn to them, with a sort of timeless beauty best appreciated by riding a bicycle around the few sights, swinging in a hammock, reading a book and chatting with locals and travellers alike.

The islands were an important link for supply lines between Saigon and Laos during the French colonial era. In order to bypass the rapids and waterfalls in the Mekong River, the French built a narrow-gauge railway across the two islands, linked by an attractive arched bridge and terminating in concrete piers at either end. Small engines pulled cargo across the islands but the French dream of making the Mekong a highway to China never really

materialised. The bridge and piers remain but no engine has run since WWII, and most of the track has long since been carted off. A press report in early 2007 said the Lao government was planning to rebuild the historic railway, though it's hard to understand why – we won't hold our breath.

Don Khon, the larger of the two islands, is famous throughout Laos for the cultivation of coconut, bamboo and kapok. In the main village, **Ban Khon**, there are several crumbling French buildings that are about 100 years old. **Wat Khon Tai**, in Ban Khon Tai, towards the southwestern end of Ban Khon, is a Lao temple built on the former site of an ancient Khmer temple, the laterite remains of which are scattered around the site.

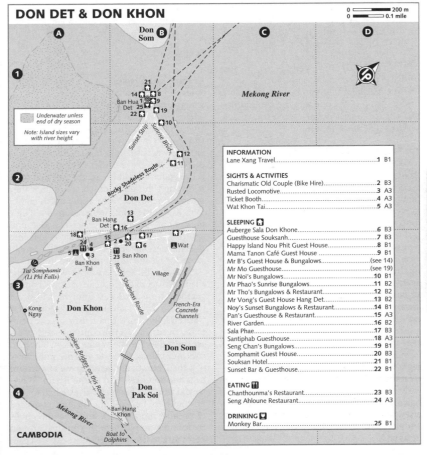

DON DET & DON KHON

0 —— 200 m
0 —— 0.1 mile

SOUTHERN LAOS

INFORMATION		
Lane Xang Travel	1	B1

SIGHTS & ACTIVITIES		
Charismatic Old Couple (Bike Hire)	2	B3
Rusted Locomotive	3	A3
Ticket Booth	4	A3
Wat Khon Tai	5	A3

SLEEPING		
Auberge Sala Don Khone	6	B3
Guesthouse Souksanh	7	B3
Happy Island Nou Phit Guest House	8	B1
Mama Tanon Café Guest House	9	B1
Mr B's Guest House & Bungalows	(see 14)	
Mr Mo Guesthouse	(see 19)	
Mr Noi's Bungalows	10	B1
Mr Phao's Sunrise Bungalows	11	B2
Mr Tho's Bungalows & Restaurant	12	B2
Mr Vong's Guest House Hang Det	13	B2
Noy's Sunset Bungalows & Restaurant	14	B1
Pan's Guesthouse & Restaurant	15	A3
River Garden	16	B2
Sala Phae	17	B3
Santiphab Guesthouse	18	A3
Seng Chan's Bungalows	19	B1
Somphamit Guest House	20	B3
Souksan Hotel	21	B1
Sunset Bar & Guesthouse	22	B1

EATING		
Chanthounma's Restaurant	23	B3
Seng Ahloune Restaurant	24	A3

DRINKING		
Monkey Bar	25	B1

INFORMATION

A couple of places offer slow internet for high prices. Otherwise, there is no bank, no medical services and not even a post office.

Lane Xang Travel (www.xplore-asia.com) has an office-cum-bar-cum-internet café in Ban Hua Det. They offer various boating options, including kayaking, rafting and sunset pleasure cruises, and can arrange all manner of transport, including a minibus across the Cambodian border and even a raft to get you to the border.

SIGHTS & ACTIVITIES

There are a few things to see while you're relaxing on the islands, all of which are best accessed on a bicycle hired for between US$0.80 and US$1 per day. The best bikes (including some bigger versions) are rented by a **charismatic old couple** on Don Khon; as he puffs on a reefer-sized rollie he'll adjust the seat to fit, check the tires and send you on your way. A booth at the south end of the bridge will charge you US$0.90 per day to cross the bridge. The ticket is also good for Tat Somphamit. This might seem steep for crossing a bridge, but it is the one way the community can ensure tourist dollars reach the village services that most need it.

Tat Somphamit (Li Phi Falls)

ຕາດສົມພະມິດ

About 1.5km downriver from Ban Khon is a raging set of rapids known locally as Tat Somphamit but referred to by just about everyone else as Li Phi Falls. Li Phi means 'trap spirit' and locals believe the falls act as just that – a trap for bad spirits (of deceased people and animals) as they wash down the river. You'll never see locals swimming here – mixing with the dead is clearly tempting fate a little too much – and it's both culturally insensitive and dangerous to do so. Water churns through the falls at a frenetic pace, especially during the wet season, and we are aware of two travellers who have drowned here in recent years.

Much less risky but thoroughly captivating is watching local fishermen edging out to clear the enormous bamboo traps. During the early rains, a well-positioned trap can catch half a tonne of fish a day. Some traps here and elsewhere in the area have an intake almost 10m long, funnelling fish into a huge basket at its end.

The falls can be reached via the main path heading southwest out of Ban Khon, or on a smaller, shaded and more attractive path that passes through the wat and avoids the trucks full of Thai tourists and their consequent dust. There are plenty of small eat-drink shops at the falls.

Railway Hike

On Don Khon you can make an interesting 5km trek across the island by following the old rail bed. Rusting locomotives sit near either end of the line; the one about 75m from the south end of the bridge sits by what was once the rail service yard. As you head south you pass stretches of primary forest, rice fields, small villages and singing birds, eventually coming to the French loading pier. Across the river to the right is Cambodia. The rail bed is quite a rocky road and tough on a bike. An alternative path runs nearer the island's western edge. The return trip, with breaks, should take about three hours by foot.

Eastern Loop Hike

A less onerous walk or cycle takes you to the waterways at the eastern edge of Don Khon where the French built a series of concrete channels used to direct logs. The logs, usually from forests in Sainyabuli Province west of Vientiane, were usually lashed together into rafts of three. To prevent them going offcourse, a Lao 'pilot' would board the raft and steer it through the maze of islands. When they reached the critical area at the north end of Don Khon, the pilots were required to guide the raft onto a reinforced concrete wedge, thus splitting the binds and sending the logs into the channels beyond. The poor 'pilot' would jump for his life moments before impact.

You can still see the walls if you go to the shaded village at the east end of Don Khon. To get there, head northwest from the bridge and turn south about 1km along, passing through a wat and following the path through rice fields to the riverbank. As you continue south you'll see the walls opposite a small village. The path continues along the river and becomes more of a road, eventually petering out at a stream near the southern end of the island. When we did this on a bike recently, we had to turn around here because the 'bridge' consisted of nothing more than a single bamboo pole. By foot it's no problem. If you turn around here you can take another, more exposed path

SOUTHERN LAOS

across the middle of the island to get back to Ban Hua Khon.

As you come downhill towards the bamboo pole bridge you'll see a sign to **Don Pak Soi**. This island is just across the channel from Don Khon and is being developed for tourism, though when we visited it didn't have much to offer beyond some mighty big fish traps.

Dolphins

Rare Irrawaddy dolphins (see below) can sometimes be seen off the southern tip of Don Khon, mainly from December until May. Boats chartered (US$5 per boat, maximum three people) from the old French pier at the south end of Don Khon run out to a small island that looks over a deep-water conservation zone. Viewing dolphins is best in the early morning or late afternoon.

Don't expect Flipper-style tricks from these dolphins. If they are there at all you'll see a brief flash as they surface to breathe, then they're gone.

SLEEPING & EATING

Seemingly every farmer on Don Det has jumped aboard the bungalow bandwagon and there are now dozens of guesthouses around the edge of the island (see Not As Same, Same As They Look, p280). The greatest concentration is in Ban Hua Det at the northern tip of Don Det, which has become the place to be if you want to socialise into the night. From here a quiet footpath known as Sunset Strip leads along the northwestern edge of the island to places which are relatively quiet and, not surprisingly, have good sunset views. The rest of the accommodation is spread along the pleasant eastern shore, known as Sunrise Boulevard. If you'd prefer to be further from the crowds, head for the quieter places on the southern shore of the island.

Note that things are changing especially fast on Don Det, so if the place you're looking at isn't listed here, that doesn't necessarily mean it's no good; it might be newer and better.

DOLPHINS ENDANGERED

The Irrawaddy dolphin (Orcaella brevirostris, called *pqa khaa* in Laos) is one of the Mekong River's most fascinating creatures, and one its most endangered. From the thousands that populated the Mekong and its tributaries in Cambodia and southern Laos as recently as the 1970s, it's now estimated there are less than 100 left. The surviving few live primarily along a 190km stretch of the Mekong between the border and the Cambodian town of Kratie.

The dark blue to grey cetaceans grow to 2.75m long and are recognisable by their bulging foreheads and small dorsal fins. They are unusually adaptable and can live in fresh or salt water, though they are seldom seen in the sea. The only other known populations are thought to be equally, if not more, at risk of extinction.

Among the Lao and Khmer, Irrawaddy dolphins are traditionally considered reincarnated humans and there are many stories of dolphins having saved the lives of fishermen or villagers who have fallen into the river or been attacked by crocodiles. These cultural beliefs mean neither the Lao nor the Khmer intentionally capture dolphins for food or sport.

In an attempt to crush these beliefs and to extract oil for their war machinery, the Khmer Rouge reportedly shot thousands of the dolphins in Tonle Sap, a large lake in northern Cambodia, during their 1970s reign of terror. Since then fishermen haven't actively targeted Irrawaddy dolphins, but general gill netting, grenade and dynamite fishing in Cambodia has inevitably taken its toll on the dolphins. Education has reduced the amount of explosive fishing, but unintentional gill netting remains a constant threat – dolphins need to surface and breath every two to three minutes, and will usually drown before fishermen even know they are in the nets. As if that wasn't bad enough, eight juvenile calves died mysteriously in early 2006, suggesting water pollution is also taking its toll.

In Laos, dolphins have been seen as far north as Sekong in recent years, but you're most likely to see them in the deep-water conservation zones between 10m and 60m deep that have been established near the border, south of Don Khon. These areas are vital to the dolphins because they act as a refuge during the dry season, when river levels drop dangerously low.

Education and conservation programmes to save the dolphins continue, particularly in Cambodia, but their survival is far from guaranteed.

NOT AS SAME, SAME AS THEY LOOK

Standards might be rising, but for now there are still plenty of bungalows on Don Khon and particularly Don Det that look basically the same and cost US$1.50 a night. There are, however, a few things worth considering when making your choice.

Bathroom As competition intensifies guesthouses are increasingly tacking basic bathrooms onto their bungalows. These can vary, so take a look. Ditto for places with share bathrooms. If you don't want to squat, look for one with a throne.

Hammock(s) Most bungalows have balconies with hammocks, but if you're a pair it's worth checking if there is room to string up two hammocks, and if the guesthouse has a second one for you.

Location If it's the hot season and you plan on sleeping in, avoid Sunrise Blvd or anywhere facing east, where the morning sun makes your bungalow pretty toasty by 8am. By the same token, places on Sunset Strip can be oven-like in the afternoons.

Neighbours Bamboo walls are paper thin. If you need privacy look for a detached bungalow.

Roof Tin roofs are hotter than traditional palm-frond thatch roofs.

Window(s) With no electricity (yet) and therefore no fans or air-con, having two windows in your bungalow/room means that air circulation (and your night's sleep) is vastly improved.

Don Khon is home to some more up-market places, pleasant eateries on the water and a less-youthful atmosphere than Don Det; staying here is definitely a more 'Lao' experience.

Virtually all guesthouses here also serve food and drinks all day.

Coming from Ban Nakasang (see opposite) boatmen will usually drop you at your guesthouse of choice if you ask.

Don Det

Seng Chan's Bungalows (Sunrise Blvd; bungalows US$1-2) These thatched-roofed and detached bungalows have two beds and two windows each and sit right on the river. Good choice.

Mr Noi's Bungalows (Sunrise Blvd; bungalows US$1.50-2) These oldish bungalows have softer than usual mattresses. You can get excellent pumpkin burgers here.

Santiphab Guesthouse (☎ 030-534 6233; bungalows US$1) Beside the north end of the bridge, Santiphab was one of the first guesthouses on Don Det and is still a good option if view and chilled atmosphere is more important than partying. The restaurant (meals US$1 to US$2.50) is a cooler place for sundowners.

Mr Phao's Sunrise Bungalows (Sunrise Blvd; bungalows US$1.50) South of the pier, Mr Phao's has a wonderfully warm, family feel to go with tasty food and bungalows with multiple windows and multiple hammocks. Good option.

Sunset Bar & Guesthouse (Sunset Strip; bungalows US$1.50) There's a fun atmosphere here and it's the bar over the river that drives it. The lào-láo mojitos (US$0.50) are pretty good.

River Garden (☎ 020-527 4785; Southern Shore; bungalows US$1.50) This three-bungalow place on the southern shore calls itself Don Det's friendliest guesthouse. That's hard to judge, but they were nice enough and it's good value.

Happy Island Nou Phit Guest House (Sunrise Blvd; bungalows US$2) The standalone bungalows with squat bathrooms aren't bad and the atmosphere is pretty good.

Mr Tho's Bungalows & Restaurant (☎ 030-534 5865; Sunrise Blvd; bungalows US$2) Just south of the pier, Mr Tho's has long been popular for the relaxed atmosphere, well-constructed bungalows and 'library'. The restaurant (meals US$1 to US$2) is above average, especially the shakes, dhal and làap.

Mr Vong's Guest House Hang Det (☎ 020-526 2591; Southern Shore; bungalows US$1.50-4) At the south end of Don Det, these bungalows aren't fantastic but Mr Vong speaks good English and is a genuinely nice guy.

Mr Mo Guesthouse (☎ 020-575 9252; Sunrise Blvd; r US$2-5) Mix of rooms with and without bathroom and nifty curtained off lattice walls, allowing more air and light in, making them brighter and cooler than most.

Noy's Sunset Bungalows & Restaurant (☎ 030-534 6020; bungalows US$3) In a prime sunset location, Noy's was one of the first guesthouses on Don Det and it's still very popular. Noy's Belgian husband has introduced some very tasty European food to the restaurant (meals US$1.50 to US$5), which is worth the extra if you want a taste of home.

Mama Tanon Café Guest House (☎ 020-546 5262; Sunrise Blvd; r US$3) Formerly known as the Rasta

Cafe, the spirit of Marley is still strong in this basic but communal place and vivacious Mama (expect to be slapped for any insolence) should appeal.

Mr B's Guest House & Bungalows (☎ 030-534 5109; Sunset Strip; bungalows US$3-4) English-speaking Mr B has reasonable bungalows in a quiet position, but it's popular more for the warm atmosphere and delicious food in the café (meals US$1 to US$2.50); the pumpkin burger (US$2) has achieved legendary status.

Souksan Hotel (☎ 030-534 5154; r US$5-15) Squeezed onto the very north tip of Don Det, the Souksan's sturdy rooms are the best on the island but are overpriced and there's not much atmosphere. All have fans that run from about 6pm to 10pm, but you need to pay US$8 for a bathroom. The restaurant (meals US$1.50 to US$3.50) has fine sunset views but it does get hot. The Lao and Chinese food isn't bad.

Almost every place serves cold Beerlao and a range of alternatives. There's also the *falang*-run **Monkey Bar** (6am-11pm), in the heart of Ban Hua Det, which had the best mix of music when we passed and organises occasional barbecue trips to surrounding islands. It's especially popular late.

Don Khon

All of Don Khon's sleeping and eating options are spread along the river either side of the bridge.

Guesthouse Souksanh (r US$2, bungalows US$3) The cheapest place on Don Khon isn't bad, with small rooms overhanging the river, and bungalows with bathroom and fan. There's a family feel and the restaurant and *kátâw* (Lao ball game) court are a bonus.

Somphamit Guest House (r US$4) Beside the river opposite Mr Bounh's, these six rooms with cold-water bathrooms are a low-budget option on the more gentrified Don Khon strip.

Pan's Guesthouse & Restaurant (☎ 020-563 1434; pkounnavong@yahoo.co.uk; bungalows US$8; 🖳) Pan's new wooden bungalows are spacious and a cut above the bamboo places. They have soft mattresses, fans, clean bathrooms, and there are plans for solar hot water. Over the track the restaurant isn't bad and information is free-flowing. Internet access costs US$6 per hour.

Auberge Sala Don Khone (☎ 020-563 3718; www .salalao.com; s/d incl breakfast US$11/21) Romantics take note: this converted French-era hospital contains Don Khon's three most charming

rooms (though only the middle room has a double bed) surrounded by an attractive garden. The remaining sturdy wooden rooms (s/d US$11/16) with terracotta tile roofs, verandas and attached cold-water bathrooms are also quite nice. Negotiation is possible and from May to September prices drop by US$3. A generator runs from 6pm to 10pm, longer if you pay for it.

Sala Phae (☎ 030-525 6390; www.salalao.com; r incl breakfast US$30) If you fancy sleeping on the river, literally, these bamboo rafts (*phae* means raft) floating on the Mekong are for you. Each supports two comfortable if slightly overpriced rooms, with bio-safe toilet in the hot-water bathroom and a small balcony.

Chanthounma's Restaurant (meals US$1-2.50; breakfast, lunch & dinner) Chanthounma's 'good food to suit your mood' lives up to the advertising, and along with charming Chanthounma, should brighten any mood.

Seng Ahloune Restaurant (☎ 030-534 5807; meals US$1-4; breakfast, lunch & dinner) The Seng Ahloune is as popular for its delicious comfort food, including great fish and chips (US$3), as its prime location over the river just south of the bridge. Vietnamese spring rolls and curries are other dishes worth trying on the epic menu. Recommended – except during the tour-group rush hour around noon. It should have four relatively plush rooms (US$10 including breakfast) open by the time you read this.

Bamboo Bar & Restaurant (meals US$2-4.50; breakfast, lunch & dinner) Adjoining the Sala Phae, this is also a floating affair and serves some interesting dishes that have had some good reports.

On the river's edge opposite Auberge Sala Don Khone is a **restaurant** (meals US$1-4; breakfast, lunch & dinner) serving decent food in a tranquil setting. The English-speaking owner is a mine of knowledge about the island.

GETTING THERE & AWAY

It seems hyperinflation has struck the Si Phan Don boatmen. Prices have tripled on the small boats ferrying passengers between Ban Nakasang and Don Det (US$1.50 per person or US$2 alone), or Don Khon (US$2 per person or US$4 alone). Boats can be hired to go anywhere in the islands for about US$10 per hour.

For Pakse (US$3, 2½ to 3½ hours, 148km), buses or *săwngthăew* leave Ban Nakasang at

281 (spu... ands)

...am and 10am. See p260 for buses
...e.

Khon Phapheng Falls
ນ້ຳຕົກຕາດຄອນພະເພັງ

South of Don Khong the Mekong River features a 13km stretch of powerful rapids with
several sets of cascades. The largest, and by
far the most awesome anywhere along the
Mekong, is **Khon Phapheng** (admission US$0.90),
near the eastern shore of the Mekong not
far from Ban Thakho. Khon Phapheng isn't
as beautiful as the towering waterfalls of the
Bolaven Plateau or the fairytale pools of Tat
Kuang Si near Luang Prabang. But Khon
Phapheng is pure, unrestrained aggression
as millions of litres of water crash over the
rocks and into Cambodia every second. Especially when the Mekong is at full flood this is
a spectacular sight, and it's probably the most
visited site in Laos for Thai tourists, who arrive by the busload. Part of the attraction is
the spiritual significance they hold for both
Lao and Thais, who believe Khon Phapheng
acts as a spirit trap in the same way as Tat
Somphamit (p278).

A wooden pavilion on the Mekong shore
affords a good view of the falls. A shaky network of bamboo scaffolds on the rocks next
to the falls is used by daring fishermen who
are said to have an alliance with the spirits of
the cascades.

GETTING THERE & AWAY
Most people book a trip through a guesthouse
to get to the falls, often taking in both the falls
and dolphins. If you're making the journey
yourself, it's best to get to Ban Nakasang and
take a *săwngthăew* from there. From Ban Nakasang to Khon Phapheng Falls you can hire a
motorcycle taxi for about US$3.50 or a jumbo
for US$10 (this is a return fare for the whole
jumbo and should include at least two hours
at the falls). Police have stopped boatman
running tourists direct from Don Khon to
the falls, though it can be arranged if you're
prepared to walk a bit at the end.

BOLAVEN PLATEAU
ພູພຽງບໍລະເວນ

Spreading across the northeast of Champasak Province into Salavan and Sekong,
the fertile Bolaven Plateau (sometimes spelt
Bolovens, known in Lao as Phu Phieng
Bolaven) is famous for its cool climate, dra-

matic waterfalls, fertile soil and high-grade
coffee plantations. It's also known for being
one of the most heavily bombed theatres of
the Second Indochina War.

The area wasn't farmed intensively until
the French started planting coffee, rubber
trees and bananas in the early 20th century. Many of the French planters left following independence in the 1950s and the
rest followed as US bombardment became
unbearable in the late '60s. Controlling the
Bolaven Plateau was considered strategically vital to both the Americans and North
Vietnamese, as evidenced by the staggering
amount of UXO (unexploded ordnance) still
lying around.

The slow process of clearing UXO continues, but in areas where it has been cleared,
both local farmers and larger organisations
are busy cultivating coffee (see *Kąaféh Láo*
p285). Other local products include fruit,
cardamom and rattan.

The largest ethnic group on the plateau
is the Laven (Bolaven means 'home of the
Laven'). Several other Mon-Khmer ethnic
groups, including the Alak, Katu, Ta-oy
(Tahoy) and Suay, also live on the plateau.
Katu and Alak villages are distinctive because they arrange their palm-and-thatch
houses in a circle. One unique Katu custom is the carving of wooden caskets for
each member of the household well in

THE KATU & ALAK BUFFALO SACRIFICE

The Katu and Alak are well known in Laos
for an annual water buffalo sacrifice (usually performed on a full moon in March) in
homage to the village spirit. The number
of buffaloes sacrificed – typically from one
to four animals – depends on their availability and the bounty of the previous year's
agricultural harvest. During the ceremony,
the men of the village don wooden masks,
hoist spears and wooden shields, then
dance around the buffaloes in the centre
of the circle formed by their houses. After
a prescribed period of dancing the men
converge on the buffaloes and spear them
to death. The meat is divided among the
villagers and each household places a piece
in a basket on a pole in front of their house
as a spirit offering.

CROSSING THE CAMBODIAN BORDER AT DOM KRALOR & VOEN KHAM

This remote border has become a popular crossing point on the Indochina circuit. It also seems to be in a permanent state of change, so keeping up with the details is difficult. When we went to press there were actually two different border points. Laos does not issue visas at this border.

The most popular route south goes via Dom Kralor and the new Chinese-built road to Stung Treng, where Cambodia issues visas on arrival (US$20). From the islands most travellers are taking a backpacker bus (minibus) at least as far as Stung Treng (US$13, two hours), and perhaps to Kratie (US$20, about six hours), Kompong Cham (US$23, 7½ to 8½ hours), Phnom Penh (US$26, 11 to 12 hours) or Siem Reap (US$30, overnight). Going to Stung Treng with this minibus is the easiest, and unless you have days to wait, the cheapest way. Getting to Stung Treng by local transport is possible but could take days and you'll probably end up on the backpacker bus anyway, for want of other options. For travel beyond Stung Treng, it's much cheaper to take Cambodian buses.

The second way of crossing the border is by boat from Voen Kham. In theory slow boats, long tails and speed boats all run down to Stung Treng from here, but competition from the minibus has in effect put them out of business. If you really want to do this, call Mr T (☎ 855-(0)12-437496) in Stung Treng and he can arrange a boat to meet you at the border; a long tail (2½ hours) should cost about US$100 per boat. There is a Lao immigration post at Voen Kham, but the Cambodian post has closed. You'll have to stop at Dom Kralor en route.

Whichever border you take you'll probably have to pay a small 'processing fee' on both sides, usually US$1 or US$2 – stock up on US$1 bills.

The final way of getting to the border is the most interesting. Lane Xang Travel (Xplore Asia; p278) run a raft from Don Det to the border (US$20), where you and your bags are met by the minivan running through to Stung Treng.

Coming north, tourist minibuses dominate the trade from Stung Treng and the trip is smooth enough. You'll cross the border at Dom Kralor, then probably have to change transport for the last leg to Ban Nakasang. Note again that, for now at least, you'll need to get your Lao visa in advance. Speak with fellow travellers or check the **Thorn Tree** (http://thorntree.lonelyplanet.com) for the latest.

advance of an expected death; the caskets are stored beneath homes or rice sheds until needed.

Among other tribes, the animistic-shamanistic Suay (who call themselves Kui) are said to be the best elephant handlers. Elephants were used extensively for clearing land and moving timber, though working elephants are hard to find these days.

The Alak, Katu and Laven are distinctive for the face tattoos of their women, a custom slowly dying out as Lao influence in the area increases.

Several **Katu** and **Alak villages** can be visited along the road between Pakse and Paksong at the western edge of the plateau, and along the laterite road that descends steadily from Muang Tha Taeng (That Heng) on the plateau to Beng, in Salavan Province. There are also a few within walking distance of Tat Lo (p286), and on Rte 20. In **Lao Ngam** (not to be confused with Muang Lao Ngam on the road to Salavan), around 40km east of Pakse,

is a large day market frequented by many tribal groups.

The plateau has several spectacular waterfalls, including **Tat Fan**, a few kilometres west of Paksong, and **Tat Lo** on Rte 20 to Salavan.

Tat Fan & Dong Hua Sao NPA

Tat Fan is one of the most spectacular waterfalls in Laos, with parallel streams of the Huay Bang Lieng plunging out of dense forest and down more than 120m. Tat Fan (pronounced *tàat fáan*) is at the edge of the 1100-sq-km Dong Hua Sao NPA and the walking trails around here are a good way to get a taste of the park. Dong Hua Sao is home to a population of tigers who are reputed to munch through the occasional unfortunate hunter, though the chances of actually seeing one are virtually nil. You're more likely to see monkeys, gigantic butterflies and, in the wet season, rare hornbills.

Tat Fan is 800m south of Rte 23 – look for the signs at Km 38. A path leads down to the top of the falls and affords fine views, though this is perilously slippery in the wet season and is often impossible. An easier viewing point is Tad Fane Resort (below), a bungalow and ecotourism operation that looks down onto the falls from the top of a cliff opposite. The resort has a couple of professional English-speaking guides who can arrange fairly easy half- and full-day treks around the edge of the NPA. These might take in Laven and Katu villages, coffee plantations, and almost always at least one other waterfall.

A half-day trek costs US$3.50 to US$5, depending on numbers, and a full-day is US$10 including lunch. When possible, the morning trek leaves at 8.30am and takes the steep descent to the top of Tat Fan, returning about 12.30pm. The 1pm trek is usually more of a stroll and swim, walking through coffee plantations to 17m-high Tat Cham Pi (which means Small Banana Waterfall, though no-one could tell us why). The large pool below is perfect for swimming, and private enough that women can usually get down to their swimwear without offending the locals. Adventure sandals are appropriate in the dry season but boots are better in the wet to deter leeches. As one guide told us, 'the flip-flop is not possible'.

Rafting operations are just beginning to venture into Dong Hua Sao. For details speak to Green Discovery or Lane Xang Travel in Pakse (both p255).

Any transport between Pakse and Paksong, or beyond, stops 800m north of Tat Fan (see opposite for details). When you arrive there's a small fee for entrance and parking if you're not staying/eating at the resort. The popularity of Tat Fan with day-tripping Thai tourists has also prompted local residents to establish a small market in the car park. Some of the goods on sale are innocent enough, such as coffee and green tea grown locally. But please don't buy the orchids, which come straight from Dong Hua Sao. Local guides report that orchids are now only marginally easier to spot than tigers in the area around Tat Fan.

SLEEPING & EATING

Tad Fane Resort (☎ 020-553 1400; www.tadfane.com; s/d/fam incl breakfast US$30/32/40) These well-built wooden bungalows sit atop a cliff overlooking the falls, though only the two larger family rooms actually have a clear view. All have a veranda and attached bathroom. The restaurant (meals US$1.50 to US$2.50), open for breakfast, lunch and dinner, has great views and serves sandwiches and cheap but tasty Thai food. In the high season (November to February) it pays to book ahead, and to bring something warm.

Paksong & Around

ຕາດຟາ/ປ່າສະຫງວແຫ່ງຊາດດົງຫົວຊາວ

Laos's coffee capital is nothing to look at, most of it having been obliterated in a storm of bombs during the Second Indochina War. But it makes a cheap Bolaven base from which to explore the plateau, has a mildly interesting market and is refreshingly cool. Plans to develop some basic tourist infrastructure are in their early stages but in the meantime Roger at **Travellers' Meeting Point Café**, on the south side of Rte 23 just as you enter town from Pakse, and the guys at Tad Fane Resort (left) are the best sources of information. Roger might also have a coffee tasting bar open by the time you arrive.

COFFEE

Coffee trees of varying sizes blanket the Bolaven Plateau and you can walk through them on the easy afternoon treks from Tat Fan (p283). Those wanting to get closer to the action can head to **Phuoi** (Phuouy), which has become the unofficial headquarters for Jhai Coffee Farmers Co-op (see *Kạa-féh Láo*, opposite). There are plans to open a modest shop selling their Fairtrade coffee by the cup and bag.

To get to Phuoi head east on Rte 23 for about 1.5km and look for the big sign pointing right (south) down a dirt road to Ban Nong Luang. This arse-jarring road runs to the southern edge of the plateau and is home to the 12 mainly Laven villages that make up the Jhai Coffee Farmers Co-op. Phuoi is 4km along, but more adventurous souls with a few hours spare might want to continue another 7km to **Ban Nong Luang**. From this village it's possible to take a local guide and walk to two fairly impressive waterfalls, the seven-tiered **Tat Tha Jet** and **Tat Kameud**. The return trip takes a while so start early. If you get stuck homestays (p48) in Ban Nong Luang are possible. Note that no-one in the village speaks English, but they should understand 'homestay' if you want one.

SOUTHERN LAOS

KĄA-FÉH LÁO (LAO COFFEE)

The high, flat ground of the Bolaven Plateau is ideal for growing coffee and the region produces some of the best and most expensive bean on earth. Arabica, Arabica Typica and Robusta are grown, much of it around the 'coffee town' of Paksong.

The French introduced coffee to the Bolaven Plateau in the early 1900s and the Arabica Typica shipped home became known as the 'champagne of coffee'. Plans to make the plateau a major coffee-growing centre died with the bombardment of the 1960s and '70s.

Business began to pick up in the 1990s and was dominated by a few plantations and companies, the largest being Pakse-based Dao Heung. For the farmers, however, earning less than US$0.50 per kg wasn't really improving their living standards. These businesses still dominate today but a fair-trade project aimed at empowering small-scale farmers is gathering steam. The **Jhai Coffee Farmer Cooperative** (www.jhaicoffee.com) is a 500-member group, which was formed in 2004 with help from the California-based Jhai Foundation and Thanksgiving Coffee in the US. Members come from 12 villages and several ethnic groups living mainly along the rough road running south from Rte 23 to Ban Nong Luang (see opposite). Machinery has been bought, and cooperative farmers have been trained in modern cultivation methods to maximise the quality of the beans. And with Fairtrade certification the farmers are guaranteed 19,000 kip per kg, more than three times what they made selling to larger wholesalers.

For now Jhai Coffee is only available in the US or online, but there are plans for a cupping lab in Paksong and for bagged bean to be sold in Phuoi, Pakse, Vientiane and Luang Prabang.

WATERFALLS

As well as Tat Fan, numerous breathtaking other cascades drop off the Bolaven Plateau within striking distance of Paksong. Most are marked by a blue sign with a painted representation of the cataract in question. **Tat Yuang** (admission US$0.50, motorbike parking US$0.30) is among the most impressive, with its twin torrents falling about 40m and flowing into lush jungle. Tat Yuang is hugely popular with daytrippers from Pakse and Thailand who like to picnic at the top, so getting there early is a good idea. It's OK to swim at the bottom – women must wear a sarong.

To get there, follow the signs right (south) off Rte 23 at Km 40 and go a further 2km along a soon-to-be-upgraded laterite road. A scenic way to Tat Fan from here is the 45-minute walk along a beautiful forest trail that starts beside the toilets at Tat Yuang.

Beyond Paksong you'll see a sign pointing north to **Tat Meelook**. Apparently these twin falls were once a popular local attraction, but we can tell you from experience that it must have been a while ago. The 3.7km trip was challenging, to put it mildly, and when we eventually arrived the falls weren't really worth it.

SLEEPING & EATING

Paksong Guest House (☎ 020-982 2006; r US$2-12) This guesthouse has rooms in three buildings, including grubby twins with shared bathroom (US$2) and better twins with bathroom (US$7); you need to pay US$9 to get hot water. Coming from Pakse, turn left after the Kaysone Monument and take the left just before the bridge (about 1.5km from Rte 23); the guesthouse is on the right opposite some noodle stalls.

Borlaven Guesthouse (☎ 030-575 8086; Rte 23; r US$5) About 2km east of town this attractive-looking wooden place is run by a young family whose pet is a young gibbon. The guesthouse is a bit out of the way, but the rooms are better value than the Paksong. If you ask ahead of time, they can supply dinner.

GETTING THERE & AWAY

Buses and săwngthăew between Paksong and Pakse's southern (Km 8) bus terminal leave frequently between about 8am and 4pm (US$1.50, 90 minutes). For Tat Fan, get off at Km 38 and follow the signs to the falls and resort (about 800m south of the turn-off).

Utayan Bajiang Champasak (Phasoume Resort)

A Thai-owned 'eco-resort', **Utayan Bajiang Champasak** (☎ 031-251294; 020-576 7678; off Rte 20) 38km northwest of Pakse is scattered through a stretch of thick jungle either side

SOUTHERN LAOS

of a small but beautiful waterfall. It's possible to stay here in one of the 14 Swiss Family Robinson–style tree houses (US$28), but they're overpriced and it's better to just stop in the restaurant (meals US$1.50 to US$4) for a tasty Thai lunch – most likely with busloads of Thai tourists.

The resort itself might seem to be more a homage to big dead trees – sliced and diced into chairs, tables, beams, posts, floor timbers, stepping stones and just about any other use you can imagine – than to live trees. But we're assured that the tonnes of timber used to build this place were taken from trees rejected by local logging operations.

An appealing elevated jungle walk leads to a 'museum village' where families of Katu, Nge and Laven attempt to entertain visitors. The families seem happy enough, and you can even stay with them for US$8 per person, but for us the whole thing was way too contrived – their museum life just felt weird.

GETTING THERE & AWAY

There is no direct public transport to Phasoume. Take any transport heading up Rte 20 towards Salavan and get off at a turn-off 400m after the Houy Cham Pa bridge, about 36km from Pakse. There's a sign in Thai, but not English. It's then about a 1.5km walk.

SALAVAN PROVINCE

Like Sekong and Attapeu Provinces to the south, Salavan is notable as much for its remoteness as any traditional tourism draws. Salavan (also spelt Saravan and Saravane) is not on the way to anywhere and roads remain some of the worst in Laos, but it is these very qualities and the lure of tough travel that have begun to attract a few hardy visitors looking to get well-and-truly off the beaten track.

There are, of course, a few attractions. The province straddles the northern edge of the Bolaven Plateau and Tat Lo, just 30km from Salavan town, is an attractive little town near some waterfalls and is the best place to base yourself. Beyond waterfalls, however, the ethnic diversity of the region is its main attraction. While more than half of the population of Salavan is ethnically

Lao (Loum and Soung), none are native to this area. The remainder of the 324,000 inhabitants belong to relatively obscure Mon-Khmer groups, including the Ta-oy (Tahoy), Lavai, Katang, Alak, Laven, Ngai, Tong, Pako, Kanay, Katu and Kado.

Actually getting into these villages, however, requires something approaching a full-scale expedition – or a fair bit of self-confidence, at least. If this appeals to you, then you could head for Tahoy (Ta-oy people, see p289) or Toumlan (Katang, see p289) for a taste of minority life.

Almost half the province is covered by natural forest but getting into the three protected areas is just as tough. **Phu Xieng Thong NPA** is accessible from Pakse (see p261), but for now the **Se Ban Nuan NPA** near to Rte 13 and particularly the **Se Xap NPA** in the far east have no tourist infrastructure whatsoever – in fact, infrastructure of any kind is extremely limited.

Just about every major branch of the Ho Chi Minh Trail cut through Salavan at some point and UXO remains a serious problem. While Salavan town no longer has piles of rusting war detritus waiting for scrap merchants, plenty of towns to the north and east do. Clearance teams head out almost every day to continue the painstaking task of finding and neutralising these weapons of war, and expect to be busy for years. Despite plenty of interest from travellers keen to walk part of the trail, so far no such operation exists.

TAT LO

ຕາດເລາະ

☎ 034

Tat Lo (pronounced *tàat láw*) is a sort of backpacker retreat with cheap accommodation, an attractive setting and things to do, but not many backpackers. Which is much of its charm. Waterfalls are the town's *raison d'être* and they give it a serenity that sees many visitors stay longer than they planned. If you're on The Southern Swing (p263) or planning to explore deeper into the province, this is the ideal base.

The town is a one-street affair, with most accommodation just east of the bridge. A **community guides office** here has information on nine different treks to surrounding sights and nearby Ngai villages (starting at US$4 per person for a four-hour trip) and is where you get hooked up with a guide. It's run by Soulideth of Tim Guesthouse (opposite), who speaks perfect English and is a mine of information on nearby attractions. He also offers **internet access** (per hour US$6) if you're desperate, and can arrange motorbike hire (US$10 per day).

WATERFALLS

There are actually three waterfalls on this stretch of river. The nearest to town is **Tat Hang**, which can be seen from the bridge and some guesthouses. It's possible to swim here – just go where the local kids do. Note that during the dry season, dam authorities upstream release water in the evening, more than doubling the waterfall volume. Check out what time the release occurs so you're not standing at the top of the waterfall then – a potentially fatal error.

Tat Lo, about 700m upriver, is a little bigger but probably won't knock your socks off. To get there, cross the bridge and walk up through Saise Guest House (below), keeping to the path by the river. The spectacular third cascade is **Tat Suong**. It's about 10km from town and you could walk there, but it's better to go by motorbike or bicycle. Head uphill past the turn-off to Tadlo Lodge (below), turn right at the power station and left where the road ends. Look (hard) for the sign pointing left to Ban Sanumnay and follow it to a parking area. It's not far from here to the stunning and precipitous edge of the falls…don't get too close.

ELEPHANT RIDES

Tadlo Lodge (below) offers rides on its two female elephants (US$5 per elephant, 90 minutes). The typical ride plods through forest, villages and streams full of slippery rocks you wouldn't dream of crossing on foot. Each elephant can carry two people and they depart from just outside the guides' office at 8am, 10am, 1pm and 3pm. You can book at the guides' office, Tim Guesthouse or Tadlo Lodge itself.

SLEEPING & EATING

Siphaseth Guest House & Restaurant (☎ 211890; r US$2-6) With newish rooms with fan and hot/cold bathroom, and more traditional bamboo rooms with share bathroom, this guesthouse is the pick. The restaurant (meals US$1.50 to US$3) is the ideal place to have a sunset drink, though the food is hit and miss. It's on the river immediately downstream of the bridge.

Saylomyen Guest House (r US$2.50) Next door to Siphaseth, the Saylomyen has simple fan-conditioned huts with balcony and an equally simple shared bathroom.

Tim Guesthouse & Restaurant (☎ 211885; 020-564 8820; soulidet@gmail.com; r US$4-6; 💻) The cane-and-wood bungalows here have shared bathroom and no views, but what they lack in luxuries is made up for in atmosphere. English- and French-speaking Soulideth has all the local information and the restaurant (meals US$1.50 to US$3), open for breakfast, lunch and dinner, serves the usual range of travellers' favourites plus seasonal specialities (ask about these), all accompanied by soft jazz. There is a book exchange, and attached to the guesthouse is a classroom (built by Soulideth) where local kids learn computer skills.

Saise Guest House (☎ /fax 211886; 020-564 2489; r US$6-60) In lush gardens on the west bank of the river, this place sprawls from Tat Hang to Tat Suong. Rooms range from cheap ('tribe bungalows' for US$6 to US$8) to overpriced (rooms in the 'blue house', about 700m upriver at Tat Lo itself). Those in between (in the 'green house'), are better value. Big, comfortable and tastefully decorated Room A2 is our pick (US$30). Others are about US$20 and most include an American breakfast.

Tadlo Lodge (☎ /fax 211889; souriyavincent@yahoo.com; bungalows s/d incl breakfast US$20/30) In prime positions on both sides of the river overlooking the lower waterfall, these well-built bungalows have balconies and clean hot-water bathrooms; discounts are possible. The open-sided restaurant (meals US$3 to US$5), open for breakfast, lunch and dinner, serves reliably good Lao, Thai and European dishes. The only downside is that until a more permanent bridge is built, it's a long, dark walk from bungalow to restaurant.

GETTING THERE & AWAY

Just say 'Tat Lo' at Pakse's southern bus station and you'll be pointed in the right direction (see p260). Tat Lo is 86km northeast of Pakse off the road to Salavan; you'll be dropped at Ban Khoua Set. There might be a *dok dok* (US$0.20), tuk-tuk or motorbike (US$0.30 to US$50) to shuttle you the last 1.8km; if not it's a pleasant, if all uphill, walk.

If you're heading to Paksong, get yourself up to Ban Beng, and catch a bus coming from Salavan. It might go all the way to Paksong, or you might need to change buses at Tha Taeng; either way, give yourself a few hours.

SALAVAN

ສາລະວັນ

☎ 034 / pop 76,493

Before it was renamed Salavan (Sarawan in Thai) by the Siamese in 1828, this area was a Champasak kingdom outpost known as Muang Mam and inhabited mostly by Mon-Khmer minorities. The provincial capital of Salavan was all but destroyed in the Indochina War, when it bounced back and forth between Royal Lao Army and Pathet Lao occupation. The rebuilt town is a collection of brick and wood buildings, though if you look carefully you'll find more old buildings around than you might expect and it's not totally without charm.

The town sits within a bend of the Se Don, which ultimately meets the Mekong at Pakse. Functionally, Salavan serves mainly as a supply centre for farmers in surrounding districts. And while it's the best place from which to explore the province, with its bus station serving anywhere in the province it's possible to go, for many travellers the tranquil rural atmosphere isn't enough of a draw and instead they stay at Tat Lo (see p286). If you do stay note that despite nearby hydroelectric power stations, power outages are not uncommon and when the power is out the water stops too.

Information

The **Lao Development Bank** (☯ 8.30am-4.30pm Mon-Fri), a little west of the market, will change US dollars or Thai baht cash; if it's closed, try the market. The **post office** (☯ 8am-4.30pm) is around the corner from the market, and next door is a **telecom office** (☯ 8am-5pm Mon-Fri) but apparently they don't do international calls.

Two unmissably large Municipal Authority buildings dominate the town, the older of which is home to the **Provincial Tourism Office** (☎ 211528; Ground fl; ☯ 8.30am-noon & 1.30-4pm Mon-Fri), where the French- and English-speaking Mr Bounthone Sinachak is well worth chatting with if you plan on heading further into the province. If you ask nicely he might give you a handy booklet with pictures of what you might see. The **Provincial Hospital** is one block north, and is OK for minor emergencies.

At the time of writing there was no internet in Salavan.

Sleeping & Eating

Most of the lodgings in Salavan have a mix of fan and air-con rooms with and without private bathrooms. There are several noodle shops around the market and at the bus station.

Silsamay Guesthouse (☎ 020-554805; Rte 20; r US$4-7; ☒) On Rte 20 just west of the bus station, the spacious rooms are nice enough with fan or air-con, TV and hot water.

Saise Guest House (☎ 211054; r US$4-8; ☒) On a rambling plot about 800m east of the market, the Saise has plenty of character but seems to be in a steady cycle of decline. Certain rooms in the newer 'Hotel' building are huge and fair value at US$8 with air-con. The older wooden building has airy but dusty fan rooms (US$4) with two or three beds.

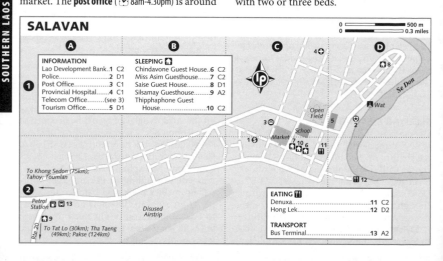

SALAVAN

| 0 | 500 m |
| 0 | 0.3 miles |

INFORMATION
Lao Development Bank..1 C2
Police...........................2 D1
Post Office....................3 C1
Provincial Hospital.......4 C1
Telecom Office.........(see 3)
Tourism Office............5 D1

SLEEPING
Chindavone Guest House..6 C2
Miss Asim Guesthouse......7 C2
Saise Guest House............8 D1
Silsamay Guesthouse......9 A2
Thipphaphone Guest
House.......................10 C2

EATING
Denuxa...........................11 C2
Hong Lek........................12 D2

TRANSPORT
Bus Terminal....................13 A2

To Khong Sedon (75km);
Tahoy; Toumlan

Petrol Station

To Tat Lo (30km); Tha Taeng (49km); Pakse (124km)

Disused Airstrip

Se Don

Open Field

Wat

School

Market

Chindavone Guest House (☎ 211065; r US$8; ❄)
Near the market right in the centre of town,
the bungalows here have large rooms with
hot-water bathrooms, TV, and both fan and
air-con. For rooms and location, if not price,
this is probably the pick.

In the same street as the Chindavone is
the **Thipphaphone Guest House** (☎ 211063; r US$3-7;
❄), with a wide variety of rooms, some with
satellite TV, and a wonderfully welcoming
manager, though she doesn't speak any English; and the **Miss Asim Guesthouse** (☎ 211062;
r US$4; ❄), where rooms aren't great; try the
others first.

The pick of Salavan's limited number of
eating establishments is **Denuxa** (meals US$1-4;
❄ dinner), which serves tasty Lao and sukiyaki
dishes and a lot of local information from the
English and German-speaking host.

Down a short dirt road at the south end
of town, **Hong Lek** (meals US$1-3; ❄ dinner), a fish
restaurant on the banks of the Se Don, serves
superb barbecued fish, fresh vegetables and
icy Beerlao, just don't forget your mosquito
repellent and phrasebook.

Getting There & Away
BUS & SĂWNGTHĂEW
For buses from Pakse see p259. Salavan's
bus terminal is 2km west of the town centre
where Rte 20 meets the rough Rte 15. Buses for
Pakse (US$2, three hours, 124km) are sched-
uled to leave five times between 7.30am and
1.30pm. Buses or *săwngthăew* leave for Sekong
(US$1.80, three hours, 93km) at 7.45am and
1.30pm. These go through Tha Taeng (US$1,
one to 1½ hours, 49km), which has dedicated
services at 10am and 11am.

Lot dai săan, trucks with wooden cabins
built on the back and seats sans legroom
crammed inside, are the only beasts capable
of tackling the roads north, east and directly
west of Salavan. They run along rough Rte 15
to Khong Sedon (US$2.50, 2½ to 3½ hours,
75km), on Rte 13, where you can pick up other
transport to Savannakhet.

In the dry season they also take on the
potholed stretches of earth that masquer-
ade as roads running to Tahoy (right) and
Toumlan (right).

AROUND SALAVAN
Upcountry Salavan Province is an adventurer's delight, partly because getting to anywhere
worth seeing is an adventure in itself.

Nong Bua
ໜອງບົວ
The lake of **Nong Bua**, near the source of the Se
Don about 15km east of town along a seasonal
road, is famous for its dwindling population of
Siamese crocodiles (*khàe* in Lao). There aren't
many left (two or three, apparently), but tourism officials are establishing a day trip to Nong
Bua by bicycle, motorbike or foot. A guide and
bicycle cost US$5 per day each; there are no
motorbikes for rent. Chances of actually seeing the crocs are slim. Instead, look at 1588m-
high Phu Katae nearby – there are plans for a
trek to the old CIA landing strip on top.

Toumlan & Rte 23
About 50km north of Salavan along bumpy
Rte 23 is the Katang village of **Toumlan**. The
area is famous for its silk weavings and Lapup
festival (see The Katu & Alak Buffalo Sacrifice
p282) usually held in late February. The town
is very poor but interesting from a cultural
point of view and because of its position on
the Ho Chi Minh Trail, which continues to
pose a threat through UXO while also providing income from the sale of scrap. There is an
ultra-basic government guesthouse in town.

North of Toumlan Rte 23 heads towards
Rte 9 and Muang Phin, via the site of **Princes'
Bridge**, named because it was built by the 'Red
Prince' Souphanouvong (who was a trained
engineer) in 1942. Unfortunately the bridge
was blown up in 1968 and has never been
rebuilt. Locals tell us that in the dry season it
should be possible to cross here with a small
motorbike and continue on to Muang Phin
on Rte 9, the journey between Salavan and
Muang Phin taking about six to eight hours.

Tahoy & the Ho Chi Minh Trail
ເສັ້ນທາງໂຮຈີມິນ
Northeast along Rte 15, which can be impassable for days during the wet season, is
Tahoy (Ta-oy) a centre for the Ta-oy ethnic
group, who number around 30,000 spread
across the eastern areas of Salavan and Sekong Provinces. The Ta-oy live in forested
mountain valleys at altitudes between 300m
and 1000m, often in areas shared with Katu
and other Mon-Khmer groups. Like many
Mon-Khmer groups in Southern Laos, they
practise a combination of animism and sha-
manism; during village ceremonies, the Ta-oy
put up diamond-patterned bamboo totems to
warn outsiders not to enter.

290 SEKONG PROVINCE •• Sekong (Muang Lamam)

Tahoy town was an important marker on the Ho Chi Minh Trail and two major branches lead off Rte 15 nearby. If you want to see war junk ask a local to take you; you might need to draw pictures of bombs or tanks to get your message across. If you come to Tahoy you'll likely have to stay. The government lets out **rooms** (US$3) in a simple building. Tahoy is tiger country and while the locals won't leave town after dark for fear of them, you'll be very lucky indeed to actually hear one.

A *săwngthăew* leaves Salavan for Tahoy (US$1.50, four to eight hours, 84km) at 2pm every second day in the dry season. Alternatively, ask Mr Bounthone Sinachak at the Provincial Tourism Office (p288) about hiring a 4WD pick-up. If you're really into adventure, follow the story of one Dutch couple who took their 4WD up an obscure branch of the Ho Chi Minh Trail beyond Tahoy in March 2006. They eventually made it to Ban Dong on Rte 9, but it took them three days and they don't really recommend it – read their account at www.landcruising .nl. All this is due to change, though, as a sealed road to the border via Tahoy is due to be completed by 2010.

SEKONG PROVINCE

Stretching from near the eastern edge of the Bolaven Plateau to the Vietnam border, this rugged and remote province is dotted with waterfalls, dissected by the impressive Se Kong and dominated in the east by the lesser-known Dakcheung Plateau, which rises 1500m above sea level. With the massive cliff walls of the southern Se Xap NPA (some are said to be more than 1000m high) and several sizable mountains in the province, Sekong could be an outdoor adventurers' paradise.

Alas, not yet. The province is among the poorest in Laos and a combination of terrible road infrastructure, virtually no facilities for tourism and a landscape that remains unsafe due to UXO dropped on the Ho Chi Minh Trail (p251) decades ago, mean much of it is off-limits to all but the most intrepid.

That's not to say there's no reason to come. There are waterfalls on the Se Nam Noy (Nam Noy River) and the breathtaking Nam Tok Katamtok waterfall (p292), which

drop more than 100m. The other reason to come is the people. By population Sekong is the smallest of Laos's provinces, but among its 85,000 inhabitants are people from 14 different tribal groups, making it the most ethnically diverse province in the country. The vast majority are from Mon-Khmer tribes, with the Alak, Katu, Taliang, Yae and Nge the largest groups. These total more than 75% of the population. Other groups include the Pacoh, Chatong, Suay (Souei), Katang and Ta-oy (Tahoy). These diverse groups are not Buddhists, so you won't see too many wats. Rather, their belief systems mix animism and ancestor worship. The Katu and Taliang tend towards monogamy but, unusually in a part of the world so traditionally male dominated, tolerate polyandry (two or more husbands).

Note that in the wet season travelling anywhere off Rte 16 can be difficult.

SEKONG (MUANG LAMAM)

ເຊກອງ(ເມືອງລະມາ)

☎ 038 / pop 24,000

Sekong is a good base from which to visit the surrounding waterfalls or embark on a river trip down the Se Kong to Attapeu. It's not, however, very exciting. Carved out of the wilderness in the mid-1980s, the unnecessarily sprawling town is set on a basic grid with government buildings in the centre surrounded by areas of concrete, wooden and wood-and-thatch stilt homes. There are no street names.

The Se Kong wraps around the town on the southern and eastern sides, while the Bolaven Plateau rises precipitously to the west. At the **town market**, tribes from outlying areas trade cloth for Vietnamese goods while others sell an ever-dwindling number of birds, lizards and small mammals hunted in nearby forest.

It's worth visiting **UXO Lao** (🕙 8am-5pm) opposite the Ministry of Finance office, just west of the market. These guys have been clearing UXO for years and have a mildly interesting display of rusting munitions and weaponry in their yard. Visitors are welcome.

Information & Orientation

Sekong sits on a grid between Rte 16 in the north and the Se Kong to the south. Almost everything you need is in the streets just east of the market. The only real information offered here is in the Pha Thip Restaurant menu, which has stacks of information on local ethnic groups, villages and handicrafts, most of it prepared by a United Nations Development Programme (UNDP) caseworker in the late 1990s.

The **Lao Development Bank** (☯ 9.30am-4pm Mon-Fri) is on the road behind Souksamlane Sekong Hotel, nearer to the market; it changes Thai baht and US dollars cash for kip only. The **post office** (☯ 8am-noon & 1-5pm Mon-Fri) is at the other end of this road; the **Lao Telecommuncations** (☎ 8am-noon, 1-5pm & 6-8pm Mon-Fri) building is next door. There was no internet when we visited.

Sleeping & Eating

Sekong isn't blessed with wonderful lodgings. Several modest restaurants and *föe* shops can be found near the market.

Woman Fever Kosmet Centre Guesthouse (☎ 211046; r US$3) Next to the Sekong Souksamlane, the simple rooms with share bathrooms here are cheap but fine and we haven't heard of any guests catching woman fever (your money actually goes to a malaria education group). Good ultra-budget option.

Phong Paseuth Guesthouse (☎ 211085; Rte 16; r US$4.50-7; 🆒) On the left as you enter town from Paksong, these simple, compact rooms with cold-water bathrooms were new and subsequently quite clean when we visited.

Sekong Souksamlane Hotel (☎ 211039; r US$5-6.50; 🆒) The fan rooms on the ground floor and air-con rooms upstairs have hot water and are decent enough, but you'll probably need to wake someone up to get anything. The restaurant opens irregularly. There is a handicrafts shop outside (see Shopping right).

Vangxang Savanh Sekong Hotel & Restaurant (☎ 211297; r US$6-7.50; 🆒) This place sits on the banks of the Se Kong at the west end of town (look for the sign from Rte 16). The rooms aren't bad, but with cold-water bathrooms aren't as good as they look. It has a popular (and sometimes noisy) restaurant. A reasonable choice.

Koki Guesthouse (☎ 211401; r US$7; 🆒) Last time we visited this place it was home to a UN worker and her family. Now it's a small guesthouse with friendly staff who don't speak any English. Rooms are small but clean and have TV and hot water. To find it, go past the bank from the direction of the market and take the first right (north).

Pha Thip Restaurant (☎ 211343; meals US$1.50-2.50; ☯ breakfast, lunch & dinner) Opposite the Sekong Souksamlane Hotel, this simple place is the best choice for food. It has a variety of tasty Vietnamese, Lao and Western dishes (try the deep-fried fish with vegetables), heavenly fruit shakes and a hugely informative menu. Lovely Vietnamese owner Nang Tu speaks some English and is hoping to offer rooms (for about US$4) soon. Recommended.

The **Somview Restaurant**, just down a lane beside the Pha Thip Restaurant, is a good place for a sunset drink.

Shopping

The cheapest place to buy tribal textiles is the market (where a sarong-sized textile of recent manufacture should cost about US$10), but the selection is not as good as in the following shops.

Sekong Ethnic Store (☯ 8am-6pm) A ramshackle bamboo-thatch place on the street behind the Souksamlane Sekong Hotel and opposite the street with the Koki Guesthouse, this store has a good range of textiles woven by the Alak, Katu, Nge and Talieng tribes, plus a few baskets and other tribal products. It's a good place to sort out the different colours and patterns of the various tribes. Mention the tribe and the owners will show you, for example, Katu cloth and its typically broad bands of red and black with small white beads sewn into the fabric, or Alak designs with their more refined stripe. Rare Alak or Nge loincloths – long, narrow, heavy beaded affairs – can occasionally be found on sale for as much as US$200. To find the shop, look for the blue and white painted sign announcing 'Welcome to Visit Laos Year 1999–2000'.

Lao Handicrafts Shop (☎ 211039; Sekong Souksamlane Hotel; ☯ 8am-4pm) Among the piles of textiles here you might find rare (though not necessarily expensive) examples of sarongs or blankets with stylised helicopter and fighter-jet motifs alongside traditional renditions of scorpions and lizards. If it's closed, as is likely, ask someone at reception to let you in.

Getting There & Away

Sekong's dusty/muddy bus station is about 2km northwest of town off Rte 16; a jumbo there costs about US$0.50. Few buses actually originate in Sekong, rather stopping here between Pakse and Attapeu, and schedules are flexible. For Pakse (US$2.50, 3½ to 4½ hours,

SOUTHERN LAOS

DOWN THE SE KONG BY LONGTAIL BOAT

With Rte 16 improved, boats down the Se Kong to Attapeu are hard to find these days. However, you should be able to find a boatman willing to take you if you ask around at the pier beside the Vangxang Savanh Sekong Hotel early in the morning – or perhaps speak to the Pha Thip Restaurant the night before. Expect to pay about US$60 for the four- to seven-hour trip, depending on the river level.

The trip is incredibly scenic as the river parallels the eastern escarpment of the Bolaven Plateau most of the way. During the late dry season, you may have to get out and walk along a path next to the river while the boatman manoeuvres the craft through shallow rapids. The Se Kong is quite swift during the rainy season – if you're not a good swimmer, this journey may not be for you.

Remember that the cheapest boatman will not necessarily be the best – it's worth looking for someone with experience. Also, if a life jacket is provided be prepared to wear it; the last time a *falang* drowned on this trip (in very unlucky circumstances) the boatman got 10 years.

135km) there is at least one bus (usually 6am) then occasional buses/*săwngthăew* coming through from Attapeu until about 1pm. For Attapeu (US$1.50, two hours, 76km) there is one dedicated departure at 8am, then every two hours or so until about 4pm. Transport to Salavan (US$1.80, 2½ to 3½ hours, 93km) leaves intermittently from 5am 'til noon.

For transport from Pakse see p260.

Getting Around

Sekong has a couple of jumbos, look for them at the market. Pha Thip Restaurant can rent motorbikes for US$10 per day.

AROUND SEKONG

Off Rte 16 south of Sekong there are several villages and waterfalls that could be visited as part of a day trip; you'd have to hire a bicycle or motorbike in Sekong, or charter a tuk-tuk or jumbo (about US$8 for six hours). About 3.5km south of town, turn right along a rough dirt road immediately after a school. Follow the dirt road about 2.5km to the relatively ordinary **Tat Hia** (Tat Hien) waterfall. A little further along Rte 16, another path heads southeast for about 3km toward the Se Kong and two Alak villages. The first is known for its fine *sín* (traditional sarongs). Similar villages can be found at the end of dirt roads leading east 12km and 14km from Sekong.

The road at Km 14 also leads to **Tat Faek**. On the Se Nam Noi not far upriver of the Se Kong, Tat Faek is about 5m high and there are two pools in which you can swim. Swimmers should use the one above the falls, as a diabolical-sounding puffer fish known as the

pa pao is believed to lurk in the pool below. Locals report with a sort of gleeful dread how the evil *pa pao* can home in on and sink its razor-sharp teeth into the human penis with uncanny precision. (Admittedly, the women are more gleeful about this than the men.) Tat Faek is about 1.5km off the road; take the right fork after about 500m, then turn left another 800m on.

At Km 16 a long bridge crosses the Se Nam Noi and you enter Attapeu Province. Just south of the bridge a track leads east to **Tat Se Noi**, known locally as 'waterfall of the heads' (Tat Hua Khon) owing to a WWII incident in which Japanese soldiers decapitated a number of Lao soldiers and tossed their heads into the falls. The falls are about 100m wide and 7m deep.

Nam Tok Katamtok

ນ້ຳຕົກກະຕໍ່ຕົກ

All of the above falls are small fry compared with the mighty Nam Tok Katamtok. Running off the Bolaven Plateau, the Huay Katam drops more than 100m out of thick forest at what some describe as Laos's highest waterfall. And while they may or may not be bigger than Tat Fan, these falls are more impressive because you need to be something of an explorer to find them.

Turn west along the laterite road 31km south of Sekong that eventually leads to Paksong, 71km away. There are actually two falls to be seen from this road. The first is after 16km, where if you look off to the north (right) you'll see a large cascade in the distance. Nam Tok Katamtok is about 2km further on. You'll know you're getting near when you cross three bridges and climb a hill, where a 25m-long trail leads back off to the left and out of the jungle appears this spectacular drop. There is no sign and both are easy to miss, so check your odometer and slow down when you get near.

ATTAPEU PROVINCE

Attapeu is the wild east of Laos. It's frontier territory in every sense, with the rugged and densely forested regions bordering Cambodia and Vietnam as well-endowed with wildlife as anywhere in the country. Tigers aren't uncommon and species as rare as the clouded leopard have been seen in the more remote areas.

The province has hosted an important trading route since the Chenla period and Khmer-style brick *prasat* have been found in the jungles near the Vietnam border. During the Lan Xang period the area was known for being rich in gold and forest products. And in the 16th century, it saw the demise of King Saysetthathirat. Historians believe the Lan Xang regent upset the locals and members of his court in Vientiane when, on an expedition to the area, he kidnapped a local woman and hauled her off to Vientiane. After getting her pregnant he returned to Attapeu to settle things down but wound up dead instead. The town of Saisettha is named after him and he is believed to be buried under a nearby stupa (p296).

More recent history is just as violent. Every branch of the Ho Chi Minh Trail ran through Attapeu and the province was heavily bombed during the Second Indochina War. Rare pieces of ordnance are still visible, though most has been carted off for scrap – the missile launcher at Pa-am (p296) being the notable exception.

A new trail, the smooth-sealed Rte 18B to the Vietnam border, has brought Vietnamese back in numbers. In several new guesthouses and restaurants in the pretty provincial capital you'll need to speak Vietnamese to be understood.

Of the 11 ethnic groups found in Attapeu, Lave, Nge and Talieng predominate, with Lao Loum, Chinese and a fast-growing number of Vietnamese concentrated in the capital. There are less than 20 Buddhist temples in the entire province.

ATTAPEU (SAMAKHI XAI)

ຊັດຕະປື

☎ 036 / pop 19,200

Officially known as Muang Samakhi Xai but seldom referred to as such, the capital of Attapeu Province is set in a large valley and flanked by the mountains of the nearby Bolaven Plateau, 1000m above, and the two rivers that meet nearby – the mighty Se Kong and the smaller Se Kaman. Attapeu is famed in Southern Laos as the 'garden village' for its shady lanes and lush flora. While thoroughly deserved, this reputation is all the more remarkable given that Attapeu actually means 'buffalo shit' in Lao. Legend has it that when early Lao Loum people arrived they asked the locals what was the name of their town. In response, the villagers apparently pointed at a nearby pile of buffalo manure, known locally as *itkapu*. There was (hopefully) some misunderstanding, or perhaps the Lao Loum or even the villagers actually didn't like the place. Either way, with some subsequent adjustment in pronunciation, the town became Attapeu.

While Attapeu has little in the way of 'sights' it's not a shitty town. The engaging locals, cheap accommodation and riverside 'sunset' drinking spots make this a good base for exploring the wild east, a job made simpler by the recent completion of a bridge across the Se Kong and Rte 18B (the only street in town that actually has a name) to Vietnam.

Information

Attapeu Office of Tourism (☎ 211056; Provincial Office) On the northwest edge of town this office has guides (usually a staff member), though you'll find better value (less than US$20 per day) asking around town. They do have some brochures and a large-scale map.

Attapeu Travel & Tour (☎ 211204; www.offroad .laopdr.com; Attapeu Palace Hotel) The only English-speaking guide in town is Mr Yae (☎ 020-581 2112), who can arrange and lead any treks, including expeditions to Nong Fa. He also rents 4WD vehicles for US$50 per day, plus petrol.

Internet (Attapeu Palace Hotel; per hr US$6; ☺ 7am-10pm) Only one terminal, in reception. Lao Telecom say optic fibre is coming in 2008...

Lao Development Bank (☺ 9.30am-4pm Mon-Fri) About 500m southeast of the airstrip. Changes US dollars or Thai baht for kip at poor rates.

Lao Telecom (☺ 7am-5pm Mon-Fri)

Post office (☺ 8am-noon & 1-4pm Mon-Fri)

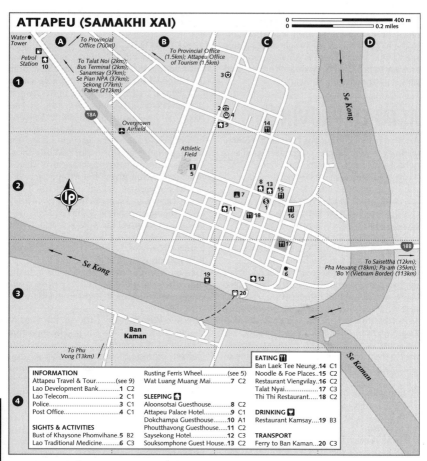

ATTAPEU (SAMAKHI XAI)

INFORMATION
Attapeu Travel & Tour............(see 9)
Lao Development Bank............**1** C2
Lao Telecom............................**2** C1
Police.....................................**3** C1
Post Office..............................**4** C1

SIGHTS & ACTIVITIES
Bust of Khaysone Phomvihane.**5** B2
Lao Traditional Medicine.........**6** C3

Rusting Ferris Wheel..............(see 5)
Wat Luang Muang Mai...........**7** C2

SLEEPING
Aloonsotsai Guesthouse..........**8** C2
Attapeu Palace Hotel..............**9** C1
Dokchampa Guesthouse.........**10** A1
Phoutthavong Guesthouse......**11** C2
Saysekong Hotel....................**12** C3
Souksomphone Guest House..**13** C2

EATING
Ban Laek Tee Neung..**14** C1
Noodle & Foe Places..**15** C2
Restaurant Viengvilay..**16** C2
Talat Nyai.................**17** C3
Thi Thi Restaurant.....**18** C2

DRINKING
Restaurant Kamsay....**19** B3

TRANSPORT
Ferry to Ban Kaman...**20** C3

Sights & Activities

Despite being a largely Lao Loum place, Attapeu town is not renowned for its Buddhist temples. The most interesting is **Wat Luang Muang Mai**, usually known as Wat Luang, which was built in 1939 and features some older monastic buildings with original *naga* bargeboards.

A couple of hundred metres west is an open field with an overgrown **bust of Kaysone Phomvihane** and a diminutive, rusting **Ferris wheel**. The latter will appeal to photographers on weekends, when children can often be seen scrambling all over it.

After a motorbike adventure (motorbikes can be hired from Souksomphone Guest House) sweat out the dust at **Lao Traditional Medicine** (3-7pm Tue & Thu-Sun), which is actually a sauna place. Look for the 'Sauna Open' sign.

Sleeping

You'll probably find several new places have opened to cater to the growing number of Vietnamese traders coming this way.

Souksomphone Guest House (211046; r US$3-7.50;) A block north of Rte 18A, the Souksomphone is the place with the mother-of-all hardwood staircases protruding from the front. The cramped rooms (which come in several varieties) are disappointing by comparison. The manager speaks some English and can arrange motorbike hire (US$10).

SOUTHERN LAOS

Aloonsotsai Guesthouse (☎ 211250; r US$3-9; ❄) Just west of the Souksomphone, this two-storey aquamarine-coloured place has clean rooms to fit a range of budgets. If you can live without air-con and Vietnamese TV the US$4 rooms upstairs are the best value.

Dokchampa Guesthouse (☎ 211061; Rte 18A; r US$5.50-7.50; ❄) A little out of town the atmosphere at the Dokchampa is pretty welcoming and the rooms aren't bad, especially those in the main building which are large and well-equipped for the cost. There's a restaurant out front.

our pick **Phoutthavong Guesthouse** (☎ 020-981 8440; r US$6-8; ❄) This new family-run place is in a wonderfully quiet location down a shaded dirt road south of Rte 18A. Rooms are clean and spacious and come with satellite TV, fan or air-con, and hot water. The best rooms are upstairs overlooking the traditional wooden houses and palm trees opposite.

Attapeu Palace Hotel (☎ 211204; atppalace@yahoo .com; r US$6-27; ❄ ▢) This 44-room monolith two streets north of Rte 18A has the best rooms in Attapeu, even if service can be a little rough. Rooms are mostly spacious and fairly clean, and anything US$12 or above has a fridge, hot water and satellite TV. VIP rooms (US$27) have a bathtub and are big enough to play football in. Breakfast is included in the rates of any room worth US$12 or more. The hotel has Attapeu's only internet connection (US$6 per hour) and is home to Attapeu Travel & Tour (see p293). The restaurant (meals US$2 to US$5.50), however, isn't great.

Saysekong Hotel (☎ 020-240 6844; r US$12; ❄) Looking more like a modern mansion than a hotel, the Saysekong manages to combine river views and well-equipped rooms to make this a reasonable choice if service isn't a major requirement.

Eating & Drinking
Noodle dishes and *fŏe* are available during the morning at **Talat Nyai** (main market), near the bridge, and other snacks can be had at any time. There are cheap noodle and *fŏe* places east of the Souksomphone Guest House, including one that specialises in tasty barbecued pork.

Restaurant Viengvilay (☎ 020-599 4153; meals US$0.50-1.50; ❄ breakfast, lunch & dinner) It might look like a garage, but the precooked food here is delicious and fantastic value at about

US$0.30 per dish, but get here by 7pm or you might miss out.

Restaurant Kamsay (☎ 020-2337594; ❄ lunch & dinner) One of several mainly bamboo places overlooking the Se Kong, Kamsay is mainly about sunset drinking but is also popular for its barbecued goat (US$2 per plate). If you buy the whole beast – they're usually tied up out front praying for a busload of vegetarians – you get to drink its blood for free.

Thi Thi Restaurant (☎ 211303; Rte 18A; meals US$1-3; ❄ breakfast, lunch & dinner) This Vietnamese-run place has, unsurprisingly, decent Vietnamese food but we found the service lacking.

Ban Laek Tee Neung (☎ 020-591 3580; meals US$3-6; ❄ lunch & dinner) This Korean barbeque-style place is uniformly considered the best dining in town. The sukiyaki is good and the various *làap* are mouth-watering. Recommended.

Getting There & Away
BOAT
Attapeu can be reached by boat from Sekong via the Se Kong (p292).

BUS
The Attapeu bus terminal is next to Talat Noi at Km 3 northwest of town. Rte 18A that runs south of the Bolaven Plateau remains impassable to most traffic, so all transport to or from Pakse goes via Sekong and Paksong. A 6am bus goes to Savannakhet (US$6.50, nine to 10 hours) via Pakse, and after that there are four other buses to Pakse (US$3.50, five to six hours, 212km) at 7.30am, 8am, 10am and 11am. You can get off any of these buses at Sekong (US$2, two to 2½ hours, 77km) or Paksong (US$2.50, four to five hours, 162km), and there might be an early afternoon bus that travels to Sekong only, but don't count on it. For Salavan you'll need to head off early, get a bus heading to Paksong, and change at Tha Taeng.

Gluttons for punishment might consider the 8am or 11.30am services which power on through to Vientiane (US$11, 20 to 24 hours, 912km). Most buses servicing Attapeu are older, naturally cooled affairs.

Getting Around
A jumbo trip around town should cost about US$0.20 per person. To/from the bus terminal costs about US$0.40. Bicycles (US$2 per day) and motorbikes (US$10) can be rented from the Attapeu Palace Hotel.

SOUTHERN LAOS

AROUND ATTAPEU

Heading east on Rte 18B brings you to **Saisettha**, a sizable village 12km from Attapeu on the north bank of the Se Kaman. There is an attractive wat in use here and the whole town has a good vibe. Continue about 3km further east, across the Se Kaman (Kaman River) and take a sharp right just beyond Ban Hat Xai Khao. **Pha Meuang**, another 3km along a dirt road, is the main attraction because the Lan Xang king Saysetthathirat is buried here in Wat Pha Saysettha – the stupa under which he is believed to lie is thought to have been built by his son around 1577. Just wandering around the village and wat is fun.

The area southeast of Attapeu was an integral part of the Ho Chi Minh Trail (p251) and as such was heavily bombed during the war. The bombers were particularly interested in the village of **Phu Vong**, 13km southeast of the capital, where two main branches of the trail split – the Sihanouk Trail continuing south into Cambodia and the Ho Chi Minh Trail veering east towards Vietnam. The village is a pleasant diversion for an hour or two, though you won't see much war junk. To get there, cross the Se Kong (US$0.10 each per person and motorbike) to Ban Kaman, then take a *săwngthăew* (US$1, 30 minutes, 13km) to Phu Vong.

Several trekking routes have been established, including some shortish hikes to waterfalls, villages and wats near Attapeu.

Pa-am

ພະອາ

A day-trip to Saisettha could happily be combined with a visit to the modest, tree-shaded village of **Pa-am**. About 35km east of Attapeu, Pa-am straddles both the small Nam Pa (Pa River) and a road that was formerly a branch of the Ho Chi Minh Trail. The main attraction is a Russian **surface-to-air missile** (SAM), complete with Russian and Vietnamese stencilling,

which was set up by the North Vietnamese to defend against aerial attack. It has survived the scrap hunters by government order and, apart from a few cluster bomb casings-cum-planter boxes, there's not much else to see – it's the trip that's most fun. Alak villagers sell textiles and basic meals are available.

When coming from Attapeu you need to cross the Nam Pa to reach the missile launcher. In the dry season you can walk, at other times there is an improvised passenger and motorbike ferry. Pa-am is easily reachable by motorbike; take Rte 18B 10km towards Vietnam and keep straight on the laterite road when the sealed road bends to the right. Otherwise *săwngthăew* run from Attapeu (US$1.20, one hour, 35km) every morning.

Se Pian NPA

ປ່າສະຫງວນແຫ່ງຊາດເຊປ່ຽນ

While **Se Pian NPA** (p2710) is most accessible from Pakse, it's also possible to get into the park from Attapeu. Community-based tourism projects have recently been established and involve village homestays and treks into the eastern reaches of the area. There are one-, two- and three-day treks concentrating on a **Tat Saepha**, **Tat Samongphak** and **Tat Saeponglai**, three impressive waterfalls along branches of the Se Pian. In the rainy season some sections are of the treks are done by boat.

For now, the only English-speaking guide in the province is Mr Yae from Attapeu Travel and Tour (p293). Prices are a bit higher than elsewhere, but having someone to translate for you makes the trip, and the almost mandatory (options are extremely limited) homestay (p48) in the pretty village of **Ban Mai**, much richer.

Another way into this part of the Se Pian NPA is by taking a boat down the Se Kong towards the Cambodian border. If you fancy the road (or river) less travelled, then this might be for you. To do it, take

---

CROSSING THE VIETNAM BORDER AT BO Y

Smooth new Rte 18B runs 113km to the border with Vietnam at Bo Y. The Lao government says 30-day visas should be available here, but they weren't when we checked – we recommend getting your visa in advance. The road and border only opened in mid-2006 and at the time of writing transport details were still fairly sketchy. We could confirm that at least three Vietnamese-run buses were operating each week from Attapeu to Pleiku via Kon Tum (US$10, 12 hours), departing Attapeu at 9am Monday, Wednesday and Friday, coming the other way Tuesday, Thursday and Saturday. Tickets were sold at the Thi Thi Restaurant (p295) in Attapeu. By the time you arrive, expect local buses or *săwngthăew* to be running at least as far as the border.

a *săwngthăew* from the bus terminal in Attapeu to Sanamsay (US$1.20, 75 minutes, 35km) along Rte 18A; *săwngthăew* leave Attapeu at 9am, noon, 2pm and 4pm, and the last one returns at 3pm. In Sanamsay find a boatman to take you to the border (about 30km, four to five hours).

This trip is more about the travel than the destination, so don't expect a pot of gold at the end (or much in the way of services, either; BYO food, water and sun protection). The journey is, however, quite a trip. The river is abutted by deep forest for much of the way and, when we passed, dozens of Chinese dredges were tearing up the river bed in search of gold, at the same time altering navigation channels and fish spawning grounds. Fortunately the government has banned this, so hopefully they will be gone by the time you arrive, though the ugly piles of dirt might not.

To get back to Sanamsay on the same day start early (hiring a jumbo or motorbike from Attapeu might be best). There's no guesthouse in Sanamsay but if you need one someone will find you a bed.

DONG AMPHAM NPA

ປ່າສະຫງວນແຫ່ງຊາດດົງອຳພາມ

Dong Ampham NPA is a 1975-sq-km protected area wedged between the Se Kaman to the north and west, the Vietnamese border to the east and Rte 18B to the south. Timber and wildlife poaching threaten the pristine environment, but wildlife researchers still report that, for now at least, this is one of the most intact ecosystems in the country. Hydroelectric projects on the Se Kaman and Se Su rivers might change this.

In the meantime anyone with a strong constitution and five-to-seven days to spare can take what would be the trip of a lifetime into the protected area and magical **Nong Fa**. This beautiful volcanic lake, similar to but larger than Yaek Lom in Cambodia's Rattanakiri Province, was used by the North Vietnamese as an R and R for soldiers hurt on the Ho Chi Minh Trail. These days it's one of the holy grails of Southeast Asian travel, much talked about by people in the know but very seldom visited.

The trip involves several days walking, staying either in Yae (Ngae) villages or camping in the forest, with a range of birds, deer, gibbons and other wildlife for company. Mr Yae at Attapeu Travel & Tour (p293) is the man to speak with; he charges US$300 for one person, less per person for groups, between November and April only. But get in quick – plans to build a proper road to Nong Fa will probably change it forever.

Directory

CONTENTS

Accommodation	298
Activities	300
Business Hours	301
Children	302
Climate Charts	302
Courses	303
Customs	303
Dangers & Annoyances	303
Embassies & Consulates	305
Festivals & Events	306
Food	307
Gay & Lesbian Travellers	307
Holidays	307
Insurance	307
Internet Access	307
Legal Matters	308
Maps	308
Money	309
Photography & Video	311
Post	312
Shopping	312
Solo Travellers	313
Telephone & Fax	313
Time	314
Toilets	314
Tourist Information	314
Travellers With Disabilities	315
Visas	315
Volunteering	317
Women Travellers	317
Work	318

PRACTICALITIES

- The *Vientiane Times* (www.vientian etimes.org.la), published Monday to Saturday, and the only English-language newspaper permitted in Laos, cleaves to the party line.

- Francophones can read *Le Renovateur*, a government mouthpiece similar to the *Vientiane Times*.

- The LPDR's single radio station, Lao National Radio (LNR), broadcasts sanitised English-language news twice daily.

- Short-wave radios can pick up BBC, VOA, Radio Australia and Radio France International. A good frequency for BBC in the morning is 15360.

- Lao National Television has two TV channels. Programming in Lao is limited so most people watch Thai TV and/or karaoke videos.

- The LPDR uses 220V AC circuitry; power outlets usually feature two-prong round or flat sockets.

- The metric system is used for measurements. Gold and silver are sometimes weighed in *bàat* (15g).

ACCOMMODATION

The range and quality of accommodation in Laos is rapidly improving. That said, once you get off the beaten track (Vientiane, Luang Prabang, Pakse and Vang Vieng) the options are more modest, typically restricted to budget-priced guesthouses and hotels and the occasional midrange offering.

Paying in the requested currency is usually cheaper than letting the hotel or guesthouse convert the price into another currency using their unfavourable (to you, at least) exchange rates. If the price is quoted in kip, you'll do best to pay in kip; if priced in dollars, pay in dollars. Because the kip is a soft, unstable currency, room rates in this book are given in the US dollar equivalent of the kip rates, calculated at 10,000 kip to US$1.

Accommodation prices listed in this book are high-season prices for rooms with attached bathroom, unless stated otherwise. An icon is included to indicate if air-con is available; otherwise, assume that a fan will be provided.

Homestays

Staying in a village home is becoming increasingly popular. Homestays are invariably in rural areas, cheap at about US$5 for your bed, dinner and breakfast, and provide a chance for travellers to experience life, Lao style. For an idea of what to expect, and what not to expect, see Feeling The 'Real Laos', p48.

Guesthouses

The distinction between 'guesthouse', 'hotel' and 'resort' often exists in name only, but legally speaking a guesthouse in Laos has fewer than 16 rooms. They typically occupy large, two-storey homes of recent vintage, but occasionally you'll find them in more historic and charismatic wooden homes. In places such as Don Det (p280) in southern Laos or Muang Ngoi Neua (p163) in northern Laos you'll come across guesthouses consisting of simple bamboo-thatch huts with shared facilities, going for as little as US$1 a night.

Facilities are improving across the country, but the most inexpensive places might still have cold-water showers or simple Lao-style bathing, where you wash yourself using a plastic bowl to scoop cold water from large jars, tanks or even 44-gallon drums. Hot water is hardly a necessity in lowland Laos, but is very welcome in the mountains.

Simple rooms in most towns average between US$3 and US$5 a night with shared bathroom. For an attached bathroom and hot shower expect to pay about US$6 to US$8; anything above this will usually also have air-conditioning and a television, with cable TV in English if you're lucky. Some guesthouses have stepped up the style and offer upscale rooms for between about US$15 and US$30.

Hotels

Hotel rooms in Vientiane, Luang Prabang, Vang Vieng, Savannakhet and Pakse offer private bathrooms and fans as standard features for between US$5 and US$10 per night. There is then a vast range of rooms with air-con, hot water and television costing between about US$8 and US$50, differentiated by their location, the city and the levels of style and service.

Small and medium-size hotels oriented towards Asian business and leisure travellers and tour groups exist in the larger cities. In Vientiane, Luang Prabang and Pakse these may be housed in charming old French colonial mansions. Whether modern or historic, tariffs at hotels such as these run from about US$25 to US$60 for rooms with air-con, hot water, TV and refrigerator.

Then there are the few top-end hotels with better décor, more facilities and personalised service, often occupying more carefully-restored colonial villas or modern, purpose-built buildings. These typically cost between US$50 and US$150, occasionally even higher.

ROOM RATES

In this guide all accommodation is listed by price order, starting at the cheapest, *not* in order of preference. We have divided accommodation by the price of a double room thus:

Budget   less than US$15
Midrange   US$16-50
Top end   more than US$50.

The overall quality of rooms in Laos has improved substantially in recent years but prices remain remarkably reasonable. By Western standards, they're a bargain. It's worth remembering this if you're trying to bargain the price down, particularly at the budget end where competition is fierce and margins are small.

For example, the farmers flogging bamboo bungalows on Don Det aren't making any money on their US$1.50 rooms, they're just hoping you'll buy some food and beer. And in Vang Vieng many rooms are actually cheaper than they were six years ago. Taking this into consideration, and understanding that international economic imperatives like inflation and the price of oil affect Laos as much as they do prices in your own country, room rates will probably go up compared with those listed in this book. When that happens please don't just assume you're being ripped off.

By all means try to get the best rate you can, that's part of travelling. But be aware of the cultural context. Generally speaking, the Lao avoid conflict as much as they possibly can and while they are happy to bargain a little, they don't usually buy into protracted negotiations/arguments over price. If the rate seems unfair to you (as opposed to being beyond your budget) by all means make a counter offer. This will usually be accepted, or not, straight away.

What is common among all hotels in Laos is that the rooms are great value compared with what you'd pay at home. Solid mid-range places, that would cost US$80 or more at home, can be had for US$15 or US$20. And at the top-end boutique luxury, that would cost two or three times as much in Europe, North America or Australia, can be had for US$80.

The trade-off, however, is in the service. Few hotels in Laos have managed to hone their service to Western standards, and English literacy is often frustratingly poor, even in the more expensive hotels. So prepare for lower standards of service than you're used to and you'll be more likely to have a good time.

Resorts

The term 'resort' in the Lao context may be used for any accommodation situated outside towns or cities. It does not imply, as it usually does in many other countries, the availability of sports activities, spa and so on.

Lao resorts typically cost about the same as a mid-range hotel, ie from about US$15 to US$50 a night. A few, such as those outside Luang Prabang, come closer to the international idea of a resort, with prices to match.

ACTIVITIES
Boating

With public boats disappearing from Laos's many waterways, do-it-yourself boating is increasingly the way to see some of Asia's most stunning and untouched wilderness. Rafting, canoeing and kayaking trips are all available, with varying degrees of comfort and cost. Operators in Luang Nam Tha, Luang Prabang, Vang Vieng, Tha Khaek, Pakse and Don Det offer guided rafting and kayaking trips, complete with the necessary equipment, along waterways in those areas.

As with bicycles, you shouldn't have any special customs difficulties bringing your own small boat to Laos. Because of the difficulties of overland transport, however, the smaller and lighter your craft is, the better.

For trained paddlers almost any of the major waterways draining from the western slopes of the Annamite Mountains towards the Mekong valley can be interesting. In the north, the Nam Ou, Nam Tha, Nam Khan, Nam Ngum and of course the Mekong River are navigable year-round. In central and southern Laos the Nam Theun (though not for long), Nam Kading, Nam Hin Bun and Se Kong as well as the Mekong are safe bets. The upstream areas of all these rivers can be accessed by road, so drop-offs and pick-ups are limited only by the availability of transport.

Several tributaries that feed into the Mekong between Vientiane and Tha Khaek are particularly recommended because they see so little boat traffic and run through spectacularly rugged limestone country. In particular the Nam Kading and Nam Hin Bun are wide and relatively clean rivers, though a proposed dam on the Nam Kading might change things there. Upstream put-in spots are limited but possible. If you'd prefer someone else looks after the logistics, both **Green Discovery** (www.greendiscoverylaos.com) and Thailand-based **North-by-Northeast Tours** (www.north-by-north-east.com) offer rafting and kayaking trips in this area.

Several companies and guesthouses on Don Det rent kayaks so it's possible to explore the islands of Si Phan Don this way – though we recommend starting upstream. Rafting is also possible here.

If you want to go local, small wooden canoes can be bought for between US$60 and US$140 without a motor; add from US$50 to US$90 for motors. Small Japanese and cheaper Chinese outboard motors of 5.5HP to 11HP can be purchased in any of the larger cities along the Mekong. These sorts of boats are suitable only for well-navigated waterways as their bulk prohibits portage around shallows or rapids.

Cycling

The overall lack of vehicular traffic makes cycling an attractive proposition in Laos, although this is somewhat offset by the general absence of roads in the first place. Bikes can be hired in the larger towns but they're generally cheap Chinese affairs unsuited to much more than pedalling around town. For any serious out-of-town cycling you're better off bringing your own bike, one that's geared to rough road conditions.

In terms of road gradient and availability of food and accommodation, the easiest long-distance ride is along Rte 13, which extends the entire north–south length of the country from Boten on the Chinese–Lao border south to Voen Kham on the Cambodian border. In the dry season this road may become very dusty even in the paved sections, and trucks – though nowhere near as overwhelming as in Vietnam or Thailand – can be a nuisance.

There are any number of other good cycling routes with less traffic. The various loops described in this book are (usually) just as good on a bicycle as they are on a motorbike, just slower. There's The Southern Swing over the Bolaven Plateau and beyond (p263); the shorter Spin Through Savannakhet (p248); and of course the original The Loop (p240) out of Tha Khaek. In northern Laos heading east along Rte 7 towards the Plain of Jars is a good trip. We wouldn't, however, recommend heading into the former Saisombun Special Zone north of Vientiane on a bicycle as the roads are punishingly steep, lodgings are few and camping is not encouraged at all.

Other cycling routes of interest – several of which remain unpaved – include: Luang Prabang to Muang Khua; Huay Xai to Luang Nam Tha; Thang Beng to Lak Sao; Muang Xai to Phonsavan; and Sam Neua to Phonsavan. The last two routes are quite remote and you might need to camp.

Hiking & Trekking

Trekking through the mountains and forests of Laos is the best way to experience what is one of the most untouched environments in Southeast Asia. Indeed, trekking has become so popular it's almost a mandatory part of any visit to Laos. And thanks to several projects aimed at getting money into poor communities, there are now more than 10 areas you can choose from; for a full rundown, see Where To Trek (p70). Each organised trek is different, but most involve walking through a mix of forest and agricultural land and staying in homes or community guesthouses in remote villages. Prices, including all food, guides, transport, accommodation and park fees, start at about US$20 a day. In most cases you can trek with as few as two people, with per person costs falling the larger the group.

While the cultural side of a trip is limited without some language skills, trekking alone is possible in most of the country. However, doing so in the northeastern provinces and the area formerly known as the Saisombun Special Zone (p129) might attract the attention of local authorities unused to seeing random *falang* wandering about

unguided. Walking off the track in most of eastern Laos can be dangerous given the amount of unexploded ordnance (p305) still lying around.

If you do go it alone and have some language skills or a phrasebook it's often possible to spend the night in a remote village, though do offer to pay for your food and bed.

Finally, you can set off on a day hike from just about any town or village in Laos. Take a hat, sunscreen and plenty of water.

Rock Climbing

The limestone karsts of Laos are perfect for rock climbing and routes have been established at two main sites, near Vang Vieng (p125) and Luang Prabang. Vang Vieng has the most established scene, with dozens of climbs ranging from beginner to very tough indeed. Climbers have compared the routes and guides here favourably with the high-profile climbing at Krabi, in Thailand.

Green Discovery (www.greendiscoverylaos.com) is the main operator and has a good reputation; their website has more detail on equipment, prices and routes.

BUSINESS HOURS

Government offices are typically open from 8am to 11.30am or noon and from 1pm to 5pm Monday to Friday. Some offices may open for a half day on Saturday but this

---

RESTAURANT HOURS

Business hours for restaurants vary according to their clientele and the food they serve.

- Shops selling noodles and/or rice soup are typically open from 7am to 1pm.
- Lao restaurants with a larger menu of dishes served with rice are often open from 10am to 10pm.
- Tourist restaurants offering both Lao and *falang* (Western) food, and open for breakfast, lunch and dinner, usually open their doors around 7.30am and serve till 10pm.
- Tourist restaurants that don't open for breakfast generally serve from 11am to 11pm.

DIRECTORY

custom was generally abandoned in 1998 when the official two-hour lunch break introduced by the French was reduced to one hour. Does this mean you can expect to find Lao officials back in their offices promptly at 1pm? Probably not.

Shops and private businesses open and close a bit later and usually stay open during lunch. On Saturday some businesses are open all day, others only half a day. Most businesses, except restaurants, are closed on Sunday.

For a list of standard business hours see the inside front cover. If hours vary from these, they are stated in the review.

CHILDREN

Like many places in Southeast Asia, travelling with children in Laos can be a lot of fun as long as you come prepared with the right attitudes, physical requirements and the usual parental patience. Lonely Planet's *Travel with Children* by Cathy Lanigan contains useful advice on how to cope with kids on the road and what to bring along to make things go more smoothly.

Practicalities

Amenities geared towards children – such as high chairs in restaurants, child safety seats for vehicles, or nappy-changing facilities in public restrooms – are virtually unknown in Laos. Thus parents will have to be extra resourceful in seeking out substitutes or follow the example of Lao families (which means holding smaller children on their laps much of the time).

Outside of Vientiane day-care centres are likewise unknown, though this is rarely a problem. The Lao adore children and in many instances will shower attention on your offspring, who will readily find playmates among their Lao peers and a temporary nanny service at practically every stop.

Baby formula and nappies (diapers) are available at minimarkets in the larger towns and cities, but for rural areas you'll need to bring along a sufficient supply.

For the most part parents needn't worry too much about health concerns though it pays to lay down a few ground rules – such as regular hand-washing – to head off potential medical problems. All the usual health precautions apply; see p331 for details. Children should especially be warned not to play with animals encountered along the way since rabies is disturbingly common in Laos.

Sights & Activities

Younger children usually don't find the historic temples and French colonial architecture of Luang Prabang and Vientiane as inspiring as their parents do, but travelling with children does tend to give you a different perspective to what you might be used to. The chicken's-eye view of a three-year-old, for example, means they tend to notice all sorts of things at ground level their parents often miss. As long as they don't try to put any of them in their mouths, this is usually no problem.

If boredom does set in, the best cure in Laos is always the outdoors. In Luang Prabang the waterfalls at Tat Sae (p159) and Tat Kuang Si (p159) can amuse most kids for days. Boat trips are usually well-received too.

Most children also take to the unique Hindu-Buddhist sculpture garden of Xieng Khuan (p98) outside Vientiane. The capital also has a few more mainstream activities, such as swimming pools and ten-pin bowling alleys (p99).

Elsewhere, the Plain of Jars (p169) invites the kind of fantasy exploration most kids are prone to.

CLIMATE CHARTS

The annual monsoon cycles that affect all of mainland Southeast Asia produce a 'dry and wet monsoon climate' with three basic seasons for most of Laos. The southwest monsoon arrives in Laos between May and July and lasts into November.

The monsoon is followed by a dry period (from November to May), beginning with lower relative temperatures and cool breezes created by Asia's northeast monsoon (which bypasses most of Laos), lasting until mid-February. Exceptions to this general pattern include Xieng Khuang, Hua Phan and Phongsali Provinces, which may receive rainfall coming from Vietnam and China during the months of April and May.

Rainfall varies substantially according to latitude and altitude, with the highlands of Vientiane, Bolikhamsai, Khammuan and eastern Champasak Provinces receiving the most.

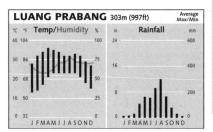

Temperatures also vary according to altitude. In the humid, low-lying Mekong River valley, temperatures range from 15°C to 38°C, while the mountains of Xieng Khuang it can drop to 0°C at night. See p17 for comment on the best times to travel in Laos.

COURSES
Cooking
Lao cooking courses are available in Luang Prabang (p147) and Vientiane (p101).

Language
Short-term courses in spoken and written Lao can be arranged in the following study centres in Vientiane. The courses are not regular so contacting the centres in advance is recommended.

Centre Culturel et de Coopération Linguistique (Map p92; ☎ 021-215764; www.ambafrance-laos.org; Th Lan Xang)

Lao-American College (☎ 021-900454; lacf@laotel.com; Th Phonkheng, Saysettha)

Vientiane College (☎ 021-414873; vtcollege@laopdr.com; Th That Luang) Opposite the WHO office.

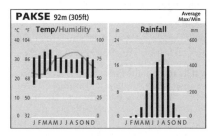

Meditation
If you can speak Lao or Thai, or can arrange an interpreter, you may be able to study *vipassana* (insight meditation) at Wat Sok Pa Luang (p101) in Vientiane.

CUSTOMS
Customs inspections at ports of entry are lax as long as you're not bringing in more than a moderate amount of luggage. You're not supposed to enter the country with more than 500 cigarettes or 1L of distilled spirits. All the usual prohibitions on drugs, weapons and pornography apply, otherwise you can bring in practically anything you want, including unlimited sums of Lao and foreign currency.

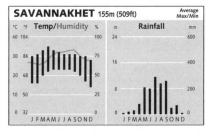

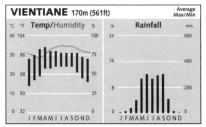

DANGERS & ANNOYANCES
Over the last 15 years or so Laos has earned a reputation among visitors as a remarkably safe place to travel, with little crime reported and few of the scams so often found in more touristed places such as Vietnam, Cambodia and Thailand. And while the vast majority of Laotians remain honest and welcoming, things aren't quite as idyllic as they once were. The main change has been in the rise

of petty crime, such as theft and low-level scams, which are more annoying than actually dangerous.

That's not to say Laos is danger free. However, most dangers are easy enough to avoid.

Queues
The Lao follow the usual Southeast Asian method of queuing for services, which is to

say they don't form a line at all but simply push en masse towards the point of distribution, whether at ticket counters, post-office windows or bus doors. It won't help to get angry and shout 'I was here first!' since first-come, first-served simply isn't the way things are done here. Rather it's 'first-seen, first-served'. Learn to play the game the Lao way, by pushing your money, passport, letters or whatever to the front of the crowd as best you can. Eventually you'll get through.

Road Travel

Better roads, better vehicles and fewer insurgents mean road travel in Laos is quite safe, if not always comfortable. It's not yet possible to totally rule out the threat from armed bandits or insurgents, though it is miniscule. And while the scarcity of traffic in Laos means there are far, far fewer accidents than the daily horror on Vietnam's roads, accidents are still the major risk to travellers.

ARMED ATTACK

With the Hmong insurgency virtually finished, travel along Rtes 7 and 13, particularly in the vicinity of Muang Phu Khun and Kasi, is as safe as it has been for decades. There have been no reported attacks on traffic for more than two years. However, you might still have an armed soldier on your bus, just to make sure. If you're still nervous – and it's true that two Swiss cyclists were murdered during an ambush on Rte 13 in 2004 – ask around in Vientiane or Luang Prabang to make sure the situation remains secure before travelling along Rte 7 to Phonsavan or Rte 13 between Vang Vieng and Luang Prabang.

ACCIDENTS

After speedboats, and assuming you'll not be walking through any minefields, the law of averages suggests travelling by road is probably the most dangerous activity in Laos. Having said that, there are relatively few reports of bus crashes and the like, and the lack of traffic and quality of roads makes collisions less likely too.

When riding in buses, you may be able to cut your risk of serious injuries if you choose an aisle seat towards the middle of the bus; these are generally more comfortable too. If you can't get an aisle seat, the right side is usually safer as it cuts down the risks in the event your conveyance is side-swiped by oncoming traffic. It's worth carrying on your person the number of your embassy in Vientiane and the number of **Aek Udorn Hospital** (☎ 0 4234 2555) in Udon Thani, Thailand, to call for help if necessary.

MOTORBIKES

As motorbikes become increasingly popular among travellers so the number of accidents rises. Ambassadors in Vientiane were not aware of any fatalities when we passed, but it's only a matter of time. More likely is the chance of earning yourself a Lao version of the 'Thai tattoo' – that scar on the inner right calf caused by a run-in with a hot exhaust pipe. For tips on motorbiking, see p328.

Speedboats

The speedboats that careen along the Mekong and Nam Ou rivers in northern Laos are as dangerous as they are fast. We recommend that you avoid all speedboat travel unless absolutely necessary. For details see p219.

Theft

While Lao are generally trustworthy people and theft is much less common than elsewhere in Southeast Asia, it has risen in recent years. Most of the reports we've heard involve opportunistic acts that, if you are aware of them, are fairly easily avoided.

Money or goods going missing from hotel rooms is becoming more common, so don't leave cash or other tempting items (such as women's cosmetics) out on show. If you ride a crowded bus, watch your luggage and don't keep money in your trouser pockets. If you ride a bicycle or motorcycle in Vientiane, don't place anything of value in the basket – thieving duos on motorbikes have been known to ride by and snatch bags from baskets. Also in Vientiane, we've had several reports of (usually) women having daypacks stolen after they've changed money near the BCEL bank on the riverfront – be especially careful around here.

Other reports involve theft on buses between Vientiane and Luang Prabang, and on the slow boat between Huay Xai and Luang Prabang. Simple locks on your bags are usually enough to discourage the light-fingered.

UXO

Large areas of eastern Laos are contaminated by unexploded ordnance (UXO) left behind by nearly 100 years of warfare. Despite heavy US bombing late in the Indochina War, the majority of UXO found today was left behind by ground battles and includes French, Chinese, American, Russian and Vietnamese materials, among them mortar shells, munitions, white phosphorus canisters, land mines and cluster bombs. US-made cluster bombs (known as *bombi* to the Lao) pose by far the greatest potential danger to people living in or travelling through these areas and account for most of the casualties. The Lao National UXO Programme (UXO Lao) reported 164 casualties in 2005, of which 54% were children and 36 people died. These statistics come only from the districts where UXO Lao is working; real figures are believed to be higher. Large bombs up to 500kg dropped by US aircraft also lie undetonated in some areas, but it's very rare that one of these is accidentally detonated.

According to surveys by UXO Lao and other non-government UXO clearance organisations, the provinces of Salavan, Savannakhet and Xieng Khuang fall into a category of most severely affected provinces, followed by Champasak, Hua Phan, Khammuan, Luang Prabang, Attapeu and Sekong.

Statistically speaking, the UXO risk for the average foreign visitor is low, but travellers should exercise caution when considering off-road wilderness travel in the aforementioned provinces. Put simply, if you walk where other people have walked you should be OK. Never touch an object that may be UXO, no matter how old and defunct it may appear.

EMBASSIES & CONSULATES
Lao Embassies & Consulates

Australia Canberra (☎ 02-6286 4595; lao .embassy@interact.net.au; 1 Dalman Cres, O'Malley, Canberra, ACT 2606)

Cambodia Phnom Penh (☎ 023-982632; fax 720907; 15-17 Mao Tse Tung Blvd, Phnom Penh)

China Beijing (☎ 010-6532 1224; fax 6532 6748; 11 Dongsie Jie, Sanlitun, Chao Yang, Beijing 100600); Kunming (☎ 0871-317 6624; fax 317 8556; Rm 3226, Camelia Hotel, 154 E Dong Feng Rd, 650041, Kunming)

France Paris (☎ 01 45 53 02 98; www.laoparis.com; 74 Ave Raymond Poincaré, 75116 Paris)

GOVERNMENT TRAVEL WARNINGS

Most governments have travel advisory services detailing potential pitfalls and areas to avoid, including:
Australia (www.smartraveller.gov.au)
Canada (www.voyage.gc.ca)
New Zealand (www.safetravel.govt.nz)
UK (www.fco.gov.uk)
US (www.travel.state.gov)

Germany Berlin (☎ 0 30 890 606 47; fax 890 606 48; Bismarckallee 2A; 14193 Berlin)

Hong Kong (☎ 0852 2544 1186; 14th floor, Arion Commercial Centre, 2-12 Queen's Road West, Sheung Wan)

Japan Tokyo (☎ 35 411 2291; 3-3-22 Nishi Azabe, Minato-Ku)

Myanmar Yangon (Burma; ☎ 01-222482; fax 227446; A1 Diplomatic Headquarters, Tawwin (Fraser) Rd, Yangon)

Thailand Bangkok (☎ 0 2539 6667; fax 0 2539 6678; www.bkklaoembassy.com; 520, 502/1-3 Soi Ramkhamhaeng 39, Th Pracha Uthit, Wangthonglang, Bangkok 10310); Khon Kaen (☎ 043 223473; fax 223849; 19/1-3 Th Phothisan, Khon Kaen)

USA New York (☎ 212-832 2734; fax 750 0039; 317 E 51st St, New York, NY 10022); Washington, DC (☎ 202-332 6416; fax 332 4923; www.laoembassy.com; 2222 S St NW, Washington, DC 20008)

Vietnam Danang (☎ 051-821208; fax 822628; 12 Tran Quy-Cap, Danang); Hanoi (☎ 04-942 4576; fax 822 8414; 22 Tran Binh Trong, Hanoi); Ho Chi Minh City (☎ 08-829 7667; fax 829 9272; 181 Haiba Trung, Ho Chi Minh City)

Embassies & Consulates in Laos

Of the 75 or so nations that have diplomatic relations with Laos, around 25 maintain embassies and consulates in Vientiane. Many of the remainder, for example Canada and the UK, are served by their embassies in Bangkok, Hanoi or Beijing. Opening hours for the embassies of neighbouring countries with valid border crossings are given here.

Principal consular offices in Vientiane (area code ☎ 021):

Australia (Map pp88-9; ☎ 413600; www.laos.embassy .gov.au; Th Nehru, Ban Phonxai) Also looks after nationals of Britain, Canada and New Zealand. The Australian embassy is set to move to Th Tha Deua, just past the Australian Club at Km 4, during the life of this book.

Cambodia (Map pp88-9; ☎ 314952; fax 314951; Km 3, Th Tha Deua, Ban That Khao; ☼ 7.30-11am & 2-5pm Mon-Fri) Issues visas for US$20.

China (Map pp88–9; ☎ 315105; fax 315104; Th Wat Nak Nyai, Ban Wat Nak; ☒ 9–11.30am Mon–Fri) Issues visas in four working days.

France (Map p92; ☎ 215258, 215259; www
.ambafrance-laos.org; Th Setthathirat, Ban Si Saket)

Germany (Map pp88–9; ☎ 312111, 312110; Th Sok Pa Luang)

Myanmar (Burma; Map pp88–9; ☎ 314910; Th Sok Pa Luang; ☒ 8.30am–noon & 1–4.30pm Mon–Fri) Issues tourist visas in three days for US$20.

Thailand Embassy (Map pp88–9; ☎ 900238; www
.thaiembassy.org/vientiane; Th Phonkheng; ☒ 8.30am–noon & 1–3.30pm Mon–Fri) Consulate (Map pp88–9; Th That Luang; h8am–noon & 1–4.30pm) Come here for visa renewals, extensions etc.

USA (Map p92; ☎ 267000; http://vientiane/usembassy
.gov; Th That Dam (Th Bartholomie))

Vietnam (Map pp88–9; ☎ 413400; Th That Luang; ☒ 8–11.30am & 1–4.30pm Mon–Fri) Issues tourist visas in three working days for US$50, or in one day for US$55.

FESTIVALS & EVENTS

Festivals in Laos are mostly linked to agricultural seasons or Buddhist holidays. The word for festival in Lao is *bun* (or *boun*). Most of festival dates change according to the lunar calendar, though even these are not set in stone and some festivals are celebrated at different times depending on where you are. All of this makes advance planning difficult. The government tourism website (www.tourismlaos.gov.la) has more details and lists the current year's dates for the larger celebrations.

JANUARY
International New Year (1–3 January) Public holiday.

Bun Khun Khao (mid-January) The annual harvest festival sees villagers perform ceremonies offering thanks to the land spirits for allowing their crops to flourish.

FEBRUARY
Makha Busa (Magha Puja or Bun Khao Chi, Full Moon) This commemorates a speech given by the Buddha to 1250 enlightened monks who came to hear him without prior summons. Chanting and offerings mark the festival, culminating in candlelit circumambulation of wats throughout the country. Celebrations in Vientiane and at Wat Phu (p268) are most fervent.

Vietnamese Tet & Chinese New Year (Tut Jiin) Celebrated in Vientiane, Pakse and Savannakhet with parties, fireworks and visits to Vietnamese and Chinese temples. Chinese- and Vietnamese-run businesses usually close for three days.

MARCH
Bun Pha Wet This is a temple-centred festival in which the Jataka or birth-tale of Prince Vessantara, the Buddha's penultimate life, is recited. This is also a favoured time (second to Khao Phansa) for Lao males to be ordained into the monkhood. Bun Pha Wet is celebrated on different days in different villages so relatives and friends from different villages can invite one another to their respective celebrations.

APRIL
Bun Pi Mai (Lao New Year, 14–16 April) Practically the whole country celebrates the Lao new year. Houses are cleaned, people put on new clothes and Buddha images are washed with lustral water. In wats, you'll see fruit and flower offerings at altars and votive mounds of sand or stone in the courtyards. Later, people douse one another and sometimes random tourists with water, which is an appropriate activity as April is usually the hottest month of the year. This festival is particularly picturesque in Luang Prabang (see p141), where it includes elephant processions and lots of traditional costuming. The 14th, 15th and 16th of April are public holidays.

MAY
Visakha Busa (Visakha Puja, Full Moon) This falls on the 15th day of the sixth lunar month, which is considered the day of the Buddha's birth, enlightenment and *parinibbana* (passing away). Activities are centred on the wat, with much chanting, sermonising and, at night, beautiful candlelit processions.

Bun Bang Fai (Rocket Festival) This is a pre-Buddhist rain ceremony now celebrated alongside Visakha Busa in Laos and northeastern Thailand. It can be one of the wildest festivals in the whole country, with music, dance and folk theatre (especially the irreverent *mǎw lám* performances), processions and general merrymaking, all culminating in the firing of bamboo rockets into the sky. The firing of the rockets is supposed to prompt the heavens to initiate the rainy season and bring much-needed water to the rice fields. Dates vary from village to village.

JULY
Bun Khao Phansa (Khao Watsa, Full Moon) This is the beginning of the traditional three-month 'rains retreat', during which Buddhist monks are expected to station themselves in a single monastery. At other times of year they are allowed to travel from wat to wat or simply to wander the countryside, but during the rainy season they forego the wandering so as not to damage fields of rice or other crops. This is also the traditional time of year for men to enter the monkhood temporarily, hence many ordinations take place.

AUGUST/SEPTEMBER

Haw Khao Padap Din (Full Moon) This sombre festival sees the living pay respect to the dead. Many cremations take place – bones being exhumed for the purpose – and gifts are presented to the Buddhist order (Sangha) so monks will chant on behalf of the deceased.

OCTOBER/NOVEMBER

Bun Awk Phansa (Ok Watsa, Full Moon) At the end of the three-month rains retreat, monks can leave the monasteries to travel and are presented with robes, alms-bowls and other requisites of the renunciate life. The eve of Awk Phansa is celebrated with parties and, near any river, with the release of small banana-leaf boats carrying candles and incense in a ceremony called Van Loi Heua Fai, similar to Loy Krathong in Thailand.

Bun Nam (Bun suang héua; Boat Racing Festival) In many river towns, including Vientiane and Luang Prabang, boat races are held the day after Awk Phansa. In smaller towns the races are often postponed until National Day (2 December) so residents aren't saddled with two costly festivals in two months.

NOVEMBER

Bun Pha That Luang (That Luang Festival, Full Moon) Centred around Pha That Luang in Vientiane, this increasingly commercial celebration lasts a week and includes fireworks, music and drinking across the capital. There is also a procession between Pha That Luang and Wat Si Muang. Early on the first morning hundreds of monks receive alms and floral offerings. The festival ends with a fantastic candlelit procession circling That Luang.

DECEMBER

Lao National Day (2 December) This public holiday celebrates the 1975 victory over the monarchy with parades, speeches etc. Lao national and Communist hammer-and-sickle flags are flown all over the country. Celebration is mandatory, hence many poorer communities postpone some of the traditional Awk Phansa activities until National Day, saving themselves considerable expense (much to the detriment of Awk Phansa).

FOOD

Virtually all restaurants in Laos are inexpensive by international standards, hence we haven't divided them into Budget, Mid-Range and Top End categories.

See the Food & Drink chapter, p74 for thorough descriptions of the cuisine and the kinds of restaurants in Laos.

GAY & LESBIAN TRAVELLERS

For the most part Lao culture is very tolerant of homosexuality, although lesbianism is often either denied completely ('Lao women don't do that, why would they?' men have been heard to say) or misunderstood. The gay and lesbian scene is not nearly as prominent as in neighbouring Thailand, though it's progressively more open. Strictly speaking, homosexuality is illegal, though we haven't heard of police busting anyone in recent years. In any case, public displays of affection – whether heterosexual or homosexual – are frowned upon.

HOLIDAYS
Public Holidays

Schools and government offices are closed on these official holidays, and the organs of state move pretty slowly, if at all, during the festivals mentioned on opposite.

International New Year (1 January)

Army Day (20 January)

International Women's Day (8 March) For women only.

Lao New Year (14-16 April)

International Labour Day (1 May)

International Children's Day (1 June)

Lao National Day (2 December)

INSURANCE

As always, a good travel insurance policy is a wise idea. Laos is generally considered a high-risk area, and with medical services so limited it's vital to have a policy that covers being evacuated (Medivaced), by air if necessary, to a hospital in Thailand. Read the small print in any policy to see if hazardous activities are covered; rock-climbing, rafting and motorcycling often are not.

If you undergo medical treatment in Laos or Thailand, be sure to collect all receipts and copies of the medical report, in English if possible, for your insurance company.

See p331 for recommendations on health insurance, and p329 for vehicle insurance.

INTERNET ACCESS

The days in which most Lao people thought the internet was some sort of new-fangled fishing device are fast disappearing. Internet cafés are popping up fast, and you can get online in most, but not all, provincial capitals. Generally speaking, if tourists go there in numbers, someone will have established a connection.

In places where there's plenty of competition – such as Vientiane and Luang Prabang – rates are usually very low, about US$0.50 to

US$1 an hour. In towns where there are only one or two places offering such services, or where they need to call long-distance to reach the server, rates will be higher; between US$3 and US$6 an hour. Broadband is spreading across the country and speeds are usually pretty fast; though in the sticks they can be excruciatingly slow.

Computers in most internet cafés have messenging software such as Yahoo! and MSN Messenger loaded and increasingly Skype, though you might need to search around for a headset.

If you're travelling with a laptop, internet cafés usually allow you to plug into their bandwidth for the same cost as using a fixed computer. To get online in your hotel you'll probably need to be in a newer mid-range or top-end hotel. Some cafés in Vientiane, Luang Prabang and Vang Vieng have wi-fi. The other option is to buy a dial-up card from minimarts in Vientiane, or from some internet cafés in the provinces, and use it in your hotel room. The only problem with this is that outside of better midrange and top-end hotels, telephones in rooms are about as rare as rocking-horse shit.

LEGAL MATTERS

Revolutionary Laos established its first national legal code in 1988, followed by a constitution two years later – the reverse order of how it's usually done. Although on paper certain rights are guaranteed, the reality is that you can be fined, detained or deported for any reason at any time, as has been demonstrated repeatedly in cases involving everything from a foreigner marrying a Lao national without government permission, to running a business that competes too efficiently with someone who has high government connections.

Your only consolation is that it's usually much worse for locals, and Lao officials generally don't come after foreigners for petty, concocted offences. In most cases you must truly have committed a crime to find yourself in trouble with the law. However, as documented by Amnesty International (and corroborated by local expats), you could easily find yourself railroaded through the system without any legal representation.

If you stay away from anything you know to be illegal, you should be fine. If not, things might get messy – and expensive. Drug possession (see p122) and using prostitutes are the most common crimes for which travellers are caught, often with the dealer or consort being the one to inform the authorities (and later take a cut of any 'action' you might be forced to cough up).

If you are detained, ask to call your embassy or consulate in Laos, if there is one. A meeting or phone call between Lao officers and someone from your embassy/consulate can result in quicker adjudication and release, though unless you are genuinely innocent (as opposed to having been set up) the diplomats can do little and will probably advise you to just cough up the cash.

Police sometimes hint at bribes for traffic violations and other petty offences. In such cases the police typically offer a choice along the lines of 'Would you like to come down to the station to pay your fine, or would you like to take care of it here and now?' Presented with such a choice, it's up to you whether to expedite matters by paying a bribe, or fight corruption in Laos by doing things by the book.

The legal age for voting and driving in Laos is 18.

Sexual Relationships

Sexual relationships between foreigners and Lao citizens who are not married are illegal. Permission for marriage or engagement to a Lao citizen must be submitted in a formal application to Lao authorities. Penalties for failing to register a relationship range from US$500 to US$5000, and possibly imprisonment or deportation. Catching men in the act, or just witnessing them leaving a bar with a working girl, is a favourite excuse of the authorities for deporting *falang* they don't like.

Otherwise, the age of consent for sexual relations in Laos is 15.

MAPS

Good maps of Laos are difficult to find. The best all-purpose country map available is GT-Rider.com's *Laos*, a sturdy laminated affair with a scale of 1:1,400,000. It's available at bookshops in Thailand and at many guesthouses in Laos, as well as online at www.gt-rider.com. At the time of research the latest edition was published in 2005. The **Reise Know-How** (www.reise-know-how.com) map also gets very good reports, though it's almost impossible to find outside Germany.

The **National Geographic Service** (NGS; Map pp88–9; Kom Phaen Thi Haeng Saat in Lao, or Service Géographique National in French; ⏱ 8-11.30am, 1-4.30pm Mon-Fri) has a series of adequate maps of Laos and certain provincial capitals. These can be purchased direct from the National Geographic Service, which is on a side street to the northwest of the Patuxai in Vientiane.

Detailed topographic sheet maps labelled in English and French and often seen on the walls of government offices are based on Soviet satellite photography from the early 1980s. The National Geographic Service has many of these maps and will usually sell them to foreigners even though they're marked *En Secret*. However, place names are often incorrect and roadways not up to date.

The NGS' 1:500,000-scale topographicals number 11 in all, although they're not all available. Other topographical maps in the series decrease in scale to as low as 1:10,000, but anything below the 1:100,000 scale maps (for which it takes 176 to cover the whole country) is overkill unless you plan to drill for oil. Furthermore the NGS usually won't sell maps of 1:100,000 or less to foreigners unless they bring a written request on company letterhead – or get a Lao friend to make the purchase for them. For all maps produced in Laos, including rare city maps, the lowest prices are available through the NGS.

Chiang Mai-based Hobo Maps has produced a series of good, if often excessively large, maps of Vientiane, Luang Prabang and Vang Vieng. These are available in book shops and some hotels in the relevant destinations. The Lao National Tourism Administration (LNTA) has also produced a few city maps in recent years, though actually finding one is only marginally more likely than winning the lottery.

Map collectors or war historians may find American military maps from 1965 – now rather rare though they may still be available from the Defense Mapping Agency in the US – of some interest. These maps seem fairly accurate for topographic detail but are woefully out of date with regard to road placement and village names. The same goes for the USA's highly touted Tactical Pilotage Charts, prepared specifically for air travel over Laos and virtually useless for modern ground navigation.

MONEY

The official national currency in Laos is the Lao kip (LAK). Although only kip is legally negotiable in everyday transactions, in reality three currencies are used for commerce: kip, Thai baht (B) and US dollars (US$). In larger cities and towns, baht and US dollars are readily acceptable at most businesses, including hotels, restaurants and shops.

In smaller towns and villages, kip is usually preferred. The rule of thumb is that for everyday small purchases, prices are quoted in kip. More expensive goods and services (eg long-distance boat hire) may be quoted in baht or dollars, while anything costing US$100 or more (eg tours, long-term car hire) is quoted in US dollars.

Despite experiencing relative stability in recent years, the kip cannot yet call itself a stable currency. As such, prices in this guidebook are given in the US dollar equivalent.

The Lao kip is not convertible to any currency outside of the Lao PDR. Because of this, the only reliable sources of foreign exchange information are those inside the country.

See p17 for an idea of the costs involved in travelling in Laos.

ATMs

Travellers on their last kip have been giving thanks that ATMs have made a tentative landing in Laos. But before you get overexcited, the ATMs are only in Vientiane and dispense a maximum of 700,000 kip (about US$70) a time, with each withdrawal incurring a US$2 fee from BCEL. If, like most of us, you also have to pay extortionate charges to your home bank on each overseas withdrawal, that doesn't work out so well. So taking your plastic into the bank itself might still work out cheaper; see right.

At the time of research ATMs dispensed cash – in Lao kip – to Visa and MasterCard accounts only, despite stickers promising access to Cirrus and Plus accounts. This might change, but don't count on it. We met one traveller who had to go to Thailand to access his cash – an expensive diversion when you consider he needed to get a new visa to come back.

Banking

Foreign residents of Laos can open US dollar, baht or kip accounts at several banks in Vientiane, including branches of six Thai banks. Unfortunately, if you already have an account at a Thailand-based branch of a Thai bank, you won't be permitted to withdraw any money in Laos; you must open a new account. Alternatively, expatriates living in Vientiane use Thai banks across the river in Nong Khai because interest rates are higher and more banking services are available.

Black Market

There is no real black market in Laos and unless there's an economic crash that's unlikely to change. Unlicensed moneychangers can be found in larger towns, and sometimes offer marginally better rates, but it's hardly worth seeking them out unless you're changing enough cash to fill a wheelbarrow (admittedly, that's not as hard as it sounds in Laos).

Cash

Laos relies heavily on the Thai baht and the US dollar for the domestic cash economy. An estimated one-third of all cash circulating in Vientiane, in fact, bears the portrait of the Thai king, while another third celebrates US presidents.

However, the vast majority of transactions will be carried out in kip, so it's always worth having a wad in your pocket. Kip notes come in denominations of 500, 1000, 2000, 5000, 10,000, 20,000 and the recently printed 50,000 kip. Small vendors, especially in rural areas, will struggle to change the 20,000 kip and 50,000 kip notes – some we met had never even seen a 50,000 kip note. Also, both of these larger notes are red, so watch you don't go handing out 50,000 kip notes thinking they're 20,000 kip.

For larger transactions the dollar and the baht are favoured. They also make carrying money less of a hassle; five 1000 baht notes – about US$135 worth – are quite a bit easier to carry than 135 10,000-kip notes. If you plan on making frequent transactions of over US$20, you can save luggage space by carrying most of your cash in baht and/or dollars, along with smaller amounts of kip.

Once you leave Laos no-one – except perhaps other travellers on their way into Laos – will want your kip, so spend it before you go.

Credit Cards

A growing number of hotels, upmarket restaurants and gift shops in Vientiane and Luang Prabang accept Visa and MasterCard, and to a much lesser extent Amex and JCB. Outside of these three towns, credit cards are virtually useless.

Banque pour le Commerce Extérieur Lao (BCEL; *thanáakháan kạan khâa taang páthêht láo* in Lao) branches in Vientiane, Luang Prabang, Vang Vieng, Savannakhet and Pakse offer cash advances/withdrawals on Visa credit/debit cards for a 3% transaction fee. Other banks may have slightly different charges, so if you're in Vientiane (where there are options) it might be worth shopping around. Advances/withdrawals can be made in Lao kip only – it's not possible to withdraw US dollars or Thai baht.

Exchanging Money

After years of volatility the kip has in recent times remained fairly stable at about 10,000 to the US dollar. Don't, however, count on this remaining the same.

Exchange rates are usually virtually the same whether you're changing at a bank or a moneychanger. Both are also likely to offer a marginally better rate for larger bills (US$50 and US$100) than smaller bills (US$20 and less). Banks also tend to offer better rates for travellers cheques, though the whole process of exchange is much more protracted. Banks in Vientiane and Luang Prabang can change UK pounds, Euros, Canadian, US and Australian dollars, Thai baht and Japanese yen. Elsewhere most provincial banks change only US dollars or baht, though you might get lucky.

The best overall exchange rates are those offered at the BCEL. Lao Development Bank has similar rates.

Licensed moneychangers maintain booths around Vientiane (including at Talat Sao) and at some border crossings. Their rates are similar to the banks and they stay open longer.

It can sometimes be difficult to change travellers cheques because the bank won't have enough kip, especially in more remote provinces, so check that the bank can cover your cheques before you sign. Hence organising your stash of cash before you leave a big town is highly recommended. If you plan on carrying US dollars or baht, stock up before you arrive in Laos. If you want to buy these currencies in Laos head to a market in a larger town or city, ask around for a money changer and don't expect great rates.

Exchange rates at upcountry banks tend to be slightly lower than what you'd get in Vientiane, despite the fact that the national bank mandates a single daily rate for all government banks. For the latest rates from BCEL, check www.bcellaos.com. For a list of exchange rates as we went to press see the inside front cover.

Tipping
Tipping is not customary in Laos except in upmarket restaurants where 10% of the bill is appreciated – but only if a service charge hasn't already been added.

Travellers Cheques
Travellers cheques can be cashed at most banks in Laos, but normally only in exchange for kip. Cheques in US dollars are the most readily acceptable, and in fact outside Vientiane they might be the only cheques accepted. Very few merchants accept travellers cheques.

PHOTOGRAPHY & VIDEO
Laos is a fantastic destination for photography and if you take the following into account there is no reason why you won't come away with some great shots – without upsetting anyone.

Digital photography is spreading fast and, particularly in popular tourist centres such as Vientiane, Luang Prabang, Vang Vieng and Pakse, the usual range of batteries, memory cards and even a limited range of cameras are available.

There are still plenty of old-school film cameras around, and Fuji and Kodak colour print films in ASA 100 or 200 are available in larger towns. A few of the better photo shops in Vientiane and Luang Prabang carry slide film, typically Ektachrome Elite or Fujichrome Sensia. For B&W film or other slide film stock up in Bangkok, where film is relatively cheap, before you come to Laos. Processing is inexpensive.

Most internet cafes have card readers and can write photos to either CD or DVD for about US$1 or US$2.

Photographing People
In rural areas people are often not used to having their photos taken, so smile and ask permission before snapping away. In tribal areas *always* ask permission before photographing people or religious totems; photography of people is taboo among several tribes. Breaking such taboos might not seem like a big deal to you, but it is to your subject. See Sleeping with Spirits (p249) for details.

Use discretion when photographing villagers anywhere in the country, and think before you shoot.

Restrictions
Lao officials are sensitive about photography of airports and military installations; when in doubt, refrain, and if you get stopped be as apologetic and dumb-tourist as you can be.

Technical Tips
As in other tropical countries, the best times of day for photography are early to mid-morning and late afternoon. A polarising filter is helpful for cutting glare and improving contrast, especially when photographing temple ruins or shooting over water.

Moisture is the biggest threat to your gear so during the rainy season (from June to October) pack some silica gel with your camera to prevent mould growing inside the lenses. Also always carry a plastic bag, at least, to keep your gear dry when the heavens open.

The wet season isn't all bad. The skies are clearer and the greens of the forest are much brighter, compared with the hot season (March to May) when you'll often find a layer of dust damping down the colours and adding glare to the skies.

Outside major cities and towns electricity is not always available. This is a problem if you need to recharge batteries, so be sure to pack enough and keep them charged. Standard camera batteries are readily available in big towns but you'll be lucky to find them out in the sticks, so carry all you'll need.

Lonely Planet's *Travel Photography* contains tips on how to get the most out of your camera.

Video
Blank videotapes in popular formats, including DV, are readily available for sale in Vientiane and Luang Prabang, and to a lesser extent in Savannakhet, Pakse and a few other provincial capitals.

DIRECTORY

POST

Sending post from Laos is not all that expensive and is fairly reliable, but people still tend to wait until they get to Thailand to send parcels. If you're heading to Cambodia, you're better off posting your parcels from Laos.

When posting any package you must leave it open for inspection by a postal officer. Incoming parcels might also need to be opened for inspection; there may be a small charge for this mandatory 'service'.

Waiting for mail to arrive, however, is not as certain, especially for packages. The main post office (p90) in Vientiane has a poste restante service. To send something here address it:

Person's Name
Post Restante
Vientiane
Lao PDR

Note that there is no home mail-delivery service in Laos; you need to rent a post-office box. Throughout the country you can recognise post offices by the colour scheme: mustard yellow with white trim. See inside front cover for opening hours.

SHOPPING

Shopping in Laos is improving fast. The growth in tourist numbers has been matched, if not exceeded, by the number of stores flogging fabrics, handicrafts and regional favourites from Vietnam and Thailand. Vientiane and Luang Prabang are the main shopping centres and in these cities it's easiest to compare quality and price. It is, however, always nice to buy direct from the producer, and in many villages that's possible.

There is a *total* ban on the export of antiques and Buddha images from Laos, though the enforcement of this ban is slack.

Bargaining

Bargaining is a tradition introduced by early Arab and Indian traders, however, in most places in Laos it's not nearly as aggressive as in other parts of Southeast Asia. Good bargaining, which takes practice, is one way to cut costs. Most things bought in a market should be bargained for and it can't hurt to try in a shop, though increasingly prices are fixed.

In general the Lao are gentle and very scrupulous in their bargaining practices. A fair price is usually arrived at quickly with little attempt to gouge the buyer (tour operators may be an exception to this rule). The amount they come down is usually less than what you see in neighbouring countries. Laos definitely has a 'two-tier pricing system' when it comes to quoting prices to foreigners, but it's nowhere near as evident as in Vietnam.

What is really important here is to remember that a good bargain is where both the buyer and the vendor end up happy. By all means try to get a fair price. But if you find yourself getting hot under the collar over 1000 kip (about US$0.10) it's time to take a reality check. In this instance both you and the seller lose face and everyone ends up unhappy. In a country as cheap as Laos, it's just not worth it.

Antiques

Vientiane, Luang Prabang and Savannakhet each have a sprinkling of antique shops. Anything that looks old could be up for sale in these shops, including Asian pottery (especially porcelain from the Ming dynasty of China), old jewellery, clothes, carved wood, musical instruments, coins and bronze statuettes. Because of the government's lax enforcement of the ban on the export of antiques, due to an overall lack of funds and personnel, you might be tempted to buy these objects. However, bear in mind not only that it is illegal to take them out of the country but that if you do so you will be robbing the country of its precious and limited heritage. For more on the fight against antiquity theft in Southeast Asia, see www.heritagewatch.org.

Carvings

The Lao produce well-crafted carvings in wood, bone and stone. Subjects include anything from Hindu or Buddhist mythology to themes from everyday life. Authentic opium pipes can be found, especially in the north, and sometimes have intricately carved bone or bamboo shafts, along with engraved ceramic bowls. The selection, though, gets smaller every year.

To shop for carvings, look in antique or handicraft stores. Don't buy anything made from ivory; quite apart from the elephant slaughter caused by the ivory trade, many countries will confiscate any ivory items found in your luggage.

Fabric (Textiles)

Textiles are among the most beautiful, most recognisable and easiest items to buy while you're in Laos. Together with a hanger that was once part of a loom, these can look great on a wall at home and, unlike many handicrafts that are ubiquitous throughout Indochina, these are unmistakably Lao.

Silk and cotton fabrics are woven in many different styles according to the geographic provenance and ethnicity of the weavers. Although Lao textiles do have similarities with other Southeast Asian textiles, Lao weaving techniques are unique in both loom design and weaving styles, generating fabrics that are very recognisably Lao.

Generally speaking, the fabrics of the north feature a mix of solid colours with complex geometric patterns – stripes, diamonds, zigzags, animal and plant shapes – usually in the form of a *phàa nung* or *sin* (a women's wraparound skirt). Sometimes gold or silver thread is woven in along the borders. Another form the cloth takes is the *phàa bjang*, a narrow Lao-Thai shawl that men and women wear singly or in pairs over the shoulders during weddings and festivals.

The southern weaving styles are often marked by the *mat-mii* technique, which involves 'tie-dyeing' the threads before weaving. The result is a soft, spotted pattern similar to Indonesian ikat. *Mat-mii* cloth can be used for different types of clothing or for wall-hangings. Among Lao Thoeng and Mon-Khmer communities in the southern provinces there is a *mat-mii* weaving tradition which features pictographic story lines, sometimes with a few Khmer words, numerals or other non-representational symbols woven into the pattern. In Sekong and Attapeu Provinces some fabrics mix beadwork with weaving and embroidery.

Among the Hmong and Mien tribes, square pieces of cloth are embroidered and quilted to produce strikingly colourful fabrics in apparently abstract patterns that contain ritual meanings. In Hmong these are called *pandau* (flower cloth). Some larger quilts feature scenes that represent village life, including both animal and human figures.

Many tribes among the Lao Soung and Lao Thoeng groups produce woven shoulder bags in the Austro-Thai and Tibetan-Burmese traditions, like those seen all across the mountains of South Asia and Southeast Asia. In Laos, these are called *nyaam*. Among the most popular *nyaam* nowadays are those made with older pieces of fabric from 'antique' *phàa nung* or from pieces of hill-tribe clothing. Vientiane's Talat Sao (Morning Market; Map p92) is one of the best places to shop for this kind of accessory.

The best place to buy fabric is in the weaving villages themselves, where you can watch how it's made and get 'wholesale' prices. Failing this, you can find a decent selection and reasonable prices at open markets in provincial towns, including Vientiane's Talat Sao. Tailor shops and handicraft stores generally charge more and quality is variable. In Vientiane and Luang Prabang several stores are dedicated to high-quality textiles, with high prices to match.

Jewellery

Gold and silver jewellery are good buys in Laos, although you must search hard for well-made pieces. Some of the best silverwork is done by the hill tribes. Gems are also sometimes available, but you can get better prices in Thailand.

SOLO TRAVELLERS

Travelling alone in Laos is very common among both men and women. Lone women should exercise the usual caution when in remote areas or out late at night (see p317).

TELEPHONE & FAX

Laos has come a long way in a short time on the telephone front. While most Lao people are still not connected, the introduction of mobile phones and, in recent years, WIN phones has allowed some truly remote villages to get connected without the need for expensive landlines.

You can make international calls from Lao Telecom offices in most provincial capitals, or if there is no Lao Telecom office, from the post office, which is usually nearby. Operators cannot place collect calls or reverse phone charges – you must pay for the call in cash kip when it is completed. A faded list of rates is usually stuck on a wall near the phone. Where a separate phone office exists, hours typically run from 7.30am to 9.30pm or from 8am to 10pm.

International calls are also charged on a per-minute basis, with a minimum charge of three minutes. Calls to most countries cost between about US$0.75 and US$1.80 per minute.

It's almost always cheaper to use an internet café (most provide international call services), if there is one. In Vientiane the telephone office has responded to competition from the internet by slashing rates to about 20c a minute. Faxes can be sent from the same Lao Telecom or post offices.

Mobile Phone

Laos has bought into mobile telephony big time. Lao Telecom and several private companies offer mobile phone services on the GSM system. Competition is fierce and you can buy a local SIM card for US$5 from almost anywhere – we bought ours from an optometry shop. Calls are cheap and recharge cards are widely available for between 15,000 and 60,000 kip each.

Network coverage varies depending on the company and the region. In our experience, Lao Telecom and another government-affiliated company, Enterprise of Telecommunications Lao (ETL), have the widest coverage. These are more expensive than Tango Lao and M-Phone, but Tango's coverage is limited to larger cities and towns.

In some areas (such as Si Phan Don where M-Phone reigns supreme), one company is so dominant that it can be hard to find recharge cards for other companies. So if you really need to make that call, buy ahead. Note that international SMS messages from Lao SIM cards often don't work.

Phone Codes

Until a few years ago most cities in Laos could only be reached through a Vientiane operator. These days you can direct-dial to and from most of the country using IDD technology.

The country code for calling Laos is ☎ 856. For long-distance calls within the country, dial ☎ 0 first, then the area code and number. For international calls dial ☎ 00 first, then the country code, area code and number.

All mobile phones have a ☎ 020 code at the beginning of the number. Similar to this are WIN phones, which begin with ☎ 030. See the inside front cover and under regional headings for area codes inside Laos.

Phonecards

In theory, Tholakham Lao (Lao Telecom), a private company, issues telephone cards *(bát thóhlasáp)* to be used in special card phone booths. In reality, they don't. These phones have been superseded by mobile phones and no-one uses them anymore; we saw two that had been converted into greenhouses.

TIME

Laos is seven hours ahead of GMT/UTC. Thus, noon in Vientiane is 10pm the previous day in San Francisco, 1am in New York, 5am in London, 1pm in Perth and 3pm in Sydney. There is no daylight saving (summer) time.

TOILETS

While Western-style 'thrones' are now found in most mid-range and top-end accommodation, if you're a budget traveller expect the rather-less-royal 'squat toilet' to be the norm. Whether you consider squat toilets an inconvenience, anatomically healthy or part of 'the real Laos', there's really no cause for alarm – they're not that bad.

Instead of trying to approximate a chair or stool like a modern sit-down toilet, a traditional Asian toilet sits more or less flush with the surface of the floor, with two footpads on either side of the porcelain abyss. Next to the typical squat toilet is a bucket or cement reservoir from which water is scooped using a plastic bowl. Firstly, toilet-goers use the scoop and water to clean their nether regions while still squatting over the toilet. Secondly, a couple of extra scoops are poured into the toilet basin to flush the waste away. The more rustic toilets in rural areas may simply consist of a few planks over a hole in the ground.

Even in places where sit-down toilets are installed, the plumbing may not be designed to take toilet paper. In such cases there will usually be a rubbish bin for the used toilet paper.

Public toilets are uncommon outside hotel lobbies and airports. While you are on the road between towns and villages it's perfectly acceptable to go behind a tree or use the roadside.

TOURIST INFORMATION

For years a visit to the Lao National Tourism Administration (LNTA) was little more than a waste of time, with a brochure or two to prove you wasted it. But things have changed. While it's still not up to the standards of map-crazy neighbours like Thailand, the LNTA now has offices in Vientiane and Luang Prabang that are well worth visiting, plus three very good websites that offer valuable pre-departure information:

Central Laos Trekking (www.trekkingcentrallaos.com)
Lao Ecotourism (www.ecotourismlaos.com)
Lao National Tourism Administration
(www.tourismlaos.gov.la)

Many offices are now well-stocked with brochures, maps (usually), house easily understood displays of their provincial attractions and employ English-speaking staff to answer your questions. Fantastic! The offices in Tha Khaek, Savannakhet, Pakse, Luang Nam Tha, Sainyabuli, Phongsali and Sam Neua are all excellent, with staff trained to promote treks and other activities in their provinces and able to hand out brochures and first-hand knowledge about them. They should also be able to help with local transport options and bookings.

However, change hasn't reached everywhere. All provincial capitals have an LNTA office but English is often rudimentary and the lack of information can be profound; in some cases visiting such an office might even be more hindrance than help. If you find the local LNTA officials to be unhelpful, you can usually get up-to-date information from a busy guesthouse (if there is one).

TRAVELLERS WITH DISABILITIES

With its lack of paved roads or footpaths (sidewalks) – even when present the latter are often uneven – Laos presents many physical obstacles for people with mobility impairments. Rarely do public buildings feature ramps or other access points for wheelchairs, nor do most hotels make efforts to provide access for the physically disabled, the few exceptions being in the top end. Hence you're pretty much left to your own resources. Public transport is particularly crowded and difficult, even for the fully ambulatory.

For wheelchair users, any trip to Laos will require a good deal of advance planning. Fortunately a growing network of information sources can put you in touch with those who may have wheeled through Laos before. International organisations with information on travel for the mobility-impaired include:

Access-Able Travel Source (www.access-able.com)
Accessible Journeys (☎ 610-521 0339; www
.disabilitytravel.com)
Mobility International USA (☎ 541-343 1284; www
.miusa.org)
Society for the Accessible Travel & Hospitality
(☎ 212-447 7284; www.sath.org)

VISAS

Getting into Laos is easier than ever and travellers from many countries can get 30-day tourist visas at most border points (see box p316).

TOURIST VISA (VISA ON ARRIVAL)

Having finally realised that people will stay for longer if they get a longer visa to start with, the Lao government now issues 30-day tourist visas on arrival at several official international border crossings and at the international airports at Vientiane, Luang Prabang and Pakse.

The whole process is dead easy. You need between US$30 and US$42 cash or the equivalent in Thai baht (travellers cheques and other currencies, including Lao kip, are not accepted); one passport-size photo of yourself; and the name of a hotel you will be staying at (pick any one from this guidebook). In theory you need the name of a contact in Laos but it's OK to leave that section blank. For airport arrivals you're also supposed to possess a valid return air ticket, but we've never heard of anyone who's actually been asked to show it.

The fee varies depending on what passport you're carrying, with Canadians having to fork out the most (US$42), and most others at US$30 or US$35. Moneychangers at these places are unlikely to be able to give you dollars in exchange for Thai baht or any other currency, so be sure to bring enough. We've seen several travellers get stuck in airport limbo because they arrived without cash to pay for their visas. In such cases the immigration officers may allow you to go into town and try to get dollars from another source. They will, however, keep your passport at the airport in the meantime. The 30-day visa is extendible, though not indefinitely (see below).

As easy as all this sounds it doesn't always go exactly to plan. We've met travellers who were only able to get a 15-day visa at a point where we'd been granted 30 days just a week before. All you can do is check that the visa is 30 days, and if not ask them why.

VISITOR VISA

If you're coming from Cambodia you'll need (for now at least) to obtain your visa in advance. In this case, the Lao embassy in Phnom Penh issues 30-day visitor visas (B3) in 24 hours for the same cost as a visa on arrival.

This visa is also what you'll get at any other Lao embassy or consulate if you don't want to wait for a visa on arrival, or are not eligible for one. In Bangkok you can get your visa in a couple of hours for an additional 200B express fee. The visitor visa is extendible up to two months.

NONIMMIGRANT & BUSINESS VISAS

A person who has a short-term professional or volunteer assignment in Laos is generally issued a nonimmigrant visa good for 30 days and extendible for another 30 days. As with the visitor visa, the application fee is around US$35.

Journalists can apply for the journalist visa, which has the same restrictions and validity as the nonimmigrant and visit visas except that the applicant must also fill in a biographical form.

Business visas, also good for 30 days, are relatively easy to obtain as long as you have a sponsoring agency in Laos. Many brokers in Vientiane (and a few in Thailand) can arrange such visas with one to two weeks notice. Business visas can be extended from month to month indefinitely, but you will need a visa broker or travel agency to handle the extensions. After the first month's extension, the business visa can be converted to multiple-entry status. Six-month business visas are also available.

While nonimmigrant and business visas may be collected in one's home country, the Lao embassy in Bangkok is a better place to pick them up. Simply make sure that your sponsoring agency in Laos sends a confirmation fax to the Bangkok embassy; if you can present the fax date to the embassy it can find your fax and then issue your visa sooner.

VISA EXTENSIONS

Getting an extension on a tourist visa is easy. Go to the **Immigration Office** (Map p92; ☎ 212250; Th Hatsady; ☉ 8am-4.30pm Mon-Fri), in the Ministry of Public Security building opposite Talat Sao in Vientiane, fill out a form, supply your passport, a photo and pay US$2 per day for the extra time you want. The whole process can be completed in one hour.

The downside is that you can only do it in Vientiane. Elsewhere, agencies and guesthouses can organise extensions, usually for about US$3 to US$4 per day. It will take a couple of days – the further you are from Vientiane, the longer it takes. You can't extend your visa indefinitely, and the Immigration office itself will suggest you cross to Thailand and come back with a new

---

VISA ON ARRIVAL – PORTS OF ENTRY

At the time of writing, these were the ports of entry where tourist visas were available on arrival. You can cross the border in other places (such as Voen Kham from Cambodia) but it's not yet possible to get a visa on arrival; see p321 for a full list of border posts.

Thailand

- Chiang Khong/Huay Xai (p218)
- Nong Khai/Vientiane (p115)
- Nakhon Phanom/Tha Khaek (p238)
- Mukdahan/Savannakhet (p247)
- Chong Mek/Vang Tao (p261)

Vietnam

- Nam Can/Nam Khan (p172)
- Cau Treo/Nam Phao (p234)
- Lao Bao/Dansavanh (p250)

China

- Mohan/Boten (p201)

visa if you try to extend longer than about 15 days.

Nonimmigrant visas, journalist visas and business visas have to be extended through the sponsoring person or organisation.

OVERSTAYING YOUR VISA

Overstaying your visa is not seen as a major crime but it is expensive. You'll have to pay a fine of US$10 for each day you've overstayed at the immigration checkpoint when you leave. Simple as that.

VOLUNTEERING

Volunteers have been working in Laos for years, usually on one- or two-year contracts that include a minimal monthly allowance. The volunteer is often placed with a government agency and attempts to 'build capacity'. These sort of jobs can lead to non-volunteer work within the non-government organisation (NGO) community.

The alternative approach to volunteering, where you actually pay to be placed in a 'volunteer' role for a few weeks or months, has yet to arrive in Laos in any great capacity. A couple of groups in Luang Prabang (p146) and Nong Khiaw (p160) need volunteers occasionally.

Check out these agencies for more information:

Australian Volunteers International (www.ozvol .org.au) Places qualified Australian residents on one- to two-year contracts.

Earthwatch (www.earthwatch.org) Places paying volunteers in short-term environmental projects around the globe.

Global Volunteers (www.globalvolunteers.org) Coordinates teams of volunteers on short-term humanitarian and economic development projects.

United Nations Volunteers (www.unv.org) Places volunteers with qualifications and experience in a range of fields.

Volunteer Service Abroad (www.vsa.org.nz) Organises professional contracts for New Zealanders.

Voluntary Service Overseas (VSO) UK (www.vso.org .uk); Canada (www.vsocanada.org); Netherlands (www.vso .nl) Places qualified and experienced volunteers for up to two years.

WOMEN TRAVELLERS

Laos is an easy country for women travellers, though you still need to be sensitive to a set of cultural mores that hasn't been watered down as much as in many parts of Thailand. Laos is very safe (see p303) and violence against women travellers is extremely rare. And while everyday incidents of sexual harassment are more common than they were a few years ago, they're still much less frequent than in virtually any other Asian country.

The relative lack of prostitution in Laos, as compared with Thailand, has benefits for women travellers. While a Thai woman who wants to preserve a 'proper' image often won't associate with foreign males for fear of being perceived as a prostitute, in Laos this is not the case. Hence a foreign woman seen drinking in a café or restaurant is not usually perceived as being 'loose' or available as she might be in Thailand. This in turn means that there are generally fewer problems with uninvited male solicitations.

That, however, is not an absolute. Lao women rarely travel alone, so a foreign female without company might be judged by Lao – male and female – as being a bit strange. And while this is less prevalent in the larger towns and cities where society is generally more permissive, in rural areas Lao men might see a woman travelling alone as a woman who wants company. Generally, though, if your bus or *săwngthăew* has other women on board, you shouldn't have any problems.

The best way to avoid unwanted attention is to avoid overly revealing clothes. It's highly unusual for most women (even in more modern places like Vientiane and Vang Vieng where they're used to seeing tourists), to wear singlet tops or very short skirts or shorts. So when travellers do, people tend to stare. Being stared at isn't much fun for the traveller, but if you try putting yourself in their shoes it's easier to understand…relatively speaking, if a woman walked down Oxford St in London or Broadway in New York wearing nothing but a bikini, people would look.

Lao people will almost never confront you about what you're wearing, but that doesn't mean they don't care. As one woman in Vang Vieng told us: 'I wouldn't say anything, but I'd prefer it if they put on a sarong when they get out of the river. It's not our way to dress like that [a bikini only] and it's embarrassing to see it.' It's good advice – if you're planning on bathing in a village or river a sarong is essential.

Elsewhere, just keep your eyes open and dress in a way that's not too different from women around you. This doesn't mean you need to get wrapped up in a *sin*, but you'll notice that shirts with at least a tiny strip of sleeve are universally popular, as are shorts or skirts that come to somewhere near the knee. Show this small measure of respect for Lao culture, and it will be repaid in kind.

Traditionally women didn't sit on the rooves of riverboats, because this was believed to bring bad luck. These days most captains aren't so concerned, but if you are asked to get off the roof while men are not, this is why.

WORK

With a large number of aid organisations and a fast-growing international business community, especially in energy and mining, the number of jobs available to foreigners is increasing, but still relatively small. The greatest number of positions are in Vientiane.

Possibilities include teaching English privately or at one of the several language centres in Vientiane, work which pays about US$5 to US$10 an hour. Certificates or degrees in English teaching aren't absolutely necessary, but they do help.

If you have technical expertise or international volunteer experience, you might be able to find work with a UN-related programme or an NGO providing foreign aid or technical assistance to Laos. These jobs are difficult to find; your best bet is to visit the Vientiane offices of each organisation and inquire about personnel needs and vacancies, then start seeking out potential employers socially and buying them lots of Beerlao. For a list of NGOs operating in Laos, see the excellent www.directoryofngos.org.

Once you have a sponsoring employer to look after the paperwork, a working visa should be ready in a few days.

Transport

CONTENTS

Getting There & Away 319
Air 319
Border Crossings 321
Getting Around 323
Bicycle 324
Boat 325
Bus, Săwngthăew & Lot Doi Saan 326
Car & Motorcycle 326
Hitching 329
Local Transport 329
Tours 330

THINGS CHANGE...

The information in this chapter is particularly vulnerable to change. Check directly with the airline or a travel agent to make sure you understand how a fare (and the ticket you may buy) works and be aware of the security requirements for international travel. Shop carefully. The details given in this chapter should be regarded as pointers and are not a substitute for your own careful, up-to-date research.

Transport infrastructure in Laos is barely recognisable considering what existed a few years ago. Huge, foreign-funded road construction projects have transformed the network of rough dirt tracks into relatively luxurious sealed affairs. The lack of potholes has ushered in a battalion of buses and scheduled services, and getting around Laos is easy and cheap, if sometimes very slow.

Many travellers are choosing to come and go via Laos's numerous land and river borders, something we've acknowledged in this book by giving detailed descriptions of all border crossings that were open to foreigners when we researched this edition. While there are many border options, flying into Laos is refreshing in that you don't need to shop around much – only a few airlines service Laos and prices don't vary much.

GETTING THERE & AWAY

ENTERING LAOS

It's possible to enter Laos by land or air from Thailand, Cambodia, Vietnam or China. Land borders are often remote and the travelling can be tough either side, but the actual frontier crossing is usually pretty simple.

Passport

The only real prerequisites for entering Laos are a passport with six months' validity

and a visa if you are crossing at one of the few borders where you can't get a visa on arrival, such as the Cambodian border at Voen Kham.

AIR
Airports & Airlines

There are only three international airports in Laos. **Wattay International Airport** (VTE; ☎ 021-512165) in Vientiane; **Luang Prabang International Airport** (LPQ; ☎ 071-212856) and **Pakse International Airport** (PKZ; ☎ 031-212844). Lao Airlines is the national carrier and monopolises the majority of flights in and out of the country, though many code-share with some of the following:

Bangkok Airways (☎ 071-253334; www.bangkokair.com; hub Bangkok, Thailand) Code PG.
China Eastern Airlines (☎ 021-212300; www.chinaeastern.com; hub Kunming, China) Code MU.
Lao Airlines (☎ 021-212051–4; www.laoairlines.com; hub Vientiane) Code QV.
Thai Airways International (THAI; ☎ 021-222527; www.thaiair.com; hub Bangkok, Thailand) Code TG.
Vietnam Airlines (☎ 021-217562; www.vietnamairlines.com; hub Ho Chi Minh City, Vietnam) Code VN.

Tickets

Unless you're in a country bordering Laos, your first mission is to find a flight to Bangkok. Luckily there are plenty of flights to the Thai capital, but fares fluctuate sharply. Generally, you'll pay less but it will take longer if you fly to Bangkok with a stop on the way. For example, if you're flying from the UK you'll probably get a better deal with airlines such as Gulf Air, Emirates, Singapore Airlines, Garuda or, for those on the breadline, Biman Bangladesh – all of which involve a stop in the airline's home city – than you would on a direct flight with British Airways or Thai International Airways (THAI). Once you're in Bangkok, there are trains, planes and buses heading to Laos.

Asia

Almost any travel agency in Asia can book you a flight to Laos. STA Travel is always a safe bet, and has branches in **Bangkok** (☎ 02-236 0262; www.sta travel.co.th), **Singapore** (☎ 6737 7188; www.statravel.com.sg) and **Japan** (☎ 03 5391 2922; www.statravel.co.jp) among others. In Hong Kong try **Concorde Travel** (☎ 2375 2232; www.concorde-travel.com).

The only flights directly into Laos come from the following four countries – all prices listed are for one-way flights.

CAMBODIA
Phnom Penh

Between Phnom Penh and Vientiane (US$145, 1½ hours) there are two flights a week with Lao Airlines (stopping in Pakse) and a daily direct flight with Vietnam Airlines.

Siem Reap

Lao Airlines flies between Siem Reap and Vientiane (US$110, 2½ hours) five times a week, stopping at Pakse (US$70, 50 minutes). From November to March there are two more flights between Siem Reap and Pakse that continue to Luang Prabang (US$135). Bangkok Airways should also be flying between Pakse and Siem Reap by the time you read this.

CHINA
Kunming

Lao Airlines shares three services a week between Kunming and Vientiane (US$120, 2½ hours) with China Eastern Airlines.

THAILAND
Bangkok

THAI has one flight daily between Bangkok and Vientiane (about 5000B, 70 minutes), while Lao Airlines has two flights in each direction (US$99); discounts are available on THAI.

> **DEPARTURE TAX**
>
> The international departure tax is US$15, payable in kip, baht or US dollars.

Some people save money by flying from Bangkok to Udon Thani in Thailand and then carrying on by road to Nong Khai, over the Friendship Bridge to Vientiane (p115). Udon Thani is 55km south of Nong Khai and Bangkok–Udon tickets on Thai Air Asia (www .airasia.com) start at about 1300B.

Bangkok Airways flies daily between Bangkok and Luang Prabang (5000B, 1¾ hours), and Lao Airlines has three flights a week for US$120.

Bangkok Airways should be flying between Bangkok and Pakse by the time you read this.

Chiang Mai

Lao Airlines has five flights a week between Vientiane and Chiang Mai (US$111, 2½ hours), via Luang Prabang (US$85, one hour).

VIETNAM
Hanoi

There are 10 flights a week between Vientiane and Hanoi – three on Lao Airlines (US$115, one hour) and the rest on Vietnam Airlines for slightly more. Lao Airlines also flies between Hanoi and Luang Prabang (US$112, one hour).

Ho Chi Minh City

Vietnam Airlines flies from Ho Chi Minh City to Vientiane (US$140, three hours) daily, via Phnom Penh.

Australia

Qantas, THAI, British Airways and several other airlines fly to Bangkok from Sydney, Melbourne and Perth, with discount fares starting at about A$900 return (once you've added in all the taxes). For online bookings also check www.travel.com.au.

Flight Centre (☎ 133 133; www.flightcentre.com.au)
STA Travel (☎ 1300 733 035; www.statravel.com.au)

Canada

Fares from Canada are similar to those from the US. **Travel Cuts** (☎ 866-246 9762; www.travel cuts.com) is Canada's national student travel agency. Also try **Travelocity** (www.travelocity.ca).

Continental Europe

Europeans can pick up discounted seats from about €550. Middle Eastern airlines are usually cheapest. The following agents are worth a look:

Lastminute (www.lastminute.com) Click through to various national sites.

Nouvelles Frontières (☎ 0825-000 747; www .nouvelles-frontieres.fr)

OTU Voyages (☎ 01-5582 3232; www.otu.fr) Specialising in student and youth travellers.

STA Travel (☎ 01805-456 422; www.statravel.de)

Voyages Wasteels (www.wasteels.fr)

New Zealand

Both **Flight Centre** (☎ 0800-243 544; www.flightcentre .co.nz) and **STA Travel** (☎ 0800-474 400; www.statravel .co.nz) have branches throughout the country. Low season fares start at NZ$1250.

The UK

It's not hard to find a bargain from London to Bangkok, with discount prices starting at about £350. Gulf Air, Emirates, KLM and Lufthansa are worth looking at. Check the weekend broadsheet newspapers, *Time Out*, the *Evening Standard* and *TNT* magazine for offers.

Recommended agencies:

North-South Travel (☎ 01245-608 291; www .northsouthtravel.co.uk) Donates some profit to projects in the developing world.

STA Travel (☎ 0871-230 0040; www.statravel.co.uk)

Trailfinders (☎ 0845-058 5858; www.trailfinders.co.uk)

Travel Bag (☎ 0870-814 4441; toll free 0800 082 5000; www.travelbag.co.uk)

The USA

Fares from New York to Bangkok range widely, with the cheapest (via places like Moscow) starting at about US$850 return in the low season. From Los Angeles it's cheaper, and more direct, with airlines like Philippine Airlines, China Airlines, Eva Air and American Airlines. Nondiscounted fares are several hundred dollars more. The following are good for online comparisons and bookings:

Cheapflights.com (www.cheapflights.com)

Cheap Tickets (www.cheaptickets.com)

Expedia (www.expedia.com)

Orbitz (www.orbitz.com)

STA Travel (www.sta.com)

Travelocity (www.travelocity.com)

BORDER CROSSINGS

Laos shares land and/or river borders with Thailand, Myanmar, Cambodia, China and Vietnam; see the colour map at the start of this guide for their locations.

In this book we give detailed instructions for every crossing open to foreigners. These details appear as boxed texts in the relevant chapters – the information in this chapter outlines these possibilities and points you to the boxes. Border details change regularly, so ask around or check the **Thorntree** (http://thorntree .lonelyplanet.com/) before setting off.

Most crossings involve changing transport at the border, even when you've paid for a 'direct' bus. Five of the crossings on the western border with Thailand involve quick boat trips across the Mekong.

It's possible to bring your own vehicle into Laos from Thailand, Vietnam and Cambodia with the right paperwork (see p323) and Lao customs don't object to visitors bringing bicycles into the country.

In Thailand, trains (www.railway.co.th /english) run to the Thai-Lao Friendship Bridge (see p115) and to Ubon Ratchathani, two to three hours from the Lao border (see p261).

Unless stated otherwise, Laos issues 30-day tourist visas (see p315) at crossings that are open to foreigners.

Cambodia

The border with Cambodia at Voen Kham is open and while it's possible to get a Cambodian visa on arrival, for now you need to get your Laos visa in advance. There are two border points, one for road crossings and the other for boats to Stung Treng. See p283 for more information.

China

You can cross between Yunnan Province in China and Luang Nam Tha Province in Laos at Boten. From Mohan on the Chinese side it's a two- to three-hour minibus ride to Mengla, the nearest large town. See p201 for more information.

Myanmar

Foreigners are not allowed to cross between Laos and Myanmar. However, with a valid visa you could try to cross at Xieng Kok, on the Mekong north of Huay Xai, though success is far from guaranteed.

Thailand

There are seven crossings to Thailand open to foreigners. Several involve taking a boat across the Mekong, or crossing the river on one of the Friendship bridges. Borders here are listed from north to south.

HUAY XAI & CHIANG KHONG

Crossing to or from northern Thailand at Huay Xai on the Laos side of the Mekong and Chiang Khong on the Thai side (p218) is popular with travellers coming from northern Thailand. This is the starting point for two-day boat trips to Luang Prabang.

THE FRIENDSHIP BRIDGE AT NONG KHAI (FOR VIENTIANE)

The Thai-Lao Friendship Bridge (p115) is 22km east of Vientiane. There are direct buses between downtown Vientiane and Nong Khai, and regular runs between Nong Khai and Bangkok.

Rapid and express trains from Bangkok's Hualamphong train station run daily to Nong Khai (11 to 14 hours). Overnight trains have sleeper carriages and make a convenient, comfortable and cheap way to get to the border while saving on a hotel room. Berths costs from 488B to 1217B; costs are higher when booked through an agent in Laos.

Plans to extend the rail line over the Friendship Bridge and 3km into Laos have been approved, so it might be possible to catch the train from the Laos side sometime in 2008.

PAKSAN & BEUNG KAN

This river crossing (p229) between Beung Kan in Thailand and Paksan in Laos, about 120km from Vientiane, is rarely used by travellers.

THA KHAEK & NAKHON PHANOM

Another river crossing (p238) takes you from Nakhon Phanom in Thailand to Tha Khaek in Laos. Travellers who use this border are often crossing directly between Thailand and Vietnam.

SAVANNAKHET & MUKDAHAN

This is the southernmost river crossing (p247) between Thailand and Laos. A bridge across the Mekong River near Savannakhet was opened in late 2006, giving travellers the option of a road or river crossing.

VANG TAO & CHONG MEK

This border (p261) 44km west of Pakse is a popular and easy entry into southern Laos. Rapid and express trains from Bangkok's Hualamphong train station run three or four times per day to Ubon Ratchathani (sleeping berths 471B to 1180B, 12 hours, 575km), from where it's three or four hours to Pakse by local transport, or faster on the Thai-Lao International Bus.

Vietnam

At the time of writing foreigners could cross between Laos and Vietnam at six different border posts. Laos issues 30-day tourist visas at most of these, but you'll need to get your Vietnamese visa in advance (see p305). The border at Sop Hun in Phongsali Province, just across from Tay Trang (32km west of Dien Bien Phu), has been going to open for years but is still firmly shut. Keep your eyes on the Thorn Tree for the latest. These borders are listed from north to south.

NA MAEW & NAM XOI

For now, the northernmost crossing is on Rte 6A between Na Maew in Hua Phan Province, Laos, and Nam Xoi in Thanh Hoa Province, Vietnam. This crossing (p188) can be difficult on both sides, especially given how expensive the infrequent transport on the Vietnam side is. It is, however, the nearest border to Hanoi and the north, so if you're adventurous and want to avoid backtracking, it's worth a shot. Na Maew is a relatively short bus ride to/from Sam Neua, where there are buses and planes to other points in Laos. No visas are issued here.

NAM CAN & NAM KHAN

This border (p172) east of Phonsavan in Xieng Khuang Province sounds better than it actually is. Even though you're a long way north of the Kaew Neua Pass crossing, the road on the Vietnam side runs so far south (almost to Vinh) before joining north–south Hwy 1 that this border is totally inconvenient.

NAM PHAO & CAU TREO

The spectacular crossing (p234) through the Kaew Neua Pass, via the low-key border posts of Nam Phao on the Lao side, and Cau Treo in Vietnam, leads to Vinh and all points north, including Hanoi. Direct buses

VIETNAM BORDER WOES

If we had a Beerlao for every email we've received from travellers who've been scammed while crossing the border between Vietnam and Laos, we'd be able to have a very big party. There are several different scams you might encounter, and plenty of lies you'll be told that won't necessarily cost you money but will most certainly piss you off.

Among the most common is the '12-hour' bus between Vientiane and Hanoi, which is in fact a 20- to 24-hour trip including several hours spent waiting for the border to open. Once across the border (mainly at Nam Phao/Cau Treo but also Dansavanh/Lao Bao) another common scam involves the suddenly rising price. You'll know this one when your bus stops and demands an extra, say, US$20 each to continue. This one also applies to local transport from the border further into Vietnam, be it by motorbike, public bus, truck or – the worst – tourist-oriented minibuses.

The nastiest part about these scams is you can't do much to avoid them, no matter how many questions you ask or assurances you seek. The best thing to do is just go with the flow and hope your crossing is trouble free, as many are. If you do come across a problem, try to keep a smile on your face (yes, we know it's hard) and get the best result – usually paying a lower amount. As attractive as it might sound, venting your frustrations through your fists makes matters much worse.

Alternatively you could tell the scammers where to go and hope for the best. And as we discovered years ago (these scams have been running forever), sometimes it will pay off. For us, it happened on Rte 8 coming from Vinh to Cau Treo. Our minibus stopped halfway up the Annamite range and the driver demanded more money. We refused, got out and the driver left. No sooner had we asked ourselves 'What now?' than a truck loaded up with bags of cement lumbered over the hill and stopped. 'To the border?' I asked. 'Yes, yes, no problem,' came the smiling reply even after I'd shown him we only had 1300d between us. Sitting atop the truck as we wound our way slowly up through the cloud forests was fantastic and almost as good as the gesture itself, which had restored some of our faith in humanity. We had the last laugh as well, when we found our greedy driver at the border trying to rip off a Canadian couple. We enjoyed telling them: 'Don't, whatever you do, go with that guy.'

between Vientiane and Hanoi take this route, but it's a long, torturously slow and uncomfortable trip. If you can take the pain, buses leave Vientiane's Northern Bus Station (p113) every day for Vinh (US$16, 16 hours) and Hanoi (US$20, 24 hours), and occasionally for Hue (US$17, at least 24 hours), Danang (US$20, at least 24 hours) and even Ho Chi Minh City (US$45, up to 48 hours).

NA PHAO & CHA LO

Even though this remote border (p241) has a nice new highway on the Laos side, we've still never met anyone who's actually crossed here. Transport runs all the way across this border from Tha Khaek to Dong Hoi in Vietnam, and back. However, no visas are available here yet.

DANSAVANH & LAO BAO

Good roads and plentiful transport make the border at Dansavanh (Laos) and Lao Bao, 255km east of Savannakhet, probably the easiest of all crossings to/from Vietnam (p250). If you're heading to/from Hué, Hoi An or anywhere in central Vietnam, it's recommended. The downside, however, is that if you want to see all of Vietnam you're in for a fair bit of backtracking.

ATTAPEU & QUY NHON

The newest crossing (p296) to Vietnam's central highlands is at Bo Y between remote Attapeu Province and Quy Nhon, though it doesn't really fit any existing travelling routes. Visas on arrival are not guaranteed.

GETTING AROUND

AIR
Airlines in Laos

Lao Airlines is the only airline in Laos. It handles all domestic flights, with Vientiane as the main hub. The Laos Air Fares map

TRANSPORT

(p324) gives you an idea of all Laos's scheduled air routes and prices, both domestic and international; for the latest fares check Lao Airlines' website (www.laoairlines.com).

Prices have been fairly steady in recent years and are reasonable value. Except at Lao Airlines' offices in Vientiane and Luang Prabang, where credit cards are accepted for both international and domestic tickets, you must pay cash in US dollars.

Lao Airlines schedules are increasingly reliable but flights still get cancelled semi-regularly. During the holiday season it's best to book ahead as flights can fill fast. At other times, when flights are more likely to be cancelled, confirm the flight is still going a day or two before.

In its previous incarnation as Lao Aviation, Lao Airlines had a bad reputation and travellers still ask whether it's safe. The answer is 'pretty much'. Almost everything about the airline – the planes, maintenance and pilots – has improved and there haven't been any serious incidents for several years. French ATR-72 planes operate most international routes and many domestic flights, though some of the domestic flights use older and less-reliable Chinese or Russian planes.

BICYCLE

The stunning roads and light, relatively slow traffic in most towns and on most highways make Laos arguably the best country for cycling in Southeast Asia. Several tour agencies

LAOS AIR FARES

and guesthouses offer mountain biking tours, ranging in duration from a few hours to several weeks (see p330).

Hire

Simple single-speed bicycles with names like Hare, Crocodile and Rabbit can be hired in most places that see a decent number of tourists, usually costing between US$0.50 and US$1.50 per day. Mountain bikes can be hired in a few places, including Luang Nam Tha, Vientiane, Vang Vieng and even Khoun Kham, for between US$1.50 and US$5 per day.

These mostly Thai- or Chinese-made bikes come in varying degrees of usability, so be sure to inspect them thoroughly before hiring. Common problems include loose seats or handlebars and broken bells. Ask and you can usually get the seat adjusted to suit your height.

Purchase

You can buy a new bicycle for between US$40 and US$100. The Chinese bikes are sturdier, the Thai bikes more comfortable. Low-quality Chinese or Taiwanese mountain bikes cost more.

BOAT

More than 4600km of navigable rivers are the highways and byways of traditional Laos, the main thoroughfares being the Mekong, Nam Ou, Nam Khan, Nam Tha, Nam Ngum and Se Kong. The Mekong is the longest and most important route and is, in theory if no longer in practice, navigable year-round between Luang Prabang in the north and Savannakhet in the south (about 70% of its length in Laos). Smaller rivers accommodate a range of smaller boats, from dugout canoes to 'bomb boats' made from junk dropped from the skies during the Second Indochina War.

Sealed roads and buses, however, mean that the days of mass river transport are as good as finished. Every time a new road is opened more boatmen go out of business, unable to compete with the price and pace of those modern conveyors of the masses – buses and *săwngthăew*. This aspect of progress means local people have access to faster and cheaper travel, and it's not our place to begrudge them that. However, from a travellers' point of view, the gradual death of river transport is a great shame. There were few things more romantic than sitting on a slow boat, tacking from one riverside village to another as the boat worked its way along the river, picking up people, produce and animals on the way.

While there are barely any regular local boats on the Mekong anymore, there are still a few places left where you can do this, if you're prepared to get right off the beaten river and seek out the adventure…and you can be certain it will be a memorable trip, one way or another. So whether it's on a tourist boat from Huay Xai to Luang Prabang or on a local boat you've rustled up in some remote corner of the country, it's still worth doing at least one river excursion while in Laos.

River Ferry (Slow Boat)

The most popular river trip in Laos – the slow boat between Huay Xai and Luang Prabang – is still a daily event and relatively cheap at about US$15 per person for the two-day journey. From Huay Xai, boats are often packed, sometimes overloaded, while from Luang Prabang there should be plenty of room; see p218 for suggestions on avoiding an overloaded boat. Boats on the Mekong see very few passengers south of Luang Prabang, but with enterprise and patience you might find a boat running south through Sainyabuli Province all the way to Vientiane. The slow boat between Pakse and Si Phan Don via Champasak has stopped.

Every river in the country has some boat traffic and chartering a boat is easy enough. Aside from the journey from Huay Xai to Luang Prabang, two of the most beautiful routes are Luang Nam Tha to Pak Tha (US$170, one to two days) and Nong Khiaw to Luang Prabang (US$120, five hours). Prices here are for whole boat charters, shared by up to 10 people.

If you get lucky enough to find a public boat, or charter one yourself, note that standards of luxury fall far short of the *Queen Mary*. Most riverboats were designed for cargo transport and facilities range from nonexistent to ultra-basic. Passengers sit, eat and sleep on the wooden decks. The toilet (if there is one) is an enclosed hole in the deck at the back of the boat.

River Taxi

For shorter river trips, such as Luang Prabang to the Pak Ou Caves, it's usually best to hire a

TRANSPORT

KNOW YOUR BOAT

Following are some of the *héua* (boats) that you may encounter in your adventures along Laos's many waterways:

- *héua sáa* (double-deck boats) – big, old boats; almost extinct
- *héua duan* (express boat) – roofed cargo boats, common on the Huay Xai to Luang Prabang route; they're slow, but called 'express' because they're faster than double-deck boats
- *héua wái* (speedboat) – these resemble a surfboard with a car engine strapped to the back; very fast, exhilarating, deafeningly loud, uncomfortable and dangerous (see p219)
- *héua hang nyáo* (longtail boat) – boats (usually roofed but not always) with engine gimbal-mounted on the stern; found all over Laos
- *héua phái* (rowboat) – essentially a pirogue; common in Si Phan Don.

---

river taxi. The *héua hang nyáo* (longtail boats) are the most typical, though for a really short trip (eg crossing a river) a *héua phái* (rowboat) or one of the small improvised ferries can be hired. The *héua hang nyáo* are around US$5 an hour for a boat with an eight- to 10-person capacity. Larger boats that carry up to 20 passengers are sometimes available for about US$8 per hour, although higher tourist prices are often applied, and prices go up with fuel consumption if you're heading upriver when the river is at full flood.

Along the upper Mekong River between Huay Xai and Vientiane, and on the Nam Ou between Luang Prabang and Hat Sa (Phongsali), Thai-built *héua wái* (speedboats) are common. They can cover a distance in six hours that might take a ferry two days or more. Charters start at US$20 per hour, but some ply regular routes so the cost can be shared among passengers. They are, however, dangerous; see p219.

Tours

With public boats hard to find, tour companies are increasingly offering kayaking and rafting trips on some of the more scenic stretches of river. The best places to organise these are Luang Nam Tha, Luang Prabang, Vang Vieng, Tha Khaek and Pakse.

BUS, SĂWNGTHĂEW & LOT DOI SAAN

Long-distance public transport in Laos is either by bus or *săwngthăew* (literally 'two rows'), which are converted pick-ups or trucks with benches down either side. Buses are more frequent and go further than ever before in Laos, and destinations that were all but inaccessible a few years ago now see regular

services. Private operators have established services on some busier routes – particularly along Rte 13 and on international routes – offering faster and more-luxurious air-con buses, known as VIP buses, which are also pretty good value at about US$2 per 100km – about 1.5 times the normal bus price.

That's not to say local buses have disappeared completely. Far from it. You can still do the main routes by local bus, and on most journeys off Rte 13 you won't have any option.

If you can't live without your air-con, it's worth booking ahead. You'll usually have to go to the bus station to do this, though increasingly guesthouses can book tickets for a small fee. For an idea of prices, see the boxed text Leaving Vientiane By Bus (p114).

Săwngthăew usually service shorter routes within a given province. Most decent-sized villages have at least one *săwngthăew*, which will run to the provincial capital and back most days. Like local buses, they stop wherever you want but are generally slower given that the roads they ply are usually unpaved. And, given that everyone is sitting on-top-of/facing each other, they're even more social than the bus.

The final type of transport is the *lot doi saan* (wooden bus). These big, rumbling trucks with wooden cabins built on the back with forward facing seats were once the mainstay of Lao transport. They can handle the worst road conditions and these days that's where you'll find them – on routes that are unpassable to anything else.

CAR & MOTORCYCLE

Driving in Laos is easier than you might think. Sure, the road infrastructure is pretty basic, but outside of the large centres there are so few vehicles that it's a doddle compared to Vietnam, China or Thailand.

Motorcyclists planning to ride through Laos should check out the wealth of information at **Golden Triangle Rider** (www.GT-Rider .com). Doing some sort of motorbike loop is becoming increasingly popular among travellers. For some tips see p328.

Bring Your Own Vehicle

Bringing a vehicle into Laos is easy enough if you have a *carnet de passage*. You simply get the *carnet* stamped at any international border (p321) – there is no extra charge or permit required.

If you don't have a *carnet* – likely the case if you bought your vehicle in Thailand, which doesn't recognise the *carnet* system – you'll need a temporary importation permit. Travel agencies on the Thai side can arrange the necessary permit for between 7000B and 8000B. If it's a Thai-registered vehicle you'll also need to fill out an Information of Conveyance form to allow for temporary export.

On the Lao side you need to arrange a temporary export permit (usually referred to by the French term *laisser-passer*) and Lao vehicle insurance. For both sides you'll need photocopies of your driver's licence, passport information page and vehicle registration papers.

When you cross into Laos, be sure to stop at Lao customs and get your temporary import papers stamped or you might be fined when you exit the country. Police in Laos occasionally stop foreign-registered vehicles and ask to see their *laisser-passer*.

Exiting into Thailand or Cambodia is fairly hassle free if your papers are in order. Vietnam is a different story. As friends of ours reported (read their account on www .landcruising.nl), some borders just don't have the necessary papers. They crossed at Na Maew but had to leave their vehicle at the border while they went 200km to Thanh Hoa to sort out the permit with the police, which took two days and copies of their *carnet*, license, registration and insurance papers. Vietnam usually won't issue permits to right-hand drive vehicles.

If you're heading to China it's virtually impossible to drive a vehicle larger than a bicycle across the border without huge cost and hassle.

Driving Licence

To drive in Laos you need a valid International Driving Permit, which you must get in your home country.

Fuel & Spare Parts

At the time of research fuel cost about US$0.80 a litre for petrol, slightly less for diesel. Fuel for motorcycles is available from

TRANSPORT

ON THE BUSES

The buses of Laos probably won't be what you're used to, so what should you expect? For starters, it will almost certainly take longer than the advertised time. The ride itself depends on how lucky you are on a given day. It could be relatively smooth, moving at something approaching 60kph on an ageing but relatively modern bus, with two seats to yourself and no karaoke. Or it might not….

The bus itself might be a relic that's so bad it makes an otherwise flat road feel like a pot-holed monster. In the course of researching this book we had several flat tires, a bus without windows driving through a storm, a bus that stopped beside Rte 13 and picked up more than 100 50kg sacks of rice from a local mill (each labelled 'Produce of Thailand') and laid them in the aisle, under the seats, and anywhere else they would fit. Funnily enough, the bus seemed to go better after that. The music might be as loud as it is bad, and you might be sharing the bus with a menagerie of farmyard animals. Things break, too. As Justine found on a remote road in Phongsali Province, attempted fixes might be as imaginative, and useless, as putting a condom into the motor.

Our advice is don't look at your watch too much and just soak it up. These sort of trips are actually more fun than they sound. They're inevitably social events and make much better stories than a few uneventful hours on a VIP bus where the only chicken to be seen has already been barbecued.

TRANSPORT

drums in villages across the country, though prices are almost always higher than at service stations; usually about US$1 to US$1.20 a litre. Diesel is available in most towns. It's best to fuel up in bigger towns at big-brand service stations because the quality of fuel can be poor in remote areas.

Spare parts for four-wheeled vehicles are expensive and difficult to find, even in Vientiane.

Hire

Chinese- and Japanese-made 100 and 110cc step-through motorbikes can be hired for between US$5 and US$15 per day in most large centres. No licence is required. Try to get a Japanese bike (the ominously named Suzuki Smash, perhaps) if you're travelling any distance out of town. In Vientiane, Pakse and Vang Vieng 250cc dirt bikes are available for about US$20 per day.

MOTORCYCLE DIARIES

There are few more liberating travel experiences than renting a motorbike and setting off; stopping where you want, when you want. The lack of traffic and stunningly beautiful roads make Laos about the best place in the region to do it. There are, however, a few things worth knowing before you hand over your passport as collateral on a rent bike.

■ The bike – Price and availability mean that the vast majority of travellers rent Chinese 110cc bikes. No 110cc bike was designed to be used like a dirt bike, but Japanese bikes deal with it better and are worth the extra couple of dollars a day.

■ The odometer – Given that many roads have no kilometre stones and turnoffs are often unmarked, it's worth getting a bike with a working odometer. That's easier said than done. The good news is that almost any bike shop can fix an odometer in about 10 minutes for about US$3 or US$4. Money well spent, we think, as long as you remember to note the distance when you start.

■ The gear – Don't leave home without sunscreen, a hat, plastic raincoat or poncho, bandana and sunglasses. Even the sealed roads in Laos get annoyingly dusty so these last two are vital. At dusk your headlight will act as a magnet for all manner of suicidal bugs, but unfortunately their aim isn't so good and more often than not they end up smacking into your face. This soon gets tedious and you might find yourself doing a Corey Hart and wearing your sunglasses at night. Helmets are a good idea (ask for one if they don't offer), as is wearing pants and shoes, lest you wind up with the ubiquitous burnt leg.

■ The problems – Unless you're very lucky, something will go wrong – budget some time for it. However, short of a head-on with a *săwngthăew* it shouldn't be the end of the world. On this research trip we had several problems of varying magnitude. A puncture cost us US$0.60 and half an hour to fix – just push your bike to the nearest puncture repair shop, most villages have one. On The Loop (p240) both rear shock absorbers broke. That meant an alarmingly uncomfortable 70km or so to Lak Sao, but once there two new shocks and labour cost US$10 and were fixed in 30 minutes. And then there was the throttle cable breaking in the middle of nowhere on the Bolaven Plateau, which is a reflection of how helpful people will be when you're in trouble. Within 10 minutes five men appeared out of nowhere and set about fixing it. An hour later they'd disconnected the front brake, wrapped the throttle cable around the brake lever (my new throttle!), refused any money and wished me well. Great stuff.

■ The responsibility – You can ride a motorbike in Laos without a licence, a helmet or any safety gear whatsoever, but for all this freedom you must take all the responsibility. If you have a crash there won't be an ambulance to pick you up, and even when you get to the hospital facilities will be basic. Carrying a basic medical kit and phone numbers for hospitals in Thailand and your travel insurance provider is a good idea. The same goes for the bike. If it really dies you can't just call the company and get a replacement. Laos doesn't work like that, so you'll need to load it onto the next pick-up or *săwngthăew* and take it somewhere they can fix it. Do not abandon it by the road, or you'll have to pay for another one.

It's possible to hire a self-drive vehicle, but when you consider that a driver usually costs no more, takes responsibility for damage and knows where he's going, it seems pointless. Informal charters can be arranged almost anywhere, with small Japanese pickups going for between US$40 and US$100 per day, depending on where you're going; the rougher the road, the higher the price.

The following Vientiane-based companies have good reputations:

Asia Vehicle Rental (AVR; Map p92; ☎ /fax 021-217493; www.avr.laopdr.com; 354-356 Th Samsenthai, Vientiane) Undoubtedly the most reliable place to hire vehicles, with or without drivers. Offers 4WDs, vans, sedans. Recommended.

LaoWheels (☎ 021-223663, 020-550 4604; laowheels@yahoo.co.uk) One engaging man and his van. Christophe Kittirath speaks fluent French, good English, knows the country inside out and is a good driver. Highly recommended.

Elsewhere, larger hotels usually have a van for rent or can find one, or ask at the local tourism office.

Insurance
Car-hire companies will provide insurance, but be sure to check exactly what is covered. Note that most travel insurance policies don't cover use of motorcycles.

Road Conditions
While the overall condition of roads is poor, work over the last decade has made most of the main roads – originally laid out by the French as part of a network that covered Indochina – quite comfortable. Some, however, remain challenging, particularly in the wet season. These include Rte 3 between Huay Xai and Luang Nam Tha, which is being rebuilt by the Chinese, a section of Rte 1C between Vieng Thong and Phu Lao junction, and pretty much all of Rte 18, which cuts across the far south to Vietnam.

Elsewhere, unsurfaced roads are the rule. Laos has about 23,000km of classified roads and less than a quarter are sealed. Unsurfaced roads are particularly tricky in the wet season when many routes are impassable to all but 4WD vehicles and motorbikes. Wet or dry, Laos is so mountainous that relatively short road trips can take forever; a typical 200km upcountry trip could take more than 10 hours.

Road Hazards
Try to avoid driving at dusk and after dark; cows, buffaloes, chickens and dogs, not to mention thousands of people, head for home on the unlit roads, turning them into a dangerous obstacle course. Unsigned roadwork – often a huge hole in the road – is also a challenge in fading light.

Road Rules
The single most important rule is to expect the unexpected; Western-style 'tunnel vision driving' just doesn't work here. Driving is on the right side, but it's not unusual to see Lao drivers go the wrong way down the left lane before crossing to the right – a potentially dangerous situation if you're not ready for it. At intersections it's normal to turn right without looking left, and while changing lanes people almost never look behind because the person behind is responsible for avoiding whatever happens in front of them.

HITCHING
Hitching is possible in Laos, if not common, though it's never entirely safe and not recommended for women as the act of standing beside a road and waving at cars might be misinterpreted. If you are hitching, cars with red-on-yellow (private vehicle) or blue-on-white (international organisations and embassies) number plates might be the best ones to target. Long-distance cargo trucks are also a good bet.

LOCAL TRANSPORT
Apart from in Vientiane and, to a lesser extent, in Savannakhet and Pakse, you'll seldom need local transport because towns and cities are small enough to walk and cycle around.

Bus
Vientiane is the only city with a network of local buses (p115), though they're not much good to travellers.

Jumbo, Săam-lâaw, Sakai-làep, Tuk-tuk
The various three-wheeled taxis found in Vientiane and provincial capitals have different names depending on where you are. Larger ones are called *jąmbǫh* (jumbo) and can hold four to six passengers on two facing seats. In Vientiane they are sometimes called tuk-tuk as in Thailand (though traditionally in Laos this refers to a slightly larger vehicle than

TRANSPORT

TRANSPORT

the jumbo), while in the south (eg Pakse and Savannakhet) they may be called *sakai-làep* (Skylab) because someone, probably on opium at the time, once thought they looked like the famous space station that crashed to earth. But wait, there's more…these three-wheeled conveyances are also labelled simply *thaek-sii* (taxi) or, usually for motorcycle sidecar-style vehicles, *săam-lâaw* (samlor or three-wheels). Whatever you call it people will usually know what you're after. The old-style bicycle *săam-lâaw* (pedicab), known as a *cyclo* elsewhere in Indochina, is an endangered species in Laos. If you can find a *săam-lâaw*, fares are about the same as for motorcycle taxis.

Fares vary according to the city and your bargaining skills. Locals generally pay about US$0.25 per kilometre on trips no longer than about 20km. However, in Vientiane and other towns that see plenty of tourists, serious bargaining is required.

Taxi
Vientiane has a handful of car taxis that are used by foreign businesspeople and the occasional tourist, though in other cities a taxi of sorts can be arranged. They can be hired by the trip, by the hour or by the day. Typical all-day hire within a town or city costs between US$35 and US$45 depending on the vehicle and your negotiating powers. By the trip, you shouldn't pay more than about US$0.50 per kilometre, but will often be asked to.

TOURS
A growing number of tour operators run trips in Laos and it's cheaper to book directly with them rather than through a foreign-based agency. A common two-week tour might take in Vientiane, Luang Prabang, the Xieng Khuang (Plain of Jars), Savannakhet and Champasak; the better operators can customise itineraries. More specialised tours are also becoming popular, with rafting, kayaking, cycling, trekking, motorcycling and even photographic tours all available.

The following are worth investigating:

Asian Trails (www.asiantrails.com)

Asian Motorcycling Adventures (www.asianbiketour .com) Some regular and customised off-road trips, including the Ho Chi Minh Trail.

Carpe Diem Travel (www.carpe-diem-travel.com) Environmentally and socially responsible tours, focussing on pro-poor tourism and feeding some money back through sponsorship projects.

Exotissimio (www.exotissimo.com) Large company with a mix of pure sightseeing and adventure tours.

Gecko Travel (www.geckotravel.com) Mix of small group tours for newbies and those seeking more adventure, plus a photographic tour. Not the cheapest but good feedback.

Green Discovery (www.greendiscoverylaos.com) Biggest adventure tourism operator in Laos. Well-organised kayaking, trekking, cycling, rock climbing and rafting trips. Easy to book locally and fair value.

Inter-Lao Tourisme (www.interlao.com) Vientiane-based agency that subcontracts to several larger international tour operators.

Lane Xang Travel (XPlore Asia; www.xplore-asia.com) Popular with backpackers for their cheap adventure tours, especially from Pakse and Si Phan Don.

Lao Youth Travel (www.laoyouthtravel.com) Multi-day tours between Vientiane, Vang Vieng and Luang Prabang, plus trips to minority villages further north.

Paddle Asia (www.paddleasia.com) Kayaking and rafting on a host of rivers.

Spiceroads (www.spiceroads.com) Specialises in cycling tours.

Tiger Trail (www.tigertrail-laos.com) Established Luang Prabang-based company with big range of tours, including trekking, rafting and kayaking. No tigers, though.

Health Dr Trish Batchelor

CONTENTS

Before You Go	**331**
Insurance	331
Vaccinations	331
Internet Resources	332
Further Reading	333
In Transit	**333**
Jet Lag & Motion Sickness	333
In Laos	**333**
Infectious Diseases	334
Traveller's Diarrhoea	337
Environmental Hazards	338
Women's Health	340
Traditional Medicine	341

Health issues and the quality of medical facilities vary enormously depending on where and how you travel in Laos. Travellers tend to worry about contracting infectious diseases when in the tropics, but infections are a rare cause of serious illness or death in travellers. Pre-existing medical conditions such as heart disease and accidental injury (especially traffic accidents), account for most life-threatening problems. Becoming ill in some way, however, is relatively common. Fortunately, most common illnesses can either be prevented with common-sense behaviour or be treated easily with a well-stocked traveller's medical kit.

The following advice is a general guide only and does not replace the advice of a doctor trained in travel medicine.

BEFORE YOU GO

Pack medications in their original, clearly labelled, containers. A signed and dated letter from your physician describing your medical conditions and medications, including generic names, is also a good idea. If carrying syringes or needles, be sure to have a physician's letter documenting their medical necessity. If you have a heart condition bring a copy of your ECG taken just prior to travelling.

If you happen to take any regular medication, bring double your needs in case of loss or theft. In Laos it can be difficult to find some of the newer drugs, particularly the latest antidepressant drugs, blood pressure medications and contraceptive pills.

INSURANCE

Even if you are fit and healthy, don't travel without health insurance – accidents do happen. Declare any existing medical conditions you have – the insurance company *will* check if your problem is pre-existing and will not cover you if it is undeclared. You may require extra cover for adventure activities such as rock climbing. If your health insurance doesn't cover you for medical expenses abroad, consider getting extra insurance – check lonelyplanet.com for more information. If you're uninsured, emergency evacuation is expensive; bills of over US$100,000 are not uncommon.

Find out in advance if your insurance plan will make payments directly to providers or reimburse you later for overseas health expenditures. (In many countries doctors expect payment in cash.) Some policies offer lower and higher medical-expense options; the higher ones are chiefly for countries that have extremely high medical costs, such as the USA. You may prefer a policy that pays doctors or hospitals directly rather than you having to pay on the spot and claim later. If you have to claim later, keep all the documentation. Some policies ask you to call back (reverse charges) to a centre in your home country where an immediate assessment of your problem is made.

VACCINATIONS

The only vaccine required by international regulations is yellow fever. Proof of vaccination will only be required if you have visited a country in the yellow-fever zone within the six days prior to entering Southeast Asia. If you are travelling to Southeast Asia from Africa or South America you should check to see if you require proof of vaccination.

Specialised travel-medicine clinics are your best source of information; they stock all available vaccines and will be able to give specific recommendations for you and your

HEALTH

RECOMMENDED VACCINATIONS

The World Health Organization (WHO) recommends the following vaccinations for travellers to Southeast Asia:

- Adult diphtheria and tetanus – Single booster recommended if you've had none in the previous 10 years. Side effects include a sore arm and fever.
- Hepatitis A – Provides almost 100% protection for up to a year; a booster after 12 months provides at least another 20 years' protection. Mild side effects such as headache and a sore arm occur for between 5% and 10% of people.
- Hepatitis B – Now considered routine for most travellers. Given as three shots over six months. A rapid schedule is also available, as is a combined vaccination with Hepatitis A. Side effects are mild and uncommon, usually a headache and sore arm. Lifetime protection occurs in 95% of people.
- Measles, mumps and rubella – Two doses of MMR required unless you have had the diseases. Occasionally a rash and flulike illness can develop a week after receiving the vaccine. Many young adults require a booster.
- Polio – In 2002, no countries in Southeast Asia reported cases of polio. Only one booster is required as an adult for lifetime protection. Inactivated polio vaccine is safe during pregnancy.
- Typhoid – Recommended unless your trip is less than a week and only to developed cities. The vaccine offers around 70% protection, lasts for two to three years and comes as a single shot. Tablets are also available; however, the injection is usually recommended as it has fewer side effects. Sore arm and fever may occur.
- Varicella – If you haven't had chickenpox, discuss this vaccination with your doctor.

Long-term travellers

These vaccinations are recommended for people travelling for more than one month, or those at special risk:

- Japanese B Encephalitis – Three injections in all. Booster recommended after two years. A sore arm and headache are the most common side effects. Rarely, an allergic reaction comprising hives and swelling can occur up to 10 days after any of the three doses.
- Meningitis – Single injection. There are two types of vaccination: the quadrivalent vaccine gives two to three years protection; meningitis group C vaccine gives around 10 years protection. Recommended for long-term backpackers aged under 25.
- Rabies – Three injections in all. A booster after one year will provide 10 years protection. Side effects are rare – occasionally a headache and sore arm.
- Tuberculosis – Adult long-term travellers are usually recommended to have a TB skin test before and after travel, rather than vaccination. Only one vaccine is given in a lifetime.

trip. The doctors will take into account factors such as past vaccination history, the length of your trip, activities you may be undertaking, and underlying medical conditions, such as pregnancy.

Most vaccines don't produce immunity until at least two weeks after they're given, so visit a doctor four to eight weeks before departure. Ask your doctor for an International Certificate of Vaccination (otherwise known as the yellow booklet), which will list all the vaccinations you've received. In the US, the yellow booklet is no longer issued,

but it is highly unlikely the Lao authorities will ask for proof of vaccinations (unless you have recently been in a yellow-fever affected country). See Recommended Vaccinations (above) for possible vaccinations.

INTERNET RESOURCES

There is a wealth of travel health advice on the internet. For further information, **lonelyplanet.com** (www.lonelyplanet.com) is a good place to start. The **World Health Organization** (WHO; www.who.int/ith/) publishes a superb book called *International Travel & Health*, which is revised annually and is available online at no cost. Another website of general interest is **MD Travel Health** (www.mdtravelhealth.com), which provides complete travel health recommendations for every country and is updated daily. The **Centers for Disease Control and Prevention** (CDC; www.cdc.gov) website also has good general information.

FURTHER READING

Lonely Planet's *Healthy Travel – Asia & India* is a handy pocket-size book that is packed with useful information including pretrip planning, emergency first aid, immunisation and disease information and what to do if you get sick on the road. Other recommended references include *Traveller's Health* by Dr Richard Dawood and *Travelling Well* by Dr Deborah Mills – check out the website (www.travellingwell.com.au).

IN TRANSIT

DEEP VEIN THROMBOSIS (DVT)

Deep vein thrombosis (DVT) occurs when blood clots form in the legs during plane flights, chiefly because of prolonged immobility. The longer the flight, the greater the risk. Though most blood clots are reabsorbed uneventfully, some may break off and travel through the blood vessels to the lungs, where they may cause life-threatening complications.

The chief symptom of DVT is swelling or pain of the foot, ankle, or calf, usually on just one side. When a blood clot travels to the lungs, it may cause chest pain and difficulty in breathing. Travellers with any of these symptoms should immediately seek medical attention.

To prevent the development of DVT on long flights you should walk about the cabin, perform isometric compressions of the leg muscles (ie contract the leg muscles while sitting), drink plenty of fluids, and avoid alcohol and tobacco.

JET LAG & MOTION SICKNESS

Jet lag is common when crossing more than five time zones; it results in insomnia, fatigue, malaise or nausea. To avoid jet lag try drinking plenty of fluids (nonalcoholic) and eating light meals. Upon arrival, seek exposure to natural sunlight and readjust your schedule (for meals, sleep etc) as soon as possible.

The winding mountain roads in Laos can be beautiful, but they're also a problem if you suffer from motion sickness. The section of Rte 13 between Vang Vieng and Luang Prabang is particularly bad, and we heard from one guy who was ill for three days after that making this trip. Antihistamines such as dimenhydrinate (Dramamine) and meclizine (Antivert, Bonine) are usually the first choice for treating motion sickness. Their main side effect is drowsiness. A herbal alternative is ginger, which works like a charm for some people.

IN LAOS

AVAILABILITY OF HEALTHCARE

Laos has no facilities for major medical emergencies. The state-run hospitals and clinics are among the worst in Southeast Asia in terms of the standards of hygiene, staff training, supplies and equipment, and the availability of medicines.

For minor to moderate conditions, including malaria, **Mahasot International Clinic** (☎ 021-214022) in Vientiane has a decent reputation.

For any serious conditions, you're better off going to Thailand. If a medical problem can wait until you're in Bangkok, then all the better, as there are excellent hospitals there.

For medical emergencies that can't be delayed before reaching Bangkok, you can call ambulances from nearby Nong Khai or Udon Thani in Thailand. **Nong Khai Wattana General Hospital** (☎ 0066 4246 5201; fax 4246 5210) in Nong Khai is the closest. The better **Aek Udon Hospital** (☎ 0066 4234 2555; www.aekudon.com) in Udon Thani is an hour further from the border by road. **Lao Westcoast Helicopter** (☎ 021-512023;

HEALTH

HEALTH ADVISORIES

It's usually a good idea to consult your government's travel-health website before departure, if one is available:

Australia (www.dfat.gov.au/travel)
Canada (www.travelhealth.gc.ca)
New Zealand (www.mfat.govt.nz/travel)
UK (www.doh.gov.uk/traveladvice)
US (www.cdc.gov/travel)

MEDICAL CHECKLIST

Recommended items for a personal medical kit:

- antifungal cream, eg Clotrimazole
- antibacterial cream, eg Muciprocin
- antibiotics for skin infections, eg Amoxicillin/Clavulanate or Cephalexin
- antibiotics for diarrhoea, eg Norfloxacin or Ciprofloxacin; Azithromycin for bacterial diarrhoea; and Tinidazole for giardiasis or amoebic dysentery
- antihistamines for allergies, eg Cetrizine for daytime and Promethazine for night
- anti-inflammatories, eg Ibuprofen
- antinausea medication, eg Prochlorperazine
- antiseptic for cuts and scrapes, eg Betadine
- antispasmodic for stomach cramps, eg Buscopa
- contraceptives
- decongestant for colds and flus, eg Pseudoephedrine
- DEET-based insect repellent
- diarrhoea 'stopper', eg Loperamide
- first-aid items such as scissors, plasters (Band Aids), bandages, gauze, thermometer (electronic, not mercury), sterile needles and syringes, and tweezers
- indigestion medication, eg Quick Eze or Mylanta
- iodine tablets (unless you are pregnant or have a thyroid problem) to purify water
- laxative, eg Coloxyl
- migraine medication (your personal brand), if a migraine sufferer
- oral-rehydration solution for diarrhoea, eg Gastrolyte
- paracetamol for pain
- permethrin (to impregnate clothing and mosquito nets) for repelling insects
- steroid cream for allergic/itchy rashes, eg 1% to 2% hydrocortisone
- sunscreen and hat
- throat lozenges
- thrush (vaginal yeast infection) treatment, eg Clotrimazole pessaries or Diflucan tablet
- urine alkalisation agent, eg Ural, if you're prone to urinary tract infections.

laowestcoast.laopdr.com; Hangar 703, Wattay International Airport), will fly emergency patients to Udon Thani for about US$1500, subject to aircraft availability and government permission. **Si Nakharin Hospital** (☎ 0066 4323 7602/6) is further away in Khon Kaen but is supposed to be the best medical facility in northeastern Thailand. From any of these hospitals, patients can be transferred to Bangkok if necessary.

Self-treatment may be appropriate if your problem is minor (eg traveller's diarrhoea), you are carrying the appropriate medication and you cannot attend a recommended clinic. If you think you may have a serious disease, especially

malaria, do not waste time – travel to the nearest quality facility. It is always better to be assessed by a doctor than to rely on self-treatment.

Buying medication over the counter is not recommended, as fake medications and poorly stored or out-of-date drugs are common in Laos.

INFECTIOUS DISEASES
Dengue Fever

This mosquito-borne disease is becomingly increasingly problematic throughout Laos, especially in the cities. As there is no vaccine it can only be prevented by avoiding mosquito bites. The mosquito that carries dengue bites day and night, so use insect avoidance measures at all times. Symptoms include high fever, severe headache and body ache (dengue was once known as 'breakbone fever'). Some people develop a rash and diarrhoea. There's no specific treatment, just rest and paracetamol – do not take aspirin as it increases the likelihood of haemorrhaging. See a doctor to be diagnosed and monitored.

Filariasis

This is a mosquito-borne disease that is very common in the local population, yet very rare in travellers. Mosquito-avoidance measures are the best way to prevent it.

Hepatitis A

A problem throughout the region, this food- and water-borne virus infects the liver, causing jaundice (yellow skin and eyes), nausea and lethargy. There is no specific treatment for hepatitis A, you just need to allow time for the liver to heal. All travellers to Southeast Asia should be vaccinated against hepatitis A.

Hepatitis B

The only sexually transmitted disease that can be prevented by vaccination, hepatitis B is spread by body fluids, including sexual contact. In some parts of Southeast Asia, up to 20% of the population are carriers of hepatitis B, and usually are unaware of this. The long-term consequences can include liver cancer and cirrhosis.

Hepatitis E

Hepatitis E is transmitted through contaminated food and water and has similar symptoms to hepatitis A, but is far less common. It is a severe problem in pregnant women and can result in the death of both mother and baby. There is currently no vaccine; prevention is by following safe eating and drinking guidelines.

HIV

According to Unaids and WHO, Laos remains a 'low HIV prevalence country'; Unaids reported a range of between 1000 and 1800 as of 2001. However, it's estimated that only about one fifth of all HIV cases in Laos are actually reported. Heterosexual sex is the main method of transmission in Laos.

The use of condoms greatly decreases but does not eliminate the risk of HIV infection. The Lao phrase for 'condom' is *thæng anáamái*. Condoms can be purchased at most *hâan khǎi yáa* (pharmacies), but it is worth bringing your own condoms from home.

Influenza

Present year-round in the tropics, influenza (flu) symptoms include high fever, muscle aches, runny nose, cough and sore throat. It can be very severe in people over the age of 65 or in those with underlying medical conditions such as heart disease or diabetes; vaccination is recommended for these individuals. There is no specific treatment, just rest and paracetamol.

Japanese B Encephalitis

While a rare disease in travellers, at least 50,000 locals are infected with Japanese B Encephalitis each year in Southeast Asia. This viral disease is transmitted by mosquitoes. Most cases occur in rural areas and vaccination is recommended for travellers spending more than one month outside of cities. There is no treatment, and a third of infected people will die while another third will suffer permanent brain damage.

Malaria

For such a serious and potentially deadly disease, there is an enormous amount of misinformation concerning malaria. You must get expert advice as to whether your trip actually puts you at risk. Many parts of Laos, particularly populated areas, have minimal to no risk of malaria, and the risk of side effects from the antimalaria medication may outweigh the risk of getting the disease. For some rural areas, however, the risk of contracting the disease far outweighs the risk of any tablet side effects. Remember that malaria can be fatal. Before you travel, seek medical advice on the right medication and dosage for you.

Malaria is caused by a parasite transmitted by the bite of an infected mosquito. The most important symptom of malaria is fever, but general symptoms such as headache, diarrhoea, cough, or chills may also occur. Diagnosis can only be made by taking a blood sample.

Two strategies should be combined to prevent malaria – mosquito avoidance, and

HEALTH

antimalarial medications. Most people who catch malaria are taking inadequate or no antimalarial medication.

Travellers are advised to prevent mosquito bites by taking these steps:

- Choose accommodation with screens and fans (if not air-conditioned).
- Impregnate clothing with Permethrin in high-risk areas.
- Sleep under a mosquito net impregnated with Permethrin.
- Spray your room with insect repellent before going out for your evening meal.
- Use a DEET-containing insect repellent on exposed skin. Wash this off at night, as long as you are sleeping under a mosquito net. Natural repellents such as citronella can be effective, but must be applied more frequently than products containing DEET.
- Use mosquito coils.
- Wear long sleeves and trousers in light colours.

MALARIA MEDICATION

There are a variety of medications available. The effectiveness of the Chloroquine and Paludrine combination is now limited in most of Southeast Asia. Common side effects include nausea (40% of people) and mouth ulcers. It is generally not recommended.

Lariam (Mefloquine) has received much bad press, some of it justified, some not. This weekly tablet suits many people. Serious side effects are rare but include depression, anxiety, psychosis and seizures. Anyone with a history of depression, anxiety, other psychological disorder, or epilepsy should not take Lariam. It is considered safe in the second and third trimesters of pregnancy. It is around 90% effective in most parts of Southeast Asia, but there is significant resistance in parts of northern Thailand, Laos and Cambodia. Tablets must be taken for four weeks after leaving the risk area.

Doxycycline, taken as a daily tablet, is a broad-spectrum antibiotic that has the added benefit of helping to prevent a variety of tropical diseases, including leptospirosis, tick-borne disease, typhus and melioidosis. The potential side effects include photosensitivity (a tendency to sunburn), thrush in women, indigestion, heartburn, nausea and interference with the contraceptive pill. More serious side effects include ulceration of the oesophagus – you can help prevent this by taking your tablet with a meal and a large glass of water, and never lying down within half an hour of taking it. It must be taken for four weeks after leaving the risk area.

Malarone is a new drug combining Atovaquone and Proguanil. Side effects are uncommon and mild, most commonly nausea and headaches. It is the best tablet for scuba divers and for those on short trips to high-risk areas. It must be taken for one week after leaving the risk area.

Derivatives of Artesunate are not suitable as a preventive medication. They are useful treatments under medical supervision.

A final option is to take no preventive medication but to have a supply of emergency medication should you develop the symptoms of malaria. This is less than ideal, and you'll need to get to a good medical facility within 24 hours of developing a fever. If you choose this option the most effective and safest treatment is Malarone (four tablets once daily for three days). Other options include Mefloquine and Quinine but the side effects of these drugs at treatment doses make them less desirable. Fansidar is no longer recommended.

Measles

Measles remains a problem in some parts of Southeast Asia. This highly contagious bacterial infection is spread via coughing and sneezing. Most people born before 1966 are immune as they had the disease in childhood. Measles starts with a high fever and rash and can be complicated by pneumonia and brain disease. There is no specific treatment.

Melioidosis

This infection is contracted by skin contact with soil. It is rare in travellers. The symptoms are very similar to those experienced by tuberculosis sufferers. There is no vaccine but it can be treated with medication.

Opisthorchiasis (Liver Flukes)

These are tiny worms that are occasionally present in freshwater fish in Laos. The main risk comes from eating raw or undercooked fish. Travellers should in particular avoid eating uncooked *pąa dàek* (an unpasteurised fermented fish used as an accompaniment for many Lao foods) when travelling in rural Laos. The *pąa dàek* in Vientiane and Luang Prabang is said to be safe (or safer) simply because it is usually produced from noninfected fish, while the risk of infestation is greatest in the southern provinces.

A rarer way to contract liver flukes is by swimming in the Mekong River or its tributaries around Don Khong (Khong Island) in the far south of Laos.

At low levels, there are virtually no symptoms at all; at higher levels, an overall fatigue, a low-grade fever and swollen or tender liver (or general abdominal pain) are the usual symptoms, along with worms or worm eggs in the faeces. Opisthorchiasis is easily treated with medication. Untreated, patients may develop serious liver infections several years after contact.

Rabies

This uniformly fatal disease is spread by the bite or lick of an infected animal – most commonly a dog or monkey. You should seek medical advice immediately after any animal bite and commence post-exposure treatment. Having a pretravel vaccination means the postbite treatment is greatly simplified. If an animal bites you, gently wash the wound with soap and water, and apply iodine based antiseptic. If you are not vaccinated you will need to receive rabies immunoglobulin as soon as possible.

Schistosomiasis

Schistosomiasis (also called bilharzia) is a tiny parasite that enters your skin when swimming in contaminated water – travellers usually only get a light, symptomless infection. If you are concerned, you can be tested three months after exposure. On rare occasions, travellers may develop 'Katayama fever'. It can occur some weeks after exposure, as the parasite passes through the lungs and causes an allergic reaction – symptoms are coughing and fever. Schistosomiasis is easily treated with medications.

STDs

Sexually transmitted diseases most common in Laos include herpes, warts, syphilis, gonorrhoea and chlamydia. People carrying these diseases often have no signs of infection. Condoms will prevent gonorrhoea and chlamydia but not warts or herpes. If after a sexual encounter you develop any rash, lumps, discharge or pain when passing urine seek immediate medical attention. If you have

been sexually active during your travels have an STD check on your return home.

Strongyloides

This parasite, also transmitted by skin contact with soil, rarely affects travellers. It is characterised by an unusual skin rash called larva currens – a linear rash on the trunk which comes and goes. Most people don't have other symptoms until their immune system becomes severely suppressed, when the parasite can cause an overwhelming infection. It can be treated with medication.

Tuberculosis

Tuberculosis (TB) is very rare in short-term travellers. Medical and aid workers, and long-term travellers who have significant contact with the local population should take precautions, however. Vaccination is usually only given to children under the age of five, but adults at risk are recommended pre- and post-travel TB testing. The main symptoms are fever, cough, weight loss, night sweats and tiredness.

Typhoid

This serious bacterial infection is also spread via food and water. It gives a high, slowly progressive fever and headache, and may be accompanied by a dry cough and stomach pain. It is diagnosed by blood tests and treated with antibiotics. Vaccination is recommended for all travellers spending more than a week in Southeast Asia, or travelling outside of the major cities. Be aware that vaccination is not 100% effective so you must still be careful with what you eat and drink.

Typhus

Murine typhus is spread by the bite of a flea whereas scrub typhus is spread via a mite. These diseases are rare in travellers. Symptoms include fever, muscle pains and a rash. You can avoid these diseases by following general insect-avoidance measures. Doxycycline will also prevent them.

TRAVELLER'S DIARRHOEA

Traveller's diarrhoea is by far the most common problem affecting travellers – between 30% and 50% of people will suffer from it within two weeks of starting their trip. In over 80% of cases, traveller's diarrhoea is caused by a bacteria (there are numerous potential

HEALTH

culprits), and therefore responds promptly to treatment with antibiotics. Treatment with antibiotics will depend on your situation – how sick you are, how quickly you need to get better, where you are etc.

Traveller's diarrhoea is defined as the passage of more than three watery bowel-actions within 24 hours, plus at least one other symptom such as fever, cramps, nausea, vomiting or feeling generally unwell.

Treatment consists of staying well hydrated. Rehydration solutions like Gastrolyte are the best for this. Antibiotics such as Norfloxacin, Ciprofloxacin or Azithromycin will kill the bacteria quickly.

Loperamide is just a 'stopper' and doesn't get to the cause of the problem. It can be helpful, for example if you have to go on a long bus ride. Don't take Loperamide if you have a fever, or blood in your stools. Seek medical attention quickly if you do not respond to an appropriate antibiotic.

Amoebic Dysentery

Amoebic dysentery is very rare in travellers but is often misdiagnosed by poor-quality labs in Southeast Asia. Symptoms are similar to bacterial diarrhoea, ie fever, bloody diarrhoea and generally feeling unwell. You should always seek reliable medical care if you have blood in your diarrhoea. Treatment involves two drugs; Tinidazole or Metronidazole to kill the parasite in your gut and then a second drug to kill the cysts. If left untreated complications such as liver or gut abscesses can occur.

Giardiasis

Giardia lamblia is a parasite that is relatively common in travellers. Symptoms include nausea, bloating, excess gas, fatigue and intermittent diarrhoea. 'Eggy' burps are often attributed solely to giardiasis, but work in Nepal has shown that they are not specific to this infection. The parasite will eventually go away if left untreated but this can take months. The treatment of choice is Tinidazole, with Metronidazole being a second line option.

ENVIRONMENTAL HAZARDS
Food

Eating in restaurants is the biggest risk factor for contracting traveller's diarrhoea. Ways to avoid it include eating only freshly cooked food, and avoiding shellfish and food that has

---

DRINKING WATER

- Never drink tap water.
- Bottled water is generally safe – check the seal is intact at purchase.
- Avoid fresh juices – they may have been watered down.
- Boiling water is the most efficient method of purifying it.
- The best chemical purifier is iodine. It should not be used by pregnant women or those people who suffer with thyroid problems.
- Water filters should filter out viruses. Ensure your filter has a chemical barrier such as iodine and a small pore size, ie less than four microns.

---

been sitting around in buffets. Peel all fruit, cook vegetables, and soak salads in iodine water for at least 20 minutes. Eat in busy restaurants with a high turnover of customers.

Heat

Many parts of Southeast Asia are hot and humid throughout the year. For most people it takes most people at least two weeks to adapt to the climate. Swelling of the feet and ankles is common, as are muscle cramps caused by excessive sweating. Prevent these by avoiding dehydration and excessive activity in the heat. Take it easy when you first arrive. Don't eat salt tablets (they aggravate the gut) but do drink rehydration solution and eat salty food. Treat cramps by resting, rehydrating with double-strength rehydration solution and gently stretching.

Dehydration is the main contributor to heat exhaustion. Symptoms include feeling weak, headache, irritability, nausea or vomiting, sweaty skin, a fast, weak pulse and a normal or slightly elevated body temperature. Treatment involves getting out of the heat and/or sun, fanning the victim and applying cool wet cloths to the skin, laying the victim flat with their legs raised and rehydrating with water containing a quarter of a teaspoon of salt per litre. Recovery is usually rapid, though it is common to feel weak for some days afterwards.

Heatstroke is a serious medical emergency. Symptoms come on suddenly and include weakness, nausea, a hot dry body with a body temperature of over 41°C, dizziness, confusion, loss of coordination, seizures and eventually collapse and loss of consciousness. Seek medical help and commence cooling by getting the person out of the heat, removing their clothes, fanning them and applying cool wet cloths or ice to their body, especially to the groin and armpits.

Prickly heat is a common skin rash in the tropics, caused by sweat being trapped under the skin. The result is an itchy rash of tiny lumps. Treat by moving out of the heat and into an air-conditioned area for a few hours and by having cool showers. Creams and ointments clog the skin so they should be avoided. Locally bought prickly heat powder can be helpful.

Tropical fatigue is common in long-term expats based in the tropics. It's rarely due to disease and is caused by the climate, inadequate mental rest, excessive alcohol intake and the demands of daily work in a different culture.

Insect Bites & Stings

Bedbugs don't carry disease but their bites are very itchy. They live in the cracks of furniture and walls and then migrate to the bed at night to feed on you. You can treat the itch with an antihistamine. Lice inhabit various parts of your body but most commonly your head and pubic area. Transmission is via close contact with an infected person, although body lice can come from contaminated bedclothes. They can be difficult to treat and you may need numerous applications of an anti-lice shampoo such as Permethrin, or in the case of body lice, with medicated creams or ointments. Pubic lice are usually contracted from sexual contact.

Ticks are contracted during walks in rural areas. They are commonly found behind the ears, on the belly and in armpits. If you have had a tick bite and experience symptoms such as a rash (at the site of the bite or elsewhere), fever or muscle aches you should see a doctor. Doxycycline prevents tick-borne diseases.

Leeches are found in humid forest areas. They do not transmit any disease but their bites are often intensely itchy for weeks afterwards and can easily become infected. Apply an iodine-based antiseptic to any leech bite to help prevent infection.

Bee and wasp stings mainly cause problems for people who are allergic to them. Anyone with a serious bee or wasp allergy should carry an injection of adrenaline (eg an Epipen) for emergency treatment. For others pain is the main problem – apply ice to the sting and take painkillers.

Parasites

Numerous parasites are common in local populations in Southeast Asia; however, most of these are rare in travellers. The two rules to follow if you wish to avoid parasitic infections are to wear shoes and to avoid eating raw food, especially fish, pork and vegetables. A number of parasites can be transmitted via the skin by walking barefoot including strongyloides, hookworm and cutaneous larva migrans.

Skin Problems

Fungal rashes are common in humid climates. There are two common fungal rashes that affect travellers. The first occurs in moist areas that get less air, such as the groin, armpits and between the toes. It starts as a red patch that slowly spreads and is usually itchy. Treatment involves keeping the skin dry, avoiding chafing and using an antifungal cream such as Clotrimazole or Lamisil. *Tinea versicolor* is also common – this fungus causes small, light-coloured patches, most commonly on the back, chest and shoulders. Consult a doctor for treatment.

Cuts and scratches become easily infected in humid climates. Take meticulous care of any cuts and scratches to prevent complications such as abscesses. Immediately wash all wounds in clean water and apply antiseptic. If you develop signs of infection (increasing pain and redness) see a doctor. Divers and surfers should be particularly careful with coral cuts as they become easily infected.

Snakes

Southeast Asia is home to many species of both poisonous and harmless snakes. Assume all snakes are poisonous and never try to catch one. Always wear boots and long pants if walking in an area that may have snakes. First-aid in the event of a snakebite involves pressure immobilisation via an elastic bandage firmly wrapped around the affected limb, starting at the bite site and working up towards the chest. The bandage should not be so tight that the circulation is cut off, and

HEALTH

AVIAN INFLUENZA (BIRD FLU)

In 2004, Laos, along with a number of other Southeast Asian countries, reported an outbreak of Avian influenza (bird flu). The strain in question, known as 'Influenza A H5N1' or simply 'the H5N1 virus', was a highly contagious form of Avian influenza that has since spread as far as Turkey to the west. Throughout the region, government officials scrambled to contain the spread of the disease, which wreaks havoc with domesticated bird populations.

While the Avian influenza virus usually poses little risk to humans, there have been several recorded cases of the H5N1 virus spreading from birds to humans. Since 1997, there have been about 250 reported cases of human infection, with a fatality rate of about 30%. The main risk is to people who directly handle infected birds or come into contact with contaminated bird faeces or carcasses. Because heat kills the virus, there is no risk of infection from properly cooked poultry. In February 2007 Laos reported its first human case of the H5N1 virus, no other human cases have been reported since this book went to print.

There is no clear evidence that the H5N1 virus can be transmitted between humans. However, the main fear is that this highly adaptable virus may mutate and be passed between humans, perhaps leading to a worldwide influenza pandemic.

Thus far, however, infection rates are limited and the risk to travellers is low. Travellers to Laos should avoid contact with any birds and should ensure that any poultry is thoroughly cooked before consumption.

the fingers or toes should be kept free so the circulation can be checked. Immobilise the limb with a splint and carry the victim to medical attention. Do not use tourniquets or try to suck the venom out. Antivenom is available for most species.

Sunburn

Even on a cloudy day sunburn can occur rapidly. Always use a strong sunscreen (at least factor 30), making sure to reapply after a swim, and always wear a wide-brimmed hat and sunglasses outdoors. Avoid lying in the sun during the hottest part of the day (from 10am to 2pm). If you are sunburnt stay out of the sun until you have recovered, apply cool compresses and take painkillers for the discomfort. One percent hydrocortisone cream applied twice daily is also helpful.

WOMEN'S HEALTH

Pregnant women should receive specialised advice before travelling. The ideal time to travel is in the second trimester (between 16 and 28 weeks), when the risk of pregnancy-related problems are lowest and pregnant women generally feel at their best. During the first trimester there is a risk of miscarriage and in the third trimester complications such as premature labour and high blood pressure are possible. It's wise to travel with a companion. Always carry a list of quality medical facilities available at your destination and ensure you continue your standard antenatal care at these facilities. Avoid travel in rural areas with poor transportation and medical facilities. Most of all, ensure travel insurance covers all pregnancy-related possibilities, including premature labour.

Malaria is a high-risk disease during pregnancy. WHO recommends that pregnant women do *not* travel to areas with Chloroquine-resistant malaria. None of the more effective antimalarial drugs are completely safe in pregnancy.

Traveller's diarrhoea can quickly lead to dehydration and result in inadequate blood flow to the placenta. Many of the drugs used to treat various diarrhoea bugs are not recommended in pregnancy. Azithromycin is considered safe.

In the urban areas of Southeast Asia, supplies of sanitary products are readily available. Birth control options may be limited though so bring adequate supplies of your own form of contraception. Heat, humidity and antibiotics can all contribute to thrush. Treatment is with antifungal creams and pessaries such as Clotrimazole. A practical alternative is a single tablet of Fluconazole (Diflucan). Urinary tract infections can be precipitated by dehydration or long bus journeys without toilet stops; bring suitable antibiotics.

TRADITIONAL MEDICINE

Throughout Southeast Asia, traditional medical systems are widely practised. There is a big difference between these traditional healing systems and 'folk' medicine. Folk remedies should be avoided, as they often involve rather dubious procedures with potential complications. In comparison, traditional healing systems such as traditional Chinese medicine are well respected, and aspects of them are being increasingly utilised by Western medical practitioners.

All traditional Asian medical systems identify a vital life force, and see blockage or imbalance as causing disease. Techniques such as herbal medicines, massage, and acupuncture are utilised to bring this vital force back into balance, or to maintain balance. These therapies are best used for treating chronic disease such as chronic fatigue, arthritis, irritable bowel syndrome and some chronic skin conditions. Traditional medicines should be avoided for treating serious acute infections such as malaria.

Be aware that 'natural' doesn't always mean 'safe', and there can be drug interactions between herbal medicines and Western medicines. If you are utilising both systems ensure you inform both practitioners what the other has prescribed.

HEALTH

Language

CONTENTS

Other Languages	342
Script	343
Tones	343
Transliteration	344
Pronunciation	345
Accommodation	346
Conversation & Essentials	346
Directions	347
Health	347
Emergencies	347
Language Difficulties	347
Numbers	348
Places & Land Features	348
Shopping & Services	348
Time & Dates	349
Transport	350

The official language of the LPDR is Lao as spoken and written in Vientiane. As an official language, it has successfully become the lingua franca (a universally understood linking language) between all Lao and non-Lao ethnic groups in Laos. Native Lao is spoken with differing tonal accents and with slightly differing vocabularies as you move from one part of the country to the next, especially in a north to south direction, but it is the Vientiane dialect that is most widely understood.

Modern Lao linguists recognise five basic dialects within the country: Vientiane Lao; northern Lao (spoken in Sainyabuli, Bokeo, Udomxai, Phongsali, Luang Nam Tha and Luang Prabang); northeastern Lao (Xieng Khuang and Hua Phan); central Lao (Khammuan and Bolikhamsai); and finally southern Lao (Champasak, Savannakhet, Salavan, Attapeu and Sekong). Each of these can be further divided into various subdialects; the differences between the Lao spoken in the neighbouring provinces of Xieng Khuang and Hua Phan, for example, are readily apparent to those who know the language well.

All dialects of Lao belong to the Thai half of the Thai-Kadai family of languages and are closely related to languages spoken in Thailand, northern Myanmar and pockets of China's Yunnan and Guangxi Provinces. Standard Lao is indeed close enough to standard Thai (as spoken in central Thailand) that for native speakers the two are mutually intelligible. In fact, virtually all of the speakers of Lao west of the Annamite Chain can easily understand spoken Thai, since the majority of the television and radio programmes they tune in to are broadcast from Thailand.

Among educated Lao, written Thai is also easily understood, in spite of the fact that the two scripts differ (to about the same degree that the Greek and Roman scripts differ). This is because many of the textbooks used at the college and university level in Laos are actually Thai texts.

Even more similar to Standard Lao are Thailand's northern and northeastern Thai dialects. There are actually more Lao speakers living in Thailand than in Laos, so if you're travelling to Laos after a spell in Thailand (especially the northeast), you should be able to put whatever you learned in Thailand to good use. (It doesn't work as well in the opposite direction; native Thais can't always understand Lao, since they've had less exposure to it.)

For information on food and dining in Laos, see p74. For a more in-depth guide to Lao than we have room for in this guide, get a copy of Lonely Planet's *Lao Phrasebook*. If you plan to travel extensively in any Lao Sung areas, Lonely Planet's *Hill Tribes Phrasebook* could also be useful.

OTHER LANGUAGES

In the cities and towns of the Mekong River valley, French is intermittently understood. In spite of its colonial history, French remains the official second language of the government and many official documents are written in both Lao and French. Shop signs sometimes appear in French (alongside Lao, as mandated by law), though signs in English are becoming more common. As in Vietnam, the former colonial language is increasingly viewed as irrelevant in a region that has adopted English as the lingua franca of business and trade, and among young Lao students English is now much more popular than French. Lao over the age of 50 may understand a little English, but to a lesser extent than French.

Many Russian-trained Lao can also speak Russian, though the language has drastically fallen from favour. The Russian Cultural Centre now offers more English courses than it does Russian, and the most popular event at the centre is an evening satellite TV programme of English-language shows. The occasional Lao who studied abroad in Cuba or Eastern Europe may be able to speak Spanish, German, Czech, Polish or even Bulgarian.

It pays to learn as much Lao as possible during your stay in the country, since speaking and understanding the language not only enhances verbal communication but garners a great deal of respect from the Lao people you come into contact with.

SCRIPT

Prior to the consolidation of the various Lao *meuang* (principalities) in the 14th century, there was little demand for a written language. When a written language was deemed necessary by the Lan Xang monarchy, Lao scholars based their script on an early alphabet devised by the Thais (which in turn had been created by Khmer scholars who used south Indian scripts as models!). The alphabet used in Laos is closer to the original prototype; the original Thai script was later extensively revised (which is why Lao looks 'older' than Thai, even though it is newer as a written language).

Before 1975 at least four spelling systems were in use. Because modern printing never really got established in Laos (most of the advanced textbooks being in Thai, French, or Vietnamese before the Revolution), Lao spelling wasn't standardised until after the Pathet Lao takeover. The current system has been highly simplified by transliterating all foreign loan words according to their sound only, and not their written form.

Lao script can therefore be learned much more quickly than Thai or Khmer, both of which typically attempt to transcribe foreign borrowings letter for letter, regardless of the actual pronunciation.

One peculiarity of the post-1975 system is that it forbade the use of the Lao letter 'r' in words where it was more commonly pronounced as an 'l', reportedly because of the association of the 'r' with classical Thai; although the 'r' was virtually lost in Laos (converting to 'h' in some cases and to 'l' in others), in many parts of Thailand it is still quite strong. Hence the names of former Lao kings Setthathirat and Phothisarat came to be rendered as Setthathilat and Phothisalat in post-1975 Lao script. Eventually the government loosened its restrictions and although the nasty 'r' is still not taught in the school system, it is once again allowed to be used in signage and in historical documents.

Other scripts still in use include *láo thám* (*dhamma* Lao), used for writing Pali scriptures, and various Thai tribal scripts, the most popular and widespread being that of the Thai Neua (which has become standardised via Xishuangbanna, China).

The Lao script today consists of 30 consonants (formed from 20 basic sounds) and 28 vowels and diphthongs (15 individual symbols used in varying combinations). Complementing the consonant and vowel symbols are four tone marks, only two of which are commonly used in creating the six different tones (in combination with all the other symbols). Written Lao proceeds from left to right, though vowel-signs may appear in a number of positions relative to consonants: before, after, above, below or 'around' (ie before, above *and* after).

Although learning the alphabet isn't difficult, the writing system itself is fairly complex, so unless you are planning to have a lengthy stay in Laos you should perhaps make learning to speak the language your main priority.

TONES

Basically, Lao is a monosyllabic, tonal language, like the various dialects of Thai and Chinese. Borrowed words from Sanskrit, Pali, French and English often have two or more syllables, however. Many identical phonemes or vowel-consonant combinations are differentiated by their tone only. The word *sao*, for example, can mean 'girl', 'morning', 'pillar' or 'twenty' depending on the tone. For people from non-tonal language backgrounds, it can be very hard to learn at first. Even when we 'know' the correct tone, our tendency to denote emotion, emphasis and questions through tone modulation often interferes with uttering the correct tone. So the first rule in learning and using the tone system is to avoid overlaying your native intonation patterns onto the Lao language.

Vientiane Lao has six tones (compared with five used in standard Thai, four in Mandarin and nine in Cantonese). Three of the tones are level (low, mid and high) while three follow pitch inclines (rising, high falling and low falling). All six variations in pitch are relative to the speaker's natural vocal range, so that one person's low tone is not necessarily the same pitch as another person's. Hence, keen pitch recognition is not a prerequisite for learning a tonal language like Lao. A relative distinction between pitch contours within your own voice is all that is necessary. Pitch variation is common to all languages; non-tonal languages such as English also use intonation, just in a different way.

Low Tone

Produced at the relative bottom of your conversational tonal range – usually flat level, eg *dii* (good). Note, however, that not everyone pronounces it flat and level – some Vientiane natives add a slight rising tone to the end.

Mid Tone

Flat like the low tone, but spoken at the relative middle of the speaker's vocal range. No tone mark is used, eg *het* (do).

High Tone

Flat again, this time at the relative top of your vocal range, eg *héua* (boat).

Rising Tone

Begins a bit below the mid tone and rises to just at or above the high tone, eg *sǎam* (three).

High Falling Tone

Begins at or above the high tone and falls to the mid level, eg *sâo* (morning).

Low Falling Tone

Begins at about the mid level and falls to the level of the low tone, eg *khào* (rice).

On a visual curve the tones might look like this:

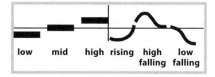

low mid high rising high falling low falling

TRANSLITERATION

The rendering of Lao words into the Roman alphabet is a major problem, since many of the Lao sounds, especially certain vowels, do not occur in English. The problem is compounded by the fact that because of Laos's colonial history, transcribed words most commonly seen in Laos are based on the old colonial French system of transliteration, which bears little relation to the way an English speaker would intuitively write a Lao word.

A prime example is the capital of Laos, Vientiane. The Lao pronunciation, following a fairly logical English-Roman transliteration, would be Wieng Chan or Vieng Chan (some might hear it more as Wieng Jan). Since the French don't have a written consonant that corresponds to 'w', they chose to use a 'v' to represent all 'w' sounds, even though the 'v' sound in Lao is closer to an English 'w'. The same goes for 'ch' (or 'j'), which for the French was best rendered 'ti-'; hence Wieng Chan (which means Sandalwood City) finishes up as 'Vientiane' in the French transliteration. The 'e' is added so that the final 'n' sound isn't partially lost, as it is in French words ending with 'n'. This latter phenomenon also happens with words like *lâan* (million) as in Lan Xang, which most French speakers would write as 'Lane', a spelling that leads most English speakers to incorrectly pronounce this word like the 'lane' in 'Penny Lane'.

Many standard place names in the Roman alphabet use an 'x' for what in English is 's'. This 'x' represents a Lao letter that historically was pronounced 'ch' but eventually became 's' in the Lao sound system. There's no difference in the pronunciation of the two; pronounce all instances of 'x' as 's'.

There is no official method of transliterating the Lao language (the government is incredibly inconsistent in this respect, though they tend to follow the old French methods). This book use a custom system of transliteration based on the Royal Thai General Transcription system, since Thai and Lao have very similar writing and sound systems. The only exceptions are where there may be confusion with terms that are already in common use (eg Vientiane vs 'Wieng Chan', Luang Prabang vs 'Luang Phabang').

The public and private sectors in Laos are gradually moving towards a more internationally recognisable system along the lines of Royal Thai General (which is fairly readable across a large number of language types).

PRONUNCIATION
Vowels
Lao vowels can be written before, after, above and below consonants – in the following vowel chart we demonstrate this by using 'x' to represent any consonant.

◌̆	**i**	as in 'it'
◌̂	**ii**	as in 'feet' or 'tea'
ໄx, ໃx	**ai**	as in 'aisle'
x◌	**aa**	long 'a' as in 'father'
xະ	**a**	half as long as **aa** above
ແx	**ae**	as the 'a' in 'bad' or 'tab'
ເx ະ, ເ ◌̆x	**e**	as in 'hen'
ເx	**eh**	as the 'a' in 'hate'
ເx̂, ເx̂	**oe**	as the 'u' in 'fur'
◌̀x, ◌̂x	**eu**	as in French *deux*, or as the 'i' in 'sir'
x̥	**u**	as in 'flute'
x̥	**uu**	as in 'food'
x◌ย	**aai**	as the 'a' in 'father' + the 'i' in 'pipe'
ເx̂◌	**ao**	as in 'now' or 'cow'
◌̊	**aw**	as in 'jaw'
ໂxະ, ◌̂ x	**o**	as in 'phone'
ໂx	**oh**	as in 'toe'
ເx̂ອ	**eua**	diphthong of 'eu' and 'a'
xʲx, ເx̂ย	**ia**	as the 'i-a' sound in 'Ian'
x◌x, x̂◌	**ua**	as the 'u-a' sound in 'tour'
x◌ย	**uay**	'u-ay-ee'
x̂◌, x̂◌	**iu**	'i-oo' (as in 'yew')
xʲ◌	**iaw**	a triphthong of 'ee-a-oo'
ແx◌	**aew**	as the 'a' in 'bad' + 'w'
ເx◌	**ehw**	as the 'a' in 'care' + 'w'
ເx̂◌	**ew**	same as 'ehw' above, but shorter (not as in 'yew')
ເx̂ย	**oei**	'oe-i'
xອย	**awy**	as the 'oy' in 'boy'
ໂx̂ย	**ohy**	'oh-i'

Consonants
An 'aspirated' consonant is produced with no audible puff of air. An 'unvoiced' or 'voiceless' consonant is produced with no vibration in the vocal chords.

ກ	**k**	as the 'k' in 'skin'; similar to the 'g' in 'good', but unaspirated and unvoiced
ຂ, ຄ	**kh**	as the 'k' in 'kite'
ງ	**ng**	as in 'sing'; used as an initial consonant in Lao
ຈ	**j**	similar to 'j' in 'join' or more closely, the second 't' in 'stature' or 'literature' (unaspirated and voiceless)
ສ, ຊ	**s**	as in 'soap'
ຍ	**ny**	similar to the 'ni' in 'onion'; used as an initial consonant in Lao
ດ	**d**	as in 'dodo'
ຕ	**t**	a hard 't', unaspirated and unvoiced – a bit like 'd'
ທ, ฐ	**th**	as in 'tip'
ນ, ໝ	**n**	as in 'nun'
ບ	**b**	as in 'boy'
ປ	**p**	a hard 'p' (unaspirated and unvoiced)
ພ, ผ	**ph**	'p' as in 'put' (but never as in 'phone')
ຝ, ฝ	**f**	as in 'fan'
ມ, ໝ	**m**	as in 'man'
ຢ	**y**	as in 'yo-yo'
ລ, ຫຼ	**l**	as in 'lick'
ວ, ຫວ	**w**	as in 'wing' (often transliterated as 'v')
ຮ, ຫ	**h**	as in 'home'

LANGUAGE

ACCOMMODATION

hotel
  hóhng háem
  ໂຮງແຮມ

guesthouse
  hǎw hap kháek
  ຫໍຮັບແຂກ

Excuse me, is there a hotel nearby?
  khǎw thôht, mîi hóhng háem yuu kâi nîi baw?
  ຂໍໂທດ ມີໂຮງແຮມຢູ່ໃກ້ນີ້ບໍ່

Do you have a room?
  mîi hàwng baw?
  ມີຫ້ອງບໍ່

How many persons?
  ják khón?
  ຈັກຄົນ

one person
  neung khón (khón diaw)
  ນຶ່ງຄົນ (ຄົນດຽວ)

two persons
  sǎwng khón
  ສອງຄົນ

How much ...?
  ... thao dǫi?   ... ເທົ່າໃດ
  per night
  khéun-la   ຄືນລະ
  per week
  qathit-la   ອາທິດລະ

air-conditioning
  qe yǎn   ແອເຢັນ

bathroom
  hàwng nâm   ຫ້ອງນ້ຳ

blanket
  phàa hom   ຜ້າຫົ່ມ

double room
  hàwng náwn tiang khuu   ຫ້ອງນອນຕຽງຄູ່

fan
  phat lóm   ພັດລົມ

hot water
  nâm hâwn   ນ້ຳຮ້ອນ

key
  kájqe   ກະແຈ

room
  hàwng   ຫ້ອງ

sheet
  phàa pǔu bawn náwn   ຜ້າປູບ່ອນນອນ

single room
  hàwng náwn tiang diaw   ຫ້ອງນອນຕຽງດຽວ

soap
  sábuu   ສະບູ

toilet
  sùam   ສ້ວມ

towel
  phàa set tǒh   ຜ້າເຊັດໂຕ

(I/we) will stay two nights.
  si phak yuu sǎwng khéun
  ຊິພັກຢູ່ສອງຄືນ

Can (I/we) look at the room?
  khǎw boeng hàwng dâi baw?
  ຂໍເບິ່ງຫ້ອງໄດ້ບໍ່

Do you have other rooms?
  mîi hàwng ìik baw?
  ມີຫ້ອງອີກບໍ່

cheaper
  théuk-kwaa
  ຖືກກວ່າ

quieter
  mit-kwaa
  ມິດກວ່າ

CONVERSATION & ESSENTIALS

Greetings/Hello.
  sábqai-dǐi   ສະບາຍດີ

Goodbye. (general farewell)
  sábqai-dǐi   ສະບາຍດີ

Goodbye. (person leaving)
  láa kawn pǫi kawn   ລາກ່ອນໄປກ່ອນ

Goodbye. (person staying)
  sǒhk dǐi (lit: good luck)   ໂສກດີ

See you later.
  phop kǫn mai   ພົບກັນໃໝ່

Thank you.
  khàwp jǫi   ຂອບໃຈ

Thank you very much.
  khàwp jǫi lǎi lǎi   ຂອບໃຈຫລາຍໆ

It's nothing/You're welcome.
  baw pęn nyǎng   ບໍ່ເປັນຫຍັງ

Excuse me.
  khǎw thôht   ຂໍໂທດ

How are you?
  sábqai-dǐi baw?   ສະບາຍດີບໍ່

I'm fine.
  sábqai-dǐi   ສະບາຍດີ

And you?
  jâo děh?   ເຈົ້າເດ້

What's your name?
  jâo seu nyǎng?   ເຈົ້າຊື່ຫຍັງ

My name is ...
  khàwy seu ...   ຂ້ອຍຊື່ ...

Glad to know you.
  dīi-jąi thii hûu káp jâo ດີໃຈທີ່ຮູ້ຈັກເຈົ້າ
Where are you from?
  jâo máa tae săi? ເຈົ້າມາແຕ່ໃສ
I'm from ...
  khàwy máa tae ... ຂ້ອຍມາແຕ່ ...

DIRECTIONS

Which ... is this?
bawn nîi ... nyăng? ບ່ອນນີ້ ... ຫຍັງ
  street/road/avenue
  thanŏn ຖະໜົນ
  city
  méuang ເມືອງ
  village
  muu bâan ໝູ່ບ້ານ
  province
  khwăeng ແຂວງ

Turn ...
lîaw ... ລ້ຽວ ...
  left
  sâai ຊ້າຍ
  right
  khwăa ຂວາ

Go straight ahead.
  pąi seu-seu ໄປຊື່ໆ
How far?
  kąi thao dąi? ໄກເທົ່າໃດ
near/not near
  kâi/baw kâi ໃກ້/ບໍ່ໃກ້
far/not far
  kąi/baw kąi ໄກ/ບໍ່ໄກ
north
  thit nĕua ທິດເໜືອ
south
  thit tâi ທິດໃຕ້
east
  thit tąawén àwk ທິດຕາເວັນອອກ
west
  thit tąawén tók ທິດຕາເວັນຕົກ

HEALTH

I'm not well.
  khàwy baw sábąai ຂ້ອຍບໍ່ສະບາຍ
I need a doctor.
  khàwy tâwng-kąan măw ຂ້ອຍຕ້ອງການໝໍ
I have a fever.
  pęn khài ເປັນໄຂ້
I have diarrhoea.
  lóng thâwng ລົງທ້ອງ
It hurts here.
  jép yuu nîi ເຈັບຢູ່ນີ້

EMERGENCIES

Help!
  suay dae! ຊ່ວຍແດ່
Fire!
  fái mài! ໄຟໄໝ້
It's an emergency!
  súk sŏen! ສຸກເສີນ
Go away!
  pąi dóe! ໄປເດີ້

Call a doctor!
  suay tąam hăa măw hâi dae!
  ຊ່ວຍຕາມຫາໝໍ ໃຫ້ແດ່
Call an ambulance!
  suay ôen lot hóhng măw hâi dae!
  ຊ່ວຍເອີ້ນລົດໂຮງໝໍ ໃຫ້ແດ່
Call the police!
  suay ôen tam-lùat dae!
  ຊ່ວຍເອີ້ນຕຳຫລວດແດ່
Could you help me please?
  jąo suay khàwy dąi baw?
  ເຈົ້າຊ່ວຍຂ້ອຍໄດ້ບໍ່
I'm lost.
  khàwy lŏng tháang
  ຂ້ອຍຫລົງທາງ
Where are the toilets?
  hàwng sùam yuu săi?
  ຫ້ອງສ້ວມຢູ່ໃສ

allergic (to)
  phâe ແພ້
anaemia
  lŏhk lêuat nâwy ໂລກເລືອດໜ້ອຍ
asthma
  lŏhk hèut ໂລກຫືດ
diabetes
  lŏhk bąo wăan ໂລກເບົາຫວານ
malaria
  khài paa ໄຂ້ປ່າ
pregnant
  thĕu pháa-máan ຖືພາມານ
  (mĭi thâwng) (ມີທ້ອງ)
toothache
  jép khàew ເຈັບແຂ້ວ

LANGUAGE DIFFICULTIES

Can you speak English?
  jâo pàak pháasăa ąngkít dâi baw?
  ເຈົ້າປາກພາສາອັງກິດໄດ້ບໍ່

A little.
náwy neung
ໜ້ອຍນຶ່ງ
I can't speak Lao.
khàwy páak pháasǎa láo baw dâi
ຂ້ອຍປາກພາສາລາວບໍ່ໄດ້
Do you understand?
jâo khào jai baw?
ເຈົ້າເຂົ້າໃຈບໍ່
(I) don't understand.
baw khào jai
ບໍ່ເຂົ້າໃຈ
Please speak slowly.
kálunáa wâo sâa-sâa
ກະລຸນາເວົ້າຊ້າໆ
Please repeat.
kálunáa wâo mai boeng dọu
ກະລຸນາເວົ້າໃໝ່ ບຶ່ງດູ
What do you call this in Lao?
ạn-nîi pháasǎa láo waa nyãng?
ອັນນີ້ພາສາລາວວ່າຫຍັງ

NUMBERS

0	*sǔun*	ສູນ
1	*neung*	ນຶ່ງ
2	*sǎwng*	ສອງ
3	*sǎam*	ສາມ
4	*sii*	ສີ່
5	*hàa*	ຫ້າ
6	*hók*	ຫົກ
7	*jét*	ເຈັດ
8	*pàet*	ແປດ
9	*kâo*	ເກົ້າ
10	*síp*	ສິບ
11	*síp-ét*	ສິບເອັດ
12	*síp-sǎwng*	ສິບສອງ
20	*sáo*	ຊາວ
21	*sáo-ét*	ຊາວເອັດ
22	*sáo-sǎwng*	ຊາວສອງ
30	*sǎam-síp*	ສາມສິບ
40	*sii-síp*	ສີ່ສິບ
50	*hàa-síp*	ຫ້າສິບ
60	*hók-síp*	ຫົກສິບ
70	*jét-síp*	ເຈັດສິບ
80	*pàet-síp*	ແປດສິບ
90	*kâo-síp*	ເກົ້າສິບ
100	*hâwy*	ຮ້ອຍ
200	*sǎwng hâwy*	ສອງຮ້ອຍ
1000	*phán*	ພັນ
10,000	*meun (síp-phán)*	ໝື່ນ(ສິບພັນ)
100,000	*sǎen (hâwy phán)*	ແສນ(ຮ້ອຍພັນ)
1,000,000	*lâan*	ລ້ານ

first	*thíi neung*	ທີນຶ່ງ
second	*thíi sǎwng*	ທີສອງ

PLACES & LAND FEATURES

Buddhist temple
  wat ວັດ
cemetery
  paa sâa ປ່າຊ້າ
church
  sìm khlit ສິມຄລິຕ
forest
  paa ປ່າ
jungle
  dong ດົງ
mountain
  phúu khǎo ພູເຂົາ
park/garden
  sǔan ສວນ
rice field (wet)
  náa ນາ
river
  mae nâm ແມ່ນ້ຳ
sea
  thaléh ທະເລ
stupa
  thâat ທາດ
swamp
  beung ບຶງ
trail/footpath
  tháang thíaw/nyaang ທາງຫຼວງ/ທາງຍ່າງ
waterfall
  nâm tók tàat ນ້ຳຕົກຕາດ

SHOPPING & SERVICES

Where is the ...?
... *yùu sǎi?* ... ຢູ່ໃສ
I'm looking for (the) ...
khàwy sâwk hǎa ... ຂ້ອຍຊອກຫາ ...
  bank
  thanáakháan ທະນາຄານ
  barber shop
  hâan tát phǒm ຮ້ານຕັດຜົມ
  bookshop
  hâan khǎai nǎng sěu ຮ້ານຂາຍໜັງສື

hospital
hóhng măw ໂຮງໝໍ
museum
phiphithaphán ພິພິທະພັນ
pharmacy
hâan khǎai yqa ຮ້ານຂາຍຢາໆ
post office
pqi-sá-nìi (hóhng sǎai) ໄປສະນີ (ໂຮງສາຍ)

I want to change ...
khàwy yàak pian ... ຂ້ອຍຢາກປ່ຽນ ...
  money
  ngóen ເງິນ
  travellers cheques
  sek dôen tháang ເຊັກເດິນທາງໆ

I'm looking for ...
  khàwy sàwk hǎa ... ຂ້ອຍຊອກຫາ ...
How much (for) ...?
  ... thao dqi? ... ເທົ່າໃດ
I'd like to see another style.
  khǎw boeng ìik
  bàep neung ຂໍເບິ່ງອີກແບບນຶ່ງ
Do you have something cheaper?
  mǐi thèuk-kwaa nìi baw? ມີຖືກກວ່ານີ້ບໍ່
The price is very high.
  láakháa pháeng lǎai ລາຄາແພງຫລາຍ

(latex) condoms
  thǒng yqang anáamái ຖົງຢາງອະນາໄມ
sanitary napkins
  phàa anáamái ຜ້າອະນາໄມ
soap
  sá-buu ສະບູ
toilet paper
  jîa hàwng nâm ເຈັ້ຍຫ້ອງນ້ຳ
toothbrush
  pqeng thǔu khàew ແປງຖູແຂ້ວ

telephone
  thóhlasáp
  ໂທລະສັບ
international call
  thóhlasáp ḷawaang páthêt
  ໂທລະສັບລະຫວ່າງໆປະເທດ
long distance (domestic)
  tháang kqi
  ທາງໄກ
open/closed
  pòet/pít
  ເປີດ/ປິດ

TIME & DATES

today
  mêu nìi ມື້ນີ້
tonight
  khéun nìi ຄືນນີ້
this morning
  sáo nìi ເຊົ້ານີ້
this afternoon
  baai nìi ບ່າຍນີ້
all day long
  talàwt mêu ຕລອດມື້
now
  diaw nìi/tqwn nìi ດຽວນີ້/ຕອນນີ້
sometimes
  bqang theua ບາງເທື່ອ
yesterday
  mêu wáan nìi ມື້ວານນີ້
tomorrow
  mêu eun ມື້ອື່ນ

Sunday
  wán qathit ວັນອາທິດ
Monday
  wán jqn ວັນຈັນ
Tuesday
  wán qngkháan ວັນອັງຄານ
Wednesday
  wán phut ວັນພຸດ
Thursday
  wán phahát ວັນພະຫັດ
Friday
  wán súk ວັນສຸກ
Saturday
  wán sǎo ວັນເສົາ

January
  dqwan mángkqwn ເດືອນມັງກອນ
February
  dqwan kqmpháa ເດືອນກຸມພາ
March
  dqwan mǐináa ເດືອນມີນາ
April
  dqwan méhsǎa ເດືອນເມສາ
May
  dqwan pheutsápháa ເດືອນພຶດສະພາ
June
  dqwan mithúnáa ເດືອນມິຖຸນາ
July
  dqwan kqwlakót ເດືອນກໍລະກົດ
August
  dqwan sínghǎa ເດືອນສິງຫາ
September
  dqwan kqnyáa ເດືອນກັນຍາ

LANGUAGE

October
dẹuan túláa
ເດືອນຕຸລາ
November
dẹuan phajík
ເດືອນພະຈິກ
December
dẹuan thánwáa
ເດືອນທັນວາ

TRANSPORT

Where is the ...
... yùu sǎi?
... ຢູ່ໃສ
  airport
  doen bìn
  ເດີ່ນບິນ
  bus station
  sathǎanii lot pájạm tháang
  ສະຖານີລົດປະຈຳທາງ
  bus stop
  bawn jàwt lot pájạm tháang
  ບ່ອນຈອດລົດປະຈຳທາງ
  departures/flights
  thîaw
  ກ້ຽວ
  taxi stand
  bawn jàwt lot thaek-sǐi
  ບ່ອນຈອດລົດແທກຊີ

What time will the ... leave?
... já àwk ják móhng? ... ຈະອອກຈັກໂມງ
  aeroplane
  héua bìn ເຮືອບິນ
  bus
  lot ລົດ
  boat
  héua ເຮືອ
  minivan
  lot tûu ລົດຕູ້

Also available from Lonely Planet:
Lao Phrasebook

What time (do we, does it, etc) arrive there?
já pai hâwt phûn ják móhng?
ຈະໄປຮອດພຸ້ນຈັກໂມງ
Where do we get on the boat?
lóng héua yuu sǎi?
ລົງເຮືອຢູ່ໃສ
I want to go to ...
khàwy yàak pại ...
ຂ້ອຍຢາກໄປ ...
I'd like a ticket.
khàwy yàak dâi pǐi
ຂ້ອຍຢາກໄດ້ປີ້
How much to ...?
pại ... thao dại?
ໄປ ... ເທົ່າໃດ
How much per person?
khón-la thao dại?
ຄົນລະເທົ່າໃດ
May I sit here?
nang bawn nǐi dâi baw?
ນັ່ງບ່ອນນີ້ໄດ້ບໍ່
Please tell me when we arrive in ...
wéhláa hâwt ... bàwk khàwy dae
ເວລາຮອດ ... ບອກຂ້ອຍແດ່
Stop here. (lit: park here)
jàwt yuu nǐi
ຈອດຢູ່ນີ້

taxi
  lot thâek-sǐi ລົດແທກຊີ
samlor (pedicab)
  sǎam-lâw ສາມລໍ້
sǎwngthǎew (passenger truck)
  sǎwngthǎew ສອງແຖວ
tuk-tuk (jumbo)
  túk-túk ຕຸ໊ກ ຕຸ໊ກ

I'd like to rent a ...
khàwy yàak sao ... ຂ້ອຍຢາກເຊົ່າ ...
  car
  lot (ǒh-tǒh) ລົດ(ໂອໂຕ)
  motorcycle
  lot ják ລົດຈັກ
  bicycle
  lot thìip ລົດຖີບ

Glossary

For a list of Lao words for different food and drink, see p80.

ąahaan – food
anatta – Buddhist concept of nonsubstantiality or nonessentiality of reality, ie no permanent 'soul'
anicca – Buddhist concept of impermanence, the transience of all things
Asean – Association of South East Asian Nations

bâan – the general Lao word for house or village; written Ban on maps
bąasïi – sometimes spelt basi or *baci;* a ceremony in which the 32 *khwăn* (guardian spirits) are symbolically bound to the participant for health and safety
baht – *(bàat)* Thai unit of currency, commonly negotiable in Laos; also a Lao unit of measure equal to 15g
BCEL – Banque pour le Commerce Extérieur Lao; in English, Lao Foreign Trade Bank
bịa – beer; *bịa sót* is draught beer
bun – pronounced *bųn,* often spelt boun; a festival; also spiritual 'merit' earned through good actions or religious practices

corvée – enforced, unpaid labour

dhamma – (Pali) truth, teachings, the teachings of the Buddha, moral law; dharma in Sanskrit
Don – pronounced *dąwn;* island
dukkha – Buddhist concept of suffering, unsatisfactoriness, dis-ease

falang – from the Lao *falang-sèht* or 'French'; Western, a Westerner
főe – rice noodles, one of the most common dishes in Laos

hăi – jar
hăw tại – monastery building dedicated to the storage of the Tripitaka (Buddhist scriptures)
hét bun – 'making merit', mostly by alms-giving to monks
héua – boat
héua hang nyáo – longtail boat
héua phái – rowing boat
héua wái – speedboat
hùay – stream; written Huay on maps

jao – pronounced *jâo;* lord or prince
Jataka – (Pali-Sanskrit) mythological stories of the Buddha's past lives; *sáa-dók* in Lao
jẹhdii – a Buddhist stupa; also written Chedi

jịin háw – Lao name for the Muslim Yunnanese who live in Northern Laos
jumbo – a motorised three-wheeled taxi, sometimes called tuk-tuk

kháen – a wind instrument devised of a double row of bamboo-like reeds fitted into a hardwood soundbox and made air-tight with beeswax
khào – rice
khào jịi – bread
khào nĭaw – sticky rice, the Lao staple food
khào-nŏm – pastry or sweet; sometimes shortened to *khanŏm*
khúu-bąa – Lao Buddhist monk
khwăeng – province
khwăn – guardian spirits
kip – pronounced *kìip;* Lao unit of currency

láap – a spicy Lao-style salad of minced meat, poultry or fish
lák méuang – city pillar
lám wóng – 'circle dance', the traditional folk dance of Laos, as common at discos as at festivals
Lao Issara – Lao resistance movement against the French in the 1940s
lào-láo – distilled rice liquor
Lao Loum – 'lowland Lao', ethnic groups belonging to the Lao-Thai Diaspora
Lao Soung – 'high Lao', hill tribes who make their residence at higher altitudes, for example, Hmong, Mien; also spelt Lao Sung
Lao Thoeng – 'upland Lao', a loose affiliation of mostly Mon-Khmer peoples who live on mid-altitude mountain slopes
lingam – a pillar or phallus symbolic of Shiva, common in Khmer-built temples
LNTA – Lao National Tourism Administration
LPDR – Lao People's Democratic Republic
LPRP – Lao People's Revolutionary Party

mae nâm – literally, water mother; river; usually shortened to *nâm* with river names, as in Nam Khong (Mekong River)
măw lám – Lao folk musical theatre tradition; roughly translates as 'master of verse'
meuang – pronounced *méuang;* district or town; in ancient times a city state; often written Muang on maps
múan – fun, which the Lao believe should be present in all activities
Muang – see *meuang*
muu bâan – village

náang síi – Buddhist nuns
naga – *nâa-kha* in Lao; mythical water serpent common to Lao-Thai legends and art
nâm – water; can also mean 'river', 'juice', 'sauce': anything of a watery nature
néhn – Buddhist novice monk; also referred to as *samanera*
NGO – nongovernmental organisation, typically involved in the foreign-aid industry
nibbana – 'cooling', the extinction of mental defilements; the ultimate goal of Theravada Buddhism
NPA – National Protected Area, a classification assigned to 20 wildlife areas throughout Laos
NVA – North Vietnamese Army

pạa – fish
pạa dàek – fermented fish sauce, a common accompaniment to Lao food
Pathet Lao – literally, Country of Laos; both a general term for the country and a common journalistic reference to the military arm of the early Patriotic Lao Front (a cover for the Lao People's Party); often abbreviated to PL
pha – holy image, usually referring to a Buddha; venerable
phàa – cloth
phàa bjang – shoulder sash worn by men
phàa nung – sarong, worn by almost all Lao women
phàa salòng – sarong, worn by Lao men
Pha Lak Pha Lam – the Lao version of the Indian epic, the Ramayana
phansăa – Buddhist Lent beginning in July, which coincides with the beginning of the rainy season; also *watsa*
phĭi – spirits; worship of these is the other main religion of Laos (and exists alongside Buddhism)
phúu – hill or mountain; also spelt phu

săa – the bark of a mulberry tree, from which paper is handcrafted
săaláa lóng thám – a *sala* (hall) where monks and lay people listen to Buddhist teachings
săam-lâaw – a three-wheeled pedicab; also written *samlor*

sabại-dịi – the Lao greeting
săinyasạat – folk magic
sakai-làep – alternative name for *jumbo* in Southern Laos due to the perceived resemblance to a space capsule (Skylab)
sala – pronounced *săa-láa*; an open-sided shelter; a hall
samana – pronounced *săamanáa*; 'seminar'; euphemism for labour and re-education camps established after the 1975 Revolution
samanera – Buddhist novice monk; also referred to as *néhn*
săwngthăew – literally, two-rows; a passenger truck; also written *songthaew*
se – also spelt *xe;* Southern Laos term for river; hence Se Don means Don River, and Pakse means *pàak* (mouth) of the river
shophouse – two-storey building designed to have a shop on the ground floor and a residence above
sĭi – sacred; also spelt *si*
sim – ordination hall in a Lao Buddhist monastery; named after the *sima*, (pronounced *siimáa*) or sacred stone tablets, which mark off the grounds dedicated for this purpose
soi – lane

tàat – waterfall; also *nâm tók;* written Tat on maps
talàat – market; *talàat sâo* is the morning market; *talàat mèut* is the free, or 'black', market; written Talat on maps
thâat – Buddhist stupa or reliquary; written That on maps
thaek-sĭi – taxi
thanŏn – street/road; often spelt Thanon on maps; shortened to 'Th' as street is to 'St'
tuk-tuk – see *jumbo*

UXO – unexploded ordnance

Viet Minh – the Vietnamese forces who fought for Indochina's independence from the French
vipassana – insight meditation

wat – Lao Buddhist monastery
wihăan – (Pali-Sanskrit vihara) a temple hall

Behind the Scenes

THIS BOOK

This 6th edition of *Laos* was researched and written by Andrew Burke (coordinator) and Justine Vaisutis. Professor Martin Stuart-Fox wrote the History chapter, Dr Trish Batchelor wrote the Health chapter and Steven Schipani penned the Ecotourism in Laos boxed text in the Environment chapter. The previous edition was authored by Joe Cummings and Andrew Burke.

This guidebook was commissioned in Lonely Planet's Melbourne office and produced by the following:

Commissioning Editors Carolyn Boicos, Kalya Ryan
Coordinating Editor Louise Clarke
Coordinating Cartographer Csanad Csutoros
Coordinating Layout Designers Mark Germanchis, David Kemp
Managing Editors Melanie Dankel, Katie Lynch
Managing Cartographers David Connolly, Julie Sheridan

Assisting Editors Elizabeth Anglin, Gennifer Ciavarra, Margedd Heliosz, Charlotte Orr
Assisting Cartographer Anneka Imkamp
Assisting Layout Designer Jacqui Saunders
Cover Designer Annika Roojun
Colour Designer David Kemp
Language Content Coordinator Quentin Frayne
Project Manager Chris Love

Thanks to David Burnett, Sally Darmody, Bruce Evans, Nicole Hansen, Yvonne Kirk, Rebecca Lalor, Chris Lee Ack, Adrian Persoglia, Averil Robertson, Celia Wood

THANKS
ANDREW BURKE

There are many to whom I owe a *khàwp jài lǎi lǎi* for their help in making this book possible. In Laos, Paul Eshoo in particular was a huge help and his dedication to village tourism is inspiring.

LONELY PLANET: TRAVEL WIDELY, TREAD LIGHTLY, GIVE SUSTAINABLY

The Lonely Planet Story

The story begins with a classic travel adventure: Tony and Maureen Wheeler's 1972 journey across Europe and Asia to Australia. There was no useful information about the overland trail then, so Tony and Maureen published the first Lonely Planet guidebook to meet a growing need.

From a kitchen table, Lonely Planet has grown to become the largest independent travel publisher in the world, with offices in Melbourne (Australia), Oakland (USA) and London (UK). Today Lonely Planet guidebooks cover the globe. There is an ever-growing list of books and information in a variety of media. Some things haven't changed. The main aim is still to make it possible for adventurous individuals to get out there – to explore and better understand the world.

The Lonely Planet Foundation

The Lonely Planet Foundation proudly supports nimble nonprofit institutions working for change in the world. Each year the foundation donates 5% of Lonely Planet company profits to projects selected by staff and authors. Our partners range from Kabissa, which provides small nonprofits across Africa with access to technology, to the Foundation for Developing Cambodian Orphans, which supports girls at risk of falling victim to sex traffickers.

Our nonprofit partners are linked by a grass-roots approach to the areas of health, education or sustainable tourism. Many projects we support – such as one with BaAka (Pygmy) children in the forested areas of Central African Republic – choose to focus on women and children as one of the most effective ways to support the whole community.

Sometimes foundation assistance is as simple as restoring a local ruin like the Minaret of Jam in Afghanistan; this incredible monument now draws intrepid tourists to the area and its restoration has greatly improved options for local people.

Just as travel is often about learning to see with new eyes, so many of the groups we work with aim to change the way people see themselves and the future for their children and communities.

Others who selflessly offered their friendship and expertise include Steven Schipani, Martin Rathie, Grace Nicholas and Tom Greenwood, Tom Morgan, Bridget McIntosh, Virginia Addison and Annette Monreal in Vientiane; Rachel and Joe Murphy in Vang Vieng; Jan Burrows, Suthep and Somkiad in Tha Khaek; 'Uncle Lee' in Ban Kheun Kham; Oudomxay Thongsavath and Khaisy Vongphoumy in Savannakhet; Craig and Natasha in Salavan; Buali, Emma Townsend-Gault, Phu Vong, Alan and Sririporn and Alex Azis in Pakse; Patrizia Zolese in Champasak; Eric Meusch and Mr Yai in Attapeu; and Bill Robichaud and Jim Johnstone in the middle of nowhere. And to all those guys who appeared from nowhere to fix my bike when the throttle cable snapped, a big thank you!

Several travelling companions made the journey more fun, particular thanks to Andrew Williamson, Frank Zeller, Paul and Simon, Stewart and Ingrid and Jon and Penny.

A special thanks to Justine Vaisutis for sharing my passion for Laos and going the extra miles in the name of research, and to Kalya Ryan and the various editors and cartographers at LP HQ who put up with me. Last but not least, a very big thanks to my wife, Anne.

JUSTINE VAISUTIS

Huge thanks first and foremost to Andrew Burke for being such a great colleague and a mate and to Anne for hospitality and great conversation. In Laos I owe a huge debt to Steven Schipani, Khamlay Sipaseuth, Bill Tuffin, Rob Tizard, and Tony Donovan and Bounby. Cheers to the travellers I met, particularly Fabien Rocha, and Jen and John for laughs and *lào-láo*. A special cheers goes to Katie Horner, my wonderful, witty travelling companion.

Big thanks to Kalya Ryan, Louise Clarke, Liz Anglin and Csanad Csutoros in-house for all their work and support.

At home thanks to Aidy, Mum, Dad and Bill, and eternal gratitude to Simon Sellars for being such a staunch ally through thick and thin.

PROFESSOR MARTIN STUART-FOX

Over the years, many Lao friends have provided me with invaluable information about Lao history, politics, society and culture. I have also learned much from the work of other scholars, for the serious study of any country is always a collaborative project. My friends and informants are far too numerous to be individually named, but I would like to mention the late Claude Vincent, Drs Mayoury and Pheuiphanh Ngaosrivathana,

Khamsing Khammanivong, Dr Somphou Oudomvilay, Dr Grant Evans, Dr Michel Lorrillard, and my former student, Martin Rathie.

OUR READERS

Many thanks to the travellers who used the last edition and wrote to us with helpful hints, useful advice and interesting anecdotes:

A Aleksi Aaltonen, Marion Algermissen, Megan Andrews, Raymond Ang, Patrick Antony, Neta Aran, Mary Atchison, Simon Atley, **B** Michel Baird, Josh Baker, Robert Baldwin, Marakusch Bengali, Assaf Bental, Catherine Benton, Freddy Bernaerts, Delbert Blake, Jarni Blakkarly, Lucas Blanco, Adrienne Bonde, Ryan Bovard-Johns, Max Branner, Alex Braun, Hollis Bromley, David Bruggen, Richard Burgio, Yvonne Butler, **C** Peter C, Darling Carl, Michael Chun, Andrew Cook, Jordi Cored, Barbara Crossette, Ian Cruickshank, Dugan Cummings, Liz Curran, **D** Alan Dainton, Emily Dalton, Jennifer Daly, Julia Damsell, Peter Danelski, Amit Dankwerth, Stuart Davis, Stuart & Pam Davis, Jeroen Decuyper, Luca Demichelis, Paul Diamond, Angela Dolan, Shawn Dolgin, John Paul Douglas, Margret Dowse-Brudow, Vivienne Duncan, Andrew Duy, **E** Jenny Earp, Kathleen Ellen, Daniel Emeny, Bettina Engel, Thomas Engel, Martin Engeset, Barbaba Erzinger, **F** Anne Fahey, Christopher Feierabend, Michael Firth, Sarah Foster, Bart Friederichs, Simon Fry, **G** Roel & Debby Geeraedts, Joshua Geisinger, Mordechai Gemer, Jeff Gilbert, Mark Given, Siow Yune Goh, Emma Gordon, Michele Gorman, Marval Grabner, Fredrik Graffner, Ann Graham, Ifat Granat, Charlotte Green, Oliver Gressieker, Marie-Adele Guicharnaud, **H** Harold De Haan, Moishe Hahn-Schuman, Judith Ham, Kelly Hardwick, Heinrich Hasper, Damien Hatcher, Regan Hawkins, Celine Heinbecker, Jess Hemmings, Aly Hendriks, Ann Hendrix, Jane Hennessy, Coleman Higgins, Rebecca Hill, Claire Hillier, Anna Hingorani, William Holloway, Sarah Horgan, Caroline Howard, Mario Hozic, Michael Huelsmann, **I** Renee Imbesi, Tobias Imboden, **J** Gill James, Luke James, John Jenks, Anne Jones, Kerry Jones, Rowan Jones, Rowan & Anna Jones, **K** Moran Karpol, Hugo Kearney, Fenneke Keijzers, Frank Kempster, David Kerkhoff, Paul Khoo, Sebastian Kiesow, Jan Kipping, Manfred Klement, Markus Kloss, Benjamin Knor, Joelle Kolman, Jennifer Konesavanh, Jutta Konig, Ilkka Koskinen, Jochem Kramer, Olga Kroes, **L** Penny Laurence, Claus Bang Lauridsen, Dan Lavelle, Andrea Lewis, Brian & Lorna Lewis, Kay Littlehales, Charles Locher, Inka Lofvenmark, Chris De Looze, Heinz Lutin, **M** Gary M, Hugo Mader, Simonette Mallard, Renzo Marcanzin, Lucy Marland, Robert Mcadam, Larry Mcgrath, Maureen Mcinroy, Jose Mejias, Royce De Melo, Rubina Menghrani, Regina Meyer, Marc Micklewright, David Miller, G P Mitchell, Ivy Mohchung, Forsk Moldova, Akos Molnar, Jon Moslet, Bob Muirhead, **N** Sigrid Norde, Enid Nuttall, **O** Rory O'Brien, Karin Ohlin, Dax Oliver, Karolina Olofsson, Ian Omaonaigh, **P** George Palmer, Trentus Paton, Darren Pearce, Patrick & Belinda Peck, Norm Peltier, Tom Peters, Franko Petri, Natalie Phanekham, Sengchanh Phomphanh, Katrina Pitt, Ian Playdon, Meike Plehn, Daniel Plewman, Ben Ploeger, Eugene Prahin, Janet Preston, F Primetzhofer, **R** David Ragg, Keith Reid,

Kymm Reid, Sarah Riches, Katja Rieger, Drew Roddy, Jesper Rogner, Hauke Rohwer, Zanchi Romana, Nicola Ronald, Kevin Rose, David Rostron, Stephanie Rozak, Janne Rueness, **S** Julie Sanderson, Regula Schmidhauser, Heiko Schmitz, Jo Schollaert, Frank Sharman, Jeffrey Sheather, Josh Shultz, Chelise Simmons, Megan Sinnott, Anneke Sips, Jan Skoglund, Heidi Smith, Jason Smith, Kathryn Smith, Julia Sobol, Eskil Sorensen, Blair Stafford, Karen Stafford, Julie Stapleton, Jonathan Stephens, Kathryn Stephens, Rebecca Stewart, Maria Strom, Lasse Svensson, Edward Sylvester, **T** H Taeed, Ka Lun Tam, Jasper Termeer, Willow Tesseneer, Olivier Tessier, Patrick Thurston, Daniel Tinsley, Kristin Tracz, Sam Trousdale, Nina Tschopp, Elaine Turner, **U** Josu Ugarteburu, Lamngeunh Uprajay, **V** Mart van Amerongen, Annemiek Verbeek, Janice Viekman, Maarten De Vries, Paul De Vries, **W** Rolf Wahlstrom, Steve Waller, Tom Walton, Giles & Sophie Watkins, Veronique Wattiaux, Wolfram Weidemann, Dean Wells, Stephen Wesley, Jon White, Stefan Wicki, Manuela Wieser, Terry Williams, Martin Wundsam, **Y** Lisbet Young, Fiona Youngwood, **Z** Sigrid Zundorf

ACKNOWLEDGMENTS

Many thanks to the following for the use of their content:

Globe on title page © Mountain High Maps 1993 Digital Wisdom, Inc.

SEND US YOUR FEEDBACK

We love to hear from travellers – your comments keep us on our toes and help make our books better. Our well-travelled team reads every word on what you loved or loathed about this book. Although we cannot reply individually to postal submissions, we always guarantee that your feedback goes straight to the appropriate authors, in time for the next edition. Each person who sends us information is thanked in the next edition – and the most useful submissions are rewarded with a free book.

To send us your updates – and find out about Lonely Planet events, newsletters and travel news – visit our award-winning website: **www.lonelyplanet.com/contact**.

Note: we may edit, reproduce and incorporate your comments in Lonely Planet products such as guidebooks, websites and digital products, so let us know if you don't want your comments reproduced or your name acknowledged. For a copy of our privacy policy visit www.lonelyplanet.com/privacy.

Index

A
accommodation 298-300
activities 19, 25, 300-1, *see also individual activities*
air travel **324**
  to/from Laos 319-21
  within Laos 323-4
Akha people 50, 55, 202, 206, 209, 213
Alak people 51, 282, 283
Ang Nam Ngum 120
Angkor era 28, 60, 255, 262, 265-8
animals 64-7
Anou, Chao 31
antiques 312
archaeological sites
  Heuan Hin 249
  Hintang Archaeological Park (Suan Hin) 186
  Ho Nang Sida 268
  Hong Tha Tao 268
  Kuruksetra 267
  Muang Kao (Old City) 267
  Uo Moung (Tomo Temple) 270
  Phu Asa 270
  Plain of Jars 169-71, 9
  Wat Phu Champasak 265-8, **265**, 7, 179
architecture 56, 57
area codes 314, *see also inside front cover*
arts 55-6
ATMs 309
Attapeu Province 293-7
Attapeu (Samakhi Xai) 293-5, **294**
Australian Embassy Recreation Club 100, 111
avian influenza (bird flu) 340

B
bạasii 55, 6
bathrooms 314
Ban Dong 250
Ban Hang Khong 274
Ban Hat Khai 119
Ban Hua Khang 186
Ban Huay 274

000 Map pages
000 Photograph pages

Ban Khon 277
Ban Khoun Kham (Ban Na Hin) 230
Ban Lak Ha-Sip Sawng 120
Ban Luang Khon 195
Ban Mai 296
Ban Na 118-19, 162
Ban Na Lae 201
Ban Nakham 207
Ban Nam Di 197
Ban Nam Sang 219
Ban Nong Luang 284
Ban Pa Sak 195
Ban Pakha 213
Ban Pako 116-17
Ban Phanom 159
Ban Phapho 270-1
Ban San Tai 189
Ban Saphai 260-1
Ban Singsamphan 262
Ban Sop Houn 160-2
Ban Tha Heua 120
Ban Thak 172
Ban Tham Buddha cave 185
Ban Thin Hong 158
Ban Wang Wai 189
Ban Xang Hai 158
Ban Xang Khong 158-9
Ban Xieng Maen 146
Ban Yo 213
Baw Nyai 171
bedbugs 339
beer gardens 110
Beerlao 77, 12
Beung Kan 229
bicycle travel, *see* cycling
bird flu 340
birds 67
Bo Y 296
boating 300, *see also* kayaking, rafting
boat travel 219, 300, 325-6
  Ang Nam Ngum 120
  Mekong River 21, 134, 156-7, 217-19, 225, 259, 175
  Nam Ou 156, 161, 212
  Nam Tha river trip 201-2, 176
  Se Kong 292, 179
  Tha Bak 233
  to Cambodian border 296-7
  to/from Attapeu 292
  to/from Hat Sa 212

  to/from Hongsa 225
  to/from Huay Xai 217-19
  to/from Luang Prabang 156
  to/from Pakse 259
  to/from Si Phan Don 276
  to/from Tham Kong Lo 232
  to/from Vientiane 113
  to/from Xieng Kok 209-10
  Vat Phou 274
  within Si Phan Don 274, 281
Bokeo Province 214-20
Bolaven Plateau 282-3
Bolikhamsai Province 228-42
bomb boats 233
bombs 182
books 18-20, *see also* literature
border crossings 321-4
  with Cambodia 283, 321
  with China 201, 321
  with Myanmar 321
  with Thailand 115, 218, 229, 238, 247, 261, 322
  with Vietnam 172, 188, 234, 241, 250, 296, 322-3
Boten 200, 201
Boun Neua 213
Boun Tai 213
Bouphavanh, Bouasone 47
boxing 62
Buddha sculptures 56-8, 95, 98-9, 120
Buddhism 52-3
Bun Awk Phansa 307
Bun Bang Fai 306
Bun Khao Phansa 306
Bun Khun Khao 306
Bun Nam 102, 275, 307
Bun Pha That Luang 101, 307, 9
Bun Pha Wet 306
Bun Pi Mai 306
Bun Pi Mai Lao (Lao New Year) 141
Bun Suang Heua 275
bus travel 326, 327, 329
business hours 301

C
camps, re-education (*samana*) 43, 183, 186
canoeing 300
car travel 326-9
carvings 312

catfish, Mekong 217
Cau Treo 234
cell phones 314
Cha Lo 241
Chaloen Suk 203
Champasak 262-5, **264**, **269**
Champasak Historical Heritage
    Museum 256
Champasak Province 255-86
Chenla kingdom 27, 134, 235, 255,
    293
Chiang Khong 218
children, travel with 302
Chinese New Year 78, 306
Chong Mek 261
chopsticks 80, 81
Christianity 55
cinemas 111
circus 111
climate 17, 302, 303
coffee 76-7, 284, 285
coffin cave 181
community service 146
conservation 68
consulates 305-6
costs 17, *see also inside front cover*
    accommodation 299
courses 303
    cooking 80, 101, 147, 303
    language 303
    textiles 147
    Vipassana meditation 101, 303
    weaving & dyeing 101, 147
crafts 58
credit cards 310
crocodiles 289
culture 46-62
    arts 55-6
    ethnic groups 50-2
    etiquette 46
    food 79-80
    immigration 52
    population 49
    religion 52-5
    sport 60-2
    women's issues 52
currency 309, *see also inside front cover*
customs regulations 303
cycling 300-1, 324-5
    Loop, the 240
    Luang Nam Tha 197
    Luang Prabang 148
    Sekong 292
    Southern Swing, the 263
    Vang Vieng 125

D
Dakcheung Plateau 290
dams 65, 71
dance 59
dangers 303-5
    bombs 305
    caving 123
    drugs 122-3, 128
    kayaking 122
    rafting 122
    road travel 304, 329
    speedboats 219, 304
    terrorism 304
    theft 304
    tubing 122
    ununexploded ordnance
        (UXO) 305
Dansavanh 250
deep vein thrombosis (DVT) 333
deforestation 71-3, 207
dehydration 338
dengue fever 334-5
departure tax 320
diarrhoea 337-8
digital photography 311
Dinosaur Museum 244
disabilities, travellers with 315
dolphins, Irrawaddy 279
Dom Kralor 283
Don Daeng 268-70
Don Det 276-82, **277**
Don Kho 260-1, **180**
Don Khon 276-82, **277**
Don Khong 272-6
Don Pak Soi 279
Dong Ampham NPA 70, 297
Dong Hua Sao NPA 283-4, **179**
Dong Natad 70, 247-9
Dong Phu Vieng NPA 70, 249-50
drinks 76-8
driving 326-9
drug use 122-3, 128
DVT 333

E
ecolodges 72
    Kingfisher Eco-Lodge 271
    Tad Fane Resort 284
    Utayan Bajiang Champasak
        (Phasoume Resort) 285-6
economy 26, 47-9
ecotourism 72
    Nam Ha Ecotourism Project 198,
        207
electricity 298

elephants 66, 118, **8**
    Ban Phapho 271
    Elephant Festival 224
    elephant trekking 224
    Hongsa 224-5
    Kiet Ngong 270
    Phu Khao Khuay NPA 119
    Tat Lo 287, **8**
email services 308
embassies 305-6
emergency services, *see inside front
    cover*
endangered species 66-7
environmental issues 63, 68, 69, 207
    fishing 69
    habitat loss 71
    hunting 69
    hydropower projects 71
ethnic groups 50-2, *see also* tribal
    groups
etiquette 46, 77, 79-80, 303, 311
exchange rates, *see inside front
    cover*

F
Fa Ngum, Chao 28
Fairtrade 285
fabric, *see* textiles
fax services 313-14
festivals 19, 306-7, *see also individual
    festivals*
filariasis 335
film industry 44
fishing 73, 217
fitness centres 99
fõe 75
food 74-84, 307, **11**, **12**
    cooking courses 80
    customs 79-80
    festivals 78
    vegetarian 78-9, 109
(Former) Saisombun Special Zone
    129-31
Fort Carnot 216
French rule 32-3
Friendship Bridge 247

G
gay travellers 307
geography 63
geology 63
giardiasis 338
glossary 351-2
government 26
guesthouses 299

H
handicrafts 58, 6
Hash House Harriers 99
Hat Sa 212
Haw Khao Padap Din 307
Haw Pha Kaeo 95, 173
health 331-41
heatstroke 338-9
Heritage House 146
Heuan Hin 249
Heuanchan 139
hiking, see trekking
Hin Khana 119
Hintang Archaeological Park (Suan Hin) 186
history 26, 27-45
  Angkor era 28, 60, 255, 262, 265-8
  books 18-20
history continued
  Chenla kingdom 27, 134, 235, 255, 293
  First Indochina War 35
  French rule 32-3
  independence 33-4
  Lan Xang kingdom 28-31
  Lao Issara 34
  Lao PDR, formation of 41
  LPRP, formation of 36
  Pathet Lao 35
  prehistory 27-8
  recent developments 43-5
  revolution 41-3
  second coalition government 37-9
  Second Indochina war 37-41
  secret army 38-9
  Tai-Lao migration 27-8
  US involvement 36-41
  WWII 33-4
hitching 329
Hmong market 171
Hmong people 51
Hmong resistance 26, 38-9, 129-30, 181
Ho Chi Minh 33
Ho Chi Minh Trail 250-2, 289-90
Ho Nang Sida 268
holidays 307
homestays 48, 298
  Ban Hat Khai 119
  Ban Kong Lo 232
Hong Tha Tao 268
Hongsa 224-5

000 Map pages
000 Photograph pages

hot springs, see mineral springs
hotels 299
hospitals 333
Htin people 51
Hua Don Daeng 269
Hua Phan Province 182-9
Huay Bo 162
Huay Bon Nature Trail 119
Huay Khi Ling 119
Huay Sen 162
Huay Xai 214-19, **215**
hunting 73
hydropower projects 71

I
immigrants 52
immigration regulations 319
Indochinese Communist Party (ICP) 33
insurance
  car 329
  health 331
  motorcycle 329
  travel 307
internet access 307-8
internet resources
  government travel warnings 305
  health 333
  news 20, 44
  travel information 20, 44
Irrawaddy dolphins 279
itineraries 15, 21-5, **21-5**
  Loop, the 240
  Savannakhet 248
  Southern Swing, the 263
  West Vang Vieng Loop 125

J
Japanese B encephalitis 335
jet lag 333
jewellery 313, 6
Jhai Coffee Farmer Cooperative 284, 285
jumbo 116, 329-30

K
Kasi 129
Katang people 51, 249
kátâw 61
Katu people 51, 282, 283, 290
kayaking
  Luang Nam Tha 197
  Muang Ngoi Neua 162
  Vang Vieng 124, 9
Kaysone Phomvihane 35
Kaysone Phomvihane Memorial 98
Kennedy, John F 37

Khamu people 51
Khammuan Limestone area 239
Khammuan Province 228-42
Khamtay Siphandone 274
Khamu people 27, 39, 51, 54
Khmaboui, Queen 186
Khon Phapheng Falls 282, 180
Khoun Kong Leng 239
khwăn 55
kickboxing 62
Kiet Ngong 270-1
Kong Le 37
Kuruksetra 267

L
làap 74, 12
Lak Sao 233-4, **233**
lakes
  Ang Nam Ngum 120
  Khoun Kong Leng 239
  Nong Bua 289
  Nong Fa 297
  Nong Luang 248
  Nong Tang 181
  Tha Falang 241
Lamet people 51
language 342-50
  courses 302
  food vocabulary 80
  glossary 351-2
langur 65
Lao Bao 250
Lao boxing 62
Lao Huay people 220
Lao Loum people 50
Lao National Culture Hall 98
Lao National Day 307
Lao National Museum 97-8
Lao National Theatre 111
Lao Patriotic Front (LPF) 36
Lao People's Revolutionary Party (LPRP) 36
Lao Soung people 51
Lao terms 342, 351
Lao Thai people 50-1
Lao Thoeng people 51
lào-láo 77
Laven people 283
legal matters 308
Leria, Giovanni-Maria 30
lesbian travellers 307
Li Phi Falls 278
Lisu people 51
literature 18, 59-61, see also books
Lolo people 51

Long Cheng 130-1
Loop, the 240
lot doi saan 326
Luang Nam Tha 195-200, **196**
Luang Nam Tha Museum 195
Luang Nam Tha Province 194-210
Luang Prabang 134-58, **136**, **138**, 8,
    12, **176**
    accommodation 149-51
    activities 146-8
    drinking 154
    entertainment 154-5
    food 151-4
    internet access 137
    medical services 137-8
    shopping 155
    tourist information 139
    travel to/from 155-7
    travel within 157-8
    walking tour 147-8, **148**
Luang Prabang Province 134-64

M
Mabri people 220
Magha Puja (Makha Busa) 306
Mahaxai 240
mail services 312
malaria 335-6
maps 308-9
markets 78
    Luang Prabang 155, 12
    Vientiane 113
massage 96, 99, 147
mǎw lám 59
measurements 298, *see also inside*
    front cover
medical services 333-4, *see also* health
Mekong catfish 217
Mekong River 63-4, 255, 175, *see also*
    boat travel
melioidosis 336
Mengla (China) 213
Mien people 51
mineral springs
    Baw Noi 171
    Baw Nyai 171
    Muang La 192
    Muang Vieng Thong 189
Mines Advisory Group 167
mobile phones 314
Mohan 201
money 17, 309-11, *see also inside*
    front cover
Monkey Forest 248
motion sickness 333

motorcycle travel 304, 326-9
    Loop, the 240
    Savannakhet 248
    Southern Swing, the 263
    Vang Vieng 125
    West Vang Vieng Loop 125
Mouhot's Tomb 159
mountain bikes, *see* cycling
Muang Houn 192
Muang Kao (Old City) 267
Muang Kham 171
Muang Khanthabuli (Savannakhet)
    242-7, **243**, 178
Muang Khong 274
Muang Khoun (Old Xieng Khuang)
    172, **169**
Muang Khua 213-14
Muang La 213
Muang Lamam (Sekong) 290-2
Muang Long 209
Muang Ngoen 225
Muang Ngoi Neua 162-4
Muang Phin 252
Muang Phu Khoun 129
Muang Saen 274
Muang Sing 70, 203, **203**, 175, 177
Muang Sing Exhibitions Museum 205
Muang Sui 181-2
Muang Vieng Kham 189
Muang Vieng Thong 189
Muang Xai (Udomxai) 190-2, **191**
múay láo (Lao boxing) 62
Mukdahan 247
Museum of Tribes 211
museums
    Champasak Historical Heritage
        Museum 256
    Dinosaur Museum 244
    Haw Pha Kaeo 95, 173
    Kaysone Phomvihane Memorial 98
    Lao National Museum 97-8
    Luang Nam Tha Museum 195
    Muang Sing Exhibitions Museum
        205
    Royal Palace Museum (Ho Kham)
        139-41, 176
    Savannakhet Provincial Museum 244
music 59, 60, 111

N
Na Maew 322
Na Phao 241
Nakai 240
Nakai-Nam Theun NPA 69
Nakhon Phanom 238

Nam Bak 164
Nam Beng 192
Nam Can 172
Nam Don 241, 242
Nam Don Resurgence 242
Nam Et/Phu Loei NPA 189
Nam Ha Ecotourism Project 198, 207
Nam Ha NPA (NPA) 70, 198
Nam Hin Bun 232
Nam Houn 160
Nam Houng 221, 222
Nam Kading 229, 233
Nam Kading NPA 229-30
Nam Khao 189
Nam Khan 172
Nam La 203
Nam Lik 25
Nam Noen 188-9
Nam Ou 64, *see also* boat travel
Nam Pa 296
Nam Pak 192
Nam Phak 213
Nam Phao 234
Nam Phoun NPA 220
Nam Sam NPA 185
Nam San 228
Nam Song 121, 122, 125, 9, 11, 174
Nam Tha 201-2
Nam Tha river trip 201-2, 176
Nam Theun 233
Nam Tok Katamtok 292-3
Nam Tok Tat Khu Khana 119
Nam Xoi 188
Nameo 188
National Protected Areas (NPAs) 69, 70
    Dong Amphan 70, 297
    Dong Hua Sao NPA 283-4, 179
    Dong Phu Vieng 70, 249-50
    Nam Et/Phu Loei 189
    Nam Ha 70, 198
    Nam Kading 229-30
    Nakai-Nam Theun 69
    Nam Phoun 20
    Nam Sam 185
    Phu Hin Bun 70, 230-1
    Phu Khao Khuay 70, 118
    Phu Xang Hae NPA 250
    Phu Xieng Thong 70, 261-2
    Se Pian 70, 271-2, 296-7
    Se Xap NPA 290
New Year, Lao 141, 306
newspapers 90, 298
Nong Bua 289
Nong Fa 297
Nong Haet 171

Nong Khiaw 160-2, **161**
Nong Luang 248
Nong Pet 171
Nong Tang 181
Nosavan, General Phoumi 37

O

opisthorchiasis (liver flukes) 336-7
opium 206
Ou Tai 213

P

pa pao 292
pqa béuk 217
Pa-am 296
Pak Beng 192-4, **193**
Pak Kading 229
Pak Lai 223-4, **233**
Pak Mong 164
Pak Nam Noi 213
Pak Ou caves 158, 11, 176
Paksan 228-9
Pakse 255-60, **257**
  accommodation 256-8
  activities 256
  attractions 256
  drinking 259
  emergency services 255
  entertainment 259
  food 258-9
  internet access 255
  tourist offices 255
  travel to/from 259-60
  travel within 260
Paksong 284-5
Pao, General Vang 38-9
papermaking 197
passports 319
Pathet Lao 35, 187
Patuxai 97, 173
Pavie, Auguste 32
petang 61, 10
Pha Bang 29, 30, 53, 135, 139, 176
Pha Luang 119
Pha Meuang 296
Pha That Luang 91-4, 7
Pha That Sikhottabong 238-9, 178
Pha Xai 119
Pha Xang 220
Phasoume Resort 285
Phetsarat, Prince 34

phìi 54
Phomvihane, Kaysone 41, 43
Phon Hong 120
phonecards 314
Phongsali 70, 210-13, **211**, 5
Phongsali Province 210-14
Phonsavan 165-9
photography 311
Phouma, Souvanna 36, 37, 41
Phoumsavan, Nouhak 35
Phra That Khong Santi Chedi 145
Phu Asa 270
Phu Hin Bun NPA 230-1
Phu Khao Khuay NPA 70, 118
Phu Khong 262
Phu Noi people 50, 210
Phu Si 143-4
Phu Vong 296
Phu Xang Hae NPA 250
Phu Xieng Thong NPA 70, 261-2
Phuoi 284
Plain of Jars 169-71, **169**, 9
planning 17-20, *see also* itineraries
plants 67-9
politics 26
  books 18-20
  modern 47-9
population 49
postal services 312
Princes' Bridge 289
public holidays 307
Pung Xay 119

R

radio 298
rafting 300
  Dong Hua Sao 284
  Luang Nam Tha 197
  Luang Prabang 148
  Pakse 255
  Si Phan Don 278
  Vang Vieng 124-5
re-education camps *(samana)* 43,
  183, 186
religion 52-5, *see also individual*
  religions
resorts 300
restaurants 78, 307
river trips, *see* boat travel
rivers 63-4, *see also individual rivers*
rock climbing 301
  Vang Vieng 125
Royal Lao Government 36
Royal Palace Museum (Ho Kham)
  139-41, **140**, 176

S

sǎam-lâaw 329-30
safety 303-5
  bombs 305
  caving 123
  drugs 122-3, 128
  kayaking 122
  rafting 122
  road travel 304, 329
  speedboats 219, 304
  terrorism 304
  theft 304
  tubing 122
  ununexploded ordnance (UXO) 305
Sainyabuli 221-3, **221**
Sainyabuli Province 220-5
Saisettha 296
Saisombun Special Zone (Former) 129-31
sakai-làep 329-30
Salavan 288-9, **288**
Salavan Province 286-90
Sam Neua (Xam Neua) 183-5, **184**
Sam Tai 185
Samakhi Xai (Attapeu) 293-5, **294**
samana, *see* re-education camps
Samsenthai 29
Sangha 53
Savang Vatthana, King 186
Savannakhet (Muang Khanthabuli)
  242-7, **243**, 178
Savannakhet Province 242-52
Savannakhet Provincial Museum 244
sǎwngthǎew 326
Say Vong Savang, Prince 186
Sayasone, General Chummaly 43, 47
Saysetthathirat, King 293, 296
schistosomiasis 337
sculpture 56-8
Se Ban Nuan NPA 286
Se Don 255
Se Kaman 296
Se Kong 290, 179
Se Nam Noi 292
Se Pian NPA 70, 271-2, 296-7
Se Pon 250
Se Su 297
Se Xap NPA 290
Second Indochina War 37-41, 130-1,
  171, 181, 250
secret army 38-9
secret war 130-1
Sekong (Muang Lamam) 290-2
Sekong Province 290-3
Sepon Kao 250
Sepon (Xepon) 250-2

Setthathirat 30
shooting 99-100
shopping 312-13
silk, *see* textiles
Si Phan Don (Four Thousand Islands) 272-82, **273**, 10, 180
Siphandone, General Khamtay 43
Sisavang Vong, King 143
Sleeping Wall 125
snakes 339-40
solo travellers 313
Songkan (Water Festival) 141
Souphanouvong, Prince 35, 41
Southern Swing, the 263
special events 19, 306-7
speedboats 219, 304, 326, *see also* boat travel
sport 60-2
stupas, *see also* temples
  Pha Meuang 296
  Pha That Luang 91-4, 7
  Pha That Sikhottabong 238-9, 178
  Phra That Khong Santi Chedi 145
  That Banmang 181
  That Chom Phet 172
  That Chomsi 144
  That Dam 97
  That Foun 172
  That Ing Hang 247, 177
  That Phum Phuk 195
su khwăn 55
Suan Hin 186
Suay people 283
Sui Reservoir 248

T
Ta Ong 272
Tad Fane Resort 284
Tahoy 289-90
Taksin 31
Taliang people 290
Ta-oy people 289
Tat Fa 119
Tat Faek 292
Tat Fan 283-4, 179
Tat Hang 287
Tat Hia 292
Tat Jao 221
Tat Kameud 284
Tat Kuang Si 159, 6
Tat Lak Sip-Et 192
Tat Lang 170
Tat Leuk 119
Tat Lo 286, 287
Tat Meelook 285

Tat Mok 163
Tat Nam Neua 186
Tat Namsanam 230
Tat Sae 159-60
Tat Saepha 296
Tat Saeponglai 296
Tat Saloei 185
Tat Samongphak 296
Tat Se Noi 292
Tat Somphamit (Li Phi Falls) 278
Tat Suong 287
Tat Tha Jet 284
Tat Wang Fong 229
Tat Xai 119
Tat Yong 192
Tat Yuang 285
taxes 320
taxis 330
tea 76-7
telephone services 313-14
temples, *see also* stupas
  architecture 57
  Haw Pha Kaeo 95, 173
  tour 25
  Wat Aham 143
  Wat Ban Boung Kham 268
  Wat Ban Khon 225
  Wat Ban Luang Khon 195
  Wat Ban Phong 181
  Wat Ban Vieng Tai 195
  Wat Chom Phet 146
  Wat Choumkhong 145
  Wat Don Kho 261
  Wat Hai Sok 101
  Wat Ho Pha Bang 141
  Wat In Paeng 101
  Wat Jan Tak Sa Po 248
  Wat Jom Khao Manilat 215
  Wat Jom Thong 274
  Wat Kang 123, 163
  Wat Khok Kho 193
  Wat Khon Tai 277
  Wat Long Khun 145
  Wat Luang 256, 178
  Wat Luang Muang Mai 294
  Wat Mahapot 202
  Wat Mai Suwannaphumaham 143
  Wat Manolom 143
  Wat Nam Kaew Luang 206
  Wat Neua 163
  Wat Nong Sikhunmeuang 145
  Wat Nyutthitham 262
  Wat Ong Teu Mahawihan 96
  Wat Pa Huak 144
  Wat Pa Phai 145

Wat Pa Phon Phao 145
Wat Pha Baht Phonsan 119
Wat Pha Baht Tai 145
Wat Pha Mahathat 145
Wat Pha Phutthabaht 144
Wat Pha Saysettha 296
Wat Phia Wat 172
Wat Phu Champasak 265-8, **265**, 7, 179
Wat Phu Khao Kaew 274
Wat Phuang Kaew 274
Wat Phuthawanaram 262
Wat Rattanalangsi 244
Wat Sainyaphum 244
Wat Salibun Nyeun 225
Wat Sensoukarahm 145
Wat Si Amphon 97
Wat Si Bun Huang 221
Wat Si Muang 96, 173
Wat Si Phan Don 221
Wat Si Phoum 172
Wat Si Saket 94-5
Wat Si Suman 123
Wat Si Vieng Song 123
Wat Sin Jong Jaeng 193
Wat Sisavang Vong 221
Wat Sok Pa Luang 96-7
Wat Sop 148
Wat Tai 163
Wat Tham Fai 256
Wat Tham Xieng Maen 145
Wat That Luang 143
Wat That Luang Neua 91
Wat That Luang Tai 91
Wat Wisunarat (Wat Visoun) 142-3
Wat Xieng Jai 205
Wat Xieng Kang 143
Wat Xieng Maen 146
Wat Xieng Muan 144-5
Wat Xieng Thong 141-2, **142**, 5, 175
terrorist activity 304
textiles 58, 313, 7, 180
  Ban Phanom 159
  Ban Saphai 260-1
  Ban Xang Khong 158-9
  courses 101
  Don Kho 260-1, 180
  Luang Prabang 147, 155
  Muang Sing 206
  Pa-am 296
  Sam Neua 183
  Sam Tai 185
  Sekong 291
  Vientiane 112-13

INDEX

Tha Bak 233
Tha Falang 241
Tha Khaek 234-8, **235**, 178
Thai Dam people 51, 54, 55, 206
Thai Lü people 57, 224
Thai Neua people 51, 182
Thai Pa people 51
Thai-Lao Friendship Bridge 115, 322
Thalat 120
Tham Davadeung 201
Tham Hoi 123
Tham Jang (Tham Chang) 123, 174
Tham Kang 162
Tham Kong Lo 231
Tham Loup 123
Tham Nam 124
Tham Nam Eng 202
Tham Nang Aen 241
Tham Non (Sleeping Cave) 125
Tham Pha 181
Tham Pha Ban Tham 240
Tham Pha Chan 242
Tham Pha Kaeo 162
Tham Pha Pa (Buddha Cave) 239, 177
Tham Pha Thok 160
Tham Phu Kham 123, 174
Tham Phu Khiaw 274
Tham Piu 171
Tham Piu Song 171
Tham Sa Pha In (Tham Phanya Inh) 241
Tham Sang 123
Tham Than Kaysone 187
Tham Than Khamtay 187
Tham Than Nouhak 187
Tham Than Souphanouvong 187
Tham That 181
Tham Xang (Tham Pha Ban Tham) 240-1
Tham Xieng Liap 241
Tham Xieng Muang 187
That Banmang 181
That Chom Phet 172
That Chomsi 144
That Dam 97
That Foun 172
That Ing Hang 247, 177
That Phum Phuk 195
That Xieng Tung Festival 207
theft 304-5
tigers 66, 12
time 314

000 Map pages
000 Photograph pages

tipping 311
toilets 314
Toumlan 289
tourist information 314-15
tours 330, see also boat travel,
  ecotourism, itineraries
traditional medicine 341
transport 319-30
travellers cheques 311
travellers with disabilities 315
trekking 70, 204-5, 301
  Don Khon 278
  Dong Ampham NPA 70, 297
  Dong Hua Sao NPA 283-4
  Dong Natad 70, 247-9
  Dong Phu Vieng NPA 70
  Luang Nam Tha 197
  Muang Ngoi Neua 162
  Muang Sing 70
  Nam Ha NPA 70, 198
  Nam Lan Conservation area 213
  Nong Khiaw 160
  Phongsali 70
  Phu Hin Bun NPA 70, 230-1
  Phu Khao Khuay NPA 70
  Phu Xieng Thong NPA 70, 261-2
  Se Pian NPA 70, 271-2, 296-7
  Tat Lo 286
  Tha Khaek 236
  Vieng Phoukha 70, 202
tribal groups 27-8, 50-2
  Alak 51, 282, 283
  Hmong 51, 10
  Htin 51
  Katang 51, 249
  Katu 51, 282, 283, 290
  Khamu 51
  Lamet 51
  Lao Huay 220
  Lao Loum 50
  Lao Soung 51
  Lao Thai 50-1
  Lao Thoeng 51
  Laven 51, 283
  Lisu 50
  Lolo 50
  Mabri 220
  Mien 51
  Phu Noi 50, 210
  Suay 283
  Taliang 290
  Ta-oy 289
  Thai Dam 51, 54, 55, 206, 175
  Thai Khao 51

  Thai Lü 57, 224
  Thai Neua 51, 182
  Thai Pa 51
tubing
  Muang Ngoi Neua 162
  Vang Vieng 125-6, 174
tuk-tuks 116, 329-30
turtles 248
TV 298

U
Udomxai (Muang Xai) 190-2, **191**
Udomxai Province 189-94
unexploded ordnance (UXO) 167,
  290, 305
Uo Moung (Tomo Temple) 270
Utayan Bajiang Champasak
  (Phasoume Resort) 285-6

V
vaccinations 331-2
van Wuysthoff, Gerrit 30
Vang Pao, General 130-1
Vang Sang 120
Vang Tao 261
Vang Vieng 121-9, **121**, **124**, 9, 11, 174
Vat Phou 274
Vatthana, King Sisavang 37
vegetarian travellers 78-9, 109
video systems 311
Vieng Kaew 224
Vieng Phoukha 70, 202
Vieng Xai 187-8
Vientiane 85-116, **88-9**, **92**, **117**
  accommodation 102-5
  activities 99-101
  attractions 91-9
  drinking 109-10
  entertainment 110-12
  food 105-9
  internet access 90
  medical services 90
  shopping 112-13
  tourist offices 91
  travel to/from 113-15
  travel within 115-16
  walking tour 100-1, **100**
Vipassana meditation 101, 303
Visakha Busa 306
visas 315-17, see also passports
Visoun, King (Wisunarat) 29, 53
Voen Kham 283
volunteering 160, 317
Vong, King Sisavang 34
Vongsa, Suriya 30

W

walking, *see* trekking
water 76
waterfalls
  Hin Khana 119
  Khon Phapheng Falls 282, 180
  Nam Tok Katamtok 292-3
  Nam Tok Tat Khu Khana 119
  Pha Xai 119
  Tat Fa 119
  Tat Faek 292
  Tat Fan 283-4, 179
  Tat Hang 287
  Tat Hia 292
  Tat Jao 221
  Tat Kameud 284
  Tat Kuang Si 159, 6
  Tat Lak Sip-Et 192
  Tat Lang 170
  Tat Leuk 119
  Tat Lo 287
  Tat Meelook 285
  Tat Mok 163

Tat Nam Neua 186
Tat Namsanam 230
Tat Sae 159-60
Tat Saepha 296
Tat Saeponglai 296
Tat Saloei 185
Tat Samongphak 296
Tat Se Noi 292
Tat Somphamit (Li Phi Falls) 278
Tat Suong 287
Tat Tha Jet 284
Tat Wang Fong 229
Tat Xai 119
Tat Yong 192
Tat Yuang 285
wats, *see* temples, stupas
Wattay International Airport 115, 319
weather 17, 302, 303
weaving, *see* textiles
weights 298, *see also inside front cover*
West Vang Vieng Loop 125
wildlife 64-8, *see also* National
  Protected Areas

wine 77-8
Wisunarat 29
women travellers 317-18
women's issues 52
  health 340
  solo travellers 313
work 318
WWII 33-4
Wuysthoff, Gerrit van 93

X

Xainya Chakkaphat 29
Xam Neua (Sam Neua) 183-5, **184**
Xe Pian NPA (Se Pian NPA) 70, 271-2,
  296-7
Xe Xap NPA (Se Xap NPA) 290
Xepon (Sepon) 250-2
Xieng Khuan (Buddha Park) 98-9,
  8, 173
Xieng Khuang (Muang Khoun) 172,
  169
Xieng Khuang Province 164-82
Xieng Kok 209-10

INDEX

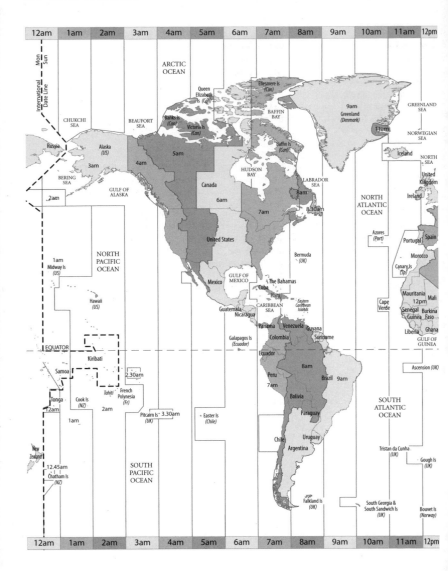

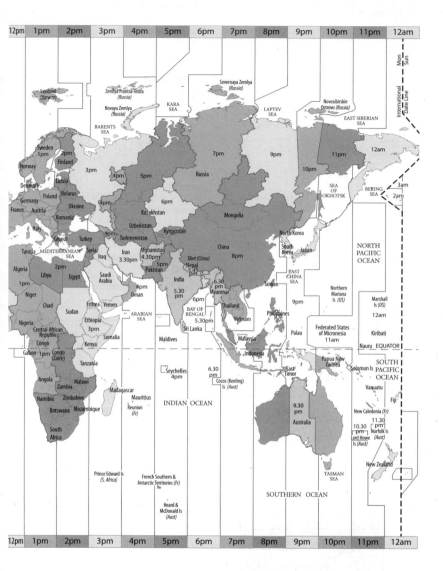

| 12pm | 1pm | 2pm | 3pm | 4pm | 5pm | 6pm | 7pm | 8pm | 9pm | 10pm | 11pm | 12am |

Svalbard (Norway)

Zemlya Frantsa-Iosifa (Russia)

Novaya Zemlya (Russia)

KARA SEA

Severnaya Zemlya (Russia)

BARENTS SEA

LAPTEV SEA

Novosibirskie Ostrovo (Russia)

EAST SIBERIAN SEA

Mon | Sun

International Date Line

Sweden 1pm

2pm

Finland

Norway

3pm

Latvia

7pm

9pm

11pm

12am

Denmark

4pm

5pm

Russia

10pm

SEA OF OKHOTSK

BERING SEA

3am

2am

Germany Poland Belarus

France Austria Ukraine

Italy Romania

4pm

Kazakhstan

Mongolia

NORTH PACIFIC OCEAN

Greece Turkey

Tunisia MEDITERRANEAN SEA Syria

Uzbekistan

6pm

Kyrgyzstan

North Korea

Japan

South Korea

EAST CHINA SEA

Turkmenistan

Iraq Iran 3.30pm

Afghanistan 4.30pm

Tibet (China)

China

8pm

Taiwan

Algeria Libya 2pm

Egypt

Saudi Arabia

Pakistan

Nepal 5.45 pm

India

6.30 pm

Northern Mariana Is (US)

Marshall Is (US)

1pm

Niger

Chad

Oman

4pm

5.30 pm

6pm

Myanmar 5.30pm

Thailand

9pm

12am

Nigeria Sudan

Eritrea Yemen

ARABIAN SEA

BAY OF BENGAL

Vietnam

Philippines

Federated States of Micronesia 11am

Kiribati

Central African Republic Ethiopia 3pm

Sri Lanka

Nauru EQUATOR

Congo Kenya Somalia

Maldives

Malaysia

Palau

Gabon 1pm Congo (Zaire)

Tanzania

Indonesia

Papua New Guinea

Solomon Is

SOUTH PACIFIC OCEAN

Angola Zambia Malawi

Seychelles 4pm

6.30 pm

East Timor

Vanuatu

Namibia Zimbabwe Mozambique

Madagascar Mauritius Reunion (Fr)

Cocos (Keeling) Is (Aust)

New Caledonia (Fr)

Fiji

Botswana

INDIAN OCEAN

9.30 pm

11.30 pm

South Africa

Australia

10.30 pm Norfolk Is (Aust)

Lord Howe Is (Aust)

Prince Edward Is (S. Africa)

French Southern & Antarctic Territories (Fr)

New Zealand

TASMAN SEA

Heard & McDonald Is (Aust)

SOUTHERN OCEAN

| 12pm | 1pm | 2pm | 3pm | 4pm | 5pm | 6pm | 7pm | 8pm | 9pm | 10pm | 11pm | 12am |

MAP LEGEND

ROUTES

Primary	Mall/Steps
Secondary	Tunnel
Tertiary	Pedestrian Overpass
Lane	Walking Tour
Under Construction	Walking Trail
Unsealed Road	Walking Path
One-Way Street	Track

TRANSPORT

Ferry	Rail
Bus Route	Rail (Underground)

HYDROGRAPHY

River, Creek	Canal
Intermittent River	Water
Swamp	Lake (Dry)
Mangrove	Lake (Salt)
Reef	Mudflats

BOUNDARIES

International	Regional, Suburb
State, Provincial	Ancient Wall
Disputed	Cliff
Marine Park	

AREA FEATURES

Airport	Land
Area of Interest	Mall
Beach, Desert	Market
Building	Park
Campus	Reservation
Cemetery, Christian	Rocks
Cemetery, Other	Sports
Forest	Urban

POPULATION

CAPITAL (NATIONAL)	CAPITAL (STATE)
Large City	Medium City
Small City	Town, Village

SYMBOLS

Sights/Activities
- Beach
- Buddhist
- Christian
- Monument
- Museum, Gallery
- Point of Interest
- Pool
- Ruin
- Taoist
- Zoo, Bird Sanctuary

Eating
- Eating

Drinking
- Drinking
- Café

Entertainment
- Entertainment

Shopping
- Shopping

Sleeping
- Sleeping
- Camping

Transport
- Airport, Airfield
- Border Crossing
- Bus Station
- Cycling, Bicycle Path
- General Transport
- Parking Area
- Petrol Station
- Taxi Rank

Information
- Bank, ATM
- Embassy/Consulate
- Hospital, Medical
- Information
- Internet Facilities
- Police Station
- Post Office, GPO
- Telephone
- Toilets

Geographic
- Mountain, Volcano
- National Park
- Pass, Canyon
- River Flow
- Spot Height
- Waterfall

LONELY PLANET OFFICES

Australia
Head Office
Locked Bag 1, Footscray, Victoria 3011
☎ 03 8379 8000, fax 03 8379 8111
talk2us@lonelyplanet.com.au

USA
150 Linden St, Oakland, CA 94607
☎ 510 893 8555, toll free 800 275 8555
fax 510 893 8572
info@lonelyplanet.com

UK
72-82 Rosebery Ave,
Clerkenwell, London EC1R 4RW
☎ 020 7841 9000, fax 020 7841 9001
go@lonelyplanet.co.uk

Published by Lonely Planet Publications Pty Ltd
ABN 36 005 607 983

© Lonely Planet Publications Pty Ltd 2007

© photographers as indicated 2007

Cover photograph: Bun Pi Mai Lao (New Year Festival), Hat Muang Khoun, Carol Ann Wiley/Lonely Planet Images. Many of the images in this guide are available for licensing from Lonely Planet Images: www.lonelyplanetimages.com.

All rights reserved. No part of this publication may be copied, stored in a retrieval system, or transmitted in any form by any means, electronic, mechanical, recording or otherwise, except brief extracts for the purpose of review, and no part of this publication may be sold or hired, without the written permission of the publisher.

Printed by Toppan Security Printing Pte. Ltd., Singapore.

Lonely Planet and the Lonely Planet logo are trademarks of Lonely Planet and are registered in the US Patent and Trademark Office and in other countries.

Lonely Planet does not allow its name or logo to be appropriated by commercial establishments, such as retailers, restaurants or hotels. Please let us know of any misuses: www.lonelyplanet.com/ip.

80025 75540

Although the authors and Lonely Planet have taken all reasonable care in preparing this book, we make no warranty about the accuracy or completeness of its content and, to the maximum extent permitted, disclaim all liability arising from its use.